I AM A I

Unfolding the Flower

This book is dedicated to the Nameless Desert God,
Bob Dylan,
Moody Blues, and last but not least the
Grateful Dead:
You not only left a candle in the window; you left a door open.
Thank you is not enough.

AuthorHouse™
1663 Liberty Drive
Bloomington, IN 47403
www.authorhouse.com
Phone: 1-800-839-8640

First published by AuthorHouse 9/2/2010

ISBN: 978-1-4490-9627-4 (e)
ISBN: 978-1-4490-9626-7 (sc)

Library of Congress Control Number: 2010923975

Printed in the United States of America

This book is printed on acid-free paper.

Introduction

This is a book about everything.

It is about the truths/laws that define the physical universe.

It is about the Truths/Laws that define the metaphysical/spiritual universe.

It is about how these laws work together, how they define your reality, and you.

It is about how you must interact or work with these Truths/truths to exist or have any effect,

physical or non-physical.

This is a primer, only.

Complete schools of thought have developed around some of the ideas in this book; many of

them are ancient.

The bottom line is

the finite temporal/spatial based science paradigm used to explain physical form – the physical

universe-- is a 'special case' of an infinite and eternal paradigm that incorporates everything –

the metaphysical/spiritual universe.

This makes perfect sense, if all things come from

GOD.

Signs of the Times Department:

Truth has been known to fracture individual realities.

Table of Contents

CHAPTER 7

CHAPTER 8

CHAPTER 9

CHAPTER 10

Prologue

"Use of clay determines a pot
Use of the pot is determined where the clay is not."[1]
Tao Te Ching

"Unless you become as a little child, you can not enter the kingdom of Heaven."[2]
Jesus

"The mind has nothing to do with thinking because its fundamental source is empty. To discard false views, this is the great causal event."[3]
Buddha

"Look onto the lilies of the field, they toil not..."[4]
Jesus

'The eyes do not see him, speech can not utter him, the senses can not reach him...in meditation the personal self is revealed."
Upanishads

'Whosoever works for me alone ... free from attachment (to outcome), and without hatred toward any creature -- that man, O Prince, shall enter onto me.'
Bhagavad-Gita

"Love God with all your heart, with all your mind, and with all your soul."[5]
Jesus

"Sit in your cell as you would in Paradise."[6]
St. Romuald

"Simply do this: Be still, and lay aside all thoughts of what you are and what God is; all concepts you have learned about the world; all images you hold about yourself. Empty your mind of everything it thinks is either true or false, good or bad, of everything it judges worthy, and all ideas of which it is ashamed. Hold onto nothing. Do not bring with you one thought the past has taught, nor one belief you ever learned before from anything. Forget this world, forget this course, and come with wholly empty hands unto your God."[7]
A Course in Miracles©

---

1 Shape clay into a vessel; It is the space within that makes it useful. -- Tao Te Ching, Feng Translation.
2 And he said: "I tell you the truth, unless you change and become like little children, you will never enter the kingdom of Heaven." -- Matthew 18:3, New International Version Bible.
3 Lotus Sutra, Buddha
4 "Consider how the lilies grow. They do not labor or spin. Yet I tell you, not even Solomon in all his splendor was dressed like one of these." -- Luke 12:26-28, New International Version Bible.
5 "Love the Lord your God with all your heart and with all your soul and with all your mind and with all your strength." -- Mark 12:30, New International Version Bible.
6 Saint Romuald's Rule
7 A Course In Miracles, Workbook for Students, Lesson 189

"Know the Truth and the Truth will set you free."[8]
Jesus

"Use the Force Luke!"
Obe wan Kenobe

---

8 "Then you will know the truth, and the truth will set you free." -- John 8:30, New International Version Bible.

Chapter 1

An Overview

1.1 - What to Believe

I AM A I is a metaphysical science textbook. A mystic works with metaphysical laws just as a technician works with physical laws. The lab for this 'science class' is you-behind-the-eyes or you-between-the-ears – your mind.

Here is an example of how this works. To paraphrase a quote from the Buddha, you are not to believe anything you read, hear, or see in this book unless something deep down inside you quietly responds and says; "Yes, that's true." It does not matter if you think it may lead to some kind of divine revelation or come from a Divine source. Do not believe it unless something quietly responds deep inside you; a quiet connection is made within you. Quietly means; there is no emotional content. Emotion may occur after the 'event', and the 'event' itself occurs without emotion.

Truth, being the laws of Creation, is at the very core of our being. When we hear a symbolic reference to it, our mind makes the connection to Truth and something deep inside us responds. This can be looked upon as a form of sympathetic resonance.

Now and then, *I AM A I* will refer to this quiet response as 'truth ringing' or 'truth bell' inside you. If any information from this book comes along and that bell does not immediately ring, let it go for now. You may however, want to set the information aside on a shelf within you and wait; do not make any judgments. It could be your perceptions are not open enough for that Truth to enter.

'Higher' Truths will not be perceived unless some 'lower' truths are perceived. For example, it is recommended to teach basic math operations (+, -, /, x, etc.), before you teach trigonometry. After a student learns the necessary math operations, then trigonometry is possible.

********************  ********************

17

Exercise and Labs 1A and B: Truth Recognition and Personal Notebook

Exercise and Lab 1 Part (A)

If you choose to use this information in its originally intended class format, get a notebook. The inside of the notebook cover should be divided into four parts. Each quarter has a different label. One label would be *In*, one label would be *Out*, one label would be *Mine*, and one label would be *After*.

What do these labels mean? Please refer to Figure 1-1. Whenever that 'truth bell' rings within you from something inside the book, you would make a slash mark under *In*. If you heard something outside the book that rang that bell, you would make a mark in the *Out* box. When you realize something inside yourself, by yourself, and the bell rings; then you would make a mark under *Mine*. *After* was for when you were done with the book and the notebook may become a journal.

➢ *This assignment is to accumulate 10 - 15 hash marks in the* In *box.*
➢ *5-10 each in the* Out *box and the* Mine *box.*
➢ *After 20 hash marks, you could stop because you may be somewhat familiar with this quiet sense.*

Figure 1-1 Keeping Record

It is understood that what you are being asked to recognize is ever so subtle. And…there are some clues that this event has been occurring on a regular basis:

♦ When hearing truth consistently, the consciousness change in the hearer can be interesting. This consciousness change expresses itself in different ways. One way can be the listener agrees with every word spoken, perhaps accompanied with a sense of peace and wholeness.

This consciousness change can occur to such a degree that the listener will not be able to say what was said. They may just have an idea of the general context. They only know; they agreed with what was said.

♦ Another reading symptom that appears is similar to hearing the truth. You are absorbed, agree with everything read, and cannot remember what is being read.

In both cases, higher priority mental operations (cognition and knowledge) are taking precedence over lower priority mental operations (memory).[1] The truth ringing mechanism can interfere with the reading mechanism.

♦ When reading truth, the consciousness change can become like a rain on the face analogy. A light rain on the face may feel refreshing, and yet, most people can only take so much of it. Too much rain can feel overwhelming.

---

1 Figure 4-4

One problem with reading truth is a tendency to put the book down. Usually, this is done to absorb what has been read. If this book is doing its job right, you may be setting this book down on a regular basis. This, in turn, can make this book slow reading.

An effect of this consistently truth ringing event can produce a consciousness change within the listener or reader. This arises when our temporal mind/matrix[2] has some points in common with, and/or is in relationship to an Infinite and Eternal Mind/Matrix.[3] By sharing the same or similar elements, a point of tangency occurs between the two and there is a communion.[4] These points of tangency determine the kind or quality of the ringing.[5] (Or, the depth of individual consciousness change is contingent on the depth of the communion.)

The main idea of this exercise is to get you to be familiar with the truth-ringing concept, that an event occurred within you, to feel it, and to learn to recognize it.

For you, the reader, a goal of the exercise may be achieved if you had a pad of paper and a pencil next to you as you are reading. Every time you read something in this book and there is a resonance or response within you, make a hash mark on the pad. By the time you reach 10 to 15 marks, you may have an idea or a feel of this response mechanism to truth. The exercise's purpose will be achieved as long as you recognize 'something' occurred.

It may not be important to know or to indicate what the concept or the thought was. Just that you recognized it happened. You can write it down if you want. However, within the oral class format it could become counter-productive to learning.

Sometimes as your writing things down, you do not hear what is being said at that moment. It tends to split individual focus. (The author is not coordinated enough to be able to write and listen at the same time.) The main idea of the exercise is to get you to recognize your own mechanism, how you respond to truth, or how truth affects you…deep inside.

When this book is used as a personal self-help, the _Out_ and _Mine_ boxes are equivalent to keeping a journal for anything. Because you probably will not be walking around with a notebook, the _Out_ box may not be marked until you come back to the notebook. ("I heard something 'heavy' today.") For this exercise, only 5-10 hash marks are required in the _Out_ box.

Again, the idea here is to recognize an event occurred. This book will cover _Mine_ later. Chapter 3 will introduce how you can perceive your own truths in an exercise and possibly 'ring your own bell'.

Chapter 4 will cover levels or depths of this 'truth ring'.

To summarize this exercise, your mind is the 'lab' and you are asked to recognize an event occurred in the 'lab'. Do not accept anything from this book unless there is a quiet response inside you. This also means do not summarily reject the idea either. The thought is to cultivate a 'watching and waiting' attitude in reference to the material of this book and your response to the material.

Exercise and Lab 1 Part (B)

When this book is used as intended for a class format, this exercise is easy to state. There is to be no talking about your personal experiences (from doing the exercises, reading the book, or while participating in the class) with anyone. The only exceptions are if talking fits within the class format (exercise feedback, meditation effects, questions, etc.)

You can talk about content and ideas presented. You are not to talk about your personal experiences from content applications.

From reading this bookstand point, the exercise is a little harder to state. This exercise can be stated as; do not share any personal experiences you have from reading or doing the

---

2 Chapter 4, Realities and the Human Matrix
3 Chapters 2-4
4 Chapters 3, 4, 7, 9, and 10
5 Chapter 4.8, Ring My Bell

exercises in the book. You can tell people about the book and describe the exercises. However, keep your personal experiences to yourself – what happens when you do the exercises. You can write about your experiences in a notebook or journal. However, do not show your notebook or journal or any entries in your journal to anyone (for as long as you are using this book).

Why do you do this? There are numerous reasons. One reason has been stated already. This is a science course and the 'lab' for this course is your mind – you behind the eyes and between the ears.

For the time being, look at your mind as being a laboratory environment. Physically, for a set of experiments to work, specific conditions must be maintained within a laboratory environment. This also applies metaphysically. Talking about personal experience affects the laboratory environment within you and therefore can affect the outcome of some of the experiments in this book.

Talking is an act of creation and it is a choice (both of these are covered in detail in later chapters). Every choice you make will have an affect on your mind's programming. This exercise is a crude way of keeping you from making some specific choices.

Look at this exercise as a shotgun approach to maintaining pristine 'lab conditions'.

The not talking exercise is also an introduction to some self-discipline that will be necessary later in this book.[6] It is an introduction to the concept of 'not doing' something can be as important as 'doing' something. What would be your intention for speaking? Could it be your saying, "Look what I did! Look what I did!" This is listening to your pride or ego. These qualities can hinder the success of future exercises, especially *ESP*. It can also foster attachments.

A number of other reasons for this exercise are:

♦ This exercise helps maintain the disinterested-interest (non-attachment) necessary for the success of the psychic exercises in Chapter 7.
♦ It relates to a Formula of Effectiveness in Chapter 5.
♦ It hinders from making premature judgments around a subject matter that you are still learning and have not yet finished learning
♦ It can also relate to the To Keep Silent rule of magic in Chapter 9.

The bottom line is; any experiences you have are between you and your Creator/ix. It really is not anybody's business except yours. An Infinite Eternal Loving God can customize everybody's spiritual curriculum to each person's needs. What you may have to learn at this moment, may not be what the person next you has to learn at this moment.

Therefore...the second part of this assignment can be translated as:

➢ *Keep silent" about what experiences you have; what you feel; or your applications involving these exercises' or their subject matter, until you are finished with this book and the included exercises.*

Those who know, do not talk
Those who talk, do not know.
Tao te Ching

******************* ☯ *******************

1.2 - Goals, Purposes, Over, Under, Around and Through View

*I*magine, for a moment, there is a huge mountain called 'All'. Surrounding the mountain is a plain. On and around the mountainsides, small villages dot the

---

6 Chapter 6, Exercises and Disciplines

surface. Metaphysical and spiritual villages reside on the snow-capped peak of the mountain shrouded in clouds and wisps of white. While at the base and on the plain leading off into the distance, is a giant forest with innumerable life forms; here resides the physical science villages. Leading up the slope of the mountain are other small villages. Though each village (at the peak, on the slope, or surrounding the mountain) has a good view of the mountain, no village can see the whole mountain.

The villages are loosely assembled into nations according to their interest. Around the base of the mountain within the 'Science' nation are the villages called Physics, Chemistry, Biology, etc. Within the mist, shrouded apex of the mountain is the 'Spiritual/Metaphysics' nation. Within it are the villages founded by Buddha, Jesus Christ, Mahavira, Moses, etc. On the borderlands of the two nations, dotting the slopes, are the villages of Scientology, Psychiatry, *ESP*, and so on.

These nations and villages are all viewing the same mountain, and yet, if not in open argument, there is disagreement about whose view is the better or more accurate view. Herein lays the state of human condition and thought around the Universe and the Divine today.

I AM A I intends to take you, the reader, on an airplane ride around the mountain 'All'. Not only does this book provide a basic overview; it provides you with a set of 'x-ray glasses' to see what is at the core of 'All'.

How does *I AM A I* do this? Any complete synthesis between thought systems/villages must find common elements in the thought systems without negating the intrinsic characteristics that make the thought systems/villages unique.

First, an examination of the strengths and weaknesses of the two largest nations/thought systems/mental constructs (physics and metaphysics -- mountain peak and base) may be helpful.

I) Science
A) Strengths
1) Language
a) Math dependent
b) Universal across time and cultures
c) Can manipulate infinities within infinities within infinities…
d) Math never changes (only our understanding of it changes)
2) Cultivates objectivity – observation: Works with obvious effects from non-visible immutable laws -- Empirical
3) Information is accumulative
B) Weaknesses
1) Empirical
a) Any perception of an event is only as good as, where the observer's position is in relationship to the event -- where they are 'standing'.
b) Any measurement of an event is only as good as the 'ruler'.
c) Only deals with the obvious observable events and does not deal with the un-obvious
d) Only deals with events outside of the observer
2) No overview
3) Life is perceived as only a chemical reaction
II) Metaphysics
A) Strengths
1) Has overview
a) Recognizes a unifying Source
b) Participation with this 'Source" is possible
2) Recognizes Life as a viable force
a) Takes science to the next step – outside or other than time/space
b) Works with un-obvious effects from invisible immutable laws
c) Works with events within the observer
B) Weaknesses

1) Not Empirical
    a) Tends to be subjective while objectivity can be lost
        i) An Infinite Eternal Love has an infinite possibilities or approaches
        ii) What ever is given to Love, it will use
    b) The individual is the laboratory
        i) Ignorance of internal conditions produces mixed results
        ii) Extensive number of variables produces distinctly different effects when two individuals execute the same exercise
2) Language
    a) Culturally based
        i) Cultures change through time
        ii) Anyone from outside the culture can misunderstand -- lose -- information
    b) Language is slippery and one sentence can be subject to a multitude of interpretations depending on the individual references of the participants
    c) The words are not the actuality. They are symbolic representations of actualities and not the actualities themselves.

❑ The science/math thought systems are accumulative (*I-A-3*). As Man learned, his thought constructs evolved. Each new construct encompassed the old one and said, "this old one is a special case of the new one".

For example, the Newtonian view of the universe did not negate Copernicus. It only said the Copernican view is a special case. When Einstein came along, he did not negate the Newtonian construct. He said Newtonian view is a special case within his universe.

No matter what thought system or construct that science/math develops to express physical form, it will always be a special case to a metaphysical thought system or construct that expresses all of Creation (*II-A-1*), physical and nonphysical.

Why? Because Creation occurs outside of time (Eternal)[7] and metaphysical laws involves the laws of the Eternal/temporal interface (*II-A-2-a*). Physical laws (science) are interested in primarily the temporal spatial aspect of Creation (*I-B-1-a>c*). One of science's 'rulers' is time, which in turn introduces limits.

❑ Traditional mystical or metaphysical thought systems/constructs are based on bursts of intuitive (enlightening) information that is translated into a human context. Except for some instances in the Covenant religions,[8] this usually takes the form of a shamanic journey.[9]

In ancient times, the mystic had to impart this 'spiritual information' in such a manner so the people could relate to it (*II-B-2*). The information translated into allegories and stories that were based on the peoples' perceptions at the time. These translations included the language idioms of the region, local cultural allegories/parables, or in the form of a continuing story (history and the Covenant). This is their major weakness – it can introduce misinformation through time.

Cultures are fluid and evolve. Therefore, information and the original ideas get lost. Anyone with an incomplete grasp of the culture (foreigner, someone from a different era or culture, child or teenager within that culture, etc.) is going to miss some information (*II-B-2-a*).

The result of this problem is that as cultures change, the meaning of words change. Information passed on by word of mouth or in allegory changes; or, it can lose the original purpose the speaker had in telling the story.[10]

❑ The beauty of the math/science constructs is that they can be passed down through generations or across cultures without losing meaning or intrinsic characteristics (*I-A-1-a>d*). (The oldest textbook used in public school today is an Euclidean geometry book.) Its empirical

---

7 Chapter 2, Postulates and Theorems
8 Judaic, Christian, Islamic religions, Chapter 10
9 Chapter 10, Concerning World Religions and Miracles
10 ibid.

nature allows anybody to see the same results if they recreate the same conditions.

❑ Science is strong in cause and effect relationships within a given set of conditions (*I-A-2*). It is weak in general connections and parallels because there is no comprehensive overview, unified field theory (*I-B-2*). Furthermore, empirical science is only as good as the ruler it uses and where you are standing when you measure (*I-B-1-a, b*). Example: what is a life unit? How do you measure a life unit? (*I-B-3*)

❑ The metaphysical constructs are comprehensive in nature. They are strong on overviews, unlike the science constructs (*II-A-1*). The science constructs are pieces of a jigsaw puzzle working toward a whole picture, while metaphysics starts with an overview and then translates it into parts of the puzzle (everyday experiences).

It is as if metaphysics is relating the information from the 'top' of the mountain down to the human condition, while physics is relating the information from the 'bottom' of the mountain up to the human condition.

Ironically, both systems have been, or are, a major influence in how we conduct our lives. The physics (science) system relates to how we individually participate with the matter around us (from walking, to throwing a ball, going to the store, etc.). In addition, it influences the choices made by Man[11] (one effect shows up as technology).

On the other hand, metaphysical thought systems have influenced our lives through world religions, psychology, and parapsychology concepts. For years, metaphysical thought systems were the major influence in Man's cultures. Today their influence has dwindled and has been displaced in many ways by physical science thought systems.

If a synthesis occurred, and metaphysics is taught -- using the logic of a mathematical format like Euclidean geometry -- a metaphysics course should not change much (*I-A-1-a*). This book is mysticism and metaphysics in a logic format using math and science as examples. Perhaps this format is appropriate today, because science and math are the language and perceptions of our technical civilization.

Another reason for using the math rationale in this book's format is because mathematics is the only symbolic logic system that Man has that enables one to juggle infinities within infinities... infinitely, and emerge with something that makes consistent sense or is workable (*I-A-1-c*).

Since physical and metaphysical creation has so many details that would boggle a human brain, it makes sense that one should use a logic system that can handle the multitude of variables that makes it up.

A synthesis between the two thought systems (science and spiritual) can be approached from a multitude of levels.

❖ One level begins with one of the definitions for truth in this book, "laws by which something works", this definition unites physics (science and mathematics) and metaphysics under a common term. The 'truths' of physical form are the laws of science (laws of motion, quantum mechanics, matrices within physical matter – crystalline, *DNA*, biology, etc.).

The truths of metaphysics are the laws of mysticism and the spiritual nature (Karma, creative vs. destructive, Creation Matrix, etc.). One of the themes of this book is the physical truths are special cases of (or are parallel to) metaphysical truths.

❖ Another level appears with Jesus' statement, "The kingdom of Heaven is within you and without you." The same can be said of the laws of physics. Gravity is 'within you and without you.' Accordingly, so are the truths/laws of motion, harmonics, thermodynamics, etc. They are all 'within you and without you'.

I AM A I is not equating the truth of physics to the Truth of God. That would be

---

[11] Mankind

ludicrous. It would be like equating a candle to the sun. What is being attempted is to show patterns, connections, or parallels. Just as a candle has some common characteristics with the sun, physics (and math) has some common characteristics with the Divine. Science and Mysticism must merge eventually, both work with a Truth Matrix -- truth framework.

❖ Another synthesis is; what color is gravity, what does it look like? The laws of science are invisible. We can only see the laws' effects; we cannot see the laws.

This idea of an invisible level sustaining the physical is a recurring mystical axiom; there is an invisible world of laws/truths behind the visible world.

❖ In addition, these laws/truths are eternally constant. Physical form is in constant flux – change. Yet, this change is determined by a set of invisible unchanging eternal laws. If these laws changed, there would be no science or mathematics.

❖ That there is a rational order underlying all things in both philosophies is another level. Just because this order is not immediately perceived by most of us does not mean that this order does not exist. This book will be using the logic of the mathematical symbol system to reflect that logical order metaphysically. This order is infinite and Eternal.

❖ Physics and metaphysics thought systems as symbolic constructs. A symbolic construct is a picture painted in ideas, words, or numbers – a model. Both physics and metaphysics are mental symbolic fabrications, created and used by Mankind, in order to help relate to the 'universe'.

Neither constructs are the actuality; they are only tools to help us understand and appreciate the actuality -- a way to order truth in the construct. This book is a mental construct that synthesizes physics and metaphysics thought systems/constructs.

In the end, it is not the philosophies, thought systems, mental constructs…that are important; it is the Truth application within the philosophies that are important. Truth is in its own web.

As stated earlier in the chapter, the construct of this book can (it is hoped) pass on ideas consistently through generations. The math formula (and the math reasoning behind the formula) in Newton's law of gravity allows the passing of the core idea we know as gravity to people separated by time, space, or cultures. At the same time, the core idea suffers a minimum amount of distortion when being passed on. The same cannot be said about words.

It is to be hoped that this book can use math reasoning to present metaphysical ideas that never leave us, which may be passed on consistently to people separated by generations. One of the reasons this can be said is many of the things in this book is not new; much of it is ancient.

The format of this book (using scientific and mathematical thinking) is about the only format that can hopefully keep mistakes or interpretations down to a relative minimum. The languages and symbols that originally made up an Euclidean geometry have come and gone, and yet, the information in that book essentially remains the same.

Because mathematical thinking and its symbol system grew hand in hand with physical science, it became the language of physical science and physical form. The logic of math language -- that came out of these symbolic forms – can also be applicable to metaphysics and it is subject to a relatively minimum amount of interpretation.

The place where errors can be introduced (other than computational) is; once you put the numbers together, interpretations are made. An example of this would be if you were an engineer dealing with stresses and such. The numbers themselves are clear, clean. The engineer makes judgment calls about what they perceive the numbers are telling them. An engineer's job is to match the numbers related to materials to the numbers of a job requirement.

Lets say I have so much weight -- so many numbers in weight (A); and I have this material that can take so many numbers of pounds per so many numbers of feet of stress (B).

Because I have this much weight (*A*) and this kind of material (*B*), that means I have to have so much material, to set up a certain way, to take that force. (*B*) must be greater than (*A*) or the project will collapse.

All the numbers are clear. It is up to the individual to interpret what the numbers are saying -- to interpret the symbolic system. The math symbol system is clear in execution and meaning. The places where discrepancies usually occur are in the interpretations, or how the numbers are manipulated. It is usually in making the translation from external form to symbol -- either entering or leaving the symbol system -- those weaknesses can occur.

This cannot be said of word language. Meanings change with culture and communication participants. How many different meanings are there for the sound, two, in words (to, too, two), and how many different meanings are there for two in math? There is only one in math. Languages have come and gone, including words that have mathematical references. Yet, the math concepts themselves have not changed.

The idea of an Eternal logic and order is not new. It is ancient. It is older than Pythagoras is. When people start applying this logic and order, they start exercising control of their own personal reality. Understanding or appreciating this order will help you as the metaphysical/spiritual student/pilgrim/operator become much more effective because you will tend to be dealing with truths instead of untruths. You will be aligning your own internal logic matrix – mind -- to the Truth Matrix.

Absolute, Infinite, Eternal Love has an Absolute, Infinite, Eternal Logic and this book uses mathematical reasoning as an example or means to approach this Eternal Logic. Mathematical thinking is used here as a way to approach metaphysics because mathematics is Man's first logic system. The first logic system he ever conceived, and is based on physical concepts that are applicable everywhere.[12]

Mathematics is the one language that would allow us to be able to talk to, or with, beings from another planet.[13] How? Because, mathematics is related to the laws of physical creation, which all physical beings have in common. If the aliens have any degree of technical expertise, they will know what π is. Concepts like π or squaring a number are universal to physical form.

However, it is not mathematics/mathematical thinking itself that is important. *I AM A I* is using mathematical logic as an introduction to a metaphysics logic format. It works very well, because as mentioned, it is our first logic system and it can juggle infinities.

There are a number of goals to this book.

$\Rightarrow$ One of the things this book attempts is to present a metaphysical logic format that can be communicated and passed on through time and space with as little misinterpretation as possible. The author hopes this book introduces a paradigm that incorporates science's jigsaw puzzle, uses science's universal math logic, and provides a synthesis with a metaphysical overview. The presented paradigm not only includes the intuitive metaphysical information passed down through religions, it includes the border 'mountain villages': psychology, *ESP*, music, etc. on the mountain of 'All' analogy.

$\Rightarrow$ Another goal is to help you, the individual, become -- using a term from thaumaturgical magic[14] -- a 'coordinated being'. The idea behind a 'coordinated being' is, when it is time to think and do, you work in Truth -- in Absolute order. When it is time not to act, you do nothing.

Most mystical exercises are a reference to this last part of not doing and getting out of thought. However, what is being presented here is that when thinking is done, if it is done in a logic order with truths, it can create a 'coordinated being'.

The "coordinated being" idea is about the inside, the outside, and the whole, of which the inside and the outside are integral to the whole. It is similar to a child learning coordination

---

12 Chapter 2.1, What Is a Postulate
13 A number of animals can count to three naturally, i.e. crows.
14 Chapter 9, Concerning Magic

of its body in conjunction with the laws of physics. There is a time to move the arm and there is a time not to move the arm.

When it is time to do something, it is working in conjunction with the laws involved, inside and outside of the operator. An example, are the simple laws of leverage of your arm. Our arm is a third class lever. Yet, the laws that determine a lever are the same in the Pleiades as well as on Earth. Coordination is motion and non-motion in terms of the laws of nature.

This is an introduction to the 'coordinated being' concept. The book will return to this idea.

⇒ Another goal of this book is to get you to be actively involved in setting up and participating in the Love's Logic system within you. This process will cause growth (when applied) whether you believe in the Love's Logic system (or this book's information) or not, because it is based on Truth. Truth – Absolute and Actual[15] -- works when applied independent of belief. When you start applying these Truths, you start participating in the Eternal aspect of the universe.

From such a logic framework, you can reform your individual personal reality, and can become more effective through the application of knowledge of universal mechanics and Eternal principles. Our human mind is a neural matrix.[16] Usually our personal logic matrix (individuality or **Individual** reality) has both truth and untruth programmed within that neural matrix, so it is erratic. We cannot always depend on what we get out of it. This course aims to give you a set of guidelines for programming and use of your own individual logic mind/matrix in harmony with a Universal Logic Matrix.

⇒ In this book, you are taught that you are not your mind. You will be taught that your mind is your vehicle in your body just as your body is your vehicle in the physical world. This book presents a broad spectrum of personal tools that can help facilitate your internal experimentation – play with the vehicle.

Application of these tools will have an effect within you. Again, the reason behind this is that this book teaches truth works when correctly applied independent of belief, as in science.

The mental tools presented are very generic in nature. You will be shown how one tool, music, can work as a spiritual or trance tool on a multitude of levels.

Because some of the personal tools taught are so basic, applications can be relevant to a multitude of individual endeavors. These endeavors may or may not be mystically or spiritually orientated; and yet, some of the tools provided can still prove useful.

Hopefully, the book's overall effect on your mind is to open your mind up to a scope and possibilities beyond what you 'thought' you had before reading the book.

Some of the things you can learn from this book are:

- How to meditate, basic types of meditation, and what they have in common
- How to do a psychic reading
- Tools and ways to use the most powerful spiritual or mystical tool we have…music
- Ways to open your mind's-eye through time and space
- How to reset your mind
- Basic mystical concepts that reoccur through out world mystical and spiritual thought systems
- How thaumaturgical magic and miracles work
- How to perceive universal truths using everyday objects
- The importance of formulating intention

This book gives you a map, and you are the traveler. This format has room for translation into individual lives as you walk the road. Just as, the book of Euclidean geometry

---

15 Chapter 4.2, What's Reality Papa?
16 Chapter 4, Realities and the Human Matrix

gives you a map of constructions; and later, you use these constructions to make your own determinations. Once you learn the geometric constructions, you perform your own operations according to your needs, be it a bridge or a what-not-shelf.

Again, you do not have to believe the information in this format. Nor does the use of the information require belief. However, if you keep doing the exercises, your participation in Truth will cause a change within you. Whether you believe in this information or not, continual application will produce an effect. You do not have to believe in gravity to walk.

When you start consistently setting up specific conditions, with Truth, and it lets Truth happen inside you.[17] That, in itself, is going to cause a change within you. It goes back to the concept; Truth works when it is applied, independent of belief.

The following is a brief summary of this book:
Truth, being Eternally constant, dictates that there is nothing new in this book. Most of the information is ancient. It is in the presentation of the metaphysical subject matter as a science class that makes this book somewhat different.

❑ The **First chapter** – this chapter -- is an introduction and overview. It introduces the idea of the mystical use of mathematical logic is not new. It does this by introducing you to Pythagoras and the Pythagorean mystery schools, plus the core concepts of western sacred geometry.

➔ *The first two exercises illustrate the field of the 'laboratory'. A third homework assignment is given – make your own mandala or yantra (meditation aid). This figure is to be made in preparation for a chanting exercise in Chapter 6.*

❑ In the **Second chapter**, a skeleton of *I AM A I*'s paradigm is introduced. Chapter 2 gives an evolution of math. Then, starting from the 'top' (God) to Creation to temporal form ('down'), this chapter gives language terms -- words -- precise meaning, treats these terms as if they were mathematical expressions, and assembles them into a set of postulates and theorems. It introduces concepts like 'Absolute Love has an Absolute Logic', a 'Truth Matrix and Creation', 'the creation of untruth', 'relationships of Truth to untruth', etc.

Using the postulate theorem format, you are introduced to some very ancient mystical or spiritual concepts.

❑ The thought construct of Chapter 2, plus its implications, continues in **Chapter 3**. This chapter continues Chapter 2's theme and fleshes out the skeleton of the previous chapter. It relates the information of Chapter 2 into physical form. In Chapter 3, physics theory and the metaphysics theory are synthesized with the introduction of the concepts involving The Correction, The Mirror, Bubbles of Temporal/spatial Reference (*BTR*s), and their matrices. Chapter 3 illustrates how all form consists of *BTR*s within *BTR*s within *BTR*s...from atomic particles to galaxies, from people to amoebas.

Chapter 3 also presents an introduction to Eternal/temporal relationships. At the end of Chapter 3, there is an introduction to Eternal-temporal interface mechanics -- time folding or time ignor-ance.

➔ *Mid-chapter a long-term homework assignment is given -- truth perception by jumping parallels.*

❑ **Chapter 4** completes the thought construct started in Chapter 2 and 3 by presenting the mechanics of the mortal mind -- giving temporal/physical form a mortal mind. This chapter examines in detail how truth and untruth exists in the human thought matrix -- mind. It discusses the realities involved, the limits of perception, and the predominant elements of our individual Bubble of Temporal/spatial Reference. Comparisons are made between the human mind/matrix's operation and a camera or the eye. This chapter also introduces levels of Truth

---

[17] This is the purpose of the homework assignments and the labs.

'ringing' within a human mind.

→   *This chapter's exercises involve some time and space exercises using the imagination to expand and open the 'mind's eye'. Another exercise introduces the concept of 'resetting' the mind.*

The rest of the book pertains to usage of the model introduced in Chapters 2-4. Chapters 2-4 are concerned with the transition from God to Man. While, Chapters 5-10 are occupied with the transition of Man to God -- applications.

❑   **Chapter 5** takes the components of the human mind/matrix, treats them as numerical values, and produces a general Formula of Effectiveness for all human situations. The formula helps explain our successes and failures, both physically and metaphysically. The chapter familiarizes the reader with the front end of their matrix (Perception/Desire Lens).

→   *An exercise is presented that helps illustrate the relationship between what you 'see' – perception -- and what you 'want' -- desire.*

❑   **Chapter 6** concerns itself with a multitude of meditation exercises and labs, both traditional and non-traditional.

→   *A short list would be: breathing, chanting and their basic categories, empty mind exercises with and without an external focus (mandalas), and several ways mentation can be used to get out of mentation. Each exercise is related back to the human matrix and its elements of Chapter 4 and the formula of Chapter 5. The exercises are referenced to what your mind/matrix is doing when performing these exercises.*

❑   Once a person has been doing still mind exercises for an extended window of time, *ESP* occurs naturally. This is the realm of **Chapter 7**. Chapter 7 simplifies *ESP* by defining all psychic phenomena or *ESP* as a communication within One Mind. We <u>perceive</u> these psychic forms as a form of telepathy – either Mind-mind or mind-mind. The chapter gives brief definitions of some of the major manifestations of *ESP* and the routes taken through the human mind/matrix (Chapter 4). Chapter 7 uses the time/space ignor-ance of Chapter 3 and clarifies most *ESP* 'mysteries'.

→   *Relating information given in Chapters 4 and 5, this chapter introduces to you a number of exercises that can help cultivate psychic information flow through your mind.*

❑   **Chapter 8** is an extension to Chapter 6. It expands on how empty mind exercises are easier when done with short bursts of blankness or emptiness. This chapter discusses the use of tools and specifically the use of music as a tool. Chapter 8 introduces a multitude of mind applications related to music.

→   *This chapter will also give labs and homework assignments to accommodate this.*

❑   All the information of the previous chapters is pulled together in the **Ninth chapter** – Concerning Magic. This chapter defines the five kinds of magic – Black, White, Grey, Silver, and Gold, plus the four rules concerning magic. Chapter 9 discusses the Eternal to temporal mechanics (Chapters 2 - 4) of magic. It relates the human mind/matrix (Chapters 4 and 5) to Truth Matrix mechanics (Chapters 2, 3, and 7). This chapter presents patterns and parallels (it parallels the magical operation to an architect building a house), and relates the operation back to the Formula of Effectiveness (Chapter 5). This chapter is the springboard to the last chapter.

→   *A short exercise with the hands that introduces energy flows through the body.*

❑   In **Chapter 10**, the concept of Gold magic is extended into miracles. This chapter presents the shamanic journey, gives a short synopsis of world religions, and what they have in common with information in *I AM A I*. This book finishes by taking the introduction and the first chapter of *A Course in Miracles* © -- a learning tool -- (*The Principal of Miracles*) and cross-references the *ACIM* material to the material in *I AM A I: Unfolding the Flower*.

1.3 - Problems with This Format

*R*ecognition of the limits of intelligence is a priority in cultivating wisdom. Both Socrates and Einstein were the first to admit they knew nothing. As with teaching physics (or anything), there are several problems or limits to the conveyance of mystical information.

♦ One problem is with words and symbolic communication. Individual people have different meanings to the same words (sometimes leaping from clarification to confusion and verse visa). This was touched on earlier.

With teaching metaphysics/mysticism/spiritual, individual realities differ[18] and the symbols not being the actuality, projections occur with language. Sometimes these projections are totally unrelated to the subject matter and they can even be distracting from the subject matter.

♦ Again, as mentioned in the previous section, another problem with words is the symbol is not the actuality. The 'map' is not the 'terrain'. For example, the word gravity has really nothing to do with the force that binds our bodies to the planet. It is only a symbolic representation of this force. It is the same with any words dealing with the concept of God and metaphysics, the words really have nothing to do with the actualities. The actualities arise when the individual starts applying the concepts behind the words.

We can talk about gravity from now until doomsday. However, until you apply gravity and the laws of motion, you will not walk. It is the same metaphysically/mystically. All kinds of metaphysical concepts (from Karma to the power of Love) can be discussed but, until you apply them, they are meaningless. It is just intellectual 'elephant shit'.[19]

♦ Another drawback to the format of this book is unfortunately or fortunately, depending on your reference, not everybody works or thinks in numbers or uses numerical logic.

♦ Another problem with the science format: it is equivalent to trying to teach physics to a teenager. Teenagers, as a group, have a working knowledge of gravity, the laws of motion, harmonics, heat, thermodynamics; all this necessary just to walk, talk, and to keep warm. They have a working grasp of physics; however, they do not have any intellectual grasp of it.

Their usual response is, "Oh, this is boring, man." Although they subconsciously know the subject matter, it is:

"I can't wait until lunch time."
"When's this class over?"
"Let's see, 12 lbs.; falling at 32 ft. per second, per second; how fast is it moving when it hits the ground from 20 ft? Who cares!!? Just don't ask me to be there, that'd hurt."

Some high-school kids really get off on physics. "Oh wow, yeah cool", and while others it is, "Oh man. I can't wait until phys ed. class or art class." Or, "Yea, no school."

If a teenager did not have a working grasp of basic physics, they would not be able to throw balls, play catch, do athletics, or pick their nose. Therefore, here is another issue with this format; it is teaching you something you already know. It is trying to teach you something when you already have some working grasp of subject. Yet, you do not know you have a working grasp of the concepts. That, which is in the 'back of your mind',[20] has to be brought forward to the 'front of your mind'.[21]

---

18 Chapter 4.2 - "What's Reality Papa?"
19 Fritz Perls said, "Everything can be broken down to 3 kinds of shit: chicken-shit, bullshit, and elephant shit."
20 Chapter 4.4, Knowledge storage
21 Chapter 4.5, Perception Lens Array

Chapter 4 explains how perceptions and desires are different sides of the same 'coin' within the metaphysics format of this book.[22] The perceptions and desires an individual has will be incorporated into part of the lab work. The necessary lab conditions for some successful labs will not be met if the individual has no desire to be there, or to learn this material. In the beginning of many of the later labs regarding meditations, internal disciplines, and psychic phenomena, individual perceptions and desires are addressed or cultivated first.

♦ There are two words you can say that clenches people's sphincters; one is God and the other is math. Another issue with this format is that some people have an emotional charge around the concepts of math, science, or logic. Just as, many people have an emotional charge around the concept of God. Usually, because they have had an experience with these subjects that has left a 'bad taste' in their mouth. An example is they have been exposed to some sort of instance where a person or group of persons has used the concepts in an apparent tyrannical manner. Thus, there is an aversion or emotional reaction.

Fortunately (for the author), the emotional charges is your personal problem and not his. And…this emotional charge will have an affect on how well you, the reader, absorb the material. It also can act as a 'double whammy' against effective information absorption.

♦ One other factor that can present a problem with the format of this book is that the information of this book is accumulative. That means, like a math book, the information in the later chapters is built upon the information in earlier chapters. If the earlier chapters are not clear to the reader, you may have a problem understanding the information that follows.

♦ Also, relating to this the idea, your absorption of *I AM A I's* material is dependent on your mind/matrix and its programming. If there is no recognition of the concepts being presented, this book will seem like gibberish.

This book (or any metaphysical/spiritual treatise) is equivalent to a 'How to Swim Book'. That book can introduce swim strokes and without the applications in the pool, it is meaningless. The 'pool' for this book is your 'head' – your consciousness. Without the applications, this book is also meaningless.

As with physics, however you plan to use this subject matter for is totally up to you. A person could tell you about the laws of thermodynamics and you could develop a solar oven or burn yourself on a match. It is your call. It is up to how you want to apply the information.

All this book can do is give a construct, a working framework, just as college physics book gives a working framework or skeleton to physical activity. It is important for you, the reader, to remember this: the mental construct or model is not the actuality. A person may know Newton's law of gravity, but it is still only a thought construct.

To summarize the problems with this format:

- Words or symbols are not the actuality. It is all in the application.
- Not everyone thinks logically or likes science or math.
- That which is the back of the mind has to be brought to the front of the mind.
- The information presented in this book is accumulative and successive chapters are dependent on previous chapters.
- Add to this the 'ringing' response of the previous section; your individual response may cause you to put the book down periodically to 'digest' the information.
- The author's language skills 'sucks'

---

22 Ibid.

1.4 - Pythagoras and the Pythagorean Schools

*T*o help illustrate how ancient some of *I AM A I*'s content is, a brief look into history is in order. Around 600 years BC, something happened that is referred to as the Axial Age. Within a 100-year period, the foundations for modern civilization, as we know it, were laid.

Within that 100-year period, there appeared through out the ancient world:

Event	Effect
The Buddha	→ Buddhism
Mahavira, the founder of Jainism	→ Jainism
The *Bhagavad Gita* (appeared in written form)	→ Hindu teachings: non-attachment and karma…yoga
The *Upanishads* (appeared in written form)	→ Hindu teachings: Divine nature and meditation…yoga
The *Tao te Ching*, Lao Tzu[23] (appeared in written form)	→ Heaven, Earth, and the Way; one of the most concise book of 'mystical secrets' that Man has
Confucius	→ The importance of social order
2nd Isaiah	→ Christianity begins here with Jesus prophecies
Zoroaster	→ The word *magic* and Good/Evil concept
Pythagoras	→ Technical civilization

There are indications that these were passed along by word-of-mouth for a very long time.

Looking at this list, one can see the roots to most thought systems used today. Most of these events appear to be of a spiritual/metaphysical nature. The two exceptions appear to be Confucius and Pythagoras. Confucius dealt primarily with social order. And…why is Pythagoras on this list?

The entire 'technical element' of 'modern' society can be laid at Pythagoras' feet.

Pythagoras is an example of a previous usage of math reasoning to mysticism. Pythagorean thinking is an integral part of our modern day culture, and yet, many of us do not know it. Here is a short history of Pythagoras for those who do not know anything other than "some of the squared legs equals the squared hippopotamus".

Concerning any right triangle, the sum of the squares of the two legs – shorter sides -- added together equals the square of the hypotenuse – longer side. Figure 1-2 triangle *abc*: (*a*) and (*b*) are the legs, and (*c*) is the hypotenuse. ($a^2 + b^2 = c^2$)

Leg (*a*) squared plus leg (*b*) squared equals (*c*) squared. This is the Pythagorean theorem. It is about all anybody learns about Pythagoras in school. And…this formula changed the world of Mankind.

Up to this time in the ancient world, it was thought that every number that existed could be expressed as a fraction, *a/b* (a rational number -- a repeating decimal). There were no exceptions. Any number in existence was expressed as a fraction. Even π (an irrational number) was expressed as a fraction.

Whether you are adding or subtracting, it does not make any difference (pardon the pun). You can have a negative three or a positive three: both are rational. Alternatively, you can have a negative 1/3 or a positive 1/3 (one is .333 to infinity and the other is -.333 to infinity), both are rational.

Then, Pythagoras came along. The sum of the squares of the legs of a right triangle[24] with *1* as each leg will equal *2*. The hypotenuse of that triangle is a number when multiplied by itself equals *2*. The Pythagorean theorem introduced the concept of a square root.

---

23 Lao Tzu literally means 'old man'

The square root of a number means there are irrational numbers; there are numbers that cannot be expressed as fractions -- non-repeating decimals. What determines an irrational number is a decimal that never repeats: like $\sqrt{2}$, $\sqrt{3}$, or π. Any square root that ends up as a non-repeating decimal is irrational.

From the Pythagorean School, comes our concept of irrational numbers. He completed a 'whole' system (rational and the irrational numbers together make up the real number system). <u>Our technical civilization today is based on this irrational number math system</u>: logarithms, radicals, etc. Ironically, the idea of square root created the imaginary number system also.[25]

With the advent of the Pythagorean theorem,

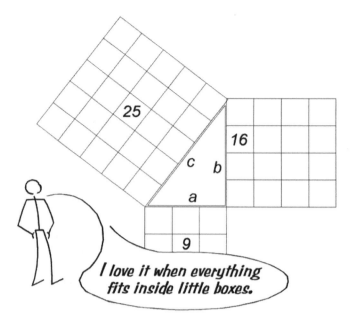

Figure 1-2, Pythagorean Theorem

mathematics makes a quantum jump in its scope and logic level. Math's logic jumps into a completely new parallel that transcends its previous logic. Herein is an excellent example of how a logic system can make cosmic like jumps, greatly exceeding its previous limits.

One book, <u>The Cartoon History of the Universe</u>,[26] tells a story of when Pythagoras (who was a vegetarian) figured out that there was this idea of irrational numbers, slaughtered 100 bulls in celebration. He had an idea of what this new concept meant. The notion of irrational numbers opened humanity's spectrum to what humanity can do with numbers. Irrational numbers made algebra, trigonometry, calculus, etc. possible.

The only thing that was missing from this number system was zero. Somebody did not think about that until that long after Pythagoras, "Oh wow, what if we had no number?"

Adding a zero, the real number system was finished, but it took humanity almost a millennium to finish what started from Pythagoras' irrational numbers.

Bear in mind most of this information that is being presented about Pythagoras is from the author's memory of things learned in college -- doing a paper. There are holes and the author encourages you to do some research on the subject matter.

Be careful though. When doing a college paper on Pythagoras the author could not find three encyclopedias that could agree on details of his life. So wherever two encyclopedias agreed the author used that in the paper.

Pythagoras was born in about the 6th century BC on the Greek island of Samos. For the first part of his life, he was chief engineer to this king on a Greek island. The king's name is unimportant. This king was very famous for the engineering marvels of his time. However, they were all Pythagoras' marvels because Pythagoras was working for the king.

Pythagoras tired of the king's court at around 40 years of age. The people were very hedonistic and he was not pleased with the 'games' of the court. Therefore, he 'split' from the king's place and he 'hung out' with Zoroaster for a while.

---

24 A triangle with a 90 degree angle.
25 Chapter 2.8 - *Postulate 7*
26 Larry Gonick, Doubleday, copyright 1990, ISBN 0-385-26520

Pythagoras spent about two to five years with Zoroaster (depending on your source). He came back to the Mediterranean and started his mystery schools. It is hard to learn anything accurate about these schools because they were one of several mystery schools of that time. Pythagorean students were sworn to secrecy. They were not to talk about what happened in the schools.

What happened inside the schools, we are not sure, but what came out of the schools is very well known.

Aristotle -- 300 years later -- dedicated a whole book to the Pythagorean schools. In some of Aristotle's books, he refers to the schools by saying 'look to my book on Pythagoreans'. Sadly -- as the author understands it, it is one of the lost books of Aristotle. That is one reason we know very little of what Pythagorean schools were about today.

The school was predominantly vegetarian.

The schools were open to both male and female. That, in itself, was relatively rare at that time. The students had to take entrance exams to enter the school. The entrance exams included math, philosophy, music, and reading.

The school -- in the end -- was a forerunner of today's colleges. They grew very influential because they produced results, and from these results, they affected the people around them. That became the downfall of the schools. This is where we are getting into the Pythagorean revolts.

The schools were influential and very effective in terms of working on things like public works. They changed people's lifestyles by having water come to their place, or having roads, or bridges and houses that would not fall down, or not having sewage in the streets.

Who became upset towards the Pythagorean schools is dependent on your history source. Some sources say it was an influential noble, but in college, the author learned the people around the schools became frightened because it was changing their lives too much. There were two Pythagorean revolts. People liked the way things were, so they burned the schools down, twice.

It is unclear what happened to Pythagoras. One source says he died in one of the schools when they burnt down the second time. Another source says that at 75 years of age he died of starvation in a temple dedicated to the muses. Since the Greek muses were regarded as sources of inspiration, that report had him dying of starvation in a temple dedicated to inspiration. Very ironic!

There are a couple of problems with studying these schools and Pythagoras.

♦ There were two Pythagorases living at about the same time. One was Pythagoras, the mystic, mathematician, and philosopher. The other Pythagoras was a very famous athletic trainer. Some of the things from one become mixed up in history with some of the things about the other. For example, Pythagorianism was predominantly vegetarian. However, the physical trainer believed in eating lots of meat. Therefore, there is this type of conflict trying to learn about these Pythagoras.

Because, there are reports about two people with the same name at the same time, perhaps this is one of the reasons there are conflicting reports regarding what happened to Pythagoras.

♦ Mentioned earlier, another reason why it is hard to learn anything about these schools is that they were one of several mystery schools of that time. The students were sworn to secrecy. Students were not to talk about what happened in the schools.

The schools themselves were forerunners to colleges, and the accomplishments of the schools are known. What happened inside the schools, we are not sure, but what the schools accomplished outside of themselves is very well known. One is, of course, the Pythagorean theorem: 'some of the square of the two legs equals the squared hippopotamus'

The schools developed the musical octave scale that we use today. This octave scale is based on pure mathematics, and it came out of those schools.

When one note is one *octave* above the next, it is twice the frequency. For instance, if I have an '*A*' note that is *440* cycles per second, the next octave up is *880* cycles per second, and the next octave above that begins at *1760* cycles per second. Usually this is done with a harp or a piano by just cutting the string length in half.

Some of the other math accomplishments of the Pythagorean schools are actually attributed to other people. However, the Pythagorean schools predate these other people. (Incidentally, a lot of stuff that came out of the Pythagorean schools is not Pythagoras' but concepts that came out of the schools themselves.) A partial list is:

- The five regular geometric solids,
- The construction of the 'Golden Section', (covered later in this chapter)
- The construction of the pentagram, and the pentacle. (covered later in this chapter)

All these are attributed to others. We know the schools worked with the five geometric solids because these ideas first showed about this time. Different sources have attributed them to Aristotle, while another source will attribute it to Plato, and yet another source will attribute them to Euclid. All these people lived at least 300 years after Pythagoras.

Figure 1-3, Regular Geometric Polygons

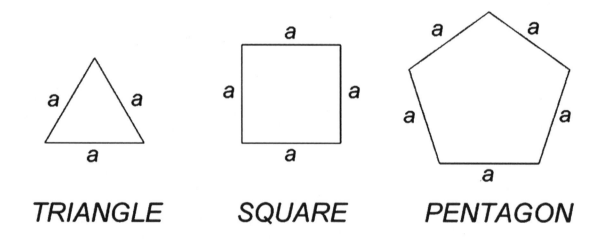

TRIANGLE SQUARE PENTAGON

What are the 5 geometric solids? The 5 geometric solids are made from regular geometric polygons: a triangle that is equilateral with side length (*a*), a square that is equilateral with side length (*a*), and a pentagon, which is five pointed and it has five equal sides length (*a*) (Figure 1-3).

Figure 1-4 shows how four equilateral triangles can form a tetrahedron (*1*), with three sides on a triangle base.

Combine the square with the triangle and you form an octahedron (The great pyramids are an aspect of the octahedron). The octahedron has eight sides that are equilateral triangles (*2*).

Assemble the square with itself and the result is obvious, it is the cube (*3*). Now, this is where things start to get sticky, because you can put 20 equilateral triangles together, to form an icosahedron (*4*). It can be seen that there are pentagon characteristics inside it.

Each solid is made out of a regular (equal sided) plane figure. An icosahedron has 20 equilateral triangles in it with 12 vertices. A dodecahedron (based on a pentagon) complements that and has 12 pentagons in it with 20 vertices.

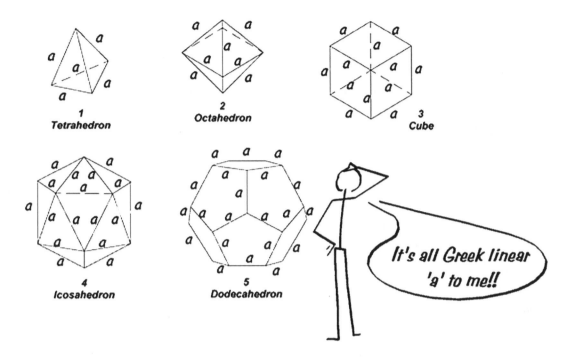

Figure 1- 4, Regular Geometric Solids

This may sound all very intellectually interesting. However, with the advent of the microscope we find that many diatoms and other microscopic sea creatures form in these shapes. Nature actually takes on these shapes.

Another major idea that came of out of the Pythagorean schools and philosophy is that 'number is immortal (Eternal)'. *Number is Eternal.* Three is eternally a three. If you take one away, the original number is no longer the concept three, the operation on the original number presented the immortal concept two. The concept of three will remain eternally the same. It will never change.

An additional Pythagorean idea that emerged from the schools is that 'everything can be expressed as number'. This idea -- that everything can be expressed as number -- is at the root of our technical civilization today. It is how we put things together. We reduce things to numbers, juggle them, and reinterpret the numbers and it becomes a bridge, computer, tape deck, or a yo-yo. It all depends on what numbers were started with, what those numbers represent, and our intention.

Now, this last idea, combined with number is immortal produces the concept that there is something immortal in everything. This implies that there is something immortal in you and me.

Pythagoras was the first western philosopher to come up with the idea of an immortal soul; and the idea was based on mathematical related reasoning. He comes up with the same concepts that other mystics have come up with, but he bases his on logical mathematical thinking.

This math reasoning is also the behind Pythagorean vegetarianism. He saw life in everything. Everything became sacred to him. What he saw obliged him to take what he knew and improve the human condition, applying his knowledge. His intention was to improve the rest of the world with it. That, in the end, is what got him in trouble. Not everybody wanted things changed.

Chapter 10 introduces Socrates' *Allegory of the Cave*. A similar thing happened to Pythagoras as did the main character in the allegory. Although he was right in the end, people fought him to death because he was trying to change something that they did not want changed.

In order to summarize what today's civilization owes Pythagoras and his schools, the contributions will be broken it down into two categories: contributions to mathematics and math related contributions.

1) Mathematical contributions
    a) Rational Numbers
        i) Math enters a whole new dimension
        ii) Made the real number set and the imaginary number set possible
    b) Everything can be expressed in number. This is at the core of our technical civilization today
    c) Number is eternal…it never changes
    d) Advanced geometry predating Euclid
        i) Construction of the Golden Section
        ii) Pentagram construction
        iii) Geometric solids
            (1) Appearance predates Euclid and Plato
            (2) Shapes of microscopic life
2) Math related contributions
    a) Octave system of music
        i) 1 octave above the previous octave is twice the frequency
        ii) Musical harmonics become math proportions
    b) Advanced public works
    c) One of the first colleges
        i) Entrance exams on numerous subjects
        ii) Co-ed
    d) First western philosopher proposing an immortal soul
    e) A spiritual respect for all life

Impressive if you consider this was all done within a 30-year period. Except for *Exercise and Lab 2* at the end of the chapter, the rest of this chapter will concern itself with the core concepts behind western sacred geometry (trivia).

1.5 - Mysticism and Mathematics

$\mathcal{T}$ he last two parts of this chapter continues the previous section and helps illustrate a logic order perceived in nature by the ancients. As stated before, the western ancients long believed that any number could be expressed as a proportion or a fraction. (And, as stated in the previous section, π was an already recognized proportion in Pythagoras' time. It is a proportion of the diameter of a circle to the distance around the circumference. The irony of this idea is that π is a proportion, and it is a proportion that cannot be expressed as a fraction. It is a definite proportion, but cannot be expressed as a rational number.)[27]

As the ancients observed phenomenon and started to express things in numbers, they noticed there were two proportions that reoccurred throughout living nature. One is π. Everything tries to approach a circle and never quite gets there. Pi is a mathematical ideal or <u>limit</u> and it does not exist in nature. Nature constantly tries to reach that perfect circle, but it

---

[27] Looking at the engineering capabilities of ancient civilizations, it can be determined how good the civilization was in engineering by their concept of π. The Hebrews value of π was three. Whereas for other civilizations -- Greeks or the Phoenicians -- it was 22/7ths.

never quite gets there.[28] A cross-section of your arm or a tree or a raindrop all approaches a circle. The orbit of a planet approaches a circle but it never quite gets there. Pi is one of these reoccurring math proportions that the ancients observed.

Nature strives towards containment that forms a circle. The concept of containment or a whole is more important than the concept of the circle. It is the containment idea shows up with the math proportion π and a circle. Mathematical representation of an abstract human concept occurs in nature. The concept of containment, of being a whole, tends to appear hand in hand with the mathematical proportion of π that determines a circle.

If these ancients noticed π is a limit to nature, what is it limiting? If there is something like a circle of containment, what is it containing? This introduces the other mathematical proportion that the ancients observed: the golden section or mean. It is referred to in this book as ϕ (Figure 1-5).

What is the mathematical expression for Golden Section? The quantity one plus the square root of five divided by two (Figure 1-5, *II*). The Golden Section proportion is that

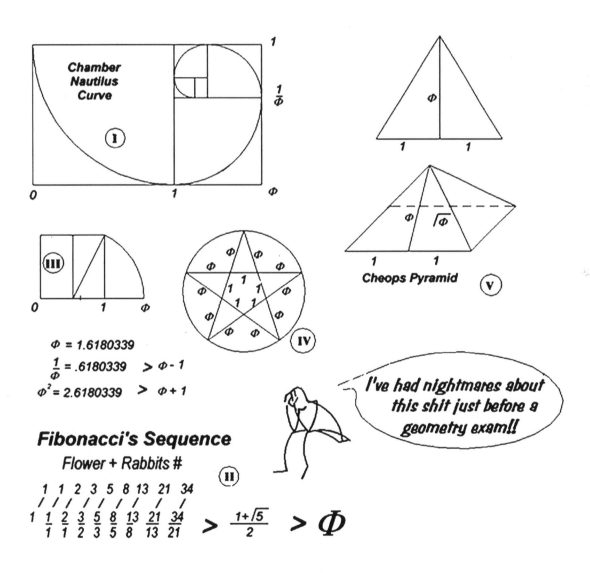

Figure 1-5, The Golden Section or Mean

---

28 Asymptotic limit

quantity to one.

The golden section is a very specific mathematical proportion. Nature emerges from itself -- extends itself -- in this proportion. It determines the spiral of a chamber nautilus shell (Figure 1-5, *I*). It is also in the spiral on pinecones, how a pinecone grows out of itself. It is also present in the multiplication rate of rabbits. It is within the number sequence of multi-flowered floweret (*II*). To restate, the golden section is the proportion in which life emerges out of itself.

This may seem intellectually interesting, and when ϕ is used in art and architecture, the golden section creates the most pleasing proportion to the human eye (*III*). Carpenters call this the 5/8 rule. It is used in the great pyramid of Cheops and the Parthenon.

One experiment that has been done in an art class is to give students a piece of paper with different rectangles of various proportions on it. Each rectangle would have a different number or letter inside it. This paper is passed around and the students are asked to note what rectangle had the most pleasing proportion to their eye; then would compare choices. Invariably, the students tended to pick the rectangle based on the golden section.

This proportion also determines the pentagram.[29] As stated previously, the pentagram and pentagon are based on a geometric construction that is attributed to Euclid. However, it was developed at least as early as the Pythagorean schools (~300 years before Euclid). The pentagram was the symbol worn by the Pythagorean students. (The students wore the pentagram on their chests, as a pendant, with the Greek letters inside meaning health.) The pentagram is not only constructed with the golden section; it contains over 200 golden sections within it.

In reference to the mystical use of mathematics, when the golden section and π are used together, it presents some unusual circumstance. The two proportions in which life physically manifests are being used. The pentacle (Figure 1-5, *IV*) is one example.

Another example of the two proportions used together is the great pyramid of Cheops (*V*).[30]

The great pyramid of Cheops is based on the golden section by dividing the side of the base in half and giving it the value of one. The face triangle's altitude is the golden section or ϕ, or 1.6180339 -- Figure 5-1, *V*. Where the pentacle has over 200 golden sections, the great pyramid has an infinite number of golden sections.

How does π relate to this? If the sides of the face

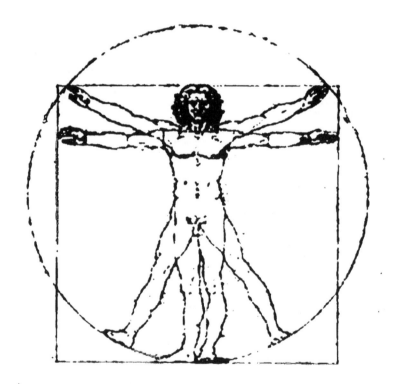

Figure 1-6, di Vinci Drawing -- Vitruvian Man

---

29 There is a geometric construction where ϕ divides a circle into ten equal parts.

30 And is around 1600 years older than the pentagram.

of the Cheops pyramid are raised a little over one minute of one degree (1/21,600 of a circle), the altitude of the pyramid divided into the base area will equal π. In the pyramid -- like nature -- π is implied just beyond the actual physical proportions that are determined by the golden section. The place of power (King's Chamber) in the pyramid is when the altitude is divided by the golden section.

All kinds of weird mathematical things happen with this number. When you multiply ϕ times itself (square it), you have your original number (ϕ) plus 1 (Figure 1-5, *III* [$\phi^2 = \phi + 1$]). The inverse of the Golden Section -- $1/\phi$ or ϕ^{-1} -- equals the golden section minus one [$1/\phi = \phi - 1$]. It is almost as if it is some kind of derivative identity number of calculus. It is really a bizarre number. Any exponential of ϕ will equal some whole number multiplied times ϕ, plus a whole number; although the original number (ϕ), is an irrational number. The whole numbers involved will be of Fibanocci's sequence (Figure 1-5, *II*).

Many disciplines and mystical studies use mathematics symbolically: numerology and such. In those systems, numbers are used as symbols that represent human archetypes or ideas. When building forms, it is more pragmatic if the mathematics of nature manifesting in form is used. That is why π and ϕ were very important to the ancients when constructing something.
Figure 1-6 gives an example of how Leonardo de Vinci divided the human body into the Golden Section.

In Chapter 3, life energy will be talked about. The use of the two mathematical proportions, in which life comes out of and contains itself, can create a life resonance condition independent of any human involvement. What does this mean? Different things can occur to something placed inside such an object.

1.6 - The Pentacle vs. the Pyramid

$\mathcal{T}$he pentacle and the pyramid use π and ϕ in different manners. The pentacle has a matrix of over 200 Golden Sections within it. The pentacle's ϕ proportions are in conjunction with one demonstrated π proportion. The pyramid of Cheops has a mathematical infinity of Golden Sections within its matrix to one implied π. A comparison of these two figures parallels a comparison between a finite matrix to an infinite matrix.
Because π and ϕ are the two proportions that living matter tends to manifest. Their usage has an effect on living matter, a sympathetic resonance of sorts. This kind of effect can be seen when living matter is placed in the different matrixes. The energy we are dealing with is subtle (life), so the effects are subtle.[31]

What is sympathetic resonance? First off, resonance is a way for an object to store energy through movement. The amount of energy that can be stored can exceed the physical capabilities of storage unit. An excellent example of this is the shattering of a glass with a high note. Another example is Tesla and his white noise generator that almost leveled New York City.
In physics, sympathetic resonance occurs in the example of two tuning forks of the same frequency (let us say *A*). Place the tuning forks on opposite sides of a room. Strike one tuning fork and the tuning fork across the room will vibrate. The two tuning forks are usually the same size (have the same math dimensions) and the same material. It does not work very well if they are the same dimensions and different material: one tuning fork is made of iron while the other is made of balsa wood.
In keeping with this though, anything tuned to *A* will also resonate: guitar strings, a harmonica reed, a chime, etc. All radio frequency telecommunications is based on sympathetic

---

31 Science has yet to devise a way to measure life.

resonance. *RF* (radio frequency) transmission through the air would not be possible without it. The front end of a *TV* is tuned to the frequency put out by the station's transmitter, and this coil capacitor combination resonates in sympathy with the transmitter.

This sympathetic resonance is concept will be returned to, and is somewhat important. Part of the purpose of this book is to help you tune your mind/matrix to the truth. Or...getting you to resonate to God's Truth.[32]

Back to the pentacle and pyramid, both have a limited low-level sympathetic resonance effect. For increased effect, the material of construction of the pentacle and pyramid should be picked such that it is conducive to life resonance (living matter for example). Remember the tuning fork made of balsa wood. Although it may have the right numbers (dimensions) as the steel, it will not work very well. A life tuning fork made of rock (like the pyramid) will be somewhat limited.

Both pentagram and Cheops pyramid have been used in conjunction with metaphysics and magic for thousands of years. In addition, there are numerous schools of thought as to why they are used. It is because mathematics is being used in a mystical manner. These proportions are tuning forks of life energy. The energy in nature manifests itself in these particular proportions and as these proportions are used within these structures, these structures start resonating to that energy. Very simple.

The pentacle's finite matrix tends to give it a passive role. The pentacle's low-level resonance limits its usage to that of a low-level amplifier or a container. Hence, the pentacle's usage in ritualistic thaumaturgical magic as a place of protection. These effects are difficult to study consistently on an empirical physical level, because internal conditions of 'magical operators' -- mages -- differ, how do you measure life's low-level amplification, and contain creative life energies.

The infinite matrix of the pyramid allows a more readily observable effect, albeit also subtle. There are documented effects on non-sentient organic matter plus its abilities to affect plant growth and putrefaction.

On sentient organisms (human beings), a different pattern of effects begins to emerge. A number of books the author remembers from old research chronicled the effects on people who have spent an <u>extended</u> amount of time (over 3 days) in the Cheops king's chamber (the focal point of the resonance). These reports indicate a change can occur with that person. The reports indicate a tendency to a fracture of their temporal reality (the author's words). This can show up as a revelation or an epiphany of sorts . This change can also manifest as a tendency toward a psychotic episode.[33] Because the pyramid is based on mathematics, it is neutral. What comes out is dependent on what goes in. 'Garbage in: garbage out.'

This why the Great Pyramid is regarded by some schools of thought as not as a tomb; but, a place of metaphysical initiation (complete with air tubes).

The mathematical basis of the pentacle and the pyramid makes them neutral. With a T-square (which is neutral), a person can build a house, or use it for cracking walnuts. Usage is dependent on the motivations of the operator. The same applies to π and ϕ.

This brings this book to the next chapter in which the logic format for this book begins. An Absolute Logic Matrix is introduced in the form of the postulates and theorems.

Everybody's logic matrix -- mind -- has elements of truth and untruth in it. As stated in the prologue (the quotation from the Lotus Sutra), "To rid yourself of all delusions (or all untruths) is the great causal event. The mind has nothing to do with thinking because its fundamental source is empty. Discard false views. This is the great causal event."

---

32 Chapter 4.8, Ring My Bell

33 As the author understands it, no one is allowed to spend an entire night in the King's Chamber of the Cheops great pyramid anymore. Again, this information comes from mostly forgotten research sources from many years ago.

However, <u>you</u> must make choices for this event to occur. <u>You</u> must make choices that foster conditions and facilitate the truth within you.

When an individual begins programming more Truths in his/her/its personal matrix, and decreases the untruths, this action is going to have and effect. That person starts participating in the Eternal aspect of Creation more, just because he/she/it is dealing in its language.

The main points of Chapter 1 are:

- The 'ringing' and silence of the first assignment.
- The concept of sympathetic resonance.
- The concept of a 'coordinated being'
- This chapter is only an introduction to the idea that the union of mathematical logic and mysticism is not new.

******************************************

Exercise and Lab 2: Creating Mandalas

This homework lesson is to make your own mandala or yantra. In the appendix, is a set of drawings. One part of that set contains templates for making your own mandala. The other part of that contains mandalas that were made from the mandala template designated *5 (easy)*. There are figures arrayed throughout this book as examples of the assignment. These figures present various shadings modes to show different effects.

A note about sketching and shading

Sketching is for people who cannot draw. You need a line, know you cannot draw it exactly, so you draw a bunch of little lines, and their accumulation presents the line you want (hopefully).

The same can be said with shading a drawing. Start lightly; and that which looks to you could be darker, lightly go over it again and again and…until you are satisfied.

The dictionary this book uses[34] defines mandala as a geometric piece of art that symbolizes the universe. Technically, a more accurate term for these figures would be a yantra.[35]

The figures made in this exercise will be used later in Chapter 6, Concerning Meditation and Disciplines. Doing the artwork, serves as an introduction to a one-point focus; and, the same artwork will be used in a later chapter as an introduction to an affirmation chant.

Since you are asked to make your own custom mandala, symbols (relevant to your intention) can be inserted into the picture.

The templates and mandalas created are provided in the Appendix are computer drawings of a mathematical construction using the proportions of π and ϕ -- pi and the Golden Section. This chapter introduced these numbers earlier. If you are going to create something, you may as well use these proportions as a structure or as something to build on. If not for aesthetic reasons, do it because of the resonant capabilities of like mathematics. Because the templates and mandalas created are based on the Golden Section, they can make some very esthetic hypnotic figures -- something that can suck your vision in and keep it there.

One part of Appendix set contains templates for making your own mandala – **Concerning the Templates**. The other part of that contains mandalas that were made from the mandala template designated *5 (easy)* -- **Concerning the Pre-drawn Figures**. These figures are arrayed throughout the book as examples, with various shadings to show different effects

---

34 American Heritage Dictionary, 3rd Edition, 1996, Houghton Mifflin Co.
35 Yantra: A Geometric meditation aid

Concerning the Templates

Templates *5 (easy)* and *5 (hard)* are based on the pentagram geometric construction that is in Euclid's geometry book. The templates *5 (easy)* and *5 (hard)* are the circles that are a result of using the golden section with π -- with a few extra circles and lines added.

Templates *4* and *8* are arranged to separate a circle into 4 or 8 sections respectively. Templates *6* and *12* divide a circle into 6 and 12 equal parts respectively. The pattern is the same with templates *7* and *14*. All still use ϕ and π.

You can use the provided computer templates to base a customized structure. To do so, take a piece of tracing paper and put it over a template. Then start, for example, with whatever line catches your eye and darken it with a pencil on the tracing paper. Pick out shapes that you see to trace and draw those out on the tracing paper.

You know you are going to make a figure, so start picking out patterns, and just follow lines. You can make a mandala squarish, anything you want. For example, Templates *4* and *8* can generate a square-like mandala/yantra. This exercise is only a starting point for you to make your own mandala, using the mathematical proportions of π and the Golden Section as guides.

This element of the assignment consists of tracing out four different mandalas with pencil using whatever templates you want.

You can 'putz' around and do that in front of the TV or something. Go over with ink the ones that you like the best. You do not have to do it 'this way', or 'that way' or any particular way. Whatever lines your eye picks out.

Please note: not drawing a line is as, or more, important than drawing a line. An example is in some of the demonstrated figures. Where there are several lines meeting, it was left open to avoid a busy-ness at that point.

A rose pattern (mandala 9)[36] was made that came out of *5 (easy)*. That was to be the logo for a Mystic Arts class. Dozens and dozens of mandalas where done, before the author finally started to see and create patterns that he really liked. He did 20 different ones before he finally got the rose.

After you trace some lines, and have some outlines of several basic mandalas, make copies of each mandala. Then go back with pencil and start shading the copies to your preference.

The author found, when teaching this, that black and white figures work better than color figures in the exercise presented in Chapter 6. The black and white simplifies the amount of data coming in to the mind.

This exercise can be just the beginning point to more mystical artwork if you wish to take this further.

Concerning the Pre-drawn Figures

If the previous element seems like too much work (which it is a lot), the pre-drawn mandalas in the appendix are available to be copied, shaded, or altered by you. It is for that purpose they are in the appendix. They can save you some work and still illustrate the one-point focus concept used later.

On the other hand, for the Chapter 6 exercise, you can research mandalas and find four different other figures you would like to work with. Remember though, the figure you choose must not be so 'busy' that it distracts. This may counteract the effect of the Chapter 6 affirmation exercise.

And...if you pick a picture or symbol (as opposed to making one), you may miss the one-point focus reference used later.

➢ *This homework assignment is to make four different mandalas to be used in a later exercise; or, find four mandalas that you can use.*

---

36 See Appendix E: Mandala Examples

➢ *Construct at least one mandala or yantra <u>without</u> symbols, words, figures, animals, etc. -- i.e. purely black and white and geometric.*

1.8 – Questions

1) How does an individual recognize truth?

2) The problem/s with reading this book are?
   a) it's a construct
   b) it's symbolic communication
   c) the math/science format
   d) the author doesn't know how to write
   e) the metaphysical subject matter
   f) all of the above

3) The oldest logic system in the world is?

4) Whom did Pythagoras spend several years with?

5) How do you square a hippopotamus?

6) The Pythagorean schools were a forerunner of what?

7) Pythagoras was the first western philosopher to hypothesize what?

8) Truth works when it is _____?

9) The two mathematical proportions that living matter tends to manifest in are?

10) What are the important things about this chapter?

11) What was the Axial Age?

12) Give a physical example of sympathetic resonance.

13) What is a thought system construct?

Chapter 2

Postulates and Basic Theorems

2.1 - What is Mathematics and Its History

*T*he core of this book is dependent on a system of postulates and theorems. This chapter presents an example of the logic system inherent within God's Creation using a math-reasoning model. As stated in the previous chapter, the words are not the reality. However, if nothing was put into words, nothing could be expressed. Some kind of symbol system has to be used to get the subject across.

First, a little math history is in order. This may help you establish a reference to math's roots.

❑ In ancient times, the major river valleys (Nile, Tigris/Euphrates, Indus, and Yellow) saw the growth of large complicated civilizations. With civilization, came commerce. With commerce, came a method of keeping track of items. Math started with literally counting beans (or pigs, or cows, or figs...). This is where basic arithmetic comes from, keeping track of physical items. As 'civilization' emerged, so did mathematics.

❑ One of these river valleys, the Nile, flooded every year on a regular basis. This was great for agriculture because it deposited a layer of fertile silt every year. However, the flooding played havoc with property markers. The Egyptians developed a way to restore land boundaries relatively quickly for plowing and sowing. And, plane geometry is born. Somebody got a bright idea of going vertical with geometry and the wonders of Egypt begin.

The Egyptians played with geometry for a couple of thousand of years. Years later, Euclid comes around and compiles a book on these geometric constructions. Math evolved from keeping track of goods to keeping track of land (both physicals).

This evolution occurred over thousands of years; it did not happen over night. Some time, in geometry's development, math transcended physical form. Meaning, some ideals expressed in math are too perfect for actual physical expression. Some examples of this are:

♦ A mathematical infinity can go any direction forever; and, if you hold up two fingers with a space in-between, there is an infinite set of mathematical points between your fingers.

♦ There is no such thing as a perfect circle or a straight line in nature. They are mathematical ideals that nature approaches but never reaches.

♦ Even in our day of technological wizardry, we deal with tolerances of error. It is impossible to get the physical form to match exactly the math ideals.

❏ Over time, while using it, Man played with numbers and made some observations. In time, it was noticed that there were numerous laws that determine how numbers work. About a thousand years after Euclid compiled his book of geometry, arithmetic laws were codified, and algebra begins. Most of this chapter's theorems' constructions can be related to the basic algebraic law of association:

If   A = B   *or*   If   A = B

And   B = C   And   B ≠ C

Then   A = C   Then   A ≠ C

❏ Play some more, combine algebra with geometry, and trigonometry along with analytical geometry unfolded.

❏ All this evolved around (and with) Man's understanding of physical form. The math understanding of those times was strong with static physical systems; and physical form is rarely static. Drop a ball and watch it speed up as it falls.

The analytical geometry expressions for explaining this were long and complicated. Then a person called Isaac Newton comes along with this thing – calculus -- that can mathematical describe a falling ball easily. Again, math's evolution is related around describing physical events.

Mathematics is the logic system of physical form.

All mathematical systems are based on an assembly of postulates and the theorems. What is a postulate? A postulate in geometry is an observation (a perception[1]). It is something somebody observes, under a given set of conditions. <u>A postulate cannot be proved or disproved.</u> It just is. Anybody who recreates the relevant set of conditions can make the same observation.

As mathematics evolved, a procedure developed for the establishment of postulates. Somebody comes up with an observation. After a couple hundred years it serves as an axiom - - if nobody can find any exceptions to it -- the axiom becomes a postulate. If one exception is found, it ceases to be a postulate.

A postulate is readily verifiable, although it cannot be proven. However, verification of a postulate is dependent on a set of conditions that apply to the postulate. The geometric postulate of parallel lines and an intersecting line is an example. (Given two parallel lines, a line that intersects one parallel line will intersect the other parallel line.) The conditions for that postulate are the parallel lines (the operator sets up the parallel lines) and the intersecting line (the operator sets up the intersecting line).

However, if the conditions are not present, it is impossible to verify the postulate. Therefore, a person cannot verify this postulate if they do not have the lines and their arrangement. (Not to mention a pencil, a piece of paper, and a straight edge.) You need to have the conditions first before the postulate is observed.

What is a theorem? One dictionary states that a theorem is a proposition that is provable based on explicit assumptions.[2] Theorems are subject to proofs or disproofs, while postulates are not. This is because they are not an observation per se, but a way of thinking about an observation or a series of observations.

For example, the Pythagorean theorem is one: $a^2 + b^2 = c^2$. One proof was made of this theorem by breaking the sides of a [*3, 4, 5*] or a [*6, 8, 10*] triangle into squares showing that this was true.

---

1 Perceptions are covered in depth in Chapter 4, Realities and the Human Matrix
2 American Heritage Dictionary, 3rd Edition, 1996, Houghton Mifflin Co.

A theorem is composed of elements of established logical thinking or perceptions. A theorem has an end-point/conclusion, a product of some form due to logical thinking. The elements that make up the logical thinking can be either postulates or previously proven theorems. Theorems are places and conclusions that an individual comes to within that logical order system. Through one form of the logic system, a theorem is derived. Nevertheless, the logic system (like math), being a complete logic system -- when folded back upon the theorem -- proves the theorem. There is a proof involved one way or another with a theorem, whereas postulates do not have a proof.

An example how postulates and theorems are at the core of math and related is:

- The concept of *1* is a postulated quality. It can be neither proven nor disproven.
- *1 + 1 = 2* is a theorem
- *2 – 1 = 1* is the proof of the theorem

The ideal being, through a logic system, a conclusion is made. Within a wholistic logic system, a proof occurs when the individual comes to the same conclusion another way. Therefore, whether you are inducing or deducing... the results are the same. The conclusion should be the same.

There is a major irony around mathematics. It goes like this: (While, giving you a preview of this chapter's format.)

Given: All mathematics is based on postulates and theorems.

Given: Theorems are ultimately based on postulates.

Then: **All mathematics is ultimately based on postulates**

and

Given: All mathematics is ultimately based on postulates.

Given: Postulates cannot be proven.

Then: **All mathematics is ultimately based on something that cannot be proven.**

Because mathematics is based on postulates, it is based on something that cannot be proven. This is cryptical, especially, with something as concise as math. This idea is also typical of the spiritual/mystical/metaphysical sciences.

To conclude this section, this chapter uses words, gives them specific definitions, and treats them as algebraic quantities. It presents a list of postulates and theorems with an accompanied reasoning. Being lazy, The writer of this book is going to leave the proofs of these theorems up to you, the reader.

This book uses the postulate and theorem format in order to introduce to you some very ancient mystical/metaphysical/spiritual concepts. As stated previously, most of the presented information is not new. The information and concepts contained within this book can be found at the core of many religions and philosophies (mystical and otherwise).

Be advised: The word 'God' is being used in this book as a generic term for the Divine. God-Goddess, to something that is All One, the concept of sexuality is *non-sequitar* to the actuality of One. The closest accurate concept may be "The Force".

Whatever you give to Love, it will use. As long as the sexuality concept does not interfere with the Love, Love will use it. Periodically this book will use pronouns (He, Him, Himself…); and…this is for convenience only, to avoid He-She-It ("he 'sheeeit'").

2.2 - Postulate 1   There is one God, the Source-less Source, the Formless Form; Absolute Will that is Eternal and Infinite in nature.

*T*his first postulate introduces a Source, a Oneness, or a fundamental singularity. This is not a new concept. History contains thousands of years of numerous religions and philosophies from places all over the world that recognizes a Source. This postulate establishes some of the qualities of that Source: formless, Eternal, Infinite, and One. From the contained definitions of terms[3] and this postulate, several theorems can be derived. Regarding Will, one can state:

Postulate 1	Given:	God is the One Source.
Postulate 1	Given:	God is Absolute Will.
THEOREM 1	Then:	**God is the one source of Will.**

or

There is no Will but God's.

or

God and Will are One.

Theorem 1 is generated from the postulated God. It expresses God as Absolute Will and the One Source. *Theorem 1* also states God is the one source of Will, there is no Will but God's. God and Will are One. The definition of terms defines *will* as intrinsic ability. God is the only One that can do anything; all abilities or anything that is possible comes from God. This will be reaffirmed later with *Theorem 11B*.

In terms of Eternity and all aspects of Eternal nature, it can be said:

Postulate 1	Given:	God is the one Source.
Postulate 1	Given:	God is Eternal.
THEOREM 2	Then:	**God is the one Source of Eternal.**

or

God and Eternity are One.

God is the one Source and God is Eternal. *Theorem 2* states God is the one Source of Eternity and all that is Eternal; or God and Eternity are inseparable -- are One. By definition of Eternity, this God is outside all temporal/spatial references. There is no beginning or end, any place, or time that it is not applicable.

There are other theorems that can be derived. (Though many of these theorems are obvious, they must be stated.)

Definition:	Given:	Infinite is boundless and without limits.
Postulate 1	Given:	God is Infinite.
THEOREM 3	Then:	**God is boundless and without limits.**

From these theorems, several corollaries can be made:

---

3 Appendix C

THEOREM 3A	Will is boundless and without limits.
THEOREM 3B	Eternity is boundless and without limits.

Infinity is boundless and without limits: God is Infinite, denotes God is boundless and without limits. Will is boundless and without limits because God and Will are One. Eternity is boundless and without limits because God and Eternity are One.

What does this mean? As the math infinity of real numbers contains infinite sets of other numbers (integers, even, odd, rational, positive, negative, irrational, etc.), let us say God's Infinity contains all infinities within it. (Fractal geometry deals with infinities that contain an infinite number of sets of infinities.)[4] Look at God's Infinity this way: God's Infinity is the One Infinity that contains <u>all</u> infinities (potential or realized).

The first postulate and the five theorems that come from it establish the qualities of the One Source: Eternal and boundless. The important idea is that they are all one thing. One quality implies the other; that one source implies one Will, Eternal ability, etc.

The first postulate and its theorems are a beginning reference to the rest of the postulates and theorems. And, be advised when dealing with such a comprehensive fundamental unity as God -- a fundamental simplicity, the question of elements or theorem parts attempts to put into separate parts one thing. What is being referred to are aspects or characteristics of this Oneness.

In some ways, to describe the Divine in any symbol system - words or math - is like trying to draw a sphere with straight lines. A sphere is one 3-dimensional non-linear object, but a description using 1 dimensional lines may have a number of linear elements (short straight lines) to express or hint at the sphere, similar to a geodesic dome. The mind of the perceiver must make a mental 'jump' in order to comprehend the whole that is being expressed.

This section introduces one ancient reoccurring concept:

Ancient truth → *There is One God, A Source, A Divine...*

2.3 - Postulate 2   God's Absolute Will actualizes as an Absolute Eternal Love.

$\mathcal{T}$he concept of Divine Love is introduced In this postulate. Because, God's Love is so far beyond any form of description, this book will not attempt to describe what that Love is. *I AM A I* 's definition for Love will focus on what Love is <u>not</u>. Love is defined as an ageless or eternal selfless state, which is intrinsically non-exclusive.[5] This is very important: Love is <u>intrinsically non-exclusive</u>.

This definition helps to reaffirm the concept of 'a whole'. There can be nothing other than this non-exclusive Oneness because if there is, it is not excluded from the whole. This postulate reinforces the secondary aspect or attribute of the Divine: its intrinsic wholeness. God's Will actualizes in Love, and Love's Absolute Ability to be whole -- One.

This concept of Eternal Love and non-exclusive wholeness presents an underlying theme, which will be carried through the rest of this work. Even though -- through our perceptions -- there can appear to be a fracture of that wholeness, patterns can be seen to form. Whatever pieces or elements we find must fit into the <u>whole</u> pattern, if it is to be true.

A Source has been established in *Postulate 1*. *Postulate 2* presents a source of what. Later postulates, theorems, and chapters will depict a pattern of manifestation. If you just sit in

---

4 Fractal geometry can boggle the brain. It is an infinity of infinities...infinitely. And, if you examine one infinitesimally small element of that infinity, <u>it will be the exact same infinity it was taken out of</u>.

5 Appendix C

Absolute Love, you will apply the rest of this work or book. If you work with this Absolute Love, you do not have to know the rest of the book. (Or, you may already know the rest of this book.) Unfortunately, must of us do not have a grasp on what this Absolute Love is, because it is way beyond our mortal limited human understanding.

The concept of Eternal Love can give one something to fall back on. Putting *Theorem 2* from the first postulate together with the second postulate, the result is:

Theorem 2	Given:	God and Eternity are One.
Postulate 2	Given:	God's Will actualizes as an Eternal Love.
THEOREM 4	Then:	**God and Love are One.**

or

There is no Love but God's.

Now that this last statement has been made, it follows:

THEOREM 4A   **Eternity and Love are One.**

Plus the corollaries:

THEOREM 5   **That which is not Love is not God.**

And its counterpart:

THEOREM 5A   .   **That which is not Love is not Eternal.**

Theorem 4A says Eternity and Love are One. Furthermore, the other theorems are obverses of this concept and are stated: that which is not Love is not God, and that which is not Love is not Eternal. This is so, because we are dealing with one thing. These obverses will become more important later as we cover the last postulate and its theorems.

Up to this point, we have Absolute Will conjoined with an Absolute Love. The definitions, and the postulates with their theorems, present an Absolute ability that is non-exclusive. However, we are dealing with a fundamental unity here, and the terms 'inclusion' and 'exclusion' are not relevant. It does become relevant when there *appears* to be a fragmentation of that unity. As stated earlier, a further examination of that *apparent* fragmentation will reveal an underlying unity.

It can be said, from the first two postulates and their theorems that Love is outside all spatial/temporal references, just as Will is. This makes it far beyond temporal – mortal -- finite human minds. This sure can put a cramp in romantic poetry.

This section introduces another ancient reoccurring truth:

Ancient truth → *God is Love.*

2.4 - Postulate 3   God's Absolute Love has an Absolute, Logical, and Eternal Mind.

*D*ue to the inadequacies of language, tension between ideas appears to occur in the concept of the unity of God and of logic. In this work, logic is defined as a gestalt[6] containing a pattern of interconnected relationships. Tension appears with the word *interconnectedness,* which implies a plurality. Part of the tension is relieved by the concept of gestalt.

Yet the definition of gestalt introduces more plural terms: something more than the sum of its parts. These tensions are brought about by the perceptual origin of words; that is, we see a plurality form a unity. Later in this book, it will be shown that perception has its limits. To facilitate clarity, reverse the sequence of the gestalt idea. The gestalt is not a result of the parts, but the parts are a result of the gestalt. This idea is in keeping with an order of manifestation proceeding from higher (God) to lower (physical form).

This postulate brings infinite Order and Logic to Love. Absolute Love has an Absolute order to it. Love and Wisdom are One. They are the flip sides of the same coin. We cannot have Love without Wisdom and vice versa. One comes from the other and/or infers the other. Beginning with this, the theorems generated are:

Theorem 2   Given: God and Eternity are One.

Postulate 3   Given: God's Absolute Love has an Absolute, Logical, and Eternal Mind.

THEOREM 6   Then: **God and Logical Mind are One.**

Join this with *Theorem 4*, to get:

THEOREM 6A   **Love and Logical Mind are One.**

Add the concept of Eternity to this and we get:

THEOREM 6B   **Eternity and Logical Mind are One.**

Throw them all together in the soup pot and it can be said:

THEOREM 6C   **Will, Love, and Logic are One in an Eternal God.**

Again, wholeness, an Absolute Complete Oneness is presented. We have the qualities of Will, Love and Logic all put together as elements of one thing. *Postulates 4* and *5* will cover some of the qualities of this Logical Mind.

Given the fundamental unity of this subject matter, these counterparts of the previous theorems also apply:

THEOREM 7   **There is no Logic but God's.**

                                        and

THEOREM 7A   **That which is not Love is not Logical and vice versa.**

---

6 Gestalt: A physical, biological, psychological, or symbolic configuration or pattern of elements so unified as a whole that its properties cannot be derived from a simple summation of its parts. American Heritage Dictionary, 3rd Edition, 1996, Houghton Mifflin Co.

In *Theorems 7* and *7A*, we have the obverse of the two previous theorems. Since God is the One Source, God is the One Source of Love/Logic; there is no Love/Logic but God's.

With this postulate and the included theorems, a divine trinity is completed -- a one in three and a three in one: just like Father, Son, and Holy Spirit; Creator (Brahman), Destroyer (Shiva), Preserver (Vishnu); Yin -- Earth, Yang -- Heaven, and the Tao -- Way; etc. The Divine Trinity is a reoccurring theme in spiritual and mystical thought systems -- the one in three and the three in one.

How is the idea of one in three and three in one possible? The very idea introduces paradoxes.

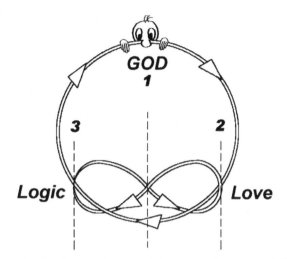

2 determines the nature of 3, as 3 generates/regenerates 2

Figure 2-1, Three in One, One in Three

Because we are defining a fundamental unity, we have to forego the words in favor of the concepts the words are trying to convey. Words and communication by words are usually dependent upon common perceptions.[7]

Figure 2-1 helps illustrate this one in three and three in one idea. In the figure, a moebius strip[8] is shown with a circle and three columns, labeled *1*, *2*, and *3*.

Column *1* represents this is one thing, the synthesis and source of columns *2* and *3*. The relationship of *2* to *3* is *2* determines the nature of *3*, while *3* generates or regenerates *2*.

This means a *2* defines a *3*. Once a *3* is defined it generates (or re-generates) a *2*. In some physical cases of this example, the *2* may, or may not, be the same identical *2* that originally defined the *3*.

In this particular representation, God's Love and Logic, it can be regarded as the same *2* (from a mortal mind's reference).

Let us look at what this means. Love defines Logic, while Logic regenerates Love. Love determines the very nature of the Logic. Once the Logic is established, it renews the Love, and this being One thing, recalls into being Love's Source.

The 3-in-1, 1-in-3 model that is being introduced here is a reoccurring pattern that repeats itself into physical form and is touched on throughout this book. Chapter 4, when covering human perceptions/desires or thoughts/emotions, returns to this idea . That chapter explains how our human mind is parallel to the Divine Mind.

Because the postulates are related in sequence for a reason, only the Will or Ability can be seen as the Causal event (*1*). Love (*2*) and Logic (*3*) are expressions, or effects, of this Ability. Stated another way: *Postulates 2* and *3* present the Absolute Ability to be Loving and Logical. Without the Will of God, Love-Wisdom would not exist.

---

7 When the common perceptions are missing, there is no communication.

8 To make a moebius strip, take a strip of paper and give the strip a half twist. Glue the ends together lengthwise with the half twist in the loop. The result, a strip of paper that started with two separate sides now has one continuous (no end) surface area.

Here are some more ancient concepts introduced in this section:

Ancient truth →   God's Love and Wisdom are One.
Ancient truth →   3-in-1, 1-in-3 nature of God.

2.5 - Postulate 4   God's Logical Mind is a matrix of Absolute Eternal Truth.

*T*his postulate introduces the concept of a Truth Matrix. To define the Truth Matrix, let us begin by examining the concept of a matrix. The root word for matrix comes from *mater*, which in some sources, means the womb.[9] A matrix is some kind of order whose gestalt has a potential to produce 'something'. (This 'something' may or may not reproduce another matrix.) Some physical examples of a matrix are the womb, DNA; a plant seed is a matrix, or the crystalline structure of solid matter that appears in metals and semi-conductors.[10] Anything that brings forth something other than itself is a matrix; it can be a door or a transition locale. The spiritual matrix idea will be expanded upon to include physical form in later chapters.

This postulate links the matrix idea with Truth. There are a couple of definitions for Truth in this work, one is, "laws by which something works". The laws of physics are part of a truth matrix and physical form is an effect of this truth matrix. The laws of metaphysics are part of the Truth Matrix.

One of the many metaphysical paradoxes that need to be addressed is the statement, "Truth is One and many". The bottom line is that Truth is One. It is our fractured perception that sees many. It is similar to looking at a circle drawn on a piece of paper through a multifaceted jewel or a kaleidoscope. There is only one circle, yet we may see many through the jewel. What we see and how we see it are actually distortions and reproductions of what is actually on the piece of paper.

On the one hand, the fractured image can be considered an illusion (a distorted or inaccurate perception). If on the other hand, the illusion is not examined and it is believed to be real, then it is also a delusion. Delusions can occur when we do not examine the illusion.

Our mortal fractured perception is like that jewel. It sees in a singularity, multiple images of that singularity. It sees both one and many. Truth is One and many; it is Eternally constant. There is only one Law/Truth and that is Love.

Due to the subject matter, and the problem with words and verbal communication, the word *Truth* and the word *Spirit* are interchangeable in this work. Truth is one and many. Spirit is one and many. They go together. However, God is the source of Spirit, while Spirit is not the source of God. (The author is unclear on whether or not this is going to make things simpler or more confusing.)

Theorem 2	Given:	God and Eternity are One.
Postulate 4	Given:	Truth is Eternal.
THEOREM 8	Then:	**God and Truth are One.**

Plus all the counterpart corollaries that go with this:

---

9 matrix: 1. A situation or surrounding substance within which something else originates, develops, or is contained;
2. The womb -- mater. Important derivatives are: mother, maternal, maternity, matriculate, matrix, matron, matrimony, metropolis, material, matter. -- American Heritage Dictionary, 3rd Edition, 1996, Houghton Mifflin Co.
10 Chapter 3

There is no Truth but God's.

and

That which is not True is not God.

Here again, is a repetition of the fundamental unity, a singularity -- a closed system. If this postulate is assembled with the concept of Eternity and Truth together, what appears is:

THEOREM 8A   **Truth and Eternity are One.**

or

That which is not Eternal is not True.

According to the definition of terms,[11] a reality is "An effect of an array of truth". The relationship of Truth to Reality is the same as the relationship of the laws/truths of physics' to physical reality (**Actual Reality**[12]). These truths (laws of physics) behind physical form are not directly perceptible: you cannot touch it, feel it, or affect them in any way. You can only feel the effects of these truths, because your body is an effect also. Yet without the Truth/truth, Reality/physical form would not exist.

Since cause and effect are linked (no cause → no effect), then it can be said:

THEOREM 8B   **That which is not True is not Real.**

Because Truth and Eternity are One (*Theorem 8A*), this logic leads us to:

THEOREM 8C   **That which is not Eternal is not Real.**

As stated earlier, the concept of Truth is one of the more elusive terms in this work to define, perhaps even more so than Love. The beginning of this section touches on some of the aspects and attributes of the Truth, and yet, there is more. No printed word or language can cover the fundamental *simplicity* of this subject matter: *One* Eternal Presence that is behind *all* form, coming from an Absolute Perfect Love, which, in turn, comes from One Absolute Cause or Will.

Again, in *Theorems 8A, B*, and *C* a unity is re-presented; this unity is Eternal, Infinite, and Boundless. This unity is the source of **Absolute** Reality (an effect of Truth). Eventually, this unity manifests into physical form.[13]

The next theorem is developed from a theorem from the last postulate, joined with a theorem from this postulate.

Theorem 6C	Given:	Will, Love and Logic are One in an Eternal God.
Theorem 8	Given:	God and Truth are One.
THEOREM 9	Then:	**Will, Love, Logic, and Truth are One in an Eternal God.**

So far, a number of things have been put together. There is presented an order of manifestation from God, to Love, to a Logical order, which consists of the Truth Matrix. With these postulates and theorems presented, Truth is not the only thing introduced. With the introduction of the matrix concept, there is a 'something' that can produce 'something else', a potential. This chapter started with God; and then went to a trinity: God, Love, Logic; and then

---

11 Appendix C
12 Chapter 4-2, What's Reality Papa?
13 Chapter 3, The Correction and the Mirror

to a Truth Matrix. What has been presented has gone from the existence of God to a potential for something.

An ancient truth introduced in this section is:

Ancient truth →   There is an order or an array to everything -- Truth (Matrix)

2.6 - Postulate 5   Creation is an Eternal effect of God's Truth Matrix.
or
Creation is an Eternal Idea within the Mind of God.

---

*T*his postulate can be expressed in at least two different ways.   One form approaches the concept from the mechanistic aspect of cause and effect.   The other is in a form that is more of an anthropomorphic reference, i.e., mind and idea.   Both are variations of the same theme.   The anthropomorphic is important for later reference.   It can lead into the mechanics of the mortal mind of Man.

The fourth postulate introduces 'something' that is potentially productive (a matrix). Creation emerges from this potential in the fifth postulate.   With this Creation, it <u>appears</u> (through the produced theorems) that God completed the Self.

Again, this book has to deal with the finite limits of words and the tensions that develop between ideas within symbolic language communication.   One tension is with the word *completed*, used in this context, is how can that which is totally whole and complete, be completed?   The source was always there.   It is from the reference of perception that there appears to be a completion.

Within the Eternal Mind of God, there is an idea.   Since this Eternal Idea has an Infinite Will or Limitless Ability behind it, it becomes an 'actuality'.   The Source is outside of time; the Mind is outside of time; Truth is outside of time; the Idea is outside of time; and so God's Creation is outside of time.   This leads to the next theorems.

Theorem 2	Given:	God and Eternity are One.
Theorem 8	Given:	God's Creation is Eternal.
THEOREM 10	Then:	**God and Creation are One.**

A significant corollary is contained in this theorem.   If God created outside of time and the creative process and its effect are outside of time, then:

THEOREM 10A   **The God-Creation process occurs in Eternity.**

or

The God-Creative process is Eternally occurring.

This theorem will become very important later in this book.   With this theorem, 'time folding'[14] and all the wonders of life, miracles, magic, and *ESP* or psychic phenomena[15] are possible and explainable.

This theorem means that God's Creation is not the big bang, as we would like to perceive it.   The God-Creative process is eternally happening.   (There may have been a temporal physical big bang as an element of it.)

---

14 Chapter 3.7, Time Ignor-ance
15 Chapters 10, 9, and 7 respectively.

The God-Creative process happens outside of time. This God-Creative process is occurring as the author is typing this text, just as this God-Creative process is occurring as you are reading this text. It is only because this Creative process is Eternally occurring that we can create as human beings. It is our participation in this Eternal God-Creative process that allows us to be, as well as to create. This book will return to this idea later.[16]

It is difficult for a finite temporal mind, which sees the creative process as linear in time, with beginning and an end, to grasp the Eternal non-linear Creative process. Our temporal perception of cause and effect to an event sees: creation at one point in time, and this creation appears not to have existed previously. A temporal mind will perceive an Eternal Creation as if it always has been. From the infinite Eternal Mind's reference, once it has created, the Creation (and all its elements) has always been.

This conundrum can make the argument between Creationists and Darwinists moot. The eternal/temporal reference of this book can have some interesting twists. When physical existence was created, it is possible for it to have been created with a complete history (with a specific future) at any point in a given time line.

Remember, we are dealing with Infinite God here; our limited mortal minds tend to project limits on an Eternal God that may not be there.

Putting the first postulate together with the fifth, this theorem occurs:

Postulate 1	Given:	God is the One Source.
Postulate 5	Given:	God created Creation.
THEOREM 11	Then:	**God is the one source of Creation.**

God is the one source of Creation and God is One with Creation (*Theorem 10*, God and Creation are One.), therefore:

| **THEOREM 11A** | **The God-Creation process is a closed system within God.** |

Again, this re-presents the already supplied fundamental unity of a singularity. Although words tend to cut and break things apart, we are still dealing with a holistic whole; a system Absolutely closed within God. God's Perfect Love, by its non-exclusive nature, leaves nothing out.

Since God is the one Absolute Source, nothing is excluded, and there is only one Creation, then:

| **THEOREM 11B** | **The God-Creation process is the only Creative process.** |

Postulate 3 introduces the idea of reoccurring patterns or parallels -- 3-in-1 and 1-in-3. It is with this theorem that these patterns and parallels will begin to show themselves. Because everything we know is a result of this Creative process and this is the only Creative process, everything we know is going to parallel, reflect, or pattern itself on this Creative process. This can make some things a little easier to understand. Later, in Chapter 3, this concept of patterns and parallels will be illustrated in more depth.

Taking a theorem from the second postulate and linking it with a theorem from this postulate, the result is:

| *Theorem 4* | Given: | God and Love are One. |
| *Theorem 10* | Given: | God and Creation are One. |

---

16 Chapters 3, 4, 9, and 10

| THEOREM 12 | Then: | **Creation and Love are One.** |

or

Creation is Love.

The last theorem begins to show the true nature of God's Creation. This Creation, from God's Truth Matrix, has the qualities of *Theorems 12* through *12C*. Combining previous theorems with this one generates:

THEOREM 12A	**Creation is God's Logic.**
THEOREM 12B	**Creation is God's Truth.**
THEOREM 12C	**Creation is Reality.**

Creation and Reality are One. This is in keeping with the definition that a reality is an effect of an array of truth. So…Creation is Reality and an effect of God's Truth Matrix.

Putting the last theorems together with *Theorem 9* derives:

Theorem 9	Given:	Will, Love, Logic, and Truth are One in an Eternal God.
Theorem 10	Given:	God and Creation are One.
THEOREM 13	Then:	**Will, Love, Logic, and Truth are One in an Eternal Creation.**

This reintroduces a very ancient idea:

Theorem 9	Given:	Will, Love, Logic, and Truth are One in an Eternal God.
Theorem 13	Given:	Will, Love, Logic, and Truth are One in an Eternal Creation.
THEOREM 14	Then:	**"God Created like unto Himself."**

or

To Create, God extended Himself.

This idea is several millennium years old, and subject to about as many interpretations. It is in the book of Genesis. It is as if God reproduced.

The erroneous idea of God Created God might occur here. Creation reflects the Mind of God, just as art reflects the mind of the artist, or ideas reflect the mind of the inventors. It is something that came from the Mind of God and in doing so, extended him. This is also saying that the Mind of God is within Creation itself -- a closed circle.

Another way to look at this is through the concept of math infinities. It was said earlier that God is the Absolute Infinity, the one Infinity that contains all infinities. Let us say God's Love is one infinity removed from this Absolute Infinity. God's Logical Mind is one infinity removed from God's Love. The Truth Matrix is one infinity removed from God's Logical Mind, and the Creation is one infinity removed from the Matrix.

The result -- Creation -- still has infinities within infinities…infinitely. Yet, Creation is a few infinities short of being God. However, from our finite limited temporal reference – mortal mind reference, these infinities can be considered the relatively the same.

This chapter began with the Absolute in the first postulate and advanced to the fourth postulate. In the fourth postulate, the potential to produce is hinted at. With the fifth postulate, production occurs and God produces a facsimile. The presented path follows from Absolute potential, to actuality, to this actuality extending itself. God extended himself.

Connecting to *Theorem 11b*, with *Theorem 14*, this idea occurs:

Theorem 11B   Given: The God-Creative process is the only creative process.

Theorem 14   Given: To Create, God extended Himself.

THEOREM 15   Then: **The only Creative process there is, is to extend God.**

A significant corollary is implied by these last several theorems. If Creation has God's Mind and the Truth Matrix within it, then:

THEOREM 15A   **Creation can Create like unto God.**

or

Creation can extend God.

The reasoning behind this is very simple. Creation was created like unto God, Truth Matrix and all. Creation can extend the God within it just because it is One to the Matrix.

Creation cannot extend what it does not have. What it can do is extend itself, and the God that is within itself. This still is a situation where infinities are within infinities... carried out infinitely. This is what this theorem means: Creation can extend the God within it. In doing so, Creation calls to attention the Source because it is all One.

If Creation can extend God, we have to have to avoid concepts and questions like, "Which came first, the chicken or the egg?" To avoid this confusion, a flow of causation needs to be established. With *Theorem 11,* this confusion can be cleared up:

Theorem 11   Given: God is the One Source of Creation.

This is saying, from God comes the Creative process. So, even if Creation has the Truth Matrix it can be said:

THEOREM 16   **Creation did not Create God.**

or

The God-Creation process is one way.

It is recognized that there is an apparent tension between the last two theorems (Creation can extend God. And, the God-Creation process is one way.) The painting did not create the artist, the clay did not create the sculptor, and the invention did not create the inventor.[17] The creative process is one way. It manifests from God to a Truth Matrix and out, an idea extension of a mind. It is very important to note that there is a flow of causation in this.

The essence of the Creator determines the essence of Creation. Since the Creator is Eternally constant, Creation cannot effect the Creator. To do so, would mean the Creator can change and that is against the previous definitions of God in this work.

With this chapter, everything starts from the first postulate and its theorems; to the second postulate and its theorems; which takes precedent over the third postulate and its theorems; which, in turn, takes precedence over the fourth postulate, etc.

All Creation stems from the Absolute Will of God. This Will was shared with Creation so Creation can create like its Creator. It is important to remember that it is impossible to create without God's Will.

Another way the circle can be perceived closed is with the idea that Creation never left the mind of the Creator (implied in *Theorem 10*).

---

17 True, the artist can let the creation <u>affect</u> him, and it does not <u>effect</u> him.

Theorem 10	Given:	God and Creation are One.
		or
		Creation never left its Creator.
Theorem 11B	Given:	The God-Creative process is the only Creative process.
THEOREM 17	Then:	**That which is Created never leaves the Creator.**
		or
		Ideas do not leave the mind of their origin or source.

Theorem 17 states the creation never leaves the creator or, in human terms, ideas do not leave the mind of origin or source. This is obvious when we look at how people create. The idea never leaves the mind of the individual artist or inventor. They only share or <u>extend</u> those ideas. The idea remains in the mind of origin. It is the extension of the idea, from the mind of the artist or the inventor, which creates the idea in physical reality.

Of course, being a mortal mind and working with limited temporal/spatial references, the inventor or artist may forget the idea. That only means that their attention and desires are not focused on the idea (at that moment in time). The idea is still -- somewhere -- within the mind of its source.

Life is an excellent example of this creation extension concept. From this work's reference point, life is the fifth interaction within a physics model,[18] the one unifying aspect or principle of physics. Unfortunately, modern science does not recognize this. It is the subtlest and yet the most powerful -- and the source of the other interactions: the source of electromagnetic, the source of gravitational, and the source of the two nuclear forces.[19] It can manipulate the other interactions from the most mundane level as a beaver manipulates wood in building a dam, to the other extreme of magic and miracles.[20]

Life is continually extending itself and, if left alone, will grow exponentially. It does not create itself, rather it is continually extending itself. For example: a mouse does not recreate a another life-form -- elephant, it just extends mouse, or a whale extends whale, or human extends human or dandelion extends dandelion. They are extending their own version of life. A mouse does not extend elephant or a dandelion does not extend a wombat.

All life is one; one aspect of physical life cannot be separated from the other. Individual life on this planet needs elements of life to exist. One element of physical life cannot leave the life sphere of its origin and remain in existence; it is dependent on other elements. It is dependent on the whole concept of Life and its related truth matrix. This Life 'spring' is Eternally occurring, because it is participating in the Eternal Moment of Creation.

As a water spring emerges from the ground, the life spring comes from outside of our immediate perception of realties. It comes out of Eternity. It has a potential to be everywhere at any time. It just needs the right physical conditions to manifest physically. The qualities of life are always the same. There may appear to be many diverse aspects, and still, they must be looked at and included as part of a whole.

What does it mean the qualities in life are always the same? Life is either here or it is not – it appears to be digital in nature. It does not change. When it is here, its qualities are always the same. When it appears not to be here, we call it inorganic or death. Life manipulates what is outside of itself to reproduce, self-organize, and extends itself. This is a continual reoccurring process, and it applies to amoebas or rock musicians.

---

18 Chapter 3.3 - Bubbles of Temporal Reference.
19 Ibid.
20 Chapters 3, 9, and 10

The concept of ideas not leaving their source is very much *A Course in Miracles* thing. Postulate 6 says something that *A Course in Miracles* also says repeatedly.[21]

This section introduces the following concepts:

Ancient truth → God created like unto self

Ancient truth → God and Creation are one and a closed system

Ancient truth → God-Creation is Eternally occurring…eternal moment

Relevant truth → Ideas don't leave mind of origin

Relevant truth → To create is to extend

2.7 - Postulate 6   I am God's Creation.

*T*his means, I am/we are all Eternal and Infinite and everything that's been covered in the fifth postulate. So, let us examine what that implies:

Theorem 10	Given:	God and Creation are One.
Postulate 6	Given:	I am God's Creation.
THEOREM 18	Then:	**God and I are One.**

This chapter went from the objective (God-Creation) to something subjective (us). We have traveled from rational theory -- cause and effect[22] -- to the writer, the reader, to the speaker, and listener. All are now part of this rational theory. God is no longer out there; no longer is God some abstract thing far removed from us. Instead, it is now at the very core of our being. There is nowhere we need to go. The quest for God often becomes convoluted, from a search without to a quest within.

This section will use theorems from the previous postulate instead of the elements that generated the fifth postulate's theorems. The main reason is because the author is lazy and does not like writing that much. If the reader cares to, you can substitute the original elements of their generation.

Creation, emanating from God's Love and all that entails, leads us to these theorems:

Theorem 13	Given:	Will, Love, Logic, and Truth are One in an Eternal Creation.
Postulate 6	Given:	I am God's Creation.
THEOREM 19	Then:	**Will, Love, Logic, and Truth are One in an Eternal Me.**

With this come all kinds of corollaries:

THEOREM 19A	**I am God's Will.**
THEOREM 19B	**I am God's Love.**
THEOREM 19C	**I am God's Logic.**
THEOREM 19D	**I am God's Truth.**

---

21 Example: Workbook, Lesson 45, 2nd paragraph, *A Course In Miracles©*
22 First five postulates and theorems

THEOREM 19E	I am Reality.
THEOREM 19F	I am Eternal.
THEOREM 19G	I am an extension of God.

Theorems 19 through *19F* present the qualities of what we are. We are Love, we are Logic, we are Reality, we are Creation, etc. Will, Love, Logic and Truth create the Eternal being, which is ourselves. I am an extension of God. You are an extension of God. We are extensions of God.

Our true potential emerges with this last corollary of *19G*:

Theorem 15	Given:	Creation can extend God.
Postulate 6	Given:	I am God's Creation.
THEOREM 20	Then:	**I can extend God.**

Here we have another complete circle. From source to identity, qualities of source to its potential, and because the system is closed, back again to the source, a very old theme.[23] Again, Life extends life. This presents itself one way in a purely physical level with birth and reproduction. Then, it presents itself another way, as our technical-medical level uses science's truth/laws to maintain life's presence, like heal.

Looking from the personal interaction reference, this extension idea appears when we extend inclusiveness (kindness and love). Extending kindness begets kindness; extending love begets love. In this extending of God, we become the tools of the Will of God. We can extend awareness of God to others. We cannot give people God; this is something that is inherent within them. What we can do is extend that awareness and give others the awareness that this God is within them. This is pretty much what most prophets of the world have been working on for thousands of years.

A recurring ancient concept introduced here is:

Ancient truth → You are the Beloved of God.

2.8 - Postulate 7   God's Creation created or mis-created an untruth.

A re-occurring idea throughout mystical thought is it was all One, and then, 'something happened'. This 'something' has been called the fall from Grace, the original sin, the first mistake, the separation, Maya, the first judgment, or the big boo-boo, they all are related to this postulate. Something happened! Something <u>appeared</u> to fracture a fundamental unity

What is this untruth? One way to express it in words is, "There's 'something' other than God".

How can, that which is absolute and One, create something 'outside' of itself? How can it create something that does not relate to One?

There is a fundamental unity. In this postulate, something occurs that <u>appears</u> to fracture that unity. Both Truth and untruth are now in Creation's mind. The concept of God's Creation mis-creating an untruth is now coexistent with Creation's Mind (Truth Matrix). Now, the Real and the unreal coexist in one mind. Paradoxes and conundrums begin to flower.

---

23 Bear in mind the extension of God that Creation presents are a few infinities short of being God. However, because Love is non-exclusive and what is being portrayed is still one thing, God makes up the difference.

God Created an Eternal 'Thought' and that 'Thought' created a thought that did not compute along Eternal Logic lines. Because God's Logic is Absolute and not exclusive, this situation created a special application of that Logic.

Definition of terms states an untruth is a law by which nothing works. Given there is a system with a set of laws/truths, an arrangement of those truths produced something, not applicable to the system. The truth was 'twisted'; and the result is not relevant to, or 'stepped out' of the existing system.

Mathematics (which is eternal and deals with infinities within infinities...) has two examples of how this can occur. These two math equivalents can help illustrate how a complete logic system can 'fold up on itself' and/or create something outside that logic system – alien to that logic system.

When one is learning algebra, we are taught that there are two math 'no-nos'. One is division by zero (*x/0*). Another math example (which is actually much closer to what is portrayed here in *Postulate 7*) is taking the square root of a negative number ($\sqrt{-1}$). Why are these labeled no-nos?

❑ Given the formula *12/2 = x*. If you divide *12* by *2*, which equals *6*; (*12/2 = 6*), through math reasoning the proof of this is *2 x 6 = 12*.

Given the formula *12/0 = x*. If you divide *12* by *0*; (*12/0 = x*), no matter what answer you come up with, there is no proof to show that this answer is true. There is no number that you can multiply times *0* to equal *12*, (*x x 0 = 12*, has no resolution). Division by zero creates something totally unrelated to, or alien to, the original logic system and makes a complete jump out of math reasoning.

❑ Any number multiplied by itself will be a positive number (*2 x 2 = 4*, or *-2 x -2 = 4*). There is no number you can multiply times itself and the result will be negative. It is only possible to take the square root of a positive number. It is impossible to take the square root of a negative number ($\sqrt{-1}$). The very concept of a square root of a negative number creates a completely new number system. This number system mathematics calls the imaginary number system, which is fitting because this book will be dealing with an **Imaginary** reality later.[24]

The math logic system recognized that this impossibility can and does occur frequently in Algebra – a condition happens that is un-relatable to anything physical or the math logic system. However, even though the concept of $\sqrt{-1}$ cannot exist, mathematics - a complete logic system - treated it as if it did exist and gave it a value.

The imaginary number system is a mirror image of the real number system. It is essentially the original real number system repeated with the value of (*i*) introduced [(*i*) being the imaginary quality of a square root of negative one, $\sqrt{-1} = i$]. Where the $\sqrt{4} = 2$; the $\sqrt{-4} = 2i$.

The real and imaginary math number systems are parallel. They have the same logic or laws of operational math in common. These laws of operational math do not change. However, because of the incorporation of this value -- the square root of negative one or (*i*) -- the simplest operations like adding, subtracting, or dividing become complicated when done in the imaginary system. (For example, $\sqrt{4} + 2 = 4$, whereas $\sqrt{-4} + 2 = 2i + 2$.)

An irony of this imaginary logic system is that it is <u>totally dependent</u> on the real number system for its values, operation, and logic. It cannot exist without the real number system; it is a 'special case' within the real number system. The real number system can exist by itself. The imaginary number system cannot exist without real numbers.

Adding, subtracting, multiplying, or standing them on their heads: *2 x 2 = 4, 2 x 3 = 6, 2 x 4 = 8*, these can be executed without the imaginary number system. However, without the concept of the square root of *4* or for that matter just the concept of *4*; the question -- what is the square root of (*-4*) -- has no relevance. The square root of negative *4* becomes the real number solution *2* (square root of *4*) multiplied by an 'impossibility' -- *i*.

24 Chapter 4.2 - "What's Reality Papa?"

The imaginary number system is a mirror image of the real. Just like any mirror image, the image is dependent upon what is in front of it. The image cannot exist by itself (except maybe, in the world of Alice in Wonderland). Remember from the beginning of this chapter that all math grew up with Man's understanding of physical form. With the advent of imaginary numbers, the mathematics involved is not relatable to anything in physical form.

With this concept of square root of negative one, it is possible to see how a logic system can 'fold up' on itself and create something other than the original. A special case of math was generated in math; and was then employed by math. This general idea will be used with the approach of this section's postulate and its theorems.

The major points presented with the concept of a square root of a negative number are:

- A comprehensive logic system created something alien or outside that logic system.
- The 'alien-ness' is a result of special application of the comprehensive logic system
- That comprehensive logic system did not exclude that 'alien-ness'.
- The 'alien-ness' created a 'mirror logic system' based on the original comprehensive logic system.
- The 'alien-ness' is dependent on a 'special application' of the original comprehensive logic system.

Now, to relate these concepts to this postulate. The first theorem in this chapter comes from putting *Theorem 8* together and *Postulate 7*.

Theorem 8	Given:	That which is not True is not God.
Postulate 7	Given:	God's Creation created or miscreated an untruth.
THEOREM 21	Then:	**The miscreation is not God.**

If this is true, then:

Theorem 9	Given:	Will, Love, Logic, and Truth are One in an Eternal God.
Theorem 21	Given:	The miscreation is not God.
THEOREM 22	Then:	**The miscreation is not the Will of God.**

If this is so, then:

THEOREM 22A	**The miscreation is not God's Love.**
THEOREM 22B	**The miscreation is not God's Logic.**
THEOREM 22C	**The miscreation is not God's Truth.**
THEOREM 22D	**The miscreation is not God's Infinity.**
THEOREM 22E	**The miscreation is not Eternal.**

or

The miscreation is temporal.

Theorem 9 presents Will, Love, Logic and Truth are one in Eternal God. Add *Theorem 21* -- The miscreation is not of God -- we developed *Theorems 22* through *22E*. Miscreation is not the Will of God, it is not God's Love, it is not God's Logic, and it is not God's Truth. The miscreation is not God's Infinity, it is not Eternal, or most important, with *22E*: the miscreation is temporal. All of a sudden, there is something that has nothing to do with God.

What is this relationship of the Infinite and Eternal to the finite and temporal? A quick look at the qualities of a mathematical infinite set[25] and a mathematical finite set may prove helpful here. Infinite and finite or Eternal and temporal can be considered mutually exclusive terms.

Either something is mathematically infinite or it is not. If something is not infinite, it is finite. The same can be said with finite. If a mathematical set is not finite, it is infinite. Eternal and temporal have a similar relationship. If something is not Eternal, it is temporal and vice versa.

The qualities of one may contain the qualities of the other. For example, a mathematical infinity can contain an <u>infinite</u> number of finite sets. The size of these finite sets is not important. They could be incredibly large (a *1* with a gazillion zeros after it) or be zero.

<u>All</u> of these finite sets can be contained in the infinity. A very large mathematically finite set may exhibit qualities in common with the infinite set, and yet, some of the qualities of the mathematical infinity will be beyond any finite set.

<u>This is important.</u> An Infinite Eternal concept (God) can contain an infinite number of finite temporal/spatial concepts (be it particles, stars, life forms, temporal matrices, etc.[26]) This demonstrates a one-way action: one can contain the qualities of the other, while the other cannot contain all the qualities of the first -- a basic duality.

This implies that any and all temporal/spatial references are contained in the Infinite and Eternal. At the same time, many very large bubbles of temporal/spatial references can reflect <u>some</u> of the Infinite and Eternal qualities.

The first six postulates and theorems portrayed an eternal constancy. The untruth has introduced a temporality (changes). Yet, this temporal condition is parallel to the Eternal (as the imaginary number system is parallel to the real number system). This brings us to a *kicker* of a theorem:

Theorem 8B	Given:	That which is not True is not Real.
Theorem 22C	Given:	The miscreation is not God's Truth.
THEOREM 23	Then:	**The miscreation is not Real.**

What a preposterous preponderance! According to this postulate, a mistake happened; yet, with *Theorem 23*, the mistake did not really happen. We have some tricky concepts here. Something happened and it created an event outside of God, Creation, and Reality; and from God's reference that <u>something does not exist</u>.

Up to this postulate, everything is One; now there is an apparent fragmentation of sorts. Since this fragmentation originated from a unity, an examination of the relationship between the unity and the apparent fragmentation may give some clarity to this confusion. For example:

Theorem 15A　　　　Given:　Creation can create like unto God.

It is important to remember that this stems from Creation having the Truth Matrix.

Postulate 7　　　　Given:　Creation miscreated an untruth.

---

25 Mathematical sets will be covered in more detail in Chapter 4, Figure 4-5, Algebraic Sets
26 Chapter 3

THEOREM 24   Then: **The untruth came from the Truth Matrix.**

or

There is an element of Truth that caused the untruth.

We already introduced this concept with the mathematical creation of imaginary numbers. We showed how doing a very specific operation could generate the imaginary number system. The real and imaginary numbers coexist in mathematics and are separate through the value (*i*). One is but a shadow of the other caused by <u>an operation</u> in the other.

As with the relationship of real to imaginary numbers, the Eternal can stand by itself, whereas the temporal is totally dependent on the Eternal to exist. All physical forms are temporal, constantly changing, and are totally dependent on the laws of physics. Yet, the laws of physics remain Eternally constant and determine the physical forms. If the laws of physics were not constant, there would be no continuity to physical form.

The temporal condition is parallel to the Eternal. They co-exist, and later this book will go over how they co-exist. The Eternal and the temporal are separated by an operation of creating an untruth, as the real number system is separated from the imaginary number system by the operation of taking a square root of a negative number.

It is within this postulate that the paradoxes around the Divine really start to appear. This latest paradox, Truth within the untruth, is not new; on the contrary, it is very, very old.
<u>Truth does not change; it remains Eternally constant</u>.

What this postulate means to Creation and how this 'miscreation' affects Creation appears in these next theorems.

Theorem 17   Given: Ideas do not leave their source.

Postulate 7   Given: Creation miscreated an untruth.

THEOREM 25   Then: **The miscreation never left Creation.**

Now there are two mutually exclusive things presented within Creation's mind -- Truth and untruth or infinite and finite. A major split in Creation's mind has appeared to occur; both Real and unreal are in its mind.

Although, that which is not real does not exist (from the reference of the Mind of God), it does appear to exist within the mind of Creation. Present within Creation is the Mind of God and something that is not the Mind of God. This is illustrated in the generation of *Theorem 26*.

Theorem 10   Given: God and Creation are One.

Theorem 21   Given: The miscreation is not God.

Theorem 25   Given: The miscreation never left Creation.

THEOREM 26   Then: **The miscreation has generated a duality within Creation.**

Until this postulate, there is no duality. There is one singular holistic whole. Now, Eternal and temporal, Love and not love, Logic and not logic, Truth and untruth, Real and unreal are all in one mind. If we accept the statement, "that which is not real does not exist", then:

THEOREM 26A   **The miscreation has generated an unreal duality within Creation.**

or

The duality does not exist.

or

The miscreation has generated a delusion of duality within Creation.

Again, paradoxes are being introduced and words are folding back on themselves, the duality does not exist from God's reference. However, as long as the untruth is believed real within the mind of Creation, the duality exists from Creation's reference. A delusional state becomes the effect of miscreation of untruth.

If that does not confuse you yet; wait, there is more. Now let us see how God's Love affects this situation:

Definition:	Given:	God's Love is not exclusive.
Postulate 7	Given:	God's Creation miscreated an untruth.
THEOREM 27	Then:	**God's Love did not exclude the miscreation.**

or

The miscreation was included within God's Love.

That means that Love included the unreal. An untruth, temporal and unreal in nature was included into the Eternal and Real. Just as, mathematics did not exclude imaginary numbers.

In the dictionary, the word *correct*, means; to remove, remedy, or to counteract; to adjust so as to meet a standard of a required condition; to make adjustments; to compensate.[27]

Given this definition of correct, then it can be stated that the non-exclusion of the miscreation can be perceived as God correcting for the untruth.

THEOREM 27A   **God corrected for the untruth.**

Since God and Truth are one, it also can be stated:

THEOREM 27B   **Truth corrects for untruth.**

This is not that weird; of course, truth corrects untruth! It does not take a rocket scientist to figure out that one. What is weird or unusual is the sequencing, or rather the lack of sequencing. We are used to temporal thinking with a linear concept of cause and effect. That is, we think something occurs and then something occurs next.

Because we are dealing with an Eternal God, there is no time lapse between the miscreation of the untruth and the correction. They co-exist and occur together from the temporal reference point. One immediately calls forth the other. The mathematics equivalent is the math thought system adjusted to include the concept of imaginary numbers. As soon as a square root of a negative number is present, so is the imaginary number system.

Postulate 1	Given:	God is Eternal.
Definition:	Given:	Eternity is outside of time.
Theorem 27	Given:	God corrected for the untruth.
THEOREM 28	Then:	**The correction works outside of time.**

---

27 American Heritage Dictionary, 3rd Edition, 1996, Houghton Mifflin Co.

Here we have another allusion to the nature of this relationship of Eternal and temporal, True and untrue, Real and unreal. They <u>do and do not</u> exist in the same time reference. As said before, the laws of physics determine all temporal form and change, and yet, they themselves are eternally constant.

This Truth and untruth existing together is stated in *Theorem 28A*, which is a simple extension of *Theorems 24, 27B,* and *28*. Truth creates and corrects untruth, and to do so Truth and untruth must somehow co-exist together. So…as mentioned earlier:

THEOREM 28A   **Truth and untruth coexist.**

The Correction is present with the untruth. Since all that which is temporal and finite can exist within an Eternal and Infinite reference, this theorem can be stated another way:

THEOREM 28B   **The correction (Eternal) and the miscreation (temporal) coexist.**

A way to understand how the Eternal and temporal co-exist is through an example used previously, that the laws (eternally constant) of physical form co-exist with physical form (temporary) itself. Gravity co-exists with a rock, the sun, the planet, the tree, a bug, or the bird in the tree eating a bug.

The laws are Eternally constant and co-exist with the form itself. This aligns with the delusion concept. Even though we are in a dream or a deluded state, the laws of physical creation have not changed. We can dream of flying, but in no way did we alter gravity.

When the dream is gone, the laws are still there. If we try acting out the dream without an application of an appropriate law of physics or metaphysics, the correction brings us 'back to earth' so to speak.

Where all this 'pseudo logic' is leading us is pretty obvious:

Definition: Given: Physical form is temporal and finite in nature.

Theorem 22E   Given: The miscreation is temporal.

THEOREM 29   Then: **Physical form is related to an aspect of the miscreation or**

                                 untruth.

So, everything we perceive to be real is not. This is an old truism, an adage of mystical/metaphysical teachings for the last several millenniums. Physical form is not part of Reality, of what is really True. The physical form is temporal, and temporal time is unreal.

This is not an easy pill to swallow. Reason tells us one thing and our senses another. Then again, how many times have one or both led us astray. What is there to trust then? The answer to that has been stated all through this work and now it will be stated directly in this theorem:

Theorem 28A   Given: Truth and untruth coexist.

Theorem 29   Given: Physical form is an aspect of, or related to the untruth.

THEOREM 30   Then: **Truth coexists with physical form.**

Physical form is temporal. To see Truth within the form, one must look for the Eternal. What immediately satisfies this idea (as stated repeatedly) are the physical laws themselves. If the physical laws did change, there would be no continuity of form -- no science or mathematics.

Imagine a chicken on her nest hatching a clutch of eggs. One egg hatches and it is a chick; another hatches and it is a butterfly; another hatches and it is a rhinoceros; another hatches and it is a jar of peanut butter. It is this continuity or constancy of the Eternal within the temporal that must be looked at as Real, not the form itself.

Even at that, many times we do not objectively see the form. We see our memory associations or our mental/emotional projections around the form and not the form itself. It is in seeing our projections/perceptions and not the actuality that we fool ourselves. Fortunately, or unfortunately (depending on your reference) Truth is unaffected by our perceptions and beliefs.

Where all this is leading to is a very ancient concept, and to another synthesis between science and mysticism. Since the physical eye only sees that which is physically related and it is stated that which is physical is unreal; the 'visible' world is the unreal. This makes the visible world of ours a special-case-effect of an invisible world, a world of truths.

Some people within the physical sciences may resist this idea and they cannot deny that gravity is invisible; we can only 'see' its effects and not gravity itself. The same applies to the Laws of Motion, thermodynamics, electronics, etc. All sciences are based on measuring effects of this invisible world on the visible, not the invisible world itself. They can only surmise the invisible world's structure.

Just as mathematics' biggest paradox is that it is based on that which can't be proven - postulates, sciences' biggest paradox is all physical science (and knowledge) is based measuring the effect (what, where, how, when…) the invisible has on the visible. Or, measure how an invisible world sustains the visible world.

Last, but not least, are these two theorems. Although they are out of sequence with the other theorems, when presented last, they help drive a point home:

Postulate 6	Given:	I am God's Creation.
Postulate 7	Given:	God's Creation created/miscreated an untruth.
THEOREM 31	Then:	**I created/miscreated an untruth.**

And the last:

Postulate 6	Given:	I am God's Creation.
Theorem 26A	Given:	The miscreation has generated a duality delusion within Creation.
THEOREM 32	Then:	**I am/we are in a generated duality delusion.**

There is another reoccurring metaphysical/spiritual theme very similar to this. That is we are all part of the Cosmic Dream state. The fractured perception has created a dream state for Creation.

Our 'waking reality' is really the Dream State. When we have dreams, the things we dream of are things that we recognize in our waking lives, and these recognitions carry over into our dreams. If we did not have the waking concepts like horse, house, walk, etc., these images in our dreams would have no meaning.

Our dream state has no effect on the laws of reality. You can dream of flying, or becoming a tornado, or turning into a dandelion seed and floating on the wind (all things perceived/programmed by the waking state). These dreams have no effect on the laws that determine the initial forms portrayed in the dream.

As a wise man once said, "Don't worry about them dreams none. They're all in your head."[28]

---

28 Bob Dylan

This section ties into numerous ancient mystical and spiritual concepts:

Ancient truth → **Something happened that <u>appeared</u> to fracture a fundamental singularity.**

Ancient truth → **There is an element of illusion or delusion in our perception of life.**

Ancient truth → **Truth and untruth coexist.**

Ancient truth → **There is an element of truth in untruth.**

Ancient truth → **Untruth exists in our mind.**

Ancient truth → **Physical form is unreal. or Life is a dream.**

Ancient truth → **Physical form is a special case of a metaphysical condition.**
or
There is an 'invisible' world that sustains the 'visible' world.

Relevant truth → **What is all encompassing has no opposite. Create an opposite and it is encompassed.**
or
Love Corrected for untruth.

Relevant truth → **Untruth is dependent and a special case of truth - independent.**

2.9 – Conclusion

*T*his is the conclusion, and a review, of a tedious set of postulates and theorems. It is recognized that there is a large amount of redundancy in this chapter and it is necessary to drive a point 'home'. We, as beings, are in an unreal schizophrenic situation. A summation of this chapter is:

♦ The first four postulates and theorems deal with the Absolute in all its Aspects and Attributes. The concepts of a mind matrix and 3-in-1, 1-in-3 will be repeated and shown relevant to physical form in later chapters.

♦ Within *Postulate 5* and theorems -- there is a Creation -- how that Creation manifests into physical life will be expanded upon. In addition, Chapter 3 will talk about how the Eternal Moment of Creation can fold time. This time folding idea will be covered even deeper when we cover *ESP* phenomena, magic, and miracles in Chapters 7, 9, and 10 respectively.

♦ In the sixth postulate and theorems, we <u>are</u> the Creation. Chapter 4 will show how the Reality of what we really are manifests in our minds. While, Chapters 5-10 show how we can explore and 'see' the evidence this Reality.

♦ The seventh postulate and theorems introduce a 'mistake', and the effect of the 'mistake' is an unreality.

In terms of the next chapters, Chapter 3 will cover the Correction and how it generates temporal physical form (Bubbles of Temporal/spatial References) and how the Mirror reflects the mistaken thinking back to our own minds in order for us to make our own corrections.

Chapter 4 shows how this Reality/Truth and unreality/untruth manifest within mortal minds -- our mind. That chapter also introduces how we can use the Truth to reduce the untruth/unreality within our minds. While Chapters 5-10 give applications within our minds.

A review of the ancient mystical truths or spiritual concepts that were introduced in this chapter are:

❖ There is a God.
❖ God is Love.
❖ God's Love and Wisdom are One.
❖ 3-in-1 1-in-3 nature of God
❖ There is an order or an array to everything-Truth (Matrix).

- ❖ God created like unto self.
- ❖ God and Creation are one and a closed system.
- ❖ God-Creation is Eternally occurring…eternal moment.
- ❖ Ideas do not leave mind of origin.
- ❖ To create is to extend.
- ❖ You are the Beloved of God.
- ❖ Something happened that appeared to fracture a fundamental singularity.
- ❖ What is all encompassing has no opposite. Create an opposite and it is encompassed. Or, Love Corrected for untruth.
- ❖ There is an element of truth in untruth.
- ❖ Truth and untruth coexist.
- ❖ Untruth is dependent and a special case of truth - the independent.
- ❖ Untruth exists in our mind.
- ❖ There is an element of illusion or delusion in our perception of life. Or…life is a dream.
- ❖ Physical form is a special case of a metaphysical condition. Or, there is an 'invisible' world that sustains the 'visible' world.
- ❖ Physical form is the 'unreal'.

Again, much of this information is not new. Mystics have been touching on these ideas for thousands of years. The core of many metaphysical and spiritual thought systems addresses this duality in one form or another: the divine-profane, the spiritual-physical, reality-illusion, Truth-untruth, Heaven-earth, etc. The rest of this book will be working with these ancient ideas.

2.10 - Questions

1. What is the casual sequence (Postulates) that makes up Creation?

2. Creation is _____ short of being God.

3. The physical world is an effect of _____.

4. God/Creation process is _____ in God's Love.

5. I am/we are what?

6. _____ is eternally occurring.

7. God's Creation did what?

8. Ideas do not leave _____.

9. God corrected for _____.

10. God's Logic contains a _____ Matrix.

11. When or where did Creation happen?

12. What kind of delusion are we in?

13. What does not exist?

14. _____ is dependent and _____ is independent.

15. What is the true potential of Creation?

16. To create is to _____.

17. What is a definition of truth?

Chapter 3

The Correction and the Mirror

3.1 - Preview of Chapter 3

*T*he previous chapter introduced the qualities of infinite eternal God, Creation, and proceeded into manifestation of temporal finite form. This chapter is going to continue that theme in detail a bit more. In later chapters, we will progress from temporal form (which is what we perceive in the human condition) to God, using the laws and principles that have been stated.

(For the rest of this book, the opposite of a value will be expressed as that value with a double line through it. For example: not Love will be expressed as ~~Love~~, untruth as ~~Truth~~ or ~~truth~~, unreal as ~~Real~~ or ~~real~~, etc)

This chapter will focus on some of the implementations of the postulates, theorems, and their concepts; and, how they apply to the physical world. Specifically:

1) *Theorem 10A*
    i)   The God-Creative process is Eternally occurring.
    ii) The time ignor-ance or folding properties of this concept.
2) *Theorems 11A an 17*
    a) The God-Creation process is a closed system within God.
    b) How this is an aspect of the Correction.
        i)   Ideas do not leave the mind of source.
        ii) How the miscreation stayed with us and the duality delusion it created.
3) *Postulate 7*
    a) God's Creation created/miscreated an ~~truth~~.
    b) *Theorem 27A* and *Theorem 28A*
        i)   God corrected for the ~~truth~~.
            (1) How part of this Correction reflects the mistake in thinking back to the mind of origin (the Mirror).
        ii) The Correction (Eternal) and the miscreation (temporal) coexist.
            (1) The nature of this coexistence.
    c) *Theorems 24* and *29*
        i)   The ~~truth~~ came from the Truth matrix. Or, an element of Truth caused the ~~truth~~.
        ii) Physical form is related to an aspect of the 'miscreation' or ~~truth~~.
        iii) How the Correction generates physical form.

The last chapter also introduced the concept of mutually exclusive terms: infinite-finite, eternal-temporal, or Truth-~~truth~~. If something is not infinite, it is finite. If something is not finite, it is infinite. The same can be said for eternal-temporal or truth-~~truth~~…

However, it was stated an infinity can contain an infinite number of finites; an eternal can contain an infinite number of temporals; Truth can contain an infinite number of ~~truth~~s. This is how they can coexist. Their relationships will be used later.

3.2 - The Correction

Ｗithin the nature of the Correction introduced in Chapter 2 lies the mechanics of physical and many metaphysical or spiritual laws. Love by definition is not exclusive. Try to divide it, and it will unite; create something that is ~~Love~~, and it will not be excluded. Love is an effect of the Will of God. Due to a complete Oneness and the inclusiveness of Love, it is impossible to split God. God is by definition a singularity, a single source, like a spring coming out of rock -- One.

When Creation uses Will, Love, and Logic to make ~~Will~~, ~~Love~~, and ~~Logic~~, it is an attempt to split from Love and the source of itself. It is an attempt to split God. This concept is *non-sequitar* to the nature of God. The result is that part of Creation's mind is in ~~Love~~ (an exclusive state); another part of Creation's mind is operating in Love and Truth (which is not exclusive). It is impossible to be separate from our selves and our source (God). Instead, we fell asleep to our true self: to God's Will, to Love, Logic, etc within us. And, just as the body of the dreamer never left the bedroom, we never left God.[1]

God and Creation's fundamental unity and its inability to be separated, conjoined with our apparently separate temporal human minds, are at the root of a lot of metaphysical contradictions and paradoxes. The Love and the unity of God's Creation can resolve many of these paradoxes in this dichotomy. Love's Correction is also not exclusive.

The Correction is a matrix that is an extension of the Truth Matrix. The Correction is called into being by the very act of the creation of an ~~truth~~. Just as, the imaginary number system is brought into existence by the square root of a negative number.

The Correction will exist as long as the ~~truth~~ exists. This Correction matrix is behind all form and is also referred to as the Mirror in the paradigm of this book.

Figure 3-1 is an illustration of how the non-exclusive nature of Love accounted for ~~Love~~. Figure 3-1 (*i*) shows that which is All-inclusive. In (*i*), Love is shown as a singularity that emerges from the Will of God and includes the Logic of God, the Truth Matrix. To the side of this representation is the miscreation of the ~~truth~~ or that, which is ~~Love~~. One is totally non-exclusive; the other is exclusive, because it is ~~Love~~. However, because Love is non-exclusive, it encompasses ~~Love~~ or ~~truth~~ and envelops it, as in (*ii*). Love "Corrects" for the ~~truth~~.

Due to its non-exclusive nature, Love does not try to overwhelm the mistake in thinking. It does not try to force Creation's true nature on itself. Instead, Love like the perfect judo master, includes and reflects the mistake in thinking back onto Creation. There is only one finite temporal mistake - there is 'something' other than God. Love, being Infinite and Boundless, generates a countless number of reflections of that idea. These reflections mirror the ~~truth~~ (and temporal limited nature of the ~~truth~~ back onto the mind of origin). Each one of these mirrored images is a bubble of temporal/spatial reference (*BTR*). Figure 3-1 (*iii*) and (*iv*) illustrate ~~Love~~ being incorporated into Love and shows temporary bubbles of temporal/spatial frames of reference materializing. There may be only one finite temporality (~~truth~~), yet Eternal Truth can reflect literally an infinite number of finite temporalities.

---

1 Theorem 17, Ideas do not leave the mind of source. Since we are an idea in the Mind of God, we can not leave our Source.

Figure 3-1, The Correction

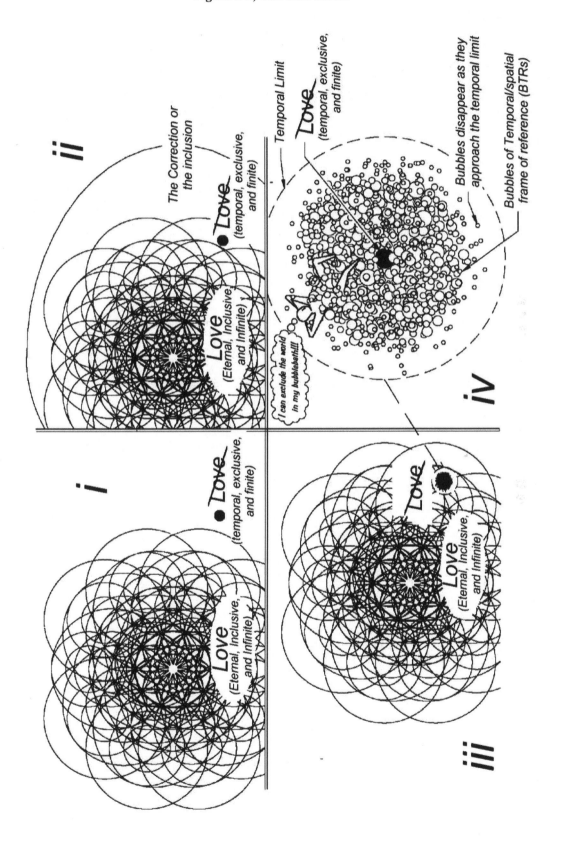

73

An analogy for this fracturing idea is to imagine a mountain, which has a large deep lake at its base. When the water is still, the reflection of the mountain is clear and whole. When the surface of the lake is disturbed, as from wind, the multitudes of mountain reflections that appear are partial and distorted. Consequently, multitudes of small partial distorted mountain images reach our eye. Each image is a partial bent part of the mountain; all the images together appear as chaos.

The essence neither of the mountain or the lake has changed. The only thing changed is the reflection -- perception. Imagine God is the mountain and Creation is the deep lake reflecting God. The partial distorted reflections are the result of a disturbance within Creation's Mind. In the model presented in this book, each reflection can be representative of a bubble of temporal/spatial reference (*BTR*).

God will not fight God (Creation). From the mortal human standpoint, these bubbles of temporalities represent the process of Creation being One. An Eternal Infinite Being perceives itself as a finite number of temporal beings. These bubbles or dream states illustrate a One Eternal Infinite Being is dreaming of a number of temporal lives (egos).

Not only do these bubbles include everybody, everywhere, all through time, people who have been and have yet to come, etc.; they also comprise all matter and the environment (stars, galaxies, grass, shoe polish, etc.). This chapter will cover how this works.

Again, it is important to recognize that this is all One thing. The Correction is not only outside of the ~~truth~~, it is also inside of the ~~truth~~ manifestation.

(Remember: the Eternal Moment of Creation, the only creative event is to extend God, and an element of Truth generated the ~~truth~~.[2] Just as, the real number system is in, creates, and sustains the imaginary number system.)

The Correction matrix –Mirror -- is an extension of an Infinite Eternal God (and an Infinite Eternal Moment of Creation -- Truth Matrix) into a temporal/spatial condition. The result is a myriad of bubbles of temporal/spatial references, of all sizes and shapes, bounded and binded by God's Love.

Creation's dreaming mind also contains matrices that incorporate the ~~truth~~; a mortal mind/matrix is developed that has both Truth and ~~truth~~ in it. However, the dreaming mind does not usually recognize the awake state. Very seldom do we remember about being awake when we are asleep.

And...just as our human sleeping/dreaming mind reflects that which makes up our waking mind,[3] our human mind/matrix (inside our personal bubble of temporal/spatial reference) reflects aspects of the Truth Mind/Matrix -- our true self.[4] One Mind/Matrix is Infinite and Eternal, and contained within it is a multitude of minds/matrices, finite and temporal. Creation's dream state is the result of the creation of an ~~truth~~ or a mistake in thinking - lake 'ripples'.

There is a math analogy: when a math mistake is corrected, the logic of the system insures every number afterward will follow. If a mistake is not corrected, then any math operation that uses the mistake is going to be in error -- be mistaken. Failure to correct the original mistake is another mistake. This is how math mistakes become compounded. The Correction's purpose is to have Creation correct the original ~~truth~~, which will correct the other temporal related ~~truths~~. Or, The Correction is there for Creation to wake itself up to the Reality of God.

First, the Mirror idea will be looked at then the Bubbles of Temporal/spatial Reference (*BTR*s) it generates.

---

2 Chapter 2.8, Postulate 7, Theorems 26A through 32
3 Like concepts of: cup, horse, lightening, cloth, car, etc. Chapter 4
4 Chapter 2, *Postulates 5* and 6

3.3 - The Mirror

*T*he previous section introduced the Correction mirrored the mistake in thinking back on Creation. This mirror concept is relatively important. The Mirror has parallels throughout a myriad of subjects. The mirror is an idea that appears repeatedly throughout physical (science) and metaphysical topics (religion) in a multitude of ways.

The Mirror is the most tangible of the unseen. Through it, perception becomes possible. It determines, assembles, and defines all *BTR* relationships. From human to a slug, from a quark to a quasar, it is the underlying template behind all form. In addition, because it has an Eternal/God reference it has time folding aspects. Time/space ignor-ance is a major element of *ESP*, the wonders of saints, and thaumaturgical magic. Within the Mirror is the Eternal/temporal interface – ~~truth~~'s reflection. All time – temporal/spatial references --, as we know it, are results of the Mirror.

In reference to the concepts that are being presented, here is a reminder about the temporal/spatial limits of language itself. We can only express or work with language on the image side of the Mirror. We are in the realm of perception, and <u>appear</u> to be outside (an image) of the Mirror that was called forth to correct the mistake. The Correction and Mirror mechanics are beyond any words (or perceptions) because it springs from a fundamental concept of unity and Love/Truth -- One.

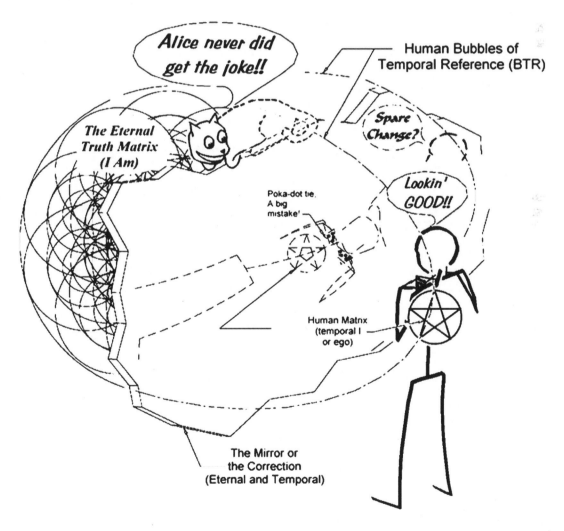

Figure 3-5, The Mirror

75

One side of the Mirror -- the Truth Matrix -- is beyond words and concepts (Figure 3-5). On that side of the Mirror, is a fundamental unity. The mirror concept is Love reflecting the mistake in thinking back to Creation -- it will not fight Creation. Love will not do anything to cause separation. It just reflects the finite/temporal back. Again, the purpose is to get Creation to correct the mistake in thinking.

What does this mean to us as mortal beings? As stated earlier, just as a dream state uses the images out of the conscious mind, a matrix containing ~~truth~~ (the human matrix) has the properties of the Truth Matrix within it.[5] The ~~truth~~ matrix cannot leave the Truth Matrix. To be more precise, the ~~truth~~ matrix is <u>dependent</u> on the Truth Matrix to exist, the same way imaginary numbers cannot exist without real numbers. Or, a perception of a reflected image is totally dependent on the mirror, the object in front of the mirror, and a perceiver.

The Divine Dream State, however, includes both the mistake and the Correction.[6] In the Mirror Eternal and temporal co-exist. This presents part of a metaphysical safety mechanism. The law of God's non-exclusive Love dictates that Creation be/is whole -- One. The apparent un-wholeness is just a state of mind and does not exist in **Absolute** Reality – a delusion.[7] Creation can only appear to be hurt in the dream. In **Absolute** Reality, it cannot be hurt at all, because it is part of God.

Inside us is the "*I Am*"[8] of God (the Creation). However, what we see from this side of the Mirror is a reflected image of that ~~Truth~~: the ego or "*I*". One side of the Mirror is the Mind of God; the other side is mistaken thinking in Creation's mind – the mortal mind of Man. The Eternal Infinite Truth Matrix has scaled itself down to a finite temporal human matrix (represented by the pentacle in Figure 3-5).

Back to the image of a mountain on a lake example: If the lake is still, the image of the mountain is clear (reversed but clear). If the lake has waves, multitudes of small partial distorted mountain images reach the eye. Each image is a bent part of the mountain, without depth. This kind of follows the (*I am*)/(*I*) relationship.

The surface of the Mirror reflects the mistaken thinking back on Creation. It reflects in two ways: active and passive. It is a passive reaction of Love and totally neutral. The active reaction of Love is to generate the image and give it a twist to help promote a change of mind within Creation.

Accordingly, we (who appear to be mortal beings) can use the Mirror spiritually in an active or passive role. The active reaction for us is to choose Truth instead of ~~truth~~. The passive reaction is for us is to be still to Love's Presence.

It was said that an infinite Eternal Mind is dreaming it is a finite number (albeit a very large finite) of temporal minds. Because there is no limit to the Mirror's comprehensive potential, it incorporates this also. This means that the Mirror not only reflects back what we choose on an individual level, it also reflects back the mind of Mankind in order for Man to see and choose as a whole and it reflects throughout time. This includes Jesus' crucifixion, governments or world wars, sciences or decimation of the environment, etc.

Choices groups of people have made are reflected back to that group of people. The history of Mankind is shaped so that Creation, at any moment of time, is influenced towards a harmonious whole and toward union with God, as an individual and as a group. This will be mentioned again periodically.

---

5 *Theorem 28A* and *30*

6 *Theorem 28*, The correction works outside of time. or The correction (Eternal) and the miscreation (temporal) coexist.

7 *Theorem 32*

8 Covenant religions, Chapter 10

Note: the <u>reality</u> of one's human-self -- with the concept of mirror -- is not directly seen. The reality of ones human-self only <u>appears</u> through the reflection. The reflection is not the actuality.

The image in a physical mundane mirror is an imperfect image of you. It is reversed. Your right hand is really your left hand in the mirror. Certain aspects become lost in the reflection. A three dimensional universe is portrayed as a two dimensional image. That which has substance and depth has no substance or depth anymore, although it appears to have depth.

Furthermore, like a physical mirror, the image may be twisted depending upon the surface quality of the mirror, or what are the qualities of the mind of the observer. In Figure 3-5, the image is rotated 90 degrees to represent that. That rotation is also in reference to the *right-angle rule,* which will be covered in a later section of this chapter.

The human mind matrix can be seen as an upside down, limited version of the Truth Matrix - the Mind of God - a parody of sorts. Just as physical form and the laws of physical form can be seen as an upside down parody of Heaven. Through the Mirror, *I Am/God* becomes *I/ego* awareness.

Other terms for the arrangement may be a parallel with a twist, a fractured symmetry, a distorted image, etc. A parody can stem from our fractured perception rather than from the laws of form itself. The underlying theme in Heaven is unity, as is true of us. Although our perception is fractured, it is possible to see a parallel of Heaven's unity within physical form; one physical universe made up of a myriad of "separatenesses". Earth appears as a skewed example of what is the actuality.

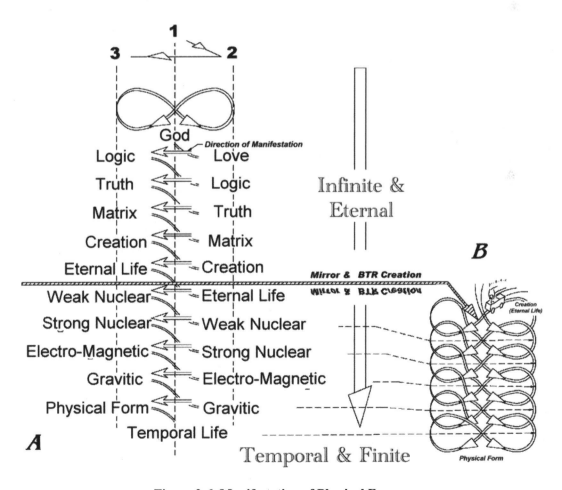

Figure 3-6, Manifestation of Physical Form

The physical follows and mimics the metaphysical just as the reflection mimics the person. The reason being is all matrices are patterned after the Truth Matrix. The Mirror matrix itself is neutral. Not only does it reflect Creation's mistake back on itself; it can also reflect its Creator, Truth, Matrix...etc. It is all contingent on the mind that is being reflected.

How does the physical laws/truths relate mutually with metaphysical laws/truths? There are a number of ways of illustrating this. One way is to show from God to physical form and the other is to show from God to Man. Figure 3-6 (*A*) is an illustration of how the concepts of the postulates manifest it to physical form. The figure has the "Three in One, One in Three" concept with the three columns of Figure 2-1.[9] As manifestation approaches the Mirror, what is column three becomes the next two column in the new level below it.
This means:

♦ Love determines the nature of Logic, as Logic regenerates Love.
♦ Logic determines the nature of Truth, as the Truth regenerates Logic.
♦ Truth determines the nature of the Matrix, as the Matrix regenerates Truth.
♦ The Matrix determines the nature of Creation, as Creation regenerates the Matrix.

This continues to the Mirror. After the Mirror, the relationships begin to pick up a fractured appearance. This is partially due to the digital nature of the relationship between infinity and finite or eternal and temporal. The ~~truth~~ presents something finite. This finite (due to the influence of the Creation Matrix) attempts to recreate the infinity, and never quite gets there. Like the concept of an asymptotic logarithmic curve[10] or nature and pi.

The moebius strip aspect (representing Creation and re-creation, Figure 3-6 [*B*]) illustrates the process of creating larger and larger *BTR*s until the *BTR*s can regenerate themselves (the moebius strip connects back up with itself so two sides of the paper are one side). With temporal life, the Creation and re-creation process of the Matrix becomes complete. Temporal life facilitates the extension principle of the Truth Matrix and Creation.[11] It 'mirrors' Eternal Life – the One.

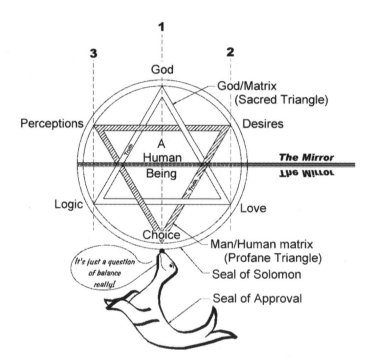

Figure 3-7 The Seal of Solomon

"As with man so is the universe, and as with the universe so it is with man". This old metaphysical adage has appeared throughout history in a number of ways. A very old example of how God and ego mirror one another is the Seal of Solomon (Figure 3-7). This figure

---

9 Two determines the nature of three, as three regenerates two.
10 A curve that infinitely <u>approaches</u> a straight line and <u>never</u> reaches it.
11 *Theorems: 11B*, The God-Creation process is the *only* Creative process; and *15*, The Only Creative process there is, is to extend God.

illustrates our human truth matrix is as an upside down reversed image of the Truth Matrix – the profane and sacred triangles. *I Am/God* became *I/ego*. Figure 3-7 comes from mystical Judaism (Kabbalah). The two intertwined triangles by themselves are known as the Star of David (symbol of Judaism). When a circle is placed around it, the symbol becomes the Seal of Solomon (a thaumaturgical magic symbol). All vertices are interrelated and are included into the whole (shown as being woven together). The labels in that figure are not the traditional kabalistic labels. They are the author's and are used in the presented thought construct -- model -- of this book.

The upright triangle of the seal reflects the Divine aspect, whereas the upside down triangle reflects the ego condition. And, there is a unity of balance shown between the triangles.

The upside down one - Man -- is a mirror image of the right side up one -- God. The circle around them completes and contains the triangles (indicating a closed system in Love[12]).

The right side up triangle, which includes Love, Truth, and the Inclusive Mind; are an independent union. Try to remove one vertex and the others will regenerate it, because they are One with God.[13] God is the Source of all.[14] This triangle is in an independent state.

The right side up triangle is one thing, a unity, and independent. God's Love and Logic cannot be touched or hurt in any way. The Love, Absolute Truth, and the inclusive Mind and the Truth Matrix are all one thing.

The triangle pointing down (dependent) is a mirror image of the triangle pointing up (independent). However, at the same time, it is distorted as a physical mirror image. Things appear upside down, backward, or distorted like a funhouse mirror. Both triangles in the Seal of Solomon are intertwined and co-exist with each other from the reference of an Eternal now.

It is important to note that we can remove one point on the upside down triangle and the other points will disappear. For example: this book has the lower triangle vertices labeled 'Perceptions', 'Desires', and 'Choice' (what enters our *Storages*[15]) -- states that separates and discriminates. This triangle is in a dependent state. Remove any one of these vertices and the other points of the lower triangle will disappear.

The human condition contains both the upside down triangle (an exclusive state of mind) and the right side up triangle (a non-exclusive state of Mind). One is related to the Eternal and Infinite; the other is related to temporal and finite. One is independent and self-sustaining; the other is dependent and non self-sustaining. Love can stand by itself because it directly comes from - is One with -- the Source; it includes everything, and is the source of the Creation Matrix. Perceptions or desires cannot stand by themselves; they are dualistic. You need something to perceive or want. If you remove any one of these points of the lower triangle, the whole thing disappears.

This is very important, for a number of reasons. One is; many of the exercises introduced later will be looking at how to affect the influence of these lower triangle points in order to access the Eternal.[16] As the upside down triangle disappears, only the right side up triangle is left. An exercise introduced later in this chapter will address a decrease in exclusive perception (~~truth~~) and an increase of Truth (Logic) within a temporal matrix (our mind).

---

12 Theorem 11A, God is the one source of Creation.

13 Theorem 6C, Will, Love, and Logic are One in an Eternal God.

14 Postulate 1, There is one God, the Source-less Source, the Formless Form. Absolute Will that is Eternal and Infinite in nature.

15 Chapter 4

16 Chapter 6: Exercises and Disciplines

3.4 - Bubbles of Temporal/spatial Reference (*BTRs*)

As mentioned previously, all the matrices of laws and interactions that make up the physical 'dream state' are weak temporal copies of God's Truth Matrix and are being created through the Eternal Moment of Creation. The Truth matrix is 'mirrored' down into simpler temporal forms. Each mirror image becomes increasingly simpler, until limits are reached (Figure 3-1, [*iv*]). Just as God's Truth is related to the Matrix, there are truths/laws associated with specific matrix arrays. This section will incorporate some elements of a current science model into the presented metaphysical model.

In ancient thought, everything (matter) was broken down and comprised of five elements: earth, air, fire, water, and spirit. In our *enlightened* age, science recognizes four interactions that create the total weave of physical form. These are weak and strong nuclear interactions, electro-magnetic interactions, and gravitational interactions. Man's science model to date has been quite useful; and it has some 'glitches'; things it cannot explain.

In this book's paradigm, there is a fifth interaction. Although, there are physical sciences dedicated to the studies of the fifth interaction, it is not yet recognized as a viable interaction. The fifth interaction is life, and some of its studies are the biological sciences. And, even in today's biological sciences, life is still regarded as only a chemical reaction.

What is physical life? In this book, life is the interaction that is representative of the Eternal Creative Moment extended into physical form, and is the source of the other four interactions. Life is that which manipulates the other four interactions to recreate and reorganize itself (extend itself into temporal form).

The relationships of these four scientific interactions and life are illustrated in two different ways with Figures 3-2 and 3-3. Figure 3-2 shows *BTRs* congealing into the physical form we perceive. Figure 3-3 illustrates a specific congealing matrix arrangement where Eternal Life manifests into temporal life. The concepts of divergent and common tangency points with this circle arrangement in Figure 3-3 will be used throughout this book.

The following is a very brief introduction to the current recognized interactions used in physics.[17]

⇒ **Weak nuclear** interactions involve the construction of atomic particles or the relationship of things called quarks. The smallest *BTR* category (and highest octave) is the weak nuclear. It is the building blocks of an atomic particle. This is the first set or category of Bubbles of Temporal/spatial Reference (*BTRs*) in this model. These *BTRs* and their interactions make up what we call protons, neutrons, electrons, mesons, and the 200+ atomic particles discovered so far. Each constructed particle in itself is another *BTR*; each has its own time/space reference with its own intrinsic characteristics.

When scientists work with this level, they perceive a limit to the smallness of size of *BTRs* (Figure 3-1 [*iv*] - temporal limits or Figure 3-2). Science calls this 'high' limit a Planck's length (h). Within the physics construct used today, no particle can be smaller than this unit. Because of this, all *BTRs* and their change are in increments or multiples of h.[18] The matrix array relationships of these *BTRs* are the simplest and each matrix exhibits itself as a particles.

⇒ **Strong nuclear** interactions are the interplay between arrays of particle *BTRs* (created by weak nuclear *BTRs*), specifically those known as the proton and the neutron. The strong nuclear matrix *BTR* array contains a number of weak nuclear arrays and is more complicated. It is what holds a group of same electrical charged particles – protons – together (which normally electrically repel) in the nucleus of an atom. It is commonly known as nuclear energy and released during a nuclear fission or fusion. It binds the nucleus (which is another larger *BTR* matrix) of an atom together.

---

17 For simplicity's sake anti-matter is going to be ignored in this book.
18 This is at the core of quantum mechanics.

Strong nuclear is the next octave of physical form manifestation. It is stronger than the weak nuclear and electromagnetic interactions, yet subtler, and except for stars and bombs, it is beyond our human perceptions (like all these interactions). This *BTR* category constitutes the nature of an element -- nucleus, how many electron *BTR*s are held in place by the nucleus *BTR*, and determines the intrinsic nature of the atomic nucleus along with atomic weight.

⇒ The next octave below strong nuclear is **Electromagnetic**. *EMF* appears as the electric field interaction between the *BTR* known as proton and the *BTR* known as electron (or proton to proton, electron to electron, etc.). The *BTR*s in this category determine the next level of manifestation. We recognize them as light and heat (other *BTR*s). *EMF* (electro-magnetic force) allows you to perceive matter.

The *BTR*s released from their (proton/electron) change of spatial arrangements or field strengths are known as light photons. These interactions of the *BTR*s (proton and electron) are what determine the shape of an atom around a nucleus or molecule (another larger *BTR*) and give the atom (or molecule) its chemical properties.

All physical matter as we perceive it is due to electromagnetic interactions. What you feel when you walk barefoot (or touch anything) are the interactions of the electrons in your feet repelling the electrons in the ground.

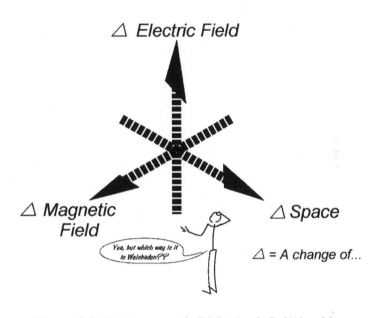

Figure 3-4, Electromagnetic Right Angle Relationships

What is the current electromagnetic theory? A changing electric field creates a changing magnetic field at right angles to the electric field and a change of space – at the speed of light -- right angles to other the two fields. (Scientists have no clear definition of what is an electric field or what is a magnetic field). The strongest element in *EMF* is the electric element. The weakest is the change of space. While some matter can stop the electric field, the magnetic field goes through everything.[19]

A change of one element automatically calls forth the other two. A change of magnetic creates a change of electric plus change of space; a change of space creates a change in electric and a change of magnetic (this is observable when something approaches light speed).

It is through the three right-angle relationships within electromagnetic *BTR*s – electric field, magnetic field, change of space at light speed -- that allow matter to take up three-dimensional space (Figure 3-4).

It is within the electromagnetic phenomena lies one of the major 'glitches' within today's science paradigm; it is the enigma of Coulomb's Law.

Coulomb's Law expresses the amount of available force created by two electric charges and is very similar to the formula expressing gravitational forces – Figure 3-10.[20] You may have experienced this electric field 'force' as static cling.

---

19 There is a magnetic field that travels all the way through our planet.

20 Instead of masses (m_1 and m_2), charge accumulations are used ($[C_1$ and $C_2]$ -- # of electrons or lack of...).

Distance (*d*) is the same as the gravity formula and measured in meters and charge is measured in coulombs (one

The formula constant (K) in Coulomb's Law is much larger than gravity's. If '1's were substituted into the gravitational formula, the resultant force would be negligible. If '1's were substituted into Coulomb's Law, the amount of force available translates to something like a million tons. Reduce all variables to 10^{-3} (equivalent to one milli-ampere at one millimeter) and still 10^6 tons are available.

The 'glitch' is no way would you have to expend that much force (electrically) to create that condition. (True creating a device that demonstrates this may be difficult.) This idea flies into the face of two science principles:

- You cannot get something for nothing.
- Nothing can be created or destroyed.[21]

The problem in using this electric field force arises with the pressure (voltage) needed to create such a condition (to keep all the repelling electrons in one place). The voltages that are required are so large; trying to use this force with closely spaced poles presents severe arcing problems.

Returning to the basic interactions, *EMF* is what determines the chemical nature of all matter as we experience it, along with the very nature of 3-dimensional space, as we perceive it.

$\Rightarrow$ **Gravity** is the weakest affinity that all *BTR*s have for each other. Be it on the particle level or the galactic, all *BTR*s have some affinity with each other. This is representative of Love binding things together. Gravity becomes apparent when the matrix arrays of the previous three *BTR* categories reach astronomical proportions (literally) and numbers.

It becomes apparent (to us) with the presence of massive systems of *BTR*s, large bodies. An example is our bodies' (a *BTR*) attraction with the planet (a *BTR*) and vice versa.

Another temporal/spatial limit can be found in gravity. When a number of *BTR*s accumulate in one place - same time and space; (too many *BTR*s in the same space at the same time), the 'lower' limit of physical creation manifests -- through gravity -- as the quantum singularity known as a black hole.

The 'low' limit of the scientific spectrum of interactions being presented manifests in gravity. While, the 'highest' limit is a Plank's length – h.

So, how does all this work? Let us look at a simple hydrogen atom. Not counting the smallest *BTR*s that make up the particles of proton and electron – weak nuclear *BTR*s, it is made of a *BTR* that is a proton and a *BTR* that is an electron. The hydrogen atom itself becomes another *BTR* comprised of the relationship of these two separate bubbles. The hydrogen atom matrix - proton/electron array -- gives the atom its own intrinsic qualities. A molecule of hydrogen (two hydrogen atoms) is a bubble of temporal/spatial reference composed of two atomic hydrogen *BTR*s.

In this example, a simple hydrogen molecule involves seven bubbles of temporal/spatial reference: four particle *BTR*s, the two atom *BTR*s they create, and the *BTR* that is created by them all -- the hydrogen molecule. (This is again, not counting the smallest *BTR*s that make up the particles of proton and electron) Each larger *BTR* is comprised of a relationship of smaller *BTR*s.

---

coulomb [C] = 6.2422 x 1018 electrons). (One ampere is one coulomb of electrons passing a given point in one second.)

21 Coulomb's Law is not the only 'glitch'. Strong nuclear and gravity raises some interesting questions as well. Given Newton's Laws of Motion and the laws of the relationship of energy to force say you "you can't get something for nothing": where is the energy coming from that accelerates the masses towards each other?

The ideas "you can't get something for nothing" or "nothing can be created or destroyed" apply to everything except the five basic interactions that define physical form: weak nuclear, strong nuclear, electro-magnetic, gravity, and life. It appears that the very interactions that define the physics paradigm can defy the paradigm.

Bubbles, within bubbles, within bubbles, etc; every atom and particle in our bodies is a bubble of temporal/spatial reference. These atoms make up the *BTR*s that are the *DNA*, the individual cells, the types and systems of cells, etc., all the way up to the human body that is another *BTR*.

All physical form is comprised of relationships or interactions between these *BTR*s, which in turn creates another *BTR*. The universe is a bubble of temporal/spatial reference made up of a finite (albeit a <u>very, very, very</u> large finite that approaches infinite) number of *BTR*s. The same is true with our bodies.

Bubbles, within bubbles, within bubbles, within bubbles...to the bubble that is the physical universe. Some of the bubbles are very stable and their temporal reference spans eons. Other bubbles' temporal reference is so short that they are almost impossible to detect from the human *BTR* reference. Some bubbles contain a bubble of sentience (life) while others carry none (rock).

<u>Notice</u> that the particle *BTR*s determine the nucleus *BTR*s, which determine the atom

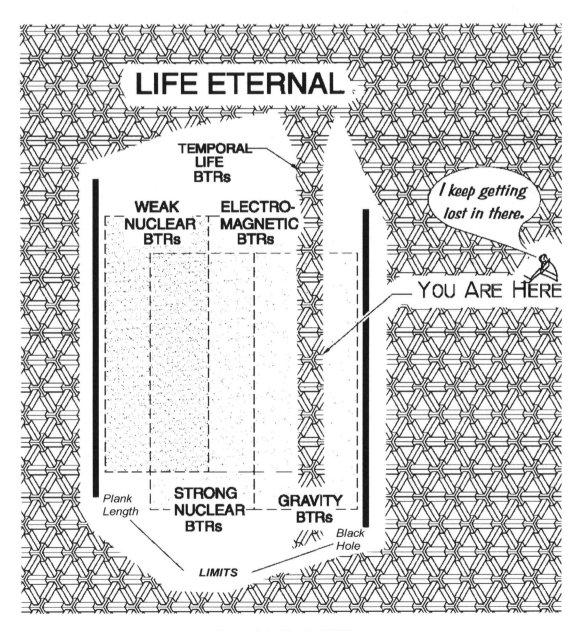

Figure 3-2, Physical BTRs

83

*BTR*s, which determine a molecule *BTR*...a planet *BTR*.

Each of these scientific interactions involves dualities. With gravity, there is the duality of the two separate pieces of matter. Electromagnetics are the interactions between electric charges -- plus to minus, plus to plus, or minus to minus. With strong and weak nuclear forces, there is a duality between nucleus particles and the duality involved with a change of state (matrix array), respectively. In scientific theory, each of these interactions is accompanied by a photon *BTR* of some sort. This photon *BTR* is what science recognizes as the interaction (the force of gravity, light, nuclear glue, etc.).

As shown in Figure 3-2, the different scientific interactions can be considered as an octave or part of a spectrum of a total system resonance. The smaller the *BTR*, the faster the rate of change, and can be looked at as a higher frequency. For example, each atomic particle *BTR* has an intrinsic nature; a proton *BTR* matrix has specific qualities, just as an electron *BTR* matrix has its own intrinsic qualities.

However, the changes those *BTR*s go through take up very small increments of time and space. In contrast, a planet *BTR*'s changes take up very large increments of time and space.

There appears to be a direct relationship between spatial size and temporal 'size'; an increase of spatial involves an increase in temporal and a decrease of temporal involves a decrease in spatial.[22]

These increments of change of a *BTR* determine the nature of the force/interaction perceived, light, gravity, atomic energy, etc. (or its position within the interaction spectrum). The nature of the incremental change of a proton to an electron determines the nature of the light we see. The change of our body in relationship to the planet determines the gravity we feel.

There are laws/truths they have in common; and there are sets of laws/truths that are only associated with each interaction. Another analogy is in Figure 4-1, The Electromagnetic

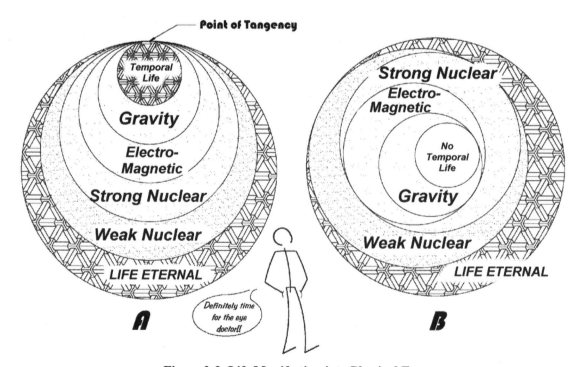

Figure 3-3, Life Manifesting into Physical Form

---

22 As spatial ⇑ ~ temporal ⇑, as spatial ⇓ ~ temporal ⇓

Spectrum. One end of the spectrum contains gamma rays while the other end contains radio waves. Both, are a form of electromagnetic energy, and yet; gamma rays act a lot differently than radio waves.

It is as if each physics interaction category, with its *BTRs*, is a special case within a whole system. Each special case has a set of truths/laws that pertain to it. These sets of truths form the *BTR* and the reality (environment) of the *BTR*.[23] Each interaction (gravity, *EMF* [electro-magnetic force], nuclear, etc.) almost acts as a separate octave within the total resonant system. Some truths/laws of particle physics are not considered pertinent to the movement of planetary bodies, just as some truths/laws of magnetism are not considered applicable to ballistics.

To continue the music analogy: each interaction and where it is in the spectrum of *BTRs* has its own sets of octaves, overtones, and harmonics.

⇒ **Life Force** is the fifth interaction in the paradigm presented by this book. Figure 3-2 shows the interaction that includes the *BTR* spectrum is the Eternal **Life Force** -- Creation. Actually, life is the spectrum; the scientific interactions are equivalent to octaves or bands within the life spectrum. Life makes the others possible through the Precious Moment of Creation and springs from the Eternal Matrix. It is possible to perceive life (and the Creation Matrix) at work extending itself all over this planet.

Figure 3-3 illustrates the relationships as a circle, within a circle, within a circle, etc. Each circle can be looked on as an array (a matrix) of *BTR* relationships. Within Figure 3-3 model, each circle can rotate and can revolve around the circle it is in. The result is points of tangency can change.

For example: let us say that Figure 3-3 (*A*) is a frog and (*B*) is a stone. For the frog to exist there must be an array of specific sub-atomic particles – *BTRs*. These sub-atomic particles must have an array that forms specific atomic particles -- *BTRs*. These atomic particles must be arrayed so they form specific *DNA* molecules -- *BTRs*. All these molecules must be arrayed in a specific manner for the frog (a *BTR*) and the environment (a *BTR*) that spawned it - life -- to manifest. The circle that contains everything is Life Eternal.

This revolving circle model can have five separate tangent points to each other (*B*) or they can have one tangent point in common (*A*). And, some of the circles can share common tangent points while other circles are separate.

When the points of tangency of these arrays are right,[24] Eternal Life manifests and extends itself in temporal form (frog). If the points of tangency are not right, then there is matrix form but no temporal life manifestation (usually the matrix is crystalline). These points of tangency in Figure 3-3 (*A*) are illustrative of specific *BTR* matrices arrays presented by the region of temporal life's physical conditions in Figure 3-2.

For every *BTR*, there are truths/laws, realities, and matrices associated with the structure of that *BTR*. The realities involved will become important when the human *BTR* is covered.[25] This revolving circle within circle model and the points of tangency will also be used again in this book. It presents a useful example for illustrating numerous relationships on a number of other topics.

Please note, as stated earlier, that with the Bubbles of Temporal/spatial Reference having relationships with other *BTRs*. There are logic arrays or small relevant truth/law matrices present as well. For example: separately the *BTRs* (proton and electron) that make up a hydrogen atom have nothing to do with the element at all. If they were just passively added together, they would form a neutron *BTR*.

Dynamically, their matrix relationship forms something new with intrinsic qualities -- hydrogen. It is the matrix array of the interactions within the *BTR*, which gives each *BTR* its innate characteristics or qualities.

---

23 Definition of terms - reality is the effect of truth and Chapter 4.2, 'What's Reality Papa?'
24 The *DNA BTR*, the planet it is on, what physical laws that are in support of the *DNA*, etc.
25 Chapter 4, Realities and the Human Matrix

One example how a matrix determines the qualities exhibited by its constituent matrices is carbon matrix arrays. Carbon matrices can exhibit the qualities of soot, peat, activated charcoal, coal, or diamond; it is all the same element -- carbon. The matrix of the atoms determines the qualities presented by the material. Constructed of the same material yet exhibiting different characteristics, the matrix array of the component matrices also determines the qualities exhibited by the material.

Another example of this is the iron crystalline structure -- matrix; it is strong and malleable. Add an insignificant amount of carbon atoms to the matrix; and, the iron matrix exhibits the qualities of steel. Control how the crystalline matrix forms – tempering – and the resultant matrix exhibits the properties of hardened steel. Add a few chromium atoms to the matrix; and, the resultant matrix exhibits the qualities of stainless steel.

These are examples of how the matrix array of the atoms – constituent *BTR*s -- determines the qualities presented by the material – the resultant *BTR*.

Examining the periodic table of elements, it can be seen that these element/particle matrices become increasingly more complicated. As the matrix becomes more complicated, the *BTR*'s physical form becomes larger (the atom) and exhibits different intrinsic qualities – the qualities of the elements. This is in spite of the fact that they have the same basic constituents.

Combinations of atomic matrices form a matrix of a molecular chemical compound. These matrices are another aspect of the Truth Matrix extending itself into physical form, all the way to the *DNA BTR* matrix extending life into physical form. As said earlier, *BTR* matrices become more involved, their time reference becomes slower. The time reference of a planet *BTR* is slower than that of an electron *BTR*.

Also, the speed of temporal/spatial rate of change of the molecule *BTR*s (stored kinetic energy) determines the nature of the matrix that determines our perception of the substance (solid, liquid, or gas).

When solid matter changes phase to a liquid, the matrices arrays has changed, giving the substance different qualities.

Ice has different qualities than water. A pure silicon crystal has different qualities than molten silicon. The same can be said when the substance changes phase to a gas (where the molecular crystalline matrix is non-existent). Each state (with its ability to hold more energy) has a looser matrix array of relationships that give that substance its intrinsic qualities in that state.

If the matrix is sophisticated enough to be a host to life -- as in a *DNA* molecular matrix, then life (or the Creation Matrix) starts using the *BTR*s around it to extend itself and its host matrix. For life to manifest into form there must be matrixes of specific *BTR*s to use, to recreate its vehicle (the conditions must be right). Each life *BTR* is a matrix; a logic arrangement of *BTR*s reproducing something else other than the parts. It becomes a recreating gestalt.

In solid matter, if the molecular matrix is not sufficiently complicated enough to become a life vehicle, the matrix usually appears as a crystalline type (with its own form of intrinsic qualities). These molecular matrices give rocks, metals, jewels, semiconductors, etc., their own uniqueness.

With the inclusion of the matrix concept, matter is not only bubbles – *BTR*'s, within bubbles, within bubbles… but also matrices, within matrices, within matrices… This compounding of matrices manifests all the way up to intelligent life, galaxies, and the universe. The more intelligent the life, the more elaborate is its logic matrix.

And…each *BTR* matrix array is a limited <u>mirrored</u> aspect of the Truth Matrix. This means the situation is such that there are not only *BTR*s, within *BTR*s, within *BTR*s… and matrices, within matrices, within matrices…but mirrors, within mirrors, within mirrors…(Which, makes physical form a kind of Cosmic funhouse.)[26]

---

26 Those who find their way out of the 'funhouse' get to go Home.

For most individuals, the physical *BTR*s and their arrangement are not considered relevant to their personal growth. "Knowing is not controlling." For one thing, we are dealing with *BTR*s/matrix within *BTR*s/matrix, within *BTR*s/matrix...to the nth degree, until it would 'blow' our finite mortal mind.

The bubble of temporal/spatial reference you need to be aware of is the one that contains your own temporal matrix - **Individual Reality**.[27] In operating your matrix along lines of Truth, the system -- Love -- will take care of the rest. This is for the later chapters to cover.

In keeping with the previous paragraphs, please note there are non-physical (metaphysical) *BTR*s as well as physical *BTR*s. A partial list may include: personal thought/emotional sets, temporal ideas of governments and cultures, demons, etc. Some of these metaphysical *BTR*s will also be addressed in later chapters. This section's primary focus is the introduction of Bubbles of Temporal/spatial Reference *BTR*s.

3.5 - Mirror Mechanics, Connections, and Parallels

*I*n the previous section, the concept of patterns and parallels was introduced. The Creation matrix, in extending itself into an increasingly limited medium (physical form); it creates limited fracture versions of itself (mirrors God/Creation). These fractured or limited versions show up in the simplest of things like a water molecule. A water molecule[28] can be seen as a very limited physical model of the 3-in-1, 1-in-3 concept in Figure 2-1.

There are many other examples of mirror patterns or parallels occurring throughout physical and metaphysical form. A partial list is:

1) Newton's third law of motion:
   a) Every action has an equal and opposite reaction.
   b) Whatever force is extended, becomes mirrored back on the source.
2) Karma:
   a) As you do, shall be done to you.
   b) Idea is throughout world religions and mystical thought systems
3) Mathematics' real number line.
   a) Mirrored around *0*
   b) The region of *1>0>-1*, where all multiplication operations produce smaller products instead of larger products (produces a reverse mirror image).
   c) The relationship of the imaginary number system as it mirrors the real number system with a distortion factor of *i*.
4) In psychotherapy, it appears in the laws of projection.
   a) Everything we 'see' mirrors what is in our mind.
   b) What we see in other people is a mirror to how we see ourselves (and vice versa).
5) The concept of mirrored light in physics.
   a) Beside the obvious reflection
   b) In reflecting, the angle of incidence equals the angle of reflection.
6) The mirroring of the Truth Matrix with the human matrix.
7) In other physics concepts of

---

27 Chapter 4.2 - 'What's Reality Papa?'

28 The water molecule -- consisting of two hydrogen atoms and one oxygen atom -- is a highly electrically polarized molecule. Interestingly, due to its matrix arrays (solid, liquid, or gas) water is one of the most unique substances in the universe.
- Distilled water is the universal solvent. Given enough time, it will dissolve anything.
- Distilled water is the perfect dielectric insulator (stops electron flow but allows electric fields to pass through). However, because it is a universal solvent, it will dissolve part of whatever container it is in. As soon as distilled water has impurities within it, it is no longer distilled water, and stops being an insulator -- it conducts.
- Most substances when changing phase from liquid to solid become denser than the liquid and sinks. Ice is less dense than liquid water and floats. If it were not for this idiosyncrasy, the oceans would have frozen from the bottom up and there would be no life as we know it on this planet.

a) Fractured symmetry and super-symmetry.
b) Matter and anti-matter

Let us examine variations of the mirror mechanics as perceived by the '*I*' or mortal human truth matrix. One excellent example of the mirror mechanics and the parallels involved is comparing Newton's laws of motion paralleled to Karma.

There are three principles in Newton's Laws of Motion (which, are related to gravity). In the first law of motion, called inertia, nothing happens to a body unless it is influenced from the outside. Take a wood block, set it on a table, and it will not move unless something moves it. Accordingly, once you choose to move it, it keeps going until something slows it down (usually caused by friction). In space, if you pushed it, the block would go on forever.

The second law of motion is the relationship of force to mass and the rate of acceleration of the mass. You put so much force on a little body, it moves farther and faster than a big body does with the same amount of force (Force = mass x acceleration). The second law of motion expresses what energy is entailed in moving a mass (block) at what speed. This law/truth illustrates there is a relationship.

In the third law of motion, whatever force you apply will be reflected back on you. If you throw a bowling ball while standing in a wagon, the effort will push the wagon in the opposite direction. Here is an excellent example of the mirror. This concept is used to make rockets work. We as people use this relationship between force and reaction everyday and we do not know it.

If you are leaning against a wall with your hand with 20 pounds of pressure, the wall must be exerting exactly 20 pounds of pressure for your hand not to move.

When we lose our balance, we use the third law of motion to regain it. We put our arm into the direction we are losing our balance and the opposite reaction of pushing the mass of our arm one way pushes the mass of our body in the other direction. It is almost as if we are leaning into the fall, but we are not. We are pushing the mass of our arm one way, which pushes our body the other direction, so we are back on balance.

This is one aspect of the mirror on a purely physical level. Whatever you do physically is reflected back to you physically.

The metaphysical parallel to this law is Karma. Karma is eastern religions' law of metaphysical cause and effect. Essentially, Karma states that whatever you chose to do; the universe will reflect that choice on you. In the Bible, it is expressed in sayings like, "As you sow, so shall you reap." Karma can work on both physical and metaphysical levels.

As with the block example, no obvious action produces any obvious effect (although inaction is an action). However, if you make a choice, that choice is reflected back on you. The effect is dependent on how forceful the choice, its contents (the physical and metaphysical levels of level of ~~truth~~ and perception involved), and your intent.

The Correction idea manifests in Karma, with this Mirror aspect, since it reflects the choices you make back on yourself. This is done in order for you to choose Truth and reunion with God.

When you have done something nasty, that nasty comes back to you.
"Hmm. That didn't work! I don't know if I want to do that one again!"

Krishna in the Bhagavad-Gita talks about karma.[29] It is written that Krishna said the only choice that does not evoke Karma -- the one thing you can do that will have no effect back on you -- is to choose to unite yourself with the Source/Divine/God. In addition, this choice must be made with no attachment to the outcome. Only this action is karma-less.

This is type of action is something that Bhagavad-Gita stresses, and it must be done with non-attachment to the outcome.

This action bypasses the karmic mechanism, because the Mirror mechanism is meant to reflect your choices back on you, for you to choose God or not choose ~~truth~~. When you

---

[29] A dialogue between an archer -- Arjuna -- and his chariot driver -- Krishna -- before a battle against Arjuna's relatives.

begin by choosing God, your actions do not reflect back because you are already doing what the Mirror intends

It is like the Mirror is set up to reflect what you do back on you to choose God. When you choose God immediately, you short-circuit the Mirror.

You must, however, do this with non-attachment, because from a human perception and a human matrix -- mortal mind -- reference, you do not know what the Source is. Because you do not know what the Source is, you must not have any attachment to the outcome – preconceived ideas -- or you will cloud the process.[30]

There are many reasons for the non-attachment. To begin with, you do not know what God is, or all the ramifications coming from the 'choice' of God. You may also recognize this: that no preconceived mortal ideas of God should be in the way to interfere with the mechanism. These preconceived ideas can come from attachments to the outcome.[31]

How can you can choose God and not know what God is? Ask a monk. To choose to be in union with the whole is essentially the same thing. You must recognize there is a whole, and, or a Source. Recognize you do not know everything about that Source or what it entails. It is something much greater than its apparent parts like yourself. One example of this is recognizing, "A wise man is someone who knows, he knows nothing."

That was Socrates thing; I am the wisest man, because I know I know nothing.[32] While, everybody around him thought they knew something. He could lead anybody into a contradiction to prove they did not know anything. He figured he was wiser because he knew he knew nothing, while everybody else thought they knew something and did not.

If you think you know all about something, it hampers your ability to learn anything new in relationship to it. Especially if, that knowledge is based on your limited perceptions.

Recognition of ignorance is the beginning of wisdom.

It can be seen that Karma and the Newton's third law of motion are the same thing; they are flip sides of the same coin. One tends to operate on a physical level, while the other tends to operate on a metaphysical level. Both illustrate the Mirror. There is something there!

Whatever you do (both physically and metaphysically) will reflect back on you.

There are many other examples of how physical laws are parallel to metaphysical laws.

❑ One example is the right-angle rule. A right-angle rule is when the effects of a choice are translated into a different direction (vector) other than the original direction or its opposite (as in laws of motion or Karma). Imagine that you had to walk to the door in front of you. However, if there is a right-angle rule involved, you may have to walk directly to the wall on your left to get the door in front of you.

As stated earlier, the right-angle rule is a major influence present in electro-magnetic propagation. A changing electric field produces a changing magnetic field at right angles to the electric field. Plus, there is a change of space that accompanies this and it is at right angles to the other two fields. Again, it is through the right-angle rule of electro-magnetic propagation that matter, as we know it, has three-dimensional space.

The right-angle rule also is the primary explanation of how a gyroscope works. The mystery of a gyroscope is; when you push down on one side of the gyroscope, the force of that push is translated ninety degrees in the direction the gyroscope is spinning. This right-angle translation is produced by the angular momentum of the moving mass (Figure 3-8, Gyroscope).

---

30 See also "disinterested-interest" of Chapters 5, 6, 7, 8, and 9

31 Chapter 4, Realities and the Human Matrix

32 Socrates is not generally known as being a mystic. And, it is recorded that he stood for 24 hours unmoving. In addition, he walked barefoot even in the snow. These actions do not fall in to the realm of the non-mystical or 'normal stream of consciousness'.

This right-angle rule parallel is a very important factor when dealing with spiritual growth, especially when we start getting into concepts of Zen, deep meditation; of going into non-action, stillness, and no perception. Entering the spiritual journey/Mirror and coming out the back/God side into the Universe by doing nothing. Whew, what a conundrum!

The right-angle rule gives everything a twist. In fact, Karma or the third law of motion can be seen as a double

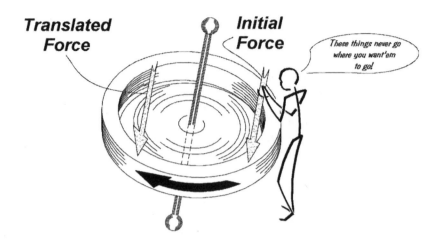

Figure 3-8, Gyroscope

application of the right-angle rule. If we try to do something, outside us towards 'what we perceive' is being with God, it tends to go in a different direction. We tend to become caught up in our perceptions of external affairs. However, if we make no effort and are still in God, our spiritual progress starts to begin. It is another right-angle twist to things. "You can't go this way (what <u>appears</u> to be the direct route). You must go that way (what appears to be the wrong direction)."

❏ Another parallel connection between physics and metaphysics is evident in harmonics and sympathetic resonance paralleled to human communication and to spiritual learning. Let us look at the concept of sympathetic resonance. [33]

To review, a simple physics experiment is to use two *C* tuning forks, both are made of the same material, and the mathematics that determine the frequency of the tuning forks are the same. [34] Separate these two tuning forks. Put one on a table in a room, and excite it. Put the other on a table across the room. When one tuning fork is excited, the other untouched one will start to resonate. This is sympathetic resonance.

All electromagnetic communication through the air is due to sympathetic resonance. The 'front' end of a radio is tuned to a station transmitter. When receiving a program, the 'front' of the radio is in sympathetic resonance with the radio transmitter.

This sympathetic resonance concept present in physics can be seen as a parallel to working with symbols in communication. If a person shares the same symbols and has made similar choices as another -- like the same mathematics of the two tuning forks being the same -- then you get a resonance of matrices between the two individuals; an idea is shared.

"Oh, like wow man, I can really resonate with what you're saying."

If however, there is a difference between the symbols; if one tuning fork is an *A* tuning fork and the other is a *C* tuning fork or the radio is not tuned to the station, there would be no resonance and hence no communication. (Kind of, like when one person is talking apples and another is hearing oranges.)

There is another example of physical and metaphysical parallels or connections regarding sympathetic resonance. The magic law of sympathy used in voodoo. This may

---

33 Chapter 1.6, The Pentacle vs. the Pyramid
34 Has the same mathematical dimensions

involve a lock of hair or a picture of a person on the voodoo doll. The idea is the object (doll) is in sympathy with the person. What will happen to the doll, will happen to the person.[35]

❏ Fluid laws. This parallel the author observed once, sitting up on top a tall building and watching people. When the streets are crowded, people will move like Bernoulli's principle: if a fluid is not moving, it pushes out equally on all directions of the container - square or sidewalk. Once the fluid starts moving, there is less pressure on the side and more of a flow. (This is what makes an airplane fly.)

This can be seen with people in a plaza where there is a craft fair -- they are all milling and bouncing around. However, if you now look at a city street like in New York City where everybody is busy and intent on a destination, you see these flows of people with very few people off to the side. It can be seen how fluid motion can be a parallel to the movement of people in crowded situations.

❏ There is the laws of thermodynamics. The laws of thermodynamics have parallels in the metaphysical and human condition. One immediately obvious: is heat flows to where heat is not. Cold does not flow -- the heat/energy flows. Energy flows from where there is some to where there is an absence. Same as with knowledge: knowledge flows from where there is some to where there is none. It is a direct parallel to thermodynamics. Knowledge does not flow the other way. It goes the one way only. Lack of knowledge does not create knowledge. Knowledge creates knowledge.

Lack of knowledge determines which direction knowledge will flow. Lack of knowledge does not flow to knowledge.[36] Knowledge flows to lack of knowledge. It is a flow of energy. Look at knowledge as energy, or heat: you must bring the lack (the pot) to the source of heat. When you move a hot pan to a table, you had better have a potholder. Otherwise, the heat transfers to your hand.

You already know that is not very bright -- it tingles and it 'smarts'. The heat or energy is flowing from the pan to your hand. Normally, you cannot make your hand hotter than the pan. This physical law is illustrates how light flows to darkness but darkness cannot flow to light?

Why does darkness not flow to light? Darkness is the absence of light. Darkness cannot do anything. It is inert. It is like saying the darkness can put out a candle. It cannot. In fact, one match -- the slightest amount of light anywhere -- illuminates it. Darkness cannot fight light; it must give way. This we will go into a little bit more when we get into magic and psychic laws.

❏ Mathematical reasoning is used throughout this book. Here is a mathematical parallel to the spiritual generation of physical form. Physical form is at/the result of/or just above the zero area of a spiritual Mandelbrot equation. Numbers plugged into a Mandelbrot equation either become infinite or they become *0*. Mandelbrot equations generate fractals.

Look at these fractals and you will see a recurring black spot in them – the *0* area. The area above (or encompassing) the black spot is like physical form (from a Divine perspective). Fractals are referred to in this book in numerous places.

You have been introduced the concept of parallels and connections between the physical and non-physical. Next, is a lab or an exercise of thinking in parallels.

********************  ********************

Exercise and Lab 3: Truth Perception

Working with patterns and parallels allows for a broader scope of perception. This is an exercise in mentally jumping parallels through truth perception and cognition using

---

35 What is being presented is over simplified and does not take into account other factors -- variables.
36 Except maybe in government or politics.

something around you. This exercise can help give your limited mortal mind another dimension.

This assignment is one truth a day for an extended period – 10 weeks to a year. This 'truth' is to be entered into a notebook. This 'truth' is not to be something you read or you are told. It is to be picked up from an everyday object around you. Pick an object, any object around you. Examine it and ask questions.

Ask: Who?, What?, Where?, When?, etc. Then ask, "What is this like?"

Pick an object that is around you! Break it down in to function and ask questions like who, what, where when, why, how, etc. After answering some of these questions, make a parallel to something that is much grander or bigger than the original object. Take an everyday object and parallel it in to Life, People, the World…

The end product – what goes in the journal -- should appear something like; "*A _____ is like a _____. Because of _____.*" Your explanation should be only about two sentences. Enter this observation in a journal or notebook.

Some common parallels that may prove useful for this exercise may be:

- Light: almost any thing dealing with light can parallel to truth, knowledge, or education.
- Air: parallels into change, life, or people.
- Water: can parallel into life, softness, people, or flexibility.
- Food: can make parallels into learning, growth, people, and survival.
- Fire or chemical reactions: make great metaphysical parallels into change, both passive and active, or people.
- Tools and utensils: can parallel the human condition.
- Anything that deals with earth or soil: can parallel into that which is solid, basic, or unmovable.

The author learned this exercise as a high school sophomore in Mr. Zehren's English class, the class had to do one truth a day and put it down in a notebook. The author had Mr. Zehren everyday (5 days a week) for two semesters; so, the fifteen-year-old author had to do this exercise for nine months.

Being lazy, the author seldom did his until he got to class. He must have gotten over thirty truths looking at or through the classroom windows. Some examples of this are:

- ❑ Some people are like windows and let knowledge or truth into our lives.
  - The glass and the teachers teaching in the classroom.
- ❑ Some people are like windows and let fresh air in our lives.
  - Opening the window and the 'changes' we like. (laughter, joy, 'warm fuzzy', etc.)
- ❑ Some people are like shades and block the light/knowledge coming to us.
  - Pulling down the shades for *A-V* purposes and some unpleasant inter-personal interactions.
  - When the light is blocked from without us, perhaps it is to have us watch the movie within us.
  - If this is a cosmic lesson plan, whose hand really controls the shade?
  - The teacher directing a student to close the shade.
  - Watching the internal movie.

Be advised that adding modifiers like *some* can make your truths more accurate or comprehensive. For example, saying, "Some people are like windows…" is more accurate than, "People are like windows…" Not everybody is like this. In saying *some*, there will always be someone somewhere acting like this (if not just a parent to a child). The modifier can help make your 'truth' more accurate and comprehensive.

Here is an example on how to do this. The author did this exercise with another person and this is how it turned out.

Pick an object! The person the author demonstrated this to picked an on-off switch on an in-line power supply and amplifier mounted on the cord of a microphone.[37] The power supply uses a battery. It has a little clip on it so it can mount on the belt or shirt. (Whew! Not something very simple.)

Once you pick an object like this and mentally examine it, start going in parallels. The best thing to do for beginners is stay in generalities with simple things (unlike microphone switches). Do not try to get too specific. The lesson can be easier to learn if you stick to simple things like windows, spoons, pencils, etc. And…anything around you can be used for this exercise!

Whatever you do, give it the **K.I.S.S.** (**K**eep **I**t **S**imple **S**tupid).

Again, start asking questions about the object. Who, what, when, where, why, how, sequencing of relationships, etc., and make a list. (Be careful with 'why'. Because, you can also ask 'why not'.)

❑ For example, who would use this?
  • Somebody who wishes to record.
❑ Who would make that switch?
  • Somebody who wishes to eat.
❑ How does it work or what is it?
  • It is something that aids the microphone in the transmission of sound to a tape recorder.
  • It is a go/no-go device
❑ When is it used?
  • When you wish to record on a tape recorder.
  • You do not use it when you want to play the tape recorder; it might give feedback.
❑ Without that on-off switch, amplifier, or battery, the mike system will not work.

The next thing to do is examine some relationships. The microphone is recording, but what is it recording?

The mike can record a myriad of things: music, words and discussions, or nonsense and noise. At the time, the microphone was being used to record the author's words. The mike, switch, and amplifier are totally neutral in terms of what they let through to the tape recorder or not.

The sound is coming from the source, through the medium of the air. The mike takes the sound, changes it to electrical energy, which travels down the wire into this battery back and amplifier. It is amplified by the battery (which is engaged by the switch) and then is picked up by the tape recorder. The mike, amplifier, on-off switch, and cord are a whole transducer assembly. It transduces sound to electricity. What the on-off switch and amplifier are doing is allowing change of electrical signals (created by sound), from the mike to the tape recorder; again, it is a go/no-go device.

The object was mentally dissected. What does it do, how is it used, and what is it for? Next, is to jump into parallels. Ask what else does this, or what is this like? For example, what else acts a go/no-go device between an amplifier between what is done on one end, as the mike (a transducer), and how it is received on the other, as the tape deck?

The mike and the tape deck have a specific relationship, one is sending and one is receiving. The mike's inline amplifier switch is there to facilitate that. If we look at the mike, amplifier, and tape deck as being all in one person, then we can say our grasp of language acts

---

37 We were recording this at the time.

as an amplifier switch or transducer of what we hear to ideas we recognize. This go/no-go device is like the individual's grasp of language.

When it was said, "Some of the squared legs equals the square of the hippopotamus."[38] That may have been nonsense to you until it was explained. The individual's grasp of language translates what went in and determines what is recognized. From the mike (author's words), through an amplifier (language/perception), to the tape deck (cognition).[39] "Oh, I got it." Click! One go/no-go device facilitates a flow of electrons; the other facilitates a flow of ideas.

Who or what can act also like an on/off switch to the flow of ideas? How about a language translator; someone who allows the flow of ideas between two languages?

So it can be said, *"A translator is like a switch – a go/no-go device -- to the flow of ideas."*

Because, without a language translator, ideas do not flow. Ideas flow with a language translator.

That is only one parallel to this mike/amplifier/recorder go/no-go array. It is possible to have other parallels.

As was just done; extend the everyday object into comprehensive generalities, things that tend to be all encompassing: Life, God, humanity, growth, people, etc. The more inclusive this truth is, the better. This exercise will help facilitate the 'ring' necessary for part of the first homework assignment -- the *Mine* box.[40] Through this exercise, you can generate that 'ring' inside you.

The truth 'ringing' is facilitated as the individual begins assembling the truths perceived, and applying them.[41] A mystical operator or metaphysical student's goal should be making their truth matrix similar to the Absolute Truth Matrix, rebuilding their human matrix. Or, more accurately, reprogramming their existing human mind/matrix so it is similar to the Absolute Truth Mind/Matrix – create common tangent points. Having their matrix store 'absolutes' they perceive, helps facilitate this.[42]

A review of this exercise: you select an object and you examine it for what, where, when, how and maybe why and, the sequencing of events that determine its use. Just examine for the facts that you see in it.

Okay. Suppose we have a container with us (a plastic one-liter container with a snap top) and it holds water right now, but it can hold other things. It is made of plastic; it has a removable top,

Assuming the liquid is for human consumption (which is what it was used for), the liquid -- no matter what it is -- has water in it. The liquid in the container could be plain water as the one the author had in his hand, juice with water and other nutrients in it, or wine. One way or another, whether it is water or juice or whatever, the container is holding a liquid with a life-giving element (water).

The exercise is for you to look at it, determine whatever it is for, and in the end, jump parallels into your perception of life. So...what, in the human system, is life giving or is a vessel for life giving? (The parallels can go in different directions. For this example, it will be narrowed down and given a direction.)

What is it or what something is necessary for peoples -- as a whole, something we need within us, outside us, for our learning or growth? What else is like this vessel that holds water? This -- the water -- is something that is absolutely necessary whereas the vessel can hold a liquid that is not absolutely necessary, like wine. So, what in our lives is as a vessel that

---

38 First chapter
39 Chapter 4.4 and 4.5, The Human Matrix - Storages and The Perceptual Lens Array
40 Chapter 1.1 - What To Believe
41 Chapter 4.8, Ring My Bell
42 Chapters 9 and 10

can be used for something we absolutely need, or just to hold something that we use and do not absolutely need?

How about knowledge? It holds truth (or truth applications[43]).

In one way, knowledge (truth applications) based on **Absolute** and **Actual** Reality[44] are truths essential for survival, and we cannot do without them. Otherwise, we would not be able to walk, talk, eat, and survive.

Yet, there is knowledge that is based on Absolute and Actual Truths -- essential -- and knowledge that is based on relative truths (society or politics) -- not essential. We can take both in. Some examples are the fantasy book sitting over there or playing with the computer on the Internet. These are not essential for survival within a human system; and, it is knowledge that we take in.

So we can say, "*Knowledge is like a container. Some things in our knowledge are necessary to survive while other things held by our knowledge are not essential to survival.*"

With this exercise, hopefully you can see how you can take anything, jump into parallels, and you see something way beyond a mere jug of water.

Now, as to storage and categorizing of the truths that you pick up from these parallels: after a while, you will notice some parallels that apply to all or everybody. And, you will see other parallels will apply to some cases and not to others.

Some of the determining factors will be:

- your wording,
- individual perceptions
- what truth is stored in your knowledge already.

Next to each truth formulated in this exercise, mark the categories of the truth. The categories are *absolute* (**A**), *unknown* (**?**), or *relative* (**R**).

A ⇒ The *absolute* category is when the parallel appears to apply to everything you see.

R ⇒ The *relative* category is applicable when you see it pertains to some things, while not to others.

? ⇒ The *unknown* category is when you are not sure.

If you find one exception to a truth in the *absolute* category, it becomes a *relative* truth. Use the geometric postulate analogy: if one exception is found to a postulate, it ceases to be a postulate.

However, exceptions must be examined just as carefully as the original truth. What may be an exception in one way may not be an exception when perceived in another way – where you are 'standing'. For example, what you may be seeing as an exception may be due to how you are perceiving -- looking at it. The changing of your perception can cause the exception to disappear.

Be like the 'fair witness' concept, presented in *Stranger in a Strange Land*.[45] When a woman, Ann, who was a fair witness, was asked the color of the house on the hill, she turned to Jubal and said, "It's white on this side, Jubal." Be objective. Recognize what you see is on

---

43 Chapter 4
44 Ibid.
45 A science fiction book by Robert Heinlein, Copyright 1961... A fair witness was trained in observation to such an extent that whatever a fair witness said happened, was accepted in a court of law as fact.

'this side'. Just because one side of a house is white does not mean the whole house is white. Then look around to the other side, it might be black.

24 ounces, 700 milligrams (markings on the plastic container).

Like the plastic container, changing where you stand changes what you see. On one side is metric measure and it says 700 milliliters, which is speaking one language. Look on the other side, it says 24 ounces -- which is speaking another measure language, and both languages have to do with the same thing, volume. Two symbol systems, one is from Napoleon and the other from English; and yet, the two symbol systems are talking about the same thing -- quantity.
So...

The same knowledge can be expressed through multiple symbol systems – languages.

Be like the 'fair witness'. By being open and not shut anything out, observe like the 'fair witness'. Being honest with yourself more than anything else; get rid of your preconceived notions, be open. "In the eyes of a child..."
There may be some truths you may not want to believe, or not even want to recognize. We can recognize and not want to believe it. But, we must recognize it at least. (Recognized -- re-cognized -- or not, the Truth still exists.)
That is what is meant by an honest frame of mind, dispassionately. If we refuse to re-know the Truth, it will not do us any good. We must re-know it, re-cognize its existence, if not believe it. This is one of the ways Cognitive Input programs our Knowledge.[46]

This is the assignment:

➤ *The assignment for this exercise is a truth/day taken from an everyday object and to enter it in a notebook for an extended period of time -- ten weeks to a year.*
➤ *State what was the original object, and then, state the 'truth' perceived. The format: A/Some _____ is like a _____. Because they both: __2_ sentences__.*
➤ *In the margin before your truth enter the category you perceive it to be in:* **A**bsolute, **R**elative, *or* **?** *(you do not know).*
➤ *In addition, five slashes are required in the cover of the notebook for the* <u>Mine</u> *category of Exercise and Lab 1a.*

There are multitudes of advantages of learning this exercise. Some of the advantages produced by doing this exercise everyday over an extended window of time -- months -- are:

1) Learning to think in parallels adds another dimension to your mind.
It takes what your mind does automatically in the 'background' and brings it to the 'front' of your mind to use.
This exercise can expand your perceptual window on things. You can see beyond the object at hand, as you begin thinking in parallels.

2) Things become simpler as you start thinking in parallels.
Looking at things, one sees things become increasingly complicated: *BTR*s within *BTR*s within *BTR*s..., matrices within matrices within matrices..., mirrors within mirrors within mirrors..., etc. With so many variables, the diversity can give the mortal brain a cramp. However, once you begin thinking in parallels, things can get simpler instead of more complicated. The similarities and connections can be seen. You can begin to generate a more non-exclusive mind or a mind with Love in it.
Again, you are starting to put your human mind/matrix to work and reprogramming it according to the lines of the Absolute Truth Matrix. As the mind becomes increasingly non-

---

46 Chapter 4, Realities and the Human Matrix

exclusive, an individual begins to see more. This effect makes it possible to relate all the information in this book into reoccurring themes.

3) Since absolute truth is invulnerable and unchangeable, this exercise can give one a place to 'stand'.

This can be important in a sea of changes. Keeping to absolute truths can be like standing on a rock in troubled seas. This also can be useful when doing and questioning *ESP* experiments.

4) This exercise facilitates comprehensive truth storage within the mind.

This is why you categorize. When Sherlock Holmes first meets Watson in the story, *A Study in Scarlet*,[47] Watson and Holmes are students together at a University. Watson sees that Sherlock Holmes is equivalent to a genius, and is very much learned in a number of different subjects: chemistry, forensics, ballistics, etc. He also learns Holmes is very ignorant on other subjects like astronomy. This is in an antithesis of the popular concept of the times (the enlightened man).

The *enlightened man* had to know a little bit of everything. Watson asked Holmes, how it is that he could be so learned in one field and completely ignorant of another.

To paraphrase Holmes' response: I look at my mind like an attic. Most people store anything they come across, throw it in their attic, and their attic becomes one big clutter. I choose to store only specific things in my attic. I don't want my attic cluttered.

If a person uses this concept with the Absolute Truth and starts storing in their 'attic' only Absolute Truth – that which they can find no exception to, this lesson will start producing results over time.

This exercise can expand your understanding and knowledge base. When we use these parallels between metaphysical and physical, we begin to generate an inclusive mind through Truth. Love's Truth is all-encompassing. We input Absolute Truth into our human matrix. The more absolutes we input and connect together, the more our human matrix becomes similar to the Truth Matrix.[48] The Truth in our minds will have an affect by aligning itself with the Truth Matrix.

It is the truth in the matrix that defines the matrix; while the matrix defines the exhibited quality of the material. The water molecule defines a snowflake or an iceberg. In addition, though each snowflake is different, all snowflakes have common variables in their formation.

The matrix of personal beliefs and philosophies are defined by the truth in them. Absolute Truth defines its own matrix. Your philosophies are important in that they help you array the truth within your mind. As new truths are learned, the philosophy must change (to accommodate it). Either that, or be in some form of denial of that truth.

This exercise facilitates truth storage in your mind and helps you assemble a comprehensive truth matrix within you.

5) The "Know the truth and the truth will set you free" mechanism.

How does this work? A review of some of the previous material may be helpful here. In Chapter 2 and this chapter, you were introduced two concepts:

❑ You were introduced to the concepts of infinite and finite or eternal and temporal as being mutually exclusive.
  ⇨ If something is not infinite, it is finite. If something is not finite, it is infinite.
  ⇨ If something is not eternal, it is temporal. If something is not temporal, it is eternal.
❑ You were introduced to the concept that a logic system can create something alien to that logic system.
  ⇨ In mathematics, the concepts of division by zero ($^x/_0$) and taking the square root (or even root) of a negative number ($\sqrt{-1}$).

---

47 A Study In Scarlet by Sir Arthur Conan Doyle
48 Chapter 2.5 - *Postulate 4*, God's Logical Mind is a matrix of Absolute, Eternal Truth.

⇨ These two examples are how a logic system can create something that is outside of the logic system.

The postulates and theorems focus on an infinite/eternal Mind manifesting a finite/temporal condition; and, it can go the other way as well. This means, if a finite/temporal mind – mortal mind -- creates something alien to it, that creation will automatically be infinite/eternal – Divine Love -- related in some way.

When a finite/temporal mind – mortal mind -- programs itself with eternals and absolutes, it becomes easier to for that mind to create something that is alien to that mind, or to 'exit' the mortal mind.

In the bible, it is written that Jesus said, "Know the truth and the truth will set you free." Because Truth is constant, this is just as true now as it was in Jesus' time. Once truths are accumulated, they start appearing in/assembling themselves into matrices they are normally in. Again, as the water molecule defines the nature of a snowflake; so does the nature of the truth define the nature of the thought construct -- philosophy.

When absolute truth starts assembling with other absolute truth (this absolute truth together with this absolute truth together with this absolute truth) within a mortal mind, a 'whirrr click' can occur inside a person; a cognitive jump occurs. This 'whirrr click' (a specific 'ringing' of the individual matrix/mind[49]) is an instant change of a mental/emotional state -- consciousness. This change tends to be comprehensive in scope when you are dealing with absolutes.

You perceive the truth matrix involved. Any truth you learn regarding that particular subject matter afterward, you can 'see' where or how it fits.

This change of state can give a quiet peace and an understanding of whole things based on comprehensive truth - a comprehensive 'quiet understanding'.

Alternatively, it can also be an epiphany.

In both cases, the matrix the truth is in becomes part of the individual mind matrix; an alignment occurs.

In the end, you are starting to reprogram your mortal truth matrix with comprehensive truths – eternals -- through your cognitive input (Chapter 4, Realities and the Human Matrix). You are starting to align yourself with the Absolute Truth Matrix (although, at the time, you may not know such a concept existed).

After this has happened a number of times, and a number of 'quiet understandings' have been stored in your mental matrix. One 'quiet understanding' (based on absolute truth) assembles with another 'quiet understanding', with another 'quiet understanding', and with another 'quiet understanding'... the 'whirrr click' (the cognitive jump) is going to be a religious experience, independent of whether you believe in God or not.

Because, God is the source of all Absolute Truth. In the end, you are just following the Truth to its Source. So, if you keep on working with comprehensive or Absolute Truth within an honest framework of mind, you are going to end up with a religious experience of some sort, because God is the Source of the Absolute Truth.

Or, in other words, when you start assembling Absolute Truths together, you get these peaceful points of knowledge, which -- when assembled -- bring you to God whether you believe in God or not.[50]

Belief in a system is not that important to the process. It is the truths in a belief system that facilitates the process.

What is being described here is a mechanism. This is how the mechanism "Know the truth and the truth will set you free" works.

---

49 "Ring' as in *Assignment 1*. This event will also be covered in depth in later chapters.
50 *Chapter 9,* building 'thought forms'. Stated simply, it is assembling the truth.

6) An old spiritual axiom is. "There is nowhere you need to go to learn the Truth. Everything is right there in front of you."

If you really learn this lesson -- how to think in parallels from a simple common object to something all encompassing, everything you need to know is right there in front of you. The student of mysticism or metaphysics needs only be aware and have their eyes open.

Everything you need to know is right in front of you in common everyday objects. You just have to look at the object, learn to jump in parallels, and everything you need to know is available to you. This lab works best when you make no judgments as the objective observer.

Be aware of your ignorance because your ignorance is going to be part of the lab.

This exercise is relatively important and when done within a formal class format, these journal entries would be a significant grade element. At first, the exercise may take some time. And...after practice the time it takes to 'perceive truths' will shorten.

One possible exercise for formal classroom groups may go this way; have the class pair up and talk to each other. Each person does a truth of his or her own. Then, they work out a truth together. Then, the whole group hears these truths from the separate groups.

********************  ********************

3.7 - Time Ignor-ance

*G*od's Eternal Love is not exclusive. Love recognizes that for temporal mortal minds, time is an apparent issue. Because it is dealing with temporal mortal mind references, Love uses - through the Mirror - these references to facilitate the Correction. From the Eternal reference, the concept of time is *non-sequitar*; Love will use it and Love is not limited by it. This is where the temporal mind can get boggled.

In the Eternal/temporal relationship, there are the two sides. One part is the Love Truth Mind/Matrix and is Eternal. On the other hand, the human mind/matrix or an ~~truth~~ mind/matrix has both some Truth and ~~truth~~ in it; and for the most part, is temporal and finite. Time is an effect of a mind separated from the Eternal God. Time from a temporal mind's reference is a series of cause/effect events (*BTR* changes) put into sequential order using an objective *BTR* reference (a reoccurring change: clock, planet rotation, heartbeat... another *BTR*).

The Eternal condition within the temporality is really Truth and the Correction on the physical level.[51] This Correction is referred to as the Mirror. God's Love reflects a mistake in thinking back into Creation's face (so to speak). Since this is a closed system in God,[52] the mistake will be corrected. It is only a question of time. Which, from Eternity's reference, (and just like the ~~truth~~) is a special case of Love's application and does not really exist.[53]

In addition, from an Eternal reference, the mistake has already been corrected.

Let us examine and review how the cause and effect relationship of the Mirror works. Figure 3-9.1 (*A*) shows cause and effect mechanism that the physical level truth works on. While the metaphysical mechanism -- (*B*), can operate on a different level.

In Figure 3-9.1 (*A*), the cause/effect relationship is in the customary time sequence we are used to, first the cause within a time sequence then an effect. The smaller the *BTR*s the quicker or closer the effect is (temporally). This cause/effect temporal proximity is limited by the speed of light within the current science model. The larger the *BTR*s are, the time window begins to expand. However, there is an increment of transpired time between cause and effect; the effect always follows the cause within the science model and the mortal mind ($+\Delta T$ occurs – a positive change of time).

---

*51 F*igures 3-1 to 3-5

52 Theorems 11A and *27*, The God-Creation process is a closed system within God. And God's Love did not exclude the miscreation. Or, the miscreation was included within God's Love.

53 Theorem 23, The miscreation is not Real.

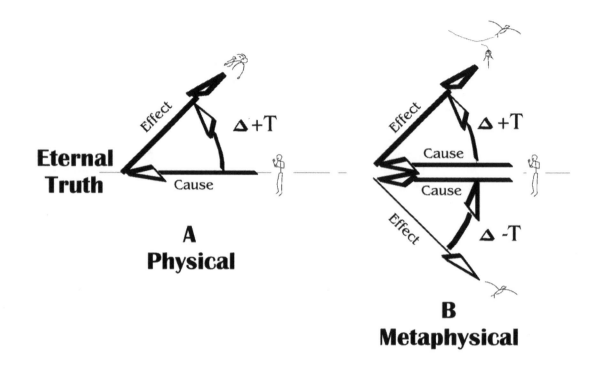

Figure 3-9.1 Cause, Effect, and Change of Time

The metaphysical operation is not limited to this; it can use both (+ΔT and -ΔT). The cause initiates and the effect can occur <u>anywhere</u> on a time line; the effect can show up in the future as with the science model or the effect can also manifest in the past. Truth can adjust the whole time line (as in Figure 3-9.1 [*B*]).

God's Love has complete control of this arrangement; it is a closed system in Love. The Eternal Moment of Creation[54] is present, in control, and remains the same in every moment, everywhere, and all moments at once (all *BTR*s). Because the Eternal is present in (and has access to) all moments at once, the Eternal Correction and the Mirror mechanics is not limited by time and can transcend time.

A choice made in one time and space (*BTR*) can be reflected back in another time and space (*BTR*). In addition, this reflection can occur before, after, or during the instigating choice.

In this model, <u>a choice you make now cannot only affect the future; it can affect the past</u>. High thaumaturgical magic and miracles work with this.

As stated earlier, the tendencies are such that the larger the *BTR*s involved, the greater +ΔT (change of time) to react. An electromagnetic photon and electron cause/effect interaction is much quicker than a planet's cause/effect interaction is to its sun.

The Eternal Moment of Creation within physical creation of the physical universe takes into account the choices of every mortal living being that has ever existed within that physical creation. In this last particular example, ΔT is very large. As ΔT becomes smaller (approaches *0*), the closer the influence of Eternal Moment of Creation (+ΔT realm of quantum mechanics physics or the $\pm\Delta T$ realm of metaphysics: *ESP*, thaumaturgical magic, and miracles).

With miracles, the $\pm\Delta T$ can become varied. The Precious Eternal Moment of Creation manifests or becomes conspicuous at the moment of time we have made our choice.

---

54 *Theorem 10A*, The God-Creation process occurs in Eternity. or The God-Creative process is Eternally occurring.

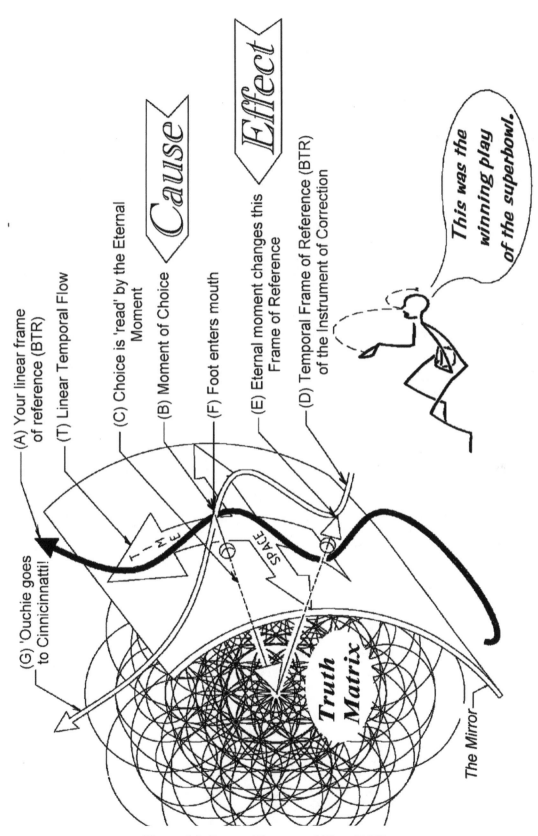

Figure 3-9, Instant Karma and Time Folding

What does this mean? There is no one moment or place in physical space and time where you can say 'Creation is here (or not here)'. Creation is all: past, present, future, and in any point in space. It was stated in the previously that all physical creation could be created at once.

Within this model, the conflict between evolutionists and creationists can be *non-sequitar*; physical creation could have been created in any moment of time with a complete past (a history) and a future. Mortal minds tend to underestimate an Eternal God.

The details of history can be changing as much as the future details through choices, although the general theme or framework remains the same. This is Absolute Love at work – a closed system.

This dynamic system allows for both predestination and free will. It allows Love to give us our free choice and for God to maintain the 'lesson plan'. The nonlinear (Eternal) is capable of arranging/rearranging the past and the future (the Mirror) around our choices (linear time as we perceive it) in order to facilitate the Correction.

'Instant Karma' is an excellent example in how the Mirror folds time. 'Instant Karma' is when a choice (such as 'bad mouthing' someone) is made, an immediate correction presents itself; making you wish you had not opened your mouth.

If you examine the 'Instant Karma' phenomena, the sequence of the physical/temporal elements that are reflected back to you may start to occur <u>before the choice that needed correcting is made</u>.

For example, Figure 3-9 portrays the Mirror similar to Figure 3-5. On one side of the Mirror, it is infinitely Eternal. On the other side of the Mirror, is a time line of a sequence (*T*) along with some spatial positioning.

The relationship between the Eternal and the temporal represent the two sides of the Mirror. The Truth Matrix is Eternal. The ~~truth~~ or a human matrix, which has both Truth and ~~truth~~ in it, is temporal and finite. The Eternal Correction occurs within and outside of the temporality (the two sides of a mirror).

In Figure 3-9 two time lines are presented, you (*A*) and the instrument of correction (*D*). Say your *BTR* is on time line *A* and you make a choice of some sort at point (*B*). 'Instant Karma', as mentioned before, is when you do or say something and a series of changes occur that immediately pushes that choice into your face. In such an instance, you may eat your words.

Examining the time line that created the action of your words being pushed in your face, Karma's correction action may begin before you made your choice. In this correction mode, you make a choice (*B*) and this choice, in this now, is on your time line (*A*).

This choice is 'read' by the Eternal now (*C*). The Eternal now effects the correction to time line (*D*) at point (*E*). This is the time line of the instrument of correction, be it a book, car and driver, a cow, etc. Because the Eternal has access to all temporal references (*BTR*s), it is not limited to an effect occurring after the choice is made. It can mirror the choice to (*D*) back at (*E*).

So the adjusted (*D*) moves along its own time line and it meets you at (*F*) and says, "Ha, eat your words, sucker!" This can be in the form of: the book falling off a shelf, somebody cutting in front of you in traffic, or the cow stepping on your toes.

However, the correction <u>may</u> have started before you made a choice or knew you had a choice to be made.

For example, let us say you are in a library, back in an aisle of books. You are with somebody and you are discussing a book. You say to the other person, "Ah, I've heard of that book and that book sucks".

In the meantime, somebody is in the next aisle over, which is not paying attention to anything you are doing, and is putting another book back on the shelf. As this stranger replaces their book, it pushes the book you are talking about off the shelf; it falls down, and hits your foot. This occurs right after the moment that you made your statement.

I am sure most of us have had something similar to this happen to us. A situation occurs that as soon as you open your mouth, something happens to make you eat your words.

The Mirror had begun to correct your judgment (*B*) at sequence of events at (*E*), before you made the judgment. Karma's actions started: with the stranger choosing to be there before the words were said, the other book being present before the words were said, the person the next aisle over putting the other book on the shelf, and pushing off the book that hit you.

This is how the Correction works on the Eternal level. Our mortal mind learns in a temporal sequence so the Eternal Love presents the lesson in temporal sequence. Eternal Love starts a sequence of events that ends up correcting (or reflecting) what you are doing the moment after you make your choice. Part of the sequence could have temporally started before you even existed in your body.

Another example is making some gross statement about somebody while you are walking in a canyon. Right after you say it, a little pebble that has been up there for millions of years, falls down and hits you on the head.

As mentioned previously, this collapsing of time -- done by the Eternal Correction and the Mirror mechanism -- is also the basis of most *ESP* phenomena, magic, and miracles. The metaphysical operator is working in the Eternal now and changing a sequence of events, collapsing time at that point of now (*B*). We will get into this more in later chapters.

The time collapsing idea allows everything to be covered because it can always go back in the sequence or other sequences; while, knowing future sequences. This allows Absolute Love to always 'have us'; it is a closed system, bounded by God's Love. The rest of this system is closed to us from most temporal perspectives. From the Eternal Correction perspective, everything is an open book (with the general plot determined and yet still being written).

The Eternal can access any earlier time and put into effect something that will bring results later in the time sequence. It is kind of like the movies *The Lathe of Heaven*, *12 Monkeys*, *Timecop*, or *Terminator*. A general theme of these movies is that something is changed in the past, and effects a change in the future and the central character is the only one who knows things have changed.

In the end, the choices you make cannot only affect your future, but can affect your past as well. Karmically, this concept can be mind-boggling. Within this model, that means some of the things that happen to you when you where a child may be a result of your choices made in adulthood.

You make a choice or a decision, and because the Correction works off the Eternal level, karma can either go forward in time or back earlier in the time line or both. This can occur for every choice that you make, from moment to moment. Again, this also allows everything to be covered by Love. The Love-Logic of God in its completeness allows nothing to be excluded.

Again, *I AM A I* will return to this idea with *ESP*, magic, and miracles. Two excellent *ESP* examples that serve for right now are premonitions and déjà vu. Within this model, premonitions are 'you' in the future telling 'you' in the past that 'something' is about to go down. Déjà vu is simply; you have just accessed a future memory (Chapter 7).

The last two chapters comprise a mental construct/model/paradigm. Just as the formula for gravity is a construct.

The construct is a sweeping generality. When working with a problem involving gravity, a person must refer back to the formula construct periodically. The construct is not the actuality. It is only something to help the human minds understand the relationships of the actuality. The same can be said of these last two chapters.

A physics teacher would refer back to the formula and its elements (quantities of the two respective masses, distance between the respective masses' center of

$$F = K\frac{m_1 \times m_2}{d^2}$$

Figure 3-10 Gravity Formula

103

gravity, the inverse square law, multiplication of a constant, etc.) to illustrate points to their students. *I AM A I* will be referring back to elements of this mental construct in these last two chapters to help illustrate some relationships in the rest of the book.

3.8 - Questions

1) How did Love correct for the mistake?

2) What is a *BTR*?

3) What is being reflected back on us and how?

4) A metaphysical parallel to Newton's laws of motion is _____.

5) What are the five interactions that make up physical form?

6) Time can be _____ by eternity.

7) Truth can be found where and how?

8) Love will not fight _____.

9) What coexists with physical form?

10) What will happen if we begin to store Truth within our minds?

11) Physics and metaphysics are what to one another?

12) The Seal of Solomon represents what when related to the Universe and to Man?

13) Physical form, as we know it, is made up of _____, within _____, and within _____.

14) Where do we have to go to learn the Truth?

15) Perceive a truth: A _____ is like a _____?

16) What is mirrored back to what?

Chapter 4

Realities and the Human Matrix

4.1 - Review and Preview of Coming Attractions

A brief review of the information so far is: Chapters 2 and 3 developed a thought-construct or model that involved a progression from a Divine Source into matter and physical form.

Chapter 2 concerned itself with a logic construct that dealt with a primary causation (God/Divine) through a set of postulates and theorems. A skeleton of this book's metaphysical model or paradigm was laid out.

The third chapter fleshes the presented skeleton in; it presented how Truth manifests in parallels, as it manifests physical form. That chapter integrated today's science model into the furnished metaphysical model and showed their relationship. The concept of bubbles of temporal/spatial reference (*BTR*s) was introduced and how that correlates to the present science model. The previous chapter also concerns itself with the Correction and how it reflects – mirrors -- back choices to the mind of origin through these physical forms (*BTR*s). It showed how Newton's Third Law of Motion and Karma are related to the Mirror.

The third Chapter referred to the idea that Love will not fight Love. God's Love, with the Mirror, acts like the perfect judo master. The Mirror takes what we choose and reflects it back on us with a twist. In addition, Chapter 3 showed how Love/Truth (and the Eternal Moment it resides in) with the Correction, and with the analogy of the Mirror, has the ability to ignore time. Love will speak through mortal minds using time because that is the mortal minds' frame of reference, and Love is not limited by the mortal mind's temporal references.

The flow of Chapters 2 and 3 went from up to down, going from God to physical form. Chapter 4 chapter concerns itself with the mortal mind that inhabits the physical form. This chapter will finish the established mental construct by examining the human mind/matrix and how the information of the previous chapters applies to us (in the human condition). This chapter will look at the bubble of temporal/spatial reference that contains the human mind/matrix. It will also introduce usage of this mortal matrix to help foster a remembrance of our union with God.

Later chapters will include various spiritual disciplines and examine how they relate to the temporary temporal mortal mind/matrix of ours. Many of the disciplines, tools, or exercises -- provided in later chapters -- would help weaken one (or more) vertices of the inverted triangle of Figure 3-7.[1] Once that is done enough, the inverted triangle in Chapter 3 becomes less of a factor and the Eternal triangle assumes priority.

An example of this is in the Truth exercise (Chapter 3.6 - *Exercise and Lab 3*) which begins to address ~~truth~~ elimination, by increasing truth in the human condition -- knowledge. If we start to expand the exclusive mind to be open and non-exclusive (increase the amount of truth, which is in keeping with the Love aspect), it also works toward weakening the lower triangle of Figure 3-7. The lower triangle is dependent (constantly in need of enforcing/re-enforcing) and dissolves when brought to truth. Once the inverted triangle is removed or weakened, the only real thing is the Eternal triangle.

In addition, the concept of learning to think in parallels in *Exercise and Lab 3* was also important. Extended application of Exercise *and Lab 3* can give your mind another dimension in its operation. That exercise brought a mechanism your mind does in the background ('back of the mind') and brings it to the foreground ('front of the mind'). It introduces to your consciousness something your mind does automatically in the background. We can use these truth parallels and the other information to foster our return to, or remembrance of, our Source.

In order to work with the mind, the human mortal mind mechanism has to be examined along with the human condition. This chapter is going to look at what and how we perceive. Chapter 4 covers what our "ego's" working mechanism is, the flows involved in our mind/matrix's operation, and how our mind works.

4.2 - 'What's Reality Papa?'

*T*heorem 32 states: I am/we are in a generated duality delusion. What is the nature of this delusion or duality? What makes up the bubble of temporal/spatial reference we call the human condition, the ego, and its perception of its surroundings? What does it mean to be a 'you and me'? How does Truth and ~~truth~~ array itself in us? Can we change this?

Definition of Terms state that a reality is an effect of a set of truths. Chapter 3 asserts that every *BTR* has a set of laws/truths that are applicable to the *BTR*. With a set of laws/truths matrix, comes realities[2] and another matrix of relationships. Changes in sets of truths being applied, changes a reality and the *BTR* qualities (and vice versa: change a *BTR* and it changes truths applied).

The human *BTR* and its mind/matrix may become clearer if we look at the realities involved first. We could get lost if we try to examine the myriad of truths that are applicable to a human *BTR*. When we look at realities, we are looking at matrices of truths -- this helps simplify things.

The model presented by this book has these truth sets broken into five basic groups or categories. They are:

First $\Rightarrow$ **Absolute** Reality - God's Truth/Laws of Creation, the Eternal Laws, or the primary causation presented in Chapter 2. Since Creation is an effect of the God's Truth Matrix, it can be said Creation is **Absolute** Reality.

Second $\Rightarrow$ **Actual** Reality - laws of physics and *BTR*s, the laws of temporal/spatial form, Chapter 3 introduced those physically related truths/laws and how they generate physical form.

Third $\Rightarrow$ **Individual** Reality - the mortal mind/matrix and its truths/laws, the laws/truths that are relevant to our personal *BTR*, the laws/truths of personality *BTR*, and its mechanism. This chapter will go into some of this in depth.

Fourth $\Rightarrow$ **Consensual** Reality - truths/laws of Mankind, all language, A *BTR* created by the agreed upon perceptions as true by a number of individual *BTR*s.

---

1 Seal of Solomon
2 Definition of terms

Fifth $\Rightarrow$ **Imaginary** Reality - laws/truths by which nothing works, ~~true~~ referenced *BTR*s, 'truths' that sustain an ~~truth~~[3], laws of nonsense, This is the category where everything that does not fit in the other four category resides.

❑ ***Absolute*** Reality: *Postulate 5* and *Theorem 12C* infer that **Absolute** Reality is an effect of Absolute Truth. It sustains, and is at the very core, of Creation's existence. Creation is an effect of the Truth Matrix while **Absolute** Reality is the effect of Absolute Truth, and since this all one, God's Creation <u>is</u> **Absolute** Reality. Since, we are God's Creation[4] that means there is an element within us that is **Absolute** Reality.

❑ ***Actual*** Reality: Perceptions on the physical level involve the laws of physics -- the truths that determine physical form. This is an aspect of **Actual** reality. This begins with the five basic levels of *BTR* interactions -- gravity, electromagnetic force, nuclear -- both strong and weak, and life force.[5] In addition, science covers all the known basic physical laws of mechanics, thermodynamics, harmonic motion, etc.

  The science laws/truths that make up an **Actual** reality, like **Absolute** Reality, are not directly perceivable. We can only perceive the <u>effects</u>. The <u>effects</u> of the laws of physical form are readily observed objectively and yet, are at the core of all subjective data; they involve both the objective and subjective. If that does not confuse you, nothing will.

  Metaphysical truths to **Absolute** and **Actual** realities are the spiritual, *ESP* , mental and emotional laws. Through them, work the mechanics of the God-Creation relationship and the Correction.

  Absolute laws are <u>at the very core of our being</u>, just as **Actual** laws are at the very core of our physical bodies. These laws are happening everywhere, every when, and have the potential to be happening all at the same time. They are "within you and without you". The laws of motion, of thermodynamics, of harmonics, of gravity, and of quantum mechanics -- all are potentially everywhere, at once. There are no bubbles of temporal/spatial reference in **Absolute** Reality -- because it is Eternal. However, *BTR*s cannot exist without **Absolute** Reality manifesting through a relatively eternal and constant set of laws/truths, as an **Actual** reality.

  Actual reality is an effect of and contained in **Absolute** Reality. To use physical references, the *BTR*s that are grass, galaxies, goldfish, and the kitchen sink are all forms. They are all actualities, part of an **Actual** reality. These actualities come in many different shapes or sizes, in different times, in a multitude of spaces. However, they all are a result of a special case of the **Absolute**, which, in turn, comprises the laws of nature and of form, the **Actual**. **Actual** reality includes everything physical: grass, quasars, paper bags, pencils, doughnuts, etc.

  Figure 4-3 (*A*) illustrates how **Absolute** reality/matrix contains **Actual** reality. (While [*B*], is referenced to how the realities relate to our mind's storage – Chapter 4.4.) In turn, Figure 4-3 (*A*) shows **Actual** reality/matrix contains **Individual, Imaginary,** and **Consensual** realities/matrices. While the **Individual** reality/matrix, -- though encased by **Actual** reality -- contains **Consensual** and **Imaginary** realities/matrices.[6] This representation is in keeping with the matrix within matrix, within matrix… concept introduced in the previous chapter.

❑ ***Individual*** Reality: Within **Individual** reality, the borders between the other realities become blurred or mutable. Language will be used as an example of how these realities can become blurred or are mixed.

  Your **Individual** reality concerns itself with your personal bubble of temporal/spatial reference. Our mind *BTR* is a human truth mind/matrix relationship inhabiting a physical body, which has its own *BTR*. Our human mind/matrix's programming contributes to our personality.

---

3 Theorem 24, The untruth came from the Truth matrix. or There is an element of Truth that caused the untruth.
4 Postulate 6
5 Chapter 3.3 - Bubbles of Temporal/Spatial Reference (*BTR*s)
6 This is an arrangement very similar to Figure 3-3.

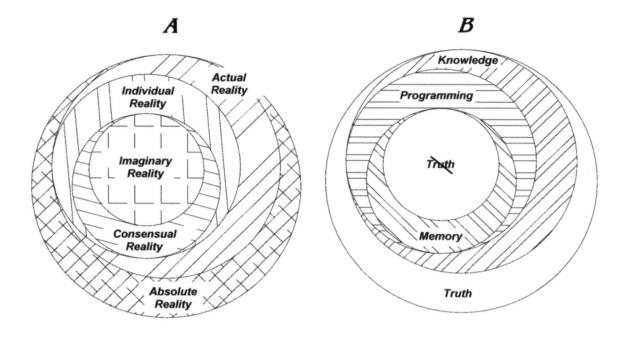

Figure 4-3 Storage Priorities

Individual reality manifests as a relationship of the human mind/matrix components and mechanics to its physical *BTR* – body --and environmental *BTR*s. This chapter will be covering this human mind/matrix in depth later, so the book will be brief here.

Individual reality can be seen as a combination or composed of all the other realities. **Individual** reality's interaction with **Actual** reality is based on a perceptual window that uses six senses -- the five physical senses, and the one metaphysical sense (*ESP*). Later in this chapter, this book will address our perception mechanism, and in Chapter 7 discuss the sixth sense.

As **Individual** reality is comprised of a hodgepodge of the other realities, symbolic communication used by **Individual** realities can involve all five realities. The following definitions will show how communication or language manages this.

❖ *Language and Absolute Reality*
First off, without God and the Eternal moment of Creation (**Absolute** reality), no thing would exist.

❖ *Language and Actual Reality*
Actual reality consists of *BTR*s. Remember from Chapter 3, that all the physical form *BTR*s we are familiar with are really *BTR*s, within *BTR*s, within *BTR*s, etc. Each bubble contains a truth matrix relationship, which makes for matrices within matrices, within matrices, and so on. **Actual** reality consists of a constant flow or dance in changes of these forms, *BTR*s, or matrix relationships.

For example: in physical form, nothing endures, whether it is mountains, trees, or stars. It is a dance of temporal forms (*BTR*s), weaving in and out of relationships with one another. These *BTR*s are interdependent and interrelated to each other on the physical level and may have different time references. However, they are all working off the same set of constant laws.

Actual reality is necessary as the medium or vector for communication/language. There must be air and specific movements of air for the spoken word. There must be a light transmitter and a light receiver for any visual communication. Something must serve as a vector for an idea to be communicated, be it book, RF (radio frequency electro-magnetics), smoke signals, or whatever.

Language can fit into **Actual** reality in another way. **Actual** reality can also occur as accurate symbolic communication – true speaking. In true speaking, as with mathematics, there is an accurate symbolic representation of actual form -- the tree, the bush, the pencil, three, etc.[7]. Saying a word is an actuality, the voice, and the vibration is an actuality of oral communication – application of physical truths, as well as the word itself having an actual objective reference. The word *tree* is based on an actual item or concept, a tree.

We are using different laws of harmonics -- **Actual** reality laws/truths-- from the resonant cavities in our head to tightening the vocal cords to produce different pitches and tones in our voice. However, true speaking must represent an actuality outside the speaker. For example: I say the tree, and there has a got to be a tree that I am referencing. What is not an **Actual** reality communication is saying, "The sun is not yellow, it's chicken!" [8]

These symbolic forms – words -- are relatively accurate symbolic <u>representations</u> of **Actual** reality events. Because they are representations, they are not the event itself. And, without the event, that symbolic representation or portrayal of the event would not exist.

In addition, the time reference of communication in an **Actual** reality may not be relevant. For instance, we can talk about some symbol of the past or of the future. However, the word or symbol must have an accurate physically actual reference apart from the individual at some time or other. True communication is based on this aspect of **Actual** reality. ("Promise to tell the truth, the whole truth, and nothing but the truth so help you God?")

However, language/symbol systems are temporal; they can come and go. The words meaning "run" or "rotten" 3000 years ago in Assyria may not exist today. We have different symbols to mean the same thing. For example, we now have the symbol *3*, which is Arabic. Two thousand years ago, this number was represented by three vertical lines in the Roman system (*III*). Other peoples had different symbols for the number three. They still are symbolic forms for the same actuality (the concept 'three').

The temporal nature of **Actual** reality manifests on the mortal mind mechanics level as well. We can only hold the symbol (a *BTR*) for a *BTR* so long in our own finite/temporal awareness. We can only think a thought for so long; the thought has a beginning and an end. How long can you hold the thought 'radish' in your mind? Or, you can speak a word and that word does not go on forever.

On all **Actual** reality levels: metaphysical forms, physical forms, symbolic form, thoughts and feelings -- the temporal forms come and the temporal forms go. They <u>are</u> all bubbles of temporal/spatial reference. Most perception of *ESP* phenomena is a form of **Actual** reality mechanics.[9]

Here this book is entering the world of mental and emotional symbolic forms (non-physical *BTRs*) that have objective actualities such as the thought: tree; the thought: jump; the thought: run. These are forms, too. We, as beings, have mental and emotional forms, as well as our physical forms, and these make up our **Individual** reality.

However, most of these mental and emotional forms are constructed forms and are put together from other realities. The construct that we put together is of our own creation; and, what we put together becomes real for us – our personality.

❖ *Language and Individual Reality*

In reference to communication, as **Actual** reality determines the vector of communication (aural, visual, electromagnetic, or *ESP*...), **Individual** reality determines the use, message, and mode of communication. It determines what symbol system will be used

---

7 Though the symbol that indicates a tree is far removed from being the actuality of the tree; the word is a symbolic communication representation of an objective physical event.

8 Bob Dylan...

9 Chapter 7.

(language, mathematics, body language, telepathy, etc.). In addition, **Individual** reality determines the arrangement of symbols -- the message.

Communication is an interaction between two **Individual** realities. It is the act of sharing ideas. It is very similar to two molecules sharing an electro-magnetic photon (one is pitching and one is catching). At times, the communication can be one way, as in the relationship between author and reader, or a sun going nova and its orbiting planets. At other times, an idea (a symbolic *BTR*) can leave an **Individual** reality, be received and absorbed by a catching **Individual** reality, and that **Individual** reality responds to the original with an extension of an idea of their own (through a symbolic *BTR*).

Usually this is done through a **Consensual** reality. A physics parallel could be even heat distribution within a material. This interaction we call two-way communication.

To create is an idea extension of a matrix,[10] specifically the mind/matrix of a human *BTR* within an **Individual** reality. The talker is extending something from his or her mind to another person's mind. The listener's matrix perceives the idea through a symbol system, correlates it to their mind/matrix. They respond and make an extension of their own, with an idea of their own, and the roles are reversed.

This, of course, is the ideal situation. We all know that, due to the nature of words and **Individual** realities, communication does not operate that cleanly. What limits this exchange is the symbol system (words), vector mediums (clarity), and the perceptions of the respective individual matrices, which must be in some kind of agreement (have realities in common). The perceptual windows of their individual matrices must see the same thing. Try talking about advanced management techniques to a two-year-old.

Communication – language -- is an interaction consisting of an exchange of non-physical *BTR*s between human/sentient *BTR*s (**Individual** realities, singular or in sets). Which, brings us to...

❑ *Consensual* Reality: **Consensual** reality is the reality of agreement; it is a reality of consensus. It occurs when a group of **Individual** realities assembles, and agrees that a specific perception is real. Then, it becomes real for them. For example all social, political, cultural laws, mores, etc., are aspects of a **Consensual** reality.

The problem with a **Consensual** reality is that if someone disagrees, the 'reality' falls apart. That person can be considered a threat to that **Consensual** reality. When that happens, they keep shooting the messenger, nail them to a tree, give them a cup of hemlock, 'barbecue their butt', etc. This is usually done with the intention of preserving a status quo (the existing **Consensual** reality).

Some significant factors that determine the nature of **Consensual** realities are:

- Physical environment: **Actual** reality, where you are in the world, the solar system, or in the galaxy.
- Time: whether an individual is at a time when man is a hunter-gatherer or today. Hunter-gatherer societies had very different **Consensual** realities than we have now. People in different times have made other agreements because of their own distinct perceptions.
- How much Absolute Truth and actual truth is involved within the agreement. The more Absolute Truth and actual truth within the agreement, the more solid a **Consensual** reality is. The more it will work within a holistic picture and last through time.
- The numbers and perceptions of the **Individual** realities involved.

❖ *Language and Consensual Reality*
How does communication tie into a **Consensual** reality? **Consensual** reality can be considered a gestalt of **Individuals**' realities (*BTR*s). It is within **Consensual** reality that communication symbols and symbol systems are born. In truth, communication cannot exist

---

10 Chapter 2, To create is to extend

without a **Consensual** reality. What is there to talk about if no one is around, if there was no agreement over the meaning of words?

An agreement must be made on definition and arrangement of language symbols. If there is no agreement, then the communication will be distorted (if it happens at all).

Teacher, *"One and one is two."*
Student, *"Right, one and one is two! Wow, cool man! One and one is two! What's a two?"*[11]

A **Consensual** reality can be a combination of **Absolute, Actual, Individual,** and it can have elements of **Imaginary**, all at the same time.

In terms of **Individual** reality, some of the first things we learn from our parents are based on a **Consensual** reality, language for example. The parents and child come to some sort of agreement on meanings for actions and words. (What does crying mean? What does grab mean? What does kiss mean? What does *no* mean? Etc.)

Consensual reality is a major variable of our **Individual** reality (a major mind/matrix-programming factor). Concern about the police officer in the car behind us or what our neighbors think of us are two examples.

❑   *Imaginary* Reality: An **Imaginary** reality has no objective reference in the other four realities. It has ~~truth~~ at its core. If it does not work off physical laws, it cannot physically exist. If it does not work off society laws, it is outside of that society. That which does not work with in individual truths and laws is not relevant to us.

In **Imaginary** reality, there is a discrepancy between the symbolic use and the actualities involved. It is not accurate: i.e. fantasy, illusion, delusion, etc. In **Imaginary** reality, there can be a conflict in terms. In many ways, the very term **Imaginary** reality is a conflict in terms – an oxymoron.

❖   *Language and Imaginary Reality*

How does **Imaginary** reality relate to communication? **Imaginary** reality is taking actual symbolic realities and arranging them so they do not convey an actuality. A true symbolic communication, as in math, has direct actualities outside the communicated or spoken. If I say three, there is a concept three outside of whatever language I use.

The opposite of this is a symbolic representation that has no reference to any actuality, like: "The sky was yellow, and the sun was blue."[12] Or, two plus two is five. **Imaginary** reality can be expressed in a form of symbolic communication, but this communication is not an accurate representation of the *BTR*s symbolized.

These **Imaginary** realities can be shared, like with a fantasy book. In fact, a **Consensual** reality can have elements of shared **Imaginary** realities. An **Imaginary** reality is not limited to one person's belief. It does not make any difference if one person believes it, or many; they are both in **Imaginary** realities extended into a **Consensual** reality.

Imaginary reality can also manifest as an inaccurate use of symbolic representation in reference to actual *BTR*s. That means mixing a little ~~truth~~ with truth and twisting things.

Fisherman: *"It was thaaaaaaaaat big!"*
Wife: *"Hmmp! After it was cleaned, we got one fish taco."*

Imaginary reality includes fiction books, deception, politics, thoughts, dreams, imagination, and a significant amount of entertainment. In all of these, there is some form of actuality involved to sustain it.[13] The actualities can be put together in inaccurate sequences or they can be assembled to give the illusion of one thing when it is really another. For example:

---

11 Bill Cosby, on kindergarten...
12 Scarlet Begonias, Grateful Dead from the Mars Hotel, Copyright 1973 by Ice Nine Publishing, Inc. Lyrics by Robert Hunter.
13 Theorems 24 and *28A*: There is an element of Truth that caused the untruth. & Truth and untruth coexist.

looking at a movie and seeing a city of an old civilization, when in truth it is just a painted backdrop behind the actors or a *CG* effect (computer graphics).

To review this section: there are five basic reality categories. These realities are tied to earlier material -- the concepts involved with *Postulates 3* and *4*. Specifically, the concept of 'logic contains a matrix of truths/laws'. The following is the list of realities with the logic and truths/laws that have been presented.

- ◆ **Absolute** – Logic of God (Truth/Laws of Creation)
- ◆ **Actual** – Logic of physical (truths/laws of science and math) and metaphysical (the Correction and the Mirror)
- ◆ **Individual** – Logic of our being and is a combination of all of the above and below (truth/laws of being)
- ◆ **Consensual** – Logic of agreement (truths/laws of Man)
- ◆ **Imaginary** – Logic of illogic (truths/laws of the unreal)

Absolute and **Actual** are the laws of physical reality and the physical forms themselves. The **Absolute** and **Actual** make up the physical survival level of an individual's bubble of temporal/spatial reference. Unless we actively participate in **Absolute/Actual** reality, we would not exist or be able to survive. We would not eat, breath, stay warm, that kind of thing. **Absolute/Actual** consist of all that is true within and without of us.

Referring to Figure 4-3 (*A*), note again pattern or parallels here. **Absolute** Reality determines **Actual** reality. **Actual** realty (physical *BTRs*) determines the **Individual** reality (*BTR*). Also, the individuals' **Individual** realities determine **Consensual** and **Imaginary** realities. It is like the box within a box within a box concept.[14]

Please note: The truths of **Absolute**, **Actual**, and some elements of **Individual** reality are independent. The truths, laws, and realities can stand-alone. They have no need to be enforced or re-enforced. Nobody has to enforce the law of gravity. In addition, they work when applied, independent of belief; you do not have to believe in Newton's Laws of Motion to walk.

Whereas, **Imaginary**, **Consensual**, and other elements of **Individual** realities are dependent. The truths, laws, and realities cannot stand-alone. They are in constant need of being enforced or re-enforced. They are subject to beliefs.

Consensual and **Imaginary** realities may have no objective existence outside of the human condition (mortal mind *BTRs*). They both are derived from the people that have influenced us, who and where we hang out, with group beliefs, our choices, etc.

Also notice; from true speech comes fantasy, from truth comes ~~truth~~, and from real numbers come imaginary numbers. There is a relationship here; a pattern is forming. One is an offshoot of the other; the second – dependent -- springs from the first – independent; and is a special operation in the first.

Reviewing the language/communication reference to the realities:

- ◆ With **Absolute** Reality ⇒ Creation, allows everything -- communication/communion -- to be possible.

- ◆ **Actual** reality ⇒ has two language references: one is the physical/metaphysical vector of information (sound, light, *ESP* , etc.). The second is an accurate symbolic reference to an actual *BTR* (symbols are in accurate reference to actualities).

- ◆ **Individual** reality ⇒ chooses the vector, symbol system, and content of the communication.

---

14 With this circle, within circle, within circle…model of Figures 3-3 & 4-3 there can be -- mathematically – infinities, within infinities, within infinities…of tangent point combinations. This includes common tangent points as well as divergent.

- ◆ **Consensual** reality ⇒ determines symbol systems and the symbol's meanings.

- ◆ **Imaginary** reality ⇒ is composed of an inaccurate symbolic reference to an existing *BTR*, or a symbolic reference to non-existing *BTR*s.

Next to cover is our human perceptual window that we have on these realities.

4.3 - Limits of the Perceptual Window

*E*xamining the limits of the five physical senses (sight, smell, touch, sound, and taste) used by our **Individual** reality *BTR* to perceive **Actual** reality, we can 'see' the narrowness of our personal perceptual window, the limits our **Individual** reality's *BTR*s, and the limits of our mind. The boundaries of **Individual** realities are based on a perceptual window into **Actual** reality that uses these five physical senses. These senses determine how we physically 'see' others and how we physically 'see' ourselves. There are many limits to our perceptual window (to how we 'see' things). To get an idea of the boundaries of our individual bubble of temporal/spatial reference's perceptual window, this book will examine only one physical sense, sight.

❑ The first limit in our physically seeing something is the amount of the available electro-magnetic spectrum we use. The electro-magnetic spectrum, Figure 4-1, is represented as a long band – broken into frequencies or wavelengths categories – this spectrum spans radio waves to visible light to gamma and cosmic rays. This spectrum includes ultraviolet and x-rays. It covers radar, microwaves, heat, and the very narrow band in the middle, is visible light -- which is what we see with our eyeballs.

Out of this whole band, we humans use only a small, very limited section of the spectrum to see things. Whereas, a pit viper (rattlesnake) can see in infrared (heat) and many insects can see in the ultraviolet range.

The question marks on either end of Figure 4-1 connote frequencies not readily associated with the *EMF*[15] spectrum. The high end (right side) covers wavelengths that approach a Planck width. On the low end (left side), are frequencies that are measured in cycles per minute as in bio-frequencies and cycles measured by hundreds of thousand years (with wavelengths measured in light years) like the magnetic field of the earth. Also, on the left side of the spectrum, there is direct current, which has no cycles.

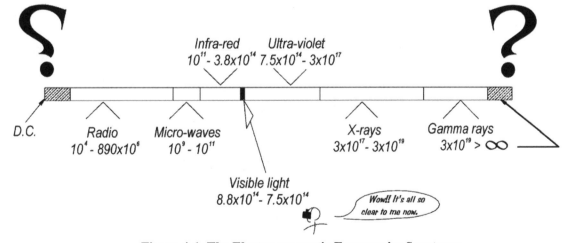

Numbers are in cycles per second

Infra-red
10^{11} - 3.8×10^{14}

Ultra-violet
7.5×10^{14} - 3×10^{17}

D.C.

Radio
10^{4} - 890×10^{6}

Micro-waves
10^{9} - 10^{11}

X-rays
3×10^{17} - 3×10^{19}

Gamma rays
$3 \times 10^{19} > \infty$

Visible light
8.8×10^{14} - 7.5×10^{14}

Wow!! It's all so clear to me now.

Figure 4-1, The Electro-magnetic Frequencies Spectrum

---

15 Electro-Magnetic Frequencies

Man can create machines (tools) to perceive these other elements of this spectrum. These machines are only translators that convert the rest of the spectrum to a form that we can perceive.

One of the reasons that we see only that very narrow spectrum is most probably for survival purposes. If we saw all the light that was available, it would be very difficult to differentiate anything. You would not know what to do. You would be overwhelmed. It is not necessary to see gamma rays for survival. We do not need to see radio waves for physical existence.

So the first limit of our sight window is the narrowness of the spectral band that vision uses. We are using a very narrow band of available light.

❑ The second limit to our sight window is spatial limits. One example of a spatial limit is something can be either too big or too small for us to see. We cannot see an entire mountain, nor can we see the entire planet from where we stand. We cannot see a microbe. Something can be too small or too big to be perceived.

Also, part of this spatial limit is our distance away from an object. We can be too close or too far away from an object to see the whole thing. We cannot see all of Andromeda, a galaxy light years away. We can only see some light from it. The opposite of this is something can be too close to us, like or own face. Unless we have a mirror or a camera (tools), we cannot see our own face completely.

Included in this spatial limit, is also the relative velocity between the perceived object and the perceiver -- how fast or how slow is each moving in reference to each other. It is like sitting and trying to watch grass grow or see a bullet go by -- you cannot see either.

Therefore, spatial limits to our visual perception are relative: size, distance, and velocity (rate of change). The observer *BTR* must be in 'synch' to the object *BTR*.

❑ The third limit is the temporal limit of our visual perceptional window -- time. When the *BTR* of an object enters our *BTR*, we see only that particular instant of the object. We do not see what happened to that object before it entered our *BTR*. Nor, do we see what happens to the object after it leaves our *BTR*. There is a sequence of events, a series of temporal/spatial changes or moments, which led up to any now.

For example, you are walking down the road and you find a small rock. You never saw this rock fall out of the mountain, or the rock matrix (that formed it in the earth to become the parent rock); or the rock matrix decomposing to become that stone. Nor, can you see that stone being turned into sand many years from now. You cannot see all the changes that the rock's *BTR* went through before it got to your *BTR*. You may only know you stubbed our toe on the rock.[16]

When we perceive in time, we see only one aspect of the sequential ordering of a series of temporal/spatial events. In order for us to relate to this sequential ordering of spatial events, we use another event as an objective reference: a clock, the sun, the moon, the stars, a lifetime, etc. Our minds use this to record an order of events, or a series of *Now*s (a *BTR*s' interaction with our *BTR*). We use this objective reference in order to relate one *now*, to another *now*, and mark their relationship in our *BTR*'s perceptual sequence.

Our perspective is always from this *now*. It is a dance of *BTR*s, and we see only the *BTR*s that are in step with our *BTR* (when the perceiver and the perceived share the same temporal/spatial reference, *BTR* elements). Physical sight cannot see into the past or into the future. We cannot see any other event -- anywhere -- within that sequence at any time. We can only see the present (the Eternal Now) in what appears to be a sequence of events. We cannot see all events that lead to this *now* -- this moment in the sequence.

For example, the clothes you are wearing now. You cannot see the clothes being sewn up, or by whom. Nor can you see the manufacturing of the material that makes up the clothes.

---

16 Think about this when breaking open a rock; the part of the rock you exposed has not seen light for millions of years.

In addition, you cannot see all the effects of the choices you make, which are future (or past) events. Let us say you see that rock, and you kick it in the road. You cannot see what will happen from that rock being kicked. You kick it in the road. A truck drives over it, causing it to fly up and crack the windshield of the following car tomorrow. Or, as was said before, you cannot see the rock turn to sand. You cannot see all the events/changes that will make up its bubble of temporal/spatial reference. You cannot see all effects of your choices. You cannot see all the events that will make up a future *now* (of your *BTR*).

These first three limits -- spectrum, spatial, and time – in some ways are conjoined. We can only see a specific spectrum of light leading from an event. We only see that light if the object is the right size, distance, and speed. We cannot see all events that lead up to the event we are observing, nor all the events that lead away from it. In other words, the *BTR*s of the observer and the observed must have the same temporal/spatial reference (share a number of common *BTR*s).

❑ This brings us to the fourth limitation to our visual perceptional window: our information-processing unit, our minds, and our mortal mind/matrix. Our brains are a limited finite electro-bio-chemical computers interfaced with our bodies. Our brains are only <u>so</u> big. There are physical limitations to our brain *BTR*. Consequently, there are only so many neural connections available to process the information that comes in through the eyes.

An example is to take a little tip of a leaf of grass or a single grain of sand, and all we see is its form and color. Our brain cannot grasp all the myriad of quantum mechanic interactions emitting these little photons that hit our eyes (that allows us to see the blade of grass). Our brain cannot fathom all the changes, weaves, or patterns of *BTR*s (the molecules and atoms) are going through to make up one cell of this leaf.

Our brain tends to run on general structures, parallels, memory, and statistical norms, which make up our processing unit. This is a storage saving device. What we see is dependent on our intelligence and our ability to store. Our mind depends on what it has in storage and memory to relate to incoming data. You see the green grass, but if you were a baby, you would have no concept of grass or green; nor, would you even have a label for it.

So, the problem with our processing information unit (brain/matrix) is very similar to what part of the electromagnetic spectrum that we see. There is a specific window of acceptance. We cannot see things that are too complicated, which is equivalent to very high frequency. At the same time, our mind cannot see things that are too simple for it to grasp, which is equivalent to a very low frequency. An example of something <u>both</u> too simple and too complicated to perceive is God. God is too complicated (Infinite) for the human mind to grasp, and at the same time, too simple (Eternal).

To review, the four basic limits to our visual perception are:

- *EMF* bandwidth
- Spatial
- Temporal
- Information processing

If we objectively look at all the limiting aspects of our perception, using sight as an example of one perceptual tool into **Actual** reality, it becomes very clear we cannot see much. And…that is just one sense, sight.

An analogy to this is with two people talking about population and planetary conditions, is roughly equivalent to two amoebae living on a beach pebble and discussing how crowded their neighborhood has become. Furthermore, there are elements they are not aware of; they do not know a storm, a crab, a high tide, or a little child with a shovel and pale is coming.

Our mind is finite; too limited to be depended on, and most decisions that are made with our temporal matrix are made from insufficient data (in ignorance). Because these decisions are made out of ignorance, in the long term they are not conducive to our survival as beings.

Our mortal perceptions are so limited that most conclusions we make are likely to be in error, just because we cannot see everything. This can be a scary thought. Be advised, these limits are only a continuation of the theme on limits of temporal/finite qualities compared to the Infinite/Eternal qualities.[17]

Here an interesting question presents itself. Given the mortal mind is so limited; spiritually, what use does it have? Remember from Chapter 2.7 how a 'logic system' can create something 'alien' to that 'logic system'; how a real number operation can create something not relevant to the real numbers.

This can go the other way as well. A finite/temporal mind – a mind immersed in a continual stream of mental/emotional events – can create something 'alien' to it. Remember; finite-infinite and temporal-eternal are mutually exclusive terms. So anything 'alien' to a finite/temporal mind, must be involved with the infinite/eternal in some way.

The finite mortal mind can be used to 'step outside' finite mortal concepts.

This chapter, so far, has introduced the realities we inhabit and our <u>objective</u> physical perceptual limits to **Actual** reality. The next thing to cover is our mind, its processing unit, and its <u>subjective</u> perceptual limits along with its mechanics.

Subjective perception entails what we see of the immediate and what we see of the whole. It entails what picture we put together from the perceived elements; our desires (long term and short term) of the moment; and what we remember -- our storage and programming.

Now this book is beginning to open the 'can of worms' that makes up our **Individual** reality or our truth matrix -- the human/sentient mortal mind/matrix.

4.4 - The Human Matrix - *Storage*

$\mathbb{W}$e are in a duality delusion.[18] Before the individual or the human truth mind/matrix is examined, remember this duality delusion; two minds become apparent within Creation (us). The human mind/matrix of ours contains both Truth and ~~truth~~ within it. One Mind is a Matrix we share with God.[19] The other is a mirror image of the Absolute Truth Matrix. One Mind is Eternal and Infinite; while, another mind is finite and temporal. Like a mirror image, our mortal mind/matrix lacks the substance or depth of the original Mind/Matrix. .

Two mind matrices in one being: the Absolute Truth matrix (which is of God and which we share with God, Absolute, and Eternal) and the other is finite and temporal. One will be dropped eventually just because it is temporal in nature.

As stated in Chapter 3, the one mind/matrix is portrayed as an upside down image of the other because one stems from the other.[20] The lower human matrix is parallel to the upper Truth Matrix, as real and unreal numbers are parallel to each other.

Absolute Truth is in both minds and it allows us to make a jump from one – eternal mind -- to the other – temporal mind. Without Absolute Truth being in both, we would not be able to make a jump. Just as, mathematics is the same in the real numbers and imaginary numbers.

Figure 4-2 illustrates an overview of the human mind's general construction. The figure shows a perceptual lens and what the categories of storage are within the human mind matrix.

---

17 Chapter 3.1, Review of Chapter 2

18 Chapter 2.8, *Postulate 7, Theorem 32*: I am/we are in a generated delusion of duality.

19 God's Truth Matrix is like electricity: it eludes definition and, in the end, is not relevant to how to work with it. Science does not <u>really</u> know what electricity is, and we can make computers.

20 Chapter 3.4, Figure 3-7, Seal of Solomon

This figure is a rough block diagram that will be used as an introduction to the model of this book. The basic components of our mortal mind matrix are:

- ❑ A *Storage* matrix – the 'back' of the mind -- subconscious
- ❑ A *Perceptional Lens Array* matrix – the 'front' of the mind -- conscious
- ❑ A *Focus Control* matrix (the man in Figure 4-2) – in between the 'front' and 'back' where we experience the mind and exert control

This section will examine the *Storages* first, later sections will look at the matrix's *Perceptional Lens Array*, and then this book will present an overview of the two along with their interface with *Focus Control*.

The word 'storages' is used for lack of a better term. Other terms may be 'matrices of accumulation' or 'collections of specific information'. Figure 4-3 relates *Storages* to the realities involved. The five storages that will be discussed and that are related to the five previously presented realities are:

- ❖ *Truth* – **Absolute**
- ❖ *Knowledge* – **Actual**
- ❖ *Programming* – **Individual**
- ❖ *Memory* – **Consensual**
- ❖ ~~*Truth*~~ – **Imaginary**

From the postulates and theorems, the human mind/matrix must contain *Truth*. *Truth* is Eternally constant and all existence and realities derive from it. *Truth* is at the very core of our matrix because it is our connection to God; plus, it encompasses the laws by which everything else works. Because it is at the very heart of our matrix, it is positioned at the top of Figure 4-2. It is also shown as <u>a</u> place within this matrix model that **Absolute** reality resides/manifests.

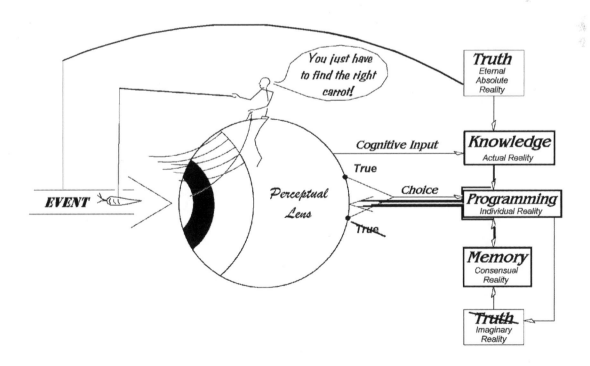

Figure 4-2, Temporal Matrix Storages

117

As the postulates and theorems imply, we have Truth and ~~truth~~ rattling around inside our heads. ~~Truth~~ is temporal in nature. It is the area of the ~~real~~ within us and part of the original mistake. It is where fantasies and delusions are within us. It is also the place of **Imaginary** reality. *Truth* is shown at the top of Figure 4-2, and *~~Truth~~* is placed at the bottom of the diagram.

Between *Truth* and *~~Truth~~*, three categories of storage are shown. The category next to *Truth* is *Knowledge*. *Knowledge*, as it used here, is not something that is intellectually known. *Knowledge* is something that is or becomes inherent in us. We apply *Knowledge* every time we are walking, we are talking, we are driving, etc. *Knowledge* is the storage of truth applications.

It is the place where all skills are stored (both acquired and inherited). We tend to work from *Knowledge* without thinking. There is 'little to no' perceived mentation involved. *Knowledge* stores truth applications and is *Truth*'s interface into the rest of the storages.

In this model, all survival is dependent on *Knowledge*. This is the storage of all truth applications and skills, inherent and acquired; how we interface with **Actual** reality.

Knowledge has a number of parts in it. One part is permanently hardwired[21] and is our read only memory, ROM in computer terms. Part of *Knowledge* is contained in the DNA matrix, knowledge relative to the body's functioning -- heart beating, breathing, and organs working. Much of that *Knowledge* is dependent upon the information contained in the genetic code. *Knowledge* includes the operational knowledge of the body.

This autonomic aspect is a manifestation of *Truth* within *Knowledge*. The neutral effect of *Truth* in this storage area allows our continuing existence in the temporal condition. *Knowledge* is the area where **Actual** reality manifests. Ironically, because *Knowledge* stores truth applications and it is neutral, <u>*Knowledge* stores the 'truth' applications that create ~~truth~~ also.</u>[22] These are the 'truth' applications that allow ~~truth~~ to exist.

Figure 4-2 shows two inputs leading into *Knowledge*, *Truth* and the Cognitive Input. These two inputs, a 'read only memory' (*Truth*) and a 'programmable read only memory', which is storage of 'cognitive jumps' or truth applications, which is used to program knowledge into us. The hardwiring (body stuff) is already in *Knowledge*. And...*Knowledge* can be programmed.

This book will work with the Cognitive Input a lot. To help understand the Cognitive Input of Figures 4-2 and 4-4, look at the word recognition – re-cognition. From the Cognitive Input into *Knowledge* comes our re-cognition of things. Recognition means to re-cognize or re-know something. This input allows us to interact with the outside world. Without recognition, nothing would be familiar and we would be totally dysfunctional in the physical world. The Cognitive Input serves as the 'view finder' of our mind/matrix (Figure 4-2.1, Camera).

This Cognitive Input is a very high priority path; it is a path used in survival. Any organism that has a sensory array to its environment has a cognitive input into the mind. Be it worm or man; it is present. When this high priority path is preoccupied, other lower priority mental operations fall to the wayside.

A 'cognitive jump' was introduced previously. What is a 'cognitive jump'? To begin with, a cognitive jump is a number of truth applications that are assembled to become a greater truth application. Because Truth is One and is in a Matrix, truth <u>appears</u> to assemble itself. Cognition is when a truth assembly (matrix) is in accord with truth applications in *Knowledge*.

One example of a major cognitive jump within us is when the light bulb goes on in our head. We assemble some truths like pieces of a puzzle and then we start putting those puzzle pieces together. When we get enough of these puzzle pieces assembled, we begin to see the

---

21 Hard-wired: Have, relating to, or implemented through logic circuitry permanently connected within a computer or calculator and therefore not subject to change by programming. ~ The American Heritage Dictionary, Third Edition, Copyright 1996, by Houghton Mifflin Company.

22 *Theorems 24* and *28A*: There is an element of Truth that caused the untruth. & Truth and untruth coexist.

whole picture and there is a 'whirrr…click'. A mental jump goes on in our head when we see the whole picture from the pieces. We could have been collecting those pieces over a period of time -- our whole life -- and not know it.

Once that click happens, that light goes on. As in a jigsaw puzzle picture analogy, we can see where future data can lie. When other pieces appear, they make sense how they fit. We 'see' it now. This is an example of how cognition and *Knowledge* can contribute to a jump in our mind/matrix operation, like an epiphany, or, "I get it now! It's so simple!"; that kind of thing.

However, cognition can make subtle jumps too. One of the ways it can subtly jump is in working through repetition of an operation, like learning to walk. When we learn that aspect, we repeat it and repeat it until the truth applications are eventually programmed into *Knowledge* cognitively; patterning the knowledge into the brain. One is very subtle and the other one is mind-blowing.

The 'mind-blowing' one is like the Archimedes' "Eureka!" when he figured out displacement volume of a body in his bathtub.

The 'mind-blowing' can carry a radical change in consciousness along with it, like an epiphany. How radical the change in consciousness will be is dependent upon how much Absolute Truth is in the puzzle pieces and how much truth is in the individual mind. The more comprehensive the truth that is in the puzzle pieces – truths without exception, the heavier and deeper the consciousness change (ringing) is going to be. This was touched upon briefly when the Truth exercises in *Labs 1* and *3* (Chapters 1 and 3) were introduced. This 'ringing' concept will be returned to at the end of this chapter.

Knowledge is *Truth*'s representative within the physical body. Within *Knowledge* can be Truth and perceived truth; one is inherent within it and one is programmed in it. What is programmed is totally dependent upon how we focus the *Perceptional Lens Array* – the 'front' of the mind. However, what is inherent always comes from the Truth.[23]

A review of *Knowledge* storage input/output feeds:

- ❖ *Knowledge* Inputs
  - • *Truth*, (Chart 4-4, *A3*)
  - • Cognitive Input, (Chart 4-4, *B5*)
- ❖ *Knowledge* Output
  - • *Programming*, (Chart 4-4, *B1*)

This *Knowledge* aspect of storage is shown in Figures 4-2 and 4-4 as one of the three major storage elements – interfaces -- between *Truth* and ~~*Truth*~~. From *Truth*, via *Knowledge* and its influence on the rest of the mind/matrix, <u>most</u> *ESP* and spiritual phenomena manifest.

ESP involves a communication or communion between the One Eternal Mind to a mortal mind. It involves an interface from that One Eternal Mind to a mortal mind. *ESP* abilities are naturally inherent within us and Chapter 7 discusses the different ways *ESP* phenomena can manifest.

We have *Truth*'s representative in the matrix, which is presented in Figure 4-2 as *Knowledge*. ~~*Truth*~~'s representative in this model is *Memory*. It is what we usually think of as storage in our mind. *Memory* is ~~*Truth*~~'s representative by being a limited perceptional record of an event from a different temporal reference (past) and does not exist in the current temporal reference (*now*) – a mental 'photograph'.

---

23 A reminder: the definition of truth in this book is the laws by which something works. God's Truth is capitalized because by it, everything works. When perceived, it tends to come into the storages through the cognitive input. When talking about the temporal matrix, the author will not capitalize truth because it will usually be in reference to how our temporal bubble works. This can also mean **Actual** reality truths, something equivalent to an individual's perception, or how a **Consensual** reality works.

Memory's function is to store perceptions (perception/desire sets or mental/emotional sets, Chapter 4.5). We cannot control whether our *Memory* is going to store, because it will, but to some extent, we can control what it might store. What we desire it to store. Just like *Knowledge*, which stores skills and the truths behind those skills – truth applications, *Memory* is totally neutral. It is going to store, but we can put some stuff in it that we want. *Memory* is shown as the place that **Consensual** reality tends to reside within us, Figures 4-2 and 4-4.

Event/perception *Memory*, objective and subjective, may begin in storage as singular neural connections or an array of singular neural connections (as all *Storages* do). Over time, that data is contained in part of our matrix array or can be contained in the whole matrix network. It was once thought that the memory of an event would be in one section of the brain. Researchers found out later that memory can be in the whole brain; removing a section they thought relevant did not have any effect on it. That means that the memory is not in just a localized assembly of neural connections. The *Memory* is contained in the whole network, as it was put together – the matrix. This involves the neural matrix of our brain. It can also include the molecular matrix of the body as well – body memory.

Memory is shown having two inputs, one from *Programming* and one from ~~*Truth*~~. It has only one output, into *Programming*.

Again, the *Memory* operation, like *Knowledge*, is completely neutral in its execution. It is constantly going, constantly recording. We have some control of it, and there is stuff that goes into our *Memory*, which we have no control (we do it sub-consciously). It just goes in, whether we want to remember it or not.

To review *Memory* storage input/output feeds:

❖ *Memory* Inputs
 • ~~*Truth*~~, (Chart 4-4, *A17*)
 • *Programming*, (Chart 4-4, *B2*)
❖ *Memory* Output
 • *Programming*, (Chart 4-4, *B3*)

Figure 4-2 shows between *Truth* and *Knowledge* and ~~*Truth*~~ and *Memory*, and in the middle is the center box, the *CPU*, or the central processing unit of our mortal mind that is labeled *Programming*. *Programming* includes our patterns of thinking, our conditioned responses, or our behavioral patterns. *Programming* is storage of choices, and our patterns of choices. *Programming* stores choices; it is where our **Individual** reality presents itself and is the net result of the choices that have been made.

What doe this mean? Let us focus on thinking patterns. When we are first born, we have *Knowledge* for breathing and heartbeat and organ function and potential to gain more *Knowledge*. Therefore, an aspect of *Truth* is already in our bodies. These other *Storages* -- *Programming*, *Memory*, and ~~*Truth*~~ -- are relatively empty when we are first born, as an empty slate or blackboard. There is no *Memory*, little to any *Programming* and, there is little to no ~~*Truth*~~ that we have programmed into ourselves.

It is similar to the field of grass analogy. When we start using our *Programming*, it is as if we start making paths within a field of grass. As we repeat the choices of the directions we travel, we create a pattern of paths in the field. Once these patterns are made, we tend to keep walking on these paths – think in these paths. Soon, these paths are established trails. We tend not to go off them. Although the rest of the field is there, we keep following the paths, because we are used to following that path. Other people may follow the paths you established or we may have learned this path from someone else

We can change our movement through the 'field' at anytime. These patterns are not written in stone; they can be changed. It is a question of re-cognition and choice. A major influence to these patterns of thinking is from attachments (perception/desire patterns). (more on that later)

Be advised, Figures 4-2, 4-4, and Chart 4-4[24] are flow charts of increasing detail. Note that this model is demonstrating statistical tendencies. These are generalities about how our system works. Like a block diagram breakdown of an electronics computer -- RAM, programmable ROM, and CPU -- you have similar flows within an electro/bio-chemical mind/matrix computer. What this model is trying to do is show you general tendencies within the mind.

Figure 4-2, Figure 4-4, and Chart 4-4 have arrows showing relationships between the elements of the drawing. These arrows indicate direction of influence or having priority.

Including Choice (*II*), numerous inputs influence *Programming*. The arrows in those drawings illustrate how *Knowledge* affects our *Programming* and how *Memory* affects our *Programming*. In addition, the arrows show how our body affects *Programming* (Figure 4-4).

❖ The four inputs into *Programming* are:
  • *Knowledge* (Chart 4-4, *B1*)
  • *Memory* (Chart 4-4, *B3*).
  • Choice (*II*) (Chart 4-4, *B6*)
  • Body Interface (Chart 4-4, *D5*)

❖ In addition, *Programming* has four outputs:
  • Whatever ~~true~~ that enters *Programming* goes to ~~*Truth*~~. (Chart 4-4, *A19*)
  • It feeds into *Memory*. (Chart 4-4, *B2*)
  • *Knowledge* and *Memory* travel through *Programming* and all together influence *Focus Control*. (Chart 4-4, *D3*)
  • Body Interface (Chart 4-4, *D5*)

There is a similarity between *Knowledge* and *Memory*. Many times *Knowledge* and *Memory* are programmed through repetition, as in a language. You hear and choose to repeat words and phrases over and over. Remember the math flash cards and how we used to learn: 2 x 2 = 4 (a language)? We remember and then know -- with the indirect influence of Cognitive Input from the perceptual lens – something; we choose to do something repeatedly. This repetition of choice perception/desire information affects *Programming* and can affect *Knowledge*.

With the first patterns of choices we made as a child, we begin to wire our adult behavior. Or...using the grass analogy, it is the first time we cut the path. Our current programming begins in the early stages of our childhood.

To summarize *Storages* and their interactions:
Knowledge <u>directly</u> affects *Programming*. The cognitive jump <u>indirectly</u> affects *Programming*, through *Knowledge* (Chart 4-4, *E5*). *Memory* <u>directly</u> affects *Programming* when we remember the taste (a perception) of a food dish. *Memory* influences whether you have it again (Chart 4-4, *B3*) and there is a constant interchange of information between *Memory* and *Programming* (Chart 4-4, *B4*). ~~*Truth*~~, we have chosen, <u>indirectly</u> affects *Programming* through *Memory* (Chart 4-4, *A18*).

The indirect influences to *Programming* are *Truth* that comes through *Knowledge*, and ~~*Truth*~~ through *Memory*. Direct influences to *Programming* are Choice (*II*) (from the perceptual lens), *Knowledge*, our *Memory*, and the body interface. All of them are an affect on *Programming*.

Essentially, what we are looking at is something very similar to those circles inside of circles of Figure 4.3 (*B*). Figure 4-3 (*B*) shows *Truth*, which contains everything and is non-exclusive, as the outside circle. The next circle in is *Knowledge*; inside that, is *Programming*. Inside *Programming* is our *Memory*. At the very core of your *Memory* is where the ~~*Truth*~~

---

24 Chart 4-4 is based on Figure 4-4 and it illustrates paths, patterns, and loops; examples of our mind/matrix flows; or a more detailed matrix flow breakdown. The upper left side deals with basic paths and priorities. The lower left shows truth routes through these paths. The upper right shows the paths truth can take through the mechanism. And the center column illustrates the paths and loops that are involved with some 'everyday' states of consciousness.

accumulates. It cannot exist anywhere else except in *Memory*. *Memory* involves something that does not exist in the *now* anyway. It is pictures or perceptions of a past event. It is not the event itself, nor is that event occurring now.

Figure 4.3 (*B*) depicts *Truth* being on the outside. (It can also be depicted at the core. Again, there is a problem with a mortal mind's use of words and temporal symbols. *Truth* is at the core by the fact it is all-inclusive, it is like the seed to everything. *Truth* can be depicted both at the core of everything or with everything within it. And...that can be confusing to depict.)

Figure 4-3 (and the thought construct being introduced) portrays *Truth* as a large circle that encompasses everything – a closed system; and then goes inward to the one circle (*Truth*), that is totally exclusive, and does not hold anything. Kind of, like the Russian doll within doll within doll toy.

Please note that Figure 4-3 is similar to the physical *BTR*s drawing (Figure 3-3). There are balances and points of tangency in the arrangement. Figure 4-3, as in Figure 3-3, portrays a dynamic situation. Imagine the circles are rotating and points of tangency are changing. This occurs when our matrix is in change. Again, mathematically, there are infinite within infinite...possibilities of tangency points

Figure 4-3 depicts *Truth* attached to *Knowledge* at one point. *Knowledge* is shown attached to *Programming* at a different point than *Truth*. *Programming*, *Memory* and ~~*Truth*~~ are all depicted as attached at other points of tangency.

The general rule-of-thumb is that the more actual truth present in the mind and *Programming*, the more functional you will be with things of the physical world outside of you. Simply because, you are dealing with the laws by which things work and you work. The more you use them the better you tend to function. The more ~~Truth~~ that enters your *Programming*, the more dysfunctional you will be with what is outside you.

Using Figure 4-2, the flow that we have touched on is an objective event occurs, goes through our perceptual lens. Truth and ~~truth~~ are mutually exclusive and are shown separated within the drawings. We make a choice – both true and ~~true~~ -- and that choice goes into *Programming*.

Truth also can take the short cut through re-cognition to *Knowledge* (Chart 4-4, *I1*) and then affect *Programming* (as in Chart 4-4, *I4*). Please notice the arrow demonstrating how *Programming* output can refocus the perceptual lens (through *Focus Control*, Figures 4-4 (*I*) and Chart 4-4, *D2*), and loops back to the 'front of the mind' and influence the nature of the choice – a feedback loop.

Whenever we make a choice, it will contain truth, ~~truth~~, or both. We also can make a choice to 'not make' a choice at any moment. These are the only choices we can make. However, all these choices affect our *Programming*.

To review the storages and have them cross-referenced to Chart 4-4:

1) *Truth* and its matrix
    a) Input
        i) God (Postulates and Theorems)
    b) Output
        i) Everything (Chart 4-4, *A10*)
2) *Knowledge* and its matrix of truth applications
    a) Inputs
        i) *Truth* (Chart 4-4, *A3*)
        ii) Cognitive (Chart 4-4, *B5*)
    b) Output
        i) *Programming* (Chart 4-4, *B1*)
3) *Programming* and its matrix of choices
    a) Inputs
        i) *Knowledge* (Chart 4-4, *B1*)
        ii) *Memory* (Chart 4-4, *B3*)

iii) Choice (Chart 4-4, *B6*)
iv) Body Interface (Chart 4-4, *D5*)
b) Outputs
i) *Memory* (Chart 4-4, *B2*)
ii) Focus Control (Chart 4-4, *C1*)
iii) ~~Truth~~ (Chart 4-4, *A19*)
iv) Body Interface (Chart 4-4, *D5*)
4) *Memory* and its matrix of perception/desires set
a) Inputs
i) *Programming* (Chart 4-4, *B2*)
ii) ~~Truth~~ (Chart 4-4, *A17*)
b) Output
i) *Programming* (Chart 4-4, *B3*)
5) ~~Truth~~ and its matrix of ~~truth~~s
a) Input
i) *Programming* (Chart 4-4, *A19*)
b) Output
i) *Memory* (Chart 4-4, *A17*)

This introduces the 'back' of the mind model. The next step is to break down the *Perceptional Lens Array* matrix – the 'front' of the mind -- into its basic components and how the 'front' interfaces with the *Storage* matrix – the 'back' of the mind. How our mortal 'mind's eye' work?

4.5 - The *Perceptional Lens Array* Matrix

An overview of our 'mind's eye' -- the mechanics of the front of the human mind/matrix – can be shown with a camera analogy (a data acquisition device) as in Figure 4-2.1. A camera has a number of parts:

- a lens for bending light – adjusting to distance
- an aperture that determines how much light will hit the receiving area
- a receiving area – film
- a shutter; which, is a go/no-go (do-it or not-do-it) mechanism.

Our eyes have a similar set up: a lens, an aperture (iris), receiving area (retina), and a shutter (eyelids). Most information gathering mechanisms have the same basic setup:

1) Something that aims and prepares the information[25]
a) Camera: Lens and aperture
b) Eyes: Lens and iris
c) Mind: *Perceptional Lens Array* – 'mind's eye'
2) Something that receives the information
a) Camera: Film
b) Eyes: Retina
c) Mind: *Storages*
3) A go-no-go control
a) Camera: Shutter
b) Eyes: Eyelids
c) Mind: Choice
4) Something that can preview the information
a) Camera: View finder and photographer

---

25 Ironically, the image that reaches the film and our retinas is upside down. Again, here is a repeat of the idea that there is a reversed or distorted image of the actuality.

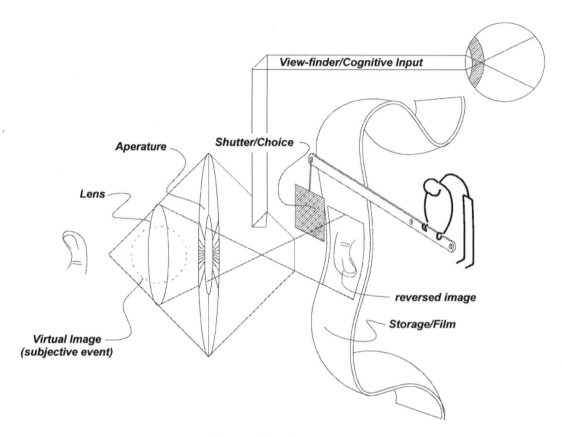

Figure 4-2.1 Camera

b) Eyes: The mind and you
c) Mind: Cognitive Input

Just as the front of a camera or our eyes let in arrangements (qualities) and quantities of light, its absence (no light), and a combination of the two (shadow); so does your mind's *Perceptual Lens Array* let in arrangements and qualities of God (Truth/truth), Truth/truth's absence (~~truth~~), and a combination of the two.

The illustration Figure 4-4 The Human Matrix – a flow chart -- is at the end of this section and is a more detailed version of Figures 4-2 and 4-2.1. The figures within Chart 4-4 represent paths, loops, and influences present within Figure 4-4. All of these figures help illustrate the various paths and connections involved within this book's presented mind model. The human figure in Figures 4-2 and 4-2.1 is represented in Figure 4-4 in the *Focus Control Buss*. The *Focus Control Buss* is shown placed between the perceptual lens – 'front' of the mind -- and *Storages* – 'back' of the mind -- within Figure 4-4.

These figures, Figure 4-4 and Chart 4-4, are to be used as objective references only. They can help demonstrate flows and internal relationships. The 'receiving' area – *Storages* – has already been covered. This section concentrates on the 'focusing' device – *Perceptual Lens Array* -- of the mind.

Looking at Figure 4-4, the *Perceptual Lens Array* is shown composed of a relationship of elements. The illustration shows vertices that make up the elements of the *Perceptual Lens Array* and are labeled as:

♦ Event (*V*)

124

- Perception
- Desires
- Beliefs
- Faith
- Attachments
- True
- ~~True~~
- Choice (*VI*)

Figure 4-4 also shows that between the initiating Event (*V*) and the Choice (*VI*), with the other seven vertices, there are eight triangular areas of influence formed by these vertices. They are labeled:

Δ Attitude (or intention)

Δ Imagination

Δ Reason

Δ Emotions

Δ Cognition

Δ Habit

Δ Judgment

Δ Forgiveness

The nine vertices and the eight triangular relationships between these vertices are also shown with four pairs of triangular relationships -- squares. Three of the pairs – squares -- are shown influenced by a separate *Storage* effect through *Focus Control* (*IV*) and one pair – square -- by *Focus Control* only (*III*).

- Δ Attitude and Δ Imagination $\Rightarrow$ influenced by *Programming*
- Δ Reason and Δ Cognition $\Rightarrow$ influenced by *Knowledge*
- Δ Emotion and Δ Habit $\Rightarrow$ influenced by *Memory*
- Δ Judgment and Δ Forgiveness $\Rightarrow$ influenced by *Focus Control Buss*

Storage's influence disperses in the *Focus Control* (*I*) and each *Storage* matrix has a primary influence to a pair of triangles – squares (labeled *Knowledge*, *Memory*, and *Programming* Influence [*IV*]).

Reason and Cognition triangular areas are shown as influenced by what is in *Knowledge* (*IV*). While Attitude and Imagination triangular areas, tend are shown influenced by *Programming* (*IV*). The major shown influence on the triangular areas of Emotions and Habit is *Memory* (*IV*).

First, the mind's general assembly and operation will be examined -- an overview of the operational break down of the perceptual mechanism. Then, each area will be disassembled into its basic components.

The front part of the *Perceptual Lens Array* contains a 'Perception/Desires Lens' formed between the Perception and Desire vertices. Consider this similar it to the lens of a camera; the 'lens' determines how things are brought into focus (Figure 4-2.1).

A camera lens adjusts for distance. Our mind's lens determines our general outlook and the way we focus on things – scope of focus. To understand this arrangement, remember some of the limits of our perceptual window and the limitations of the amount of information we receive physically.[26]

---

26 Chapter 4.3, Limits of the Perceptual Window

Like your eye or a camera, the mind's lens has limits. Hold a pencil before you and try to focus on both the pencil and something in the distance: a wall, a lamp, a tree, etc. Either you are looking right at the pencil before you or you change your eye focus and see the 'whatever' behind the pencil (which is just something in the foreground). You cannot see both clearly.

When looking beyond the pencil, you are only aware of the pencil's existence (with form, color, and the three-dimensional relationships with what is around it). The pencil itself is fuzzy and double imaged. The same happens to whatever is in the background, when our eyes focus only on the pencil. This idea also applies to a camera or the mind.

What does this mean? It means our mind cannot focus on two things at once. It can multiplex – a short time here, a short time there, a short time here, a short time there… It can also appear to take in two things, like the camera, by opening the focusing lens so one element is a part and in the foreground of a larger element; a pencil was in the foreground of a larger picture. One may look at this as using a form of peripheral mental focus of specialized vision.

The Perception/Desire Lens in Figure 4-4 is shown as the front part of our mind matrix, just as a camera or our eyes has a lens . It is illustrated as having two elements, Perceptions and Desires. The relationship between these two can determine whether we are focusing on something right in front of us or yesterday's lunch. You cannot do both at once. (You can focus on the underline details of a pencil or the underline details of a room; you cannot do both.)

Our perceptions and desires control the focus aspect that determines how far our vision will look, whether we are looking up front or in back – our scope of vision. Just as, a glass lens determines whether the camera is focusing on a nearby flower or a mountain range.

Passively, the first triangle (with the external event) and the Perception/Desire Lens forms our Attitude to any external event. While actively, it forms our intention to any external event.

To continue with the overview, behind a camera's glass lens, there is an aperture. This aperture determines how much light will expose the film; it matches the data volume to the storage capabilities. In Figure 4-4, the *Perceptual Lens Array* is shown with an Aperture array consisting of three vertices: 'Faith', 'Beliefs', and 'Attachments'. These elements determine what we let in; what goes through our 'mind's eye'. Our mind's Aperture has similar effects – focusing effects -- as the front Perception/Desire Lens, but is much more general in its usage.

Memory and *Knowledge* control the Aperture, more so than the Perception/Desire Lens, which is primarily controlled by *Programming*. However, because in this model all are interconnected, the Aperture can have some affect on Perception/Desire Lens.

A physical science parallel to their connections is diffraction; the bending of light around an object. If something is not visually clear, you can stick two fingers up and make a thin slit (an aperture) and look through it to see better. This is because the aperture the fingers make is so small, it is bending light; and, acting somewhat like a lens by bending the light slightly. The slit helps refocus the light coming to the eyes slightly. It is this way an aperture can imitate focus.

Our mind's Aperture setting tends to be determined by patterns of previous choices than the Perception/Desire Lens. Our values tend to show up in this Aperture area.

Again, remember that this whole *Perceptual Lens Array* being presented is a dynamic situation. Figure 4-4 has separated the elements in the array, and essentially, they all can affect each other either directly (represented by the arrows of influence that is between the vertices within the *Perceptual Lens Array*) or indirectly. This is a holistic system. Both the Lens and the Aperture can be interdependent; and, a change of focusing of the Perceptual Lens can have an effect on the Aperture, and re-adjustment of the Aperture can have a change on the Perceptual Lens.

To continue the overview and return to the camera analogy; part of the light coming into a camera, past the aperture, is split and enters the viewfinder. The viewfinder of our mortal mind is the Cognitive Input (Figure 4-2.1 and Figure 4-4, *VII)*. As in operating a camera, if the image is not right, we tend to refocus. If the mind's image is not according to the patterns in the

Storages (*Memory*, *Programming*, and *Knowledge*) or if there is no Cognitive Input (it is not in our viewfinder), then we have a tendency to refocus until there is some re-cognition.

Remember, Truth and ~~truth~~ are mutually exclusive. As with Eternal and temporal or infinite and finite, you are in either one or the other. Figure 4-4 shows this separation as two elements within this model, True and ~~True~~. In physics, this is similar to light broken into packets of energy – photon or no photon. Truth automatically enters *Storage* through the Cognitive 'viewfinder' (*VII*).

After the perception of an event goes through the *Perceptual Lens Array* Aperture, it then goes the Choice (*VI*) of True and ~~True~~ -- the shutter -- and to you. Just like the shutter of a camera, it is either go or no-go, one or the other, but not both. However, as in a camera, light (photon) and dark (absence of photon); truth and ~~truth~~ proceed through the shutter/Choice when operated.

From the choice of True and ~~True~~, the result goes into *Programming*, which is analogous to the film of the camera or the retina; it is stored.

This concludes the overview of the *Perceptual Lens Array*.

You have been given an overview; now to cover the individual elements of the mind's *Perceptional Lens Array* in detail and some of the triangular relationships shown. As stated earlier, the top part of the front Lens has been labeled Perception; the bottom part Desires. Perception and Desires in the model of this book are interrelated and interdependent. They are the 'flip' sides of the same coin.

Remember the mirror; the construction of our mortal mind is a weak mirror image of what is the construction of God's Mind. *Theorem 6A* states, "Love and Logic are One" within the Mind of God. The distorted reflection, or parallel, to that is the concept that our perceptions and desires are really one thing within our being.

Our desires can affect our perceptions and our perceptions can affect our desires. They are one thing. What we see defines what we want, and what we want defines (or re-defines) what we see. They are linked. We cannot want that which we cannot conceive in our mind, a perception.

There may not be a physical image, and if there is no image or perception, then there is no desire for it. When the desire comes up, some perception is involved too.

♦ **What are desires?** Basically, desires boils down to, "What do I want (or don't want)?" To help understand the relationship of Perception to Desires, look at all desire as being 'a perception of a lack' (or a lack of perception) internal or external to oneself -- something is 'missing'. Truth is One. A weak parallel to this is; if there is something perceived missing in truth, the truth matrix corrects for it. Desire can be looked as a weak aspect of the Correction. Desire is the urge to correct a perception of lack.

Desire is always object related, dualistic. It is object referenced somewhere; that object can be external; bicycle, a lawn, food, a clean pair of underwear, etc. Or, it can be an archetype within your own mind: happiness, contentment, peace, etc. Desire is perception orientated.

At times, you may have had desires without a perception of what that is before... a sort of feeling. It can be more of a feeling that there is something else (some unformed perception), and you want this 'something else'. It can also be more like not wanting something, not desiring something, a dissatisfaction. "I do not desire this." "I do not desire that." "There is something else."[27]

This is an unfocused perception along with a desire. An unfocused desire for 'something' has with it unfocused perceptions. It can be a desire for 'something else', but the 'something else' is not clear. If 'something else' is not clear, neither is the desire. So they are both vague, but they are both together. Still, they are not separated.

---

27 That also could be an aspect of Truth way back in your head calling you, saying, "There's something else here. Come see."

Bottom line is we do things because we want something. We will never do something if we have no desire. Without desire, nothing would be done. Even, when we do something we do not want; there is something we perceive we <u>do</u> want. We think we can get it by doing the odious chore, so we do it anyway. We may not like going to work, but we want to eat, we want to be warm and dry, or we need or want the money (or some other perception we think money can deliver).

Desires can be either positively or negatively charged. You can want or not want something. In Chapter 5, when constructing the Formula of Effectiveness, desires will be treated as absolute values (positive).

◆ **The other side of desire is perception.** Perception is also dualistic; there is a perceiver and the perceived. It also is object-related. Perception is a mental assembly of truth effects – a matrix. It may be through direct sensory data – 'objective event' -- or involve a mental picture or image of something – 'subjective event'. Moreover, it could be assembled through other senses – sensory data -- than sight too, like hearing. (All five senses pass through our body, to the 'objective event', into the *Perceptual Lens Array*.)

Through hearing, we get a picture: a mental construct or a matrix of cognitive associations. We hear noise; then, we assemble a picture together. We hear a sound of bottles and cans rattling around early in the morning and that sound is associated with a perception of the garbage collectors.

Perception and Desire – mind/heart -- are one thing. A change of heart effects a change of mind; a change of mind effects a change of heart. A change of perception brings about a change in desire; and... a change of desire brings about a change of perception.[28]

Another way to look at it is, when the author changed his behavior from child behavior to adult behavior. When the author was a teenager and trying to be so mature (and not being very good at it), he noticed that when he stopped looking at things as a child would look at them, his desires for those things fell away. As the author's mind saw further, the things the author wanted from what he saw as a child, disappeared.

Of these two components to the Perceptions/Desires Lens, Perception is the guide or the leader of the perceptual lens, and the Desires are the drive and the 'heart' of it.

An analogy to the mind vehicle and the perception/desire relationship is with a car. *Storage* determines the nature of the vehicle, whether it is a go-cart or a tank. Perception is like the steering wheel and the gears of a car; they are what, where, and how a car moves. Desire is the fuel. Choice can be analogous to the brake and accelerator. Cognition serves as the windshield – view. Together they make up the bulk of the mechanism of a car.

The mechanical of a car determines the direction and the velocity, acceleration, etc. However, mechanical cannot do diddly-squat without the fuel application. Desire is the fuel, the drive that makes the car go. If you have just the gas with no other mechanism, you are not going far. On the other hand, if you have just the vehicle mechanism and no gas, you are not going far again. You need them both. Desire provides energy while Perception guides the energy. We, as the drivers of our mind vehicle, are constantly using this relationship.

This Perception/Desires relationship forms the Lens and gives us a general outlook on things. It tends to be the steering mechanism of our *Perceptual Lens Array*. It reflects our general viewpoint.

When we work with inclusive perceptions, more Truth enters the Lens. When we start to see the whole picture – expand perceptions -- and are not exclusive, we start working with Truth more. The mind's lens opens to distance.

Conversely, if we start being more and more exclusive and our *sight* is more limited (i.e., I only want to see what I 'want'), then our choices tend to have more ~~truth~~. The lens sees only that which is 'close'. This is how the Perception/Desires Lens acts as the general steering mechanism of this array.

---

[28] Very similar to the relationship that magnetic fields have to electric fields, Chapter 3

- An increase in perception increases the scope of our 'mind's eye' vision – opens the mind; it opens the lens to distance.
- An increase in desire decreases the range of our 'mind's eye' vision – closes the mind; it brings the Lens focus up close.

With this Perception/Desires Lens relationship, one opens – to distance or scope, and the other closes – to distance or scope.

When desires are few or at medium to low volume, perceptions are the major guide and the predominant lens influence. When desires are many or at high volume, they can totally drown out perceptions, like when somebody sees red -- they do not see anything except their anger, and the focus of their anger. When desires are at a very high volume, it narrows and confuses perceptions. As emotions get very high in volume, one may see nothing except that which is the object -- perception -- of the emotion.

This desire/perception relationship is a flexible relationship and it is constantly adjusting and moving. It changes from one event to another. When you look at the tobacco can, your mind's Perception/Desires Lens focuses one way. When you look at a person, it focuses a very different way. When you look out at the sky and the hill, again you see something different. Your Perception/Desires Lens is constantly refocusing or changing. Just as a photographer is mindful of adjusting the camera lens for distance in each picture or your eye is constantly refocusing for distance.

When the mind's Lens starts to crystallize into patterns of focusing, it reflects our behavior patterns (*Storages*). When taken to extremes of crystallization, we experience psychoses and neuroses.

The triangles that comprise the Lens and are derived from the points in Figure 4-4's representation of the *Perceptual Lens Array* are next to be examined. This segues into the Aperture.

Attitude (or intention) $\Delta \Rightarrow$ Figure 4-4 shows how the points Desires, Perceptions, and Objective Event form the Attitude triangle. Passively (from an observer's viewpoint), this triangle comprises the first thing an objective event encounters, our attitude.

Actively, it forms your intent; what are your intentions to any event. If you are to create – extend an idea, this involves the intention elements of that creation.

Reason $\Delta \Rightarrow$ The Perception/Desires Lens and the Attitude triangle were looked. The next area to look at is the second part of the lens array -- the Aperture. The top triangular relationship is labeled 'Reason'. Its vertices are shown as our Perceptions, our Beliefs, and our Faith. The Reason triangle is where truth assembles itself into a thought matrix.

One vertex of the Reason triangle is Perception and that has been covered. Perception is the major input into this upper triangle as Desires are the major input to the lower Emotion triangle.

♦ Another vertex in the Reason triangle is Faith; what is faith? Demonstrating this to someone for this book, the author asked someone to hand him a pencil. (At the time, she first moved, hesitated, then gave it to him, and laughed because he pulled this trick on her before.) How did she know she could move that? It was an act of faith.

Within the presented model, Faith is truth application. *Knowledge* is storage of truth applications. Faith determines the truth applications that are to be stored.

Just because something happened once – an application, it does not necessarily mean that it will happen again – be applied again. You can choose not to apply truth. As with the demonstration, she first reached, then hesitated. She had a feeling about it afterwards, when her hand started to move. She hesitated because she started thinking about it. Even starting to move her hand to the pencil was an act of faith; she was applying numerous physical laws/truths. The author said, "Hand me the pencil", she moved and then hesitated for a minute, because she remembered he did this trick before. She thought about it; she perceived something from *Memory* and *Programming*, and had an emotional response. Later, she reactivated her faith, handed it to him, and then laughed.

This book is trying to pull faith out of its ivory tower to show that it is a part of our everyday life. We apply and use it all the time. It is not something way out there in some religious nether-land. In this model, we are applying truth – using faith -- and it enters *Knowledge* constantly.

In terms of this work, Faith is the *application of a truth/knowledge* without thought or feeling, although it is much more.

Spiritual faith is application of God's knowledge (*Truth* storage) in the back of our minds (Chart 4-4, *A2* or *C5*) – at the core of our being. Some religious faith is an application of a knowledge that appears contradictory to our immediate cognitive associations and *Knowledge* storage. Religious faith is an application of knowledge pertaining to Absolute Truth, when the perceived truth may not agree – an apparent reality conflict.

In the application of Truth, the Eternal moment of Creation can be working through you (or you are working in parallel to it, depending on the 'truths' involved). Since, that moment is far beyond anything words can describe; faith will be kept to the truth application level.

The Faith vertex is also relevant to the thaumaturgical magic rule, "To Will".[29]

♦ Faith and Perceptions, as two of the vertices of the Reason triangle, have been presented. The last vertex to look at is Belief. Faith, as mentioned before, is the application of *Knowledge* without mentation. You just do it. You know, and you do it. Belief is an application of *Knowledge* with mentation and emotions.

As Beliefs become more exclusive -- this Aperture, like the aperture of a camera -- grows smaller and lets in less light/truth. When Beliefs become more non-exclusive, the Aperture starts approaching infinity: you increasingly take in more and more.

Beliefs determine what we are open or not open to, what will come through, and what will not come through.

And...in Figure 4-4, the Beliefs area it is roughly a nebulous area generated by the other elements -- vertices, Perceptions, Desires, Attachments, and Faith. The interaction of the other four elements defines Belief. Beliefs are usually related to something that has already gone through the mind matrix a number of times and reflects a pattern of choices (*Programming*). In addition, there is an involvement of previous perceptions (*Memory*).

Again, Belief is an application of *Knowledge* with mentation (a perception matrix). It has thinking in it, whereas Faith tends to be an application of *Knowledge* without thought.

Another difference between Faith and Beliefs shows up in the truth applications (faith) in Absolute Truth. Figure 4-4 portrays this as a line from Faith to *Truth*. *Truth* makes up the Creation Matrix with its consequent link to God. With this link to Absolute Power, anything is possible. You can believe you can fly, but you will never get off the ground without some kind of help or some relevant truth application. Faith in Truth (or an application of truth as in Bernoulli's principle in **Actual** reality) makes flight a possibility.

Mystic operators apply higher priority Truths – **Absolute** reality Truths. When arrayed properly, **Actual** reality truths must follow. Herein lay the wonders of the Magi, Saints, and our hi-tech society. It is all a question of what Truths/truths are being applied.

Faith in Truth -- **Absolute** and **Actual** realities' truths -- ensures long-term survival. Beliefs constitute the human condition. You can believe in God, but that belief does not mean diddly-squat if you do not apply God's Truth or the truth/laws of the situation.

These three vertices conjoined (Faith, Perception, and Belief) form the triangle of Reason. This triangle represents the 'logic' of our perceptual lens; it is the basic logic behind the tendencies of our choices.

Emotion $\Delta \Rightarrow$ Figure 4-4 illustrates the lower triangle in the Aperture as 'Emotion'. Trying to put a finger on what are emotions is like trying to put a finger on a point of a moving wheel. (As

---

29 Chapter 9, Concerning Magic

soon as you touch that point, it moves out from under your finger.) In many ways, the Emotion triangle is the mirror image of the Reason triangle. The three vertices of the shown Emotion triangle are Desires, Beliefs, and Attachments.

♦ Desires and Beliefs vertices have been covered. The Attachments vertex remains. Attachments are long-term repeated chosen desires and perceptions, or preferred (desired) desires and perceptions. Like Desires and Perceptions, Attachment is also aligned to something other than itself (object orientated). With Attachments, it is as if the Desires are exponentially magnified.

As Faith is application of *Knowledge* through Perception, Attachments are repeated applications of *Memory* and Desires. It is through the Attachment connection that fear is inserted into the matrix.

What we want, Desire; what we are open to, Belief; and our history of preferred wants, Attachment; conjoin to form this Emotion triangle. Emotion, unlike Reason or Perception; is what we feel and how we feel (experience). Emotions are subtler and less perceptible than Reason and Perception.

Emotions can be delicate or very powerful. They can be in the background, or can be like a wave breaking over you. Emotion is a non-verbal, non-symbolic experience of feelings and these emotions can affect the body chemical balances through *Programming* (Chart 4-4, D5-7).

This is part of the survival mechanism. Fear creates chemical changes almost immediately in the body, and part of this is geared towards the survival of the body – fight or flight. These changes can occur almost immediately. There are also changes due to emotion, which affect the body over time.

Since emotion can cause chemical changes in the body, it makes sense that repetition of specific mental/emotional sets can produce long term changes in the body. Herein lays the connection between mental/emotional dis-ease and/or sickness. Conversely, it also makes sense a change or a correction of mental/emotional sets can alter the body condition. Here also begins the field of attitudinal healing.

A
{ 2, 4, 6, 8, 10, ... }

D
{ All real numbers }

B
{ 1, 3, 5, 7, 9, ... }

E
{2, 2.215, 3, 8.2788, ... }

C
{ 1, 2, 3, 4, 5, 6, 7, 8, ... }

Figure 4-5 Algebraic Sets

The Emotion triangular relationship affects Belief and therefore, can affect Perception and Reason. Again, recognize one element can affect the others. Even though they are shown represented as separate elements, a dynamic interaction is happening here all the time.

The Reason and Emotion triangles share a common vertex, Belief. Yet, they are joined in other ways. Just as perceptions and desires are the flip sides of the same coin, so are thoughts and emotions.

One way to explain how thoughts and emotions (or perceptions and desires) are linked is through an algebraic analogy (Figure 4-5). In algebra, a situation can occur where there are specific sets of numbers. Let us say:

- Set *A* contains all even numbers: *2, 4, 6, and 8…∞.*
- Set *B* has all odd numbers: *1, 3, 5, 7, and 9…∞.*
- Set *C* is all whole numbers: *1, 2, 3, 4, 5, 6, 7, 8, 9, 10…∞* -- all the positive integers to infinity.
- Set *D* is the set of real numbers.
- Set *E* is a group of specific numbers like *2, 2.215, 3,* etc.

Notice the elements of set *A* can fit into sets *C* and *D*. This relationship is called a subset. Set *A* is a subset of sets *C* and *D*, but not of *B* and *E*. Set *B* is a subset of *C* and *D* but not of *A* or *D*. Whereas, sets *A, B, C,* and *E* are all subsets of *D*. All the elements of these sets can be found in set *D*.[30]

Now, look at Figure 4-6. Instead of sets of numbers, look at a set as being an emotion. With an emotion, a matrix pattern of thought or reasoning has developed. Figure 4-6 shows Emotion *L* (lust), Emotion *A* (anger), and Emotion *F* (fear). Emotion *L* has a given set or matrix

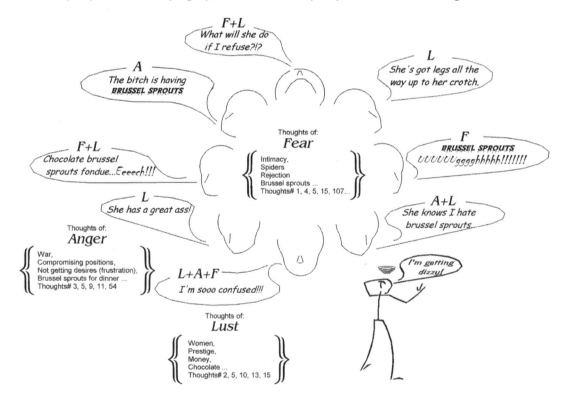

Figure 4-6 Mental/Emotional Sets

---

[30] Please note all but one of these sets presented are infinite. Here again, we have the condition of infinities fitting into infinities... The infinities of sets *A* and *B* fit into the infinity of set *C*, which, in turn, fits in the infinity of set *D*.

132

of thoughts that we have programmed into it, and are associated with this emotion. If you experience Emotion L, you experience these sets of thoughts.

Conversely, if you start a pattern of thought that is in this set, Emotion L automatically occurs. One calls forth the other. The thoughts and feelings make a regenerative circle. Every emotion BTR has a matrix of thought BTRs. Change the elements of thought matrix and the emotion changes. Specific thoughts determine an emotion and this emotion regenerates that set of thoughts, and so on.[31]

Changing perception changes the cycle. You can break the cycle or pattern if you stop entertaining the thoughts of Emotion L. Over a period of time, Emotion L will disappear. It can be waited out, and without thought to feed it, it disappears over time.

Change the thought and the emotion changes. Change the thought or do not entertain any thoughts in the thought matrix connected to this emotion, and the emotion goes away. Conversely, if the emotion goes away, the emotion's thoughts are not there. You are not entertaining them. They are not in your mind. However, entertain one thought in that emotional set and the emotion returns.

It must be mentioned that emotion may have to be waited out. Emotion has, for lack of a better term, a quality similar to inertia. Once you get it moving, it takes a while for it to stop.

Part of this emotional inertia appears as chemical changes it may produce in the body. When you cease working with the set of thoughts, you may have to wait awhile for your body to go back to a chemical balance again. Adrenaline and other chemicals are generated with strong emotions. You can stop the thinking process but, because your body has inertia and operates chemically, you may have to wait for it to slow down and stabilize. Sometimes breathing exercises can help facilitate this. (Breathing exercises will be instituted in a later chapter.)

Because of this inertia, this slowness of reaction, it is relatively difficult to change the thought set of a strong emotion. There are ways to do that, however. One simple way is to start thinking of something else that interests you, change perceptions and distract the mind. (Remember, that it cannot think of two different things at once.) Once this done, the emotion eventually dissipates; for no thoughts are being entertained that is in that emotional set. However, entertain one thought in that emotional set and the emotion returns.

One can distract the mind and forget about an incident by reading an engrossing book. When you have stopped reading, and have one thought in that emotion and it becomes, "That asshole!"

Emotional sets such as Emotion L have been introduced. Instead of putting specific thoughts into this set, this example will use numbers to represent thoughts as Figure 4-6 does. Let us say Emotion L has thoughts: 2, 5, 13, 10, and 15. Let us say Emotion A has thought elements 3, 5, 9, 11, 54. Let us say Emotion F has thought elements that are 1, 4, 5, 16, and 107.

There are thought elements in Emotion A that are common to Emotion F and Emotion L, like thought 5. An example of this can be: wanting something very badly, and at the same time being afraid of getting it, while getting angry if you do not get it.

You entertain a thought that is in Emotion A and experience Emotion A and its related thoughts. At the same time, because the thought 5 is also an element of Emotion F, entertain thought 5 and Emotion F can occur as well (with its related thoughts).

Let us say we have thought 5 triggered by lust. Because thought 5 is in anger also, we will start feeling anger as well. Since thought 5 is also an element in fear, fear also begins to occur with the other two emotions.[32] This is how we can have one thought and have multiple emotions; they are sharing thoughts/elements from different mental-emotional sets.

---

31 Again, similar to the 3-in-1, 1-in-3 relationship in Figure 2-1

32 Later, when covering miracles, Chapter 10, with *A Course in Miracles*, presents how all-exclusive emotional sets are subsets of fear. Just as in Figure 4-5, all the numerical sets presented are subsets of the set of real numbers.

Here is where things can get confusing because three emotions have been called up in a short period. In addition, when these three emotions come in, all their thought matrix elements can enter in as well. We may have started with lust and thought 5; when anger showed up we could start having thoughts 3, 5, 9, 11, and 54. When fear showed up, we may have started entertaining thoughts 1, 4, 5, 15, or 107... The result can be a general confusion, a hodge-podge of thoughts and emotions.

All these thoughts are parading before our attention while we are experiencing a multitude of emotions. We have these different feelings and thoughts, and unless we sort them out, it is going to twist us out of shape. We have to sort these things (perceptions/desires or thought/emotions) out; otherwise, we would literally get irrational. Alternatively, the mind or being can also freeze from an overload of emotions and their related thoughts.

This thought/emotion relationship is set up in childhood -- from birth. We start filling our *Programming* with choices of emotions and sets of thoughts early in childhood. When our thinking was forming, our mental-emotional relationships were forming with them. We started to "cut the paths in the field of grass".

The association between emotions and thought matrices or sets of thoughts forms the 'software' and wiring of our *Programming* and *Memory*. This early childhood programming determines a large part of our adult responses to many things.

This circle mentioned -- of emotion to elements of thoughts, back to emotion, to elements of thoughts -- can be seen when we fantasize or daydream. Certain thoughts feel good to us. Because they feel good to us, we think them some more (or more like them). The more we feel, the more we dwell on the thoughts. This is roughly equivalent to a mental masturbation. We are doing it because it feels good.

This is a feedback circle and it can be a very limited circle. In many ways, it can lead to a dead end. This may be a mistake from a spiritual growth perspective. It is possible to see people do this with anger. They have angry thoughts and they like feeling angry, so they feed the anger and have more angry thoughts. They are being angry just to be angry. Or...sad, driving themselves into a circle of being sad until it becomes a downward spiral. In both cases, they are regenerating these feelings because there is 'something' that they are getting from these feeling; something they want.

Excessive daydreaming <u>tends</u> to go nowhere constructive. When the mind is preoccupied with destructive emotions with exclusive thoughts, it gets into this downward spiral, away from Truth. Keep thinking the same thoughts while experiencing the same feelings and soon it is in the 'pits'.

While we are feeling something or having emotions, we are continually thinking thoughts (in the thought matrix) that constitute these mental/emotional sets and they travel round and round and round. Every time a mental/emotional set goes around one circle, through Perceptions and Desires, it then passes through Choice (Figure 4-4, *II*) and then to *Programming*; and then, that choice then affects *Programming*.

Programming affects the Perception/Desire Lens through the focus control and subjective event, through the lens array, back to choice, etc., again a circle or a feedback loop. Every time a thought goes around, it goes through our Choice (*II*) and contributes to *Programming*. More and more circles, and each time it makes the circle; it influences *Programming*. This is as if deepening the path in the field of grass analogy mentioned earlier.

Imagination $\Delta \Rightarrow$ The third triangle in Figure 4-4 to look at in the Aperture is Imagination. This triangle's vertices are our Perception, Desire, and Belief. All three points have been covered previously. They interact by affecting what we see, want, and are open to both objectively and subjectively. The Imagination triangle not only has Perception and Desire as two vertices. It also has a leg in common with Emotion and a leg in common with Reason. The Imagination triangle becomes a meeting ground for Reason and Emotion.

For a moment, look at the arrows in Figure 4-4. The arrows there represent the same as the arrows in *Storage*. They show direction of influence. In the upper triangles, Faith directly affects truth to be chosen, Belief, and Perception, but is not <u>directly</u> affected by them.

They can indirectly affect Faith indirectly through *Knowledge*, how we focus, and through previous choices that have gone through the *Programming* circle.

{Like in the previous Faith demonstration; she first moved to pick up the pencil (cognition and choice), then she saw what she was doing (a cognition/choice program cycle) and she did not do it (made another choice). Finally she went through another program cycle, did it (applied *Knowledge* -- faith), and reflected (another cycle) and laughed.}

As stated earlier, of the four forward triangles (Attitude, Imagination, Reason, and Emotion), each vertex, except for the Event and Faith, directly influences the others. Attachments can affect Desire as well as Desire can affect Attachment. In addition, Desire can affect Perception and Belief, and can also be affected by them. The same can be said of Perception's vertex to Desire and Belief, and the Belief vertex to Perception, Desire, and Attachment.

In Figure 4-4, Imagination is shown as a triangle where all the arrows meet and have a dynamic tension. It can be seen that we can steer choices, with our imagination, to True or ~~True~~ categories. Manipulating this triangular area is called controlled imagination or visualization. In using controlled imagination, we visualize or manipulate our 'mind's eye' – manipulate the 'subjective event'.

As mentioned earlier, this Imagination triangle is meeting ground for Reason and Emotion. An example of how these two can meet in imagination is in an example the author picked up somewhere. If a ten-foot long two-inch thick by twelve-inch wide wood board was on the ground and you were asked to walk it, you would have an easy time. However, put that same 'two by twelve' ten feet up, where you see you would be hurt, and you cannot walk that 'two by twelve' easily.

You start imagining falling, which creates fear and other emotions with their perceptions. You do not want to fall; in fact, you desire not to fall. (Desire is either wants or not wants, but they can both be very strong.) You do not want to be hurt. Your wanting to cross is counter-balanced with not wanting to be hurt or falling.

The way to get across on the board, when it is up in the air, is for you to see (visualize) yourself walking across it and getting across it safely, or visualize it on the ground. In addition, you would maintain your balance as if the board was on the ground. Therefore, you can use your Imagination to bring your Perceptions together with your Desires to complete the task.

We can refocus the Imagination triangle -- with Perception -- to see ourselves walking across. Apply this and you walk across, no problem. This is through faith/truth-application in your ability to walk, actually. Although you have the fear, you set it aside, or maintain focus on one thing only (the application of the vision/perception), so fear is not allowed to be a major influence. This is where faith/application comes in again also.

Up to this point, all this information is referenced to an 'objective event' – something outside of us. In addition, Figure 4-4 shows the 'subjective event' occurs in the imagination. This whole mental/emotional mechanism being presented is a matrix (matrices within matrices actually). Truth and the Eternal Moment of Creation expresses itself through this mental/emotional matrix. The result, this matrix is constantly creating. Left to itself, it is constantly extending that which is in *Storage* – that which defines focus. This is the 'parade' of thoughts that pervade our consciousness.

We will come back to this Imagination triangle and the 'subjective event' with an exercise at the end of this section.

Cognition $\Delta \Rightarrow$ Using Figure 4-4, we have covered the Lens and part of the Aperture. The next triangles to be covered are 'Cognition' and 'Habit'. The Cognition triangle is very important. Any organism that has any type of physical sensory array must have a Cognitive Input into its mental storage (*VII*). It is through cognition it perceives its environment. In addition, cognition is related to the first lab that was introduced.[33]

---

33 Chapter 1.1 - *Lab #1*

The Cognition triangle's three points are Faith, Beliefs, and True. Faith and Beliefs were covered previously.

♦   The True vertex is where all truth that makes it through the Perceptual Lens accumulates. From this vertex, the truth automatically enters *Knowledge* through the Cognitive Input – a survival input. This True vertex also includes the true that sustains the ~~true~~.

This Cognition triangle defines our awareness. This triangle covers growth and learning; it is where truth appears to assemble.[34] This assembly process begins in the Reason triangle and finishes in the Cognition triangle. When learning is based on truth, it goes directly through the Cognitive Input and enters *Knowledge*. The Cognitive Input is your mind's viewfinder; through this the mind re-cognizes. Cognition (Figure 4-4, *VII*) bypasses Choice (*VI*). Cognition can appear over time and it can jump. A cognitive jump is the "aha" thing mentioned earlier.

As shown, Cognition (*VII*) is the only way for the mind to affect input into *Storages* without going through *Programming*. The True point vertex directly enters *Knowledge*. It is shown in Figure 4-4 as the line from Truth to *Knowledge*.

When we hit that "Oh, I get it now!" -- it goes right into our *Knowledge*, bypassing *Programming* and Choice (*VI*). This is also the case with re-cognition. Cognition (*VII*) is the minds viewfinder's direct input into *Knowledge.*

Whereas with Choice, the Choices we make go into *Programming* (*II*) and then the *Programming* influences the refocus of the perceptual lens (and then can re-influence Cognition (*VII*), etc.).

The Cognition triangle, involving Faith, Belief, and True, can cause truth to use the Cognitive Input and/or it can also lead to truth being an element of Choice and therefore enter *Programming* (*II*). The Cognitive triangle and the Reason triangle are shown influenced by what is in *Knowledge* storage – previous truth applications. Through the Cognition triangle all of our automatic cognition patterns occur -- cognition and re-cognition. The similarity between the cognition and habit is that recognition is a repetition of a previous cognitive path. When we re-cognize something, we re-know something.

Again, Cognition may seem to have a very intellectual connotation until we compare it to the idea of recognition -- which is re-cognizing. This process is ongoing. When it is not occurring, it can tend to lead to a state of confusion. We recognize a cup, a paper clip, or a rubber band. This is governed through *Knowledge* and previous cognitive jumps.

Cognition and Reason triangles are governed by your *Knowledge* storage. We know what a paper clip is. We know what a rubber band is.

The following exercise helps demonstrate to you the high priority nature of the Cognitive input.

Exercise and Lab 4: Eye Exercise or 'Surfing' the Mechanism

It is mentioned in this chapter that there are many mental paths and feedback loops. Because we are dealing with a temporal mind, each path or loop takes '*x*' amount of time to occur. Some happen quicker while others take longer to occur. For example, the loop from an Event, to our re-cognition of the Event's existence, to our focusing, and re-cognizing the Event itself (Chart 4-4, *N5*), takes a specific amount of time. This time lapse can be used.

Remember the Cognitive path is a high priority path. It is a survival path. When it is in constant use, lesser priority mental paths must give way.

There is an eye exercise where you focus on one physical thing and move the eyes quickly from one item to another item. The eyes are on the item long enough that you recognize a perceptual change has occurred, but not long enough for complete recognition of

---

34 Truth is always present in a matrix relationship. When truth appears to assemble, it is truth's matrix relationship we perceive.

the item to occur. Not long enough finish the process or to allow any other mind/matrix operation.

Moving the eyes to 'something', the mind/matrix is refocusing until there is re-cognition. After the cognition, a number of loops can occur. Moving and refocusing the eyes before the re-cognition loop is complete; calls for a mind refocus. Constantly focusing the eyes on separate things for a period of time means your mind/matrix is constantly refocusing and little ~~truth~~ is chosen during that moment; nor, is a 'subjective event' (thought) allowed to occur. Done quickly enough, and no mentation occurs. If you find yourself thinking, while doing the exercise, you are not moving the eyes fast enough or you are not bringing your focus to bear on the objects.

Because little ~~truth~~ is chosen for a period of time and consequently not dampening the mind/matrix, a slight 'ringing' or a consciousness change occurs.[35]

There is a direct relationship between time length of an empty mind and consciousness change; the longer the time the great the change. (By empty mind, there is choice but very-little-to-zero perceptual input into *Programming*.) This is one of many direct relationships, which will be covered in later chapters.

In this exercise, you are to change your perception input faster than the cognition/knowledge/you loop can operate. You are to change your physical focus faster than your mind/matrix operates. In doing this, 'surfing' the changes in your mind, you are preoccupying the mechanism and very-little-to-zero Choice input enters *Programming*. You are using the temporal operating limits of your mortal mind/matrix to step out of your usual mental operation.

The result is; because the Cognitive path is a high priority path, an extended cognitive preoccupation resets the mind. After doing this exercise, your mind starts over. It disrupts previous mentation.

This eye exercise can be a tool to reset manually your mind. It causes a reset in your *Programming* storage. To do this exercise:

> *First, take a moment and notice how you are feeling and the nature of your most recent thought processes.*
> *Do this exercise for <u>one minute</u>. Move the eyes to one thing, to another, to another…*
> *Afterward, take another moment and notice where your 'head is at'.*
> *Assignment: Do this exercise for one minute on 10 separate occasions.*
> *Record your perceptions/feelings in your journal or notebook.*

Deep meditation can also cause your mind to reset. This exercise can manually reset your mind and the mind resets naturally. Naturally, there are numerous ways the mind resets itself:

- One is laughter. Laughter reset involves *Knowledge* storage. The moment *Knowledge* resets, the joy of Eternal Creation – *Truth* – passes through. We experience this as laughter.
- Another is crying. Crying occurs when the reset involves *Memory* storage. As *Memory* resets the ~~*Truth*~~ within bleeds through and it manifests within you as crying.
- Any rapidly changing cognitive input tends to reset *Programming* (the eye exercise uses this).
- Sleep resets the mind on all levels.

This book will return to some of the elements of this eye exercise in later chapters.

********************* *********************

---

35 End of this chapter

Habit $\Delta \Rightarrow$ To return to Figure 4-4 and the presented *Perceptual Lens Array* model, the upper triangle was covered – Cognition. Figure 4-4 shows the lower triangle is Habit. Habits are established patterns of Desires related to Choices. Habit's three vertices are shown as Beliefs, Attachments, and the ~~True~~.

♦   The ~~True~~ vertex is where ~~truth~~ accumulates that pass through the Perceptual Lens. Remember that True and ~~True~~ are mutually exclusive and they are shown as separate vertices. In addition, because all ~~truth~~ is dependent on a set of truths, the ~~True~~ vertex affects the True vertex with the set of 'truths' that sustains the ~~truth~~. This is shown as an arrow from ~~True~~ to True.

Habit is an established pattern of choices and it represents automatic *Programming* responses on a non-survival level, whereas Cognition tends to be of survival level (because it 'keys' into *Knowledge* and involves **Actual** reality).

What are examples of each one? Okay. Catch! (the author tossed a pencil to someone and she missed.) She missed; and she recognized a pencil was coming. The author asked her to catch it, and she even opened up her hand to do it. This started on a cognitive level, without thought. Habit is a repetition of established patterns of choices, "Got a cigarette?" The habit triangle is where you have automatic *Programming* responses that tend to be on a non-survival level, "I have a craving for chocolate". It really has nothing to do with survival.

Habit <u>tends</u> to be physically oriented. It tends to be orientated around our Desires, Emotions, and Attachments, which also can be physically orientated. All these are part of our Habits,

It was mentioned that part of the cognitive input might involve repetition. This functions for the truth level and it can go the other way, with habit or the ~~truth~~. The difference between the two is that *Knowledge* is a function of repetition of cognitive jumps, whereas habit is a repetition of choices or perception/desire sets. Again, one tends to work on a survival level, while the other does not.

Look at Figure 4-4 and imagine a sectional line going from the Event, through Belief, through Choice, and bisecting *Programming*. Now imagine the line as a mirror, splitting the matrix right down the middle horizontally, and you can almost see that the top parts and the bottom parts are like mirror images of each other. (Actually, they are more like a distorted mirror image of each other.) This way, cognition and re-cognition can appear to be like habit.

Both can be a function of repetition: one tends to lead up to the truth and the other to ~~truth~~. However, cognition goes a little deeper than habit. It deals with learning on a survival level, truths. When habits are exercised, about the only thing being learned is keeping the habit, perception/desire set. You do not have to have habits for survival; they can help, but are not necessary. Habits <u>tend</u> not to be survival orientated, whereas cognition and re-cognition is. That is not saying though that some survival patterns cannot become habits eventually.

Habits and emotions are kind of like baser processes, and reason and cognition are more sophisticated or refined -- subtle. Emotion is a little cruder than reason. However, they appear to be a mirror image of each other (something that will constantly be repeated). They go together, as the two sides of the mirror. They are like two sides of the same coin.[36] Pardon the mixed metaphors.

It is interesting to note that repetition through habit tends to create a downward spiral (meaning an accumulative increase of ~~truth~~ is in the choice) and can lead the matrix to a dysfunctional condition, i.e. neuroses, psychoses, etc (Chart 4-4, *G19*).

Conversely, a repetition through cognition tends to create an upward spiral (an accumulated increase of truth within the choice) that can lead the matrix to a highly functional state and illumination (Chart 4-4, *J6*). Most of us are just plodding along somewhere in between the two.

---

36 Chapter 2.4, Figure 2-1, Three in One, One in Three

The last two triangles in Figure 4-4 to cover are the Forgiveness and Judgment triangles. As mentioned in the beginning of this section, they are related to the shutter on the camera. A shutter is a 'go or no-go' mechanism – 'go' meaning acceptance and 'no-go', non-acceptance. These triangular relationships can work in a number of different ways.

Judgment $\Delta \Rightarrow$ You suspend Judgment and you wait, that is 'no-go'. Nothing is chosen or there is usually a refocus of the 'mind's eye'. Giving the mechanism free reign and making a Judgment, it's 'go'. You make a choice; it goes into *Programming*, so it is a 'go'.

So, if you are not making a Judgment, your mind might still be acting in some way; because, it may be collecting information. It is operating even if you are consciously applying it, or not. The 'choice' may be to 'not make a choice' or to refocus.

If the matrix is refocusing, Cognition (*VII*) and the assembly of relevant truths entering *Storage* initially influence the refocusing (*IV*). This in turn, is directly linked with *Knowledge*, previous cognitive jumps, and then to *Programming*. Usually you refocus the lens to the Event until there is Cognition (*VII*), then to Choice (*VI*) (a go). You let the matrix run to focus until there is some kind of agreement or correspondence between *Storages* and the *Perceptual Lens Array*. We discern this way.

If your *Storage* to the Event relationship does not make sense (*VII*), this is usually a no-go. This situation happens until your perception lens runs to a cognitive assembly (a relationship between truth from Event and truth assemblies in *Storage*). Then, it is a go. A Judgment or Choice (*VI*) is made, which goes into *Programming* (*II*).

Forgiveness $\Delta \Rightarrow$ Judgment is to make a decision to accept a perception. That decision may have a mixture of True and ~~True~~ in it. Forgiveness shown coming after Judgment in Figure 4-4 because it cancels previous judgments. Our human matrix is a gestalt of the choices/judgments we have made in our lifetime. This includes not only up to that point of time of our current perception, but also includes the time folding aspect of your whole temporal life of choices.[37] More simply: our personality is the net result of all the choices or judgments we make.

With forgiveness, you alter the whole system before you even have to make the choice. When forgiveness kicks in, there is nothing to judge.

With the Forgiveness triangle, one of two things can happen. One is where we approach correction of previous judgments. Within the Forgiveness triangle, a correcting truth to the 'truth' of the ~~truth~~ is applied before Choice (*VI*).

In the second, the True and the ~~True~~ that makes it through the lens array (due to focus) are such that; when brought together before or at Choice, the truth can relegate the ~~truth~~ (and the 'truth' of the ~~truth~~) to the special case that it is. When this occurs, the ~~truth~~ disappears before the truth (Chart 4-4, *N7*). No ~~truth~~ enters Programming through Choice (*II*). We participate in the Correction when we do this.[38]

This is roughly equivalent to a camera lens turning everything into a white light, while eliminating all shade or light variations. Using the math analogy, it is equivalent to squaring an imaginary number thereby converting the imaginary number back into the real number system.

Through our *Storages,* we can see our previous judgments/choices as we refocus them into the perceptual lens (*IV*). We may say, "I do not want to do this" or "I want to see this differently". "I do not want to judge that." Forgiveness can act like a no-go -- it does not allow things through, and consequently, no ~~truth~~ enters *Programming*. In addition, it can correct previous judgments/choices as they travel through the array.

Now, a review or another dynamic overview of material covered in this section.

---

37 Chapter 3.7 - Time Ignor-ance
38 Chapter 3.2, The Correction

❑ An 'objective event' (Figure 4-4, *V*) is affected first by the triangle of Attitude that is made up of the Event, Perception, and Desires. Within this dynamic overview, the objective event encounters this Attitude triangle, which determines the clarity of the event.

As perceptions approach infinity, and desires approach one at a medium to low level, then we will have a tendency to have more truth passing through the lens. However, if perceptions approach zero, and desires approach infinite, then our choices will tend to contain ~~truth~~.

❑ The event now proceeds to the Aperture, which affects the volume of truth and ~~truth~~ the choice is going to have.[39] What are we open to? As faith approaches infinite and perceptions approach infinite and/or desires approach one and attachments approach zero, the Aperture opens up; then, the choice will tend to contain more Truth/light.

Conversely, if faith approaches zero, perceptions approach zero, and/or desires approach infinite, and attachment approaches infinite, our choice tends to contain more ~~truth~~ (less truth, i.e. dark) because the Aperture is closing. As these values change, what the choice contains, the truth and ~~truth~~, changes. This is going to be important later when we start talking about exercises and a Formula of Effectiveness.

Belief is the part of the Aperture that is linked with Faith and Attachment. Belief is very flexible; it changes as Faith changes and Attachment changes. As stated earlier, if Faith approaches zero, and the Attachments approach infinite, then the Aperture is small – very little Belief -- and very little Truth/light will be present in the choice. Conversely, if Faith approaches infinite and Attachment approaches zero, the Aperture of Belief opens to infinite. Anything can be done if you have the faith.

As the Aperture opens to infinite, Choice (*II*) tends to align with the whole, which is determined by Truth and God's non-exclusive Love. As Faith decreases and Attachment increases, the Beliefs tend to be more rigid and consequently the Aperture becomes very narrow. The Choice (*II*) content tends to lean toward self and exclusiveness, or towards ~~truth~~.

If these vertices are treated as numerical values, with Perceptions equal to Desires and Faith equal to Attachments, any choice can contain erratic information or contradictions. When that happens, we usually refocus until some 'sense' is made. Our 'vision' can get blurry and recognition becomes difficult. So the values can be all equal, and when they are, it usually calls for refocusing of the array. The next chapter will help illustrate the mind's mechanism that is portrayed in this chapter by showing what happens when substituting numerical values into some of the elements of this presented mind model.

❑ From Beliefs, the information separates to True and ~~True~~ and a Choice is made – go or no-go. The choice will contain both and enters *Programming*. The True automatically enters the Cognitive Input to *Knowledge* also; as well as, the 'truth' that sustains the ~~truth~~ that has made it so far.

******************** 🌓 ********************

Exercise and Lab 4.1: Time/Space Imagination Exercises

The 'mind's eye' model presented so far is a matrix relationship; as so are its *Storages*. These matrices assembled (*Perceptional Lens Array*, *Storages*, and *Focus Control*) form another matrix array, which is a temporal form or a weak facsimile of the Mind/Matrix of God. In imitation to the Eternal Moment of Creation within the Mind of God, this temporal mind is always creating. What it creates is dependent on what is in *Storage*, which determines the 'mind's eye's' focus (*IV*) -- *Perceptional Lens Array*. This constant creation in time manifests a parade of thoughts. This is the 'subjective event' and is shown in the Imagination triangle of Figure 4-4.

---

39 Just as a camera's aperture or the iris of our eye adjusts for volume of light.

Using this book's model, a majority of people's minds are running on automatic. One thought after another without exercising any influence on the process.

From this point on, most of the exercises in this book involve taking control or playing with your 'subjective event' one way or another. In most traditional meditations, there is a disengaging or stilling of the *Perceptual Lens Array* - the 'subjective event'. These visualizations are concerned with maintaining an individual's focus on one thing – internal event -- and not letting it stray.

What this visualization exercise is going to do is somewhat different. Instead of stilling the lens, you are going to be actively refocusing the lens, playing with the lens, and opening your *Perceptual Lens Array*, your 'mind's eye'. It introduces to you how to match your 'subjective event' to an 'objective event'.

This exercise works predominantly with the Reason and Imagination triangles of the lens array. The desire element comes in with you wanting to 'see' further (or to find out, "What happens if I do this?"

The power of the imagination is incredible. Some of the plusses and minuses it has are mentioned in the previous 'board on the ground' example.

Plusses ⇨ Imagination can be a useful tool. Remember the board example: if you imagine you are going to fall, you will have a hard time walking the board. Whereas, if you focus your imagination on walking across successfully, as if the board was on the ground, you will not have much of a problem. "Where your head goes, your body will follow." This is true for diving, tumbling, wrestling, golf, tennis, and martial arts.

This axiom applies to the mystic arts, metaphysical, and spiritual as well. Where your head goes, your body is going to follow. Remember the Mirror, your Bubble of Temporal Reference will reflect what is in your mind. A change of 'mind' changes the reflection. It is this concept that is at the core of attitudinal and spiritual healing, as well as magic.

Another of the plusses of doing the following imagination exercises is; instead of imagining something that is not there, you will learn to imagine something that is there or is most likely there. You are going to imagine something that is there and you cannot physically see, but will attempt to see it with your 'mind's eye'. You will attempt to align your 'mind's eye' with the **Actual** reality around you without direct physical perception -- align your 'subjective event' with an 'objective event'.

An additional effect of these particular exercises is that they use imagination to expand the temporal/spatial perception of your mortal mind; they can expand your mind and its temporal space perception of your environment.[40]

Minuses ⇨ The drawbacks to the use of imagination are that there is a similarity between some *ESP* phenomena and imagination and it is very close in appearance. It can be confusing. Until the individual can perceive the difference between how the two feels, inside one's self, it can lead to confusing results when doing *ESP* exercises.

Another minus to using imagination is that whatever you imagine or visualize is going to be based on a temporality; it is subject to time. Whether you are using symbols, words, or images, they are limited to your temporal matrix. They are limited to whatever you have in your head, in your *Storage*.

Imagination – visualization -- is a tool. Like any tool, a tool's use is dependent on the skill of the user. And...like any tool, we can think we are dependent on it and not try to grow further.[41]

Here is another temporal limit to visualization. An individual can only hold a specific image in the head for so long. In the end, the serious spiritual or metaphysical pilgrim is going to need to step out of their mind's temporality and be with God Eternal. A spiritual pilgrim needs to withdraw into a deeper meditation (experience) and leave temporal perception behind (whether it is truth-based or imagined).

---

40 Remember the limits presented previously in this chapter.
41 Chapter 8.1, Tools

Exercises in later chapters tend not to be limited by our storages - previous perceptions and desires.[42] Those exercises are simple and non-specific. When you start playing with imagination, the exercises become specific and limited. Your perceptions, storage, and focus control limit imagination use.

A side effect of this exercise is it gets you to use actively what is in your *Storages*. It is possible to use what is in your *Knowledge, Programming, Memory*; storages to recognize what you see, remember, what you know, and to play with it or assemble it; to match something inside you to something outside of you.

With this imagination exercise, you review from what you already know, or have seen, and project it in your mind.

Imagination Exercise: Space

The first exercise is a space exercise. Sit yourself in a comfortable position alone, or with people. (In a class format, the author would have you listen to the sound of his voice as the author walked around you. He would have you look at something specific in front of you while he talked, and would ask you not to let your eyes stray.)

❑   Use your perception and imagine yourself behind the eyes. Then use your perception and imagination, slowly looking out and around the room, in a circle, without moving the eyes. Your eyes should still be looking in front and not moving. The images presented in this book are from the viewpoint of talking somebody through this while in a condominium in San Jose, California.

Example: construct an image of the picture on the wall over to the left of you. What you would see if you were looking in that direction? Then move your perception around and imagine the other pictures. With your 'mind's eye', see the fan on the ceiling. Move your perception behind you and imagine the television and *VCR*. Keep it moving around to the curtain and imagine the open window behind you.

Using imagination, you can see the chair behind you and to the side, and the lamp next to it. Bring the perception around and imagine the sofa. Keep moving your perception until it starts coming back into your visual range. The idea is for you to make slowly a full circle sweep around the room, using perception, and your imagination, <u>without moving your eyes or head</u>. Look around with the 'mind's eye', without moving the physical eyes. Use your imagination to <u>roughly</u> fill in the blanks. Recognize what is there around you and imagine it as if you were looking directly at it.

Avoid too much detail; form or shape is all that is needed. You can throw in some color or light if needed.

❑   Once you have established the horizontal plane that you first looked around, the next step is to jump up with your mind and leave that plane. With much of our perception or our awareness of the outside world, it appears that we are looking from behind the eyes and between the ears. The next step is you are to imagine that you are not there anymore (behind the eyes). Imagine now, you are looking from the reference of standing in that room; although, you are sitting.

Now, using this change in perceptional placement, make another circle around the room. This circle will be in a plane slightly above the first circle and your perception of the previous items will be slightly elevated, at a different angle. So, this next step is to imagine what you would see if you were standing in that room and just turning around.

❑   After you slowly go around once more, the next step is to imagine you-behind-the-eyes is up on the ceiling and looking down around you, like being on a stepladder. If you were doing it with the author, you would be looking down on both you and him, he would be talking and you

---

42 Providing the individual pre-forms intention first, as in Chapters 5, 6, 7, 8, and 9.

would be sitting there. Look down behind you and see what you saw twice before from a different perspective – as if you were on the ceiling.

So now, slowly look around you (and down around you), as with the previous part, and make a full circle. This circle gives a different perspective, because of the altitude you have given yourself.

The general idea is for you to use your imagination to perceive something that you have not perceived in that way before (or not often). When the author was a kid, he stuck his head over a bed, lying on his back and looking upside down. He saw the whole room as being upside down. He imagined he could walk on the ceiling as if was the floor.

This exercise is similar. With this exercise, you are not physically moving yourself to see. You are just placing your awareness on the ceiling; you are now looking at things from a different perspective.

❑ The next step is for you to imagine yourself passing through the roof until you are just past the roofline, outside the house. Imagine you are sitting on the peak of the roof. In class, the author would have you look with the x-ray vision of imagination into the room and see him talking and you sitting. Now, you are to raise your perception and imagine the things around you. You can see in the next room. You can see up the stairs. You can see the front door. You can see the back door. You can see a neighbor's house. You can see in your neighbor's house. 'Color' it in with them watching *TV* if you hear the *TV*, or whatever.

You can look up and out and see the roofs of a multitude of other buildings: just as if, you were sitting on the roof. Make a horizontal circular sweep at that level, just as you did when you first started, slowly moving your imaginary perception around. Imagine what you would see, if you were sitting on the roof; you know what is out there. You know there are other roofs. You know where the road is. You know there are cars out there. Make a general sweep of the area all the way around. As you are looking around, *slightly* 'color' in the details with your imagination. Do not let yourself get distracted by providing small details. Recognize the actualities that are around you in your imagination.

❑ Next step is for you to use your imagination and move your awareness up into another horizontal plane. Now, imagine you are a mile up, looking down. Imagine what you would see if you were in an airplane or helicopter. Pictures of looking from this perspective are common these days.

You know that in that one little house below you in the colored pattern of rooftops and roads we are sitting and talking. Then there are all these houses next to us. If you look up, you can see the streets, the cars, the traffic, the lights, etc. As you start bringing your awareness up, you can look at the hills around you. You can start looking around and imagine seeing down the valley towards Gilroy, towards the south and southeast. Then move your awareness around towards the east and imagine you can see the valley, over the hills, across the way. Bring your awareness up and as you are moving from east towards the north, imagine you can see the hills starting to disappear in the distance and you see the beginning of the bay. Then bend your awareness back down the bay and look at downtown San Jose. Bring your awareness up and across, across the San Francisco Bay, and back around to the west until you start imagining seeing the hills again. See the ocean appearing behind the hills. See all the other structures and all the cities below the hills.

The idea is for you to make a slow sweep with your awareness. Vaguely filling in the blanks with what you know/recognize is there, using your own imagination.

❑ The next position to try is a hundred miles up. Now you can see the whole coast going from Mexico to Alaska and the curvature of the earth. See the patterns of white clouds passing over the different blues of the ocean and the multitude of land hues. Perhaps remember some satellite photos and apply that perspective as you are doing this. Accuracy is not important; expanding your perception is what is important in these exercises.

You can keep on doing this exercise until you are standing on the moon or standing outside the solar system. You can keep on moving your visualization perspective out further and further. This exercise can increase your perception and helps open up your 'mind's eye'; it opens your mind's perception without using your physical eyes. This exercise increases or expands your perceptual awareness and helps open the Aperture of the *Perceptual Lens Array*.

Where this exercise can take you, is totally limited by how much truth is in your mind already and your imagination.

The first exercise expanded perception; we traveled up and out. And, you can go small. A suggestion is go out first and then bring yourself back in; and, just do not stop. It becomes quite useful when coming back in to keep going. The first exercise went large and out; you can also go in and small.

Take an eraser on a pencil. We are taught in school that there are a bunch of atoms set up in it so there is some kind of web or weave of material -- matrix. We are going to go smaller, and we are going to slip into the space between the weave of our body material with our imagination. We are going to go smaller and smaller so at first we can barely slip between the molecules. Now as we pass them and keep getting smaller we see the molecules are huge behind us.

We get smaller and smaller, and things become more blurry because they are much farther away. We can keep doing this and imagine ourselves in the vast amount of space between particles. Just as, we would find ourselves in a vast amount of interstellar space, if we went up and out.

This is the same exercise, but going in different directions. Instead of imagining going out, you go in. Either way, you are guiding your imagination by what is in your *Knowledge* and *Memory*. You are the driver – the operator. You are using the *Focus Control Buss* and your faith, applying your *Knowledge* without a direct physical interface (senses).

Imagination Exercise: Time

With this time exercise, it may be helpful to look at a corner of the room where two walls and a ceiling meet, or two walls and a floor meet. Pick a three dimensional space that is defined by some long-term physical structure. If outside, look at something like a big old tree or a rock face. The idea is to pick something that is relatively solid and unmovable. Use your imagination to construct a small one-foot cube next to it. (Again, the imagery here is from doing this indoors in San Jose.)

❑   As you imagine looking from or at that cube, move back in time to that which you know has occurred already. Start from this moment, and as you move back in time, watch us come in to the room. The light in that corner is going to change as the sun is moving across the sky, imagine this as you go back in time. Use your imagination to move the sun across the sky and it is moving the shadows in the room.

Do this and keep going back in time with your imagination, until it starts getting dark again as you are going from this morning and into last night. Envision seeing the cube as it was last night and dark - maybe, during that time, a bug flies through the cube or a spider walks through it. Before you went to bed, the cube is filled with lights from the lamps. Imagine the reflections of the lamps off of the mirrored surface of the drapes. Again, maybe another fly or bug crawls through the space.

If you were sitting in that upper corner, you can imagine last night and yourself or people watching *TV* below you. Use your perception and imagination and stay as an observer from that corner.

Observe the changing light of sunset, and from that corner, watch the room and the day go back in time. From getting home from work and maybe walking below the cube, to coming from the bedroom and making coffee this morning. All are done in reverse below the cube, like a movie running backwards.

You can recognize many things as happening around or to that cube. You can do it from being an observer of the cube or seeing from the cube's perspective. You know air is, and has, moved through it. Once you get the alternation of light and dark down with your imagination, start speeding up the cycles of the sun, going further back in time - days, weeks, years...

❑   In that corner, nothing much is happening right now because it is isolated and away from everything -- the one the author was looking at anyway (a wall/wall/ceiling corner). Use your mind and start speeding up the cycles of the sun, day and night. Visualize what you would see going back in time, blurs of people movement and no people.

Imagine that a number of bugs have gone through that cube. A lot of wind or air has gone through it, many reflections, a lot of light over a period of days, and numerous people have passed underneath while furniture has moved. Keep on going back and back until you get to the point to where this building is being built.

❑   Man defined that space we are looking at, by those three corners. Watch the building -- kind of like watching a movie backwards -- being disassembled around that space to where there is nothing but dirt below it. Go further back, and the area under the imaginary cube is a field -- like the movie, _Time Machine_ based on the H. G. Wells book.

Where we were at it was a field and, prior to that, a plum orchard, and before that a bog. Imagine these vistas are happening below you as they go through their transitions. Recognize all kinds of 'critters' have passed through that cube.

❑   Now, keep on going back. Because the surface of the Earth is moving with the tectonic plates, the landmass we are on is moving westward (or toward the cube we are visualizing.) Eventually, if you go back far enough, you can visualize the land retreating from that cube and the cube is above the ocean (as you are suspended above the ocean). You can watch the continent retreat from the cube.

From the perspective of being in the cube, the space you occupy is staying the same as you watch the continent retreat across the ocean. Included with all this stuff are tons of bugs flying through (especially when you are in the grass or bog) tons of air, wind, rain, and storms. One can visualize all kinds of things that probably happened. Trees died in that cube, fell, and then new plants reoccupied the space.

This is where you -- the operator -- guide the visualization. You are actually creating this experience of guiding it for yourself and using imagination to roughly color in details and expanding your perception through time.

We went backwards. We can go forward in time, also. The book will stay away from the concept of any apocalyptic change. We will take it, as we recognize things to be now.

Be advised though; cities built on top of the rubble of other cities is an old theme. Usually in the past, the cities were razed and destroyed; then new cities built on top. Troy was like that. There was something like seven levels (maybe more) of the city of Troy. Crete is famous for that because they had so many bad earthquakes.

Cities were destroyed and they rebuilt the next city on top of the last one. Some devastation would occur -- economic, social, or ecological. Then the next city would be built on top of the last.

❑   We sit in that cube, and watch from its perspective all the people going through this room underneath the cube daily. Several families have occupied the house and you can imagine the changes eventually until the building starts getting old and starts sagging. It will be torn down and then the cube is above the rubble. Then you can start to visualize someone building something else. There may be an I-beam going through that cube for a big office building or an apartment building, or it is sitting above a car parking lot. You can visualize that cube in a big chunk of concrete, farther along in the future. Could be a landing pad. The exercise's direction is dependent on your imagination. You know it will change and something else will happen.

❑   Keep going further forward in time. Again, using the continent tectonic plate movement thing, imagine the hills to the east moving towards that cube as all those changes are happening below the cube. All this man-stuff has been built and has come down, built, come down, built and come down, as well as changes in vegetation, while the hills are growing and approaching that cube. Soon, that cube is going to be buried in the hills. You can imagine this, and set up a panorama of time in your own mind.

It is important to stress that when doing these imagination exercises -- you should imagine or visualize as much perceived or recognized possible actualities as possible; using natural landmarks can help. Visualize the general picture - a whole picture. Do not let your mind stray off into the imagined details and try to make things up. Use your imagination to only lightly color in some of the details; just enough for you to recognize that the objects or changes exist.

These time and space exercises can expand your perception. They can open up windows within your mind and more. They can give you a broader perspective on things. These imagination exercises use the *Perceptual Lens Array*, Cognition, *Knowledge*, Focus, and 'subjective event' feedback loop of your mortal mind.

With this expanded perception, true choices can begin to become simpler and not so complicated - you see a bigger picture. Again, be aware of the existence of a myriad of details, but do not use the imagination to dwell on them. Use the imagination to sketch in only general forms and shapes.

It is very important for you to be the observer only. You are watching these things unfold, like a little child -- no judgments, because any judgment made will tend to cloud the exercise. You have been shown how limited your perceptions are to begin with, and when you are judging something, you are constricting them further. In addition, given our perceptions are limited; most judgments made will be in error because these judgments are made from incomplete data. Cultivate a 'disinterested-interest' in what you are doing.

Once you have learned both the time and space exercises, then you can put the two exercises together and travel in time and space to jump around. You can leave the earth, looking down at it at any particular time.

For example, anchor yourself in the cube and anchor the cube in time and space. In the time it takes to snap the fingers, the earth is rapidly moving away from you in deep space (about 90 miles a second) and will not approach the cube for another year. Nor, will it show up on the planet in the same place it did before for many years.

The main idea behind these exercises is to get you to match a 'subjective event' - your mind's imagination, to an 'objective event' - something around you; to visualize something you can not immediately physically see.

➢ *With the space exercises, inside and out, and the time exercises, forward and back; the assignment is to do three of each, preferably in a different location with each application. For example, do the space exercise one time watching TV. Another time do it sitting in the yard, and another time sitting in a restaurant. Vary where you physically are and do the exercises in different locals.*
➢ *Do each one for 5-10 minutes,*
➢ *Make an entry in the workbook regarding where the exercise was done, distance, perceptions, and feelings afterward.*

➢ **Optional space exercises:** *From wherever you happen to be, while keeping the eyes still, explore your surroundings with your imagination. For example, if sitting at home, explore the house or apartment with your mind without turning your head. From that central perception point, place all the windows, floors, and walls around you and be aware of the furniture and other items. Increase your awareness in larger circles and be aware of things like the line of buildings across the street, in relation to you. Look around you with your 'mind's eye' and do not move your head. Do this for one minute once a day in different familiar settings for a week or longer.*

➤ *Look at the wall in front of you. Now imagine what you would see if that wall was not there. What would be the view? What would some of the items you would see? What buildings or vistas you would see?*[43]

➤ **Optional Time Exercise:** *As with the optional space exercise, pick a familiar place; somewhere you have spent some time. Without moving your head, imagine the surroundings at a different time. For example, if on a bus during 'rush hour', imagine that you are on that bus (and what you would see) running over the same route it is traveling now but at 3 a.m. If in the living room at home, imagine the living room as it would look when everybody is asleep or gone away for the day's activities. The same can be done to the working environment. Do this for one minute once a day in various familiar settings for a week.*

********************  ********************

---

43 Thank you Superman comics.

148

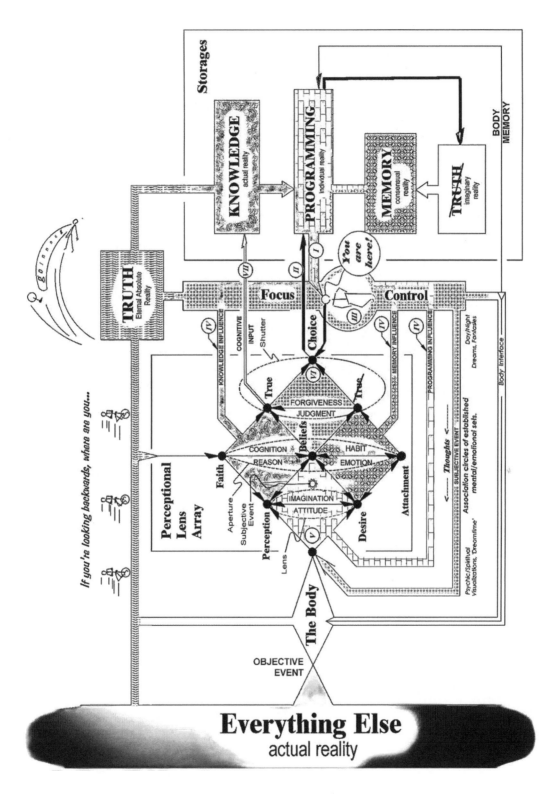

Figure 4-4, The Human Matrix

149

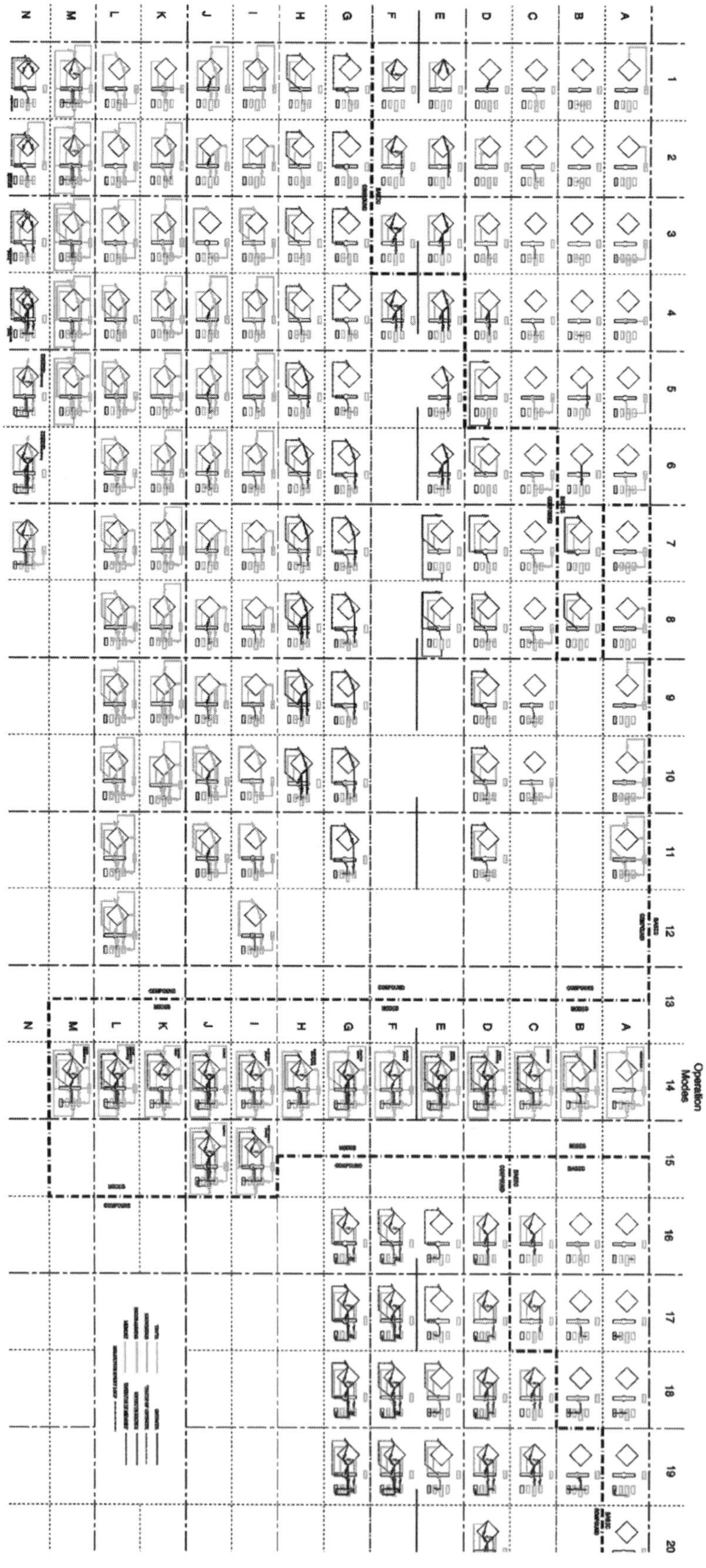

Chart 4-4

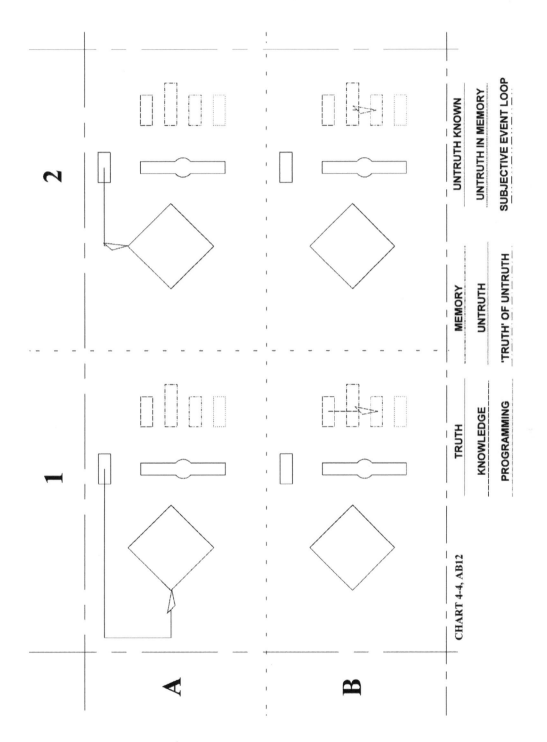

CHART 4-4, AB12

151

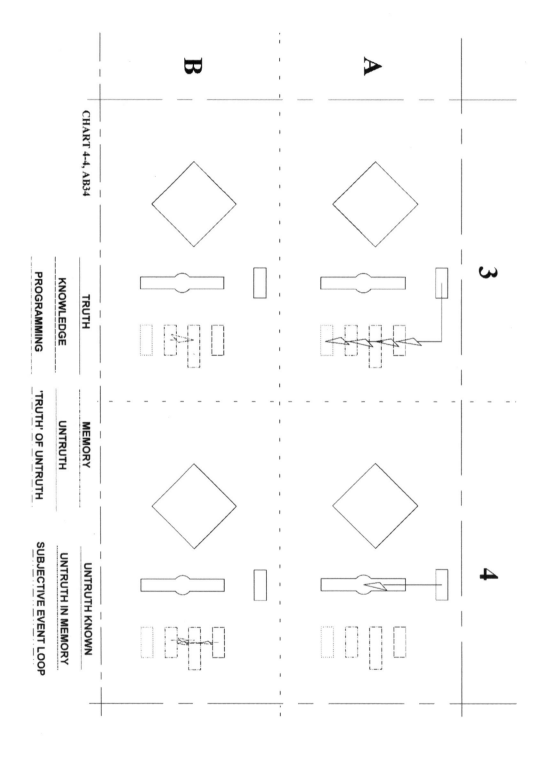

CHART 4-4, AB34

A

B

3

4

TRUTH — KNOWLEDGE — PROGRAMMING

MEMORY — UNTRUTH — 'TRUTH' OF UNTRUTH

UNTRUTH KNOWN — UNTRUTH IN MEMORY — SUBJECTIVE EVENT LOOP

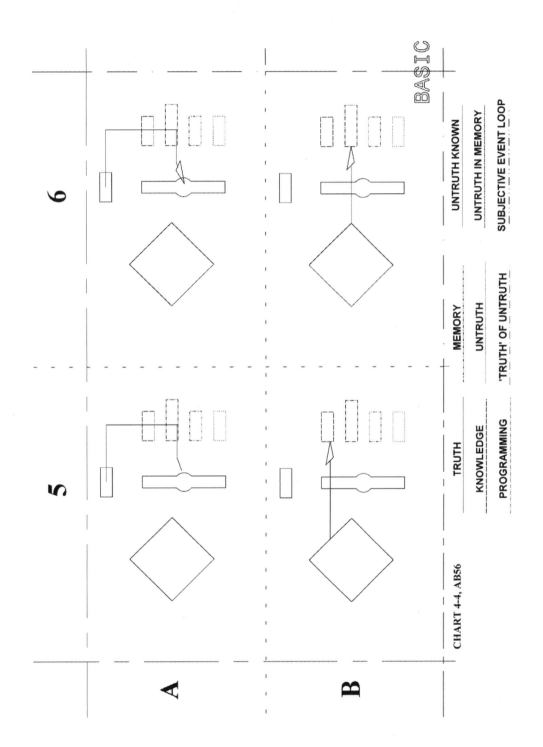

CHART 4-4, AB56

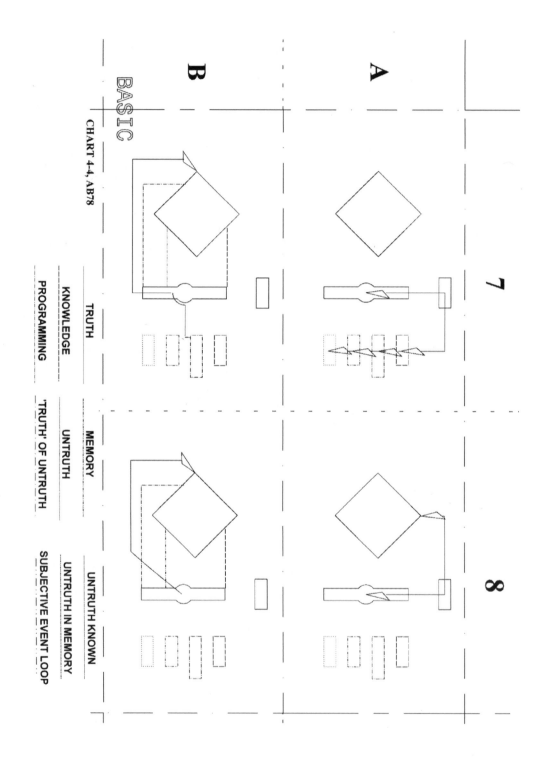

BASIC

CHART 4-4, AB78

A	**7**	**8**
B		

TRUTH — MEMORY — UNTRUTH KNOWN

KNOWLEDGE — UNTRUTH — UNTRUTH IN MEMORY

PROGRAMMING — 'TRUTH' OF UNTRUTH — SUBJECTIVE EVENT LOOP

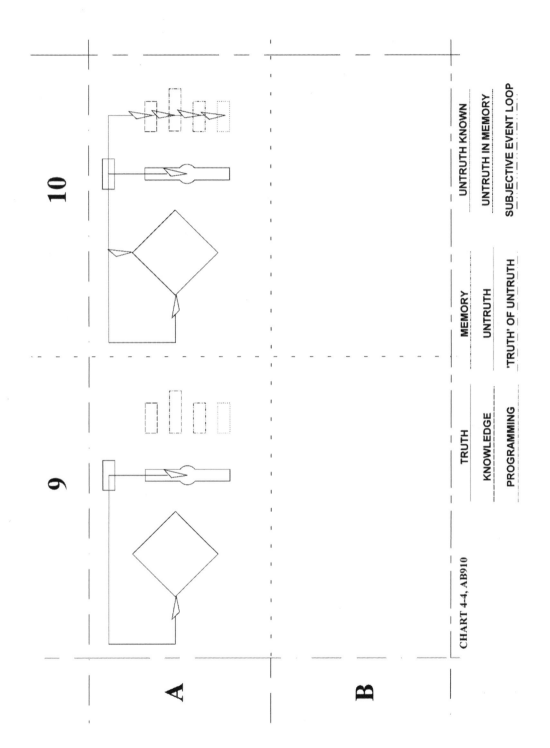

CHART 4-4, AB910

| 9 | 10 |

| A | | B |

TRUTH	MEMORY	UNTRUTH KNOWN
KNOWLEDGE	UNTRUTH	UNTRUTH IN MEMORY
PROGRAMMING	'TRUTH' OF UNTRUTH	SUBJECTIVE EVENT LOOP

155

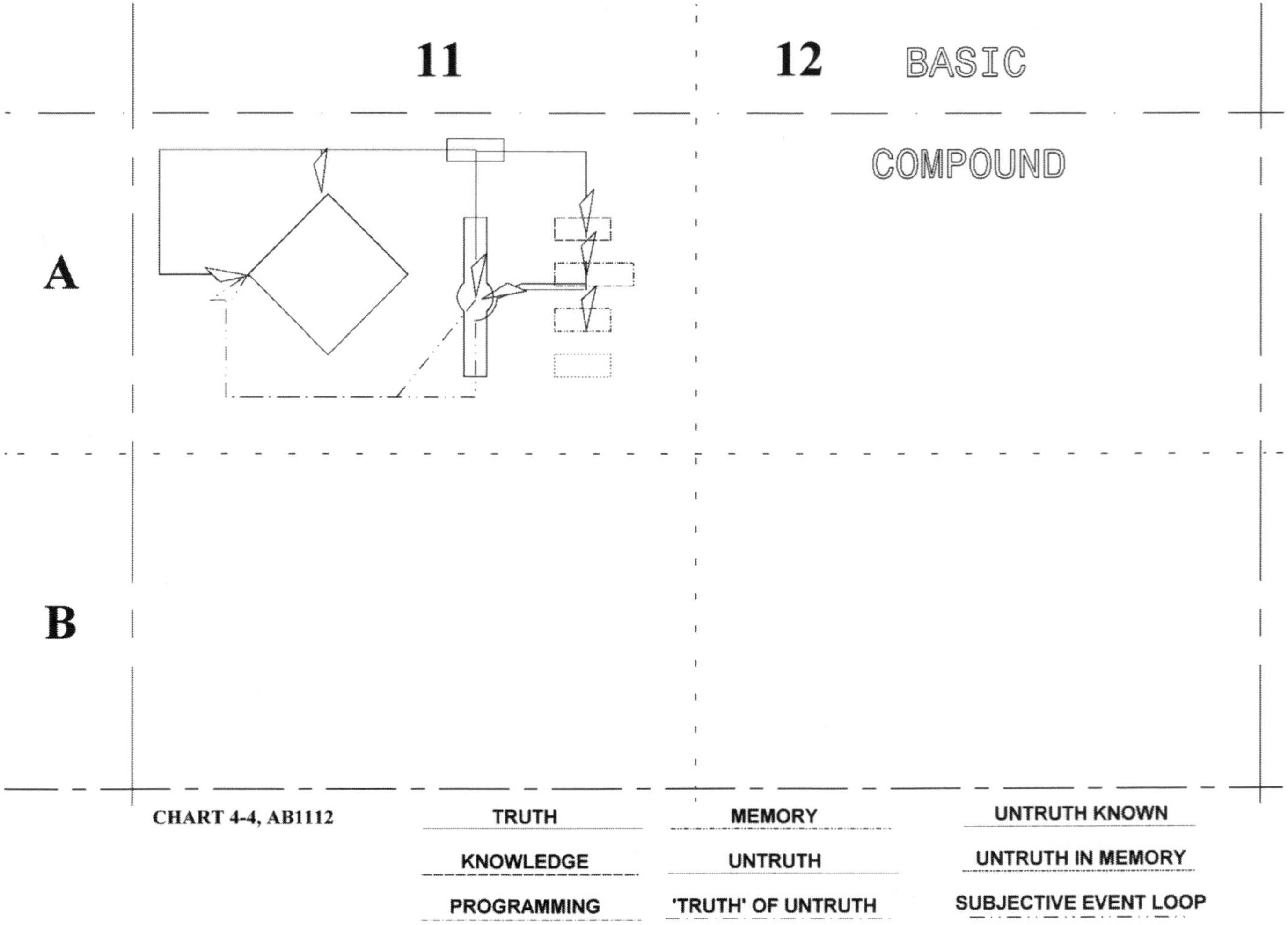

A

11   12   BASIC

COMPOUND

B

CHART 4-4, AB1112

TRUTH	MEMORY	UNTRUTH KNOWN
KNOWLEDGE	UNTRUTH	UNTRUTH IN MEMORY
PROGRAMMING	'TRUTH' OF UNTRUTH	SUBJECTIVE EVENT LOOP

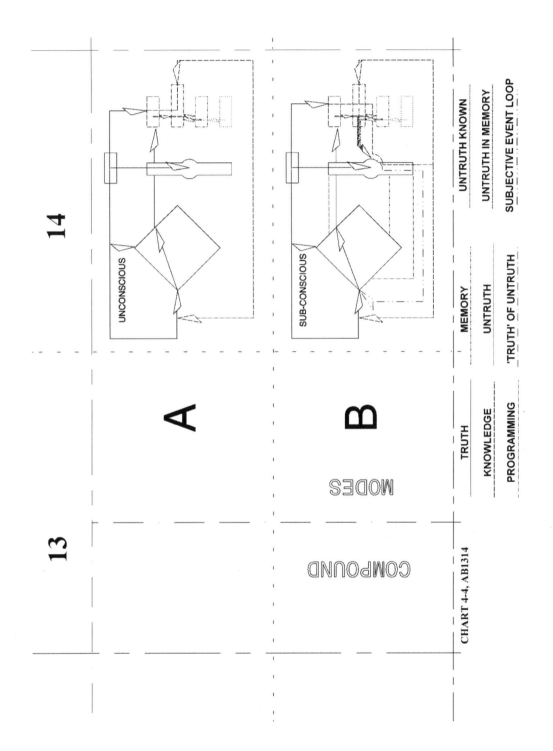

14

13

A

B

UNCONSCIOUS

SUB-CONSCIOUS

MODES

COMPOUND

	TRUTH	MEMORY	UNTRUTH KNOWN
	KNOWLEDGE	UNTRUTH	UNTRUTH IN MEMORY
	PROGRAMMING	'TRUTH' OF UNTRUTH	SUBJECTIVE EVENT LOOP

CHART 4-4, AB1314

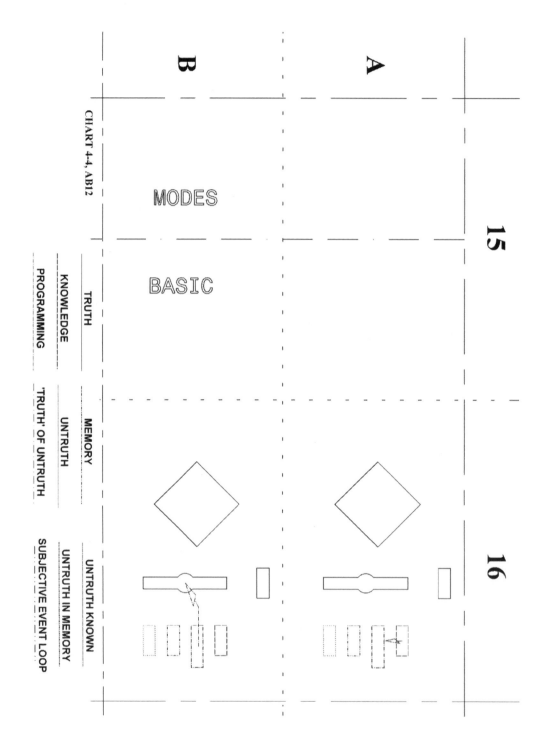

CHART 4-4, AB12

B

A

15

16

MODES

BASIC

PROGRAMMING	KNOWLEDGE	TRUTH
'TRUTH' OF UNTRUTH	UNTRUTH	MEMORY
SUBJECTIVE EVENT LOOP	UNTRUTH IN MEMORY	UNTRUTH KNOWN

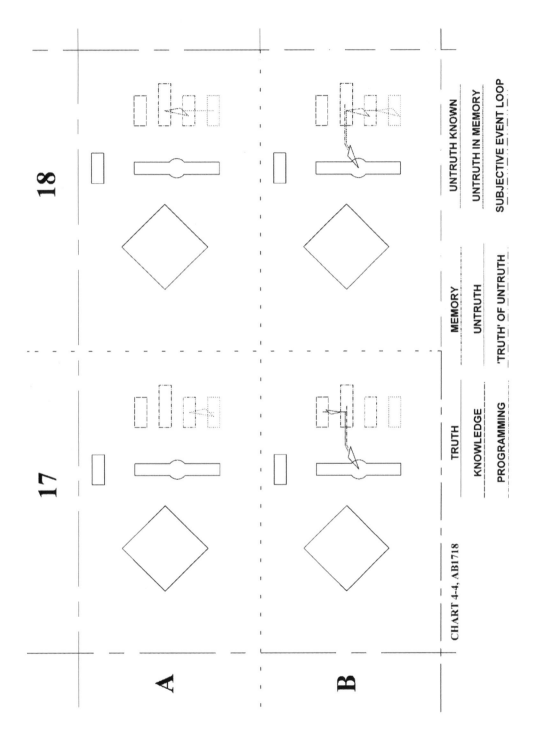

CHART 4-4, AB1718

TRUTH	MEMORY	UNTRUTH KNOWN
KNOWLEDGE	UNTRUTH	UNTRUTH IN MEMORY
PROGRAMMING	'TRUTH' OF UNTRUTH	SUBJECTIVE EVENT LOOP

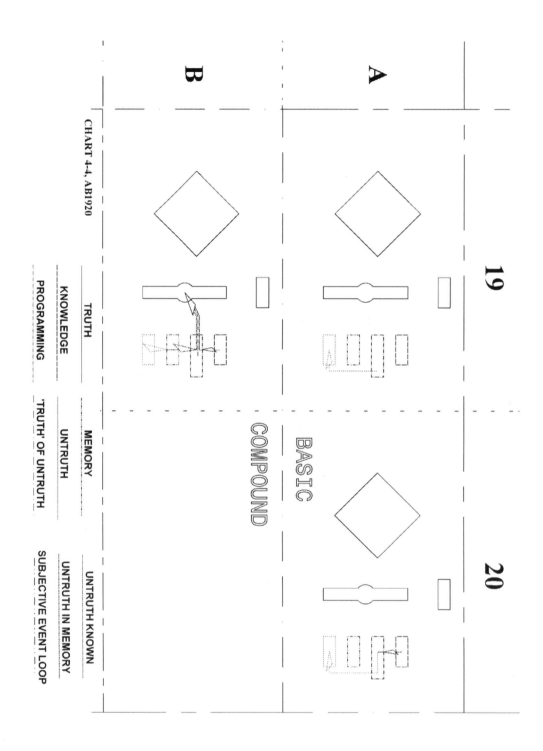

CHART 4-4, AB1920

B

A

19

20

BASIC COMPOUND

TRUTH — KNOWLEDGE — PROGRAMMING

MEMORY — UNTRUTH — 'TRUTH' OF UNTRUTH

UNTRUTH KNOWN — UNTRUTH IN MEMORY — SUBJECTIVE EVENT LOOP

160

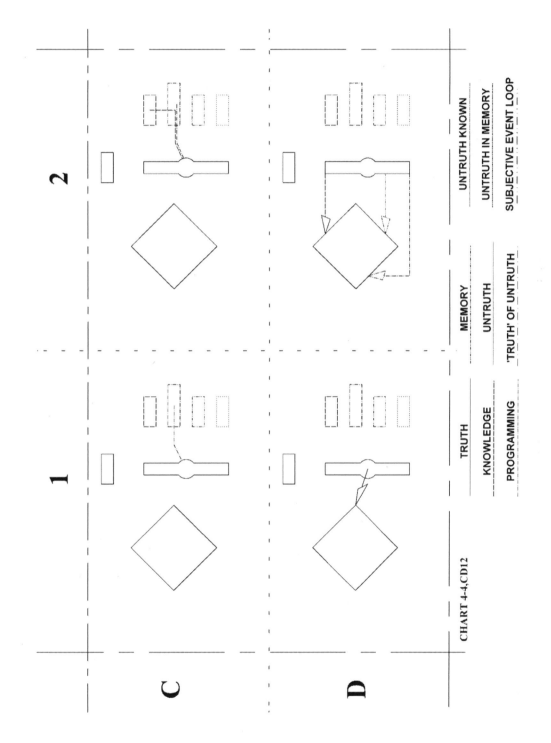

CHART 4-4,CD12

	TRUTH	MEMORY	UNTRUTH KNOWN
	KNOWLEDGE	UNTRUTH	UNTRUTH IN MEMORY
	PROGRAMMING	'TRUTH' OF UNTRUTH	SUBJECTIVE EVENT LOOP

161

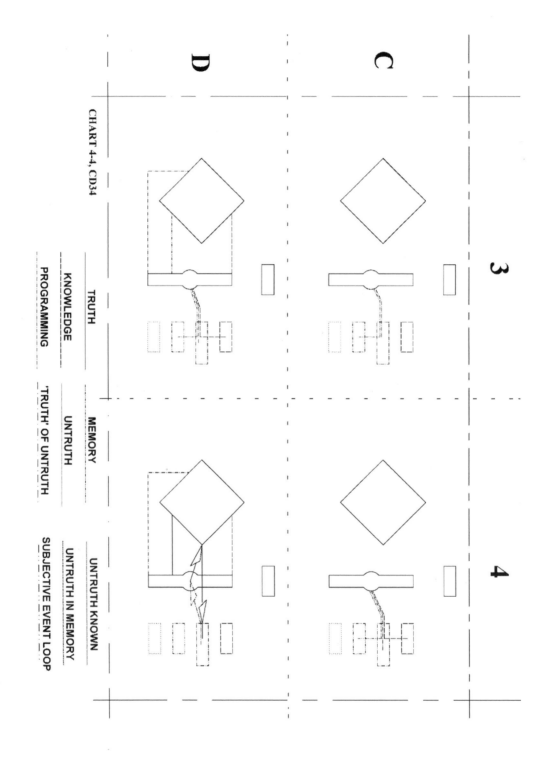

CHART 4-4, CD34

C

D

3

4

TRUTH	MEMORY	UNTRUTH KNOWN
KNOWLEDGE	UNTRUTH	UNTRUTH IN MEMORY
PROGRAMMING	'TRUTH' OF UNTRUTH	SUBJECTIVE EVENT LOOP

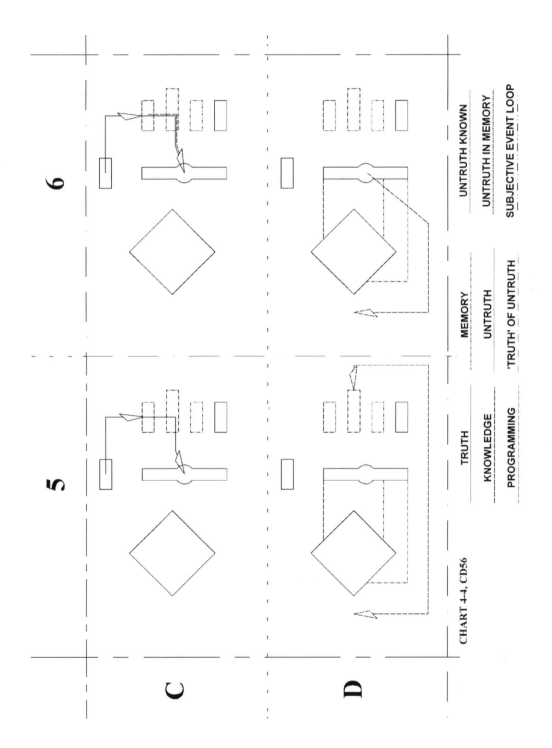

CHART 4-4, CD56

163

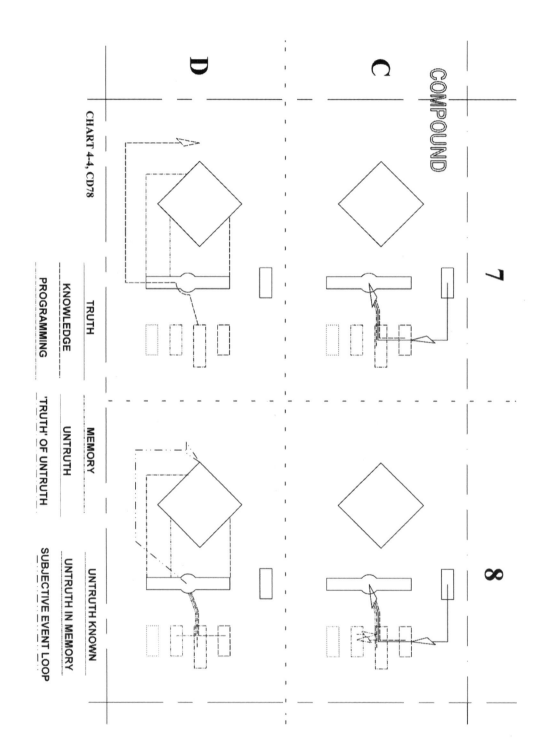

COMPOUND

7

8

C

D

TRUTH — KNOWLEDGE — PROGRAMMING

MEMORY — UNTRUTH — 'TRUTH' OF UNTRUTH

UNTRUTH KNOWN — UNTRUTH IN MEMORY — SUBJECTIVE EVENT LOOP

CHART 4-4, CD78

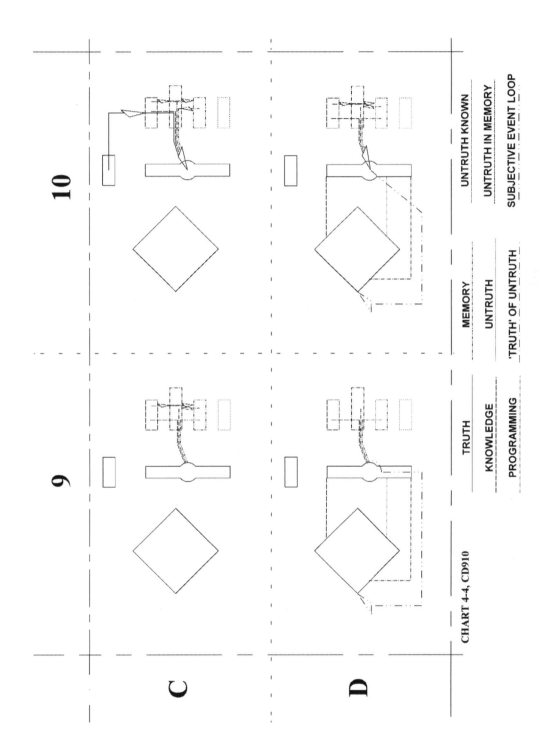

CHART 4-4, CD910

165

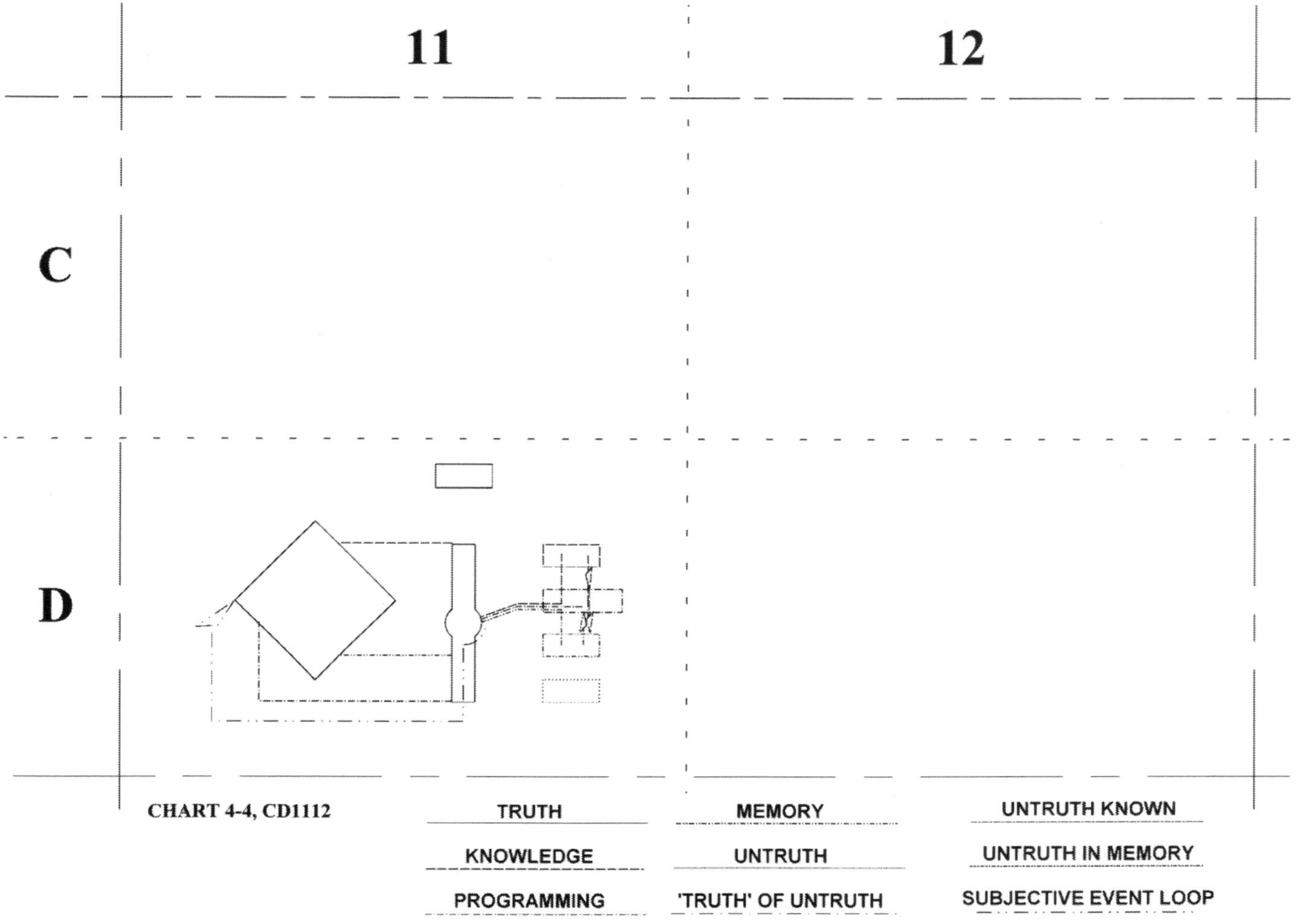

C

D

11

12

CHART 4-4, CD1112

TRUTH	MEMORY	UNTRUTH KNOWN
KNOWLEDGE	UNTRUTH	UNTRUTH IN MEMORY
PROGRAMMING	'TRUTH' OF UNTRUTH	SUBJECTIVE EVENT LOOP

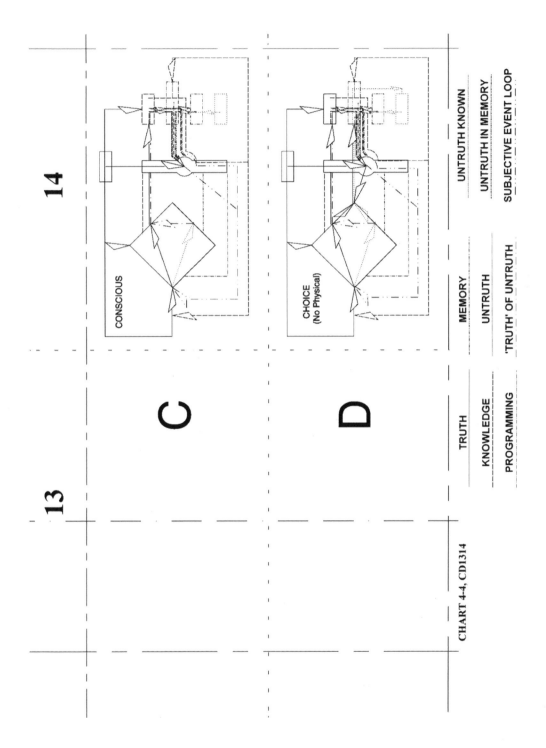

13   14

C

CONSCIOUS

D

CHOICE
(No Physical)

TRUTH   UNTRUTH KNOWN

KNOWLEDGE   UNTRUTH IN MEMORY

PROGRAMMING   SUBJECTIVE EVENT LOOP

MEMORY   UNTRUTH

'TRUTH' OF UNTRUTH

CHART 4-4, CD1314

167

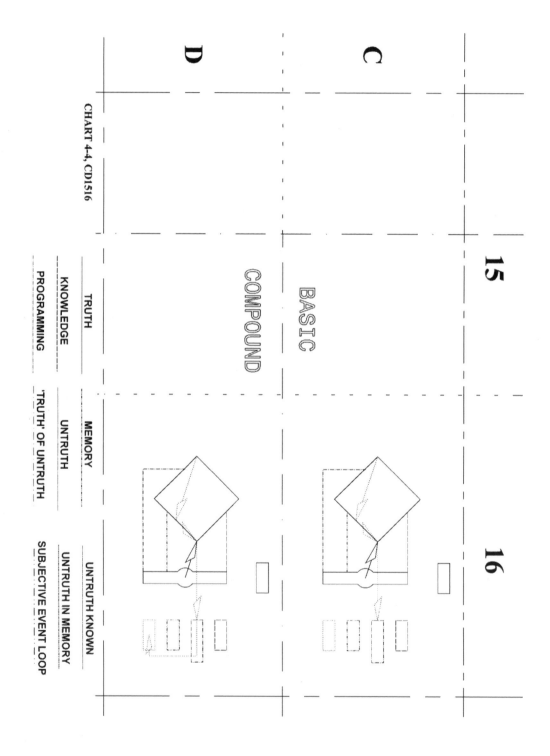

C   15   16

D

BASIC

COMPOUND

CHART 4-4, CD1516

TRUTH	MEMORY	UNTRUTH KNOWN
KNOWLEDGE	UNTRUTH	UNTRUTH IN MEMORY
PROGRAMMING	'TRUTH' OF UNTRUTH	SUBJECTIVE EVENT LOOP

168

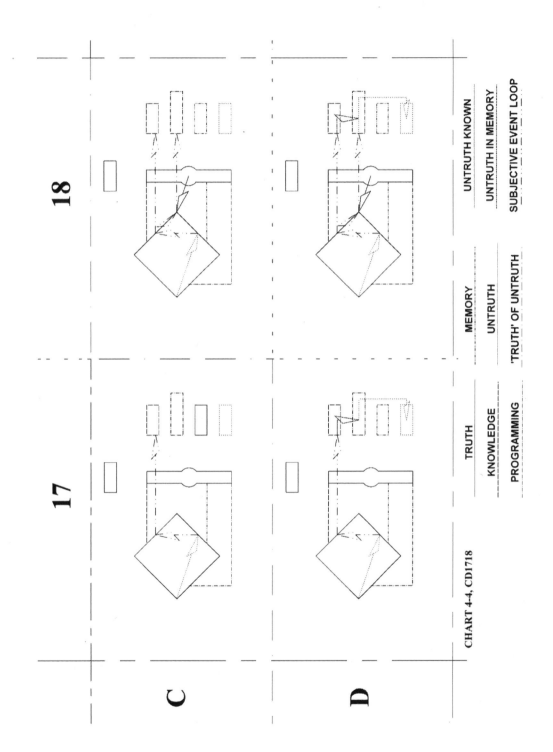

17 18

C D

TRUTH   MEMORY   UNTRUTH KNOWN

KNOWLEDGE   UNTRUTH   UNTRUTH IN MEMORY

PROGRAMMING   'TRUTH' OF UNTRUTH   SUBJECTIVE EVENT LOOP

CHART 4-4, CD1718

169

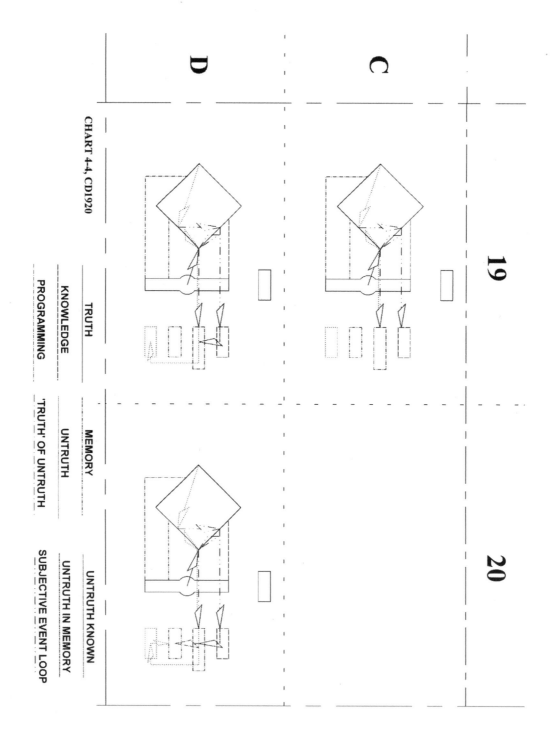

CHART 4-4, CD1920

C   19   20

TRUTH	MEMORY	UNTRUTH KNOWN
KNOWLEDGE	UNTRUTH	UNTRUTH IN MEMORY
PROGRAMMING	'TRUTH' OF UNTRUTH	SUBJECTIVE EVENT LOOP

D

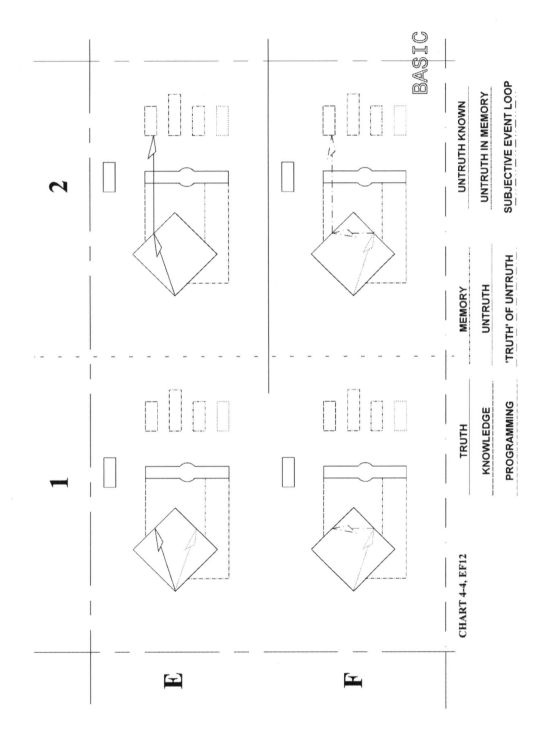

BASIC

CHART 4-4, EF12

TRUTH	MEMORY	UNTRUTH KNOWN
KNOWLEDGE	UNTRUTH	UNTRUTH IN MEMORY
PROGRAMMING	'TRUTH' OF UNTRUTH	SUBJECTIVE EVENT LOOP

171

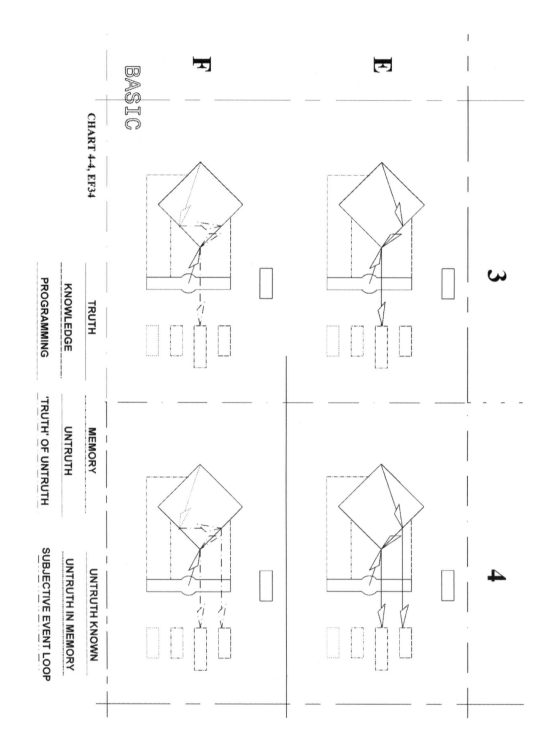

BASIC

CHART 4-4, EF34

| | E | 3 | |
| | F | | 4 |

TRUTH — KNOWLEDGE — PROGRAMMING

MEMORY — UNTRUTH — 'TRUTH' OF UNTRUTH

UNTRUTH KNOWN — UNTRUTH IN MEMORY — SUBJECTIVE EVENT LOOP

172

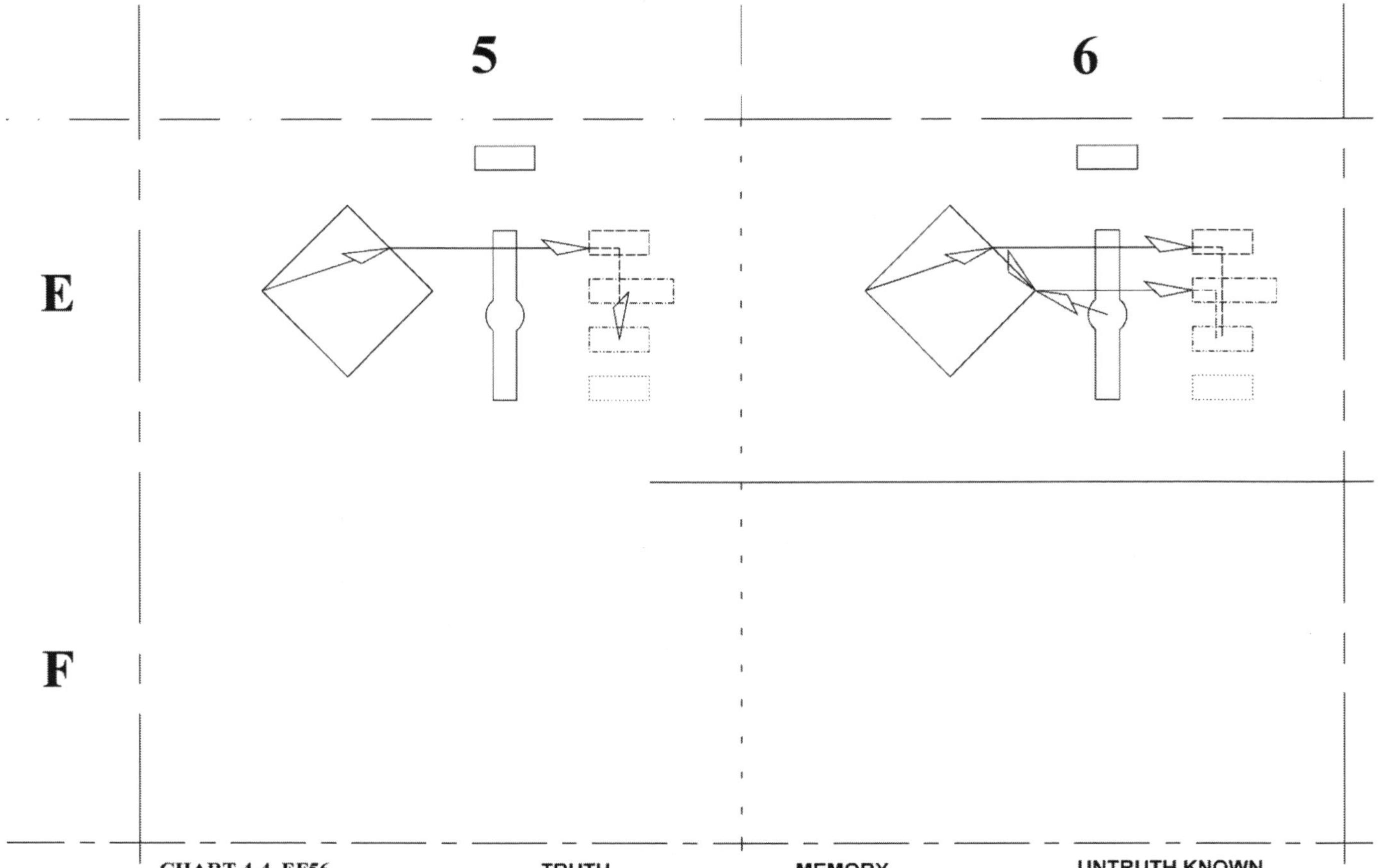

CHART 4-4, EF56

5	6

TRUTH	MEMORY	UNTRUTH KNOWN
KNOWLEDGE	UNTRUTH	UNTRUTH IN MEMORY
PROGRAMMING	'TRUTH' OF UNTRUTH	SUBJECTIVE EVENT LOOP

E

F

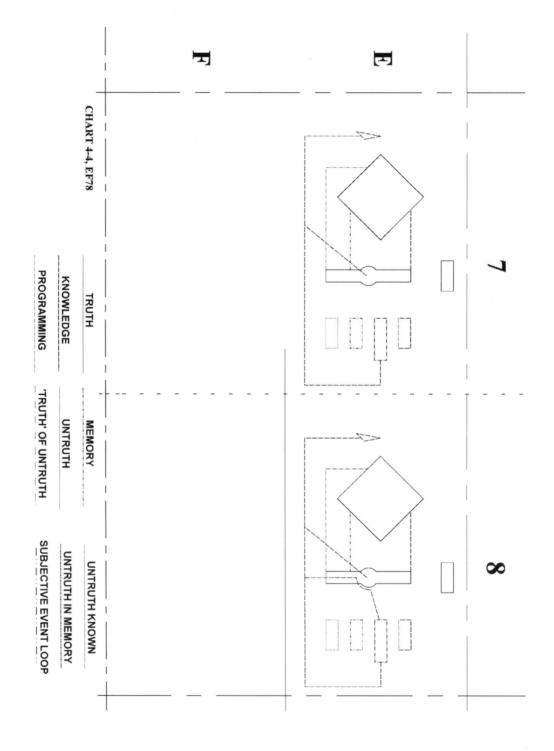

CHART 4-4, EF78

TRUTH	MEMORY	UNTRUTH KNOWN
KNOWLEDGE	UNTRUTH	UNTRUTH IN MEMORY
PROGRAMMING	'TRUTH' OF UNTRUTH	SUBJECTIVE EVENT LOOP

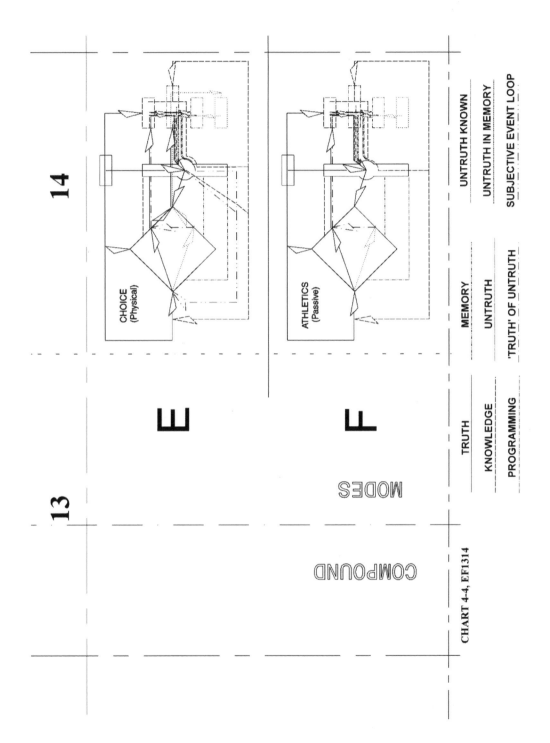

13

14

E

CHOICE
(Physical)

F

ATHLETICS
(Passive)

MODES

TRUTH

MEMORY

UNTRUTH KNOWN

KNOWLEDGE

UNTRUTH

UNTRUTH IN MEMORY

PROGRAMMING

'TRUTH' OF UNTRUTH

SUBJECTIVE EVENT LOOP

COMPOUND

CHART 4-4, EF1314

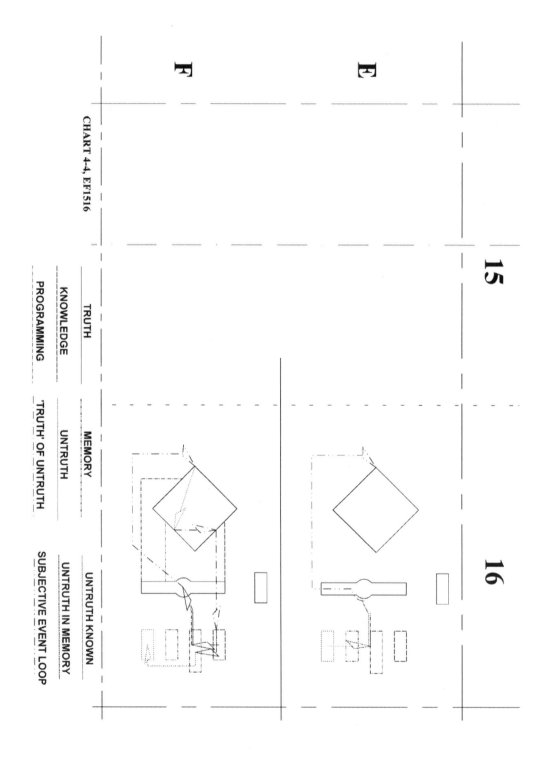

F   E

15   16

CHART 4-4, EF1516

TRUTH   MEMORY   UNTRUTH KNOWN

KNOWLEDGE   UNTRUTH   UNTRUTH IN MEMORY

PROGRAMMING   'TRUTH' OF UNTRUTH   SUBJECTIVE EVENT LOOP

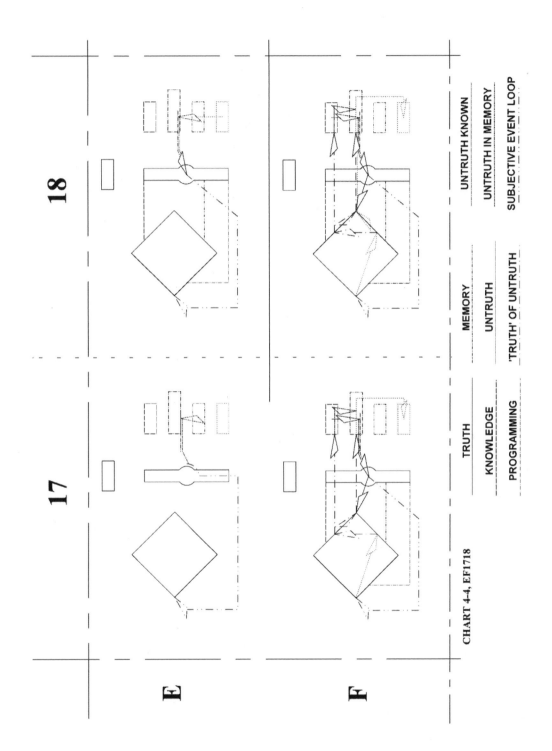

CHART 4-4, EF1718

TRUTH

KNOWLEDGE

PROGRAMMING

MEMORY

UNTRUTH

'TRUTH' OF UNTRUTH

UNTRUTH KNOWN

UNTRUTH IN MEMORY

SUBJECTIVE EVENT LOOP

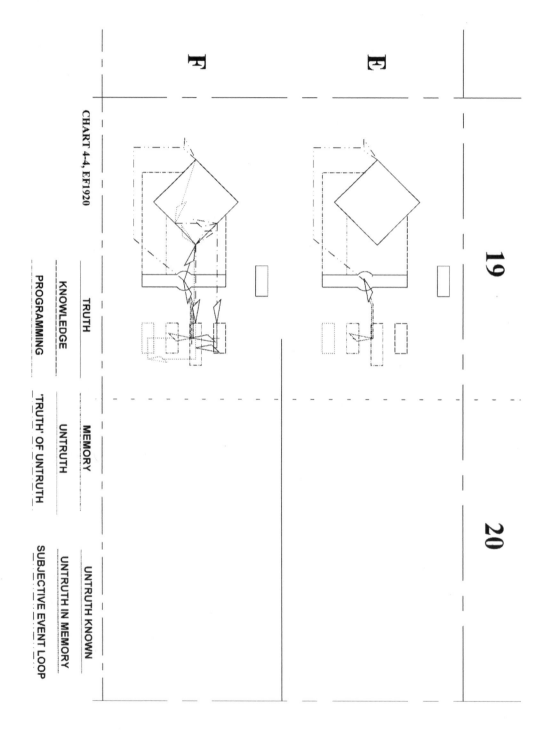

CHART 4-4, EF1920

E

F

19

20

TRUTH — KNOWLEDGE — PROGRAMMING

MEMORY — UNTRUTH — 'TRUTH' OF UNTRUTH

UNTRUTH KNOWN — UNTRUTH IN MEMORY — SUBJECTIVE EVENT LOOP

178

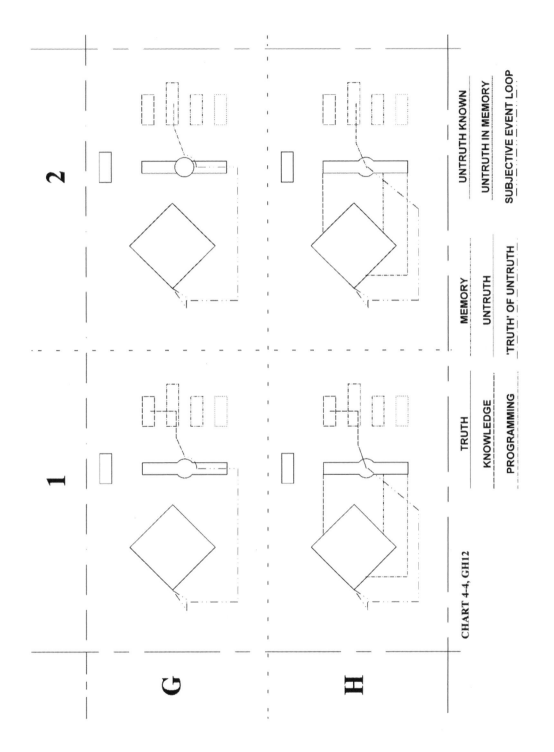

CHART 4-4, GH12

179

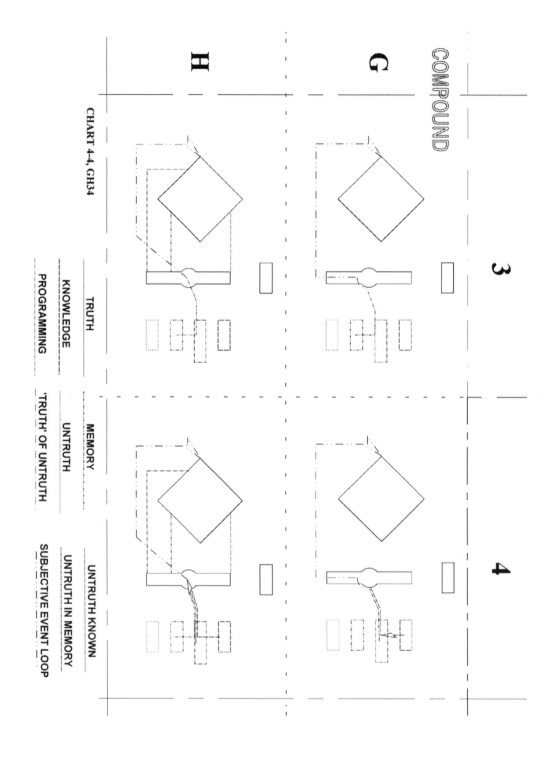

COMPOUND

G

H

3

4

TRUTH

KNOWLEDGE

PROGRAMMING

'TRUTH' OF UNTRUTH

MEMORY

UNTRUTH

UNTRUTH KNOWN

UNTRUTH IN MEMORY

SUBJECTIVE EVENT LOOP

CHART 4-4, GH34

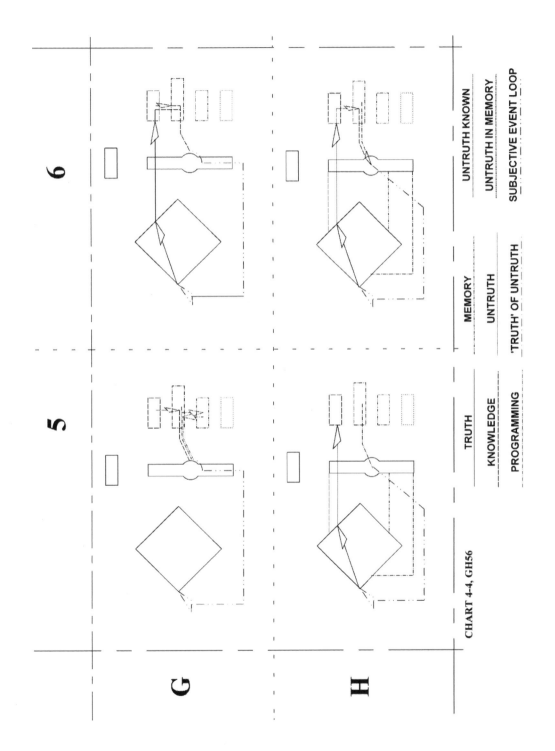

5

6

G

H

TRUTH

KNOWLEDGE

PROGRAMMING

MEMORY

UNTRUTH

'TRUTH' OF UNTRUTH

UNTRUTH KNOWN

UNTRUTH IN MEMORY

SUBJECTIVE EVENT LOOP

CHART 4-4, GH56

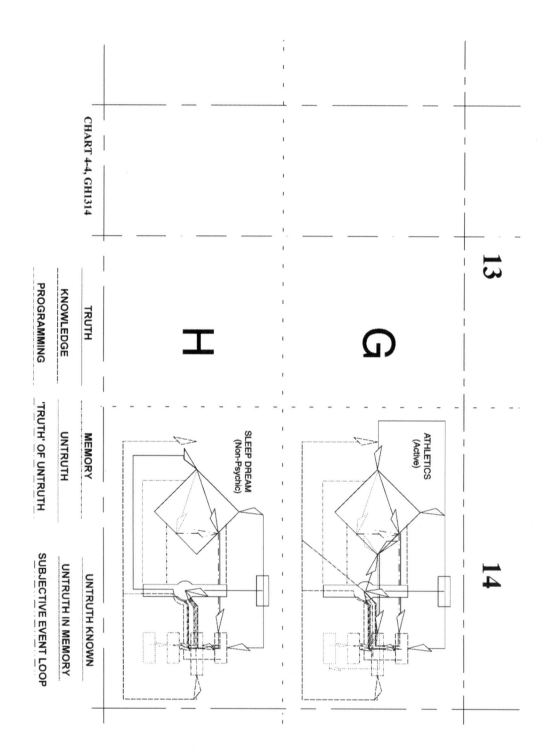

CHART 4-4, GH1314

13

14

TRUTH — KNOWLEDGE — PROGRAMMING

H

G

MEMORY — UNTRUTH — 'TRUTH' OF UNTRUTH

UNTRUTH KNOWN — UNTRUTH IN MEMORY — SUBJECTIVE EVENT LOOP

SLEEP DREAM
(Non-Psychic)

ATHLETICS
(Active)

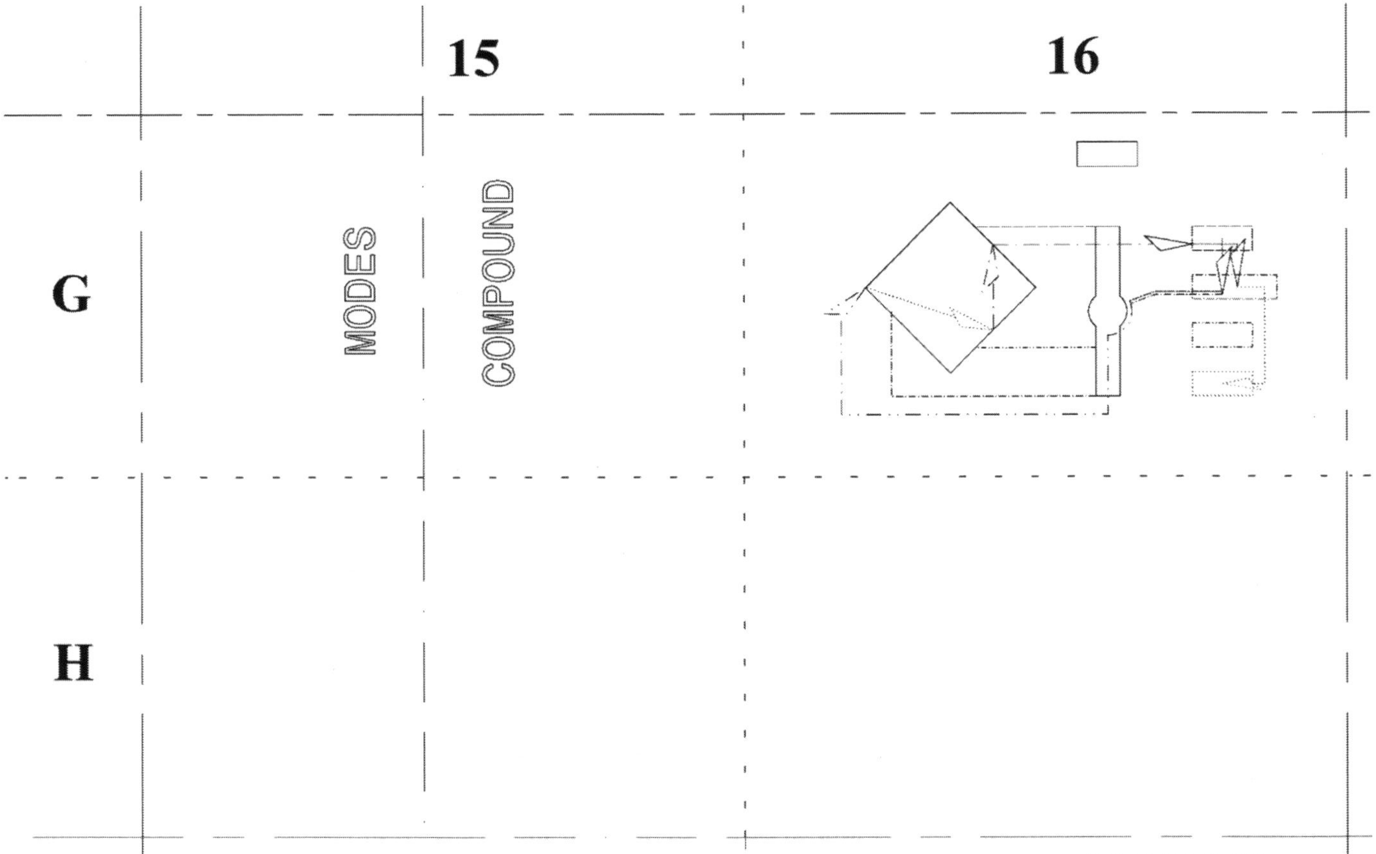

15   16

G

H

MODES

COMPOUND

TRUTH	MEMORY	UNTRUTH KNOWN
KNOWLEDGE	UNTRUTH	UNTRUTH IN MEMORY
PROGRAMMING	'TRUTH' OF UNTRUTH	SUBJECTIVE EVENT LOOP

CHART 4-4, GH1516

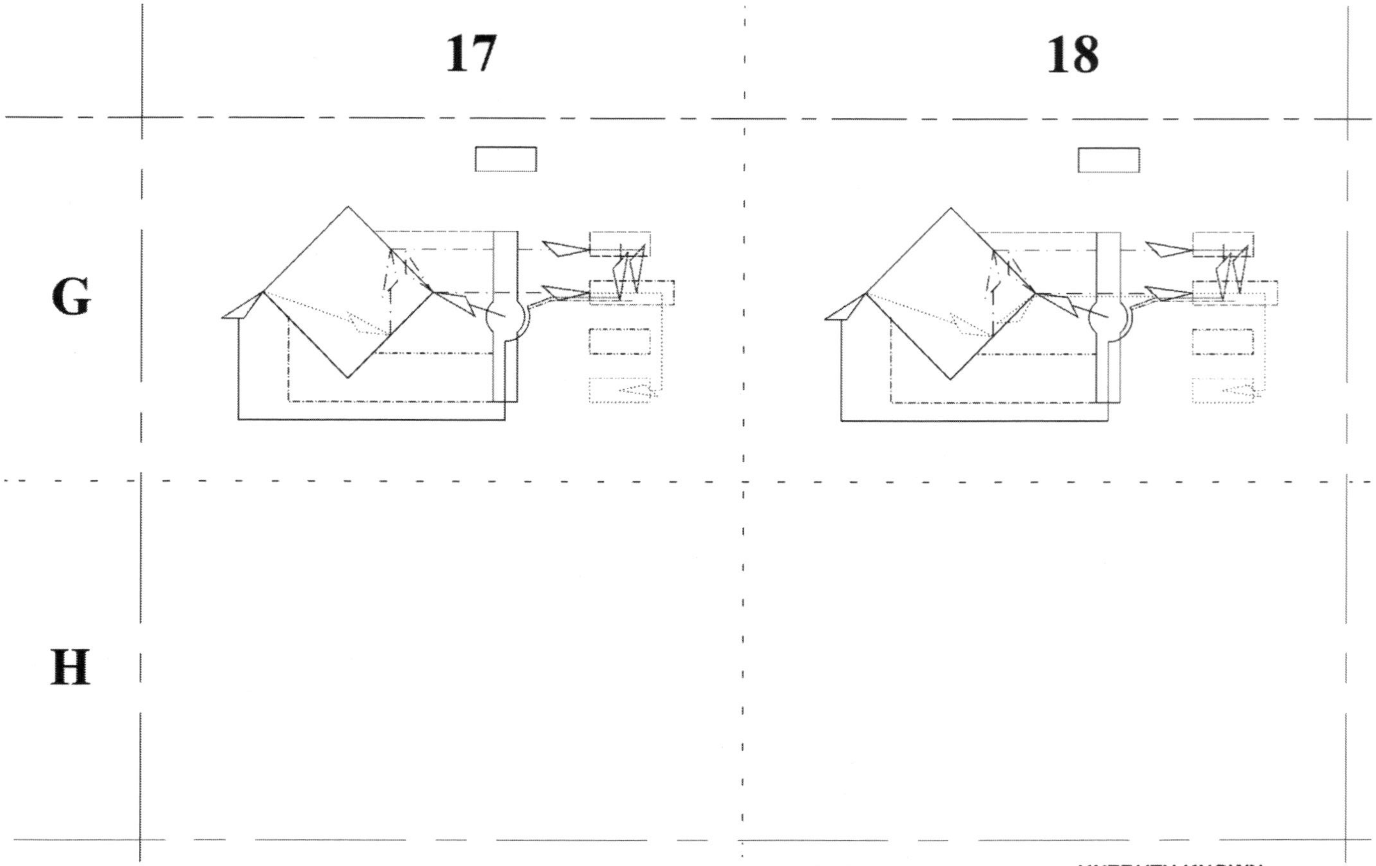

G

H

17

18

CHART 4-4, GH1718

TRUTH

KNOWLEDGE

PROGRAMMING

MEMORY

UNTRUTH

'TRUTH' OF UNTRUTH

UNTRUTH KNOWN

UNTRUTH IN MEMORY

SUBJECTIVE EVENT LOOP

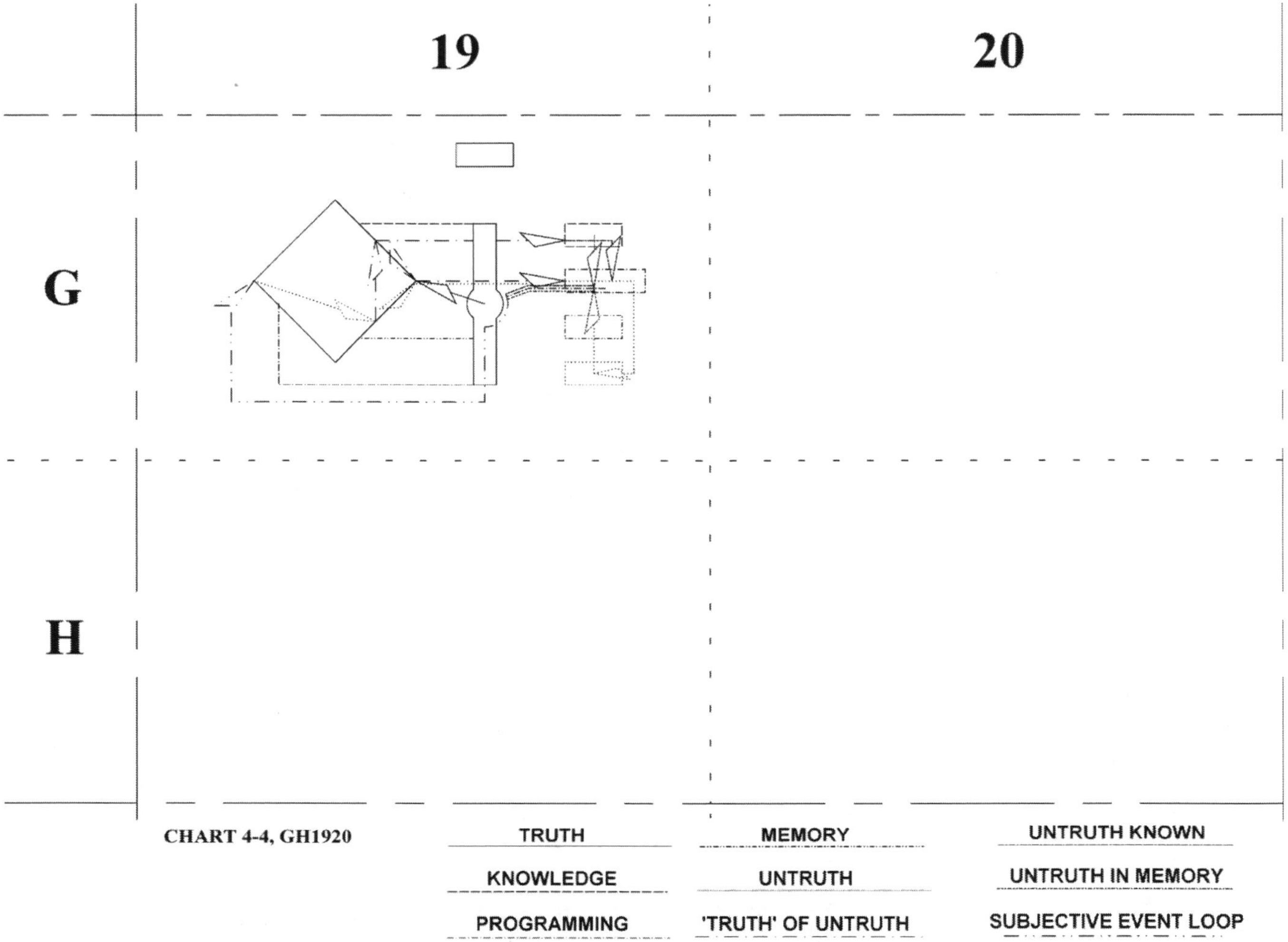

20

19

G

H

CHART 4-4, GH1920

TRUTH	MEMORY	UNTRUTH KNOWN
KNOWLEDGE	UNTRUTH	UNTRUTH IN MEMORY
PROGRAMMING	'TRUTH' OF UNTRUTH	SUBJECTIVE EVENT LOOP

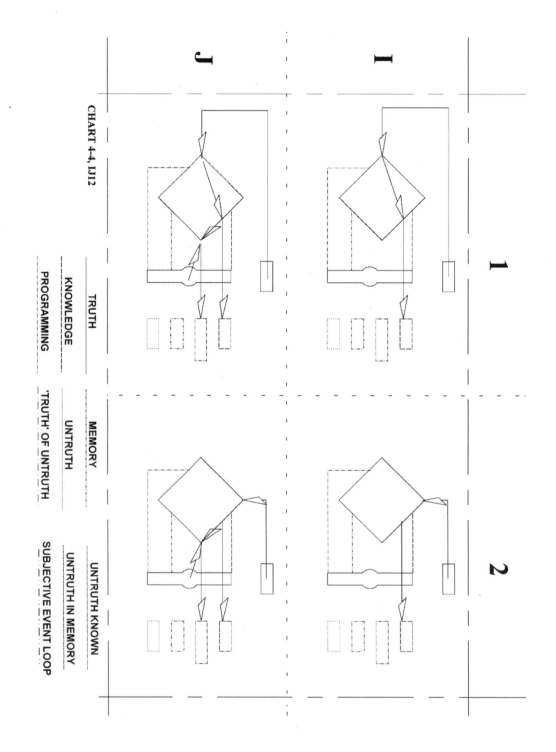

CHART 4-4, IJ12

	TRUTH	MEMORY	UNTRUTH KNOWN
	KNOWLEDGE	UNTRUTH	UNTRUTH IN MEMORY
	PROGRAMMING	'TRUTH' OF UNTRUTH	SUBJECTIVE EVENT LOOP

I

J

1

2

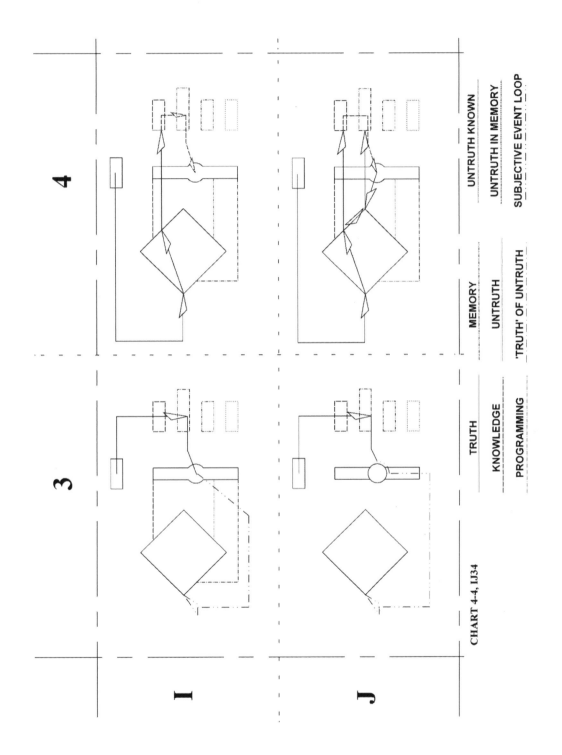

CHART 4-4, IJ34

TRUTH

KNOWLEDGE

PROGRAMMING

MEMORY

UNTRUTH

'TRUTH' OF UNTRUTH

UNTRUTH KNOWN

UNTRUTH IN MEMORY

SUBJECTIVE EVENT LOOP

187

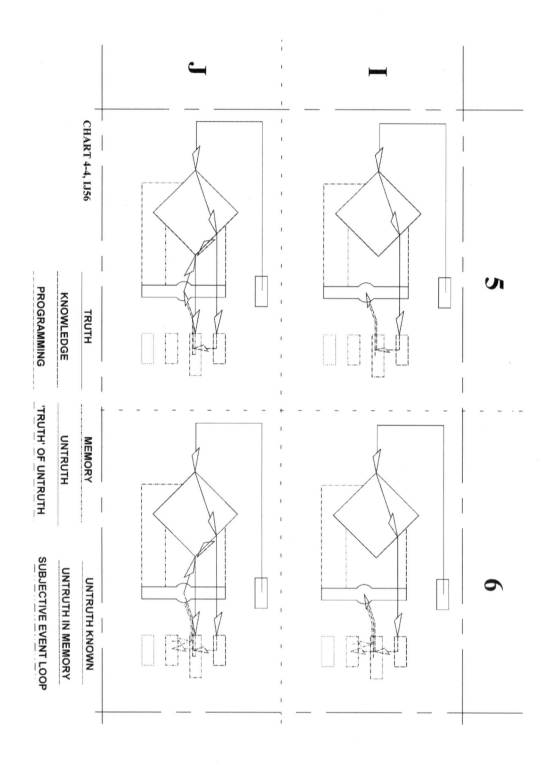

CHART 4-4, IJ56

	5	6
J		
I		

TRUTH	MEMORY
KNOWLEDGE	UNTRUTH
PROGRAMMING	'TRUTH' OF UNTRUTH

UNTRUTH KNOWN
UNTRUTH IN MEMORY
SUBJECTIVE EVENT LOOP

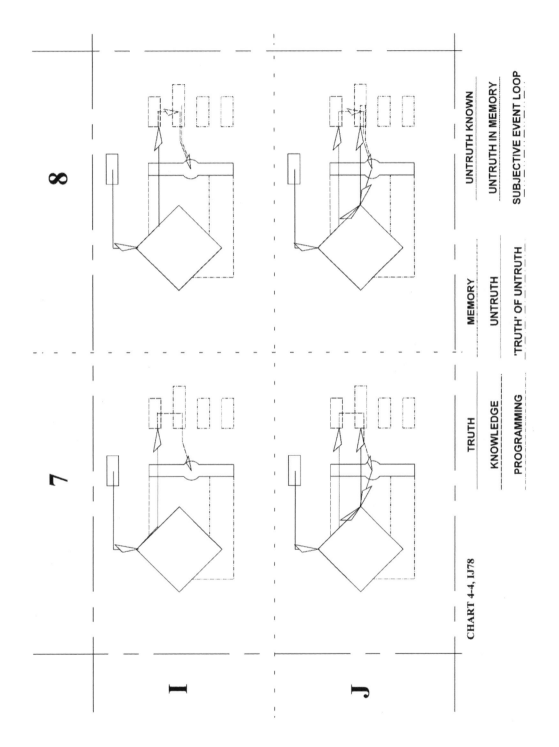

7   8

I

J

CHART 4-4, IJ78

TRUTH   MEMORY   UNTRUTH KNOWN

KNOWLEDGE   UNTRUTH   UNTRUTH IN MEMORY

PROGRAMMING   'TRUTH' OF UNTRUTH   SUBJECTIVE EVENT LOOP

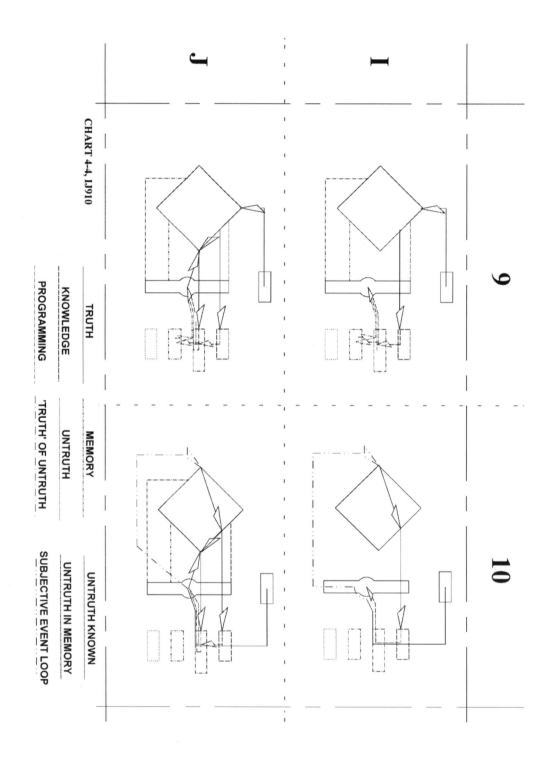

CHART 4-4, LJ910

	9		10
I			
	TRUTH	MEMORY	UNTRUTH KNOWN
J	KNOWLEDGE	UNTRUTH	UNTRUTH IN MEMORY
	PROGRAMMING	TRUTH OF UNTRUTH	SUBJECTIVE EVENT LOOP

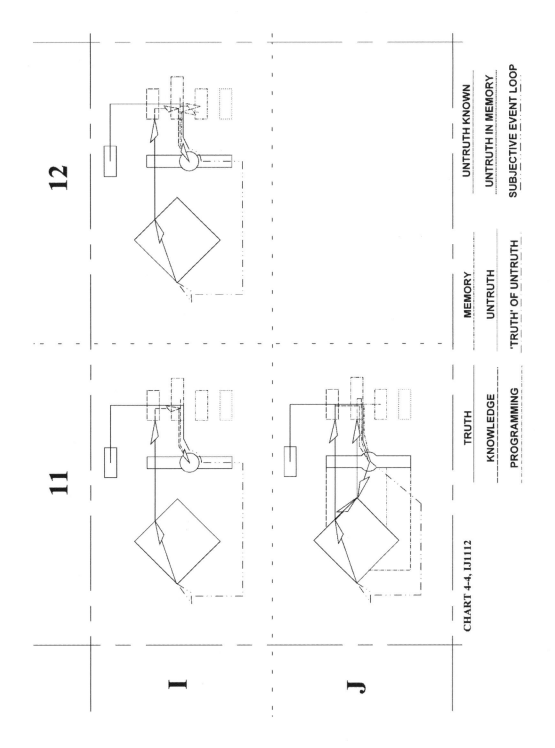

11

12

I

J

TRUTH

KNOWLEDGE

PROGRAMMING

MEMORY

UNTRUTH

'TRUTH' OF UNTRUTH

UNTRUTH KNOWN

UNTRUTH IN MEMORY

SUBJECTIVE EVENT LOOP

CHART 4-4, IJ1112

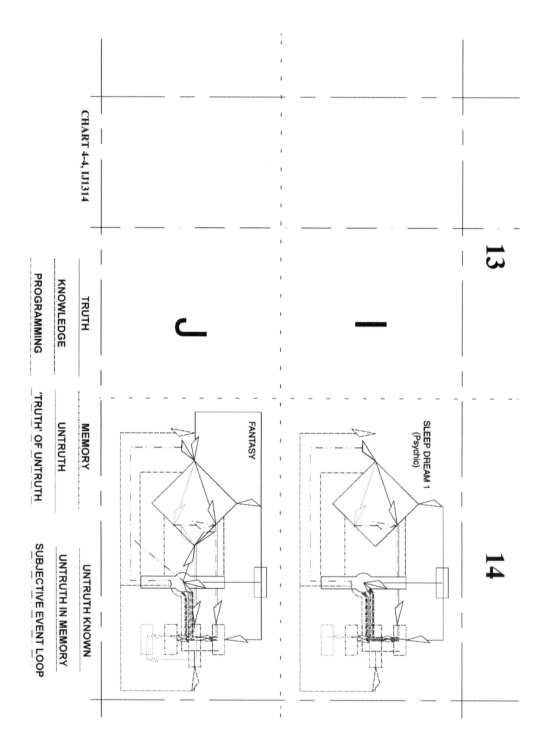

CHART 4-4, IJ1314

13

14

J

I

TRUTH — KNOWLEDGE — PROGRAMMING

MEMORY — UNTRUTH — 'TRUTH' OF UNTRUTH

UNTRUTH KNOWN — UNTRUTH IN MEMORY — SUBJECTIVE EVENT LOOP

FANTASY

SLEEP DREAM 1 (Psychic)

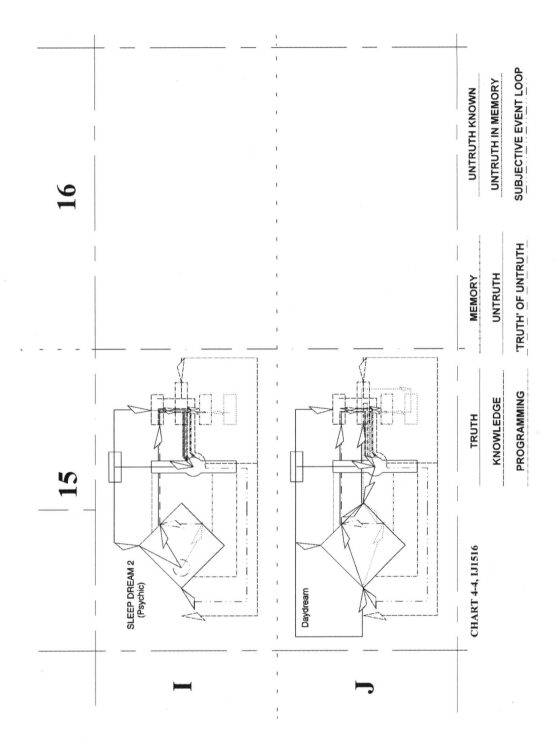

15   16

I

SLEEP DREAM 2
(Psychic)

J

Daydream

CHART 4-4, IJ1516

TRUTH	MEMORY	UNTRUTH KNOWN
KNOWLEDGE	UNTRUTH	UNTRUTH IN MEMORY
PROGRAMMING	'TRUTH' OF UNTRUTH	SUBJECTIVE EVENT LOOP

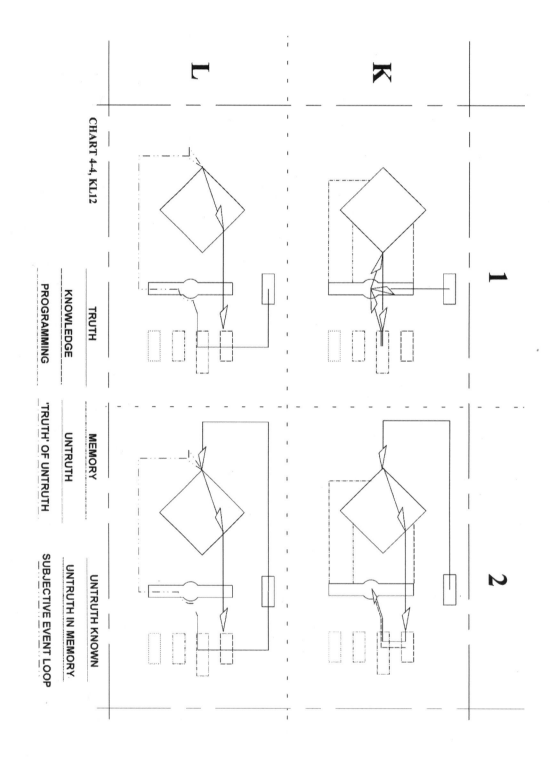

CHART 4-4, KL12

	1	2
K	TRUTH / KNOWLEDGE / PROGRAMMING	UNTRUTH KNOWN / UNTRUTH IN MEMORY / SUBJECTIVE EVENT LOOP
L	MEMORY / UNTRUTH / 'TRUTH' OF UNTRUTH	

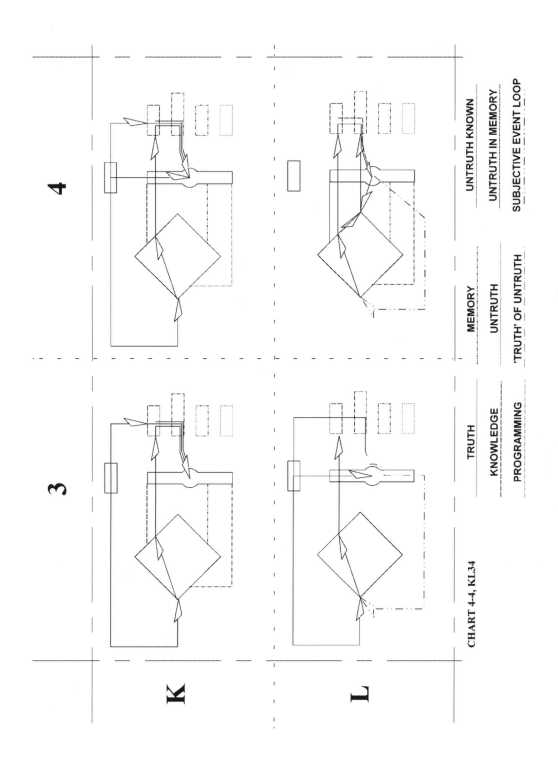

3

4

K

L

TRUTH	MEMORY	UNTRUTH KNOWN
KNOWLEDGE	UNTRUTH	UNTRUTH IN MEMORY
PROGRAMMING	'TRUTH' OF UNTRUTH	SUBJECTIVE EVENT LOOP

CHART 4-4, KL34

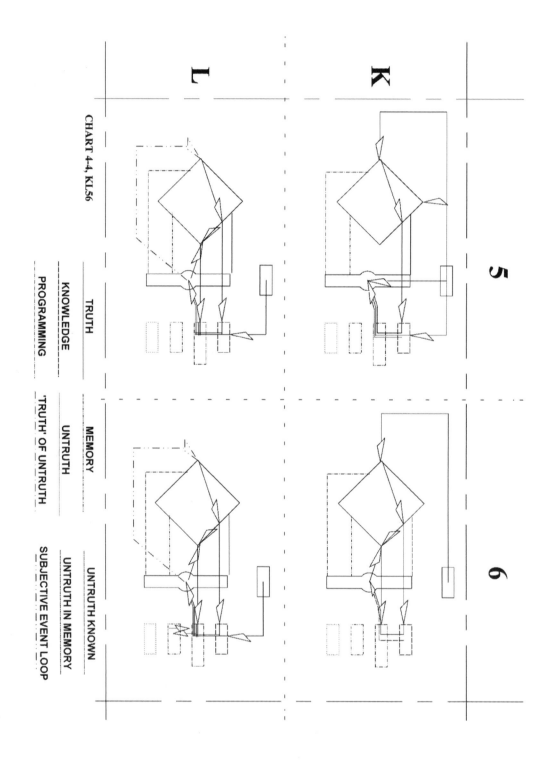

CHART 4-4, KL56

K   5   6

L

	5	6
K	TRUTH	UNTRUTH KNOWN
	KNOWLEDGE	UNTRUTH IN MEMORY
	PROGRAMMING	SUBJECTIVE EVENT LOOP
L	MEMORY	
	UNTRUTH	
	'TRUTH' OF UNTRUTH	

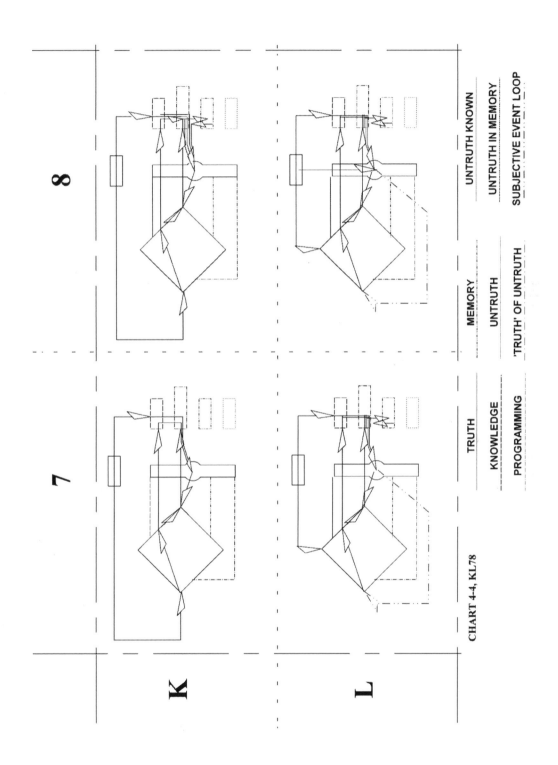

CHART 4-4, KL78

UNTRUTH KNOWN	
UNTRUTH IN MEMORY	
SUBJECTIVE EVENT LOOP	
MEMORY	UNTRUTH
'TRUTH' OF UNTRUTH	
TRUTH	KNOWLEDGE
PROGRAMMING	

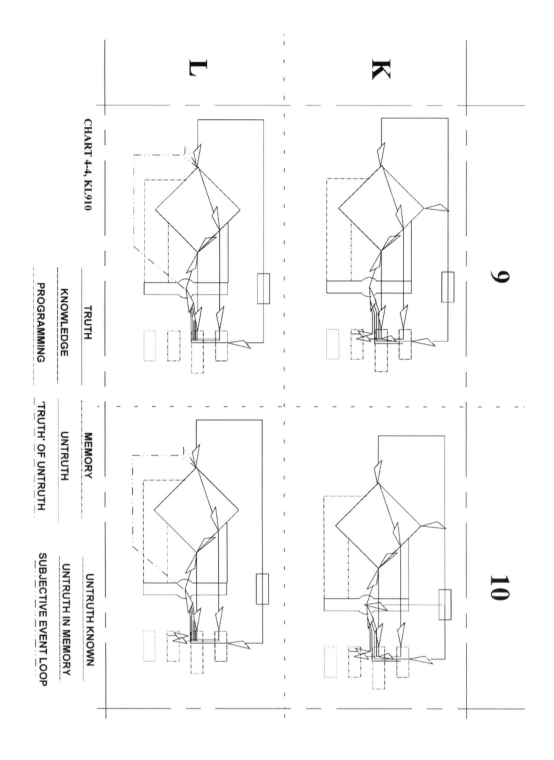

K

9

L

CHART 4-4, KL910

10

TRUTH
KNOWLEDGE
PROGRAMMING

MEMORY
UNTRUTH
'TRUTH' OF UNTRUTH

UNTRUTH KNOWN
UNTRUTH IN MEMORY
SUBJECTIVE EVENT LOOP

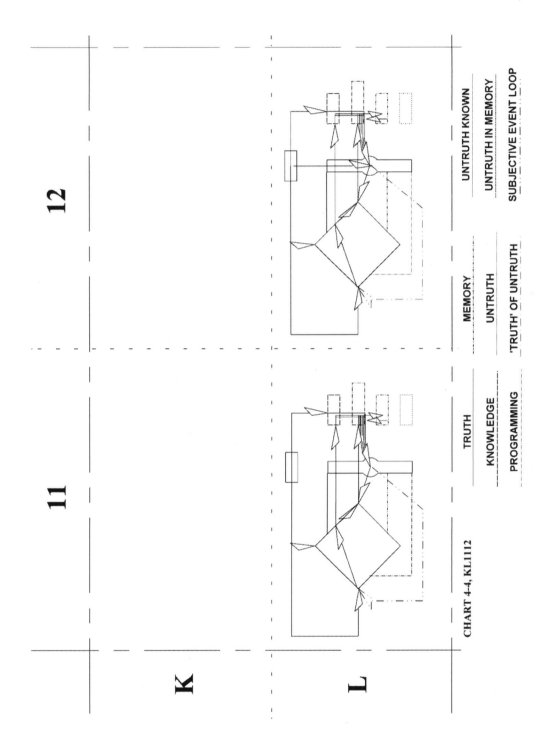

CHART 4-4, KL1112

TRUTH   MEMORY   UNTRUTH KNOWN

KNOWLEDGE   UNTRUTH   UNTRUTH IN MEMORY

PROGRAMMING   'TRUTH' OF UNTRUTH   SUBJECTIVE EVENT LOOP

11   12

K

L

CHART 4-4, KL1314

	TRUTH	MEMORY	UNTRUTH KNOWN
	KNOWLEDGE	UNTRUTH	UNTRUTH IN MEMORY
	PROGRAMMING	'TRUTH' OF UNTRUTH	SUBJECTIVE EVENT LOOP

L

K

14

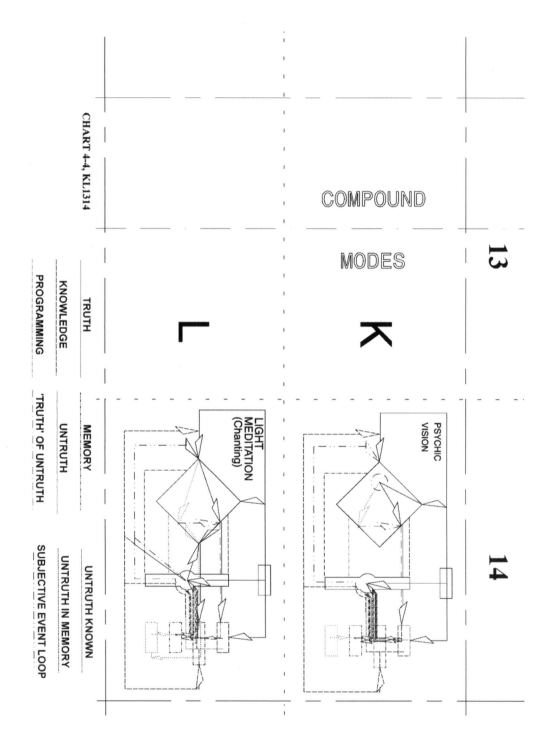

LIGHT MEDITATION (Chanting)

PSYCHIC VISION

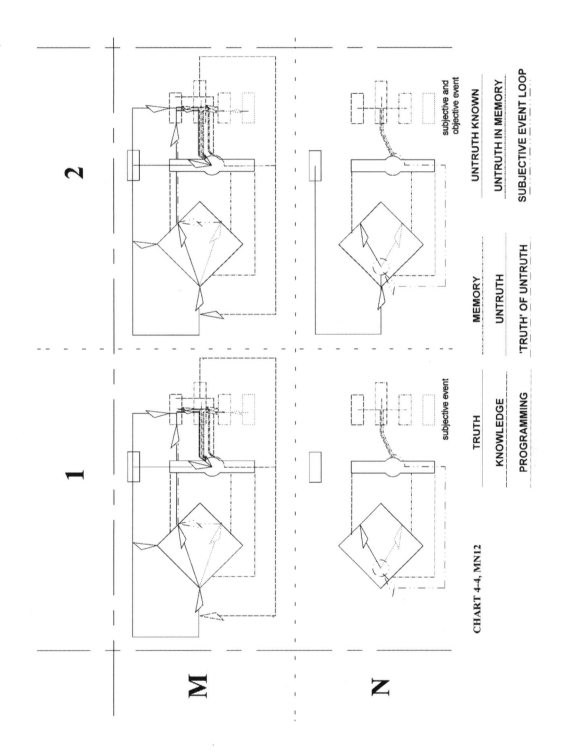

CHART 4-4, MN12

TRUTH	MEMORY	UNTRUTH KNOWN
KNOWLEDGE	UNTRUTH	UNTRUTH IN MEMORY
PROGRAMMING	'TRUTH' OF UNTRUTH	SUBJECTIVE EVENT LOOP

subjective event

subjective and objective event

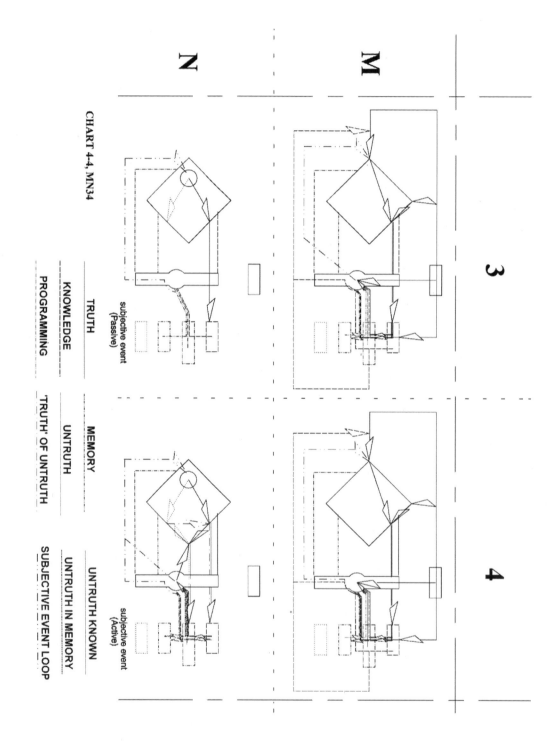

CHART 4-4, MN34

M	3	4
N		

TRUTH
KNOWLEDGE
PROGRAMMING

MEMORY
UNTRUTH
'TRUTH' OF UNTRUTH

UNTRUTH KNOWN
UNTRUTH IN MEMORY
SUBJECTIVE EVENT LOOP

subjective event
(Passive)

subjective event
(Active)

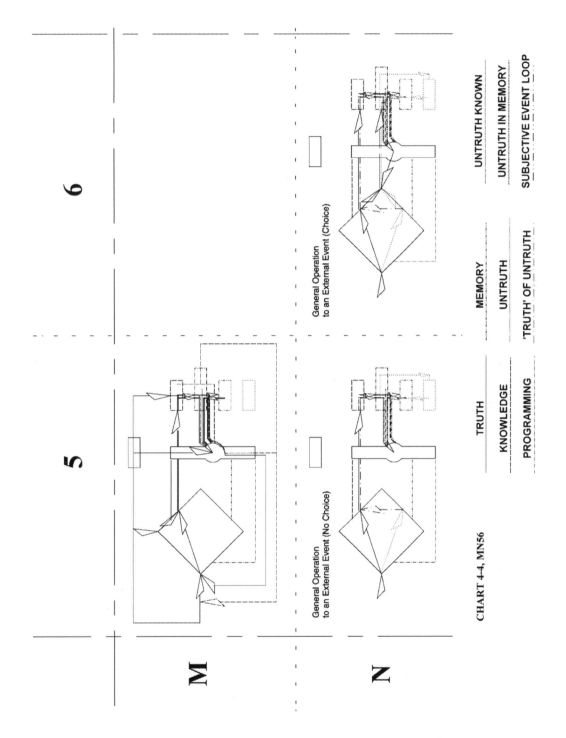

5

M

General Operation
to an External Event (No Choice)

6

General Operation
to an External Event (Choice)

N

CHART 4-4, MN56

TRUTH	MEMORY	UNTRUTH KNOWN
KNOWLEDGE	UNTRUTH	UNTRUTH IN MEMORY
PROGRAMMING	'TRUTH' OF UNTRUTH	SUBJECTIVE EVENT LOOP

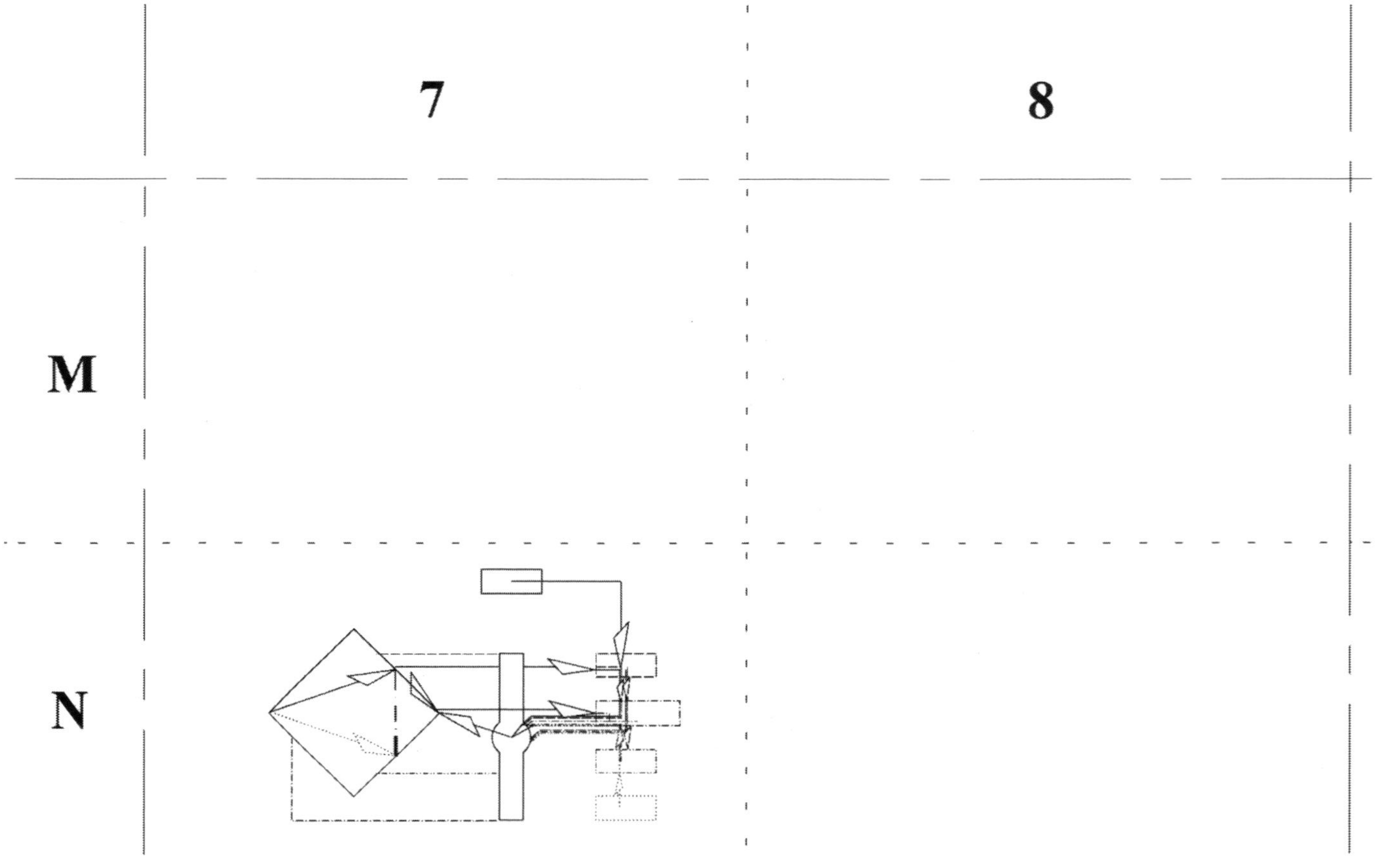

M

N

7

8

CHART 4-4, MN78

TRUTH
KNOWLEDGE
PROGRAMMING

MEMORY
UNTRUTH
'TRUTH' OF UNTRUTH

UNTRUTH KNOWN
UNTRUTH IN MEMORY
SUBJECTIVE EVENT LOOP

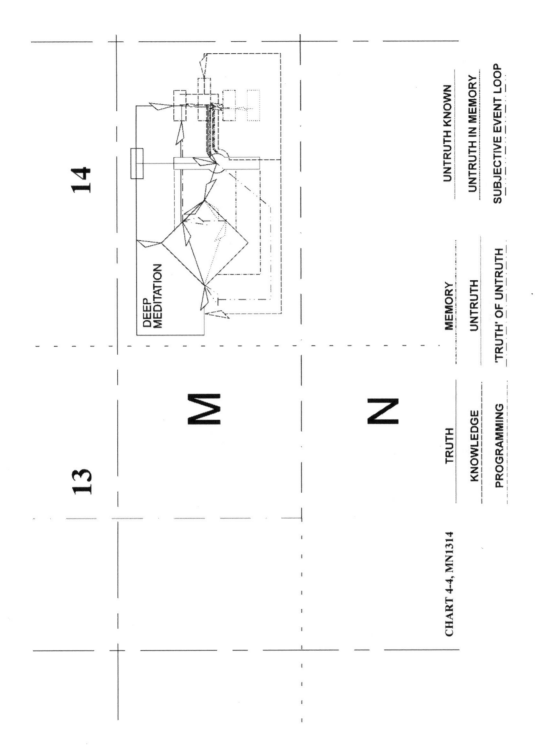

13　14

M

N

TRUTH　　MEMORY　　UNTRUTH KNOWN

KNOWLEDGE　　UNTRUTH　　UNTRUTH IN MEMORY

PROGRAMMING　　'TRUTH' OF UNTRUTH　　SUBJECTIVE EVENT LOOP

DEEP MEDITATION

CHART 4-4, MN1314

205

4.6 - Focus Control and Feedback Loops

*E*arlier in this chapter, the perceptual lens (*Perceptual Lens Array*) – the 'front' of the mind -- was covered: its elements, the internal influences of the elements, how information flows through the *Perceptual Lens Array*, and enters *Storages* through Choice (*II*) and Cognition (*VII*) – the 'back' of the mind. All of this activity passes through and around the *Focus Control Buss* of Figure 4-4, (*III*), "You are here."

The term buss is an electronic term. It is a place where data passes through and is sometimes temporarily stored. In Figure 4-4, it means this is an interface between the storage and lens. It takes what is in *Storage* (*I*) and uses it to focus the *Perceptual Lens Array* (*IV*). Using the camera analogy, with the *Focus Control Buss* we adjust the Lens and Aperture (*I* & *IV*) of our mind. We adjust what we focus on and what we will let in. Also from the *Focus Control Buss,* we control the Shutter (*VI*), what the picture will consist of with choice.

The mind model that is being depicted is a neutral <u>mechanism</u> – it operates on its programming and storage according to desires. Or, as it has been put another way, "garbage in, garbage out".

Using the earlier car analogy, the focus control is the driver's seat of the mind vehicle. It is through this focus control we exercise control of our mind/matrix; and, how we experience our minds. This is where life resides in the mortal matrix. We are the operators of a truth matrix vehicle (*III*). We are not our *Storage*. We are not our perceptual lens. We are not the mortal mind/matrix, or our ego vehicle. *Postulates 5* and *6* and their theorems say, "We are the Creation of God."

You are the Beloved of God. And…we are much more than these words or this book can convey. However, words and the perceptions words convey can be instrumental to understanding some of the relationships and what this truly means.

Through the *Focus Control Buss*, God/Love/Truth -- which is at the very core of everything and us – is allowed to manifest within us. The control buss, you (*III*), has Creation in it. It is the dynamic controller/passenger of this whole system; it is the 'driver's seat' of your mortal mind vehicle. It adjusts this 'mind's eye' mechanism -- *Perceptual Lens Array* -- to focus and refocus.

As mentioned previously in this chapter, the Eternal Moment of Creation manifests temporal forms indirectly through this mind matrix mechanism with the 'subjective event'; the Eternal Moment of Creation – you -- can take a direct control from the Focus Control.

You are an interpreter, controller, an observer, and more. Within the *Focus Control Buss*, who we really are -- God's Creation -- resides. Here is where we exercise control of this mortal mind/matrix vehicle. It is where we dwell in the Mirror and the Correction. And…who we really are is none of these. We come from Truth.

It is the 'go/no-go' of the Choice (*VI*) shutter, exercised through you within *Focus Control*, that determines when and what this lens array is choosing, or not. It determines whether there is a flow or not into *Programming* (*II*). Flow – 'go'; 'no go' -- no flow. You can stop the choice and there will be no flow through Choice (*II*). If there is truth in the perception, it can also flow through pure cognition without a choice (*VII*).

You are the dynamic interface – driver and experiencer, because you are constantly making choices from the *Focus Control Buss*, ([*VI* & *II*] Chart 4-4, *D1* and/or *D4*). Your 'choices' continually affect the whole system. With every thought that enters your head, you have a choice whether you want to accept it or not. With everything you see or feel, you have a choice whether you want to embrace it, wait, or not.

The *Focus Control Buss* is where our consciousness is shown in Figure 4-4 to reside in this model; this is where our conscious awareness <u>tends</u> to lie. The model of Figure 4-4 demonstrates how our conscious awareness mechanism can have both Truth and ~~truth~~ programmed into it and how they both make up part of what we <u>think</u> is us.[1] Our conscious awareness can be outside of this process, also. Some of the later exercises aim at exposing you to this.

---

[1] As stated in Chapter 2's postulates and theorems

Here is a review on how a specific storage block has an influence on a particular area of the lens array (*IV* in Figure 4-4). For example, the upper focus control loop is a reflection of what is in *Knowledge*. This *Knowledge* tends to affect Reason and the Cognition triangles (*IV*). The lower focus control loop affects the Emotion and Habit triangles, and tends to be influenced by *Memory* storage (*IV*). While, *Programming*'s major affect reflects in the two triangles Attitude and Imagination (*IV*).

The line (*I*, Figure 4-4) that enters the *Focus Control Buss* from *Programming* is shown broken into three different patterns. The matching patterns are shown leaving the buss and going to the respective perceptual lens represent focus controls (*IV*). With like patterns, Figure 4-4 (*IV*) illustrates how the different *Storages*/matrices influence the various portions of our *Perceptual Lens Array* matrix.

Figure 4-4 shows how these three *Storages* influence how we see and how we focus on these things. Whether directly or indirectly, *Storage*'s influence, through these loops, involves similar paths. Figure 4-4, *I* or Chart 4-4, *C1-4* shows how *Storage* affects the *Perceptual Lens Array* shown as separate lines of influence that come from our *Programming* (*IV*) and are influencing *Focus Control* and us (Figure 4-4, (*III*) or Chart 4-4, *C4* or *C9*).

Note also, that these loops are primary tendencies. This is still one system because they are all interrelated. Together they form a dynamic whole – a gestalt, called our personality.

Again, the stress here is that this is a flexible dynamic system. *Programming* influence, with its *Knowledge* and *Memory* bias, enters the *Focus Control Buss* (Chart 4-4, *C4*). The *Focus Control Buss* then breaks down that influence from the three basic *Storages* (*I*) and reflects the *Storages*' influence into their related triangle pairs – squares -- (areas of influence, Figure 4-4, (*IV*) and Chart 4-4, *D3*). What you have programmed (previous cognitions, choices,/judgments, and memories) aligns your perceptual lens and influences the nature of future choices are to be made.

This is not that strange -- of course our programming affects our focus; the 'back' of the mind determines the focus of the 'front' of the mind. Within this model, one can see the psychological laws perceptual psychology and of projection forming. Everything we 'see' reflects what is in storage and the programming of the 'back of the mind'.

Figure 4-4 shows the focus controls leaving the focus buss (through us) and influencing the respective elements of the perceptual lens, ([*IV*], Chart 4-4, *D2-3*). These focus controls direct the nature of the *Perceptual Lens Array*.

They can cause the array to focus in various behavior modes:

❖ Passively
  • They determine the basic operating function of the lens array (Chart 4-4, *B14*).
  • They determine the relaxed state of the mind/matrix (Chart 4-4, *D3* or *C14*).
  • Produce a 'subjective event' creation loop; daydream (Chart 4-4, *N3*).
❖ Actively
  • They can bring what is in Storage to focus on an external event (Chart 4-4, *N5* or *F14*).
  • Create a 'subjective event' loop; problem solving thinking and visualizing (Chart 4-4, *N4*).
  • Determine the nature of a *ESP* event (Chart 4-4, *I14-15* or *K14*).
❖ Combinations of the above.

These controls come from the *Focus Control Buss*, adjusted by us (*IV*), (which in turn is influenced by what is in [*I*], Storage, Chart 4-4, *D2-3*). The Cognitive Input ([VII], Chart 4-4, *B5*) guides focusing and refocusing. If there is no cognitive input, this mind/matrix model tends to refocus the perceptual lens until there is a cognitive input.

Choices enter *Programming* (*II*) and recycles to the front, through the *Focus Control Buss*, to influence the perceptional array again ([*I* & *IV*], Chart 4-4, *D3*). This is done either through the focus control loops and/or the 'subjective event' loop[2], such as fantasies or problem solving (Chart 4-4, *D8* or *D9*).

The focusing of these three pairs of triangles – squares -- influences the flow from the Event, to True and ~~True~~, then through to Choice (*VI*) (Chart 4-4, *E4*). This choice effects the *Programming* (*II*), in turn, feeds back through (*I*) to the focus control loops (*IV*), to the array, influencing future choices (Chart 4-4, *D4*) and so it goes and goes and goes...

As with *BTR*s within *BTR*s..., matrices within matrices..., patterns and parallels within patterns and parallels..., this model presents feedback loops within feedback loops.

The major factors here are how much Truth and ~~truth~~ perceived, chosen, focus/refocus, plus repetition.

Although continual repetition influences the whole, repetition through the bottom half of the diagram can lead to some nasty results. As mentioned earlier, without cognitive direction or reasoning based on truth, it can lead to some unwanted ~~Truth~~ Storage re-enforcement and some nasty programming loops like bad habits, compulsive behavior, or worse. Neuroses, psychoses, aberrant or compulsive behavior can result; because the matrix flows tend to go in downward spirals, away from Truth. Usually, this occurs when there is no effort to guidance or refocus.

When an excess of lower array influenced repetitive choices enter the *Programming* storage (*II*), ~~truth~~ accumulates and becomes a major factor in the matrix (Chart 4-4, *D19*). Truth is "laws by which something works". If you are not working in the laws of an event – working with truth, means your mind/matrix will be increasingly dysfunctional to that event.[3] This is a down side of the temporal human condition.

A downward spiral has been mentioned, away from Truth to ~~truth~~. At the same time, repetition can be a beginning route for learning. You can do an upward spiral using cognition, toward Truth.

In learning through repetition -- we do something repeatedly -- then, a cognitive jump is made. "I got it." With that cognitive jump -- the loop going from True to *Knowledge* (*VII*) – is the final leg of learning (Chart 4-4, *B5*). If you repeatedly choose to do something, to apply some truth, eventually you will come to this point. As mentioned earlier, <u>the flow of truth with a cognitive jump -- through the lens array -- will bypass Choice (*II*) on the last leg of its journey and go directly into *Knowledge* (*VII*)</u>.

True, you may have to choose the repetitive act for it to go through *Programming* and have specific focuses to start the process. When the flows repeatedly make a journey through the upper part of the lens array, Choice (*II*), and *Storage* several times, eventually it will make a jump through the cognitive input into *Knowledge* (*VII*), bypassing Choice (*II*). However, you have to 'focus' on making the repetitive choice for that jump through the cognitive input to occur.

"So it goes, and so it goes." This is a route of Truth into *Knowledge*. This is also the route of the epiphany.

When the cognitive loop affects *Knowledge*, *Knowledge* then affects *Programming* (Chart 4-4, *E5*). Knowledge has priority over *Programming*. This is survival; *Knowledge* is truth/law applications. Notice that the line of influence between *Knowledge* and *Programming* is one way, just as the effect of *Truth* to *Knowledge* is one way. *Truth* influences/has-priority over *Knowledge* (Chart 4-4, *A3*), which in turn influences/has-priority over the *Programming* (Chart 4-4, *B1*), and then *Knowledge* -- through *Programming* -- back to the lens array, back to choice and cognition, etc (something similar to Chart 4-4, *I12*).

With this particular mind model, an interesting thing can occur with the Forgiveness-Judgment triangles. If the Perception/Desire Lens is focused using Absolute Truth, we tend to 'see' the whole picture. There is nothing to judge or forgive, it becomes a no-go condition; and

---

[2] The 'subjective event' [←Thoughts ←] line in Figure 4-4 is a way of portraying special focus setups of the other controls (*IV*)

3 Chapter 5

yet, there is a flow through into *Storage*. The reason is there is a flow through is that truth from the lens array flows into pure cognition ([*VII*], Chart 4-4, *I12*).

Do you see what is being said? It is possible to act without thinking and using the perceptual lens only through the cognitive loop, with minimum to no choices.

This type of cognitive input can be related to the 'ringing' mechanism of the first exercise.[4] Absolute Truth is within us as well as everything else. When Truth is perceived and it travels through the *Perceptual Lens Array*, and it is also at the very source of our being; a number of connections can occur through Cognition, to *Knowledge*, to the *Focus Control*, and consequently to you.

Since you happen to be between the two (Figure 4-4, *III*), you can experience the connection as a resonance or a consciousness change. The greater the truth perceived and the less ~~truth~~ is present, the greater the 'ring'. This will be covered in detail later in this chapter.

It is possible to get an idea of how this whole *Perceptual Lens Array-Storage* model process works, by illustrating the development of the lens usage. With a little exercise of the imagination, we can run a baby through into adult programming. First, the newborn baby gets light, color, form, and other sensory input and has no initial reference. It just focuses on random objects, and has no recognition of objects because there are no cognitive jumps that have been made yet. It has some vague desires and wants. Its immediate perceptions are of the surroundings affecting it. It has very poor perceptions, or understanding, or any sense whatsoever of what is happening, or what 'is'. Consequently, because of the unfocused or limited perceptions its desires or wants/not-wants are very simple.

The repetitive cycles of forms (light, color, composition, etc.) go through a number of choices and cognitive jumps, which then go into *Knowledge* (along with *Memory*), and which affects the *Programming*, and *Programming* begins to use focus control. "Red! Like color red! Green food, ugh!"

Once the baby begins to use this cognitive loop, and after it has some kind of storage to work from, it begins to use the *Focus Control*. The patterns of choices that the baby starts making, through the *Focus Control*, begin to show up as behavioral programming tendencies; the baby learns the word *no*.

Every individual truth matrix at this point is beginning to grow. The baby is beginning to program his/her *Storage*. He is learning to exercise his/her control, and beginning to influence how this information is coming into him/her/it. Using the field of grass analogy, the baby is beginning to cut the main trails that will make up its mind's paths.

4.7 – Thinking, the Subjective Event, and more Loop d' Loops

*T*his chapter has looked at the major operational paths and loops truth takes a number of times. The next focus is on the ~~truth~~ paths a little bit more (shown in the upper right of Chart 4-4). It has been mentioned that ~~truth~~ is created by and dependent on a specific set of 'truths'. Because God's Creation is the only way to create,[5] their relationship is a very finite limited mirrored version of the 3-in-1 1-in-3 of Chapters 2 and 3. A specific 'truth' determines the nature of the ~~truth~~ and ~~truth~~ regenerates that 'truth'. This is important. Because ~~truth~~ is dependent on a set of 'truths', address the set of 'truths' and ~~truth~~ is addressed.

It has been shown, there are two ways truth enters *Storage* from the *Perceptual Lens Array*, through Cognition (*VII*) and Choice (*II*) (Chart 4-4, *B5, 6,* and *E4*). Accordingly, there are two basic ways ~~truth~~ can enter *Storage*. Through the 'truth' that sustains the ~~truth~~; it enters through Cognition (*VII*) (Chart 4-4, *B6* and *F3*); in addition, it becomes an element of Choice (*II*). Through Choice (*II*) comes a 'double whammy' though. Not only is ~~truth~~ directly chosen (Chart 4-4, *C16*), but also, so is the 'truth' that sustains the ~~truth~~ (Chart 4-4, *F3*) chosen. All ~~truth~~ that enters *Programming* goes directly into ~~Truth~~ storage.

---

4 Chapter 1.1, *Lab 1*
5 *Theorem 11B*, The God-Creation process is the *only* Creative process.

The truth inputs from the *Perceptual Lens Array* into *Storage* are expressed in Chart 4-4, *C19*. So eventually, truth that makes it through the *Perceptual Lens Array* – the 'front' of the mind -- ends up affecting *Knowledge, Programming, Memory,* and *Truth* – the 'back' of the mind, either directly or indirectly.

Truth affects *Memory* now from two directions in this model. Combining Chart 4-4, *B2* with *D19* produces an effect similar to Chart 4-4, *D20*.

Chart 4-4, *A19, 20,* and *D19, 20* illustrate how, once it enters *Storage,* Truth is 'fed' in the mortal mind/matrix. A change of this loop from *Programming,* and the truth entering changes. Once truth (and the consequent 'truth' that goes with it) has been established in the mind/matrix *Storages,* it affects the matrix numerous ways. These ways are both direct and indirect, primarily indirectly. Directly, *Truth* affects *Memory* (Chart 4-4, *A17*).

Indirectly, *Truth* works through *Memory* and in turn, *Memory* affects *Programming* (Chart 4-4, A18). At the same time, whatever 'truth' sustains the truth, which is in *Knowledge,* has an effect on *Programming* (Chart 4-4, *A16*). Moreover, *Programming* then affects *Focus Control* and what the *Perceptual Lens Array* will let through. Thereby, producing an effect leaving *Storages* going to *Focus Control* (*I*) similar to Chart 4-4, *B19*.

The truth that enters *Storage* and the ways truth's influence leaves *Storage* to *Focus Control* (*I*) combine to form more feedback loops. These loops are very similar to truth's feedback loops (Chart 4-4, *I-M/1-12*). These feedback loops can be consciously directed (Chart 4-4, *F19*) or just allowed to happen (Chart 4-4, *G19*). The mortal mind/matrix vehicle mechanism, along with these truth and truth loops, combine to form our personality.

This presented model illustrates how truth and truth are separate in *Storages.* Both Truth and truth can affect *Programming* (Chart 4-4, *A3* and *B18*), in different ways, which then can refocus the perceptual lens. So again, feedback circles occur and the entire process may look something like Chart 4-4, *D14.*

Here is another review of the flows, between and within, the *Storages* and the *Perceptual Lens Array* presented so far. An objective event (*V*) occurs and goes through our perceptual lens, which is focused by our *Programming* (Chart 4-4, *D3*) and reaches True and True ([*VI*], Chart 4-4, *E1*). Whatever truth applications existing within the array, enter directly in to *Knowledge* ([*VII*], Chart 4-4, *E2*).

We make a choice (*VI*), something that contains true, true, or both (Chart 4-4, *E3* and *C16*). This choice feeds into *Programming* (*II*) that in turn can feed into *Memory* (Chart 4-4, *B2*) and directly into *Truth* (if there is any truth in the choice [Chart 4-4, *D16*]).

Directly, the patterns of our truth perceived applications start to build up in *Knowledge* -- storage of truth applications. *Knowledge* is also affected directly, through the patterns of truth 'applied' that facilitates the choice event – how the 'front' of the mind is focused. Choice (*II*) affects *Programming, Memory,* and *Truth* directly and *Knowledge* is indirectly affected by what is 'allowed' to come through the lens.

Whatever truth is applied through the lens (by a particular focus), starts automatically to accumulate in *Knowledge* (Chart 4-4, *B5*). (Again, it must be pointed out that the 'truth' of the truth enters *Knowledge* also, [Chart 4-4, *F2*]). However, if we make a choice both for true and true, the choice for both also shows up in *Programming* (Chart 4-4, *E3* and *C16*). Eventually – directly or indirectly – the effect of choices will accumulate in *Knowledge, Programming, Memory,* and the *Truth* storages.

The storages (and what they will store) *Knowledge, Programming,* and *Memory* are neutral in their operation as interfaces between *Truth* and *Truth.* If there is any truth chosen, it is stored directly in the *Truth* storage (Chart 4-4, *D16*). In addition, if any of the truth that enters *Knowledge* through Cognition (*VII*) is a 'truth' that supports a truth (Chart 4-4, *F2*), this also reinforces *Truth* (Chart 4-4, *A20*).

One example of how these cycles of circles run is when somebody comes up to you on the street. Cognition tells you a person is before you (Chart 4-4, *E2*). Their features are referenced to what is in *Knowledge* and *Memory* (Chart 4-4, *B4*), and either you recognize them or do not recognize them *Knowledge* → *Memory.* (If no recognition, a refocus ensues

[Chart 4-4, *D3*].) If there is a match in *Memory*, *Programming* refocuses your lens from *Memory* (your previous perceptions of them) and *Knowledge* (Chart 4-4, *G8*). Also included in this refocus is your *Programming* itself (previous choices) and current perceptions/desires (what you do or do not see/want from them [Chart 4-4, *D10*]). Then, conversation may ensue. Several loops occurred here before any conversation started.

If you do not know them, you refocus and go into *Programming* and the familiar patterns of previous choices (Chart 4-4, *D3* or *C9*) appear. How do you treat strangers? Do you like how they look? This again refocuses your perceptual lens. Again, several loops occurred before any interaction happens.

In addition, in the case of a stranger, there can be some *Memory* if they remind you of someone. It is possible they remind you of a perception of person or an event. Again, whatever you use from your *Storages* (*I*) can affect this focusing and refocusing of the perceptual lens (*IV*). The whole procedure just mentioned may look like Chart 4-4, *N6*.

This last example was in reference to an 'objective event'; but, what about 'subjective events'? It was stated earlier that the *Perceptual Lens Array* is a matrix with a number of components – a gestalt. This matrix, being a mirror image of the Creation Matrix (a temporally limited finite version), is creating also. It is constantly creating or recreating temporal thoughts. In this model, a thought is a perception, perceptional scenario, or an array of cognitive associations. How and what thoughts that are created (or recreated) are contingent on how the *Perceptual Lens Array* is focused and by what is in *Storage* (*I*) guiding it. If creating is to extend, it can be said thoughts – 'subject events' -- are extensions of *Storage*.[6]

Figure 4-4 shows a 'subjective event' loop (← Thoughts ←), which is another type of feedback loop within this whole system. This 'subjective event' loop – shown as Chart 4-4, *B7* for passive (automatic) and Chart 4-4, *B8* for active (thinking) – is really a specialized representation of Chart 4-4, *D3*, Focus Control loops (*VI*).

The 'subjective event' loop is only a specific focus of the perceptual lens matrix (Chart 4-4, *D10* or *D11*); where a 'subjective event' is created (shown in the Imagination triangle of Figure 4-4, Figure 4-2.1 virtual image, or Chart 4-4, *N1*). The 'subjective event' loop is shown in Figure 4-4 to suggest specific focusing patterns of *IV*.

One aspect of the 'subjective event' loop can be passive or automatic, such as daydreams and night dreams (as in Chart 4-4, *J15* and *H14* respectively). It also can take a dynamic form; it can be *ESP* and spiritual visualization, when you are using reason, (Chart 4-4., *I14* and *C14*), or active fantasizing. The 'subjective event' is another way more programming loops become involved.

The 'subjective event' loop can involve some meditations, but not all. This loop can involve psychic and spiritual visualization that some meditations use. It is when working something out, putting a puzzle together in your head, as in reasoning; and, also used when you are doing *Exercise and Lab 3: Truth Perception* and *Exercise and Lab 4.1*.

When you are trying to reason something out, you are using the subjective feedback loop. "Okay, I have that conclusion (cognition), now let me run (refocus) that back through and see (perceive) how it relates to..." The subjective loop is being used to figure something out. In this case, the subjective feedback loop would be on an active mode.

Let us look at the passive or automatic aspect of this 'subjective event' loop first, daydreams and night dreams. These are predominately based on and/or influenced by what is in *Knowledge, Programming*, and *Memory* storages. For the most part, with dreams, there is a free flowing of cognitions, desire sets, and perceptual elements – stored in *Knowledge, Programming*, and *Memory*.

A perception, and a desire along with it, comprises a subjective element. We see that arrangement with daydreaming. The daydream is created in the *Perceptual Lens Array,* within the Imagination triangle, through the array, and we make a choice, go.

---

6 *Theorems 14, 15,* and *15A*: God Created like unto Himself. or To Create, God extended Himself; The Only Creative process there is, is to extend God; Creation can Create like unto God. or Creation can extend God. The mind/matrix being a very limited parallel to God's Love/Logic/Mind-Matrix extends what is in it.

Earlier, *I AM A I* referred to the use of this loop like this as a form of mental masturbation. There is a free flow of desire sets and perceptual elements and usually the free flow is guided by a desire or desire gratification. With daydreams, the figure in the *Focus Control Buss* plays the observer of what is happening by choosing to let the 'machine' run on automatic. It is kind of like choosing to watch a movie or a TV that is happening on the inside (Chart 4-4, *J15*).

Most choice options are not actively exercised in the free flowing that makes up daydreams and night dreams. We are usually just observing -- the only choice we usually are making (with daydreams) is allowing it to happen. <u>Again, this choice to allow it to happen also tends to show up in patterns of storage (*Programming*)</u>. Which then, will tend to show up in patterns of how the lens focuses in the future because of how *Storage* affects the lens array, and so on, and so on, etc? Circles within circles within circles, etc...again.

In night dreams, you are an objective observer or participant and <u>most</u> choice is removed (Chart 4-4, *H14*). Night dreams are another example where the patterns of previous choices have an indirect relationship, as it does with cognition (*Knowledge*).

Night dreams tend to show the patterns that have already been generated in the mortal mind/matrix when awake, through the Dream State. Like the patterns of recognition -- a clown, a wheelbarrow, horse -- night dreams contain these patterns of recognition and in turn, patterns the perceptional lens. This is guided somewhat by the desires you have around these perceptions or what these perceptions represent to you. Change what you want (from what you are seeing in the dream), and the dream can change.

Night dreams can have some *ESP* elements because it can be affected by the Truth. Usually, daydreams do not.

The daydreams that have *ESP* aspects are called visions. For the most part, daydreams are just the mind/matrix running on automatic; there is no *ESP* involved with them; they just feel good. Most of the time, daydreams are just the free running of the perceptual lens into storage, and from storage, feeding back through the lens, Chart 4-4, *J15* -- mental circles. Daydreams happen according to the current desires you maybe having – what you want or do not want.

In active visualizing (taking direct control of the parade of perception/thought), you are <u>not</u> just the objective observer. You put yourself right into it, are constantly consciously creating, refocusing, and making choices (Chart 4-4, *J14*). Like many loops and *Exercise and Lab 4.1*, the dynamic aspect of this feedback loop or specific lens arrangement is based on *Knowledge* and *Memory* storage, *Knowledge* storage more because it has priority over the other storages (Chart 4-4, *B1* or B4). *Knowledge* uses and references what is stored in *Memory*.

This is problem solving. Instead of letting the mind/matrix free-run or letting the choice spiral go down, we are guiding it upward to a point, using truth, and assembling truth, through perception and desire. This means imagination may be involved because Perceptions, Desires, and Beliefs form the Imagination triangle.

Again, this all contingent on what has already been programmed in the mind/matrix -- *Storages*. With visualization and problem solving, we enter a realm of major mind/matrix manipulation or operation. We use the focus mechanism to manipulate perceptions or symbolic forms of an objective reference – as math can manipulate physical form. This can be done without direct manipulation of the objective itself. We are putting it together in our head before we go and do it outside of our heads. Again, these active visualizations are indicative, as in dreams -- passive, of our *Programming* and *Storage* patterns.

That is how we visualize. And...how we visualize is dependent on what is already in our head.

A word about *ESP* and spiritual events: They come from Truth and depending on the type of psychic exchange can manifest through several routes (Chapter 7).

Whatever is in *Storage* determines the *Perceptual Lens Array* (*I & IV*) focus. If the *ESP* information takes the form of a perception (clairvoyance, clairaudience, a sense, etc. Chart 4-

4, *I2*), that which determines the <u>perception</u> of the message, comes from *Storage*. The *ESP* information is entering the matrix and being 'clothed' by how *Storage* arranges the *Perceptual Lens Array*. This accounts for how *ESP* messages can be disjointed. The *Storage* and *Perceptual Lens Array* and their interface may not have the language or 'clothes' to cover the 'message'.

Truth manifesting in *Storage* type of perceptual *ESP* event is first 'colored' by *Knowledge*, and that *Knowledge* becomes 'colored' by *Programming* (Chart 4-4, *B1*) as it travels. It becomes colored by what we know (patterns of cognition) and what we have programmed (patterns of choices) into us. Therefore, the *ESP* or spiritual information becomes interpreted into systems and ideas that we tend to understand. They will tend to assume forms that are recognized and established already in your *Storages* and their interface (Chart 4-4, *B4*).

One example is an image from the book of Revelations: a figure with a sword coming out of its mouth.[7] A sword, at the time of the vision, was a common instrument of war, destruction, and conquest. It implies something that is very solid, that cuts, and holds an edge.[8] Truth is indomitably solid and whatever 'edge' it has, never changes. Relate this to what comes out of the mouth is words. A spiritual figure with a sword emerging from its mouth can be analogous to waging war, destruction, and conquest with words of Truth.

In this book's presented model, every individual possesses a thought system and *ESP* information will appear through that system. Numerous systems of patterns of thinking within our individual mind/matrix have already set been up. *ESP* information will come through those patterns/systems/paths of thinking that already exist.

One part of an *ESP* exercise, is to create a conscious mental setup or construction; then, letting the Truth <u>use</u> the setup. There is one form of *ESP* introduced in Chapter 7 where the *ESP* information appearance is due to a non-active passive 'listening'; while, another form actively provides a medium for the information to appear.

The difference between the two ideas is Truth is using what system of patterns is already setup in the mind/matrix (passive, Chart 4-4, *I7, I8, I10, and I11*). While in the other, an individual is consciously setting up a system to facilitate this flow of Truth (dynamic, Chart 4-4, *L4-12*). Chapter 7 has a number of examples concerning the second case.

An example of the first case, is of prophetic visions -- seeing the sky turn black and lightning coming through and illuminating the land. It is speaking through personal images of darkness, of lightness and quickness; it is speaking through personal images of illumination and change (and whatever perception/desire sets the individual has that are associated with these perceptions).

ESP information tends to speak to you through the patterns and ideas that are already set up. It will not speak to you through archetypes and concepts you do not understand. This is not how Love works. Love will speak to you in a way you can understand.

ESP and spiritual information that is coming down into your conscious is colored by what already is in *Knowledge*, *Programming*, and *Memory*. It <u>tends</u> occupy perceptual forms that are recognized and already established within the mortal mind/matrix.

The one major exception to this is the more we start programming Absolute *Truth* into the *Knowledge* storage area, the less <u>perceived</u> *ESP* forms come through. The more Truth we choose, the less the *ESP* shows up in <u>perceived forms</u>. The more we enter a quiet knowing -- labeled in this work as intuition -- we 'see' things less and we just know. This quiet knowing rarely uses the perceptual lens (Chart 4-4, *C10* for example). Chapter 7 will go into the three different kinds of *ESP* phenomena's manifestations more deeply.

Dreamtime in Figure 4-4 is also another form of *ESP* (Chart 4-4, *I14* or *15*). *I AM A I* is using *Dreamtime* in the Australian aboriginal reference. It can be a dynamic or passive use of the matrix through *ESP* and spiritual terms. However, and again, *Dreamtime* <u>tends</u> to come in

---

7 "In his right hand he held seven stars, and out of his mouth came a sharp double-edged sword. His face was like the sun shining in all its brilliance." -- Revelation 1:16, New International Version Bible.

8 Brass, bronze, iron, flint...You have to watch out for those double edged swords though, they can cut *you* as well as your opponent.

patterns of forms that the individuals recognize -- something that has already been established or programmed within them.

If these last three sections have left your mind spinning in circles, good. That is what is happening within the mortal mind/matrix operation: circles within circles within circles, etc. There is no way *I AM A I* would be able to cover all the variations involved and leave this book a manageable length. It would be the same way if one tried to explain the workings of a video camera or a car. There is just too much information, with a large number of interdependent relationships; and in the end, is not relevant to basic usage. You do not have to be a mechanical engineer to drive a car.

Just as long as you recognize truth's and ~~truth~~'s roles, and you can see that there are a number of elements and feedback loops involved. In addition, recognize that you can adjust these elements and adjusting these elements or feedback loops will produce an effect within you. You can exert some control on your mortal mind/matrix vehicle.

4.8 - Ring My Bell

What is the Truth recognition exercise's (Chapter 1.1, *Lab 1*) relationship to this chapter's presented human matrix construct -- model? That exercise was an introduction to the concept that truth can have a conscious altering affect within your mind and to recognize it. This change of consciousness is directly related to how comprehensive – absolute – the truth is and the length of time it is present in the mind.

Why can this be important? Remember the 3-in-1, 1-in-3 concept; specifically, Truth regenerates the Love behind it. The presence of Absolute Truth within your mind will regenerate or bring forth God's Love that determines the nature of Absolute Truth. Herein is another reference to "Know the truth and the truth will set you free".

After you have become aware of the 'ringing' affect of Truth, you may notice some instances where the 'ring' is truer or feels deeper or different from other instances. Why is this ringing different?

The only thing that dampens the effect of Absolute Truth in the mortal mind/matrix vehicle is ~~truth~~. How ~~truth~~ is arranged and the type of ~~truth~~ within the mortal mind/matrix (and thought matrix that is being communicated) determines the nature of this dampening action. Conveniently, the patterns and parallels of physics to metaphysics can help clarify this dampening action.

For example: imagine you have a thin brass tube 10 inches long and 1 inch in diameter (25 cm x 2.5 cm), as in Figure 4-7.

If you hold the tube in one hand and strike it with a metallic object like a spoon, it produces a sound. The quality of the sound is dependant on where and how you hold it. If you hold the tube at the bottom, as in Figure 4-7 (*I*), the sound made will be a clunk. The resonance is minimal and striking the tube will make a dull noise.

If you hold the tube with the whole hand (Figure 4-7 [*II*]) – in the

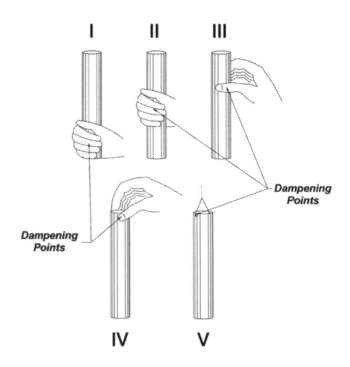

Figure 4-7, Dampening a Brass Tube

center, the result will be a clunk also, but slightly different sounding.

Hold the tube lightly, with two fingers. Hold it so; the long length on one side of the fingers is a whole number multiple of the short length (2, 3, 4, etc.) as in (Figure 4-7 [*III*]). Striking the tube like this will give a more melodious sound with harmonics.

Striking the tube, while holding it on the end (Figure 4-7 [*IV*]), will give a different sound with fewer harmonics. Put a couple of holes in the end of the brass tube and suspend it with a piece of string; then, strike it. The dampening action is minimal now. The resultant sound will be cleaner than the previous conditions, and the harmonics created will be dependent on where on the cylinder length the string is (Figure 4-7 [V].

What is happening here? The tube is a standing wave generator. It is a tuned circuit and has its own basic sound resonance frequency. That frequency is dependent on material of the tube (brass), dimensions (length, diameter, thickness), speed of sound in the material, and speed of sound in the surrounding medium (air).

Strike the tube, energy enters the tube, and is stored as a resonance. Wherever the tube is held, it will produce an attenuating or dampening action on that resonance. Holding it on the end tends to give the basic frequency, while holding anywhere else tends to produce harmonics – whole number multiples of that basic frequency. How it is held (how much of the tube material is dampened) will determine the quality of the sound; how clean it sounds.

Figure 4-7 (*I*) shows about one third of the tube material is dampened, while Figure 4-7 (*V*) shows the tube is dampened only where the string is touching the tube. The tube is dampened by a handful – compared to the total number within the tube – of molecules.

The mortal mind/matrix is like that brass tube. It resonates to Truth because Truth is at the core of the mind/matrix's existence – it is the laws by which the mind works. This is only natural; the mind has a natural resonant condition, like the tube – an energy storage condition.

This elementary mental ringing phenomenon uses the Cognitive Input. The most basic ring is consciousness. Truth and the Eternal Moment of Creation – from a temporal standpoint – is constantly exciting the mind/matrix, producing a low level of resonance or 'ring', consciousness.

The mortal human mind/matrix would naturally align to God's Truth Matrix and resonate with God itself (that is, if allowed to). What dampens this resonant action is how much ~~truth~~ is in the mortal matrix. Most of our minds/matrices are dampened so much by ~~truth~~; when truth enters, the resultant resonance is little more than a 'clunk'.

Sympathetic resonance occurs when the incoming energy has a relationship to the structure of the resonating object. The incoming energy is stored in the structure. In most cases, the wavelength has some relationship to the object's physical dimensions – length, width, thickness, etc. A 'C' tuning fork responding to a 'C' note is an excellent example of sympathetic resonance.

Sympathetic resonance of this mortal mind model involves some correlation with the incoming data to what is already in *Storage*. The resonance can be a slight 'ring' in the background or it can be a conscious altering event – depending on the dampening action, ~~truth~~.

What happens is that Truth can travel through the *Perceptual Lens Array*, through the Cognitive Input, into *Knowledge* (Figure 4-4, [*VII*]), bypassing Choice, and connects with the truth that is there. Thus, producing a sympathetic resonance of sorts -- this is the 'ringing' of the first exercise (a graphic example is Chart 4-4, *K2*).

There are many ways truth can travel through the mind/matrix as in Chart 4-4, (*I-M, 1-12*). Because, truth constitutes the very makeup of the mind. In order to simplify things, in this model, this 'ringing' effect is shown broken into five basic categories of ringing in the lower portion of Figure 4-8 (*I-V*).

In addition, in Figure 4-8 this model of the human truth mind/matrix presented is shown cross-referenced to a chakra construct – body energy center construct/model. There are many versions of the chakra construct: kundalini, raja, or hatha yoga; theosophist; Tibetan Buddhism; occult; etc. Because of this, this book will leave it up to you to do your own chakras research.

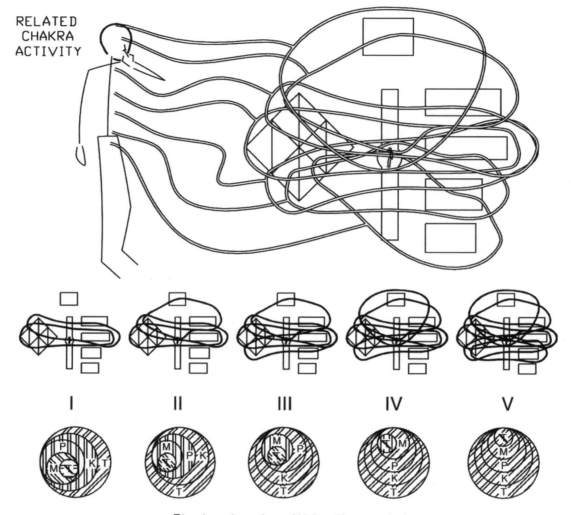

Ringing levels within the matrix

Figure 4-8, Human Matrix, Chakras, and Truth Ringing Levels

Just know that areas of this mind/matrix model ringing activity can be cross-referenced to some chakra model activity.

In the lower portion of Figure 4-8, the various ringing categories are cross-referenced to the circles within circles model presented in Figures 4-3 & 3-3, (*Life Manifesting into Physical Form and* Storage *Priorities*). The rotational alignment, circles within circles, and the circle tangency concepts of both are used again in Figure 4-8 to help illustrate the presented idea. This lower portion of Figure 4-8 shows the circles coming into a one-point tangency condition.

Here is a brief explanation of these categories or levels of ringing:

❑ The first basic category 'ring' is when a sufficient amount of truth has gone through the cognitive loop, into *Knowledge*, to facilitate recognition of symbols and forms (you know words and recognize physical matter). When an event enters the perceptual array (such as spoken truth) and whatever truth is within the words, must pass through the array. (If, focus allows it to pass through the array.) In addition, it is mixed with certain amount of ~~truth~~ (the temporal); either from within the communication (speaker) or projected on it (listener). In the process, a closed loop has formed (example Chart 4-4, *M1*).

216

This loop begins with Eternal Truth, the source of all, manifesting into physical form. The true event enters the array, usually as words or perceptions. When it is allowed to pass through the array and reaches the True point of Figure 4-4, one aspect goes directly through the cognitive loop into *Knowledge* (Figure 4-4, [*VII*]), to *Programming*, and back to us (Figure 4-4, [*I* → *III*]) in the focus buss. Along the way, this truth also is matched by truth within *Knowledge*.

At the same time, *Truth* is at the very core of our being. It directly enters *Knowledge* and it is also present with us at (*III*) of the focus control, Figure 4-4. And so, circles or feedback loops have been completed. Two continuities or reinforcements (for lack of better terms) have been established. One continuity loop exists where truth in *Knowledge* goes into physical form and back to *Knowledge* again. Another continuity loop is the truth at the core of our being, involves Cognition, *Knowledge*, *Programming*, and is in us. Whatever truth is allowed to reach us through the mind/matrix, it is matched by the Truth with in us (Chart 4-4, *A4*), acting as an amplifier or reinforcement. Truth is constantly exciting and maintaining this mortal mind system.

Remember the Truth Matrix is responsible for the Eternal Moment of Creation…us. With these feedback loops, elements of the Creation within us becomes present. We perceive or experience this as a 'ringing'.

Within the first presented category, a certain amount of ~~truth~~ also passes through the array, is chosen, and enters *Programming*. The ~~truth~~ that passes through, along with *~~Truth~~* storage, dampens this 'ringing'. This is why we can hear something and it rings true, yet we know there is something else. The combination of Truth and ~~truth~~ produces a clunk, as with the brass tube (Figure 4-7 [*I* or *II*]).

This category involves beginning metaphysical learning and a general learning operation mode of the matrix and is represented in Figure 4-8 (*I*).

❑ The second presented category shown in Figure 4-8 (*II*) is relatively similar to the first. The difference being, a significant amount of truth has been chosen already; it affects the perceptional lens focus (through *Knowledge* and *Programming*); and consequently a decrease in *~~Truth~~* storage accumulation has begun.

More truth going into *Knowledge* through Cognition (*VII*) in combination to less ~~truth~~ through the array reaches the choice, decreases the dampening action of the ~~truth~~ total and the 'ringing' is deeper. Deeper lines of communication are being constructed between Truth, *Knowledge*, and you. This basic category is equivalent to the alignment in Figure 4-8 (*II*) or Chart 4-4, *M2*.

This category involves intermediate metaphysical and spiritual learning/programming, plus beginning *ESP* phenomena. It is also in this category that some significant consciousness changes begins to occur with the 'ring'.

Because one aspect of this 'ringing' uses the high priority Cognitive Input (Figure 4-4, [*VII*]) and bypasses Choice in the *Perceptional Lens Array* (*VI*), it can have an unusual effect talked about in the first chapter. The mind is so preoccupied by this 'ringing' using the high priority Cognitive Input (*VII*) that lower priority functions, like memory, give way. This influence was introduced as the concept of agreeing with every word that was said (or read) and yet not being able to recall what was said – first exercise.

In this category, the truth ringing can produce deeper altered consciousness states and it is in this category psychic perception (*ESP*) begins to becomes a regular occurrence -- normal.

❑ The third basic category shown takes the second category the next step. After a significant amount of *Truth* is allowed to pass through the array to affect *Knowledge* and *Programming* (Figure 4-4, [*II* & *VII*]), it begins to accumulate and influence the *Programming Storage* more (which, in turn, affects the focus of the *Perceptual Lens Array* [*IV*]). When this occurs, it adds another truth continuity loop to the other two loops and affects you (Figure 4-8 [*III*]).

More *Truth* is allowed to pass through the matrix directly with less 'going around the block' (through an 'objective event'). The *Truth* within us (through *Focus Control*) matches truth

217

that comes through the array (either through the 'objective' or through 'subjective event' using Faith, *Storages*, and Cognition (*VII*)). In addition to matching the truth that is at one's disposal (through *Knowledge*), this make a three circle tangency, Figure 4-8 (*III*). *Truth* is tangent to *Knowledge* and is tangent to *Programming* at the same point. This, in conjunction with a decrease in ~~truth~~ reaching choice, causes more elements of Creation/Us to come into our awareness. We experience this as a deeper 'ringing' (Figures 4-8 [*III*] or Chart 4-4, *M3*). Notice in Chart 4-4, *M3* that the 'subjective event' and the focus loops do have a hand on focusing and allowing this to happen.

This is the category of more advanced metaphysical and spiritual learning. It is in this basic category where epiphanies are the norm, because communion with you and God has increased considerably.

Normally, we do not stay at this ringing level long. Depending on mind/matrix programming, an individual usually goes back down to a second level ring or can move on to a fourth level ring.

Please note, once a metaphysical student learns to maintain a mental/emotional or a perceptual/desire balance in this level, their spiritual growth accelerates. It is as if they are beginning to balance the Truth and ~~Truth~~ within them.

❑ The fourth basic category (Figure 4-8 [*IV*] or Chart 4-4, *M4*)) takes the third category one step further. The subject matter has transcending symbolic communication – words. In this category, the word 'ring' is very inadequate. This is a way of life, or an active participation in Creation on a regular basis here. *Truth* is passively controlling the *Perceptual Lens Array* focus (Figure 4-4, [*IV*]). This is equivalent to the 'ring' becoming a relatively constant background hum, without any objective external event to initiate it. This 'hum' can go in and out of an individual's awareness, yet it is always there, part of them.

There is an old spiritual saying, "Take one step to God and He will take three to you." The fourth basic category is a result of this saying having happened 'several times over' to the individual. A consequent permanent alteration has been made to their human mortal mind/matrix (shown in Chart 4-4, *M4* as *Knowledge's* normal line type of influence on the perceptual array being Truth's line type). Enough Truth is in the human matrix to facilitate a communion with God on a regular basis.

In this category, another continuity loop or element to the tangency has been added. It involves an increase of applications of truth within *Knowledge* -- Faith. As we assimilate and work with Truth over a period, we begin to apply it on a daily (hourly, minute to minute, etc.) basis with thought as well as deed. This application begins to bring Truth directly into the *Perceptional Lens Array.*[9] Consequently, a relatively small amount of the lesser priority ~~truth~~ passes through the array into Choice. This effect of an added level of resonance to Truth and a continuing reduction of ~~Truth~~ storage increases the effect that the Eternal Moment of Creation has on the mortal mind/matrix at that moment.

It is in this category that magic and miracles become workable.[10] It is possible to do magic from the third category 'ring', but a lot more effort is needed to produce an effect. This 'work' may be just to enter a specific consciousness state. Within the fourth category, magic begins to become more effortless, plus miracles can occur as a side effect.

On the **Individual** reality level, somewhere in this category involves the Bodhisattva Choice.[11] The individual would have to make a conscious decision to remain in physical form. Within mystical schools, this stage in individual growth has a number of references; a Bodhisattva is one. In the magic reference, it is known as the adept stage (fourth level initiate).

There is another name that is not commonly associated with this choice. After the choice, it is also known as the 'true dark night of the soul'. Why? The individual can 'see' both Heaven and earth, is able to enter both, and yet does not 'belong' to either. This dual

---

9 The line from Truth to Faith in Figure 4-4 or Chart 4-4, *A2*

10 Chapters 9 and 10,

11 The choice between merging with the Divine and leaving the body behind and that of to remain in physical form to help.

perception can lead the individual into being something equivalent to a spiritual *Steppenwolf*.[12] While the people around that person, may tend to see a saint.

Here lies a source of the 'tears' of the Bodhisattva. Another source of the Bodhisattva tears is watching (and having to allow) people create their own 'hell' with 'Heaven' eternally before them.

Fortunately or unfortunately (depending on your reference), this stage of development is rarely reached. Most people are not willing to foster the degree of selflessness and dedication necessary to reach this stage. Having tasted the 'fruits of Heaven', most people do not want to come back.

❑ The fifth category evolves from the last, and simply is: <u>no</u> ~~truth~~ passes through the perceptional array and enters *Programming*. In addition, the operator's evolution to this point has also purged most of ~~*Truth*~~ from within their storage. All, or most, of ~~truth~~ within them has been brought to Truth, Figure 4-8 (*V*).

There is a continual participation in the Eternal Moment of Creation. Miracles occur naturally without effort. That person is walking in Creation that they are and all physical creation reflects what is in their mind through the Mirror.[13] This can be referred to as the Godhead Event or a priest-king.[14]

4.9 - Conclusion

*T*his chapter threw a lot of information at you. This chapter began with the human BTR and with the realities that constitute our **Individual** reality makeup, **Absolute** Reality, **Actual** reality, **Consensual** reality, and **Imaginary** reality. This chapter introduced the temporal mind/matrix vehicle -- within the human *BTR*; the matrix's elements and its operation were given a cursory going over. Your mind is your vehicle in your body. Just as your body is your vehicle in physical existence. And…there are laws/truths to how vehicles work.

Bottom line is the more there are truth/laws of a reality within human mind/matrix vehicle; the more functional an individual becomes within that reality. The more ~~truth~~ in their choices – the less they work in the laws of a reality. The more dysfunctional they will become within that reality. This is Chapter 5 subject matter.

However, because of the nature of **Consensual** reality and **Imaginary** reality, an individual can be functional within a **Consensual** reality even though they have, generally speaking, an insignificant amount of **Actual** truth in their mind/matrix.

Conversely, Absolute Truth may make you functional in **Absolute** Reality. It also can make one dysfunctional within a **Consensual** or an **Imaginary** reality. Just because, the **Absolute** may be something that the **Consensual** or **Imaginary** reality does not recognize as real (though both must have some degree of **Absolute** and **Actual** within it in order to exist).

A problem can lie in the fact that the truths of **Absolute** Reality, **Actual**, **Individual**, **Consensual**, and **Imaginary** reality may not always <u>appear</u> compatible. For example, what man is doing with pollution to the planet -- there is a heavy discrepancy between what we say is real and what the planet is saying is real.

Other examples of this mismatching of truths to realities may be a person could be a wizard in business (a **Consensual** reality), but do not give them a screwdriver; they could maim themselves or someone else (an **Actual** reality). Or…a person could be a master craftsperson (an **Actual** reality), but take them to a bar and they are a major social embarrassment (a **Consensual** reality).[15]

This chapter concludes the third and last part of the thought construct, model, paradigm… begun in Chapter 2. The second chapter introduced God and the Loving Logical

---

12 A fiction book by Herman Hesse
13 Chapter 3
14 Chapter 10
15 "Hey Babeeee, I got something you can sit on!"

219

Mind's Creation. Chapter 2 is at the core of this thought construct -- skeleton. Chapter 3 fleshed out the implications of Chapter 2 to physical form.

Chapter 4 finishes the construct and adds a mortal mind vehicle to the form. This chapter attends to the human *BTR* and the operation of our temporal mind/matrix within the physical condition we find ourselves and is related back to information within Chapters 2 and 3.

Again, look at the paradigm presented by the three chapters as a map. A map is not the terrain. In the end, you do not need the theory of gravity to walk. You just have to know how to apply it. Maps come in handy when you get lost or are planning an itinerary. They are not considered popular literature. If maps are placed on a wall, it is for functional purposes and very seldom for aesthetic purposes.

The labs and exercises introduced in later chapters will be addressing -- some form of playing with -- this presented model of the human mind/matrix vehicle. They will have you walk some of the 'terrain' of the 'map'.

As previously stated, you may note that spiritual disciplines favor an increase in the top aspects of the *Perceptual Lens Array* and a decrease of the bottom aspects; a pattern is forming.

Later, a serious metaphysics operator – mystic -- will learn to recognize what control they have in their focusing and refocusing of their mind. When covering future labs, there will be a periodical reference back to the mental model/construct in Figure 4-4 or to Chart 4-4. These future references will show what elements of the human mind/matrix vehicle the labs are addressing.

To conclude what was covered in this chapter -- lens, storage, loops, flows, and programming patterns -- make up our mortal ego vehicle. Figure 4-4 has the ego vehicle/matrix broken down into flows, aspects, tendencies, and relationships – sub-matrices. There are the *Storages*. There is the lens array. There are choices (*VI*), which affect *Programming* (*II*), which affect *Storages*, which affect the lens (*I & IV*), which affect choices (*VI*)...etc. -- the circles, spirals, or feedback loops.

Again, it is not important to believe or remember all that this chapter previously talked about (remember the first lab assignment). You should recognize that there is some sort of focusing mechanism, some kind of storage, there is a cause and effect relationship in your perceptual lens related to what is in storage and truth, and you can exert some form of control.

You do not have to believe in or know the principles behind internal combustion engines or the basic mechanics of a car to drive. You do have to know how to steer, acceleration, braking, and the basic character of their vehicle (what it can do or what it can not do). And...you have to take the car out for a drive.

Like the car, you just need to know the basics about your mind. Perception is the view and 'steering'. Desire is the 'fuel'. Choice is the 'brake and accelerator'. The vehicle 'model' is determined by what is in *Storage*.

Applying the exercises later in this book takes your mind out of the 'garage'.

Again, a serious metaphysical/mystical/religious student should recognize that their temporal mortal mind/matrix vehicle is limited. Almost any operation performed by this vehicle is going to be temporal and finite. All growth, spiritual or otherwise, involves leaving the temporal mind/matrix as it is now behind or sublimating it to God's Eternal Matrix. It can also involve reprogramming the human mind/matrix with Truth (which again will involve the Matrix).

This process may also involve the removal of ~~truth~~ within their mind/matrix, which is also known as spiritual purification.

Our human mind/matrix is constantly producing/running; it reflects God's Matrix and Eternal Creation. We are not our temporal human mind/matrix. We are the Children/Child of an Infinite and Eternal God. Either we have to step out of our mortal mind, shut the temporal mind/matrix up, learn to ignore it, or reprogram it with Truth. In this way, we can begin to reside in the Eternal; who we really are.

Here is another tie-in to the second and third chapter, specifically, about matrices and life -- Chapter 3 talks about a proper physical matrix arrangement hosting life. (Remember life – due to its connection to the Eternal Moment of Creation and Truth – is inclusive and extends itself.) This applies to a thought matrix also. A thought is a matrix of perceptional cognitive associations. (True, this all happens literally at the 'speed of thought', and yet, within every thought there is a set of cognitive relationships.) The thought's construction and how much Truth that makes up its matrix relationship determines how much life is in that thought.

The opposite is also true. How much ~~truth~~ within a thought determines how much life is absent.

A general rule of thumb is: if a thought is non-exclusive and extends itself, it has life. If a thought is exclusive or divisive, it is un-living.

Using this concept, this book can help you to foster living thoughts of a living God and show how to reduce un-living thoughts within your mind/matrix (and their effects). This is a way we can step out of the limits imposed by our limited temporal/spatial 'mortal' mind.

The last thing to touch on in this chapter is a continuation of the patterns and parallels to two ideas that were introduced in earlier chapters (independent/dependent and the 3-in-1 1-in-3).

The first involves the relationship between two concepts -- one concept is independent, while the other concept is dependent. A partial list of what already has been covered is:

❖ God's Love can exist without His Logic, but His Logic cannot exist without His Love.
❖ Real numbers can exist without imaginary numbers, but imaginary numbers cannot exist without real numbers.
❖ **Absolute** Reality can exist without **Actual** reality, but **Actual** reality cannot exist without **Absolute** Reality.

Paralleled into Chapter 4's mortal mind model, add to this list:

❖ Perception can exist without desire, but desire cannot exist without perception.
❖ Cognition can exist without habit, but habit cannot exist without cognition.

In addition, incorporate the 3-in-1 1-in-3 concept manifesting in parallels; 2 determines the nature of 3 while 3 regenerates 2:

❖ God's Love determines the nature of God's Logic, while God's Logic regenerates God's Love.
❖ God's Truth Matrix determines the nature of Creation, while Creation regenerates the Truth Matrix.

Add Chapters 3 and 4 concepts to this and:

❖ A matrix determines the nature of a *BTR*, while a *BTR* regenerates a matrix.
❖ Perception determines the nature of a desire, while desire regenerates perception.
❖ *Storage* determines the nature of the *Perceptual Lens* (*I* & *IV*), while the *Perceptual Lens* regenerates *Storage* (*II* & *VII*).
❖ *Knowledge* determines the nature of *Programming*, while *Programming* regenerates *Knowledge*.
❖ *Programming* determines the nature of *Memory*, while *Memory* regenerates *Programming*.
❖ The 'truth' of an ~~truth~~ determines the nature of the ~~truth~~, while the ~~truth~~ regenerates the 'truth' of the ~~truth~~.

4.10 Questions

1) Desires and emotions are one with what in the *Perceptional Lens Array*?

2) The 'back of the mind' consists of _____.

3) The human *BTR* contains a what kind of mind?

4) What reality is the human *BTR* primarily concerned with?

5) Perceptions enter *Programming* directly through _____.

6) You are not your _____.

7) What is the mind and the *Perceptional Lens Array* analogous to?

8) What example is used to show the power of imagination?

9) Faith is _____.

10) Beliefs are the result of what other elements in the *Perceptional Lens Array*?

11) What function(s) does the cognitive loop serve?

12) Who controls focus?

13) What reality are all the others dependent on?

14) What are the four limits of our visual perceptional window?

15) The 'front of the mind' consists of what elements?

16) Forgiveness plays what role?

17) What are the five realities?

18) The mortal mind is a reflection or a limited copy of _____.

19) For every thought that we have, what are our options?

Chapter 5

Formula of Effectiveness and Motivational Analysis

5.1 - What is a Formula?

Chapter 2 introduced a set of postulates and theorems. Some theorems were composed from the postulates. Other theorems -- symbolic references to the relationships between the introduced qualities -- are composed of the previous postulates and the previous presented theorems. What does this all mean?

Remember that a postulate is, given a set of conditions, a readily observable perception that can neither be proved nor disproved. Chapter 2 showed the relationship of postulates to theorems and theorem creation. That chapter introduced the idea that *1* is a postulated concept and that *1 + 1 = 2* is a theorem.

The postulates introduced in Chapter 2 are applicable to **Absolute** Reality. **Actual** reality has postulates also. Science is based on postulated (observable) concepts.

These postulates represent apparent physical characteristics and some are:

- Time
- Space
- Mass
- Energy, Etc

A number of 'labels' can represent **Actual** reality postulated qualities. For example:

- Time → hours, minutes, seconds, etc.
- Space → meters, feet, cubic feet, light years, etc.
- Mass → pounds, grams, tons, etc.
- Energy → ergs, joules, kilotons of TNT, etc.

We know **Actual** reality theorems of science as formulas. A formula shows the relationships of postulated ideas (and proven theorized ideas). They start with logically proposing another provable -- through the proposed postulated qualities -- characteristic that consists of a distinct relationship between the postulated qualities. An example is the formula for velocity: velocity = distance/a unit of time. The new label is velocity and it is comprised of a relationship between two postulated labels, distance/space divided by time. Some examples of **Actual** reality theorems are:

- Velocity = Δdistance /Δtime, ($V = s\,/t$) [Δ means 'a change of']
- Acceleration = Δvelocity /Δtime, ($A = s\,/t^2$)
- Force = mass x acceleration, ($F = ma$)
- Pressure = Force /square area ($P = f\,/s^2$)
- Energy = mass x (light velocity)^2, ($E = mc^2$)

Notice how a label can contain other labels. For example, speed or velocity being expressed as one label – distance/linear space per another label unit of time -- miles/hour, feet/second, kilometers/hour, etc. Though they are labels for the same concept (movement through space), a foot is not a mile, nor is a mile a kilometer.

There are even basic conversion formulas/theorems, which show the relationship of various labels for the same quality. Some examples are:

- 1 mile = 5,280 feet: a number (1) of label (x miles) is the same as a number (5,280) of label (y feet).
- 1 kilometer = .62 miles: a number (1) of label (x kilometer) is the same as a number (.62) of another label (y miles).
- 1 kilogram = 2.2 pounds

Keeping with the matrix within matrix, *BTR* within *BTR*, truth within truth, etc. idea, it can be seen that there are labels within labels, and even formulas within formulas. Velocity (a label and a formula) is the relationship of two labels (distance per unit of time). Distance can be expressed in a number of different labels and so can time. In turn, acceleration (another label and formula) is the relationship of label/formula of velocity (feet per second) to time again (feet per second per second).

A common perception of a formula is a string of numbers that 'mean something'. Remember Chapter 1 and Pythagoras; everything can be expressed in number. A number by itself is meaningless other than being that number. You can say, "I have 5". But, you have 5 what? Five feet? Five seconds? Five doughnuts? Five eyes? Etc. It is the labels, which the numbers represent, that give the numbers meaning in **Actual** reality.

With a formula, it is the labels that the numbers represent that are the primary concern (and must match); the numbers themselves come afterward. Numbers and math's logic formula help illustrate the labels' relationships. Once the labels' relationships are straight, plugging in the numbers representative of the labels gives the answer. However, for a formula to work, the labels must match first.

Because labels can be expressed in numbers, they are subject to the logic of numbers. It is possible then to juggle the labels as if they were numbers <u>without actually knowing what the numbers are</u>. This is what basic algebra is all about. It is manipulating labels for numbers, according to the logic of numbers, without having to know the numbers themselves.

Another beauty of mathematics is the labeled numbers can represent infinities; and yet, the infinities can be juggled without knowing every number. Again, this makes mathematical logic the prime candidate for logically dealing with spiritual, metaphysical, or the Divine. Mathematical logic is used to having to deal with infinities, within infinities, within infinities…

Science books contain formulas illustrating **Actual** reality relationships. *I AM A I*, being a science book, has a formula as well.[16] This chapter's formula illustrates the relationships of the mind's elements introduced in Chapter 4.

Chapters 2 through 4 generated a mental construct/model – a paradigm. The previous chapter proposed that for any given reality/event the more truth within a mind that is immersed in that event, the more effective that mind would be in that event. Or…the more you work within the laws of a circumstance the more effective you will be in that circumstance.

---

16 The author thinks it is in the contract somewhere, "Science books must contain formulas."

This chapter takes this idea and some of the labels introduced in Chapter 4, treats their truth/law quantities as if they were numbers, and using relationships and mathematical logic, assembles them into a formula. This chapter concerns itself with general usage of the previously introduced mortal mind model through a Formula of Effectiveness.

Although the material of this chapter is in reference to metaphysical subject matter, the resultant formula is applicable to almost everything we do in our daily lives. People who do not like or understand math may hate this chapter (again). Therefore, the subject matter will be kept as short and as relatively 'painless' as possible.

5.2 - Focus over a Change of Time ($f / \Delta t$)

*I*n Chapter 4, the *Focus Control Buss* was introduced. It was stressed how we control our matrix/mind operation from this area. What is focus and what does it mean? Our focus is essentially what truth and ~~truth~~ is engaged in the mortal mind matrix at any given moment of time. This means:

❑ It was stated that the more you work in Truth the more effective you will be, because you are working in with the laws of the event. This is a <u>direct relationship</u> in math; an increase of one generates an increase in the other.

❑ Conversely, the more ~~truth~~ you work with the less effective you will be, because you are not working with the laws of the event. This is an <u>inverse relationship</u> in math; an increase of one generates a decrease in the other.

Truth has a direct relationship to effectiveness ($E : T$) and ~~truth~~ has an inverse relationship to effectiveness ($E : 1/\cancel{T}$). Given, your focus is whatever truth and ~~truth~~ are in your mind at any moment; your mind's focus can be expressed as it is in Figure 5-2, *1a*:

$$f = \left(\frac{T}{\cancel{T}} \right)$$

Figure 5-2, *1(c-e)* shows a relationship between time, focus, and effectiveness. How long you focus through a time period, is expressed as focus (f) to change of time (Δt). Effectiveness (E) is expressed as directly proportional to focus over change of time ($1\Delta t$). The longer the focus is on an event within a change of time, can increase a person's effectiveness. The less a person focuses over change of time, the less effective they will be. This is another

$$f(\ t\ ) : \ E$$

$$f(\ t\ ) : \ E$$

direct relationship:

A reminder is these elements are just being broken into direct and inverse relationships.

Now, what if your focus remains the same and your change of time varies? It is a summation -- total. It is accumulative, and if the time of focus is broken up, the mental matrix/construct – thought system -- that you are using can be forgotten when you are not using it. You may have to go back and pick up the 'loose ends'. It can be likened to your having stopped knitting a sweater. When you pick it up again, you have to remember how you started and the stitch you were using; how many stitches and rows are in the pattern and everything like that. Therefore, it is not the most effective way to do it, and it can be done that way.

The effect of focus over time tends to be accumulative. That is why for some people it may take years to finish a masterpiece; they kept returning to that one point focus. They maintained a focus on what they wanted to do.[17]

Focus is a one-point:[18] focus on what you want, on what you are going to do, focus on the event you are immersed in, or an event you wish to occur. This is similar to constructing a building. In that example, the effectiveness in the event is the completion and the quality of the building. In order for this to occur, a one-point focus had to be maintained.[19]

Within a one-point focus over a change of time, the longer your focus has T ($Truth$) within it over change of time, the more effective you become. As the change of time decreases, effectiveness will decrease. If you do not put much time into it and what truth you are using is limited, you are not going to be that effective. With the time element, energy becomes dispersed.

Conversely, if $\cancel{T}$ ($\cancel{truth}$) starts becoming a large significant number and T ($Truth$) becomes a small number, then the more you focus over time, the less effective you will become. That is because the mind/matrix is preoccupied with truths not relevant to the event. This shows focus involves the quantities/qualities of both.

Your focus is what your matrix/mind is occupying itself with. In this chapter, it will be expressed in the relationships of Chapter 4 elements with the labels in Figures 5-1 and 5-2: T_S (total $Knowledge$), P_S, (Perceptions total) C_S (Choice total), D_S (total Desires), or A_S (total Attachments). How these labels are put together will be gone into a bit more with the next sections. All of these labels help define our focus.

Note: The change of time (Δt) presented in this formula can be, dependant on the formula use, relevant to a particular task or it can be relevant to your whole life. It can pertain to long-term focus or short-term focus. In many cases, a long-term focus helps define the nature of the short-term focus (and it can go the other direction as well).

5.3 - Algebraic Manipulation of Questionable Values

$\mathcal{T}$his book's construction of a Formula of Effectiveness is referenced to how the individual's interactions relate with an external/internal event, their participation in Absolute Truth, how they respond, and their effectiveness of response. Effectiveness is really, how much creative energy is flowing through the individual.

You have at this very instant the Eternal Moment of Creation[20] within you. So, in the end, this Formula of Effectiveness is actually how much you are going to allow Creation to affect your life and what effect you have (or how much of the Eternal Moment of Creation is coming through you); how you affect the world of form around you.

This Formula of Effectiveness is for everything, not just for meditation, mysticism, and metaphysics. How the individual looks at the world and how they affect everything in it is applicable. How well one functions in the **Absolute** and **Actual** realities. It also can apply to **Individual**, **Consensual**, and **Imaginary** realities depending on what truths/laws are being applied.[21]

---

17 Old saying: The sign of being a 'master artist' is knowing when the work is done.
18 See Chapter 6
19 True, focus has to be moved or split from each aspect of construction of the structure: foundation, carpentry, plumbing, electrical, etc. All these ancillary focuses fit within a primary focus to build the structure.
20 Chapter 2.6, *Postulate 5* and theorems
21 A reality is composed of a matrix of laws or truths: Chapters 2, 3, and 4.

Ironically, because the formula represents an effectiveness interface and because of the Mirror and it is an equation, the formula can work in the other direction also. That is, the formula can also become a reference to how much an external event affects you.

First to look at is the label relationships for a very basic formula and then to break those labels into some of their constituent labels. The T/~~T~~ ratio was introduced, so to begin with, there is:

Now since anything we do in **Actual**, **Individual**, **Consensual**, and **Imaginary** realities involves the Mirror[22] introduced in Chapter 3, our effectiveness will be related to the ratio of Truth to ~~Truth~~ (T/~~T~~) plugged into the Mirror function.[23] Whatever we do will be reflected back on us either to help us (amplify) or work against (attenuate). The letter M represents this. In addition, the change of time mentioned previously (Δt) must be taken into account. These elements can be assembled and expressed in a basic formula as:

To help generate a complex formula, the basic T/~~T~~ labels can be broken in to some of its constituent element labels within the human matrix model presented in Chapter 4. For example, specific labels that have been presented so far are:

$$E = M \left(\frac{T}{\cancel{T}} \right) \, t$$

☐ *Truth* (T) – *Postulates 4, 5, 6, + 7 and theorems (A core element of Storage, which supports and is behind the existence of everything – all realities).* Chart 4-4, *A3*

☐ ~~*Truth*~~ (~~T~~) – *Postulate 7 and theorems (Another basic element of Storage that influences* **Individual**, **Consensual**, and **Imaginary** realities. In addition, to some extent, has an indirect affect on *Knowledge*). Chart 4-4, *A18*

☐ Total *Knowledge* or *Knowledge* summation (T_s) – Truth's and the 'truths' that sustain the ~~truth~~. **Actual** reality's representative in *Storage* and has priority over *Programming* and *Memory* (**Individual**, **Consensual**, and **Imaginary** realities). Chart 4-4, *B1*

These labels begin to outline *Storage*'s influence within the formula. *Truth* and ~~*Truth*~~ must be present from the postulates and theorems of Chapter 2. In addition, *Truth's* representative – *Knowledge* -- must be included for an **Actual** reality condition, which we commonly associated as 'reality'.

Next is to define the labels that determine what comes into *Storage* through the *Perceptional Lens Array* and how that array is focused (Chart 4-4, *D3*). The critical vertices mentioned in Chapter 4 are:

Perception – The 'image' of something generated by the physical senses or a 'subjective event'. Half of the front part of the *Perceptional Lens Array* -- lens. Perception opens the lens to distance, away from self.

Desires – A perception of a missing element or a missing perception in that 'image' along with an urge to 'correct' that missing element. The other half of the front part of the *Perceptional Lens Array* -- lens. Desires brings the lens up close, towards self

---

22 The Mirror being the Correction and a very special case of the Truth Matrix -- God, is the Eternal to temporal interface. Everything we see, know, feel, etc. is a function of the mirror. At the same time, all metaphysical laws that relate to physical form are a function of the mirror.

23 A math function is a predetermined math operation. For example, let's say we have function f. Let's also say function f = $2a^2 + 3$. So any number x plugged into function f will equal $2x^2 + 3$. This is expressed as f(x) or f of x.

Figure 5-1, Algebraic Quantities

ATTACHMENTS

$$A_S = A_{T_p} + A_{\overline{T}_p}$$
$$A_{T_p} = A_S - A_{\overline{T}_p}$$
$$A_{\overline{T}_p} = A_S - A_{T_p}$$

$A_S =$ Summation of Attachments - total
$A_{T_p} =$ Attachments to Truth perceived
$A_{\overline{T}_p} =$ Attachments to untruth perceived

DESIRES

$$D_S = D_{T_p} + D_{\overline{T}_p}$$
$$D_{T_p} = D_S - D_{\overline{T}_p}$$
$$D_{\overline{T}_p} = D_S - D_{T_p}$$

$D_S =$ Total (summation) desires
$D_{T_p} =$ Desires of Truth perceived
$D_{\overline{T}_p} =$ Desires of untruth perceived

PERCEPTIONS

$$P_S = T_p + \overline{T}_p$$
$$T_p = P_S - \overline{T}_p$$
$$\overline{T}_p = P_S - T_p$$

$P_S =$ Total (summation) perceptions
$T_p =$ Truth perceived
$\overline{T}_p =$ Untruth perceived

KNOWLEDGE

$$T_S = T_K + \overline{T}_K$$
$$T_K = T_S - \overline{T}_K$$
$$\overline{T}_K = T_S - T_K$$

$T_S =$ Knowledge Total (summation)
$T_K =$ Truth Known
$\overline{T}_K =$ Untruth Known (truth of the untruth)

These shitty values bug me.

CHOICE

$$C_S = T_C + \overline{T}_C$$
$$T_C = C_S - \overline{T}_C$$
$$\overline{T}_C = C_S - T_C$$

$C_S =$ Summation of Choices - total
$T_C =$ Truth Chosen
$\overline{T}_C =$ Untruth Chosen

Attachments – ~~Truth~~'s representative in the *Perceptional Lens Array* along with a record of previously established Desire/Perception patterns, ~~truth~~ applications – one part of the aperture. This closes the aperture.

Faith – *Truth*'s representative in the *Perceptional Lens Array* as well as being truth applications – the other part of the aperture. Faith opens the aperture.

The last label to be mentioned is that which connects the *Perceptional Lens Array* to *Storage*. The Cognitive Input (Figure 4-4, *VII*) can be predominantly ignored here because it is automatic and is predetermined by the four just mentioned. The one we have immediate control over is:

Choice – The major programming influence into *Storage* from the *Perceptional Lens Array*. Choice (Figure 4-4, *II*) is a completion of a major programming loop (*Storage* to *the Perceptional Lens Array* back to *Storage*. Chart 4-4, *B6* – shutter.

As mentioned before (and will be stressed again), the more truth involved within your actions, the more effective those actions will be. The more ~~truth~~ in your actions, the more ineffectual you will be. This comes from the simple definition of truth, "laws by which something works". Whatever reality/s you are working in, the more you work in the laws of those reality/s, the more effective you will tend to be in those reality/s.

All of the labels to be covered represent aspects of these two elements -- truth and ~~truth~~. Let us deal with some simple relationships within the presented mind labels, through these two elements.

Figure 5-1 shows relationships of parts to totals using labels of the human matrix, such as the relationship of total perceptions (P_S) to truth perceived (T_P) and ~~truth~~ perceived ($\mathcal{T}_P$), or knowledge total (T_S) to truth known (T_K) and ~~truth~~ known ($\mathcal{T}_K$)[24]. Using these elements of Figure 5-1, and direct or inverse relationships, Figure 5-2 assembles a formula. Let us look at Figure 5-1 and some simple relationships of parts, to wholes.

Total knowledge (T_S) contains not only how much truth known (T_K), but also how much ~~truth~~ you know ($\mathcal{T}_K$) which, is the 'truth' that sustains ~~truth~~. What does this mean? In the perception of any given event, how much and what truth applications within *Knowledge* you have, is going to be a major influence to your effectiveness.

Knowledge total is expressed as Truth summation (T_S). This refers to the total truths known by you that make up the event.[25] T_S is going to be equal to the truth that you know (T_K) that makes up the event, plus the ~~truth~~ you know ($\mathcal{T}_K$) that makes up the event. This is expressed in Figure 5-1 as $T_S = T_K + \mathcal{T}_K$. Therefore, the total knowledge relative to an event is the truth you know plus the ~~truth~~ you know -- which is common sense.

KNOWLEDGE

$$T_S = T_K + \mathcal{T}_K \qquad T_S = \text{Knowledge Total (summation)}$$
$$T_K = T_S - \mathcal{T}_K \qquad T_K = \text{Truth Known}$$
$$\mathcal{T}_K = T_S - T_K \qquad \mathcal{T}_K = \text{Untruth Known (truth of the untruth)}$$

---

24 The 'truth' applications that sustains truth and enter *Knowledge* through the Cognitive input.

25 There may be truths you do not know that make up an event, also. This would reflect in the 'numeric' quantity of *Knowledge*.

Doing some algebraic juggling or playing with this formula, we can say that the truth that you know (T_K) is equal to the total knowledge summation (T_S) minus the ~~truth~~ you know ($\not{T}_K$). We started with $T_S = T_K + \not{T}_K$. Flipping it around, algebraically, we can say $T_K = T_S - \not{T}_K$.

Taking this the next step further we can say $\not{T}_K = T_S - T_K$. This simply states the ~~truth~~ we know ($\not{T}_K$) equals the total knowledge of an event (T_S) minus the truth we know of the event (T_K).

These are showing some basic relationships here and demonstrating how these labels can be mathematically manipulated.

This algebraic dance was done around *Knowledge* storage, the truth, and ~~truth~~ known and the same thing can be done around the elements within the perceptual lens. The total perceptions (P_S) that you have, in relationship to an event, equals the truth perceived (T_P) plus the ~~truth~~ perceived ($\not{T}_P$) related to that event: $P_S = T_P + \not{T}_P$.

PERCEPTIONS

$$P_S = T_P + \not{T}_P \qquad P_S = \text{Total (summation) perceptions}$$
$$T_P = P_S - \not{T}_P \qquad T_P = \text{Truth perceived}$$
$$\not{T}_P = P_S - T_P \qquad \not{T}_P = \text{Untruth perceived}$$

Now, let us play around with this as we did with the last one, and we get the truth perceived (T_P) equals total perception (P_S) minus the ~~truth~~ that you perceive ($\not{T}_P$): $T_P = P_S - \not{T}_P$. Bringing this back full circle, the ~~truth~~ that you perceive ($\not{T}_P$) equals total perceptions (P_S) minus the truth that you perceive (T_P): $\not{T}_P = P_S - T_P$.

A reminder, the idea is to introduce you some very straightforward algebraic relationships here. To introduce, what is considered to us, as humans, some very abstract terms that can be expressed in an algebraically relationship to each other.

CHOICE

$$C_S = T_C + \not{T}_C \qquad C_S = \text{Summation of Choices - total}$$
$$T_C = C_S - \not{T}_C \qquad T_C = \text{Truth Chosen}$$
$$\not{T}_C = C_S - T_C \qquad \not{T}_C = \text{Untruth Chosen}$$

Figure 5-1 shows summation of choice (total choice = C_S) also broken into two components. The two components are truth chosen (T_C) and ~~truth~~ chosen ($\not{T}_C$). As with the associations of T_S to T_K, the figure shows C_S relationships. There is not only $C_S = T_C + \not{T}_C$, but also $T_C = C_S - \not{T}_C$ and $\not{T}_C = C_S - T_C$.

ATTACHMENTS

$$A_S = A_{T_P} + A_{\not{T}_P} \qquad A_S = \text{Summation of Attachments - total}$$
$$A_{T_P} = A_S - A_{\not{T}_P} \qquad A_{T_P} = \text{Attachments to Truth perceived}$$
$$A_{\not{T}_P} = A_S - A_{T_P} \qquad A_{\not{T}_P} = \text{Attachments to untruth perceived}$$

As was done with the others, Attachments can be similarly looked at. Examining attachments, there are total attachments (A_S) equals attachments to the truth that we perceive (A_{Tp}) in addition to our attachments to the ~~truth~~ that we perceive ($A_{\mathcal{F}p}$). Again, it is a very simple relationship: $A_S = A_{Tp} + A_{\mathcal{F}p}$.

When we can play with this, as was done previously, we get attachments to the truth perceived (A_{Tp}), equals attachments to the total (A_S), minus attachments to the ~~truth~~ we perceive ($A_{\mathcal{F}p}$): $A_{Tp} = A_S - A_{\mathcal{F}p}$. Once more, we do a little juggling; and we get: attachments to ~~truth~~ perceived (A_{Tp}) equals attachments total (A_S) minus attachments to the truth we perceive (A_{Tp}): $A_{\mathcal{F}p} = A_S - A_{Tp}$.

Stepping away from the math logic for a moment, what does this attachment concept mean in real life?

In our lives, we have a total number of attachments related to our perceptions. For example, you can have attachments to what you are doing and related subjects. Examples of Attachments total are having an attachment for tobacco, or chocolate, or a person, or a feeling for a person, a lifestyle, etc. All these attachments have an influence on the choices we make and how we act towards any given event.

This is illustrated by a little child doing a 'sleepover' at some other child's house, but not wanting to do it without 'blankey' – their blanket. That is an attachment and affects the nature of the event (the pajama party).

The last element to be looked at is desires. As we did with T_S, P_S, C_S, and A_S, our desires total (D_S) equals desires of the truth that we perceive (D_{Tp}) and the desires for the ~~truth~~ that we perceive ($D_{\mathcal{F}p}$): $D_S = D_{Tp} + D_{\mathcal{F}p}$. If we play with this formula, as we did with the others,

DESIRES

$$D_S = D_{T_p} + D_{\mathcal{F}_p} \qquad D_S = \text{Total (summation) desires}$$
$$D_{T_p} = D_S - D_{\mathcal{F}_p} \qquad D_{T_p} = \text{Desires of Truth perceived}$$
$$D_{\mathcal{F}_p} = D_S - D_{T_p} \qquad D_{\mathcal{F}_p} = \text{Desires of untruth perceived}$$

we can say desires for the truth we perceive (D_{Tp}) equals desires total (D_S) minus desires for the ~~truth~~ we perceive ($D_{\mathcal{F}p}$): $D_{Tp} = D_S - D_{\mathcal{F}p}$. Flip it around again and desires for the ~~truth~~ within us ($D_{\mathcal{F}p}$) equals desires total (D_S) minus desires of the truth we perceive (D_{Tp}): $D_{\mathcal{F}p} = D_S - D_{Tp}$.

How do these labels of T_S, P_S, C_S, D_S, and A_S relate to the labels of T and $\mathcal{F}$ that was presented earlier? It can be seen that T (*Truth*) is reflected in our mind/matrix by T_K, P_S, D_{Tp}, and T_C. While, $\mathcal{F}_K$, $\mathcal{F}_P$, $\mathcal{F}_C$, D_S, and A_S reflect $\mathcal{F}$ (*~~Truth~~*) in our mind/matrix. These relationships will be examined in the next section.

The reason these relationships need to be covered is to build a formula that will reflect effectiveness of our actions. In later chapters, the book will show you what parts of the perceptual lens/mind are involved when doing exercises and will show how the lens parts relationships are interacting, influencing effectiveness.

Later exercises will also be preceded by an examination or pre-forming intent, which consequently, predetermines some of these variables. The exercises themselves will work to shut the lens array down, preoccupy it, using the system to jump out of the lens, or to refocus the lens to allow more energy/information through it.[26]

---

26 Chapters 6, 7 and 8

5.4 - Formula Construction

U p to this section, this chapter covered what makes up the quantities for the formula, as in Figure 5-1. Next is to assemble the relationships of some of these quantities so they relate to effectiveness (Figure 5-2).

As mentioned in the previous section, within the basic formula of Figure 5-2, the labels of *Truth* and ~~*Truth*~~ need to be defined within the mind/matrix labels. What makes up the truth within our mind/matrix and what constitutes having ~~truth~~ within our mind/matrix?

Remember that your effectiveness is in fact how much you let the Truth come through in what you do. Effectiveness is how the Creative energy flows within you and effects a situation or an event. Creative energy comes from God and the Matrix of the original postulates and theorems.

First, let us look at some basic relationships and how they relate to effectiveness. Figure 5-2, Part 2 helps illustrates this by showing the direct and inverse relationships.

Storages define and focus the *Perceptual Lens Array*, so the basis of the formula will be the controlling *Storages*, ~~*Truth*,~~ and *Knowledge*. How much truth we know (T_K) versus how much 'truth' we know that sustains ~~truth~~ ($\cancel{T}_K$) will be at the core of the formula.

Notice how much truth in knowledge (T_K) is shown as direct relationship [the more truth known relating to the event (T_K) the greater the effectiveness you will have on an event].

In addition, how total your perception (P_S) is has a direct relationship. It is a direct relationship in that, as the truth that you perceive increases, your effectiveness increases. In addition, total perception can regulate the 'truth' that sustains the ~~truth~~ to the special case that it is.

Conversely, Figure 5-2, Part 2 also shows the mentioned inverse relationship to effectiveness with ~~truth~~ perceived ($\cancel{T}_P$) and ~~truth~~ known ($\cancel{T}_K$) – 'truth' that sustains ~~truth~~.

The previous chapter introduces a relationship between attachments and previous desires. Attachments tend to be a repeated pattern of desires/perceptions and we start becoming attached – work -- in these patterns of desires/perceptions. These include long-term desires or short-term desires.

Because Desire and Attachment vertices in the *Perceptual Lens Array* tend to be influenced by *Memory* and

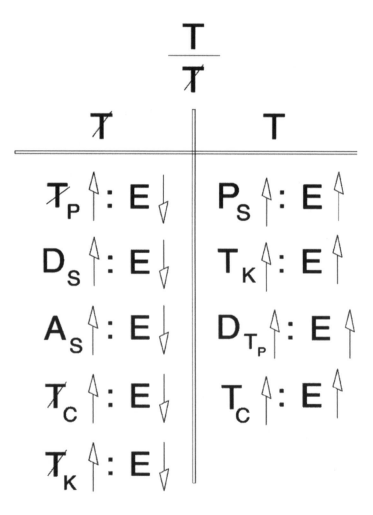

Figure 5-2, Part *2* Direct and Inverse Relationships

232

~~Truth~~ in *Storage*, then Desire and Attachment -- with a couple exceptions -- tend to work against you. First, the Desire element, then the Attachment element will be looked at.

Remember that there is a relationship between desires/emotions and perceptions/thought; perceptions and desires are really one thing.[27] The more desires, the more the perceptions that are related to those desires. The more desire/perception patterns from previous choices, the more we tend to inhibit what we are actually seeing now. Simply because, you are 'looking' at something that may not be relevant to the present event.

With total desires (and their resultant perceptions), there can be another inverse relationship to effectiveness. What is represented here is a total number of desires (D_S) over a change of time (Δt). (As mentioned earlier, all of these relationships are in reference to a change of time.)

Say a change of time is one ten-minute period. You may want one thing one moment of time in that ten minute period, then another thing the next moment of time, another the next, etc.

For example, you are working at the office. One desire you may have is to complete the work you are doing. There is something not clear with the work, so the next desire may be for clarity, and the next may be to talk to somebody to reach clarity. A later desire may be you want to go home, or have a break, or the person next to you draws your interest sexually.

You have a total number of desires that are happening within that block of time. That is what D_S is -- total desires over a change of time. As mentioned earlier, a multitude of desire summations (D_S) tends to have an inverse relationship to effectiveness. That means, as total desires increase, effectiveness decreases.

However, this occurs in a different way than attachments. The model being presented shows all attachments (with one exception) work against you, but not all desires work against you. Because -- for reasons covered in a later section -- you want desires for the truth we perceive (D_{Tp}) to be at least one, and desires for the ~~truth~~ perceive ($D_{\overline{T}p}$) one or less (preferably 0).

Technically, desires summation (D_S) – for mundane applications -- can never be zero. Because, if desires ever become 0, you will have no desire to be effective. You will do nothing. That means desires for truth perceived (D_{Tp}) is a direct relationship.

This relationship can be looked at in different ways. If you are an artist (a painter), you have an idea of a 'something' you want to do. You may have the picture represented through the body (with sketches – truth application within **Actual** reality), and then your mind's eye lens starts working the idea to bring the picture into color and form. As you are doing this, you are making constant perceptions and judgments on those perceptions, "Oh, I want red here. I don't want this line." When you go from Truth to manipulation of form and matter, there is a constant perception/desire flow happening. The long-term desire may be to want to create. While, the short-term desires inside the 'wanting to create' may involve details like form and color.

As mentioned before, as total desires decrease, your effectiveness will increase – an inverse relationship. While desire for truth perceived (D_{Tp}), is a direct relationship.[28]

Both of these Desire inverse and direct relationships are shown in Figure 5-2, Part 2.

The next relationship to effectiveness to look at is Attachments. The relationship of total attachments (A_S) to effectiveness is shown as an inverse relationship in Figure 5-2 Part 2. The total attachments you have over a change over time (Δt), the less effective you become. How do we know this?

First off, these are repeated observations made long ago in a multitude of disciplines. The Bhagavad-Gita,[29] the Buddha, The Bible,[30] and the Upanishads mention non-attachment.

---

27 Chapter 4.5 The *Perceptional Lens Array* Matrix

28 Remember that Truth is *1* and ∞, infinite.

29 Basic theme of the '*Gita*': Whatever you do to be in union with God and doing it with no attachment to outcome, only this is karma-less. All other actions generate karma.

This non-attachment theme is ancient. It is so old it is ridiculous. Many spiritual teachings work with this concept, this non-attached state.

This old theme of non-attachment works into the effectiveness formula, and will become a relatively important variable as (A_S).

In 'real life', non-attachment becomes relevant because, <u>our effectiveness – in any situation – is inversely proportional to our attachment to the outcome.</u> This is an old metaphysical axiom and applies with everything we do. Simply because, you have an expected outcome that you try to make happen instead of working with the event as it is now.

With attachments, you are limiting your options. You are doing all kinds of things. Attachments are patterns of desires we have chosen. With those desires come the thoughts and perceptions associated with the desires usually taking up space and 'cluttering up' the mind/matrix in the 'now'. This flow of information will tend to accumulate a larger amount of ~~truth~~ being chosen.

Your temporal mind is limited. It can only hold so much and focus has limits. With attachments, you have created an interference, of a sort, of other unrelated perception/desire sets flowing through you; splitting your focus.

Please notice; the top half and the bottom half of the human matrix (Figure 4-4) is appearing to have polar qualities, regarding effectiveness. Also notice; that the two vertices at the bottom of Figure 4-4 -- Desires and Attachment – tend to have an inverse relationship to your effectiveness.

The last set of relationships to look at in Figure 5-2, Part *2* is easy to understand. They are truth chosen (T_C) and ~~truth~~ chosen ($\overline{T}_C$). These two are like the other variables. The more truth chosen (T_C) passing through the mortal mind's lens is a direct relationship and will increase effectiveness, while the more ~~truth~~ chosen ($\overline{T}_C$) would be an inverse relationship and will decrease effectiveness.

Next is to assemble all these relationships into a formula. Figure 5-2 (*2 & 4 a-m*) illustrates the direct and inverse relationships and how they can fit together. How much truth we know (T_K) reflects how much *Truth* is in the matrix and therefore is placed in the numerator because it will aid us. While how much ~~truth~~ we know ($\overline{T}_K$) reflects how much ~~truth~~ is in the matrix and is reflected in the denominator, and will work against us. Both of these expressions [(T_K) and ($\overline{T}_K$)] are shown at the core of the *T/T̶* expression.

Now, to review the relationship total perceptions (P_S) and ~~truth~~ perceived ($\overline{T}_P$) to effectiveness (E). Total perceptions (P_S) is shown as having a direct relationship to *Truth* in the mind matrix [Figure 5-2, (*4j*)]. As total perceptions increases, *Truth* increases (all other variables being ignored). This will put total perceptions in the numerator of this formula.[31] At the same time, because total perceptions (P_S) augments/magnify the base number [truth known (T_K)]; total perceptions (P_S) is shown having an exponential relationship to truth known (T_K) as in Figure 5-2, (*4o*):

$$T : \left(T_K\right)^{P_S}$$

The two combined are shown as an exponential expression[32] for a number of reasons. One is what happens when numerical values (both exponential and base numbers) fall into the zero to one range. This will be touched upon later in this chapter.

Another reason is that matter and Life occupy space and extends exponentially. An example is volume of a three dimensional space. A cube of *x* dimensions has a volume of x^3.

---

30 Christian: "Be in the world, but not of it" or "In the eyes of a child…", Jesus.

31 Total perceptions does not exclude truth perceived.

32 As opposed to multiplication T_P x T_C, or addition $T_P + T_C$

Double the side of the cube $2 \times (x)$ and the volume is $[2 \times (x)]^3$. Doubling the size of a cube multiplies the volume of the cube by 8.

In keeping with simple statistical records of life operating and extending itself exponentially, the choice is the author's to represent P_S to T_K, relationship exponentially. Whatever total perceptions (P_S) is, is going to increase the value of *Truth* (T_K) within the mind/matrix.

Conversely, as ~~truth~~ perceived (T_P) increases, effectiveness decreases [Figure 5-2, (2)]. This places ~~truth~~ perceived in the denominator of the formula. As in the case of total perceptions (P_S), ~~truth~~ perceived (T_P) augments/magnifies the ~~truth~~ known (T_K); ~~truth~~ perceived (T_P) is again shown having an exponential relationship to ~~truth~~ known (T_K) as in Figure 5-2, (4r):

$$\frac{1}{T} : \frac{1}{(T_K)^{T_P}}$$

Chapter 4 introduced how desires and perceptions are linked. Because Perceptions are the guide and Desire is the drive, Desire in both the numerator and the denominator is shown as an exponent to Perception. What we see is going to be augmented by what we want.

Figure 5-2 (4i) illustrates the direct relationship desire for truth perceived (D_{Tp}) has to truth (T) being present. While Figure 5-2, (4p) shows it becoming an exponent in the formula:

$$T : ((T_K)^{P_S})^{D_{T_P}}$$

As mentioned, desires and perceptions are linked, or are the 'flip sides of the same coin'. An increase of desires present increases perceptions related to those desires. Some, or all, of these perceptions may not be relevant to the event. The increase in total desires tends to fracture our perceptions of an event, or seeing things that are not there or pertinent. Usually that means an involvement of desire for ~~truth~~ perceived (D_{Tp}).

Conversely, to the previous expression, the desire total (D_S) is shown having a similar function in the denominator. It is directly proportional to how much ~~truth~~ is in the mind/matrix. The desire for ~~truth~~ is going to augment the amount of truth is in the mind. As well as, any desire for truth perceived (D_{Tp}) that is not relevant to the event might bring up truths that do not pertain to the situation. Plugged into the formula, D_S acts as in Figure 5-2 (4s):

$$\frac{1}{T} : \frac{1}{((T_K)^{T_P})^{D_S}}$$

It was mentioned earlier the inverse role Attachments have to effectiveness. Figure 5-2, (4d) illustrates total attachments (A_S) inverse relationship to truth within the mind. It has been mentioned repeatedly that attachments are patterns of desires. It can go a little deeper than that. A more accurate definition would be a pattern of desires/perceptions that we consistently desire. Kind of like the relationship of velocity ($V = s/t$) to acceleration ($A = s/t^2$).

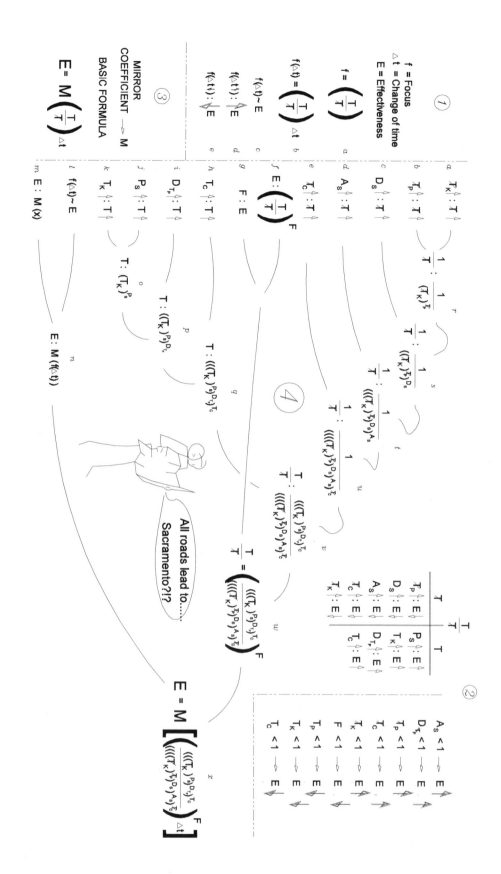

Figure 5-2, Formula Construction

236

Desire for ~~truth~~ perceived and total desires ($D_S + D_{Tp}$) has an inverse relationship to effectiveness; so do attachments. Since desire is the root of attachment, attachments have been given an exponential role to the D_S expression. Attachments augment/magnify desires.

The denominator now reads $\bcancel{T}_K$ to the $\bcancel{T}_P$, to the D_S, to the A_S power as in Figure 5-2, (4t):

$$\frac{1}{T} : \frac{1}{(((\bcancel{T}_K)^{\bcancel{T}_P})^{D_S})^{A_S}}$$

Now, for the Choice function. Remember that Choice is representative of a go/no-go device – a shutter. Figure 5-2 shows how Choice relates to perceptions, *Truth*, and effectiveness. Again, it is shown as being exponential to the desire/perception/knowledge expression. Truth chosen (T_C) is shown as a direct relationship to *Truth* in the mind/matrix [Figure 5-2, (4h)] as with total perceptions (P_S), desire for truth perceived (D_{Tp}), and truth known (T_K) [Figure 5-2, (4i-k)]:

$$T : (((T_K)^{P_S})^{D_{Tp}})^{T_C}$$

Together, total perception (P_S), desire for truth perceived (D_{Tp}), and truth known (T_K) defines what truth is in your *Perceptual Lens Array*. While truth chosen (T_C), connects what is in the *Perceptual Lens Array* back into *Storage* thereby completing a program or a truth loop.[33] This aids in defining what *Truth*'s role is in the individual mind/matrix and characterizes the numerator of the expression $T/\bcancel{T}$.

For the same reason, the ~~truth~~ chosen ($\bcancel{T}_C$) is shown in a similar position in the denominator of the expression being constructed.

This resultant expression defines what ~~truth~~ is coming through your *Perceptional Lens Array*. As with what was done with the numerator, ~~truth~~ chosen ($\bcancel{T}_C$) connects what is in the *Perceptual Lens Array* back into *Storage*; completing a ~~truth~~ loop,[34] defines the amount/role of ~~truth~~ within our mind/matrix, and defines the denominator of the expression $T/\bcancel{T}$. This, again, is expressed exponentially and is shown in Figure 5-2, (4u):

$$\frac{1}{T} : \frac{1}{((((\bcancel{T}_K)^{\bcancel{T}_P})^{D_S})^{A_S})^{\bcancel{T}_C}}$$

These derived numerator and denominator expressions, when put together, form the basis of the expression $T/\bcancel{T}$ as in Figure 5-2, (4v):

$$\frac{T}{T} : \frac{(((T_K)^{P_S})^{D_{Tp}})^{T_C}}{((((\bcancel{T}_K)^{\bcancel{T}_P})^{D_S})^{A_S})^{\bcancel{T}_C}}$$

---

33 Example: Chart 4-4, *J4*
34 Example: Chart 4-4, *D19*

Though this expression gives a foundation for our formula, there is still something missing. This expression may characterize truth and ~~truth~~ present within our mind and yet this only defines what is there to be applied and does not necessarily mean they are applied. This makes Faith (*F*) the next variable to introduce, the application itself.

In order to insert faith into the formula, please recognize that faith is defined as application of truth. This can be knowledge of truth (T_K) <u>and</u> it can be knowledge of the 'truth' that generates and sustains ~~truth~~ ($\mathcal{T}_K$). Faith in truth can increase your effectiveness and at the same time, faith in ~~truth~~ can decrease effectiveness. This places Faith as a variable that affects both the numerator and the denominator of the above expression. How much truth and ~~truth~~ are being applied.

Like the construction of both the numerator and the denominator, when Faith changes, its result is shown in this book as having an exponential effect on the truth/~~truth~~ relationship. Plugging faith (*F*) into the ratio generated so far gives the expression seen in Figure 5-2, (*4w*):

$$\frac{T}{\mathcal{T}} = \left(\frac{(((T_K)^{P_S})^{D_{T_P}})^{T_C}}{((((\mathcal{T}_K)^{\mathcal{T}_P})^{D_S})^{A_S})^{\mathcal{T}_C}} \right)^{F}$$

Now, the expression of *T/$\mathcal{T}$* has a definition.

5.5 - Plugging in to the Mirror Function and the Final Formula

*F*irst there is a need to review material in Chapters 2 and 3 to re-examine the Mirror function. In Chapter 2, *Postulate 7* states, "God's Creation created/miscreated an untruth". With this postulate came a number of attendant theorems including 27A, "God corrected for the untruth". The chapter also mentions that this Correction by Absolute Love did not exclude the 'mistake', but rather, used it by reflecting the mistake back to the Mind of origin, Creation. This allows Creation to 'see' what it is doing and to correct it.

Chapters 2 and 3 also mention that this Correction matrix – Mirror -- was called into being automatically by the creation of the ~~truth~~. It will exist as long as the ~~truth~~ exists. Both the Mirror and the ~~truth~~ involve a temporary temporal condition. And...if God and Creation – the source of the Correction -- are Eternal, then the Correction – Mirror -- has an Eternal root as well.

Chapter 3 details the Mirror aspect of Chapter 2's Correction matrix. It is the interface between Eternal and temporal conditions. The Mirror contains the existence of Truth and ~~truth~~ together (*Theorem 28A*, Truth and untruth coexist.). Chapter 3 outlines how all physical form, a temporal condition, is the result of a set of eternal laws/truths (gravity, electro-magnetic, etc.). The framework of that chapter states that these laws/truths are part of the Correction, and only a mere reflection of God's Laws/Truths. The Mirror makes up every 'thing' we know (and do not know).

Chapter 3 also makes a parallel between Karma and Newton's Third Law of Motion; and, how both are the Mirror in action. Karma reflects back to us, Creation, all ~~true~~ thoughts/actions. This makes the Mirror function in our formula the Karmic Correction Conundrum.

Everything covered up to this point in this chapter is now plugged into the Mirror function or the Karmic Correction Conundrum. This is the universe's reaction to the variables in the formula; what is in our mind.

This Karmic correction factor is the Correction in Chapters 2 and 3 -- the postulates and theorems -- and is *Truth* ("to everything else", Figure 4-4). This function is totally comprehensive and includes what has been set up from the past that leads to the Correction application in any moment of time. <u>It is present in 'every-where' and 'every-when'</u>.

This means not only is the Mirror reflecting what is in your mind back to your *BTR*, but also it is reflecting what is in other people's minds back to people's *BTR*s around you, and creating the *BTR* that incorporates everybody's event.

This includes all the people around you, the culture you are in, where you happen to be at the time, when you happen to be at that time, etc. It also includes what the Mirror is reflecting back to the mind of Mankind as a whole – the entire environment. The Mirror contains the environment in which you find yourself.

This Correction factor in the formula is the Mirror, reflecting back to the whole of Man as well as you the individual.[35] <u>Love does not exclude.</u> All the formula variables will influence how the Mirror is going to be reflecting your personal choices back on you and affect your effectiveness.

How the Mirror or the Karmic coefficient (*M*) works is related to what realities do the truth/laws you are working with in order to create. Are you working with the Truths of **Absolute** or the truths of **Actual**, **Imaginary**, **Consensual**, or **Individual** realities? The Mirror concept (*M*) reflects particular elements (~~truth~~) of the formula back on the individual. Specifically, exclusive elements are reflected in order for you to foster a non-exclusive mind. It can multiply the exclusive elements (the denominator) back on the ratio and thereby increase ineffectiveness.

The Mirror's coefficient mathematical expression is not important because it transcends mathematics. It is only important that you know it exists and it is in directly related to where 'your head's at' and your environment. It reflects elements of *T/F* back to the mind that is containing them. Thereby, either amplifying or attenuating effectiveness.

The Karmic coefficient (*M*) is this formula's 'fudge factor'.

With this Karmic coefficient and plugging change of time (*Δt*) covered previously in this chapter, the final formula is Figure 5-2, (*4x*):

$$E = M \left[\left(\frac{(((T_K)^{P_S})^{D_{T_P}})^{T_C}}{((((T'_K)^{T_P})^{D_S})^{A_S})^{T_C}} \right)^F \right]_t$$

Figure 5-3, Formula of Effectiveness

If this was a pure mathematical formula and we just plugged numbers into the *T/F* ratio, what numbers we put into the ratio would determine the final number. That number would vary in size accordingly to what numbers we chose.

The greater the numerator and the lesser the denominator, the greater will be the final number. The greater the denominator and the smaller the numerator, the less the final number will be. With this human matrix formula, the greater the *T/F* ratio the more effective we would be in an event. The smaller the *T/F* ratio, the less we would be effective in an event.

Remember, that this formula is only relevant on this 'side' of the Mirror. The next section on formula usage will touch on using, manipulating, or transcending or 'stepping' out of the formula.

5.6 - Formula Application and Usage

$\mathcal{T}$his formula can 'boggle the brain'. It is only meant to serve as a guideline. Because, even though we are dealing with a finite mind, the mathematics involved has the potential to work with infinities. (This is by the very nature of mathematics.)

---

35 Chapter 3

The combinations of all the variables involved would make it prohibitive to cover them all. Instead of covering details, this section covers particular areas of interest. Specifically, this section will cover what happens to exponentially arranged numbers when the numbers are greater than one; when numbers are between *1* and *0* or are *0*; and how these cases affect a ratio (fraction i.e. *T/F*).

Furthermore, consider all variables in the formula (P_S, D_S, A_S, etc.) as being absolute values, that is; they are all positive. No negative numbers are used.

This section's primary focus will be on:

1) Exponential relationships, for any $(x)^{(n)} = y$
   a) When an exponent is greater than *1*, $(n > 1)$
   b) When an exponent is less than *1*, $(n < 1)$
   c) When an exponent is *0*, $(n = 0)$
   d) When the base number is greater than *1*, $(x > 1)$
   e) When the base number is less than *1*, $(x < 1)$
   f) When the base number is *1* or *0* , $(x = 1,$ or $x = 0)$
2) Fractions - Numerator conditions, for any *a* of *a /b*
   a) When a numerator increases $(a \uparrow)$
   b) When a numerator is *1*, $(a = 1)$
   c) When a numerator is *0*, $(a = 0)$
3) Fractions - Denominator conditions, for any *b* of *a /b*
   a) When a denominator is greater than *1*, $(b > 1)$
   b) When a denominator is less than *1*, $(b < 1)$
   c) When a denominator is *1*, $(b = 1)$
   d) When a denominator is *0*, $(b = 0)$
4) Combination of the numerator and denominator, for any *a /b = y*
   a) When the numerator is greater than the denominator, $(a > b)$
   b) When the denominator is greater than the numerator, $(a < b)$

1a & **1d** $\Rightarrow$ For any exponential expression, $[(x)^{(n)} = y]$; If both *x* and *n* are greater than *1* $(x > 1$ and $n > 1)$ and if either *x* or *n* increases, *y* will increase, **{For any $(x)^{(n)}$ = y, and x and n > 1, if x $\uparrow$ or n $\uparrow$; then y $\uparrow$}**. *y* increases -- $[(2)^{(2)} = 4, (2)^{(3)} = 8, (3)^{(2)} = 9...]$.

1b & **1d** $\Rightarrow$ For any exponential expression, $[(x)^{(n)} = y]$; any *x* greater than *1* $(x > 1)$ and any *n* less than *1* $(n < 1)$, as *n* approaches *0*, *y* decreases and approaches *1*. The expression $x^{1/2}$ is really $\sqrt{x}$, the square root of *x*. Let us take the formula $(x)^{(n)} = y$. If the exponent (*n*) is less than one and it gets smaller (approaches *0*). For any $x > 1$, if *n* approaches *0* $(n < 1)$ *y* will approach *1* **{For any $(x)^{(n)}$ = y and x > 1 and n < 1, if n $\downarrow$; then y $\rightarrow$ 1}**. *y* decreases and approaches *1* -- $[(2)^{(1/2)} = 1.414, (2)^{(1/3)} = 1.259, (2)^{(1/4)} = 1.189...]$.

1a & **1e** $\Rightarrow$ For any exponential expression, $[(x)^{(n)} = y]$; any *x* less than *1* $(x < 1)$ and any *n* greater than *1* $(n > 1)$, as *n* increases, *y* will decrease and approach *0*. **{For any $(x)^{(n)}$ = y and x < 1 and n > 1, if n $\uparrow$; then y $\rightarrow$ 0}**. *y* decreases and approaches *0* -- $[(1/2)^{(2)} = .25, (1/2)^{(3)} = .125, (1/2)^{(4)} = .0625...]$.

1b & **1e** $\Rightarrow$ For any exponential expression, $[(x)^{(n)} = y]$; any *x* less than *1* $(x < 1)$ and any *n* less than *1* $(n < 1)$, as *n* approaches *0*, *y* increases and approaches *1*, **{For any $(x)^{(n)}$ = y and x < 1 and n < 1, if n $\downarrow$; then y $\rightarrow$ 1}**. *y* increases and approaches *1* -- $[(1/2)^{(1/2)} = .707, (1/2)^{(1/3)} = .793, (1/2)^{(1/4)} = .840...]$.

1c $\Rightarrow$ Here mathematics <u>appears</u> to make an intuitive jump and gets slightly strange. For any exponential expression, $[(x)^{(n)} = y]$; <u>and for any x</u>, if $n = 0$; y will be *1*. That means <u>any number to the zero power will be *1*.</u> **{For any $(x)^{(n)} = y$ and any x, if $n = 0$; then $y = 1$; $(x)^{(0)} = 1$}**.

There is a proof for this and still it can be hard to understand. It can be seen with ***1b*** & ***1d*** and ***1b*** & ***1e***, because all the numbers around (and leading up to) this condition points to this.[36]

1f $\Rightarrow$ For any exponential expression, $[(x)^{(n)} = y]$; and any *n*, if *x* is equal to *1* the resultant number will be *1*. It doesn't matter what n is. **{ For any $(x)^{(n)} = y$ and any n and if $x = 1$, then $y = 1$; $(1)^{(n)} = 1$}**. -- $[(1)^{(1/2)} = 1, (1)^{(3)} = 1, (1)^{(.840)} = 1...]$.

1f $\Rightarrow$ For any exponential expression, $[(x)^{(n)} = y]$; for any *n* not equal to *0*, if *x* is equal to *0* the resultant number will be *0*. **{For any n and if $x = 0$, then $y = 0$; $(0)^{(n)} = 0$}**. -- $[(0)^{(1/2)} = 0$, $(0)^{(3)} = 0, (0)^{(.840)} = 0...]$.

We have looked at what happens to sets of numbers when base numbers and exponents are zero, equal to *1*, greater than *1*, or a number less than *1* -- fractions. Now, to examine the numerator and denominator relationships on individual levels and together.

2a & ***4a*** $\Rightarrow$ For any *a /b = y* and any constant *b*, if the numerator increases (*a* ↑); the larger the resultant number, (*y* ↑). The greater the numerator is in any ratio, the greater the resultant number will be; *y* <u>increases</u>. **{For any $a/b = y$, and b is constant if a ↑; then y ↑}** -- $[1/2 = .5, 2/2 = 1, 3/2 = 1.5...]$.

2b, ***3a***, & ***4b*** $\Rightarrow$ For any *a /b = y* and the numerator *a* equals one (*a = 1*), if *b* is greater than or equal to 1 (*b ≥ 1*); *y* will be less than (or equal to) *1* (*y ≤ 1*). *y* <u>decreases</u> and is a fraction. **{For any $a/b = y$ and $a = 1$, if $b ≥ 1$, as b ↑; then $y ≤ 1$; y ↓}** -- $[1/2 = .5, 1/4 = .25, 1/10 = .1...]$.

2b, ***3b***, & ***4a*** $\Rightarrow$ For any *a /b = y* and the numerator *a* equals one (*a = 1*), if *b* is less than or equal to 1 (*b ≤ 1*); *y* <u>increases</u>. **{For any $a/b = y$ and $a = 1$, if $b ≤ 1$-- b ↓; then $y ≥ 1$; y ↑}** -- $[1/.5 = 2, 1/.25 = 4, 1/.1 = 10 ...]$.

2c $\Rightarrow$ For any *a /b = y* and any *b*, if *a* is equal to *0*, then *y* is equal to *0*. The numerator will be zero, making the whole expression zero. When you divide zero by any number, the answer will always be zero. <u>*y* is non-existant.</u> **{For any $a/b = y$, if $a = 0$; then $y = 0$}** -- $[0/2 = 0, 0/4 = 0, 0/10 = 0...]$.

3c $\Rightarrow$ For any *a /b = y* and any *a*, if *b* is equal to *1*; then *y* is equal to *a*. The resultant will be what is in the numerator; <u>*y* equals *a*</u>. **{For any $a/b = y$, if $b = 1$; then $a = y$}** -- $[2/1 = 2, .25/1 = .25, 10/1 = 10...]$.

3d $\Rightarrow$ For any *a /b = y* and any *a*, if *b* is equal to *0*; then mathematics is no longer relevant. This was covered in the 2nd chapter.[37] <u>The formula is no longer relevant.</u> **{For any $a/b = y$, if b**

---

36 An example is:
- $4^1 = 4$, $4^{.1} = 1.148$, $4^{.01} = 1.014$, $4^{.001} = 1.001$....etc.

or for any number less than one:
- $.4^1 = .4$, $.4^{.1} = .9124$, $.4^{.01} = .9908$, $.4^{.001} = .9990$....etc.

37 Chapter 2.8 - *Postulate 7*

= 0; this is a math 'no-no'}. The formula and math's logic just stepped out of mathematics. Strangely enough, this will actually be encouraged for some advanced applications.

4a $\Rightarrow$ For any $a/b = y$ and any a or b, if a is greater than b; then y is greater than *1*. <u>y will be greater than *1*</u>. **{For any $a/b = y$, if $a > b$; then $y > 1$}** -- [$2/1 = 2$, $8/4 = 2$, $10/2 = 5...$].

4b $\Rightarrow$ For any $a/b = y$ and any a or b, if b is greater than a; then y is less than *1*. <u>y will be less than *1*</u>. **{For any $a/b = y$, if $b > a$; then $y < 1$}** -- [$1/2 = .5$, $4/20 = .2$, $2/5 = .4...$].

How does all this apply to the Formula of Effectiveness? This translates to; the more you work with or apply the laws/truths of the situation the better off you will be. The more you work in the laws/truths not relevant to an event, the more dysfunctional you will be. Our effectiveness is a ratio of these two.

The idea that is presented is to increase numerically the formula's ratio T/F any way you can. The greater the T/F expression becomes the greater your effectiveness in any event.

When the numerator is greater than the denominator, effectiveness increases (**4a**). The greater the numerator is to the denominator, the greater the effectiveness. If the denominator is less than *1* (**3b**), then instead of decreasing the numerical value of the numerator/denominator ratio, it just makes the T/F expression that much greater (thereby improving your effectiveness).

Conversely, an increase in denominator has the opposite effect of an increase of the numerator. The larger the denominator is; the farther up 'shit creek' you are going to be (with or without a paddle). If the denominator is greater than the numerator (**4b**), the less effective you will be. Again, as above, if the numerator is a fraction, your effectiveness will be even that much less.

Looking at how you can adjust each element in the formula individually can help illustrate these formula relationships and applications. It can help show you how you can use the mortal mind as the vehicle it is. In addition, exercises presented in previous chapters will be cross-referenced to these mind elements.

The first thing to look at is these applications of truth (whatever these truths may be), and then address each element individually in the numerator first and then the denominator.

Faith (*F*)

Faith is the exponent to the T/F expression. This cannot be stressed enough. You can have two theoretical physicists discussing gravity and crunching numbers in a room; and until they apply gravity, they 'ain't' leaving that room. All their mental constructs of gravity do is help define future applications and understanding. While, these 'constructs' have little to do with the actual applications themselves. It will not help them walk.

The greater faith/application in the truth of any event, the greater will be the result (**1a**). The greater faith/application in the ~~truth~~ of any event will produce a lesser result. Faith augments both. Whatever is in your mortal mind/heart will have no effect until you apply it.

Truth Known (T_K)

Exercise and Lab 3[38] works on increasing this component. It does this by introducing to the mind the perception of comprehensive truths. The more comprehensive the truths – absolute, the more the mind approaches the Absolute Truth. The assignment also introduces a parallel framework to help store these truths.

There are many other ways this variable can be tweaked. Many traditional methods involve reading philosophical and spiritual material -- study. Another method may involve knowledge of self; have a working knowledge of how your mortal mind/heart works.

Ironically, an element of this variable involves recognition of how much you do not know, your ignorance. <u>It is in the recognition of ignorance that wisdom begins.</u> This

---

[38] Truth perception assignment of a truth a day.

recognition allows T_K to be an open variable instead of a constant. The greater the truth known the greater the result (**1d**).

This is the truth you are skilled in, the truth in your 'attic'[39] that you have to work with.

Total Perceptions (P_S)

Exercise and Lab 1a[40] begins opening this P_S element up by introducing to you the effect truth has in your mind. It introduces you to the connections your mind makes.

Exercise and Lab 3 also helps in increasing this P_S component by expanding your perception from an everyday objects into a bigger picture. It helps extend your 'mind's eye' into a larger mental picture.

While, *Exercise and Lab 4.1*[41] works on increasing or opening P_S and your perception of your physical surroundings. It works on increasing T_K by getting you to recognize your spatial and temporal relationship to your surroundings. Opening P_S involves you extending your perception into your surroundings.

This variable will increase with anything you do that helps you 'see' farther. There are multitude ways of doing this on numerous levels, from reading a newspaper or a scientific discourse to spiritual prose or poetry. The increase of P_S can involve perceptions that produce epiphanies to going to school and learning math. The increase of this as with **1a** and **1d** contributes to increasing the numerator.

Desire for Truth Perceived (D_{Tp})

This has not been addressed yet in any exercises; and…this one is relatively obvious. Your effectiveness will be linked to what you want or not want of the truth/laws involving any event. Bottom line: with this variable, you have to want to have an effect to be effective.

If you do not want anything, you will have no effectiveness. This equivalent to making $D_{Tp} = 0$. When this is done, **1c** is applicable. This would convert the whole numerator to *1* and effectively neutralize any other numerator components. If the denominator is greater than *1*, it will create a fraction condition as in **4b**. So…Desire for truth perceived should be greater then *0* and ideally equal to *1*; $D_{Tp} = 1$.

Desire can work for you in a number of ways. For example, in the spiritual sense, a desire for God or union with God and recognizing that you do not know what that God is nor have a vague perception of what that God may be, reduces the tendency to have ~~true~~ perceptions ($\cancel{T}_P$). At the same time, it can increase truth perceived and truth known (T_P & T_K).

Truth Chosen (T_C)

This variable involves the go/no-go device of the mind. What truth that is chosen or not chosen will be dependent on what is known (T_K) and what is seen (P_S). Again, the increase of this element as in **1a** and **1d** contributes to increasing the numerator.

The numerator was examined. Tweaking (P_S) and truth known (T_K) within the mind -- increasing their values, increases the value of the numerator. Many thought systems or philosophies (ancient and contemporary) work on an increase of these values with study.

Because there are so many variables in this formula, the primary focus of this chapter will be to reduce the denominator component. There are numerous ways to address this and many are found in world religions. One of this book's approaches is using the denominator's exponential relationships.

Please remember, exponential refers to how many times you will multiply a number by itself. Both the numerator and the denominator increase exponentially. Numbers cascade on each other with exponents. Life is exponential on this planet. It reproduces exponentially. The numerator and denominator of this formula express this by having exponential relationships in it.

---

39 Sherlock Holmes analogy, *Exercise and Lab 3*

40 "Do not believe anything unless…"

41 Time and space visualization exercise

The denominator has a similar effect to the numerator, but in reverse. How many ~~truths~~ you know is going to work against your effectiveness in an event. This makes sense just because do not have a grasp of the laws pertaining to the event or are working with laws irrelevant to the event. The effect of the ~~truth~~ you perceive is increased by the amount of ~~true~~ choices you make and the desires you have. Any thing you do to reduce this denominator will help you.

If the denominator is less than *1* (*3b*), it increases the numerical ratio (*T/F̶*) by dividing the numerator with a fraction. This may occur if $F̶_K$ is a fraction.

Previous homework and lab assignments have worked on decreasing the denominator – ~~truth~~ – within your mind.

Exercise and Lab 1B works with discouraging the re-enforcement or extension of ~~truth~~ by not talking.

Exercise and Lab 4 works with discouraging the creation of ~~truth~~ by preoccupying the mind to such an extent that no dependant ~~truth~~ is re-enforced.

Looking at the denominator and tweaking or reducing those elements can have a dramatic effect on the *T/F̶* ratio and whatever values that are placed in the numerator. These exponential relationships hint at how we can tweak the condition of *T/F̶*. The smaller the denominator the more effective you will be as in *2a*, *3b*, and, *4a*. Most spiritual and mystical thought systems involve some sort of tweaking of these variables and usually refer to it as a period of purification.

It is interesting to note here that reducing one ~~truth~~ element will help reduce the others. Remember that ~~truth~~ is dependent. Specially, if $F̶_K$ is reduced there is nothing there to support the apparent ~~truth~~ anomaly and the ~~truth~~; or, the truth special case dissolves into the greater truth it is a part.

As each denominator variable is examined, the case of the previous chapter's Figure 4-8 (*V*) – God-Head event -- will be cross-referenced to the formula.

~~Truth~~ Known ($F̶_K$)

This is the base number of the whole denominator exponential expression. The smaller $F̶_K$ is, the less the denominator exponential expression is, and the better for you.

Ideally, $F̶_K$ should be reduced to *1*, less than *1*, or *0* for maximum effectiveness.

Figure 4-8 (*V*) reference →

If $F̶_K = 0$, then there is not any ~~truth~~ known or the 'truth' that brings the ~~truth~~ into existence is non-existent. All ~~truth~~ within the individual has been brought to the Truth.

~~Truth~~ Perceived ($F̶_P$)

Due to the very nature of the temporal/spatial condition, this number will never be *0*. The very nature of the temporal/spatial condition has an ~~truth~~ reference.[42] In addition, perception is dualistic; there is the perceiver and the perceived. If everything is one, what is there to perceive?

This number will always be some positive number, *x*. And, as stated previously, this number will reduce automatically, when ~~truth~~ known ($F̶_K$) is reduced.

Figure 4-8 (*V*) reference →

This will always be a positive number, *x*. This will produce the condition of *0* to any power which equals *0* (*1f*). Zero to any power is zero. That means the result is still *0*, $(0)^{(x)} = 0$. The base number to the other denominator exponants still remains *0*.

Desire Total (D_S)

Because the desire for truth perceived must have a value (D_{Tp}), the value of total desires (D_S) will never be *0*. This total desire component will have some non-zero numerical value, *y*.

---

42 *Theorem 29*; Physical form is related to an aspect of the miscreation or untruth.

Desires can work for you or against you. It has been repeatedly said, that desires and perceptions are the 'flip' sides of the same coin. An increase in the desires (D_S) is going to bring sets of perceptions with them. Most of these perceptions may not be relevant to the event. Therefore, an inordinate amount of desires can increase the amount of ~~truth~~ or non-relevant truth perceived. These desires can fracture your perception of the event by introducing perceptions that are not relevant to the event.

In the realm of the everyday (mundane or 'real world') simplifying desires like when we prioritize (arrange sets of desire/perceptions to be applied), inhibits the introduction of ~~true~~ perceptions and desires ($\mathcal{F}_P$ & $D_{\mathcal{F}p}$). This increases our effectiveness to any job at hand.

In almost all cases, within any block of time that makes up an event, there will be a number of desires occurring. It is best to keep these desires few; this D_S variable should be kept to a very low number and relevant to the event. Ideally, this D_S variable should just consist of the desire for truth perceived (D_{Tp}). $D_S = D_{Tp}$; 1.

Figure 4-8 (V) reference →

If the only desire is truth perceived (D_{Tp}) and that desire is for God, that would make this D_S variable 1, $y = 1$. (And...this is the Infinite Eternal One of the postulates and theorems.[43]) As with $\mathcal{F}_P$, 1 is a positive number. Because the base number is 0 (from previously mentioned $(0)^X = 0$ relationship), this will produce the condition of 0 to a power of one, which equals 0 (**1f**), again. That means the result is still 0, $(0)^{(1)} = 0$. Again, the base number to the rest of the other denominator exponants still remains 0.

Attachments Total (A_S)

It is this A_S variable that many mystical and spiritual thought systems address. Whether it is Buddhism or mystical Christianity or Bhagavad Gita or shamanic practices, the non-attachment concept resurfaces repeatedly.

Because the term 'non-attachment' has been used so much in so many disciplines, its meaning tends to be watered down. What does the term 'non-attachment' mean?

Within *I AM A I*, it means executing an action with a <u>disinterested-interest</u>. This 'disinterested-interest' means you have just enough interest to keep you doing something, and at the same time, you could not care less how it turned out.

By cultivating a 'disinterested-interest' in what you do, you are reducing the A_S variable to 0 which reduces the entire denominator to 1. Remember **1c** -- if any of the denominator exponents -- $\mathcal{F}_P$, A_S, D_S, or $\mathcal{F}_C$ -- are zero (**1c**: $(x)^{(0)} = 1$) and **1f** – one to any power is one; the denominator will automatically be one. The other variables' ($\mathcal{F}_P$, D_S, or $\mathcal{F}_C$) influences on the ratio do not matter.

When the denominator is one, it creates a **3c** condition. Which means the numerator alone defines the effectiveness $T/\mathcal{F}$ ratio; it becomes $T/1$.

Desires and attachments are related. Attachments are patterns of previous desires and perceptions, so they have a major effect on the desires we experience during the event. (And...it is possible to have attachments and no desires at that moment. You can have an attachment to chocolate, but not want it <u>now</u>.)

If you have several desires concerning any event, whatever attachments you have greatly increase the effect of those desires. What this means is your desires and your attachments augment each other. The more attachments you have, the more desires you have toward your attachments. They are being powered against each other and it becomes a big exponential mass/mess. Can you see this?

The more desires you have, the more attachments you create. Desires over time are attachments. Therefore, attachments and desires over time, in the denominator react. The desires of ~~truth~~ perceived ($D_{\mathcal{F}p}$) during Δt, increase. Thereby increasing the desires total (D_S) so that this ratio's denominator can become a very large number.

This non-attachment's 'disinterested-interest' is important in terms of successful experiments and exercises later. One of the objectives in presenting this Formula of Effectiveness is to prepare you for spiritual, psychic, or mental exercises. Many of the

---

43 Boggles the brain

exercises of this book must be executed with a 'disinterested-interest' for them to be successful. Therefore, a non-attached state must be cultivated ahead of time.

Ideally, in almost all cases, this attachment variable should be tweaked to 0, $A_S = 0$. Your effectiveness in almost all situations will be inversely proportional to your attachment to the outcome.

Figure 4-8 (V) reference →

Up to this point in the book, attachments have been portrayed to have a detrimental affect. And…what if you are attached to God? Meaning, you are attached to God's Love, God's Logic, God's Truth, etc. If you are at-One-ment with God, that is definitely being attached to God. Here is the one exception to attachments inverse relationship. In this case, attachments total would equal one -- God, $A_S = 1$. As with T_P and D_S in the previous examples A_S would be a positive number, 1.

Because the base number is 0 (from previously mentioned relationship $(((0)^{X)1)} = 0$), this will produce the condition of 0 to the one power which equals 0 (**1f**), again. That means the result in the denominator is still 0, $(0)^{(1)} = 0$. Here again, the base number to the last exponant still remains 0.

~~Truth~~ Chosen (T_C)

As with ~~truth~~ perceived (T_P) and total desires (D_S), this number will be some non-zero value, some z. Again, this is due to the very nature of the temporal/spatial condition. This T_C number will never be 0. The very nature of the temporal/spatial condition has an ~~truth~~ reference; so, some ~~truth~~ will be chosen.

This T_C number will always be some positive number, z. As with the others (T_P and D_S), this number will reduce automatically, when ~~truth~~ known (T_K) is reduced. In addition, it will be small if T_P and D_S are reduced as well.

Figure 4-8 (V) reference →

If ~~truth~~ chosen is just the ~~truth~~ perceived (T_P), it can be expressed with the same variable as T_P; x, or $T_P = T_C$. As with T_P, this will be a non-zero positive number. Because the base number is 0 [from previously mentioned $((((0)^{X)1)1)} = 0$ relationship], this will again produce the condition of 0 to any power which equals 0 again (**1f**). That means the result is still 0, $(0)^{(X)} = 0$. This last variable turns the entire denominator expression to 0.

If $T_K = 0$, and all the other denominator numbers were non-zero numbers, this would make the denominator 0 creating a **3d** condition.

This means the formula has a division by zero in it and this formula has stepped out of math reasoning. In addition, as division by 0 creates something alien to math – **3d**, division by 0 in the metaphysical case creates something alien to the temporal mind – the Eternal.[44] This condition transcends the formula; the formula and the mortal mind it reflects are no longer relevant. <u>All bets are off</u>. Mathematical logic has stepped outside of its logic system. The individual begins to step outside the formula's limits or guidelines. This is the realm of Gold magic and miracles.[45] Only the Mirror and the Divine Source behind the Mirror is present. While, producing effects that are consistent with God's and the Mirror's intention. God/Creation – the Godhead -- is clothed in physical form.

What does all this mean? As mentioned previously, what is in the numerator is going to work for you. What is in the denominator, is going to work against you. The more truth you perceive (truth being the laws of the realities you are working in), the better off you are because it is a direct relationship as in the numerator. How much truth you perceive and know (T_K and T_P) is going to increase the effect of how much truth you choose (T_C). How much you apply the truth of knowledge, or how much faith you have, will increase your effectiveness by leaps and bounds.

---

44 Because they are mutually exclusive.
45 Chapters 9 and 10

The greater the four denominator elements of: ~~truth~~ perceived ($\mathcal{F}_P$), ~~truth~~ chosen ($\mathcal{F}_C$), desires total (D_S), and attachments total (A_S), the deeper the trouble you are likely to find yourself.

It can be seen that these -- the numerator and denominator -- are distorted reflections of each other, the numerator: T_K to the T_P, to the D_{Tp}, to the T_C: truth known, to truth perceived, to the desired truth, to the truth chosen. While the denominator is $\mathcal{F}_K$, to the $\mathcal{F}_P$, to the D_S, to the A_S, to the $\mathcal{F}_C$ power: ~~truth~~ known, to ~~truth~~ perceived, to the desire total, to the attachment total, to the ~~truth~~ chosen power. The two appear to have a polarity ratio relationship.

Again, the whole thing about these exponential relationships is; if you throw zeros in the denominator or numerator, all of a sudden things go 'bananas'. For example, if a *0* is in for ~~truth~~ perceived ($\mathcal{F}_P$) within the formula, it does not make any difference how many attachments (A_S) or ~~truth~~ chosen ($\mathcal{F}_C$) are; the effect on this denominator number will be to make the denominator *1*. If ~~truth~~ chosen ($\mathcal{F}_C$) is *0*, again the denominator is *1*. If total desires (D_S) are *0*, the denominator is *1*.

Likewise, if any of the numerator exponential variables (T_P, D_{Tp}, or T_C) are *0* as in *1c*, then the numerator is *1* (again, none of the other numerator values will matter). If any are *0*, the numerator will automatically be reduced to *1*, a *2b* & *3a* condition.

Again, if attachments (A_S) becomes *0*, the denominator, no matter what the other values are, is *1* (*1c*, *1f*, & *3c*). Effectiveness then is solely determined by how much truth is in the matrix – numerator -- and how much truth is applied, over a change of time. It is this particular A_S variable that many mystical thought systems address. This A_S variable will be addressed in later chapters before doing exercises.

This one special case must be mentioned again, when the reflection of the Mirror function is neutralized. The Krishna in the *Bhagavad Gita* said that whatever we do to unite ourselves with God, and we do this with non-attachment to the outcome (whatever it may be), is karma-less. Since we are doing, what the Mirror intends us to do; the Mirror is no longer needed; it has been 'short-circuited'.

This occurs in the case where Attachment (A_S) is *0*, while all the other denominator values are reduced. When all the denominator values have been reduced to their lowest values (specifically ~~truth~~ known ($\mathcal{F}_K$) and ~~truth~~ perceived ($\mathcal{F}_P$), there is no ~~truth~~ ($\mathcal{F}$) within the mind to reflect back.

Whatever is in the numerator/denominator expression, will be augmented (increased or decreased) by Faith. Faith, as application of knowledge, may be applying any knowledge that is in *Storage*. This can be applications of truth or the 'truth' of the ~~truth~~. Faith being Truth's (and the Eternal Moment of Creation) representative within the *Perceptual Lens Array* is where your true 'power' lies.

This includes applying knowledge that you know deep down (as a Child of God), but you may not have available in *Knowledge* storage of your human matrix. This is a spiritual aspect of faith.[46] And…it is still an application of a knowledge, Divine or otherwise.

Concerning the numerator, when a human being is increasing the absolute truth – comprehensive truth -- within their mind/matrix, they are aligning with the Truth Matrix. How aligned it becomes is dependent on how much Absolute Truth is in the numerator and how little ~~truth~~ is in the denominator. Remember that Absolute Truth is infinite. The condition of Absolute Truth in the numerator and *0* ~~truths~~ known in the denominator begins a condition of God divided by *0*.

As soon as ~~truth~~ known ($\mathcal{F}_K$) becomes *0*, this formula is neutralized. In the ideal mathematical sense, if any of the denominator exponents were *0* also, the denominator would be *1*. However, ~~truth~~ is dependent. It cannot exist without the support of truth known ('truth' of the ~~truth~~ applications). Once the 'truth' of the ~~truth~~ -- ~~Truth~~ -- is eliminated from your mind/matrix, you are as God created you. The formula or any of the denominator variables are no longer relevant.

---

46 "If you had the faith, you could move mountains.", Bible

In turn, the Mirror function will reflect all this back into the formula and thereby increasing effectiveness even more. Effectiveness then, will be on the metaphysical/spiritual level and is dependent on applications/faith of the Creation Matrix.

Putting zeros in the denominator is an extreme case and it helps illustrate a point. To use this formula for purposes of effectiveness the general rule of thumb is:

- the numerator should be as large as possible
- while the denominator should be as small as possible.

If the denominator is less than *1* then it can increase effectiveness dramatically, instead of detract (denominator greater than *1*). That means putting fractions (Figure 5-2 [2]) in the places of F_P, F_C, D_S, or A_S; and introducing radicals[47] into the denominator. The fractional values we will work with more in Chapters 6 and 7.

There is an old cup analogy. In order for a cup to be filled, it must be empty first. In order to be filled with Truth, ~~truth~~ must be removed.

Later in this chapter – a motivational analysis – and the rest of the book, the focus will be operating with tweaking aspects of this formula. In other chapters, *I AM A I* will be using the formula while playing with one point focus exercises and meditations. In addition, the book will use the condition of when some of these variables are *0*. Zero can short-circuit the whole formula; and how, this 'short-circuit' can lead to God.

This book will work on getting you to cascade the formula up at the numerator for you – approach infinite, and reduce the denominator by using ones, numbers less than one, and with zeros.

$$E = M\left[\left(\frac{(((\infty)^{\infty})^{1})^{\infty}}{((((0)^{0})^{1})^{0})^{0}}\right)^{\infty} \triangle t\right]$$ Ka-Ching!!!!!

Figure 5-4, Formula Application

5.7 - Formula Conclusion and a Book Transition

*A*ll the previous formula material helps illustrate Love's Logic. Now, after going through all that formula bovine excrement[48], you will be told, you actually do not need to know most of this stuff. Just like, you do not need to know Newton's formulas of gravity and motion in order to walk. Application is everything. The intellectual/rational only gives it order and completes the science model. The presented mind model and *I AM A I*'s paradigm and the constructed formula only comes in handy when you want to do an analysis or a projection of an event.

What does all this mean? The formula is not the actuality it represents. A college student, majoring in physics (specifically motion and mechanics), joins a track team. While running, the student trips and falls. As the student falls, Newton's laws of motion and gravity will be the last things on their mind. They will be to busy <u>applying</u> the elements of the formulas, from their direct knowledge, to cushion their fall.

Newton's formulas were left behind (within the student's mind) for direct experience and applications. If the student chooses, they can later reflect back, see what happened, and plug the event into the rational of the physical paradigm's formulas.

---

47 Square root, quad root, etc., That is why, for most purposes, truth known (or truth known) can not equal a negative number. It avoids the involvement of the imaginary number system ($\sqrt{-1}$).

48 'bullshit'

The spiritual applications of this chapter's formula have been expressed in number of ways. From Jesus', "Know the Truth, and the Truth will set you free", which addresses the numerator. To the denominator, formula application can be related to the quote from the Lotus Sutra (Buddha) in the prologue.[49] That quote addresses the removal of ~~truth~~ or attachments, leaving only Truth.

The metaphysical science construct of this book needs this formula, especially for covering the rational and applications concerning meditation, *ESP*, magic, and miracles.

This formula is necessary in order to apply the book's construct and predict movement within an **Actual** reality that the construct represents.[50] This book will be referring back to this formula when introducing exercises to note what aspect of the formula and the matrix the exercise is addressing. This can prove to be useful.

One of the biggest problems with this book's kind of 'scientific' approach to metaphysical operations is breaking down what are the conditions that make up effectiveness and recreating these conditions. The ancients rarely broke it down, even though hints of it have been in many ancient and current world religions.

This formula construct and the class/book construct are put together so that if the formula is followed, individual successful metaphysical laboratories and experiments within us become possible. Cause and effect relationships become more apparent. You will be able to see, "Yes, if I allow these conditions, this will happen." At the same time, the formula helps the metaphysical/mystical operator or student figure out what they did that was wrong; why an experiment did not work.

One example where this formula will be applicable is in the start of psychic exercises -- *ESP* exercises. When you start doing psychic and metaphysical exercises, and if these exercises are going to have any effectiveness, then certain aspects of this formula must be followed. This will help foster a set of conditions within you, conditions that will be conducive to a successful *ESP* experiment outcome. If specific quantities, in the formula, or matrix conditions were not present, doing some of these exercises would be just a waste of time.

Most of the exercises later will be referring periodically to this formula in order to get the specific effects from your matrix. This includes working with the inter-dynamics of the matrix, or just shutting it out/down and jumping out of the whole system. This can be either closing your eyeballs and going in a different direction or taking your perceptual lens for a 'walk around the block'.

Recognition of your personal temporal matrix and learning to step out of it, or consciously aligning it to the Eternal Matrix; either one will produce effects. Changing the ~~truth~~ you perceive, changing how much ~~truth~~ you know, and getting to a quiet place through faith; are all going to have an effect on you, your **Actual,** and **Individual** realities.

This, returns to the limit of the formula: why it is, in many ways, not that important. The formula and the thought construct/matrix are temporal constructs representing temporal actualities, to be used by temporal minds.

The infinities within infinities that make up God's Loving Logic dictates you must know when this information is not relevant. When **Actual** reality becomes the primary focus, much of the **Consensual** or **Imaginary** realities are not important at that moment of time.[51] The same can happen when **Absolute** Reality becomes the primary focus; then some aspects of **Actual** reality are no longer relevant. Here again, in this area, we are beginning to enter the realms of high thaumaturgical magic and miracles.

---

49 "The mind has nothing to do with thinking because its fundamental source is empty. To discard false views, this is the great causal event."

50 Any fool can shoot a gun -- hitting the target is a whole different story. A gunnery officer has to be trained in ballistics (gravity, motion, fluid mechanics, etc.) to ensure the missile goes where it is suppose to. The officer's decisions must be guided by using the equipment with those laws/truths in mind.

51 If you loose your drinking water, the first priority is to restore it. The second may be deal with whatever politics (if any) that lead up to the water's loss.

It is also important to remind you there are two separate letter cases when expressing the word Truth. Large case Truth is God's Absolute Truth(s). Small case truth is **Actual, Individual, Consensual, Imaginary** reality truths, relative truth(s). Remember *Exercise and Lab #3;* and, how you were asked to categorize the Truth/truth you have found by no exceptions verses one exception. Relative truths may have a degree of ~~truth~~ within them. This distinction can be important for this formula application.

Again, stated in previous chapters, one of the definitions for Truth/truth is laws by which something works. This means small case truth also refers to the laws by which **Consensual, Imaginary,** or **Individual** realities work. The amount of Absolute Truth chosen increases your effectiveness within the **Absolute** and **Actual** realities. This does not mean you will be effective in a **Consensual** reality. Effectiveness, using Absolutes, in a **Consensual** reality will be dependent on how much and what Absolutes are within the **Consensual** reality.

Remember the example of the businessperson or politician vs. the craftsperson and their different realities expertise presented in Chapter 4.

In conclusion, it has been stated that the formula has a limited importance. The same can be said of Chapters 2, 3, 4, and as well as the first half of 5. Within the material of these chapters, a crude map/construct has been drawn. Again, "The map is not the terrain." Eventually, the map must be put down and one's focus turns to making the journey. It can be dangerous to drive while reading the roadmap. The map comes in handy if we get lost or planning a route. Then we put it away while we are applying the information.

The rest of this chapter and the remaining chapters are more concerned with applications, making the journey. The focus of the book will change from intellectual theory to utilization of the theory. Here is where your personal confirmation of the theory can be attained by direct experience. And...here is where the real work begins.

These next chapters' focus will be on exercises and is comparable to doing any physical regime. Instead of talking about features or elements of the journey, it is time to do some walking.

5.8 – A Motivational Analysis – Pre-forming Intention

What does all this perception, desire, attachment, faith, etc. have to do with practical applications and the 'real world'? Remember that the perception/desire lens forms a triangle to any event. Passively, this triangle is your attitude to any event. With active participation, it is your intention towards any event. Changing what you see or what you want, changes your attitude or your intention.

Tweaking what you 'see' or changing what you 'want' affects the other. The perception/desire lens is one thing. This book will be using pre-forming a clear perception, clear desires, and one point focus to clear the lens up before an exercise in order to prepare the lens for the exercise. Pre-forming the perceptual lens area will boost your effectiveness (success) with psychic experiments. It really helps to have clear desires to work with truth, absolutes, with the whole, or with anything.

Future exercises will expose you to prioritizing your perceptions, attachments, and desires. Prioritizing determines what you want to do for this block of time, or what you are going to apply. *I AM A I* encourages individual conscious exploration of your 'lens' to see what is the relationship between this and that, and that to the other, etc.

The following exercise exposes you to your perceptions and your desires. To expose you to your *Perceptional Lens Array* – the 'front of your mind' -- and what is in your *Storage* – the 'back of your mind' -- that guides/focuses the front.

You will be exposed to relationships of your desires to your perceptions, and your attachments to your desire and perceptions.

It has been mentioned repeatedly, most religious, metaphysical, mystical... exercises aim at reducing the amount of ~~truth~~ (~~T~~) participation within the mind/matrix. Some aim to fill the mind with truth (*T*) using study, memorized ritual prayers, or meditation. With practice, the latter can have a large degree of success. However, for people just learning it can get kind of 'iffy' because it can introduce more perceptions, desires, and attachments, ~~truth~~.

Reducing the ~~truth~~ has a more of an immediate reaction. As stated previously, in spiritual and mystical traditions, this is usually related to some period of purification. When the ~~truth~~ is eliminated, the only thing left will be the Truth. Alternatively, to put it another way, eliminate the ~~truth~~ within you and God's Grace will fill you with His/Hers/Its/The Truth. Here is the analogy of a cup again; "A cup must be empty in order for it to be filled."

When analyzing motivations and performing all other exercises, this has to be said from the start: you must ask questions – observe -- honestly of the perceptual lens and the lens system. Do this dispassionately, without judgment, as an observer.[52] Having an objective scientific observer attitude has some advantages, "What happens if I do this?" It keeps attachment down.

You are trying to figure something out, as if it is a kid's toy or a crossword puzzle, but the puzzle is yourself. In fact, it is better to look at it as if you are just a puzzle. This approach helps cultivate the disinterested-interest concept.[53]

This attitude is very important because we have already shown, with the perceptual window bandwidth, that there are many things you do not see right now. Just saying, "I don't know right now," is an honest answer. As has been said repeatedly, recognizing ignorance (recognizing lack of truth perceived) is the beginning of wisdom. It allows space for truth to be perceived.

As was expressed in a previous chapter,[54] it is similar to the concept of the fair witness in the book *A Stranger in a Strange Land*. ["It's white on this side, Jubal."]

This attitude must be taken into almost every work/assignment/exercise that you are going to do from here on. Be objective and make very few assumptions. Just because a house is white on the side you are looking at, does not necessarily mean it is white on the sides you do not see. Therefore, be like a fair witness in doing these exercises. Be only an observer. Learn to use only the Cognitive input of your mind/matrix.

Every time you make a judgment/choice, you had better be careful, because your judgment is most likely going to be wrong or a distraction. The simple reason why a judgment may be in error is <u>there are things you do not see</u>.

If you make a judgment, observe yourself making a judgment. Be the observer of yourself, recognizing that you are making a judgment. This itself, can lead to correction. If you decide to observe instead of being attached to any outcome, then you have already changed perception and the outcome becomes different. You have altered the flow through your *Perceptual Lens Array*.

That is what this flow through the lens has been presented as -- going through the perceptual lens and making a judgment/choice. Seeing the event, re-evaluating, refocusing, the flow is not automatic anymore. Then, at that moment, you have changed your choice.

Again, all this is in reference to Figure 4-4 and Chart 4-4. Changing the flows and the choices with the exercises, is the approach of this book to get you to focus-refocus your matrix. This cannot be stressed enough, you must be aware of how much you do not know to begin with, and be very objective about it – do not be afraid of your ignorance. In doing so, you are addressing limits to T_K or T_P.

Observing the human matrix mechanism with its perceptual window (or the ego mechanism) within you, allows you to see how the accumulation of truth and ~~truth~~ occurs; how your perceptual lens inside this ego mortal mind/matrix/mechanism influences your choices.

When we cover magic subject matter, this motivational analysis will be very important, even essential. Motivations determine what category of magic is being worked: Black, White, Gray, Silver, or Gold.[55]

---

52 A disinterested-interest: This reduces the Choice input, specifically truth chosen (TC). At the same time, the major input into Storages is through the Cognitive input.
53 "The eyes of a child" concept that appears throughout a multitude of mystical thought systems.
54 Chapter 3.6, *Exercise and Lab #3*

In order to learn a new perception system, the old system must be called into questioned or recognized. To begin this exercise:

♦ You have to start asking questions about your storage and lens elements.
♦ You need to ask questions about your perceptions.
♦ You will need to start asking questions about what you want and your attachments.
♦ This may include asking questions of your questions.

******************** ☯ ********************

Exercise and Lab #5: "How Do I See _____?"

The worksheet for this exercise is in the appendix in the back of the book.

Again, (this cannot be repeated enough) the idea is to do this as a totally objective observation exercise and be careful about making any judgments/choices. Try to make none. Just watch yourself, as if you are looking at pieces while doing a jigsaw puzzle. "This piece is brown with a bit of green on it. This other piece is brown, but not the right shade. Oh, this piece over here is the right shade; and it fits."

This exercise begins as *Homework and Lab #3* did (Chapter 3.7). Look around the room and pick something, anything. Then, on the *Exercise and Lab 5* Worksheet, write down what the object is and ask, "What do I see _____?" Then, enter a short list of perceptions to answer the question. You can insert anything you want into the blank. You can say life, God, the world as a whole, your culture, your society, other people, mate, boss, friend, the table, the wall, this finger, frying pan, etc. -- any subject is applicable. [see Assignment 5 Worksheet (Sample)]

In fact, it is relatively important not to be exclusive, like the truth exercise *of Lab #3*. Moreover, like the truth exercise of *Lab #3* remember to give it the **K.I.S.S.** (**K**eep **I**t **S**imple **S**tupid). (Do not try to solve or 'see' everything and start simple.)

After you have made a short list of perceptions – what you see, go through the perceptions on the list and ask the question: "What do I want from 'the perception of _____'?" That is the other half of the same question. "What do I see and what do I want from what I 'see' or don't' 'see'." Remember, perceptions and desires are linked. An example is, "What do I see from this table and what do I want from this table?" Again, any subject is applicable.

You may be tired when doing this exercise. You may see a table as a thing to rest on. "What I want the table to do is prop me up." There are other things besides that; like not collapsing when used, hold food, to write on, etc. And…that is all you may see right at that one moment, to hold your head up. There are other things besides that; are there not? There may be many other things. You are to record the things you see about that item you picked and are seeing in one block of time.

The idea of this exercise is to explore yourself; so, making a list can be relatively informative. The list can be an objective reference and help increase the spectrum of your perceptions and desires that you will explore.

After you ask, "What do I see _____," and "what do I want from _____"; you ask, "what could there be that I do not see about _____?" So you can ask, "What could there be about this table that I do not see?"

An example is a knot in the wood of the table. Layers of the knot go through the table. You can see the rings of the knot. (Moreover, there are rings in that knot that are imbedded in that table that you cannot see.) So, what is there about the table you do not see? You cannot see the fasteners holding the table together.

55 Chapter 9, Concerning Magic

You may say; I am using it to hold me up. What you do not see right now is your use of it to hold your food up last night, or you use it to hold a piece of paper while you are writing. Recognize there are aspects that you did not see.

If you saw a table as a thing to rest on and picked that one that was most important to you at that moment of time, this was your desire influencing your perception. What do you want from the table now?

That was what you wanted at that moment, for the table to hold you up. You saw other things, but you may have not actually focused on them, so that narrowed your vision. That would illustrate how your perceptual lens works here. How perceptions have a direct relationship to the desires.

This also shows how any subject is applicable. Honest answers will affect your lens focus-refocus, how you set up and program yourself. This relates to the programming aspects of Figure 4-4 and Chart 4-4, which, in turn, controls the perceptions and desires through the focus control.

Observation and inquiry are your <u>only</u> jobs here. The idea is to show you how your perceptions and desires lead to how you are your programming your storages. For this to work, the only thing you need to do is to be honest and question. You have to be honest. Do not try to be too smart and fool yourself. Just be an observer. "I don't know right now" is an excellent answer. Because with questions of a very large subject like God, life, the world or that which is at the very core of your being, of course you do not know; and you may have to 'chew' on them.

We may have to 'chew' on the questions, and slowly turn these questions over inside until things fall into place (cognition). Again, no judgment/choice. Because, with judgment, your own ignorance can lead you astray. Judgment plus is just as bad as judgment minus. Either way, plus or minus, the flow is going to go through the Judgment triangle of Figure 4-4.

"This is a good idea", can be just as detrimental as judgments against. The more judgment (what you allow to recycle through the lens) the more things will pump through your perceptual choice mechanism, which then will affect your choice, which will affect your programming, etc., and it will go into a loop again. The idea of this and later exercises is to help reduce some of the loops that sustains or can contain ~~truth~~ (T).

To do this exercise, pick an object that is around you. Anything you put your eyes on. After you have done this exercise several times, do it towards a much broader subject. *Life* may be one, another one *God/Divine, people,* or you can pick *the world*.

To begin the exercise, look at anything in the room, like the truth exercise. Just pick up anything in the room and write down a subject. You can use anything that comes to your mind. Using what is immediately around you, makes it easier, generally speaking.

Each item is going to have a dedicated sheet of paper -- worksheet. Put one category-item at the top of each worksheet. Any item will do, it does not make any difference. An example is a ceiling fan.[56]

What do you see of this fan? Some answers might be:

- I see a hub with four blades.
- I see these blades in rotation.
- I see this assembly suspended a distance from the ceiling (or floor).
- I feel it is cooling.
- Etc.

Start making a list on the left-hand side of the worksheet of what you see in the fan. The next step, after you have written what you do see, in the other column, start writing what you do not see. Like, you do not see the electricity. You do not see the magnetic field. You do not see the 'kosmic karmic korrection konundrum'.

---

56 The *Assignment 5* Worksheet (Sample) uses a table fan. Many of the concepts are the same though.

With this list of what you see of the fan and what you do not see -- see, then you start asking, "What do I want?" from each entry. Some of these can be nothing/zero. A partial list may be:

- I want to know what the laws of motion are that governs it. That is a 'want' around a 'see'.
- You want the wind.
- You want the coolness.

You may think wind or coolness are things that you do not see. That may not be entirely true. If physically feeling is something regarded as perception -- sight, touch, feel, smell, or hearing, these are all perceptions.

The idea is to work with perception here. You may not hear the sound or the electricity, or may not have any 'wants' about them. You may want to include the electricity with any appliance and yet have no immediate desires. In addition, you may not want to be 'zapped' by the electricity – a 'want',

Like the concept of rotary, there may be no immediate wants. In addition, if the fan does not go around, it has not any effect, so you may have a 'want' about that. Or, you do not want to know what that rotary action would do if you stuck your hand there – a 'want',

The idea of this exercise is for you to see the connections between what you 'see' and what you 'want' – perception/desire sets. That is the whole goal of this exercise. The idea is to have you see that these connections exist within you and how your motivation is directly connected to what you want/want from what you 'see'/see'.

Because, technically speaking, everything you put down you may have some kind of attachment to, or some desire around, or else you would not have thought of it probably. The whole idea of this exercise is to expose you to your perceptional lens and storage.

➢ *The assignment for this exercise is to do this seven times. Use the worksheet in the Appendix.*
➢ *Make a list of what you see about them; what you do not see about them*
➢ *Write done what you want or want pertaining to what you see and see.*
➢ *Do the same exercise once with the concepts Life, the world, God, etc.*

➢ *An extra assignment that will expand this exercise is to ask questions such as, "Where do I see I am?" or "When do I see I am?" and answering with the previous chapter's Space/Time Imagination Exercise.*

********************  ********************

Before doing any exercises (either in this book or in any exercise you come across later), a motivational examination or pre-forming intention is recommended. If an exercise is to be effective, desires and attachments must be kept to a low number (the *Perceptual Lens Array* cleaned up). Most schools of thought stress no attachments to the outcome of any exercise/discipline. Remember, if attachments are *0*, the denominator of the truth/truth expression will automatically be *1*. This would increase the likelihood of a successful experiment.

An example of a simple examination would begin with a stretch of your perceptions, make them as broad or inclusive as possible. See as much as possible with your mind.[57] Then observe what you want, from what you see. Remember to just observe, be aware that desires exist. (Recognize all exercises in this book are aimed at expanding your awareness and can increase the perceptions of your "mind's eye".)

---

57 Perhaps do a short version of *Exercise and Lab # 4,* Chapter 4 – eye exercise and resetting the mind.

OBJECT: table fan

SEE

fan cage

WANT	W~~ANT~~
there to protect	to collect dust
	to rattle from vibration

body

WANT	W~~ANT~~
to be silent	to fall apart
on a stable base	to collect dust
made of good materials	
to look good	

(barely see) moving blades

WANT	W~~ANT~~
move air when not needed	hit anything but air
to be quiet	be dirty
	come in contact with my body
	move air when not needed

SEE

electricity

WANT	W~~ANT~~
to be there to operate fan	to start a fire
	to be shocked

moving air

WANT	W~~ANT~~
the air to be cool	the air to be warm
feel the moving air and be cool	

people who made the fan

WANT	W~~ANT~~
do a good job in construction	to be exploited

Assignment 5 Worksheet (sample)

With the expanded perception, be aware there are things you cannot see. Use this awareness of ignorance to foster a non-attachment to the outcome of the exercise. Mental exercises can open up for you many things. Most of these things may be outside your perceptual grasp right now. Use your recognition of your own ignorance to generate a non-attachment to the outcome of any exercise. This will increase the effectiveness of any exercise you do.

At the same time, for future exercises, you will be setting aside a 'block of time'. You are to recognize that for this 'block of time' you want only to do this exercise (whatever exercise it may be). When you drift, remember your original want for this time; and use it to bring yourself back to the exercise.

This is prioritizing your focus for a specific time window.

5.9 - Questions

1) The factors that have an inverse relationship to effectiveness are?

2) The factors that have a direct relationship to effectiveness are?

3) Desires and perceptions are _____?

4) What does exponential mean in relationship to the formula?

5) What is the result when an exponent is 0?

6) The numerator should be?

7) The denominator should be?

8) What is the Karmic Correction Coefficient?

9) This formula is:
   a) a pain   d) something that must be forgotten at times
   b) a hard and fast rule   e) all but (b)
   c) a construct

10) Most mystical/metaphysical exercises work at reducing _____ within the mind.

11) What do you see life to be?

12) What do you want from life?

257

Chapter 6

Concerning Meditation and Disciplines

6.1 - A Review and a Synthesis

*C*hapter 3 introduced how everything in physical form is comprised of *BTR*s – Bubbles of Temporal/spatial Reference – within *BTR*s, within *BTR*s, within *BTR*s...; as well as, matrices within matrices within matrices...; mirrors within mirrors within mirrors...

Chapter 4 presented a mental construct – model -- of a mortal mind/matrix *BTR*. Figure 4-4 and Chart 4-4 illustrate the constituent *BTR*s, their matrices, operational flows, and storages comprising the human mind/matrix -- *Focus Control Buss* with elements of the *Perceptual Lens Array* and *Storages*.

Chapter 5 used labels presented in Chapter 4 and presented a formula that enables us to project or predict how effective that mind/matrix construct will be to any given event. And... how any given event will affect us.

The following is a review of Figure 4-4, Chart 4-4, and the formula mind/matrix relationships (Figure 5-3), referred back to the previous labs and exercises. In addition, future exercises will be related to these figures and the formula. Aspects of these drawings (that are relevant to the exercises) will be noted.

❏ *Exercise and Lab 1A*[1] exposes you to an automatic response that pertains to hearing something as an event. *Exercise and Lab 1* exposes you to the effect Truth has on you when it is present in your mortal mind/matrix. It helps illustrate the two-way aspect of the formula of effectiveness by how something can affect you. The truth influence enters *Knowledge* storage through the Cognitive input of Figure 4-4.

Hearing involves an audio perception going through the Perceptions/Desires Lens array. It must pass through elements of this array. What does the individual want from the event (D_S)? What perceptions do they have (how do they see) around the event (P_S) and how do these perceptions flow through and how they affect the belief area? All have an effect on what makes it through the lens to the Cognitive input.

Whatever aspect of the event that makes it through the lens and has truth, ends up at the True point, and goes through the Cognitive input into *Knowledge* (Chart 4-4, *E2*) automatically. It is matched by what truth is in *Knowledge*, and adds to or compliments the information flow. The individual (Figure 4-4, [*III*]) is now receiving a number of inputs: one from

---

1 Chapter 1.1, What to Believe,

the cognitive loop; Chart 4-4, *I1*, and matched by another from the *Knowledge* output (through *Programming*), Chart 4-4, *C6*. This is the two point 'ringing' effect – shown in Chart 4-4, *K2* – that was briefly covered at the end of Chapter 4.[2]

This 'ringing' is an <u>automatic</u> movement through the matrix. Little to no choice is involved (other than to pay attention).

❑ *Exercise and Lab 1B*[3] is an exercise that works on a multitude of levels. One level is; it is a crude attempt to keep you, the learner, from making some specific choices. This exercise is a shotgun approach to reduce some programming contamination that can occur when talking. Because this is a science course and your mind is the laboratory, this exercise is a weak attempt at helping you keep a pristine lab environment. Keeping silent is an ancient practice.[4]

To talk is a choice to create. Talking is extending ideas that are in your mind. *Exercise and Lab 1B* is an attempt to keep you from making some ~~true~~ choices (F_C). It also hinders you from extending ~~true~~ perceptions (F_P). What ~~true~~ perceptions? If you are talking about your experiences around the information in this book or the exercises and you have not finished the course yet, then you are speaking from ignorance of the completed subject matter. You are making judgments around something that you have not finished yet.

Another level to *Exercise and Lab 1B* is this is an exercise in 'not doing something'. Instead of 'doing something', this is an exercise in restraint. Subtly and in the background, this exercise involves a re-cognition of an event (Cognition) and a choice not to encourage specific events (Choice and Judgment triangle).

❑ *Exercise and Lab 2*[5] is an introduction to a one-point focus (*1Δt*). In making a mandala in preparation for this chapter, there may have been moments where there was only you–behind-the-eyes, your hand, the pencil, and the paper – no thought. This is a one-point focus on a specific event. Everything else was 'tuned out'.

This particular exercise is an introduction to a focus on an external event, through cognition (hopefully with minimal 'subjective event' interference – no thinking). This one-point focus idea will be used again throughout this chapter.

Again, another aspect to *Exercise and Lab 2*, as in *1B*, is in learning about 'not doing something'. If you make a mandala from one of the templates (*IV, V, VI,* or *VI*), not making a line can be as important as making a line.

❑ *Exercise and Lab 3* (Chapter 3.5) is <u>non-automatic</u> or a deliberate exercise (unlike *Exercise and Lab 1*). This truth perception exercise is where you, the individual, begin to play with your matrix: 'subjective event' loop, lens array, and storages. This assignment has you take an item and jump into inclusive parallels to greater more comprehensive events using focus and storage.

This exercise can increase truth known, truth perceived, and truth chosen (T_K, T_P, and T_C). It also works at decreasing ~~truth~~ perceived and ~~truth~~ chosen (F_P and F_C). In addition, the assignment exercises one-point focus (*1Δt*), and it uses the 'subjective event' feedback loop dynamically.[6] (Both operations strengthen the mind/matrix's coordination.)

Truth can enter *Storage* from the *Perceptual Lens Array* from both the Cognitive input and through Choice.[7] Through Cognition, truth goes directly into *Knowledge* and then into *Programming*.[8] Through these various loops, an individual can affect one's own consciousness change and expand the perceptions by increasing the presence of truth within your mind/matrix. This exercise provides a way for you to self induce the 'ringing' change of consciousness of *Exercise and Lab 1A*.

---

2 Chapter 4.8, Ring My Bell
3 Do not talk…
4 "Those who know, do not talk. Those who talk, do not know." First line of the Tao te Ching
5 Creating Mandalas
6 Example: Chart 4-4, *L4*
7 Example: Chart 4-4, *J1*
8 Example: Chart 4-4, *I5*

When our perceptions are based on Absolutes (remember that was part of the exercise, to store Absolutes; something you perceive to be always so) this also tends to decrease ~~truth~~ participation within the finite mortal mind/matrix.

What are the desires (D_S) for this exercise? Wanting to learn, play, or grow can be the single desire here; or just curiosity works. When the author was a teenager and 'got the exercise down', he found that sometimes doing an exercise was a kind of playing. Look at it as if you are playing with words, and how things can fit together; saying, "this is like this", "this appears like this." Curiosity (want to know or experiment) and a want to play can become useful desires.

❏ *Exercise and Lab 4*[9], this exercise uses a one-point focus ($t\Delta t$) and the one-point focus is continually changing focus. The mortal mind operates in time. Therefore, there are some time constraints on it. This exercises uses the time it takes information from an 'objective event' to pass through the *Perceptional Lens Array*, through Cognition, to *Storages*, to you (Figure 4-4, *III*), and interrupts it before the route is completed.

Exercise and Lab 4 illustrates the high priority role that Cognition has within your mortal mind/matrix. It demonstrates how a continual cognition operation over a short period can interrupt other mental processes and can cause these mental processes to start over (re-set your mortal mind/matrix).

❏ *Exercise and Lab 4.1*, the imagination exercise (Chapter 4) is another way you actively use of the front part of your lens array. This exercise has you do this in several ways. By getting you to imagine something actual, but not directly seen, it can increase total perceptions (P_S), as well as truth perceived (T_P), and truth known (T_K). This exercise can also decrease ~~truth~~ perceived ($\mathcal{F}_P$) by preoccupying the mortal/mind matrix.

This exercise involves an additional exposure to a one-point focus ($t\Delta t$). *Exercise and Lab 4.1* also requires a cycle of information flowing through Choice to *Programming*, from *Programming*, through the Subjective Event, into a refocus of the perceptual lens, and back to Choice.[10]

The exercise gets you to play with your Imagination triangle within your matrix. It gets you to use imagination in conjunction with **Actual** realities of Chapter 4.2. Instead of imagining something that is not there, you are trying to imagine something you know or remember is there but you cannot physically perceive it. This exercise has you match your 'subjective event' with 'objective events'. This is an exercise in increasing perception of a reality not directly seen -- expanding your perception of a reality. The mystical term for this is "opening the mind's eye". You are trying to 'see a little further'.

A side effect of doing this exercise is it can decrease the participation of desires for ~~truth~~ perceived ($D_{\mathcal{F}p}$) [and therefore decrease total desires (D_S) as well as decrease ~~truth~~ chosen ($\mathcal{F}_C$)]. It does this by preoccupying the mind/matrix with a larger picture/perception so the desires for smaller perceptions fall away before it. Remember; desire and perception are one thing.

This exercise familiarizes you with changing your focus and manipulating the front of your mind through the 'subjective event' loop.[11]

❏ *Exercise and Lab 5* (Chapter 5.4) addresses the desires/perception area of the matrix, the front lens of the *Perceptional Lens Array*. *Labs 1, 3*, and *4* presented direct flows toward truth and toward the cognition area of the matrix array.[12]

Lab 5 exposes you to your perceptional lens' influence, how the flow of information is to be chosen. The see/want motivational exercise can disclose to you your perceptions/desires or thought/emotion sets. What do you see (T_P and $\mathcal{F}_P$)? What do you want/not-want (D_S, D_{T_P}, and $D_{\mathcal{F}p}$)? What are your attachments (A_S)? Perceiving some of your internal relationships of your

---

9 Eye Exercise or 'Surfing' the Mechanism
10 Example: Chart 4-4, *H10*
11 Example: Chart 4-4, *H7* or *H10*
12 Example: Chart 4-4, *J1*

perceptions to your desires, perceiving flows towards truth and ~~truth~~, and then to choice, was an aim of *Exercise and Lab 5*.

All the *Perceptional Lens Array* elements can appear in these labs. The flows proceed, depending on where you take it, what you believe in, what you want to work with, or what your faith is (what you apply), to the Choice input. To pre-form intentions or change motivations are choices through refocus (a choice not to accept the current focus and then refocus ensues).

Okay, choice to do what? In the final analysis, our mortal mind/matrix, at any one period of time, is representative of all the choices we have made. Our mind's programming is the net result of the choices or judgments we have made in our lives. There are variations to the hardwiring (i.e., genetic configurations). However, the manner of flows of truth/~~truth~~ ($T/\!\!\!T$), related to our choices and storages, are much the same.

<u>You can never completely eliminate Truth or truth from your finite mind/matrix.</u> You can only choose to ignore it. Your mortal mind is a very limited version of God's Mind/Matrix – Love's Logic, which in turn, is a result of an Absolute Love. Truth involves the very laws of your existence, physically and metaphysically. To say you can eliminate truth from your mind is like saying you can walk away from gravity. Truth will always be in the 'background' of your mind. It is an element of your existence.

Conversely, ~~truth~~ and the 'truth' that sustains the ~~truth~~ are quite removable; they are dependent. Temporal in nature and un-fed, ~~truth~~ has a specific window of time to exist. In a previous chapter, the cup analogy and how the mind can hold only so much was made. Elimination of ~~truth~~ within your mind/cup will automatically allow more room for truth. Since, "nature abhors a vacuum" truth will fill the space vacated by the ~~truth~~ within a mortal mind.

Given truth are the laws by which something – anything – works, this means any exercise that eliminates or reduces ~~truth~~ not only would be to your spiritual/metaphysical advantage, but to your practical everyday advantage as well.

One way this idea has been traditionally approached is by narrowing the content of the Choice option (C_S) within your mind matrix. Reducing what is in your choice will not hurt the truth. However, it can bring about a reduction of the ~~truth~~ reinforcement. Many meditations, chants, and exercises work on this.

When doing future labs and exercises from this book, you will be reminded periodically to look at the formula and see how you are plugged into it. Chapter 5 introduced the idea that when an individual plays around with the exponents of the formula, it can have a major effect.

It has been said, "If you but had faith, you can move mountains." This is a particular case where you may have an infinite amount of Absolute Truth known (T_K), to an infinite amount of Absolute Truth perceived (T_P), to the Truth chosen (T_C), to an infinite amount of faith (F) power (application of Absolute Truth -- Creation). The numerator term becomes an infinite figure with a multitude of infinities within it. This, conjoined with a *0* in the denominator, makes for God divided by *0*. Your effectiveness transcends the formula and your temporal mind/matrix – mortal mind, and then, you begin to operate with the Precious Eternal Moment of Creation within you. As stated previously, this is the working miracles and high magic area. (See Figure 5-4)

In this book's remaining exercises and labs, there will be a repeated attempt to hold the denominator value of the formula down to as small as it can be. It is encouraged to keep ~~truth~~ perceived and ~~truth~~ chosen ($\!\!\!T_P$ and $\!\!\!T_C$) to one or less. You will be asked to keep desire to one (D_S), to a single desire for a single event or for truth perceived (D_{Tp}). In addition, you will learn to work on reducing your attachments to zero (A_S). Working on all of these variables at once, helps insure the formula's denominator is small and can increase effectiveness of these or any exercises.

How does one reduce these things? One way is at the beginning of each exercise, you will be asked to look at your desires and perceptions. What do you want from this exercise or the whole spiritual trip? What do you want from doing this exercise? What is your intention?[13]

This is important. When you start your meditation exercise (or anything), it is very helpful to establish priorities. "I am going to do _____ exercise for _____ time period". It may be helpful before starting a meditation, ask yourself some questions. For example: "What do I want when I'm doing this exercise? What do I hope to achieve? What do I want from life?" The more honest you are, the better off you will be when you start.

Remember, "I don't know" can be an honest answer. <u>Recognition of ignorance is the beginning of wisdom</u>.[14]

To help keep D_S down, it is suggested that while doing these exercises that some kind of time keeping instrument be used. A watch with a beeper, a cooking timer, or a clock that strikes on the fifteen minutes, anything that keeps time and lets you know how much time has passed while your focus is elsewhere. It is suggested that you use such instruments to help prioritize your tasks; "for _____ period of time, I only want to do _____."

Remembering motivation – perception/desires -- can aid you when you drift. It helps bring you back and it gives a form of prioritizing. For example: "Well, I know I am thinking of this, but right now (in this block of time) I am meditating (or doing this exercise) and it's something I can think about later." Or, "I will ignore these thoughts for the moment. They are not what I want to do in this block of time." You can use this pre-formed "want" to help prioritize and maintain your focus. Therefore, desires are not all bad after all; they can be useful.

As mentioned in Chapter 5, one desire for truth perceived (D_{Tp}) could be very effective if truth perceived is large. It is when an individual has many desires at a very high volume (with a lot of passion) and lacks truth (no or very little T_P or T_C, and a large amount of $\mathcal{F}_P$ or $\mathcal{F}_C$), they tend to get in trouble.

Desire can be somewhat helpful because, without desire in most things, nothing happens. You will not be effective because you do not want to do anything. It is how much ~~truth~~ is within the desire ($\mathcal{F}_P$) that determines the nature of the desire, how it will work for or hinder effectiveness.

What are you 'seeing' (perceiving). What do you want? Other ways to frame the question may be:

- "Do I want to learn?"
- "What happens when I do this?"
- "Do I want peace?"
- "Do I want happiness?
- "How do I work?"
- "Do I want harmony with self, with others, with the world, or the universe, etc.?"
- "Do I want truth, or love, or God?"
- "I want to know what is this truth that I see, or this love that I see, or God?"
- "Do I know what growth is?"
- "Like... I want to be 'One' with the Universe. Dude."

On everyday mundane level, the level where most people work, desires are a necessity. For everyday life, zero desire is not effective because you will do nothing. No want, no work. Ideally, desire (D_S) should be one in most situations. It should be kept to desire for truth perceived (D_{Tp}).

It has been stated that another way to hold the denominator down is to make attachment (A_S) equal to *0*. This is doing something just to do it, with no preconceived idea of the outcome. You must cultivate a 'disinterested-interest' in each exercise you are about to do. With A_S equal to *0*, no matter what $\mathcal{F}_P$, $\mathcal{F}_C$, or D_S are, the denominator will become one.

---

13 The first triangle in your lens.
14 This cannot be stressed enough.

For most meditations, it is encouraged that you have only one clear desire when you start an exercise or meditation, with no attachment to the outcome.

One of the many things that has been repeated in this book is how limited our mortal perceptions are; we cannot see all the variables that make up an event. We do not see the whole picture, so there are bound to be holes in our perception. Working with non-attachment allows the holes to fill themselves, instead of filling them with our preferences or our creations ($\mathcal{F}_K$ or $\mathcal{F}_P$).

For everyday use and for most *ESP* exercises, it is better to keep desire/wants equal to one (or less-than-one) while being totally unattached to the outcome.

There is a 'wholeness' that you can not immediately see – One Mind. There are so many ways you can approach this oneness. It is like a mathematical circle. No matter which way you go, you end up with one. Do you understand? Peace, Love, or God, that is all One anyway. There are just these different names and labels for it. We, as people, have a variety of different attributes that we ascribe to the universe that all relate to this oneness concept – a multitude of philosophies.

In terms of philosophies, it does not matter what you pick that represents this oneness to you. It is the 'oneness' idea that is important. You could pick the universe is on the back of a turtle idea as opposed to the big bang universe concept, as long as the concept involves a Oneness. However, for these concepts to be absolutely non-exclusive (loving), the 'big bang' thinking must not exclude the symbology of 'turtle' and the 'turtle' must not exclude 'big bang' thinking. How is this possible? Working with Absolutes can regulate them both to being 'special case' approaches or perspectives. Outside these 'special cases' the concepts may cease to be relevant.

You could believe the universe could be on the back of a slug, instead of the turtle, just as long as it has the oneness/non-exclusive concept. When working with a non-exclusive Oneness concept, you are working with God's Love whether you know it or not.

In summary, to the introduction to this chapter, what we see is determined by what we know and want. When we daydream or fantasize, our minds tell us what we want to hear (or fear) based on our *Storages*. The mortal mind/matrix is limited. If it is filled with daydreams and fantasies, it does not have room for truth to be consciously present. The opposite is also true. If it is filled with truth, it will have less room for ~~truth~~.

Our conscious mind's focus can only do one thing at a time. There are moments our conscious mind can appear to be busy multi-tasking. It accomplishes multi-tasking by spending a short time focusing here then a short time focusing there, then a short time focusing here and then back to a short time focusing there, etc. In electronics, this term is called multiplexing and gives *FM* stereo radio. We can daydream while doing a physical chore. And…if we do not bring our mind's focus back to the chore periodically, preoccupation in the daydream will make us 'screw' the chore up.

Subconsciously, a part of the mind is constantly maintaining an **Actual** reality condition, breathing, heartbeat, balance, etc. Another working part involves a constant communion within *Storages* (between *Knowledge, Programming, Memory,* etc.) and the *Perceptual Lens Array.*[15]

Most of the rest of the exercises and labs in this book involve a one-point focus of some sort or another. In many ways our mental focus is like a muscle -- the more you use it the stronger it gets. Asking you to do these exercises, in many ways, is like asking you to do mental calisthenics. Just like any physical regimen, it requires self-discipline. Moreover, like any physical regimen, it may take practice (repetition over some time reference) for effects to become apparent.

Some of the general effects of a constant meditation practice can be:

- Learning some internal coordination and strength

---

15 Chart 4-4, *14 A & B*

- Learning some things about yourself
- Learning the value of not doing something
- Setting up blocks of time when ~~truth~~ reinforcement is minimal can promote the reduction of ~~truth~~ with your mind
- Altered states

6.2 – What is Meditation?

*A*ll meditation can be reduced to a single concept, a one-point focus on an event. It usually is associated with an internal event; which is the traditional perception of meditation. Meditations can also involve an external event, like a candle or drawing. Furthermore, some meditations can involve both as well, like some athletics or martial arts. With both, the meditation may be a one-point focus on the interaction between the internal and external event.

The artwork of *Exercise and Lab 2* serves as an introduction to this concept. When doing artwork, one's focus can be, at times, only on the tip of the pencil and the effect it is having on the paper. This is a one-point focus on an event. All meditations can be expressed as a variation of this theme. In the case of internal events, the focus may be on no event; and, this is still an event.

In addition, meditations involve a one-point focus over a period of time $f(\varDelta t)$ of Chapter 5. Usually, the focus is on some event, (x). The consciousness change that occurs with doing meditations (let us say y) involves a direct relationship with $\varDelta t$. The greater $\varDelta t$ is the more it will affect y. As $\varDelta t \Uparrow \Rightarrow y \Uparrow$.

An excellent example of this relationship is how one feels getting out of a car after just finishing some long distance driving; the 'buzzed' disconnected feeling you get. That one-point focus involves a constant return to a form of mental peripheral vision. In addition, there are elements of the eye exercise of Assignment 4 in the driving operation. The effect on you is a consciousness change.

One purpose of doing theses exercises is for you to observe some of the consciousness changing effects that these meditation exercises can produce. One way of doing this is:

❑ <u>Before doing an exercise</u>, pre-form your intention, cultivate a disinterested-interest, and just sit and notice how you feel: physically, mentally, and emotionally. What does your body feel like? What are your emotions right now? Notice the flavor of the thoughts you have been entertaining before the exercise. Also, establish your priorities for this coming time window; what is your intention.
❑ <u>After doing each exercise</u>, again, notice how you feel. What does your body feel like? What are your emotions right now? Notice the flavor of the thoughts (if any) you have afterward. Sit with (and notice) how you feel after doing each exercise.

These two operations (pre-forming intentions/attachments and observation of current state) are <u>part</u> of all the rest of the exercises in this book. One is to be performed before each exercise. Right after each exercise, set aside a block of time, and observe how you feel after doing the exercise – the effects. Just observe, for about 2-5 minutes. These activities are a <u>part</u> of every exercise from this point forward.

If you want, enter these perceptions into your notebook for future reference.

********************  ********************

Exercise and Lab 6: Breathing Exercises

There are many methods of doing breathing exercises. There is a complete yoga[16] around breathing exercises (Pranayama Yoga). One of the reasons breath is being covered first is because when mantras and other exercises are introduced some of them can be done in conjunction with the breath.

In addition, breath exercises introduce to you the consciousness changes that can occur with breathing. This can help with the perception of effects of mental exercises. It can help you see what elements of the effects are due to breathing and what elements are due to the mental exercise.

Breathing exercises are an excellent introduction to meditation -- focusing on an 'internal event'.

Of the many methods of working with breath, this book will focus primarily on three basic methods. (All these methods are breathing through the nose only, and not through the mouth.)

When doing these exercises, your attitude or focus is to be watching and waiting. Watch your body move. Hear and feel the air moving through you. No thought is appropriate or desired. And...wait. Wait until the allotted time period is finished. Accept no judgment. Just watch your breath and wait. When you are finished with the breathing exercises, you then enter a reflection period; you are to extend your watching and waiting period an extra few minutes.

To begin with, make your self comfortable, but not comfortable enough to fall asleep. Sit upright in a chair, sit cross-legged, lie down with your hands behind your head, or any position that allows you to be only partially relaxed. (Any position that is difficult for you to fully fall asleep in.)

The three different exercises you will be doing are:

➤ **Upper abdomen** → To learn this exercise, place your right hand on your chest and your left hand on your lower belly. The first exercise uses only the chest, and of course, the diaphragm. The only thing moving when you breathe is your chest and the top part of your shoulders. Slowly breathe deeply in through your nose. Feel the air flowing into the upper part of your abdomen. Perhaps, pulling you shoulders back to increase the intake. Then, slowly exhale through your nose. Only your right hand should be moving in and out. Your left hand should not be moving. The only thing moving is your chest and upper torso. Your stomach is not moving whatsoever. Exaggerate the body movement if you wish. Your one-point focus over a period of time ($1\Delta t$) is the air moving through you.

➤ **Lower abdomen** → The second exercise is just the opposite. You do not move your chest or your shoulders at all, and just breathe in slowly, deep from the pit of your abdomen. With this breathing version, only your stomach and the lower part of your abdomen are moving. Only your left hand should be moving in and out. Your right hand should not be moving. Make an effort not to move anything else. You may have to exaggerate your stomach movement so you can do this. Please notice how it feels when this exercise tends to pull air deep into the bottom of your lungs. Again, your one-point focus over a period of time ($1\Delta t$) is the air moving through you.

➤ **Both** →The third method is a combination of the previous two done in sequence. It is done like this. When you inhale, you slowly and deeply inhale with the stomach; only your left hand is moving at first. As you get close to the end of the inhale, you expand your shoulders and chest with air, bringing the air to the top of the chest, your right hand begins to move after the left hand is almost done. Then, begin exhaling from your stomach, your left hand goes in first. As the breath finishes, you exhale with your shoulders and chest

---

16 Yoga means 'union'. Yogas are approaches to union with the Divine.

collapsing. Again, your right hand begins to move after the left hand is almost done. It is as if you are filling your lungs up from the very bottom first and expanding your body all the way up to the top. Then when you exhale, you are squeezing it out from the bottom first and, finally, you squeeze the top.

You may get dizzy after doing these exercises for a few minutes. These are altered states of consciousness. When you couple this altered consciousness from your breath with some of the other mental exercises, it is possible to get interesting effects. One of the goals of this breath exercise is to get you to learn to maintain focus through consciousness changes ($f\Delta t$) by watching your breath. Breathe into what you are feeling. Just remember to breathe through your nose slowly to avoid hyperventilation.

When doing these exercises set a block of time aside. Use some objective time reference, like a cooking timer, a clock, a makeshift sundial, etc. This can help you maintain focus.

Your focus ($f\Delta t$) is only on breathing; you focus on the air going in and out of the body. With no thought, the idea is to just wait and observe. Watch it (air) and yourself, and if you drift, remember: what you want; what are you doing this for; and gently bring your awareness back to doing it again. Remember your pre-formed intention.[17]

These breathing and focus exercises deal predominately with the *Focus Control Buss* and somewhat limit the amount of ~~truth~~ that goes through choice in the matrix of Figure 4-4 [temporarily reducing ~~truth~~ chosen ($\mathcal{T}_C$), ~~truth~~ perceived ($\mathcal{T}_P$), and total desires (D_S)][18]. It does this by preoccupying the mind with an internal event -- breath.

In addition, it involves a manipulation somewhat of the 'subjective event' loop in your matrix. This exercise can also help you to foster an awareness of your body.

This assignment consists of:

➤ *Get into a comfortable position.*
➤ *Do a pre-form of your intention or establish your priorities, notice how you feel at that moment, and cultivate a 'disinterested-interest' in what you are about to do.*
➤ *When doing these exercises, do a breathing method for an allotted period of time (10-15 minutes for example), and then stop.*
➤ *Sit for 2-5 minutes after each period of breathing. Notice how you feel. No judgments; just kind of childlike; notice how you feel. Observe the change within you. This part of the assignment is for you to just sit and feel what changes -- if any -- have occurred inside you.*
➤ *Perhaps enter perceptions or feelings into your workbook.*
➤ *Do each breathing method three separate times (this makes for 9 total sessions). If doing a number of these exercises in one sitting, allow a period of 15 minutes between exercises.*

As mentioned previously, these breathing exercises can be applied with other meditations. Once you as an individual get this breathing down, you can do breathing while putting your focus somewhere else. You may even use the breathing in conjunction with focusing on something other than breath (like focus on a 'subjective event' in conjunction with an 'objective event' – air movement).

In addition, this exercise introduces to you the concept of breathing into what ever is happening to you or what you are feeling at that time.

Exercise and Lab 7: Mantras and Chanting

With mantras, the application of the mental focus -- ($f\Delta t$) -- is you focusing on a word, and you are using the words for a vehicle to the exclusion of everything else. More specifically

---

17 Like, "I am only going to be doing this breathing exercise for the next 10 minutes."
18 Example: Chart 4-4, *C19*

the focus is on the word and nothing else. You can also use a set of symbols – words and concepts words imply -- as vehicles to 'cruise' around in your own head.

As with the previous exercises, before you start some kind of chant or mantra session, or any other exercise, ask, "What am I doing this for?" Pre-form your intention; set your priorities. "I am only going to do _____ for this period of time."

Question your current paradigm, programming, or perceptions; "What am I seeing? What do I want from what I see? I want to know what happens when I do this."

For any new paradigm or perception to be taught, the old paradigms or perceptions are usually called into question.

As stated previously, some of the goals, reasons, and/or desires for doing these exercises are: God, union with the universe or Divine, love, kindness, harmony within yourself or with the world, truth, understanding, knowledge, a sense of 'there's something else', or just curiosity and experimenting. "What happens when I do this?" Just doing this to observe your own mechanisms is a very valid motivation – recognizing your ignorance. "I'm doing this to know me, to figure out how I work."

Any answer that revolves around the concept of 'One' or recognition of ignorance is no problem. It is clear sailing, pretty much.

What mantra syllables – words -- you use can reflect your perceptions and motivations. The author met a man who taught meditation and biofeedback in a college.[19] He said, you can use any word for a mantra, and he is right -- you can use any word whatsoever for one-point focus. He used the word hamburger. His mantra was, "Hamburger, hamburger, hamburger, etc."[20] However, what word/s you choose may reflect in the change of consciousness because your previous perceptions and desires influence it – your associations with the words

Different mantra exercises can produce different results, changes of consciousness. This is because your desire/perceptions[21] focus is in separate areas. When varying these mantras, the different desire/perceptions involved produce varied changes within the individual. The change of consciousness feels different with this mantra than it does with that mantra, and different with this other one.

That is why this book is going to give at least three different mantra forms to introduce three variations of changes of consciousness. The purpose of these exercises is to expose you to the forms and the variations in consciousness change; how you feel afterward.

When you use a mantra, you are altering the flows through your perceptual lens array. Your one-point focus over a period of time ($1\Delta t$) will be one perception – the words or the perception related to the words. An effect of this narrow focus is ~~truth~~ perceived ($\mathcal{T}_P$) and ~~truth~~ chosen ($\mathcal{T}_C$) will have a reduced participation within your mind/matrix.

Exercise and Lab 7A: Passive Chanting

The first mantra to be introduced many people know -- *OM*. It can be pronounced long ō and with m or it can be pronounced as *Aum*. This chant is conjoined with breathing, one *OM* per breath. You may want to learn to say it aloud at first.

So, inhale through the nose. Then exhale and as you exhale say, "*Aaauuummmmmmmmmmm*". (or *Ooooommmmmmmm*). The vowel part, '*aaauuu*' or ōōō, is relatively short. The last part, '*mmmmmmmm*', is long and let yourself vibrate to it. Let yourself vibrate or resonate to the '*mmmmm*' part. Learn to ride the "mmmm..." part into yourself.

One *OM* is stretched with each exhale of a breath. Then, take another deep breath and *Aaauuummmmmmmmmmm*.

There are three basic ways to chant *OM*.

♦ Aloud like mentioned in the example (one *OM*/breath).

---

19 When not teaching, he was doing biofeedback research for the Naval Postgraduate School in Monterey, CA
20 This is the basis for Transcendental Meditation (TM); the one point focus is on the repetition of a specific word.
21 D_S, P_S, T_C, $\mathcal{T}_P$, and $\mathcal{T}_C$

- ◆ Another way is to say it softly to yourself, the word gently coming out with your breath.
- ◆ The third is no vocal whatsoever, and do the word inside your mind (one *OM*/breath).

Generally speaking, the more pronounced consciousness changes occur when the *OM*s are done in stillness; there are no body applications splitting focus. You may have to learn to ride the vibration by saying it aloud first though.

Once get the hang of riding the vibration concept, say *OM* in your mind to the silence, in the stillness of your being. As you are doing that one-point focus on *OM*, you turn your awareness and everything 90 degrees away from your thought/emotional sets, away from everything and jumping into yourself with this '*mmmmmm*' vibration/sound.

As with the other exercises, before you start this exercise, set a specific block of time. You have the cooking timer (or ?) out. Do this exercise for 20 minutes.

Remember that this is the only thing you are going to do. If you start drifting, remember: "I don't want to do that now, I want to do this." And…go back to the exercise. Kind of like; a person on roller skates thinks, "I got to remember to write something down for the report. Oh, but I don't want to do that right now, I want to have fun and finish doing this."

Maintain your focus!!! Growth comes from bringing yourself back.

As presented earlier, the third method, the silent one, can be the more powerful one. This is true for most mantras (with a few exceptions). A deeper trance can ensue when the body is not involved.

A number of swimming and water analogies can be made with meditation. One trick of doing an exercise can be similar to a swimming stroke. When teaching swimming, the usually recommended action is stroke, glide; stroke, glide; stroke, and glide. This translates as work, rest; work, rest; work, rest…

With this exercise, the operators can do this inside themselves. The stroke can be in the inhale, in the '*Ooo*", or '*Aaauuu*' part, and the glide is in the 'mmmmm' part. You can learn to stroke and glide concept in your own head. Burst of focus, rest or glide, burst of focus, rest or glide, burst of focus, rest or glide, etc. Move deep inside yourself. Stroke, focus, glide. Go back deeper. Stroke, glide.

On the other hand, letting go and entering your being can serve as the glide. It is shutting everything down and riding the sound (or vibration), while empty. The stroke in this instance is the inhale and the initial sounding 'Aaauuu', the glide is the exhale and the vibrating 'mmmmm'.

Stroke-glide can be considered more active while dropping into yourself can be considered more passive. *OM* is one of the passive chants that is being introduced now; along with the stroke-glide aspect which, can be more relevant when we get into active aspects of focus as with music.

The idea that is being presented here is that <u>there is more than one way to do any one of these chants</u>. One way is like swimming, while another is equivalent to floating in the water, exhaling, and sinking rather than stroking.[22] Nevertheless, no matter which way you look at it or do it, whenever you drift, recognize it and re-evaluate or remember priorities: "What do I want? Why am I doing this?" Gently bring your focus back to doing what you want, in this case, the exercise. Your growth occurs when you catch yourself.

Remember that if you just ask yourself that question ("What do I want to do right now"), this can help you stay focused. This idea of "what do you want now" can be applied to <u>anything</u>. It is prioritizing your actions in the moment. The process of doing this involves the basic mechanics of refocusing your mind/matrix.

The *OM* exercise consists of:

---

22 An exercise taught in swimming class that shows the student that as long as you have air in your lungs; you will float.

➢ *Get into a comfortable position (but not too comfortable).*
➢ *Do a motivational analysis or establish your priorities/intention for the next block of time and cultivate a disinterested-interest.*
➢ *When doing these exercises, do an OM chant for an allotted period of time (twenty minutes for example), and then stop.*
➢ *The next part of the assignment is just to sit; after each period of chanting, sit with what you are feeling for 2-5 minutes. Notice how you feel. No judgments; child like, notice how you are feeling. Observe.*
➢ *Do a chant method three separate times with each of the three methods – aloud, softly, and silently -- (9 times total). If doing a number of these exercises in one sitting, allow a period of 15 minutes between exercises.*
➢ *Enter any thoughts or feelings into your workbook.*

Voluntary and Optional Exercises
➢ *Do the above exercise using I Am,[23] 'Iiaammmmmmmmm'.*
➢ *Something else can be added onto the chant that can alter its effect. Take the OM, together with your breathing, and go through your mind and remember a musical chord that gives you 'goose bumps'. Some musical chord or transition from some favorite song that gives you a goose bump reaction. Then you say that OM to that chord. ♫Aaauuummmmmmmmmmm♫ (breathe). ♫Aaauuummmmmmmmmmm♫ (breathe)…*

********************  ********************

Exercise and Lab 7B: Affirmation Chanting

The second mantra to be introduced is an affirmation exercise. An excellent example that is already out in world religions is the Nichrin sho-sho Buddhists chant: *Nam-Myo-Ho-Renge-Kyo*. Affirmation chanting also appears in many shamanic practices.

Essentially, Nam-Myo-Ho-Renge-Kyo means, "I will follow the chosen way to peace and enlightenment." (At least, that was what people who taught it told the author.) Still, it is an affirmation/reaffirmation chant. An affirmation chant can be done with or without devotions. It is an affirmation of a direction you want to go in chant. Affirmation chants are also known as power chants.

However, because Nam-Myo-Ho-Renge-Kyo happens to be a mouthful for non-Japanese speaking people, you may want to develop a chant that has meaning for you in your native language. Like:

- "I'm going to do this, I'm going to do this, I'm going to do this." …
- "I will _____.", "I will _____.", "I will _____.",…
- "I will follow the chosen way", "I will follow the chosen way.", "I will follow the chosen way." …
- "I will go to peace", "I will go to peace", "I will go to peace"…
- "I will go to God", "I will go to God", "I will go to God"…
- "I will be one with Creation", "I will be one with Creation", "I will be one with Creation"…

When doing an affirmation chanting session, say a number of your chosen affirmation phrases with one breath. When you run out of breath, inhale. It is even possible to say one chant phrase while inhaling. With this chant, as with the others, you may develop a rhythm with breath. Affirmation exercises can be the exception to the 'say it in silence' rule mentioned in the previous exercise.

Recognize the "I" element, using breath, along with the choosing element in the chant, and expressing it physically produces the effect. This chant is tweaking aspects of the human mind/matrix (decreasing D_S, $\mathcal{F}_P$, and $\mathcal{F}_C$ while attempting to increase T_P and T_C). An affirmation chant is playing with desire, perception, choice; desire, perception, choice; desire, perception,

---

23 Doing the above chant with the name the Nameless Desert God gave Moses on the mountain.

choice loop. The use of this exercise with constancy can affect your total *Programming* through the exercise of choice using repetition.[24] Again…it is also exercising your focus 'muscle'.

Again, you do several affirmations in one exhale and perhaps one affirmation with the inhale. Part of the effect of this chant will be due to breath.

When you do this exercise with eyes open, it is recommended to have something for your eyes to converge on in order to have a one-point physical focus. Your one-point focus over a period of time ($t\Delta t$) for this exercise is with the words and the mandala or yantra you made in *Exercise and Lab 2: Creating Mandalas.* [25]

This is only one of the ways the mandalas created in *Homework assignment 2* can be used in this course. Your eyes are to stay on that yantra or mandala (or, what ever is in front of you) as your mind stays on the words.

It is also strongly recommended that whatever you are focusing on be in black and white.[26] No other thought is appropriate. The idea is you would keep your eyes on the center of a mandala while saying something like:

- ♦ "*Nam-Myo-Ho-Renge-Kyo, Nam-Myo-Ho-Renge-Kyo, Nam-Myo-Ho-Renge-Kyo*"
- ♦ "I will do this. I will do this. I will do this. I will do this."
- ♦ "I choose peace. I choose peace. I choose peace. I choose peace."
- ♦ "I will follow the chosen way to _____. I will follow the chosen way to _____. I will follow the chosen way to _____.", etc.

It is strongly advised, for this exercise, that there is only one thing to look at and that 'something' does not move. <u>Do not let your eyes drift from that object while chanting</u>. There are a couple of advantages to doing it this way -- one is you are maintaining a physical focus as well as a mental one. In addition, there are less visual distractions this way and it decreases 'objective event' perceptions at Choice.

You may want to experiment with different chants. Then, pick one you like to do constantly. You are also encouraged to experiment with this type of chant with the eyes closed as well as open. Just to notice the difference of effect the chant has on you.

Again, doing this exercise exerts your focus over a change of time [$f(\Delta t)$]. It can strengthen your focus and resolve. All of these exercises do in the end. They are applications of the formula and the matrix. The stronger your focus is, the more effective the chant is going to be. No thought (perception) is appropriate while chanting except the chant.

This exercise is to:

➢ *Get into a comfortable position (again, not too comfortable). When doing the exercise with eyes open, hang the mandala/object on the wall at eye level and position yourself before it about 3-4 feet (1+ meter) away from it.*

➢ *Before each session, pre-form intention, cultivate a disinterested-interest, and establish your priorities.*

➢ *Perform an opening ritual like bowing before the mandala/object three times, one mantra and one bow per breath. Emptying your mind, except for the words, as you do so.*

➢ *Do the affirmation chant for at least 20 minutes.*

➢ *When done, perform a closing ritual like the opening one; again, bowing before the mandala/object three times -- one mantra and one bow per breath. This time in emptiness. (The before and after bowing ritual clearly marks a beginning and a closure to this exercise.)*

➢ *Do the affirmation chant session <u>aloud</u> at least three separate times.*

➢ *Do the affirmation chant session <u>softly</u> to yourself three separate times.*

---

24 Example: Chart 4-4, *H10*

25 Chapter 1

26 This way less information – no color – is coming into the mind from the outside. *Nam-Myo-Ho-Renge-Kyo* uses a gohonzon – a black and white calligraphy scroll.

> ➢ *With both ways, develop mantra rhythm with your breath. If the eyes are closed, focus behind the eyes, go all the way back in. With eyes open, focus the eyes on one specific thing (like the mandala) and do not let the eyes drift.*
> ➢ *Sit for 2-5 minutes after the chant session; this is in order to get a perspective on how it feels afterwards.*
> ➢ *Enter any thoughts or feelings into your notebook or journal.*
> ➢ *Do both methods with the <u>eyes open </u>looking only at the mandala or yantra three times. Then, do both methods with the <u>eyes closed</u> three times (making 12 separate chanting sessions).*

One of the reasons why this specific type of exercise is chosen is, it is an example of an active affirmation whereas *OM* is a passive and a dropping in. They are almost opposites. This exercise, instead of a dropping in, is going out, involves a participation in a specific perception/desire, and a one-point focus on the words as well as the object.

A reminder of what you are being exposed to are chants that can induce different changes of consciousness, when done over a period of time. Just like the breathing exercises, chanting can have varied effects on your mind/matrix. That is why these three types of chants exercises were picked. They have different effects.

********************  ********************

Exercise and Lab Chanting 7C: Devotional Chanting

The third mantra category is devotional, also known as a heart chakra chant. There are all types of devotional chants in world religions -- the Psalms in Judaic and Christian traditions, Hari-Krishna from India; they are all devotional. The rosary is a devotional form of mantra.

To help you understand devotional chants, one reference is that it involves a desire for union with something greater than yourself; devotional chants involve a recognition of 'something' grander than you. The earlier mantras are more steering in, steering out, this way, that way. They were dealing mostly with steering – manipulating mental direction or operation. *Exercise and Labs 7A & 7B* can be done without any concept of a Divine Being. Throw in the concept of a Divine Being and now the chant turns up the drives, turns up the fire. You are working in conjunction with the fire aspect of the spiritual, the emotional, the desires.[27]

As long as there is some sense of a Creator/Creatrix in an operation, it has a devotional element. Devotional can go so many directions. Devotional can carry in to Shamanism as well as Islam. Devotion is an element that is at the core of almost every religion. The whole concept -- recognition of something greater and the desire to be with or at one with -- is used different ways. It is the same concept; just the individual perceptions and philosophies of what that One may be change.

Devotional may also involve a degree of contemplation of the God's Glory.

Devotional mantras are also known as prayer vehicles. Psalms are prayer vehicles. <u>Prayer is a 'heart song' communion from the Created to the Creator.</u> The bible's psalms are very old 'heart songs' to God.

Some heart songs have words and there are others that are wordless. With this devotional chanting exercise, you are being introduced to the 'heart song' through a set of mantra/words. It is encouraged that you to develop your own 'heart song' to your Creator.

The 'heart song' music begins in the heart and mind -- intention, <u>not the voice</u>. The heart is singing, guided by your intention -- perception. The voice is only expressing what is in the heart.

---

27 The perception/desire analogy of how perceptions steer, while desire/emotions are the gas, Chapter 4.5 - The Perceptional Lens Array Matrix. Staying in that parallel, what happens when an engine floods; it gets to much gas. The gas/passion must be in the right proportion to the necessary operation.

One of the nice things about devotional mantras is that they tend to pre-form your intentions automatically.

In the previous two mantras, desire was kept at a low volume to little/no-strong desires at all. We kept desires singular and low volume -- one perception and one desire. When you begin to perform devotional chants, you start turning up the volume of your desire a bit (along with, introducing numerous perceptions). This is the desire for the One (D_{Tp}), and it is made stronger, more specific, or cultivated.

With this exercise, as with the previous ones, you are using words (or a series of perceptions) as vehicles. You use these word vehicles as vectors for your one-point focus. With this exercise, unlike the previous exercises, you are not only using words where the words do not mean anything, or have very simple meanings. Instead, you are including whole concepts involving perceptions/desires into the words. You are 'pumping' specific concepts through your mind.

You are turning up the volume on desires, and perceptions are increasing. And...you are still doing a one-point focus. For example, one devotional is a simple 'Glory Be'. *Glory be to the Father, Son, and Holy Spirit. Glory be to the Father, Son, and Holy Spirit*, etc.

(The author has found that many people have trouble with popular Christianity and a Christian God, due to some bad experiences. If this is the case with you, it is encouraged that you develop your own devotional mantra. You can use a mantra that is already established in a religion or something that fits with your perception of the Divine. Just saying, "*Glory be*" can work.)

The problem with most existing devotionals is they tend to be long and there is a large amount of memory work with them. Like the Rosary beads, or the prayer of St. Francis, or any one of the Psalms. It is usually a long wordy thing. You know: "*Yeah, though I walk through the valley of death, I will fear no evil because God is with me, etc.*" [28]

Hari Krishna is done as "*Hari Krishna, Hari Krishna, Krishna, Krishna, Hari, Hari, Hari Rama, Hari Rama, Rama, Rama, Hari, Hari*". Most devotionals tend to be long and wordy.

Whereas a one word devotional like Amen -- "♪*A...men, a...men, a...men, amen, amen...*♫" – can be useful. That one is relatively easy. And...as mentioned previously, most existing devotional chants involve a lot of memory work or use a book as a tool.

Like the other mantras, this chant can be coordinated with breath. This mantra is to be done with the desire at medium or low volume within yourself. It is better to avoid a devotional at a high desire volume, because it can be somewhat counter-productive if perceptions are not 'one' or focused on the whole (of which, you are a part). (To be 'one', is to unify a number of perceptions into one perception. It means to be inclusive or non-exclusive.) When perceptions start being skewed or divisive and the one desire starts getting at very high volume that is when the individual may start getting into fanaticism.

This is a condition where a person's perceptions tend to be divisive or exclusive (limiting truth perceived [T_P] and truth chosen [T_C]). When perceptions and desires are many and at high volume -- without any exercise of choice control – is a condition where the individual may also enter the psychotic realm. (Which, may not be that far from a being a fanatic.)

This assignment is:

➤ *You are to get into a comfortable position (but not too comfortable).*
➤ *Do a motivational analysis or establish priorities along with cultivating a disinterested-interest.*
➤ *You are to do a 20-minute sessions.*

---

28 23rd Psalm

- ➢ *The assignment is for you to use 'Glory Be', create your own, or find an existing devotional mantra (Hare Krishna, Lord's Prayer, Allah, rosary, Amen etc.).*
- ➢ *Do the chant for 20 minutes.*
- ➢ *Then, sit with what you are feeling afterwards for 2-5 minutes.*
- ➢ *Perhaps, enter how you feel in the workbook.*
- ➢ *Do this on three separate occasions.*

Additional note: those who have a problem with the Divine or Divine concepts can do the devotional with a reference toward the concept of Oneness, a Unity, or the Universe. You can facilitate the exercise using a verse from a song, any song you want, as a mantra. The important points of this exercise are: holistic motivation and perception, the breath, the mantras, and everything is focus, focus, focus, focus....

Those of you who feel there may be a Divine and you do not know what this Divine is, good. Use this; use the sense within you that there may be Something Else and you do not know what.

******************** ********************

Exercise and Lab 8A: Blank or Empty Mind Exercises

The previous exercises had you focus on a specific 'subjective event' with in your *Perceptional Lens Array*. This exercise is to produce a one-point focus $f(\Delta t)$ on maintaining a no 'subjective event' condition.

This assignment takes what you have been previously introduced to the next logical step. The exercise is in 'blankness'. No thoughts, zero, nothing, blank.

"null + 0 = hold that thought."

This essentially minimizes the 'objective' and/or 'subjective event' input of your mind/matrix. With this exercise, the choice is, "make no choice". [29]

At first, this idea may seem intimidating. Yet, there are many times in your life that you have had an empty mind and not recognized it. In athletics, this condition can occur in many different ways. In fact, when doing some athletics, focus must be maintained to such an extent on an 'external event' such that, if you think, you usually 'mess up', or are injured. In this case, the individual's perception becomes preoccupied – focus becomes split -- by a 'subjective event' at an 'objective event's' expense.

Many times, listening to, or playing music can help one be devoid of thought. [30]

No thoughts or perceptions -- that means attempting a zero for P_S and $\cancel{F}_C$. (Remember the Truth in your mind – *Knowledge* -- cannot be hurt by 'no thought'.) In reference to Figure 4-4, *Exercise and Lab 8* is an attempt to exert control of, reduce, or ignore the *Perceptual Lens Array*. This means no, or very few, ~~true~~ perceptions are chosen ($\cancel{F}_C$) with *0* attachments (A_S), conjoined with an extended one-point focus (an increase of Δt), with little or no 'subjective event'.

In doing this exercise of a blank mind, you as the operator must recognize that <u>no thought is acceptable whatsoever</u>. This is an effort to shut down or step out of the subjective feedback loop. If you think of something you feel is important, set it aside and think of it later. "Not now, I'm going to do this exercise". And...bring yourself back to the exercise.

Remember your priority for the moment; then, return to the exercise. Know what you want. All perceptions are approaching *0* in this exercise, and still there is a one-point desire for doing the exercise.

This practice reduces the overall activity of the human matrix – mortal mind . You are making only one judgment or choice -- no thought. Reduce perceptions and there is little to judge.

---

29 No truth chosen (T_C) or ~~truth~~ chosen ($\cancel{F}_C$) minimizing choice total (C_S)
30 Chapter 8

When you set this exercise up, as with the others, set a specific time limit at first. "I am going to work at having a blank mind for this period of time."

The idea is for you to set a specific time, a time with a beginning and an end to it, a timing device. This is to help you return and not drifting while you are doing this. Again, this is an application of a one-point desire. "There's only one thing I want to do for this period of time." This way, you bring desires to 1 (D_S) as perceptions (P_S) approach 0. This will help facilitate the reduction of the participation of any ~~truth~~ with in your mind/matrix.

Everything should be empty or blank for that window of time. When you find yourself drifting, remember your purpose and correct. You are just sitting and waiting, empty. It is not as if you have to do anything; because, there is nothing you have to do. You just wait; sit and wait until the time has passed and be empty. This can be done with the eyes open or the eyes closed.

With the eyes open, it can help if the eyes focus on only one thing. This narrows or simplifies the 'objective event'. Again, that is where the mandala that was made in the second homework assignment can come in handy. Hang the mandala on the wall, sit in front of it, and focus on the center of the mandala, not letting the eyes or mind to drift. You can also use the flame of a candle, a blue sky, the ocean, the sand of an egg timer, etc. The idea is to just focus, wait, and be empty (no thought is appropriate).

After attempting this, you will find that it is hard to keep a blank mind indefinitely. It is difficult. Your limited mortal version of the Creation Matrix is constantly working -- creating. However, using exercises of mantras and music, you will find that it can be done in distinct short bursts for a relatively long time.

When emptying the mind, there is the initial effort and then an effort to maintain the condition. What can be tried is a continual repetition of the initial effort.

Instead of exerting an effort of maintaining a blank while waiting an extended period, it is *blank*, *blank*, *blank*, *blank*; and doing a series of 'blanks' while waiting. This exercise can have a similar effect to the exercise of moving the eyes very quickly.

That particular eye exercise consisted of moving the eyes, in such a manner, that the eyes would rest on something only shortly. Then, they would move to something else momentarily, then to something else, then to something else, etc. Your eyes were not to linger on any one thing. This was to be done for a specific window of time (one minute).

The movement of the eyes tends to blank the matrix automatically as the eyes and mind work together to establish focus and re-cognition. *Exercise and Lab 4* takes advantage of the brief moment that the mortal mind/matrix takes to focus to Cognition, and moves before the process is completed, restarting that moment with each movement of the eyes.

Instead of physically using the eyes as with *Exercise and Lab 4*, use the distinct bursts of emptiness exercise and refocus consciously with your mind -- blank, blank, and blank -- bypassing the eyes/matrix mechanism, and doing it inside the head without using the eyes. This can be done in short bursts for a significant amount of time.

This 'quantum burst' type of approach cannot only used with emptiness alone, it can be used with music and mantras. Music is perfect for short periods of blankness -- blank, blank, and blank: an emptiness on each note.[31] You are not really thinking anything, just listening to the note. There is little or no subjective event. With mantras, an emptiness can be injected with each word.

Again, the longer you have a blank mind, more significant the consciousness change. For effectiveness (if effectiveness is measured as a change of consciousness and individual growth), the change of consciousness/effect will be directly proportional to how long the exercise is done over a change of time. The expression Δt is directly proportional to consciousness/effectiveness. There is a direct relationship of change of time to change of consciousness. Please be aware that the Δt variable also means how many 'sessions' you have done in total as well.

---

31 Chapter 8, Concerning Metaphysical Tools and Music Use

(The quality of the consciousness change/effectiveness will also be in direct relationship to how much Truth has been programmed in the mind/matrix – *Storages* – at the time of the exercise.)

The longer the operator has a blank mind, the 'heavier' their consciousness change is going to be.[32] As mentioned before, there are many different ways we can have a blank mind and we do not know it. Again, doing athletics is an example; specifically, when you have to focus on a ball. If you think about what you are doing, you are going to 'blow it'.[33] A significant part of the 'euphoria' of athletics can come from maintaining an empty one-point focus – empty mind/matrix.

The mind's 'subjective event' must be empty or still to allow fully an 'objective event' to pass through it. As mentioned before, your mortal mind/matrix is limited. With most things, the perceptual lens focus (your control of the array) cannot do two things at once. If you are busy thinking, then you are not watching your physical situation. You can open up your focus to allow both events to occur, to come through the array (a form of mental peripheral vision). However, when it comes time to act, the focus must be on the event that is to be acted upon – the 'objective event'.

Driving a car is an excellent example of this. A detached awareness can occur where we are aware of traffic and the 'chatter' in our mind. Our mind's eye is open enough to 'see' both. When driving, awareness does not need that much attention, we listen to the chatter/thoughts. However, when the car needs our focus, the chatter and thoughts must recede into the background.

Along with this, sometimes in driving a car, we create a long-term focus situations. The longer we do it; we get a consciousness change. Again, this is why our minds are in an altered state after doing a long drive.

As mentioned previously, there is a direct relationship between the time of focus (Δt) and consciousness change.

Another variable of the consciousness change is dependent on the individual's motivation – intention -- when they focus (what truth and ~~truth~~ are perceived [T_P & $\mathcal{F}_P$] and desires total [D_S] is in their mortal mind/matrix).

So...the major variables that influence the operator's change of consciousness with an empty mind/matrix exercise are:

- $f(\Delta t)$ focus over change of time…This includes long term as well as short term; how much you have done this exercise previously.
- How much Truth that is already in your *Storages* (*Knowledge*, *Programming*, and *Memory* specifically).
- Your intention in doing the exercise – perceptions and desires.

This is a great exercise if you have to stand around and wait for something. Waiting. Blankness and empty. The author did this exercise a lot in the army. "Hurry up and wait", is the military credo. In waiting, the author would be empty and allow no thoughts to be entertained.

That is one of the interesting things about doing mental exercises in a crowd. No one has any idea what you are doing. True, you may appear a bit 'spacey'. And…doing mental exercises is a lot subtler than doing jumping jacks or hatha yoga in a crowd.

This exercise consists of:

➢ *Because for the beginner it is hard to keep a blank mind indefinitely, the assignment is only for three to five minutes.*[34] *You are to get into a comfortable position.*

---

32 To the limit of what your mind/matrix's current programming is capable of.
33 An example of focus being split by 'subjective' and 'objective' inputs is Chart 4-4, *N2*
34 If you wish to do this longer than five minutes, you are welcome to try.

> *Do a motivational analysis or establish your priorities/intention and cultivate a disinterested-interest.*
> *Notice your 'state of mind' before hand.*
> *Do the blank mind exercise.*
> *When done, You are to sit and notice how you feel for 1-2 minutes (extending your watching and waiting time).*
> *Then afterwards, perhaps make an entry in the notebook or workbook.*
> *This is to be done on at least 5 separate occasions with the eyes closed and 5 separate occasions with the eyes open.*

Exercise and Lab 8B: Maintaining A Physical Focus <u>Only</u>

This exercise simply involves sitting in front of a mandala or any object and not let your eyes leave the center of a mandala. This is simple exercise in maintaining a physical focus only.

This exercise is for you to:

> *Sit in front of the mandala or any object as in exercises 7B or 8A*
> *Do this exercise for twenty minutes, on at least three separate occasions.*
> *Sit and observe for 2-5 minutes afterward.*
> *Enter any thoughts or feelings into the workbook.*

Exercise and Lab 9: A Possible Combination

The last exercise to be covered is a combination of all three previous mantra types and the empty mind. The idea consists of doing blank bursts (*Assignment 8A*) at relatively high frequency, at heartbeat speed or twice your heartbeat (using your own internal rhythm). Blank, blank, blank, blank, blank. This is very similar to using any word or mantra repetition introduced in previously.

The word or concept that your focus is on should be one syllable and very short such as: God, God, God, God, God… You can use the words Love, Jah, Allah, One, etc.; any short word that connotes the Divine for you can be used. As you are doing this mantra, bring the attention or focus (*↑Δt*) inside, 90 degrees away from everything. The power or stroke part of it is focusing and saying the word 'God' the rest is the short space between words. (God…God…God…God...) Again, this is very similar to transcendental meditation concepts.

This is another exercise where the use of power and rest, power and rest, power and rest…may be applicable. These rests however are for very short periods.

Alternatively, you can also float, gently float back into it, and flutter into your being; riding the word repetition – empty -- with no rests.

Here again, because a God/Divine concept is involved, a devotional element is involved this exercise. Use the love that you may feel for God or… You can use both mind bursts and love bursts as you do this mantra.

At first, try it rapid, twice your heartbeat. Later, on your own, you can do it at whatever speed you want. That speed was picked because it matches some of your internal rhythms. You may prefer to do it with each heartbeat. You, as the operator, may have to learn to experiment on your own; and play in your head with this to see how it feels.

However, if you do any degree of experimenting, stay with one general action per sitting. Meaning, do not change from chanting *OM* to *Nam-Myo-Ho-Renge-Kyo* in one sitting.

To repeat, this exercise can also be applied to instrumental music as well.[35] Remember that as you are doing any of these mantras or exercises, you are just existing -- being. Your whole attitude is just sit and wait while doing them. You have nothing to do but

---

35 Chapter 8

wait and do the chant/exercise. The intentions of introducing all these exercises are for you to explore yourself and to play with your mental mechanism.

You can use these presented mantra exercise types in a multitude of applications. That was one of the goals of the chapter, for you to custom design your meditation approaches along 'some' Eternal principles. Usually, mantras tend to involve you in relationship to some of your perceptions of the outside and yourself. And…it can go the opposite way, too ("null + 0 = hold that thought"). It is totally up to you, which way you want to take it (intentions/motivations). When you are 'playing' with these ideas and concepts, observe that there are different directions, vehicles or modalities, and ways you can take it.

In addition, remember, no matter what you do: if you do anything over an extended period of time with one point focus, there is going to be a consciousness change within you. You may not understand this change or even recognize it.

And, you do it to yourself.   Done in conjunction with regular breathing or deep breathing, this can augment the consciousness change/effect.   As stated previously, the consciousness change/effect will be proportional to time of focus; the longer the focus, the more significant the change.

Remember, always with these and other meditations, you set a beginning time and an end time. When doing a deep meditation, use a clock or a cooking timer. See what time it is, and wait until the clock rings the quarter or the half or the three-quarter or the hour or do the exercise until the cooking timer 'dings'.

An objective time reference keeps things clearer and cleaner for you.   Use time. Although from the Divine's reference, time is non-sequitar. The Divine uses it to approach us – those who experience time. You can use it also.

"Okay, I'm doing this right now.
"OOPS, I drifted. I forgot."
"I've got to bring myself back."

This can help keeps things clear. The time to stop is when the timer thing goes off. Afterwards, you can start thinking about some of the things that came into your mind while you were doing the exercise. When doing the exercise though, do not think about any thing. You can always set the distracting thoughts on a shelf and say, "Later. I'll think about that one later."

For this exercise you:

➢ *You are to get into a comfortable position (but not too comfortable).*
➢ *Do a motivational analysis or establish priorities/intention, and cultivate a 'disinterested-interest' in what you are about to do.*
➢ *Notice how you feel and how your mind feels.*
➢ *You are to do three separate 20-minute sessions. Do this exercise three separate times*
➢ *As with the other exercises, sit and observe yourself 2-5 minutes afterward.*
➢ *Enter any thoughts or feelings into the workbook.*

******************** ⚫ ********************

Up to this point, these assignments have been playing with the perceptual lens related to what choices we make. The meditation/mantra forms are manipulating the flows through the lens array. Our perceptions and our desires (motivations) are part of this manipulation with available choices -- to make choices based on truths of the whole and unity.

Many exercises using imagination, perception, and focus have been introduced. Imagination exercises today are called visualizations. Which are just other ways to play with the *Perceptual Lens Array*.

In addition, what has been touched upon previously is using the brief moment in time the *Perceptual Lens Array* takes to focus. The eye exercise was an example of doing that. It constantly caused the matrix to refocus and in doing so, no or few choices (a decrease in ~~truth~~

chosen [$\mathcal{T}_C$]) were made, which directly affects *Programming*. Other exercises can use this as well.

"Now, for something completely different".

6.3 - Additional Study: Zen and Slipping Between Thoughts: Options, Options, Options...

Again, it is brought to your attention our mortal mind/matrix is very limited. This makes stepping out of the mind a 'gilt edged' priority for anyone who is serious about growth in metaphysical or spiritual studies. (It also offers a mental coordination approach to physical studies as well.) In order to explore that which is beyond our normal perceptions we have to leave those perceptions behind.

"Get out of the house and go out on the street all alone."[36]

All the meditations that have been covered, including the mantras, the breath, and everything that has been introduced have passive and active elements in them; yet, they are still dynamic in nature. They are doing something. Some are efforts in reducing ~~truth~~ ($\mathcal{T}$) within the mind while others are efforts that increase truth (T) within the mortal mind/matrix. All the exercises up to this point in the book -- except for the recognition exercise of truth, the 'ringing' -- the operator is doing something actively. The very act of meditation is an act. Even if it is to non-act, this is an act.

With most of the previous exercises, this is a manipulation of the mind/matrix operation. These exercises use the mind's operation to alter what truth or ~~truth~~ it contains at any given moment. Essentially, the operator is setting a block of time to do 'something' within their head. What if that block of time is set aside to do absolutely nothing? Instead of manipulating the mind/matrix, recognize the limits of the mind and 'step' outside those limits. This, in turn can reduce the participation of ~~truth~~ within the mind.

You are not your mortal mind. You are God's Creation. When you leave your mortal mind behind, the only thing left will be who you really are.

Option #1

This introduces a very passive form of meditation; that was touched on with the watching waiting part at the end of each exercise. An excellent image of this meditation is the Zen or the Taoist picture of a heron on a lake. A functional stillness occurs with the passive operation of watching and waiting – being relaxed and paying attention.

St. Romuald said, "Sit in your cell as if in paradise." You do not know there is a paradise around you (or in you for that matter), but there is. (The heron is probably more cued into the paradise aspect than any human is.)

This next exercise is for your mind to be as a heron on the lake; watching and waiting in the whole paradise that is around you.

This exercise is to cultivate a functional stillness or non-action arising from just being relaxed and paying attention. While paying attention, you are to be like the heron and watching your thoughts as the heron watches the fishes, without judgment or choice, and no action. You are watching your perception/desire or thought/emotion mechanism, which is reflected by the 'subjective events' that are created by your mortal mind/matrix.

Be an objective observer of these thoughts, daydreams, and fantasies. You are watching it all inside your head as if they are fishes. You are just watching the movie go by. As one thought passes by, another one arrives. The thoughts follow each other, and you are watching them from above. Like a bird, that already has had dinner. Be like the heron watching the fish below it.

---

[36] *Trucking*, Grateful Dead

Here is an analogy to fixing a record player. After the author got out of college, He started working in analog electronic repair places: *TV* and stereo repair, p.a. systems, alarms, etc. The first three jobs (the very first chore) the author got in those electronics repair stores would be; they would give him a box full of parts and say, "This is a record player; fix it."

After putting it together though, the author would see the record player is not working properly. It was not doing what the author knew it is supposed to do. It is supposed to eject, it is supposed to play, etc. Because the author did not know what made a record player eject or play, the author would have to watch it go through the eject and reset cycles maybe 40 or 50 times. He would just sit and watch it, not doing anything except recognizing connections. He was just watching. (The author was being paid the same -- minimum wage.)

Finally, as the author observed, he saw 'this' connects to 'that', he saw that this notch goes there, and the wheel comes back. As said, the author may have had to do this at first -- watch it 30 or 40 times -- to digest what is happening with each part. Most of it was just watching, and finally in the watching; a cognitive jump occurs. "Oh, I got it! I see it now!"

Doing this inside -- watching yourself, watching the mechanism of the matrix inside you -- is a truly passive form. By not taking any active control anywhere here, you are using the focus/cognition mechanism of the mind/matrix on the mind/matrix itself, using the Cognition input only.[37] You are just watching with no judgments.

You are watching your thoughts. You are watching your reactions to thoughts. Watching what you are feeling. Watching how you are sitting. Watching the car go by. Watching your reaction to the car go by. The whole idea behind doing this is that certain reoccurring mechanisms will begin to appear to you as you are doing this. Start watching yourself, looking at your mechanisms. This exercise addresses the old Oracle of Delphi adage, "Man, know thyself". This is *a* beginning.

An excellent example of watching and waiting, in everyday life; is to watch yourself watching *TV*. Watch your reactions to watching *TV*. The *TV* itself is totally neutral. The reactions within you are what you have created through your previous programming to the *TV* programming. Whatever meaning the *TV* (and what is on it) has for you, is what you give it.

The value of this exercise is that it exposes you to your parade of thoughts. Like the *TV*, whatever meaning these thoughts have for you, is what you give them. Outside of you, these thoughts have little to no meaning.

> *"Redwoods talk to me.*
> *It's all the same,*
> *By the human name,*
> *It doesn't mean shit to a tree."*[38]

Once you cease giving these thoughts any meaning, you begin to step 'outside' of the mind's operation.

This exercise is for additional study. The exercise is to watch your thoughts. If you find yourself becoming involved with a thought-desire set, pull back and disengage. Remember why you are doing this -- your intention. It may be just to fool around or explore your own head.

Breathing exercise can help the operator relax into this exercise. Instead of watching the breath, you are watching your mind.

You are to:

➤ *Set aside three separate blocks of time (15 to 30 minutes) to watch your thoughts or reactions.*
➤ *Find a partially comfortable position.*
➤ *As in the other forms of meditations, before the one starts this passive exercise, you still should look at what are you doing this for; what do you want? What do you want? What attachments do you have on the results of the exercise?*

---

37 Chart 4-4, *B5*
38 Jefferson Airplane

➢ *Watch your thoughts and wait.*
➢ *Enter some of your perceptions of the operation in to the workbook.*

You will find the chatter -- the mind/matrix chatter -- is endless. That was brought up in earlier chapters. The human matrix, like limited mortal mirror version of the Truth Matrix that it is, is constantly creating. One is on a temporal level, and the other is on a Eternal level. Most of the time its creations are meaningless chatter, flitting from one perception/desire set to another.

One of the things this exercise is addressing is for one to see it and just watch the parade of thoughts going by. To re-cognize it is there, that it exists, and to watch it. You will begin to see some reoccurring themes within them as you are doing this. In seeing these themes, a re-evaluation may occur. In re-evaluating, perceptions, desires, and attachments may change; this may include being attached to your own mind.

The next logical application of this is to learn to ignore your thoughts; ignore the chatter. Again, this is a passive application. The reasoning for these type of actions are:

- Given: whatever meaning your thoughts have is what you give them.
- Given: whatever the thoughts say to you is going be limited by what is in your mind – programming – and are liable to be inaccurate representations – ~~true~~ – based on limited perceptions.
- Given: truth is laws by which something 'works'.
- Given: the more you work in truth of an event, the more functional you will be in the event. And…conversely, the more you work with ~~truth~~ – not in the laws of an event, the more dysfunctional you will be in that event.
- Then: learning to ignore your thoughts is can contribute to your function – effectiveness – in an event.

This exercise is more personal than the previous ones. Everybody has to learn to do this on his or her own. The author does not know how to show a person how to watch his or her own thoughts.

Option #2

Another method of meditation is used in *Lexio Divino*.[39] This method steps out of the free flowing thought-desire sets that come through the subjective input, to use mentation to get out of mentation (like mathematical operation of division by zero leaves mathematics). An easy way to do this is to use the writings in a spiritual or meaningful book – something that impacts you. Use a spiritual text, read it, and sit with it afterward.

Referring to the 'ringing' of the first exercise, it was mentioned that if Truth is perceived constantly, it could alter states of consciousness through this ringing.[40] The speaker is 'weaving' truthful symbols, and the listener is interpreting the symbols.

In that interpreting, the listener can make a mental 'jump' and leave the separate elements of the 'weave' and start to appreciate the 'cloth' of the subject matter. Kind of like seeing the <u>curved</u> sphere, that is implied by the <u>straight</u> lines of the geodesic dome. (Pardon mixed metaphors.)

The listener can leave mentation (mental constructions) and enter the presence of Truth through the mentation. The mentation in itself is limited and temporal in nature. It is being woven to imply something beyond (behind) it -- an Eternal.[41] Just as, a one-dimensional thread is woven to produce a two dimensional cloth. It is the listener that makes the jump.

Try this idea of *Lexio Divino* on your own. This idea is a method of 'weaving thought forms', pumping truths (with as much Absolutes as possible) from *Knowledge*, through the subjective event, via the *Perceptional Lens Array*, into Choice, thereby altering *Programming*;

---

39 A monastic Catholic exercise
40 Chapters 1, 3, and 4
41 Again, a logic system creates 'something' alien to the logic system.

and then, going around again.[42] Usually reading something that affects you, spiritually or inspirationally, can do this. This can start a ringing in the mind/matrix, especially if the truths are augmented/increased each time it goes through the lens array. Do this for a short time; and sit with what you feel for a short time.

In order for this to be effective though, there must be a measure of truth within the mind/matrix *Storage* to start with. A specific amount of truth applications must be present within *Knowledge* for this to work.

This exercise is to:

➢ Establish: *What do you want? What is your intention? What attachments do you have on the results of the exercise?*
➢ *Pick a piece of spiritual writing that impacts you*
➢ *Read it*
➢ *Sit with how you feel, or sit with what that writing means to you for 15 minutes*
➢ *Do this on 3 separate occasions*
➢ *Write perceptions in the journal or workbook*

Option #3

There is another way to use mentation to leave mentation, still using the weaving cloth analogy. What if you are following some threads of thought or symbols within an idea weave, and all of a sudden, there is nothing there; a hole with nothing else to grab or to follow? A Zen koan can do this, "What is the sound of one hand clapping?".

OOPS. All of a sudden, there is nothing there. It causes the mind/matrix to refocus or reset. Every time the mind refocuses, there is still a hole that prevents full operation of the array, even to cognition. The mind recognizes the words; and the words 'do not compute'.

In doing this, it is possible to slip between the threads of thought to enter another state of consciousness. A kind of slipping between the temporal thoughts and leaving temporal thought behind. As stated previously, because eternal and temporal are mutually exclusive, when an individual leaves the temporal in any way, the only thing left is the Eternal, in one 'form' or another.

Playing with these particular exercises/mechanisms are more of an auxiliary assignment to this chapter. Each individual's mortal mind/matrix is different.[43] It is totally up to you. This book is just putting it out there -- to you -- that it can be done.

An example or a spin-off of the koan idea was introduced in Chapter 4. That is, when a series of unrelated cognized perceptions (with their subsequent reasoning and logic) are put in a semi-logical order to produce a new independent irrelevant cognition.[44] This condition can cause the mind/matrix to reset completely. It is similar to pressing *Ctrl*, *Alt*, and *Delete* on the computer keyboard.[45]

As stated earlier, when the mortal mind/matrix is resetting, an element of the eternal joy of God/Creation manifests in the matrix. We experience that moment as laughter.

---

42 Examples: Chart 4-4, *I10-12* or *J10-11*
43 Due to the choices they have made and the subsequent mind/matrix programming these choices have produced.
44 As opposed to a series of unrelated cognized perceptions put in a semi-logical order -- there is no cognition, and the matrix refocuses, Chapter 4.
45 Pressing *Ctrl*, *Alt*, and *Delete* at the same time on a Windows operating system will cause the computer to bring up a screen with all programs that are running -- if pressed again, the computer will restart -- resets.

6.4 Road Signs

*I*n this chapter, some common signs, states of consciousness, or experiences are introduced. Many of these 'signs' that can occur are an effect to some of your exercises. Some can occur shortly after you start do exercises and be like a quantum leap. While others are results of long-term mind/matrix reprogramming.

All are like road signs on a journey. All should be 'looked' on as such and then keep 'moving on'. Preoccupation with a road sign can detract from the 'trip'. If you are busy watching a road sign, you are not looking where you are going; you may not see the cow in the road.

Some of these 'signs' are such that if you change your focus from what your exercise is to the 'sign', the 'sign' disappears.

Everything that has been presented in this chapter and previous chapters can initiate changes in the mortal mind/matrix operation and you may experience consciousness changes or have effects from them. Every mortal mind/matrix is like a snowflake. Even though every snowflake may be different, there are numerous elements they have in common.[46] Alternatively, your mortal mind/matrix may experience variations of such changes.

These changes/signs have been arranged into three specific categories. These categories are, basically, reflections of postulated qualities of Chapter 2. The second postulate (God's Love) forms one category and is 'heart' related. The third postulate (God's Logical Mind) forms a second category and is 'mind' related. And, since they are One, a third category is formed as a combination of 'head' and 'heart'.

Most of these may mean nothing to you. Some of these signs you may understand only after you experienced them.

I. Head
    A. Epiphanies or sudden quantum mental jumps into metaphysical or spiritual subject concepts
        1. An intense sense of beauty related to the 'whole'
        2. These also can instigate heart states
        3. Mount of Transfiguration' a major epiphany that involves exposure to the Absolute Power of God.
    B. Deep meditation states
        1. A perceived light that appears while doing a mental exercise for a period of time
            a) A light forming in the mind while in a deep meditative state
            b) A light forming in the mind while in a deeper meditative state than *a*. This light has a dark spot or 'door' in the center of it.
        2. Derivatives of the 'Precious Stillness' within the Eternal Moment of Creation
            a) Several forms of a peaceful contemplation
            b) The "velvet monkey wrench" – you are incredibly soft surrounding 'that' which is still and immovable.
        3. A visual blackout that occurs while doing an exercise for a period with open eyes and all 'visual' perception disappears (or maybe just the peripheral).
    C. An introduction to the 'Dreamtime' or psychic education (*ESP* validation)
    D. A blinding white light
        1. Getting "knocked off your ass on the way to Damascus"
        2. Usually associated with some initiation or initiatory process
II. Heart
    A. A 'bliss-out', a variety of states that comes with maintained prayer (heart-song)
        1. The Bodhisattva Choice

---

46 Water matrix (molecule), the nature of solid matrix created by a series of water matrices (molecules) when at a specific conditions: temperature, an impurity, relative humidity, etc.

        2.   The Absolute Love behind the 'Mount of Transfiguration' – The Power
    B. Bodhisattva heart flame
III. Combination
    A. A 'bliss-out' that comes with an epiphany
        1.   Compassion
        2.   Intense 'heart' spaces accompanied by holistic perceptions
    B. Bodhisattva tears

Remember it is a mistake to look for these or after experiencing them give them excessive meaning. These are effects of the 'work' and should be looked on as such. "Oh that's kind-a neat!" Then, move on. Becoming preoccupied with the 'effects' can cause you to be distracted from the work that is the 'cause'.

Or, as it is written, "My Father's house has many mansions." You can get lost in the 'rooms'.

6.5 Conclusion

$\mathbb{A}$ ll of the previous exercises and material of this book involve playing with the flow mechanics through the presented mortal mind/matrix model. These exercises help demonstrate the logical operation of the mechanism. There are many different ways to play with your mortal mind/matrix mechanism.

Some of the ways mentioned in *I AM A I* so far are:

a) To use a logic system to exit that logic system
    i)   Logic creates illogic as with a Zen koan
    ii) Mortal mind logic enters into Eternal Mind concepts using truths
b) To use the effect the presence of Truth has in your mind
    i)   Connects you to your source
    ii) Reduce ~~truth~~ re-enforcement
c) To preoccupy the mortal mind with predetermined tasks
    i)   One-point focus on an event
    ii) Exercising the mind
d) To use mortal – temporal – limits of the mind to interrupt mental operations
    i)   Preoccupying the mind with cognitive input
    ii) Using the 'can only think of one thing at a time' limit
e) To ignore or not allow the 'subjective event' – mentation
f) To manipulate the 'subjective event'
    i)   Changing desire – what you want
    ii) Changing perception – what you see
    iii) Changing attachment
    iv) Combinations of the above

A word about ritual, ritual is many times necessary for people just learning. Typically, ritual is a tool of the beginner. Chapter 8 will cover tools a little more deeply. However, for now, ritual will be touched upon here. This is because you may develop some rituals as you do some of these exercises.

The purpose of a ritual is to perform a specific operation on a regular basis. This is so that the operation becomes programmed into the mortal mind/matrix to such an extent that the *Storages* can take care of the operation with little or no effort from you in the *Focus Control*. Once the operation is programmed in, the ritual may become redundant. You do not keep going over the math flash cards after you have the numbers and the math operations down.[47]

Accordingly, for an increase of effect, you may have to set up or work with some rituals to learn some of the internal operations that have been presented in this book. You may have

---

47 $2 \times 2 = 4$; $2 + 3 = 5$; $6 - 4 = 2$, etc.

to (or want to) setup specific times and establish procedures to learn some internal coordination or principles. These rituals are tools, like the flash cards.

Do not mistake the ritual for the operation. It is the operation that is important. The ritual is only an aid to perform the operation. Rituals can help remind us to perform the operation and give the operation form, but the are not the mental operation itself. They help you array or arrange a block of time to enter a meditative or mystical state -- to perform a particular internal operation.

A goal is to be able to enter that state at any moment without the ritual. Just like, you can be able to do a multiplication operation without flash cards.

A number of swimming analogies has been made. This is because the author did a lot of swimming when young. Consequently, the author's mortal mind/matrix has been programmed with swimming concepts. To some degree, these analogies are well suited for we as beings are swimming in a Sea of Love.

Physical form is a 'precipitated' version of this Sea. Through the God's Logical Mind and the Truth Matrix it contains to a sea of *BTR*s, the Infinite Eternal Sea becomes a finite temporal sea. What we know as form can be considered condensed versions of the sea of *BTR*s, ice flows.

In order to swim, we do not have to know intellectually the truths that make up the swimming condition (fluid dynamics, laws of motion, specific gravity, etc.). It is their usage and applications are things we do need to know to keep from drowning. It is the stroke and how you move yourself in the sea that becomes important – the applications.

Just as the blood within the sea creatures -- and us -- is a specialized version of the seawater, so is our mortal being a specialized version of God's Love. It is an intrinsic part of our very being and makeup. We cannot escape it. A fish cannot escape its own blood.

As Chart 4-4 attests, there are so many different ways Truth can enter the awareness of our mortal minds. We just need to make room for it. We just need to remove a degree of ~~truth~~ for truth to make itself known. As was said in the beginning of this chapter (and book), we just have to set up the proper conditions.

This ends this chapter on exercises. The purpose of this chapter is to expose you to things you can do in your head. Once the basics are learned, experimentation is encouraged. At the same time, this brings to a close all the information of the previous chapters.

It has been shown that the mortal mind is limited and some of the aspects and the complexity of the details of its own operation may elude it. That is all right; it is the general principles and their applications that are important. You can get lost in the details. In addition, a preoccupation with details may interfere with the actual mental operation.

God is such a fundamental simplicity; your relationship with your Creator should, in time, become simpler and not be cluttered up with excessive details or rituals.

6.6 - Questions

1) What were the three basic categories of mantra chants that were introduced?

2) These exercises are aimed at reducing what elements, in the formula; and how?

3) The meditation exercises are playing with the flows through and focus of _____.

4) All exercises involve a _____ over a change of time.

5) For most of these chapter exercises, effectiveness is presented as equivalent to:

    a. the matrix   b. consciousness change
    c. choice   d. laundry service
    e. a change of time   f. all of the above

6) All exercises are to be preceded by what?

7) All exercises are to be followed by?

8) Reductions of ~~truth~~ within the mind will do what?

9) _____ can never leave the mind.

10) Name one benefit from doing a meditation practice over an extended period.

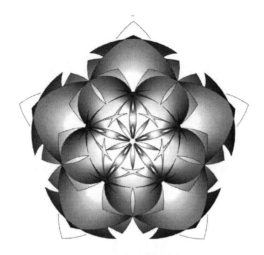

Chapter 7

Concerning ESP Events and Psychic Phenomenon

7.1 – Extra Sensory Perception Events

*G*enerally speaking, all *ESP* facilitated information transfer will be collaborated by an **Actual** reality event – be true. There are a few exceptions. If a perception involves an *ESP* event, it will occur in **Actual** reality. Errors that occur are usually with perceptions or interpretations of the operator, not the mechanics. If a perception does not occur in **Actual** reality, it most likely was not an *ESP* event. The perception was probably something created from within the mortal mind and not of something 'other' than the mortal mind.

A partial list of the psychic phenomena – *ESP* events -- to be covered in this book is:

1) Extra Sensory Perception (*ESP*)
   a) Telepathy
   b) Clairvoyance
   c) Clairaudience
   d) Geomancy
   e) Forms of Scrying
2) Magic
3) Miracles

Except for miracles, what these forms have in common is a perception of 'other-ness'. (Miracles are a correction to that perception of other-ness). Typically, *ESP* conveyed information is referenced to something outside of or away from the perceiver's mortal mind and body. This means, *ESP* can involve the *Perceptual Lens Array* – the 'front' of your mind. In addition, because how the 'back' of the mind – storages, focuses the 'front' of the mind your *Storage* becomes an influence as well.

What will not be covered in this chapter are things like channeling, spirits, telekinetics, etc. This chapter concerns itself with primary *ESP* associations. The concerns of this book are on the immediate operations of the human matrix that relate to the *ESP* expansion of the **Individual** reality into **Absolute** reality. Where channeling et al are secondary applications, they may or may not be relevant to individual growth on a daily application level.

We are in a duality delusion.[1] We 'perceive' we have separate minds and that there is a number of other mortal minds around us. Normally, these 'perceived minds' communicate through a physical medium – *BTR* array -- of some sort (visual, audio, through symbols, etc). What we associate as communication is an extension of ideas between at least two individual *BTR*s. If it is communication between individuals, communication becomes an idea mutual extending session.

This action is facilitated by a *BTR* they have in common (words, room, broadcast system, phone system, etc.). This information is carried from one individual's physical *BTR* to another by smaller *BTR*s within the large *BTR* that they share (molecules and sounds, photons or electrons, printed symbols, etc.).

The forms of psychic phenomenon and *ESP* that are presented in this chapter of *I AM A I* are an effect of a temporal/spatial mind accessing an idea through the Eternal Mind. *ESP* in this book deals with information related to a *BTR*, away from the operator's physical *BTR*, in another time/space reference (*BTR*), with no *BTR*s in common, and by way of the One Mind, which is present in all *BTR*s.

When there is a flow of information between 'perceived' minds without any discernible means of communication we call this *ESP* or telepathy. *ESP* phenomenon is a flow of information traveling via the Mind/Matrix to your mind/matrix. Within the duality delusion concept, this makes all psychic phenomena (*ESP* et al) a form of telepathy. Knowledge or information is shared between minds (mind to mind and Mind to mind).

Carried to the *nth* degree, this idea becomes the Communion with God concept of saints.

A beginning definition for telepathy is the extension of an idea between <u>apparently</u> separate minds without any physical vector of that idea – common *BTR*s. This can occur in the same moment of time, and it does not necessarily have to happen that way. The common perception of telepathy is for two or more distanced temporal/spatial minds to share an idea at the same moment. This can be misleading. <u>They do not have to share the idea in the same moment of time – have the same temporal (or spatial) references.</u>[2]

Much of psychic phenomenon in this book fits in the category of *ESP*. Extra Sensory Perception is a perception of **Actual** physical reality through non-physical means – the five physical senses.[3] Some common *ESP* manifestations are:

♦ Clairvoyance is a form of *ESP* where an individual mentally 'sees' an event that is in another spatial/temporal reference from the perceiver's physical body. The operator 'sees' an event that is occurring or will occur in another time and space. Clairvoyance tends to come to the individual through imagery.

♦ Clairaudience, instead of the information coming in imagery, the information appears to come in sounds.

♦ Geomancy tends to be a feeling the operator gets when he/she touches rocks or something of earth; it tends to be sensate. Geomancy can also be related to psychic tool usage of geometric figures.

Geomancy is not the only *ESP* that manifests in a sensate manner. Geomancy is used as a reference of an *ESP* perception through feeling, instead of hearing or seeing. Some people 'see' things using geomancy. Geomancy can refer to the material (ground, rocks, and earth) as well as; it can be a geometric figure that the operator is using to guide their perception. Geomancy can also be a feeling, like dowsing for water. This chapter will return to the sensate idea later.

---

1 Theorem 32, I am/we are in a generated delusion of duality.

2 This means what may appear as 'past lives' may be a psychic connection between two mortal minds occupying different times and in different spaces.

3 Hence it being called the sixth sense; a sense other than the five physical ones -- sight, touch, hearing, taste, or smell.

Please note that extra sensory perception can parallel physical perceptual senses: images to sight, sounds to hearing, feelings to touch, etc. Those people who are visually oriented tend to get *ESP* in images. Those people who are audio orientated tend to get their *ESP* in sounds, words, or sentences. When the author first started playing with this subject and started picking things up from people, different people would have a different 'taste' for him. *ESP* may 'mimic' a physical sense that is important to you within your **Individual** reality.

This is an excellent example of how *ESP* facilitated information becomes 'clothed' by the receiving mortal mind (next section).

The relationship between *ESP* and your physical senses in terms of which came first or what stems from what, is not important to learning this subject. You should be aware that some of the parallels between the physical senses and *ESP* senses exist. What can apply to the use of one for you; can apply to the use of the other for you.

Another form of psychic phenomena that should be mentioned is astral projection, which involves the mortal mind leaving the physical body. The temporal mind/matrix disengages from the temporal body matrix. This can occur when the mind is wide-awake while the body is very tired.

There is a sign when this engaging and disengaging of the mind with the body process is not quite complete. You have awareness and are awake but your body appears to be paralyzed; you cannot move.

There is an irony with astral projection. The mind 'appears' to leave the body; and in the paradigm of this book, it does not really 'go' anywhere. It is only participating in a different aspect or perception of the One Mind. This different aspect may <u>appear</u> as a different place in time and space or a 'place' that has no physical reference.

The one-point focus involved with learning the deep relaxation techniques of astral projection can be very useful to meditation and other mind/body mechanics. The same can be said for self-hypnosis trance techniques as well.[4]

Again, in order for this book to keep the subject matter simple, *I AM A I*'s focus is on primary applications: telepathy, *ESP*, magic, and miracles. Magic and miracles have their own separate chapters.

7.2 – Mechanics and *ESP* Forms

A review of some theory is necessary and this theory can help explain and introduce an *ESP* event. This review can also help you understand or comprehend *ESP* event mechanics.

$\Rightarrow$ There is only One Infinite and Eternal Loving Mind.[5]   This Mind IS the very core of your being.

This chapter is a natural extension of the previous chapter because psychic perception (an *ESP* event) is a side effect of having an empty mind. When you begin to step outside of your temporal – mortal -- mind/matrix, the only thing left is the Eternal Truth Mind/Matrix within you; your given natural mind takes over.[6]

All *ESP* is through the One Mind. Since the Love's Eternal Mind is yours by the nature of God-Creation relationship -- you,[7] *ESP* is working from the very core of your being. The major irony around *ESP* is being psychic is natural; it is not being psychic that is un-natural.

---

4 It is encouraged to explore some self-hypnosis techniques.
5 *Postulates 3* and *4*
6 Here is an excellent example of the *Right Angle Rule* presented in Chapter 3.5 - Mirror Mechanics, Connections, and Parallels
7 *Postulates 3, 4, 6,* and *Theorem 10*

Previous chapters have given you numerous examples of exercises for manipulating, setting aside, or working with the temporal – mortal -- mind/matrix mechanism. Operations that decrease ~~truth~~ participation within your mind/matrix were introduced. Some of these are by either preoccupying the mind with systematic operations – meditations, increasing truth's presence, expanding perceptional limits, etc.

You are not your temporal matrix – your mortal mind.[8] <u>You are not the mental/emotional sets that preoccupy the mortal mind</u>.

As has been mentioned previously, eliminate the ~~truth~~ and the truth is that which remains. Consequently, remove ~~truth~~ from the mortal mind and the Eternal Mind and consequent *ESP* events tend to manifest. This means that an *ESP* event manifests automatically or naturally in two ways. Either when you learn to still the mind, or when a sufficient amount of absolute truths are programmed into the mind.

$\Rightarrow$ From the One Infinite and Eternal Loving Mind's reference time and space is a 'special case' of the Infinite and Eternal, irrelevant, *non-sequitar*, etc.

An *ESP* event involves a communion within this One Mind; and consequently, it involves the One Mind's time/space ignor-ance. Since that One Mind is not restricted by temporal/spatial limits, that means, <u>we can have access to everything that can be known, which is at any place or at any time.</u>

This Mind is Eternally present in all of time and space and does not live in time and space. (one of those mystical conundrums to a mortal mind) What that One Mind has access to, we all can access. This means that all the knowledge (and Creation capabilities) that is in the Loving Mind/Matrix is available. *ESP* events are a form of mental participation of truth/Truth (depending on the inclusiveness) applications or experiences between a mind and the Mind. This idea can help take some of the bizarreness out of psychic phenomena.

Chapter 3.7 introduced two examples of the time/space ignor-ance qualities of an *ESP* event -- within a single mortal mind -- are with premonitions and *déjà vu*

- A premonition is 'you' in the future,[9] telling 'you' in the past,[10] something is about to 'go down'.
- With *déjà vu*, you just accessed a future memory.

One reaches from the future to the past – premonitions – while the other reaches from the past to the future – *déjà vu*. Instead of an idea shared by two apparently separate minds, these two are examples of something shared by the same mortal mind at separate times. Which, is another example of an internal communication within a single mind (Mind), and both are indicative of time ignor-ance capabilities inherent in the Eternal presence of God's One Loving Mind – the Mind within you.

ESP Event Vectors

ESP facilitated information -- how we indirectly perceive something outside us and away from us -- can come through two basic vectors:

Vector 1 $\Rightarrow$ One vector is through our internal mind/matrix vehicle. It comes from the Truth within us; it may use our *Perceptual Lens Array* or *Knowledge* storage, and it manifests to our awareness in the *Focus Control Buss* (Figure 4-4, III). Nothing outside of us facilitates this seeing. It is an internal communion and the information manifests within the mind mechanism.

Vector 2 $\Rightarrow$ The other vector *ESP* facilitated information can make itself known is through an external vehicle/vector (physical *BTR/BTRs*). This *ESP* still may involve an internal process, and the operator is using something external as a catalyst or a tool for the internal process.

---

8 Chapter 2.8, *Postulate 7, Theorems 26, 26A*, and *32*
9 A *BTR* at one temporal reference.
10 The same *BTR* at a different temporal reference.

This can vary from a simple object, like a crystal or a mirror, to complete thought systems and philosophies. Something outside of the mortal mind is used to 'trigger' or facilitate the internal accessing of information.

The second idea will be looked at first. Most forms of scrying use an external tool or 'whatever' as a vector to receive information. The operator may use a crystal ball, a black mirror, or a pool of water. The scrying vector of *ESP* also includes the *Tarot*, the *I Ching*,[11] astrology, runes, etc.

What is scrying? It is a specialized form of clairvoyance.[12] Scrying is using a physical object to see something outside and away from the operator.[13] A blank 'something' serves as a vector for an empty mind. Almost anything can be used as a vector. (Usually though, something is picked that is still and not moving – unlike lit candles.)

Here is an excellent example. When the author was in the army, a friend of the author would use the pattern of cloth. Specifically, he was the local 'hash' dealer. He would use the pattern left on a plate of hashish after the wrapping of cheesecloth was removed. He would take the cheesecloth off, look into the pattern of the cloth on the hashish, and he could perceive things or events that occurred away from him.[14] This is an example of how most people who scry use any simple object.[15]

Beginners usually do scrying, with an object. As well as, people who have a strong preference or talent for that particular 'art' do it. This is an example of an *ESP* form that involves some tool usage.

Scrying can be a very useful learning tool. Something that can help you become in touch with the psychic mechanism inside you by using objective references. Once you get in touch with that mechanism, the tool, however, may no longer be needed.

One of the biggest dangers of using a tool in the metaphysical areas (as well as physical) is to think you are dependent on it. Ideally, tools are developed to make a specific job easier.[16]

Using any external tool to learn *ESP* is very analogous to using tools to learn how to walk. A child puts their weight on the sofa or a coffee table for a while. The ideal is, though, to let the sofa or coffee table go. The *Tarot* and the *I Ching*, the crystal ball, or the black mirror are like the sofa. The ideal is to be able to do that in the 'head' without having to need anything from the outside.

Again, it does not make any difference what the operator is using to scry. It all starts and ends with their mind. The only difference between using something outside of you instead of inside is it may be easier to use something outside of you to help create the mental image when first learning. Systems like the *Tarot* and *I Ching* also give external objective references to the *ESP* event.

When a predetermined symbol system or philosophy like *Tarot* or the *I Ching*[17], runes, Astrology, etc. is used, that symbol system serves as a vector for the *ESP* operation. With thought systems such as these, life and/or the human condition is broken up into symbols of **Absolute**, **Actual**, **Consensual**, or **Individual** reality archetypes/truths. Some of the archetypes of the *I Ching* are Heaven, earth, wandering, foolishness, etc. Some of the Tarot's archetypes are strength, cycles, disruption, illumination, etc. Some Astrology archetypes are communication, beauty, stubbornness, etc.

With the scrying forms of divination that use *Tarot* cards, the *I Ching*, Astrology, etc., there is an external reference (re: "the question") other than the actual event itself (the cards -- a thought system and the 'reading').

---

11 Chapter 8, Tools and Music
12 A form of remote viewing
13 Instead of something like an image constructed inside the head – later this chapter
14 His accuracy of perceiving something not immediately present was very good.
15 Though most people pick less illegal objects.
16 Chapter 8.
17 ibid

Important: Whatever you give to Love, it will use. That means, whatever you give to Love to grow in Love, Love will use to facilitate the process.

These forms of scrying are an example of this. These are examples of giving the Universe a thought system or image, plugging a question into that thought system or image, and letting the Universe answer in the thought system or image.

A typical *Tarot* or *I Ching* 'reading' (or any thought system reading) would consist of formulating a question, giving it to Love in the form of the reading system, and letting Love answer through the given symbols or the archetypes in the system. It is helpful usually, in order to avoid confusing answers, that a question should be very specific. (If I do _____, what effect will this have on _____?)

As mentioned, Astrology can serve as another physical *ESP* vector. Astrology is based on the general precept of; "As with Man so it is with the Universe, and as with the Universe so it is with Man." -- a holistic system. The basic premise behind astrology is everything has an energy (*BTR* influence), people, planets, stars, etc. As we enter physical form through a matrix – womb, the surrounding energies imprint themselves on us.

Kind of like the analogy, of having a paint can with changing swirls of different color paint in it. Dipping a ball on a string in the can of paint and pulling it out will leave patterns of paint fixed on the ball comparable with the paint swirls at that moment. When we come out of the womb, we have these planetary energies imprinted on us.

Astrology is essentially a way of reading the patterns of relationships involving the temporal bubbles of planets and stars (the paint can and paint movement) and how they relate to individual temporal bubbles (the patterns of paint on the ball). Are they in compliment? Are they discordant? When will they compliment? Etc.

This is another example of using some external 'gizmo' to facilitate information transfer. *ESP* can also play a role in the interpretation of those astrological patterns as well.

In terms of *ESP* vectors, **vector 1** mentioned above is where the information comes from the 'inside'. This will be the focus of the rest of this chapter.

While **vector 2**, is where the individual is using something outside to focus their mind on in order to draw forth the information. The external is just something to help them. The external object is used to trigger something internal within the operator.

Your perception is limited anyway. When using these physical forms -- using an external gizmo, your perception is twice removed from the actual event.[18]

The internal **vector 1** alone is better, because that is where the process starts -- inside. The operator in **vector 2** is only using the physical object to facilitate something inside their mind.

Successful experimental results in *ESP* will come with practice and the right motivation.[19] You are using the Correction, and the Love behind the Correction. Whenever you want to see the whole picture, of which you are a part -- whenever you are inclusive (or non-exclusive) in your perceptions and desires -- God/Love will work with you.

With **vector 1**, *ESP* facilitated information uses what is already within the mortal mind/matrix to convey the 'message'. As Chapter 4 stated, information coming via the Eternal Mind – an *ESP* event -- 'clothes' the information with the mortal mind/matrix content. The One Mind uses recognized symbols, pictures, patterns, etc. established in and by the individual's programming and formulates a message for the mortal mind – one that the individual will recognize.

---

18 In using a construct like the *I Ching* or *Tarot*, the instance when psychic phenomenon may not be true presents itself. The temporal construct (*I Ching*, *Tarot*, etc.) 'reads' from this moment in time onward – the question, based on choices that have made up to that moment in time. However, having 'free choice' means that the reading can change sometime in the future; because somebody, somewhere, made a choice so the reading is no longer relevant. Admittedly, this occurs with beginners. The more skilled in the psychic one becomes, one can see a little further and be more comprehensive in vision.

19 "perseverance pays" *I Ching*

An excellent example of this is the original biblical 'speaking in tongues'. The major government at the time was Rome. The 'seats of learning' in the Roman Empire were Egypt and Greece. The Roman Empire encompassed many countries and cultures; which, tended to attract people from all over the empire to these 'seats of learning'. Consequently, many languages were spoken in relatively concentrated areas.

The apostles came from what was considered the 'boonies' to deliver their message to 'civilization'. The apostles only spoke Aramaic. The apostles stood in the public squares and spoke before a diverse crowd. Each person in the crowd would hear the message in their native language.

The Roman would hear the message in Latin. The Grecian would hear it in Greek. The Egyptian would hear the message in their language. The original 'speaking in tongues' was equivalent to a universal translating device out of science fiction.

This is an excellent instance of how Truth (outside of temporal/spatial references) becomes 'clothed' by the temporal/spatial mind receiving it so that mortal mind would have a reference on the information.

This is why *ESP* facilities are so hard to scientifically 'nail down' – a mystery. There are so many variables introduced with each mortal mind's programming, perceptions/desires, choices, etc. In addition, because most people's minds are a mystery to them, an *ESP* event that is 'clothed' by their mind has mysterious elements as well.

There is an electronics analogy. With today's electronics, most information is transmitted digitally. Where, up to today's state of the art, all telecommunications information was transmitted in analog.

What is digital and analog?

- Digital – A light switch is digital. Either it is on or it is off. A digital computer is a large multitude of transistors acting like light switches. The timing of these on/off modes conveys information.
- Analog – A rheostat type light dimmer is analog. Not only can it be off and on; it can be anywhere between the two. All physical form and all our physical senses appear as analog – sound, light, touch, etc.[20]

There are advantages and disadvantages of digital. An advantage of digital is all natural information is conveyed in an analog mode and so is the noise that is introduced in the process. Analog noise introduced in the source/receiver process is ignored by the digital.

A disadvantage to digital is in order to keep the volume of information that has to be conveyed down to a manageable level, some of the analog subtleties can get lost.

When conveying information digitally, the analog information has to be converted to a digital format to be transmitted – analog to digital converter. The information is 'juggled' – analyzed, manipulated, transmitted, etc. -- in the digital mode. Then, that information has to be converted to an analog mode for us to recognize it – digital to analog converter.

The same is with *ESP*. *ESP* information coming through an infinite/eternal medium must be translated into finite/temporal references. Love uses the receiver – your mind and its programming – to translate the information into a recognizable form like an electronics digital to analog converter.

ESP information is 'clothed' by your mind's content and programming. Alternatively, using the swirled paint can analogy mentioned earlier, dip a ball into a paint can of unmixed paints. As the ball emerges, the paint patterns on the surface of the ball are those that are on the surface of the paint can. The 'paint can' be our mortal mind; the *ESP* information – the ball – as the ball – *ESP* -- emerges it takes on swirls of 'paint' of our mind as it emerges into our awareness. The *ESP* information is 'clothed' by the mind just as the ball has paint patterns it picked up as it emerged.

---

20 An irony is that though our body operates on an analog mode, our brain tends to operate in a digital mode.

This is Love at work. Love tends not to do something very alien to you. Love is using a construct the individual has setup – through his or her own mental programming. Through this programming, Love speaks. Moreover, it is in accord with the established perception system. Most people are not knocked off their ass on the way to Damascus. Even though, that will occur, if that is what it takes for you to grow in God.

ESP facilitated information that uses the internal **vector 1** tends to manifest within our temporal minds in three basic forms.

ESP forms
An *ESP* event makes itself known in our mind may take on one of these basic forms.

1. As a perception: words, images, etc.
2. As emotions, body feelings, sensate (these are still somewhat perceptual, though the perceptions are less clear)
3. Intuition, or a quiet knowing

❑ **Form 1**: **As a perception: words, images, etc.**
This first way (**form 1**) would be if the operator received the information in words, symbols, visions, or audio. These are when they tend to parallel any one of our senses, such as vision, hearing, smelling, tasting, or sensation (as mentioned earlier in this chapter). This form of manifestation uses the perception aspect of the human matrix. There are as many different types – modalities -- as there are ways to perceive. It would be prohibitive to go into them all.[21]

The way this first form operates for any individual, will be dependent on how they have programmed their matrix. It can appear as pictures, dialogs, or monologues, complete or fractured. (The dialogue aspect is in keeping with the common perception of telepathy.)

One exercise you will learn in this chapter is -- after meditating and practicing being empty,[22] is to create a mental image with the eyes closed.[23] Then, ask a question of the image; and, its answer comes back as part of the image. (A very similar concept to using *Tarot* or the *I Ching* – giving to the Universe/Love...)

The flows of information in this *ESP* instance come from Truth through the *Storages* into a specific 'subjective event' focus.[24] **Form 1** uses the *Perceptual Lens Array* (and its focus patterns developed in *Storage*), to the Cognition path through *Knowledge*, and then to other *Storage*s; the information then flows into our awareness in the focus buss.[25]

❑ **Form 2**: **As emotions, body feelings, sensate (these are still somewhat perceptual, though the perceptions are less clear)**
The second way (**form 2**) *ESP* can appear through the *Perceptual Lens Array* is in when it involves the desire aspect of the lens. It usually manifests more as feelings -- sensate. Something may not feel right.[26] "I've got a gut feeling." Or, "I've a bad feeling about this."

This form may be just an emotion (like fear) or it can also involve another information route, the body, as with some water dowsers.

With the body example, the information flow comes from Truth through Storage to the body (which makes the *ESP* information take on an 'objective event' appearance), through the 'front' of the mind using the *Perceptual Lens Array*, from Cognition through *Knowledge*, and then into our awareness in the focus buss.

---

21 In fact, Love being non-exclusive, will customize the modality according to an individual's mortal mind/matrix programming.
22 Stilled, altered, or took control of the 'subjective event' input in the matrix.
23 Create a specific condition within your mind.
24 Examples: Chart 4-4, *H5*, *H6*, and *H7*
25 Figure 4-4, *III*. Examples: Chart 4-4, *I2* or *I7*
26 Examples: Chart 4-4, *L1* or *I10*

And…because we are all different, *ESP* facilitated information can manifest by a combination of these two forms. These first two basic forms involve the 'subjective event' of the lens – the 'front' of the mind -- and can be paralleled to perceptions/thoughts or reasoning and to desire/feelings, or emotions.

This means; **Forms 1** and **2** can relate to the Reason and Emotion triangles of Figure 4-4 as well. Both of these forms of psychic manifestation are coming from Truth and involve the *Perceptual Lens Array* (which may be through *Storage* or the way *Storage* focuses the array [subjective loop][27]), into *Knowledge* through the Cognitive Input, to *Programming*, and to us.

An important observation is the appearance of these first two forms of psychic phenomena and the imagination in the mind is about as far apart as the index and middle fingers. Psychic phenomenon has a deeper feeling to it than imagination, but there can be trouble telling them apart in the beginning. That is why caution or questioning can be important. (In addition, why using an objective system [*I Ching* or *Tarot*] may be helpful.)

ESP has a slightly 'deeper' feel to it, and the information can be questioned honestly (as much as the operator needs for clarity). The truth in the *ESP* can withstand that questioning. It is only the ~~real~~ -- the ~~truth~~ -- that cannot stand up to truth based questioning.[28]

Again, this is important; whatever you give to Love, it will use. That means; what you give to Love to grow in Love, Love will use to facilitate the process. The exercises presented in this book consist of giving Love a mental construct – image – and letting Love speak through that image.

Here is an example of using that. In one of the exercises to facilitate clairvoyance, you will construct an image. This image can be a mirror, a movie screen, a field, etc. One professional psychic teacher used the image of a flower. She would mentally plant the seed – the question, water it, and mentally watch it grow. Then, she would ask the flower questions. What is happening with that flower would be parallel or congruent to what is happening to the person who is being 'read'.

She would begin a dialogue and question the flower, and the flower would return with answers. If the flower is cramped, it was significant. The person is feeling cramped, closed in. She would question the flower to get parallel answers about the person while have a dialogue with this flower in her head.

The flower construct – the image -- along with a 'disinterested-interest' provided a medium for the information via the One Mind so that the information can effectively appear in a finite/temporal mind -- mortal mind (to use the form the human mind set up or constructed).

❑ **Form 3: Intuition, or a quiet knowing**

This form occurs naturally with empty mind exercises. Both **forms 1** and **2** take the long way around, or the 'scenic route' through your being. This form does not involve the 'subjective event' route of the matrix. It comes from the Truth within the individual and *Storage*s. Truth manifests through *Knowledge* storage, to *Programming* into the awareness in the *Focus Control Buss*.[29] The information can also go right from *Truth* directly into your awareness within the focus buss.[30]

With intuition, there are no words, no pictures, no feelings…no perceptions. You just quietly know. Unlike the first two forms of manifestation, this form of *ESP* does not go through any of the perceptual routes – through the 'mind's eye'. It does not go through the *Perceptual Lens Array* -- 'front' of the mind -- whatsoever, as the first two forms of manifestation did. There is no 'objective' or 'subjective event' representing an Objective Event – the 'reading'.

---

27 Example: Chart 4-4, *H1*
28 This questioning can be facilitated by the absolute truths acquired in Chapter 3, *Exercise and Lab 3*
29 Examples: Chart 4-4, *C5* or *C6*
30 Example: Chart 4-4, *A4*

Intuition manifests from *Truth*, through *Knowledge* and completely bypasses the perceptual lens. It just occurs. It comes from *Truth* to the 'back' of your mind to you. This is the form to go for, or work with. It is the direct route.

With the other forms, an individual can misinterpret, mislead, or introduce errors – delude oneself. The first two forms may contain perceptions and meanings attached to former judgments or choices -- *Programming*. This may involve *Knowledge* as well as mental/emotional sets that involve *Programming*, and *Memory*...

The first two forms appear as perceptual phenomena; meaning, they involve the 'subjective event' route and the *Perceptual Lens Array* (Chart 4-4, *I2* or *L1*, for example). This means the 'front' of the mind – 'mind's eye' -- as well as the 'back' of the mind may be involved. Whereas, in the case of intuition, the individual just knows. The third form involves only the 'back' of the mind. The *Programming* and *Memory* storages are not involved as much as *Knowledge*.

It is possible to misinterpret a symbol, as with *Tarot* cards or something equivalent. It is very hard to misinterpret intuition, except after the fact. You can rationalize or fool yourself about what it means after the knowledge becomes present, but not when receiving the specific input.

As the first two forms (**forms 1** and **2**) are parallel to perception or desire in the presented model, intuition (**form 3**) is an *ESP* form that works kind of parallel to cognition.

Intuition is an introduction to a psychic skill that does not travel through the perceptional lens. This skill is outside of 'words'. Unfortunately, this book has to use symbols in order to get the subject matter introduced and to do some of the labs.

With all three forms, especially with intuition, *ESP* facilitated information process can also happen as the 'objective event' being 'read' is happening. As the specific external event is happening, the individual can know certain things in reference to the event and at the same time, without physically seeing them. What does this mean?

Usually with most **forms 1** and **2** of *ESP* phenomena, *ESP* involves an awareness that something is happening in a different place or a different time.[31] This phenomenon can give awareness of something in the past as well the future. In the first two forms (**1** and **2**), the event tends not to have occurred yet, has occurred already,[32] or occurred in a different space. The 'objective event' tends not to have occurred at the same time or place as the 'subjective event' psychic 'reading'. The psychic 'reading' tends to come before, after, or at some other temporal/spatial reference other than the 'perceived' event.

However, it is very common for intuition to occur at the same time that the external event is happening (although it may be in a different space from you). Intuition can be more immediately available to the individual. Instead of the information going through the lens array one or two times (with the consequent perceptions, desires, judgments, coloration, or mental pollution), intuition can act like the Cognitive Input of the mortal mind/matrix. It is there as you are there.

When the intuitive is working, the event is happening and the individual is working off an *ESP*, psychic cognitive parallel, of their mortal mind/matrix. Their cognition is working with the One Mind. If the individual is in the same space and time as the actual event, one may be using intuition in compliment with the Cognitive Input of the External Event to the mortal mind/matrix as well.

Again, intuition is the preferred form of psychic awareness. This *ESP* form tends to manifest naturally with the cultivation of an empty mind. Since almost all mental activity involves major collaborations between *Knowledge*, *Programming*, and *Memory*, reducing the *Programming* and *Memory*, element allows for a clear path for intuition to move through *Knowledge*.

---

31 Another *BTR* separate from the operator's *BTR*.
32 Different time references.

As mentioned earlier, where and how *ESP* manifests with **forms 1** and **2,** is dependent on the individual's programming of their personal matrix – their mind. If they tend to be sensory orientated, it will tend to come as one of their favorite senses, a sense that they really like.

One person talked about smelling people; they sensed people by how they smelled. Previously, it was mentioned that, when young, the author used to sense people by their not tasting right. They tasted different. In addition, a person can perceive it as a sight, a feeling, etc. Once the individual starts doing empty mind exercises, the first two forms of psychic manifestation will tend to come through the favorite feelings or senses that they have already programmed into the matrix.

As stated in the beginning of this chapter and to be repeated here, psychic phenomenon tends to be a side effect of still mind exercises. When you start emptying your human mind/matrix and being still, that situation starts creating its own scenario. The Eternal Mind will come through, with the needed information. You can do all kinds of exercises to facilitate the psychic within (like constructing an image). However, you do not have to do those kinds of exercises.

If you do internal disciplines involving stillness of being,[33] and start expanding your mental perceptions to see the whole (increase Truth), you end up being psychic no matter what. Once you start stilling the mind, *ESP* naturally starts to occur. The more you work a still mind, the stronger the tendency of the *ESP* information to appear as intuition, and not as a perception or feeling.

When you first start to do some of this book's exercises, you may experience a fear to enter your mind, a fear of a void. Nothing. You know; that you would just drop into a black hole somewhere. Nevertheless, the truth is, when an individual empties their mind, then they will be filled.

You cannot fill a full cup, so you have to empty the cup before the cup can be filled from the One Mind.[34] Nature abhors a void and fills it with herself or you will fill it.

There will never be a void. God fills all voids and God is at the core of your being. All of those previous exercises given are like emptying a cup, and then the cup will be filled. The *ESP* phenomenon comes as a side effect of doing the emptying.

As well as the first two forms of *ESP* (**1** and **2**); the intuition method of reception (**3**) will also automatically start to grow. The more you start emptying the mind -- because there is no perceptions, thoughts, or your own programming in the way-- the preferred form, intuition, tends to emerge predominant.

With practice, the non-intuition types of *ESP* will be sublimated. The more an individual starts working with the One Mind, the more they tend to work with intuition.

With all three forms of *ESP* facilitated information, the operator will know 'something' is about to happen or is happening. In some other time/space line, an external event in **Actual** reality event collaborates the *ESP* acquired information. This collaboration is used later as measures of successful 'reading' -- effectiveness. This was touched on in the beginning of this chapter.

Teaching *ESP* is equivalent to telling you how to walk. You have to do the work and make mistakes in order to have recognition of cause and effect. [35]

7.3 - Human Matrix and the Formula of Effectiveness Relationships

As stated throughout this book, the truths/laws of physics have the potential to happen everywhere at once. They are applicable to, and perceived through, specific *BTR* conditions. Gravity is applicable and perceived in large-scale *BTR* conditions

---

33 Some of the exercises that have been presented in previous chapters, the mantras and the breath and the others; these are examples of the type of exercises being referred to.

34 "Usefulness of clay determines a cup, but usefulness of the cup is determined by where the clay is not." *Tao te Ching* (See Prologue)

35 "Every child has the right to fall on their face when learning how to walk." -Jesus…

(stars, planets, baseballs, etc.). Electro-magnetic is applicable and perceived in smaller scale *BTR* conditions.[36]

If we wish to perceive (and work with) gravity, we must setup the applicable conditions. It would do no good to begin our gravity experiment by rubbing a glass rod with cat fur (a condition that pertains to a static electricity experiment). We must work with the conditions that are relevant to that particular law/truth. Accordingly, this also applies to metaphysics -- *ESP* phenomenon.

Remember the formula of Chapter 5. A major point stressed with the formula usage is to avoid using the lower half of the mind/matrix – denominator -- when learning to work with *ESP*. The denominator becomes involved when you begin to have pre-formed perceptions with emotional reactions (desires and attachments) to the information that you are working with. This thereby, decreases your *ESP* effectiveness.

To facilitate learning this *ESP* stuff, the book will cross-reference Chapter 5's Formula of Effectiveness to the *ESP* process. The formula can be a reference that helps you figure out what you may have done wrong when an experiment does not work. The formula provides an objective reference.

Remember: When *1*s and *0*s were substituted in the denominator, the results of that complex formula began to simplify.

Because the formula is an ideal; and in the human condition, we rarely have *0* attachments or desires, it is smart to address as many variables – numerator and denominator -- as possible. The more variables that are juggled to produce effectiveness, the greater the chances are that you will have successful *ESP* experiments.

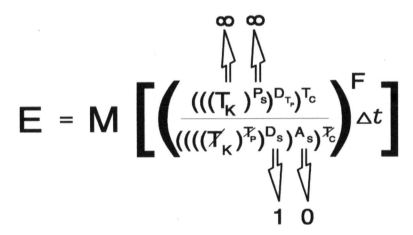

Figure 7-1, Formula of Effectiveness Applications

Perceptions (*P_S*, *T_P*, and *T_P*):

Try to 'tweak'[37] these values to infinite or be very open. When we make our perceptions as inclusive or non-exclusive as possible (remember Love is not exclusive), we are open to having true perceptions (an increase of *T_P*). Recognizing your individually ignorance is another way to keep these variables open (see truth known).

---

36 The energy stored within a molecular matrix and its release as electromagnetic *BTRs*– to burn something; moving a conducting matrix through a magnetic field – generation of electricity; the forces between electric fields – static cling of a sock to a sweater, etc.

37 An electronic term for adjusting a coil's inductance, what frequencies the coil works at.

❏   This increases the numerator, decreases the denominator of the formula, and contributes to your *ESP* effectiveness.

Choice (T_C and F_C):

Stated in Chapter 5, there is a direct relationship between choice and perceptions. When our matrix machine is in idle or on automatic, the relationship is one to one. In this case, what enters the perceptual array through the 'subjective event' is allowed a straight run, through into storage, through Choice (as in daydream). Once we start taking control or refocus, the one to one relationship changes. We can choose not to allow this automatic mode. We can 'see' but not 'choose'.

Either way, whatever choices made are based on perceptions. A decrease of ~~truth~~ perceived (F_P) causes a decrease of ~~truth~~ choices (F_C). Accordingly, an increase of truth perceived (T_P) would allow an increase in truth chosen (T_C).

❏   Playing with perception and choice like this, while plugging in the relationships into the formula, you can increase values in the numerator twice and decrease values in the denominator twice, thereby increasing an *ESP* experiment effectiveness.

Desires (D_S):

For the coming experiments, you are to generate a curiosity. Curiosity is being a desire to know within a 'disinterested-interest' condition – one desire or a fraction of a desire. Curiosity keeps desires at a low level. A mild curiosity is encouraged, and that is all. This holds total desires (D_S) in the formula down to a low value.

It is at this juncture that reducing D_S to less than one – a fraction of a desire – can be to your advantage. Chapter 5.6 - Formula Application and Usage introduced the concept of what happens with a fraction – a number less than one -- in an exponent. If the base number is greater than one, the fraction reduces the base number. A fraction in the exponent of the denominator reduces the denominator of the formula.

(In terms of the numerator, if perceptions are tweaked to infinite [$P_S > \infty$}, taking a radical – fractal exponent -- of an infinite set will still result in an infinite set.)

❏   This, in turn, keeps the denominator of the formula down also, increasing your *ESP* effectiveness.

Attachments (A_S):

As with desires, a 'disinterested-interest' implies no attachments or fears. You want to know and you could not care less about what you learn.

❏   Cultivating a 'disinterested-interest' is an attempt to put a *0* for the A_S value, turning the denominator of the formula into *1* (or close to *1*), increasing your *ESP* effectiveness.

Truth Known (T_K):

The above has shown how to 'tweak' the denominator of the formula down until it is close to one; and, 'tweaked' up the numerator. Now let us 'tweak' the numerator up even more to facilitate a successful *ESP* operation.

The category of truth known is slippery. Within us is a Mind that makes it possible to have at hand everything that can be known. We know everything through the One Mind within us; we just do not know we know everything. Since psychic information usually involves the *Knowledge* storage of the human matrix, that increases the importance of this variable.

To increase our truth known (T_K) we recognize that there is more to know than we have in our temporal *Knowledge* storage and we look for this knowledge -- to know we do not know. To access the One Mind or to receive information psychically, we are attempting to increase the value of truth known (T_K) or keep this variable open. So, to apply the formula and to increase truth known, we need to step out of what we think is in our *Knowledge* storage and become open to new knowledge – be non-exclusive.

Another way to say this is -- the operator is setting aside temporal source knowledge, in order for the eternal source knowledge (*ESP*) to be present. In just setting aside our temporal knowledge, that act automatically encourages our eternal knowledge.

❑ All of this reflects as an attempt to increase T_K and augments the numerator of the formula.

Faith (*F*):
Even if faith is only one, the operator can have effective experiments. As long as Faith is not *0* (thereby turning the formula expression to *1*) or less than *1* (incomplete applications), the chances are your experiments will be met with some degree of success.

❑ Ideally, for successful *ESP* experiments, Faith should approach infinite (*F* → ∞).

The Mirror or Karmic Correction Coefficient (*M*):
This variable represents the Mirror of Chapter 3 and is the formula's 'fudge factor'. Remember the function of the Mirror is to reflect the ~~truth~~ in our minds back to us, for us to chose/remember God.[38] This can make this variable an amplifier or an attenuator in terms of effectiveness.
Whatever ~~truth~~ is in the operator's matrix, will be reflected back on that person; <u>even if, attachments are *0*</u>. This makes it a gilt-edge priority to reduce all the ~~truth~~ variables in the denominator as well. At the same time, aligning the numerator to *Truth* is aligning the mind to the essence of the Mirror -- the Eternal Moment of Creation.

❑ The end product of reducing ~~truth~~ from all the previous examples affects this variable, and would increase *ESP* effectiveness.

So, what does this mean? How does the arrangement within the matrix in Figure 4-4, cross-reference to the formula for effectiveness of Figure 5-2 and psychic phenomena? In Chapter 4, an analogy was made between the *Perceptual Lens Array* and a camera. Also in that chapter, it was stated that the beliefs vertex of the array was equivalent to the aperture of a camera and really was a result of the mixing of the other vertices.[39]
A clear *Perceptual Lens Array* is essential for all forms of psychic information to emerge into your awareness in the focus buss. Since you are trying to <u>see</u> beyond your immediate *BTR* with maximum detail, the aperture of your lens array must be set accordingly – wide open.
A camera trying to pick out detail in weak light must have the aperture wide open to allow light to get to the film. Accordingly, the aperture of our *Perceptual Lens Array* (beliefs) must be all the way open. That means there should be no beliefs (beliefs should approach zero).
Important: <u>This means not only **no beliefs**, it also applies to **no non-beliefs**.</u>

The lens of a camera (when going for distance) is focused to infinity. Accordingly, the Perception/Desires Lens should be totally open (attempt to stretch perceptions to infinite -- P_S → ∞).[40] At the same time, a one-point desire focus is present, to bring the lens to bear on the subject (D_S and D_{Tp} → *= 1* or *> 1*).[41] This can also help reduce self-created distractions.
Reducing A_S in the formula – cultivating a non-attachment to what is happening -- is essential to learning and operating all three of the *ESP* forms of manifestation. The author and a friend of the author once discussed the necessity of a 'disinterested-interest' to facilitate an event.[42] This 'disinterested-interest' with no attachment to what is happening facilitates

---

38 Figures 3-4, 5-1, and 5-2
39 Perceptions, Desires, Attachments, and Faith.
40 Equivalent to *Lab and Homework Assignment #4*, Chapter 4.7.
41 This one-point desire is the same whether we use the physical senses or the 'sixth' sense.
42 The conversation we had was originally about magic. When I mentioned the 'disinterested-interest', he chuckled; and said, he used that to 'pick-up' women.

effectiveness in all situations. Moreover, a 'disinterested-interest' is <u>most</u> important if you want to learn psychic skills.[43] This helps you keep a mental/emotional balance as your skills evolve. It can be counter-productive to become mentally/emotionally 'wrapped up' in what you are doing, 'seeing', or your successes.

A dispassionate examination of the phenomena is encouraged, as if you are watching *TV* from very far away. Again, there is no vested interest involved, no preconceived ideas – a 'disinterested-interest'.

The dispassionate examination (or observation) of the event is almost necessary, if you are to access psychic phenomena in the perceptual, visual, or feeling modes (**forms 1** or **2**). You can question (and at times it is necessary), because as mentioned earlier, the truth can withstand all questioning and probing. Only illusion and delusion cannot stand up to honest questioning.

Remember the truth is independent and choosing or not choosing it has no effect on it. No choice will, however, affect the ~~truth~~ in the mind because it is dependent – must be enforced or re-enforced.

To summarize formula use relevant to *ESP* experiments:

❑ in order for beliefs to be open, attachments must approach zero ($A_S \rightarrow 0$),
❑ desires should be tweaked to one or less (D_S and $D_{Tp} \rightarrow 1$),[44]
❑ perceptions are open or floating ($P_S \rightarrow \infty$),[45]
❑ no (or very few) judgments are made (no choice or suspend T_C and F_C), -- observe and just use the cognitive input.
❑ Faith must approach infinite or open ($F \rightarrow \infty$).

As the lens of a camera must be focused to a distance without having the foreground in the way, so must your 'lens' (perceptions and desires) have no previous ideas or perceptions in the foreground of the *Perceptual Lens Array*. This involves no former choices or perceptions – a reduction in the *Programming* storage influence – entering through the 'subjective event'. Meditation before an *ESP* experiment can help with that.

What will be apparent is that these particular arrangements and value manipulations tend to guide automatically the information towards the True. This, in turn, will lead to the Cognitive Input. The Cognitive Input connects to *Knowledge* that works with *Truth* (where the information is originally coming from) and then to you.

Here is a review; before doing an *ESP* experiment, it is strongly recommended that:

❖ You meditate first; especially, if you are a beginning student. The stilling of the mortal mind in meditation can help foster some connection or rapport with the One Mind.
❖ You should examine yourself and make your attachments approach *0*; while desires are adjusted to *1* or less than *1* (prioritize or pre-form your intentions).
❖ Add to this, perceptions are tweaked open, and no beliefs are present to interfere with any information coming through.
❖ Co-join all this with you must apply the truth (Faith) -- that you can do it.

7.4 - Keeping Track

As stated in the beginning of the chapter, most psychic readings are in reference to an objective actual event -- **Actual** reality event, so there must be a correlation between what is happening inside the mind to outside the mind. Did it work? Did it turn out as you saw? What was different between what you saw (or what you interpreted what you saw)

---

43 *I AM A I* will be harping on this for the rest of this chapter.
44 Only that what you wish to do is desired.
45 Stretched as far as possible, reaching to infinity.

and the actuality, etc.? It can be helpful to categorize the successes or apparent successes, and failures.

As a child, the author had a strong science background. When the author first started 'playing' in his head, the author would categorize the probability of whether an experience or experiment was a success or not. Was there a true relation between what was happening in his mind and what is happening outside of his mind?

Eventually the author saw that more than yes or no categories were needed, so the author expanded to use the following categories:

❑ **Nothing**, the experiment did not work.

❑ **Possible** is a category where there <u>may</u> be a relationship between what is happening in the author's mind and what is happening outside of the author's mind. This category can include 'coincidence'.[46]

❑ **Probable** is a category where coincidence is not entirely ruled out; there is still no absolute confirmation of a psychic event. Reasoning may have played an important part in this category. This was especially true when the author was doing any *ESP* exercise that involves immediate perception of an external (objective) event.

❑ **Most Probable** is a category where the author was <u>almost</u> positive that a relationship of some sort exists between an external event and his mind/matrix. Still, the author was not completely sure.

❑ **Definite** usually transpired when something inside the author's mind occurred the same time that something happened in **Actual** reality. There was a direct one-to-one involvement. With some exercises, the author could actually feel something coming in or leaving him. This was especially true when working with magic

A true *ESP* event must have a collaborating objective correlation. If there is no collaborating objective correlation, then the event tends to be one of imagination or of mental projection and not an *ESP* event. The 'subjective' and 'objective' events must correlate, be it telepathy, clairvoyance, the use of the mind to manipulate clouds, or whatever.

If things are not clear – you do not understand what you are 'seeing', you cannot hurt this *ESP* process by asking truthful questions about the information – the content. Remember: Honest – truthful -- questioning <u>may</u> also involve questioning the perceptions of the questions, questioning the questions. Because you, as the student, should have as much as an open mind as possible, one must be aware of the perceptions involved that formulated the questions. Know one's self.[47]

This is being objective and only fair. If we are going to question the phenomena, we must question the questions also, and do it dispassionately. Observe any answers that come.

You can look at this like the jigsaw puzzle analogy. You are trying to put together the jigsaw puzzle that is yourself and the universe. What is the whole picture that is you? When you find a piece, recognize its characteristics. If you do not know where the piece goes, set it aside.

After a while, like a jigsaw puzzle, you will see relationships between the pieces you have accumulated. Some will fit together, while some pieces only appear to fit together. With perseverance, a picture that is you and the universe will start to emerge. Then it will be more apparent where each future piece goes. "Ah, yes, this piece goes here." In this way, you can observe not only your mechanics but also the *ESP* phenomena's mechanics.

---

46 This was before he found out that there is no coincidence. The coincidence idea is not in keeping with the idea of Absolute Love – nothing is excluded.

47 "Where am I coming from when I am looking at this, and asking these questions? What are my motivations? What perceptions formed these questions that I am questioning with?"

In summary of *ESP* cultivation, our mortal mind matrix is a limited and fractured replica of the One Mind Eternal Matrix. It is kind of like a distorted reflection of the One Mind Matrix, its basic template. The human mind has the One Mind within it.[48] As stated earlier, this means people can access the One Mind by going within themselves.

The psychic operator has to attune his/her mortal mind to learn to work with this Eternal One Mind. Another way to say it is to facilitate *ESP*; we have to align our temporal minds to the Universal Mind.

With practice, you will know what ESP is and what ESP is not . Moreover, when just beginning, another objective reference like categories of possibilities of success can come in handy. In the end, the *ESP* delivered information must compliment external references – have **Actual** reality references. These **Actual** reality references are your *ESP* successes.

7.5 – Cultivating Clairvoyance

As mentioned previously *ESP* **form 3** – intuition – comes naturally with empty mind exercises. This form cannot be taught; it happens as a side effect. The other two forms can be consciously cultivated however.

The Eternal Mind has access to everything. Every temporal mind has established internal communication symbols (perceptions). The Eternal Mind will talk in the symbols that the human mind relates to – 'clothes' itself in the mortal concepts present. It will talk in whatever symbols; that have been set up in the programming and are based on perceptions -- previous and current. It becomes known in a way that is familiar. Because the Eternal Mind will talk in the symbolism that the specific mind uses, this allows for 'constructed thought systems' like *Tarot* and *I Ching* as vectors for clairvoyance.

A thought 'system' is set up. The operator is talking to this thought 'system/construct', and working through this 'system'. The Universe/Love accepts this whole symbol 'system' (symbolic matrix), and the operator is letting the symbol 'system' speak back, letting the matrices do the 'work'. However, the ideal level of clairvoyance is communion with the Universe with no constructs.

As with telepathy and other *ESP* exercises, the presented clairvoyance exercises requires some kind of motivational analysis. "What is it I want from doing this? Once I find out, then what? What am I doing this for? What do I want from the exercise and from life?" The idea is to be clear, to have only one desire, to pre-form your intention. You should not be concerned about the outcome. You do not know the outcome. You are trying to get information. Doing this pre-forming your intention clears your perceptual lens.

Cultivate a passive attitude and an open mind, and again, a 'disinterested-interest' when doing these exercises. Do not become attached to what is happening. Having a 'disinterested-interest' in most forms of communication can improve your success.

Here is something from *A Course in Miracles©* that illustrates the communion mechanism that facilitates *ESP*.

Simply do this: Be still, and lay aside all thoughts of what you are and what God is; all concepts you have learned about the world; all images you hold about yourself. Empty your mind of everything it thinks is either true or false, good or bad, of everything it judges worthy, and all ideas of which it is ashamed. Hold onto nothing. Do not bring with you one thought the past has taught, nor one belief you ever learned before from anything. Forget this world, forget this course, and come with wholly empty hands unto your God.[49]

---

48 Or, this One Infinite Eternal Mind contains all mortal minds in their duality delusion. (*Theorem 26*).
49 A Course In Miracles, Workbook for Students, Lesson 189, *I feel the Love of God within me now.*

This is the communion mechanism carried to the nth degree briefly. If the word group "wholly empty hands unto _____" was substituted in (with _____ taking the place of the words "your God"), this would be an excellent example of one-point focus listening. The phrase would apply to being a good listener in a simple conversation as well as communing with God. It all depends on what the intention of the focus is.

******************** ********************

Exercise and Lab 10: Clairvoyance in a Group Format

As mentioned previously, one psychic teacher had a very down-to-earth way of saying how to do it, how to get in touch. All her workshops had element of being empty and still, cultivating a disinterested-interest, and meditating.[50] Then she would use the mental construct idea. Her favorite image was the flower example, mentioned earlier.

The person being 'read' would define the question. Usually, this would entail a dialogue between the 'reader' and the person being 'read'. She would have the 'reader' students plant the flower (the seed being the question), water it, and then watch the flower grow in their mind. Watch the flower grow until it is in full bloom. Alternatively, the operator can visualizing the seed as being the person being 'read'; visualize planting the flower; when the flower is fully-grown in its maturity, the 'reader' asks it the question.

When the author first started playing with *ESP* cultivation, the author used the image of black mirror or blackboard; the pictures would unfold in the image like a slide show. These pictures flashed momentarily on the blackboard. Whereas, with this example of this psychic's exercises, there is a dialogue occurring. Whatever communication form you use, whether it is visual, words, images, feelings, or whatever, write down the questions and write down the answers.

It is very helpful to keep the initial question precise. A previous example was, "If I do _____, what effects will this have on _____?" The clarity of the question helps define the clarity of the answer.

Remember, when you start working with this construct that you have generated in your mind, you not only ask the original question (the one on the paper), you also ask what this question is about. It may be important to ask what is behind this question also. How does the person who wrote down this question feel about this question?

Therefore, you are now asking more than one question about the question. There is the original question. There is also the question of what is it about this question that concerns the writer. Ask how the writer feels about this question. You then write down the answers that you get, from the image.

If the things that are coming to you are not clear, do not be afraid to ask the image more questions. Remember the thing about truth: it can be questioned. It will not hurt; especially, when you are trying to learn. Be quiet, listen to what the image has to say; then, do the next question.

When this exercise is done in a group setting, an example of the exercise may be:

➢ *The group meditates for fifteen minutes.*
➢ *On two pieces of paper, everybody writes down a question about their lives (or whatever) on each paper. Do not sign it. Fold the papers up so the question inside the paper is not seen. Make a mark on the outside of the paper, one that you would recognize.*
➢ *All the papers go in a hat. People take turns taking questions out of the hat. Look for your mark and do not take your own question. And...do not open the paper and read the question yet.*
➢ *Next, each operator constructs a communication image. The image you create should be one in which you feel comfortable. The image can be anything. It can be a flower, a*

---

[50] The day would begin with meditation; and before each group exercise, there would be a meditation period.

blackboard, a tree, a star, a mayonnaise jar with a Funk & Wagnall's dictionary. It does not make any difference.

➤ *After each individual has chosen their image, they then read the question on the paper. When all this is set up, everybody should be sitting there with two pieces of paper in front of them, not written by him or her, with a question on each.*

➤ *Then, sit with the paper in front of you, breathe and still your thoughts. Breathe; still the thoughts, while cultivating a disinterest or 0 attachment to the outcome. Then create your pre-determined construct or image in your mind with the eyes closed. Ask the construct the question and wait and watch what happens.*

➤ *After asking the main question, ask questions that may be relevant to the main question. Example: If the main question is something like, "Why am I not happy?", ask about home-life; what makes one happy; what does the questioner want; etc. If what is seen is not clear, ask for more information.*

➤ *After the operator generates a construct, they ask questions and write down what the image says, or what they see. Everybody would be doing this in the lab. This is done without any communication with anyone else.*

➤ *When everybody was done, the group comes back together and looks at some of the questions with the answers. The person who wrote it can say whether they feel the answer is accurate or not. It was up to them how far they want that discussion to go, because the question can be personal. Some people may not want to admit they even wrote the question. It may be just enough for them to hear someone say an answer without them having to respond. And...an objective reference to a successful ESP event can be in the response.*

********************  ********************

Exercise and Lab 11: Clairvoyance in an Individual Format

❑ This first exercise can be done traveling to a place that you have never been to, or it can refer to something you have never seen. Traveling to 'somewhere' will be used as an example on how to do this exercise. First, as stated previously, do a still mind exercise – meditate -- before the *ESP* exercise.

As you are traveling, close your eyes (first make sure you are not the driver) and create in your imagination a blackboard or a dark screen. Once this image is established, with your mind, take the name of the place you are going to and put it on the blackboard. Then, as a passive observer, watch the image that appears on the screen. What does it look like? Record aspects of that image in your memory. When you get to that place, compare the image you had with the actuality of the place.

Another option is to imagine driving up to the 'place' for the first time (though you had not arrived yet) and 'observe' the nature of the place as you visualize your arrival.

This is a form of distant or remote viewing.

❑ The second exercise is to use a newspaper, radio, or TV and pick a news item. It should be a news item on a subject that is occurring and not yet concluded. If it is a newspaper, read the article several times, while maintaining a mental and emotional distance from the subject. It is helpful to pick a news item in which you have little or no interest. Your interest in this exercise is to 'see', not in the subject matter itself.

Returning to a redundant reminder, a good part of the success of these exercises is dependent on maintaining a 'disinterested-interest' in the outcome of the 'seeing'.

After you have made yourself relatively familiar with the ideas in news item, meditate and do a still mind exercise with breathing. With your imagination, visualize an image of the original news media. If the news media was a newspaper, imagine how the newspaper would look.

Then, with your mind, form the question: What is the outcome of this subject? Ask the newspaper, TV, radio... Your job now is to passively observe or read the results.

As in the previous exercise, remember what you have read or write it down in the workbook, and keep an update on the subject through the news media or newspaper. Compare your individual reading to what actually happens.

The assignment is:

➤ *Meditate or do an empty mind exercise before the operation (5-15minutes)*
➤ *Establish your intentions and a 'disinterested-interest'*
➤ *Do each exercise three times, distant viewing and precognition.*
➤ *Keep track of successes and failures.*

The success of these exercises is dependent on several factors:

• A still mind and being.
• Your attachment to the exercise outcome; how well you can cultivate a disinterested-interest
• How much truth is in your mind/matrix.
• How much *Truth* is stored in your *Knowledge*.
• How the cognitive input to *Knowledge* is used.

Learning to open your psychic perception is like learning any other skill. You may make many mistakes at first or you may pick it up easy. No matter which -- to quote the *I Ching* -- "perseverance pays".

******************** ☯ ********************

7.6 – Cultivating Telepathy

*E*arlier sections of this chapter introduced the various forms in which *ESP* phenomena can appear. Also mentioned, it can be seen how *ESP* is from one mind (Mind) to another -- telepathy. This section will focus specifically on the mechanics and aspects of telepathy. Again, all *ESP* phenomena can be 'seen' as a form of telepathy. This applies to a psychic seeing something in a rock, to a practicing witch or shaman, or to a saint in communion with God.

Telepathy is much more common than is customarily thought. We tend not to be consciously aware of it. On the other hand, at times, we may even be subconsciously afraid of it – deny it.

Telepathy is natural. Most animals have telepathic capabilities. These capabilities can be very limited in the concepts their minds work with, but telepathy is possible with animals. All life shares in the One Mind.

Plants are empathic,[51] which is a cruder form of telepathy. Plants respond to emotions. There have been all kinds of studies on the response of plants to human emotions and even studies on various means of communication between plants. How a 'stressed plant' communicates that 'stress' to other plants for example.

The following is an example of how common telepathy really is. Perhaps, this has happened to you at least one time or another. Let us say you are at a bus station or on an airplane and you are not looking at anybody in particular, but you are aware of somebody over in the corner with your peripheral vision. You are just aware them and have only a mild interest.

Without moving your heads, the other person's awareness turns to you at the same time as your awareness is on him/her and there is this 'click' or a 'snap' that happens.[52] Usually, both of you will turn away at once, or will both turn to do something at the same time.

---

51 A communication of feelings or emotions.
52 'Click'; a connection has been made. A 'snap', if a connection has been made and broken immediately after.

It can be a shock the first time. This 'click' is the making of a bond in which telepathy is dependent; the 'snap' is the abrupt breaking of the bond.

If this happens in some social situation, like a bar or a party, and if communication is not shut down entirely, verbal or body communication can ensue. Later, this section will go into depth what is meant by bond.

Another example of how telepathy is used is in a magical love spell. In thaumaturgical magic, the most powerful love spell there is consists only of a look and a touch. It is a form of telepathic bond that is done with that look and touch.

The author has observed that many women and some men already know this subconsciously without studying magic.

One definition for telepathy is an idea or ideas shared by apparently separated minds, without any physical form -- BTRs -- of communication to foster that sharing. For telepathy to work, one way or another, the 'bond' is necessary. In some books, it is called the 'love bond'. (In addition, remember that due to the time ignor-ance of the Eternal Mind, these two people [mortal minds] do not have to have the same temporal reference – live in the same times.)

Moreover, there is a 'bond' between your mortal mind/matrix and the Eternal One Mind/Matrix. Which is not a living temporal person; it is a living Eternal Being. It cannot really be considered or compared to a human mortal mind (in fact it can appear quite un-human), and at the same time, it is at the very core of the human matrix. Our mortal mind is contained or a special case within this Eternal being.

Here, with spiritual applications, there is a problem with words. In some cases, the word 'bond' may be misleading. As you reprogram your personal temporal matrix to the Eternal Matrix, through the matching of the matrices' elements, the two start working as the same matrix.[53] An idea that is in the One Matrix appears in the other matrix.[54] When psychic phenomena manifests in this manner -- from the True Mind to a temporal mind, the word 'bond' may be misleading.

The 'word' bond is applicable to two apparently separate minds/matrices. If there is a perception of separateness, then a perception of a connection is inevitable for communication (or sharing) to proceed. This telepathic bond is simply a mental agreement or accord. Almost like the agreed radio frequency between a transmitter and a receiver.

It is called a 'love bond' for a number of reasons. Because Love is not exclusive, it unites what appears to be fractured minds and beings. Love's Mind is a common thread running through a multitude of minds. For example, mothers with their children have this 'love bond'. That is why a mom tends to know what the kid's doing, (much to the kid's dismay). At times, she is telepathically 'in tune' with what is happening with the kid through that bond.

Another problem with words is the word *love*. The number of human projections and meanings to that word 'boggles the brain'. The bond referred to here naturally occurs when two minds develop a mild 'disinterested-interest' in each other, as in the plane or bus station example.

A bond can be just between close friends, like two buddies in the army. Under adverse situations, this bond forms between them and then these communications occur where they both know what is happening in each other's minds; it clicks. Another example is with lovers, provided they are not thinking about their projections – 'baggage' -- or other things happening in their relationship.

A Course in Miracles expresses that there are only two emotions, love or fear.[55] If you are free from fear, you are in love whether you know it or not.

The mechanics of this is ever so simple. Fear is exclusive in nature; Love is non-exclusive in nature while Absolute Love is all-encompassing. At the same time, Love will not directly confront fear; it will not go where it is feared. With fear present, Love just will not be the

---

53 Figure 4-8 (*I-V*)

54 Kind of like the tuning coil of a radio is tuned to the transmitter's frequency.

55 Text, Chapter 13, The Two Emotions

major apparent influence and can appear to be absent. If fear is absent, Love and the Correction will automatically be present and will resume being the major influence.

A 'disinterested-interest' works with these mechanics. A 'disinterested-interest' entails no attachments or fear, so a 'love bond' ensues naturally. Again, a 'disinterested-interest' is at the core of learning all *ESP* phenomena and at the core of spiritual growth.

Here is an irony with *ESP*, telepathy, and some of the more advanced metaphysical applications. The desire to have a successful telepathic event can interfere with a successful telepathic event.

You must not be caught up in what you find or what you are doing. It is almost essential that you are not emotionally involved in what you discover. If you do, you can start 'losing it'. The best-case scenario for this is one deludes oneself on a minor level. The worst-case scenario; it may lead to psychotic episodes.

This 'disinterested-interest' tends to foster this love bond whether you know it or not, as with a stranger on a plane. A bond ensues. When that 'snap' happens and you both turn away, that is the bond breaking.

You both have the choice whether to 'go with it' or not go with it. Turning away reflects not going with it. To act on it, you may start physically communicating through body language (like smiling) or conversation. The bond occurs first, before any ideas can be shared telepathically between the minds. And…once emotional content or attachment ensues, the 'bond' disappears.

One analogy around the function of the love bond and telepathy in this section is a *CB* radio. When using a *CB* radio, the transmitter and receiver must be tuned to the same frequency for this communication to occur. As in the *CB* analogy, it takes two to tango; both parties must have an interest – radios turned on. In addition, there must be a listener and a talker; both listening and talking cannot be done at the same time. So again, here is another reference to a need for the individual to learn to still themselves and become receptive – to listen.

Using this 'love bond', the individual minds do not have to think alike. The Love bond acts as if it is an automatic translating device between the individuals. That is the beauty of it. Because it works through Absolute Love, the communication is translated. It goes from the perceptions of one mind and it translates over to the perceptional lens in the other's mind. The purest form of this is the speaking in tongues mentioned previously.

There is a translation device -- for lack of a better term -- in the love bond. Once the love bond is there, Love's non-exclusive nature automatically translates. It goes from applicable knowledge in one person to another's applicable knowledge through Absolute Truth. While in each individual *Storage*s, the concept being communicated is translated, clothed, or filtered through each individual's matrix and his or her programming.

It may be helpful, if both individuals have knowledge of some of the same things. An example is having mutual perceptions shared by similar cultures. A telepathic bond between a cave dweller and a New York stockbroker might be somewhat difficult, because they may not have common perceptions, values, wants, etc. They may not have common motivations. They may not have agreement on what is the world (a common **Individual** or **Consensual** reality between them). Therefore, it may be necessary (or desirable) some way or another to have some kind of common knowledge.

Basic human needs, emotions, and archetypes can serve as that common knowledge. It is difficult to have a telepathic bond with someone and communicate an understanding of human foibles though, if the other person does not recognize any human foibles.

To recap what telepathy needs.

- There must be a disinterested-interest
- There has to be a love 'bond'.
- You must learn to mentally shut up and still your mind to listen. Be still! You must have an open mind -- no preconceived ideas. It is essential with doing telepathic communication, for the operator to learn to stop thinking, to still their temporal matrix. As with any form of

dialogue, there is a time to listen and a time to talk. Or, with the CB analogy, if you want to listen you have to take your thumb off the transmit button.

Psychic, *ESP*, or spiritual phenomena can be broken down into two forms of telepathy -- passive and active (whether you are 'reading' or having a 'dialogue').

❑ **Passive** → Most of the psychic phenomena like clairvoyance and Clairaudience tend to be on the passive side of telepathy. No specific love bond or focus is involved outside of the operator. It is related to a 'bond' within the operator, between that human mind and the Eternal Mind, or you and your Source. One way to look at it is the operator has come to some kind of accord or agreement with the Universe.

How the 'bond' in passive telepathy occurs, is very dependent on the state of mind of the individual. This means how the individual has programmed their human matrix with choices made from the information flow through the perceptual lens (*Storages*). It also involves what the individual is doing to set it up the communion, or not setting it up (the focus of the *Perceptual Lens Array*).

What all the passive telepathic aspects have in common are cultivating a listening attitude, a watching and waiting, being relaxed, and paying attention with a 'disinterested-interest'.

Every thought that any person thinks is transmitted -- it is available. The volume of that transmission of perception is somewhat dependent on how much desire and emotions are involved. The stronger the desires, the stronger will be the transmission. Remember the vehicle analogy.[56] Desire is the fuel, whereas perception is the guide.

Therefore, every thought anyone thinks is transmitted out, and the volume of that transmission is dependent on how much desire or emotion is behind it. In addition, because every thought is transmitted, that means passive telepathy involves not mind reading, but mind listening.

Remember that your ability to tune into anyone's thoughts is also related to your desire. Too much desire and you will be listening to your mind instead of theirs – to what you want. The 'disinterested-interest' help cultivates a low-level desire ($D_S = 1$ or $D_S < 1$). Tuning into someone specifically is dependent on how well you can be empty and have a bond with the other person. You must have enough desire to maintain an interest. However, not enough desire to generate vested interests, attachments.

The passive telepathic listener acts like radio receiver; they are turned on, are listening, and without putting anything out -- transmitting. Everybody is speaking at once, and the telepathic listener just happens to be a tuned listener to a specific individual. That is essentially what telepathy is all about.

Every thought is transmitted. The individual does not have to pick things out of people's minds, because people are transmitting all the time. The operator has to learn to shut up and be discriminating about whom they want to listen to. That is what makes the bond -- a discrimination about who is being listened to.

The author used to have some problems with going into 'The City' (San Francisco) because there would be this miasma of feelings and thoughts. Nothing too specific; there was just this 'ugh' -- this mental/emotional soup. The first time the author noticed that, it threw him for such a 'loop' – into a confusion. To such a degree, that the author had to go back and sit up by Coit Tower for a day; he sat until the author was used to that feeling.

This is the passive aspect of telepathy. It is telepathy through *ESP* perception. Every thought we think is transmitted. The power of the transmission can be in proportion to how much emotional charge is behind the thought. A city is full of this sea of thoughts -- other people's transmissions. With *ESP* perceptions, we tend to receive it as noise.

❑ **Active** → The telepathic act should be effortless, and not limited by time/space constraints. In having a dialogue (active form), the 'speaker' instead of thinking and having the thought go out in space (like talking to oneself), their focus is on an individual (talking to someone).

---

56 Chapter 4.5, The *Perceptual Lens Array*, Ref: Thought/emotion sets.

The transmission (the active part of telepathy, how much is put into somebody's mind) is dependent on the bond and the clarity of mind the sender has achieved. If there is no bond with anybody specific, and if there is strong clear thought with one emotion, it is put out into the ether -- or whatever you want to call it. It is put 'out there'.

As with verbal dialogue, if there is to be communication, the speaker's focus must be on the awareness of the listener. Without this awareness, the speaker is talking 'at' someone and not 'to' someone. Telepathy is similar.

To learn active telepathy is very similar to going to another country and learning a foreign language. The best way to do it is to have a companion who speaks the language. Learning comes with this daily exposure.

This partner factor helps you learn to separate **Actual** realities from the **Imaginary** realities. Observing co-relations between 'objective' and 'subjective' events gives first hand experience -- something necessary for the learning process. It provides the objective reference of successful *ESP* events (beginning of this chapter).

In many ways, it is much better if the telepathic act is spontaneous. Rigid or controlled experiments are only useful in the beginning; they serve as introductions. Instead of setting up a time, it is much better to learn to work daily using an 'internal conversation' with another person.

And, for this book to do a lab in a group format, the only way a person can really verify what is happening is if that person sets up specific conditions within themselves. With the case of telepathy, a specific set of conditions must be present within the people involved; structure is needed.

Bottom line: since it is a communication within the One Mind, telepathy is natural. It is not being telepathic that is unnatural. The following experiments are meant to give direction. A serious psychic student must learn to expand from these experiments.

******************************************

Exercise and Lab 12: Telepathy

A reminder: A book telling you how to develop *ESP* or telepathy is equivalent to a book telling you how to swim. Eventually, you are going to have to put the book down and get in the water.

Many of the exercises in this book the author learned or 'played' with seriously while in the army. The author had plenty of time on his hands, so the author started 'playing' in his head. When the author was in the army, the author's telepathy partner was the previously mentioned local 'hash' dealer, who had similar interests.

When they started working together, they rarely discussed the results; and, they both agreed something was happening. Sometimes they may have orally set something up, and then they did the experiment. Other times, it was spontaneous.

Because it is a question of detached listening inside, there is no sense talking about most of the details. <u>Do it, do not talk about it.</u> Talking can cultivate attachments. Just as long as an agreement or a recognition is made, "something is happening".

Telepathy can be a much more efficient form of communication. Talking about the event can introduce all sorts of non-relevant perceptions, desires, and attachments.

Remember that both people need to have the same mindset to do it – desire or interest. It does not work if you want to do it and the person you work with does not want to. It does not do any good if one person's desires are focused on a computer and the other's are focused on the garden. The individual desires are not the same. You both have to have the same 'disinterested-interest'-- the same one desire to communicate (or no desire at all).

Part of these experiments is for you and your partner as the operators to cultivate the same desire or interest. As the 'disinterested-interested' desires meet, the telepathic bond ensues naturally. As interests increase or the desires separate, it stops.

To facilitate a group lab, conditions have to be set up so that telepathy can be perceived. (Setting up personal conditions within the perceptual lens was in previous sections.) One of the problems that scientific people have with the study of telepathy is they do not take into account the mechanics or conditions involved.

Most science assumes telepathy is mind to mind and does not look at the conditions in individuals' minds that set up the telepathic event or the necessity of a bond. These factors determine the effectiveness of telepathy. If people try to work with telepathy as they perceive it, but they do not look at the conditions that foster telepathy, there may be problems and erratic responses.

As in physics, the student gets theory about oscillating motion and resonant conditions and things like that. Then they go to lab and start playing with a weight and a string. Once they set up an experiment with a string and a weight on it, they can watch the weight go back and forth at a certain frequency (determined by the string length). This collaborates the theory that they learned.

What is being constructed with this lab is to first set up the conditions that foster telepathy, then try to get at least some experience within a group setting of telepathy occurring; that it is possible that telepathy can occur.

For the lab in a group situation, the group would meditate as a group for fifteen to twenty minutes, and then people would pair up with a partner. Avoid pairing with somebody you have a very strong interest in, either positive or negative. (Meaning, do not hook up with anybody because you want to get into his or her pants.) At the same time, do not hook up with somebody you have some aversion to or you have some negative feelings about. No strong interest, either positive or negative; the idea is to keep the individual desires and attachment levels down.

Before the experiment can start, a bond has to occur between the two participants, especially if it is not there when they first pair up. A set of conditions has to be cultivated for this telepathy experiment to work. There are a number of ways to do this:

⇒ One way to do it is to sit facing each other, not touching and not looking at each other. Be empty and mentally aware of the other's presence in front of you.

⇒ Another way is to sit next to each other (side by side and touching [shoulder to shoulder or knee to knee]) and visually looking at the same thing and be aware of each other's presence.

⇒ Another way is to sit back to back and be aware of each other's presence.

⇒ Another is to do a five-minute breathing exercise together. Then, get up and slowly walk around the room while always being aware of the presence of the other. Do this for 2-3 minutes, then sit down and do the exercise.

Whichever way, you need to be aware of the other's presence and breathe into this awareness.

There are many ways to approach this bond element. The first examples given do not include any direct eye contact. However, the experiment participants can try doing direct eye contact.

⇒ One example is a condition where the individuals sit facing each other, knees touching. They just sit, and look into each other's eyes. They could do a one-point focus exercise with the other person's eyes as the focal point, and breathe into it or just look into each other's eyes momentarily.

⇒ Another way is to have each one take their right hand, look into each other's eyes, and touch the cheek of the other one at the same time. That is, to use a physical symbolic action to foster the bond.

A mental bond can ensue so many ways. These are just a few ways it may be nurtured.

Both experiment participants need to look at their desires or fears, and recognize that they have an internal movie. They have desires around their perception of the group and the exercise itself. These perceptions/desires can, and will, interfere with the internal telepathic mechanism.

As with all exercises in the latter part of this book, a pre-forming of intention is appropriate if not essential. Remember to ask yourself something equivalent to…

- What do I want from this exercise?
- What is my intention?
- What is my motivation for sitting and doing this?
- How do I see this group/person?
- What do I want from this group/person?
- What do I want when am I doing this exercise?

The ideal is to establish a motivation (one desire) where you are doing it because you want to learn. You want to grow. You want to communicate. You want to expand yourself. Having no preconceived thought or perception is very appropriate if you do not know where you are going. It does not get in the way of 'getting there'.

Back to this experiment, the beginning of the exercise involves being still, sitting and breathing, and being empty together. Just wait, and be aware of that other person. The purpose is to calm the mind and develop a 'disinterested-interest' to communicate one way or another with this person.

Be aware of the mental/emotional drift that occurs within you. There is a chattering away or an internal movie of the temporal mental matrix always working.

Focus on breath, being empty, and still, etc. Return to being present with that person and waiting. Learn to wait with that person.

The participants will do a bonding exercise for 5-10 minutes. No thought is appropriate. If you have thoughts, think, "I don't want to think about that now"; or "I want to do this exercise instead." Breathe into waiting with that person. Cultivate a 'disinterested-interest' in communicating to that person.

Before performing the experiment, the two individuals first agree on who will be a transmitter and who will be the receiver when beginning the exercise. For a short time one experiments as a transmitter, while the other experiments in receiving. After doing a few experiments, they exchange roles.

Next is to break out a deck of cards. Playing cards are given to the transmitting people in the group. If there are 10 people, each transmitter has 10 or more cards. For small groups or couples, do not use the whole deck; use only a handful of cards.[57] Both people – receiver and transmitter -- should look at the cards chosen[58] and then the transmitter takes the cards.

The transmitter shuffles the cards. The transmitter will use the short stack of cards before them as a record of the cards and their sequence.

There are several ways for the 'transmitter' to approach this exercise:

$\Rightarrow$ **Option number one** is the transmitter holds a card. As the two experimenters face each other, the transmitter looks at the card and rotates it around in their mind, looking at the front and back.[59]

_____

57 It may help facilitate successful experiments if the cards were dissimilar: a male face card, a female face card, a red ace, a black ace, a red ten, a black eight, etc.

58 This way the receiver's mind has relevant information to work with.

59 Similar to *Exercise and Lab #4*, Imagination and Time/Space Exercises

Visualize the card in their mind; and look at what impact the card has to them. You can use symbolic meaning, like the words, 'King of Hearts' while doing this. The transmitter should cultivate the image of the King of Hearts in their mind. First, the transmitter is aware of what they are doing inside their mind with this picture of King of Hearts. Then they look at the receiving person, using their imagination, and place that perception they have of the card into the receiver's head or on the forehead.

⇒ **In the second option**, the transmitter physically looks down at that card and gets a perception in their mind of the card. Then, they look up at the other person, use the awareness of connection, and act like they are "telling' them the card in the mind. Alternatively, act inside themselves as if they already have communicated the idea. Sit with the other person with the conviction that you both know what the card is – as if you just said it.

The first example is taking the thought and putting it into the other's mind. The other example is recognizing a bond and letting the bond do the work. It is an attempt for two minds to think the same thought at once. It may help if you imagine you are one mind, and you both think this thought and have the image of the King of Hearts at the same time.

The receiver's job is to sit and wait, be totally passive with a 'disinterested-interest', and to breathe slowly. Remember this is only an experiment. Nothing of value is at stake. Minimize attachments to success on this exercise. As said earlier, attachments to successful telepathy can get in the way of telepathic act.
As if waiting for that person to say something, the receiver is sitting and waiting. Again, it cannot be stressed enough -- cultivate a 'disinterested-interest' in the desire to know what the card is. Have no fear. If you experience fear, just breathe into it and let it go.
The receiving person then says or writes the first image that comes in their head.
What may or may not help is for the receiver to be aware of the person before them and visualize a blank card, a card with no markings on the front. Then let the card color itself in.

The transmitter will keep track of which cards were used (and what order) in the card sequence. The receiver will keep track of what they are receiving and in what order in a notebook. Then, after the exercise, the two experimenters compare. Do this several times, and then switch roles. The receiver becomes the transmitter and vice versa.

One-sided successes reflect that someone was passive. A recurring event that showed up when doing these experiments in a group format was the listener may actually be 'reading' the deck of cards and saying what the next card was rather than listening to the transmitter.
Having successful comparisons definitely reflects a two-way communication, facilitated by a bond (and usually you both already know it). If one person is successful, it only tends to mean that one person may be more 'in tune' to the 'psychic' than the other may and has more of an awareness of the cards. Because telepathy is natural, this infers they may have less of an interest in the success of the experiment
Again, non-attachment to the outcome cannot be overstressed. Your very desire to want to do this and have some success can get in the way of having any *ESP* success. This again reflects back to the formula of effectiveness. If your desires and attachments start to rise, then your effectiveness is going to go down.

In conclusion, practice will increase the success rate. There are many different options to how you can play with this. This book is just giving some basic guidelines. The experiment participants can speed up or slow the rates of how they have contact with the cards as they start to get a feel for what is happening. Communication can become more spontaneous.
This experiment consists of:

➢ *Find a partner.*

- ➢ *Both participants meditate together beforehand.*
- ➢ *Both cultivate a 'disinterested-interest' and pre-form intentions.*
- ➢ *Decide ahead who will be transmitter and who will be the receiver.*
- ➢ *Assemble the cards*
- ➢ *Develop the 'bond' or its conditions. (with a previous exercise example if necessary)*
- ➢ *The transmitter looks at the card 'communicates' the card to the receiver.*
- ➢ *The receiver writes what they perceived.*
- ➢ *The transmitter goes through the stack of cards keeping them in order.*
- ➢ *After going through the stack of cards, the receiver compares their notes to the card stack order.*
- ➢ *Do this once; then transmitter and receiver reverse roles (transmitter → receiver and receiver → transmitter) and do it again.*
- ➢ *Discuss perceptions afterward and perhaps make some entries in a journal.*
- ➢ *Do this on three separate occasions, preferably at different days and at different time of day.*

7.7 Conclusion

Another caution here on the limitations of imagery use. As it has been mentioned before, the problem with imagery use and the imagination is; it is hard to discriminate between *ESP* and the imagination. What is the source of the image's answers, your matrix (your own perceptions/desires), or the Truth Matrix? This makes objectivity absolutely essential. If you start being 'crapped up', then you are going to be getting shit back. "Shit in – Shit out".

The more objectivity is lost, the more the constructed image starts answering with the operator's desires/perceptions or programming; instead of, answering about information of the objective event. When you, as a metaphysics operator, start being mentally/emotionally wrapped up; the image is going to start speaking in what you <u>want/not-want</u> to hear, instead of what is really happening with the subject matter.

Because all images are temporal forms, the imaging comes and it goes. This occurs whether it is with your own constructs within you or established constructs without you. You cannot play with the *Tarot* forever. Whatever imagery you use, whether the construct is inside of you or outside of you, it should be a springboard to the 'quiet knowing' or intuition.

Again, do not be disappointed with initial results. 'Perseverance pays.' When you learned how to walk, learned how to talk, learned how to ride a bicycle, learned how to swim -- as you persevered and practiced -- your skills increased. *ESP* is just like any other activity that you have consciously acquired.

However, when beginning these kinds of experiments, do keep some kind of record, either in your head or in your journal/workbook. Establish categories of successes. How the categories are defined is your call. However, the first and last categories covered in this chapter will be common to all -- and they are *nothing* and *definite*. Definitely, something happened and it's 'right on', or nothing happened.

The *definite* can sometimes occur with a click and you recognize it's 'right on' just when it happens or with some other signal of completion. With each person, it may be different. What you should be aware of when you start keeping track is the *definites*. Forget about the *possibles* and most *probables*. Just have them as loose categories to put other stuff in. The category that should be focused on is the 'definite' and what led up to the 'definite'.

Doing some of this telepathy stuff by yourself, without a partner, is somewhat difficult, <u>and</u> it can be done. However using psychic signs just for yourself can be dangerous. Quite often, we are too close to the subject matter, to many attachments. It is hard to look at ourselves objectively. So, it may be easier to learn *ESP* phenomena on, with, or around other people.

To ask questions about other people and on external situations can be better than it is to ask them about yourself. You can be too mentally/emotionally close to the answers. Doing it on yourself, your attachments can get in the way of your successes. This is another reason why a partner comes in handy to do experiments -- someone to play with and validation. A partner <u>can</u> give an objective reference point, providing you two are not fooling each other as well as yourselves. This is also where the *Tarot, I Ching*, Astrology, et al may be useful – an objective reference.

These lab assignments are for you to experiment with, to be aware of the different ways *ESP* emerges within yourself. They are to give you direction. You do not have to be proficient with them. Just be aware that various approaches exist.

One last thing: as you experiment with the psychic on deeper levels, it will become imperative you foster some kind of relationship with or recognition of God, Love, Truth, Creation, Universe, etc. How or whatever way you see the Creator as, is only a limited expression of the actuality. All human perceptions are on a finite temporal level and cannot encompass the Reality of Eternal Infinite God. The relationship or recognition of God's existence is important.

The reason for this spiritual reference is that just as a recognition of physical truths foster survival on a physical level, the recognition of God's Truth fosters survival on a metaphysical level. Let God's Love/Truth be your anchor and refuge. Love's Truth is Eternally constant and cannot be moved or hurt in any way. It is a rock that cannot be swayed by psychic currents.

Exercise and Lab 3: Truth Perception can give you a foundation of truth to help facilitate this.

7.8 – Questions

1. What makes an *ESP* event possible?

2. *ESP* facilitated information can come through what two vectors.

3. What are the three basic forms that *ESP* facilitated information manifests within the individual?

4. What is ignored by the Eternal Mind?

5. All *ESP* phenomena is a form of _____.

6. Explain *déjà vu* or premonitions?

7. *ESP* facilitated information is a side effect of _____.

8. Why is telepathy natural?

9. What has to be set aside to exercise psychic awareness?

10. All exercises must be done with a _____.

11. Telepathy requires what?

12. What are the drawbacks to mental imaging and dialogues?

Chapter 8

Concerning Metaphysical Tools and Music Use

8.1 – The Nature of Tools

 You are not your mortal mind! You are the Beloved of God.[60] Anything you use to grow spiritually is really a tool to help you remember who you really are. We can use many different things as tools. In addition, there are different ways we can use the same tools to aid us metaphysically, mystically, or spiritually. And...once we remember who we are, the tools may no longer be necessary.

Some previous chapters mentioned tools. In this chapter, *I AM A I* will go into tool usage a bit deeper. For physical forms, tools are created to make some jobs easier. We do not absolutely need a lathe to make a table leg. However, it sure is a lot easier and takes less time than doing it with a pocketknife or our teeth.

When we use tools over a period, we tend to forget this. Then, we think we cannot do the job because we do not have the tool. The problem with tools is although they are very useful; we can become dependent on them. We can think, "I can't do _____, because I don't have _____."

This may not always be an accurate thought and can lead to a form of tool dependency -- abuse.

Physical tools work with physical laws/truths: the nature of molecular matrices, thermodynamics, gravity, electro-magnetic, seven basic machines, etc. Most physical tools are in reference to or used to manipulate physical form: saw, fork, car, shoes, etc.

Metaphysical tools work with non-physical laws/truths: mental/emotional ideas, *ESP*, magic, spiritual, etc. A majority of metaphysical tools are used to manipulate non-physical form: memory exercises, grammar, hypnotism, meditation, etc.

In addition, physical and metaphysical tools can be combined to have an effect in either a physical or a non-physical medium or both. Some examples are:

- Math flash cards: using physical cards to program mental operations (non-physical)
- Anagrams like Roy G. Biv – colors of a rainbow -- or **E**very **G**ood **B**oy **D**oes **F**ine – music notes -- are mental constructs (metaphysical) that help us keep physical relationships straight.

---

60 Postulate 6, I am/we are God's Creation.

Just as many physical tools may contain non-physical ideals like algebra or trigonometry. Many non-physical tools may use physical objects such as in ritual or a calculator. Metaphysical tools may have some physical form aspect to it or it may not have any physical form reference. (Confused yet?)

Advanced metaphysical tools are usually in reference to a non-physical effect.[61] Conversely, most physical tools are in reference to a physical effect.

A tool itself is neutral. It is neither good nor bad. The intention of the wielder of the tool and the people around the wielder determine whatever meaning or use the tool has. You can use a hammer to build a house or you can use it to kill ants. The hammer is neutral.

In addition, tool usage dictates there are times when not to use the tool. The hammer must be put down or set aside when it comes time to carrying or cutting a piece of wood.

Many tools are 'double edged', both physically and metaphysically. Meaning, they can also 'cut' you. Recognition of this is helpful if not necessary. It is a mistake to start using a table saw without some respect for what the tool can do. If you do not respect the table saw, people may start calling you 'two-fingers'.

When using whatever tool, be mindful of these things.

1.   Recognize you are the operator of a tool.
2.   Respect what tool you are using, for it may 'cut' both ways.
3.   You are not the tool.
4.   There are times when not to use the tool.

Whatever you give to Love, It will use. This has been touched on in previously. If you use the tool to facilitate the reduction of ~~truth~~ within you with non-attachment to the outcome, Love will work with you. This means Love accepts the medium and acts through it. Because Love can act through the tool, this means tools may serve as the vector for quantum jumps in individual spiritual understandings as well.

Love speaks to you in the medium that you set up. After awhile, these tools may evolve into becoming part of your personal communion mechanism with your Creator.

Spiritual tools can help foster specific choices. These choices can be important. They change your programming. In addition, the influences these choices made expand if they are made in our daily life. (As opposed to, only making these choices when using the tool.)

Said in another way, "Going to church (a tool) doesn't make you a good Christian (a daily effect)".

8.2 A Partial Tool List

*A*s mentioned in the previous section metaphysical tools are primarily designed to produce a non-physical effect. True once the non-physical effect is accomplished, it may reach in to physical form. One example is an engineer who learned math operations – a mental operation -- with flash cards in grade school and how those math operations influences his structures built as an adult.

Anything can serve as a metaphysical tool, or can be applied in that direction. This section contains a partial list of tools that can be used for spiritual or mystical effects. There may or may not be physical elements to them. This list is so broad that there may be whole schools of thought around their usage.

⇒ **Ritual**: As mentioned in a previous chapter, typically ritual is a tool of beginners. Again, math flash cards are an excellent example. Once the mental operations are learned (math) then the ritual may not be necessary. This math ritual becomes a very useful learning tool.

---

61 The exceptions are the more advanced forms of metaphysical applications: *ESP*, thaumaturgical magic, miracles, etc.

Another way ritual becomes a useful metaphysical tool is it provides a framework to 'pump' specific truths into the mind in a prearranged sequence. Examples of this can be found in a Catholic Mass or a Magic ceremony (thaumaturgy).

Remember truth has an effect within your mind (*Exercise and Lab 1*). 'Pumping' truths through the mind will have an effect on your mind – alter consciousness. In magic, this is called weaving thought forms. *I AM A I* will return to this idea later in this chapter and the next chapter.

Religious ritual is an excellent example of compound tool use. A chalice is used in many religious rituals. A chalice is a symbol of a concept or idea; it is a tool to introduce an idea into the mind. A number of other tools like the chalice may be used throughout the ritual: flowers, knife, food, etc. These symbolic tools – ideas or concepts -- are then assembled within the ritual tool, as they are assembled within the mind.

With religious ritual, there can be elements of tools, within tools, within tools... being used.

⇒ **Chanting**: This tool was introduced in Chapter 6. Chanting is a tool that can help facilitate a one-point focus on a mental event for a prescribed time window. It is an excellent introduction to meditation. Depending on the chant and whether it is said aloud or not, there may or may not be any physical references. Saying the rosary uses beads – a physical reference; while, a silent *Om* has no physical reference.

Chanting, as in ritual, can also provide a framework to 'pump' specific truths into the mind in a prearranged sequence. Because of the constant repetition of chanting, the one-point focus of 'pumping' specific truths leaves little to no room for ~~truth~~ re-enforcement within the mind. (Remember: ~~truth~~ must constantly be enforced or re-enforced.)

Using ritual can introduce (or re-introduce) ~~truth~~ within the mind; and with chanting and the restricted number of concepts involved, this possibility can be reduced.

⇒ **Meditation**: Also introduced in Chapter 6. Meditation techniques are mental tools using one-point focus on a specific mental operation (or non-operation) for an allotted time window. Meditation techniques may or may not contain visualization elements with them.

Like chanting, the repetitive mindful preoccupation with a specific mental event can also serve as a tool to reduce ~~truth~~ re-enforcement within the mind. This is of course dependent on what exactly the 'mental operation' consists of. What is the meditation and the operator's intent.

⇒ **Visualization**: This tool introduces a specific sequence of images within the mind and can be another form of meditation. These image sequences may have different effects depending the nature of the visualization, on your intent behind the imaging, and how extensive your perceptions are. (The visualization exercises of *Exercise and Lab 4.1* works on expanding perceptions.)

Visualizations can expand perception and are excellent tools for one-point guidance of the mind into particular directions. Usually, the direction is predetermined before the exercise.

Conscious use of the imagination -- visualization -- involves a one-point focus on the creation of a *subjective* event – a visual construct.

⇒ **Music**: As touched on lightly in previous chapters, and will be covered in depth in this chapter.

⇒ **Nature**: Here is an excellent example of using something physical (outside the operator) to introduce a metaphysical effect (inside the operator). There are numerous ways this idea can be approached.

❑ One can use a physical panorama to foster a mental panorama – perception -- of the whole. Looking at the mountains or the ocean and seeing the planet and all the people on it. Be reminded of the 'wholeness' of where you are. This involves using a whole

panorama to foster an inclusive state of mind…God -- a contemplation of 'the big picture'.
- ❏ Using details to see a reflection of the whole. An example of this is observing a subsystem within a 'whole' (like giving birth or a flower) and seeing a 'whole' – seeing the panorama of life on the planet reflected in a part.
- ❏ A combination of the above.

⇒ **Art:** Creating artwork can be a useful spiritual tool. Again, intention of the operator becomes a primary variable here. Some ways art can be used as a tool is:
- ❏ Art is an excellent example of a one-point focus at a single task for an extended time window – a meditation, which reduces re-enforcement of ~~truth~~. This book has used this.
- ❏ In doing artwork, you may be creating something that 'reflects' your perception of the whole.
- ❏ The artwork may reflect your perception of a poignant aspect of the whole: form, composition, color, or something that strikes a 'chord'.
- ❏ Artwork itself is an act of creation. It is an act of extending an idea or concept from the mind of the artist into physical form and then into the mind of the observer to produce an effect.

⇒ **Athletics:** Athletics can serve as a metaphysical or mystical tool in numerous directions. Some of the ways are given in these examples:
- ❏ Use of physical movement to facilitate a mental state.
  - • One example of this is using a repetitive operation as a one-point focus for a specific window of time. Instead focusing on a repetitive chant the focus here is on a repetitive physical operation, like running.
  - • Tai Chi, on the other hand, is an excellent example of a ritual that has you go through a prescribed sequence of physical events once within a time window. Tai chi can serve as another tool for one-point focus on an event. Moreover, that one-point focus produces internal (metaphysical) effects – consciousness states.
  - • Dance is something that will be covered later in this chapter.
- ❏ Use of an internal state to facilitate physical movement
  - • Most martial arts involve an element of this. In martial arts, there can be a period of internal focus beforehand and during an operation. This internal focus defines the precision of the physical operation -- movement.
  - • In competitive sports there is an element of a one-point focus on an external event; 'keeping the eye on the ball' is an example. As mentioned in previous chapters, for a successful physical operation this focus must be maintained for an x time period – until the event is over.
- ❏ A combination of the above

⇒ **Fellowship:** Fellowship is a tool that is an accumulation of **Individual** realities sharing common perceptions. It creates a **Consensual** reality. How effective these reality accumulations are is dependent on numerous variables.

One major variable is how much Absolute Truth is involved in the common perception. The more Absolute Truth and **Actual** reality truth that is in the agreement, the more likely a **Consensual** reality will survive. Another major variable is; what is the group intent and the individuals', who make up the group, intent.

Some of the ways fellowship can contribute as a tool is:
- ❏ A church uses this tool on a spiritual level with:
  - • Using group devotionals to foster or cultivate individual devotion.
  - • When in a congregation, a church setting can help develop an inclusive mind. One way it can do this may be in recognizing a long tradition of people doing the same thing before you. Another way this may occur is give an individual a 'handle' on the comprehensiveness of Divine Love.

- With in a church setting, truth can be 'pumped' through individual mortal minds while in a group environment – pre-ordained internal sequences are inserted in the mind on a group level.
- ❑ Fellowship can serve as a support system. It can serve as a personal reinforcement of individual purpose and priorities with in a group setting. Team athletics is an excellent example of this as well.
- ❑ A school is an example of a tool that cannot only serve on a spiritual level as above, and it can serve as a secular metaphysical tool. Two examples of this are:
  - Schools provide a forum to expand individual perceptions.
  - Schools provide a self-discipline framework.

⇒ **Television:** Here is an excellent example of how anything can serve as a metaphysical tool. Like many others in this list, this one can go many directions. The metaphysical effects may or may not have spiritual references.

Again, two major variables to tool usage are the intention of the observer and what meaning (perceptions and judgments) is attributed to what is being observed.

Some of the ways *TV* can be used as a tool is:
- ❑ *TV* expands perceptions. It can serve as an individual's 'window to the world'.
- ❑ Can act as a mirror to reflect the observer's mental states. This can appear as watching yourself watch *TV*. This may involve watching your reactions and your perceptions around an event being portrayed on *TV*.
- ❑ The blocks of time created with *TV* programming can be used to time specific mental operations. An example of this is closing the eyes and doing a 'blank mind' exercises during commercials.

⇒ **Work:** The effects of work as a metaphysical tool may be similar to the effects of some of the previously listed tools.
- ❑ Like fellowship and athletics, work can foster a non-exclusive mind. Either by team concepts – working together, a vector to one point focus, or as a group whole working for Mankind.
- ❑ Just like athletics or artwork work to provide a forum to extend mental states, ideas, or concepts into physical form.

⇒ **Drugs:** With this category of tools is one of the many places where this book enters controversial realms. Drugs as any other tool are totally neutral. The intentions and perceptions of the operator determine this tool effectiveness (as with other tools).

Use of drugs is an excellent example of the 'double-edged' nature of some metaphysical tools and it is an excellent example of the danger of tool dependency. The focus of this category concerns will be "a drug connected with metaphysics for thousands of years"[62] – cannabis – and mind altering hallucinogens.
- ❑ Cannabis
  - Both hashish and marijuana turns up the 'volume' – loudness -- of thoughts. This can be very useful for self-knowledge and visualization purposes.
  - Time perception becomes altered, which 'mimics' the Eternal Moment
  - When a mental exercise is learned 'straight', doing the exercise 'stoned' is equivalent to running with weights. (If cannabis is to be used as a metaphysical tool, this procedure of learning a mental exercise 'straight' first is highly recommended.)
- ❑ Hallucinogens (mushrooms, peyote, LSD 25, etc.)
  - Typically, hallucinogens have been a drug of initiation. The 'trip' produces occasional moments of 'stepping out' of one's **Individual** reality

---

62 A definition for hashish from an old dictionary in the author's junior high school library.

- Once a person has stepped out of their individual 'box' – been initiated, these new perceptions can be brought back and incorporated into their **Individual** reality – applied in daily life.

⇒ **Self-induced trance states:** This category includes self-hypnosis, deep relaxation techniques, or sleep-learning or affirmation tapes. This is another broad category for there are many ways to enter trance states. Just as, there are many different kinds of trance states.

⇒ **Mathematical Reasoning**: This is a tool used through out *I AM A I*.

⇒ **Spirit guides and teachers:** The function of a guide or teacher is to help one through a learning phase. Once the core material of that learning phase has been acquired, the guide or teacher is no longer necessary. It is the individual's application afterward that produces effects. Therefore, it can be said that the goal of a successful teacher is to make themselves obsolete to the pupils. A teacher or guide, by definition, is meant to be a temporary learning tool.

This can include spirit guide[63] -- non-corporeal -- as well teachers having a physical form. The physical form type may be actual people or it may be an established rune system like the *Tarot* or the *I Ching*.

⇒ **Books and Other Media:** This book is a tool. Any book or form of media can serve as a spiritual tool. Like spirit guides, most books are temporary tools. They can introduce new concepts to the mind; and once the material has been assimilated and applied, they are not needed. However, they can be useful to hold information somewhere other than in your mind, a form of physical memory.

Books can also be incorporated into part of your personal practice as well. *Lexio Divino* type practices[64] use the material in books to 'pump' specific truths within the mind.

⇒ ***Tarot* and the *I Ching*:** If *ESP* becomes clothed by the mind of reception, the *Tarot* or the *I Ching* gives the mind a prearranged wardrobe. These two ancient systems (*Tarot* or the *I Ching*) use the idea whatever you give to Love/The Universe, it will use and they have two different approaches and come from two different civilizations.

❑ A legend behind the *Tarot* is that it showed up shortly after the library of Alexandria burned down and volumes of information were lost (~300 AD). The 'ancients' of the time took information relevant to the human life and the universe, put it into playing cards, and gave the cards to the people. Hopefully, that way, the information would not be lost again.

❖ The *Tarot* has two parts, the **Major Arcana** of 22 cards and the **Minor Arcana** of 56 cards.
❖ The **Minor Arcana** are depictions of archetypal changes in mundane life involving four areas of human existence – 4 suits.
- Wands…growth and change
- Cups…emotion and love
- Swords…intellect and sorrow
- Pentacles…physical matters or matter
♦ Some card examples are like the ten of pentacles, which represents physical prosperity as opposed to the ten of swords, which is 'bad news'.

---

63 A word about channeling here: if you are going to channel a spirit, why deal with anything short of God? You limit your options otherwise. Why not channel that which is inherent within you already and is any external spirit's Boss/Source?
64 Chapter 6.3

- ◆ Today's playing cards evolved from the *Tarot*'s Minor Arcana. (The page face card was removed.)
  - • Wands – clubs
  - • Cups – hearts
  - • Swords – spades
  - • Pentacles -- diamonds
- ❖ The **Major Arcana** consists of cards that are depictions of major life event archetypes. These cards can be representative of a major mundane life event or a spiritual life event. From the spiritual reference, the pilgrim (The Fool – card *0*) must go through every card **Major Arcana** to reach cosmic consciousness (card *21*)
  - ◆ These archetypes may involve Strength, the Wheel (cycles), radical change (the Tower), etc.
  - ◆ And…be aware that there are connections between the *Tarot's* **Major Arcana** and Cabalistic writings (one of the books of Moses and at the core of Judaic mysticism).

- ❑ The roots of the *I Ching* appear to be older than the *Tarot*. There appears to be a relationship between the *I Ching* (Book of Changes) and the *Tao te Ching* (The Way of Life). Both books involve Heaven – Yang -- and Earth – Yin -- the interaction or the Way of the two, and how this involves all form– the Tao[65].

There are two I Ching lines: Heaven _____ and Earth ___ ___. These two *I Ching* lines are put in arrays of three lines (trigrams) and then two of the resultant eight trigrams are assembled to be one change archetype, an *I Ching* symbol (hexagram).

An example of these lines and how they fit together is:

Line categories

Heaven line (a yang line)	———	earth line (a yin line)	— —

These 2 lines are combined to form 8 trigrams – 8 sets of 3 lines:

resultant trigrams

Heaven	Fire/Sun	The Deep/Water	Earth
———	———	— —	— —
———	— —	———	— —
———	———	— —	— —

Wind/wood	The Marsh/Mist	Mountain	Thunder
———	— —	———	— —
———	———	— —	— —
— —	———	— —	———

The 8 trigrams – 3 line figures -- are paired into 64 hexagrams – 6 line figures -- like:

Heaven Hexagram *1*	——— ——— ——— ——— ——— ———	*Earth* Hexagram *2*	— — — — — — — — — — — —

---

65 This reflects in how a group of six lines (consisting of the two line types) are arrayed.

| Peace or Harmony Hexagram *11* (Heaven below earth) | ⚊ ⚊
⚊ ⚊
⚊ ⚊
⚊⚊⚊
⚊⚊⚊
⚊⚊⚊ | Stagnation Hexagram *12* (Heaven above earth) | ⚊⚊⚊
⚊⚊⚊
⚊⚊⚊
⚊ ⚊
⚊ ⚊
⚊ ⚊ | Before Completion Hexagram *64* (Sun below the Deep) | ⚊⚊⚊
⚊ ⚊
⚊⚊⚊
⚊ ⚊
⚊⚊⚊
⚊ ⚊ |

Moreover, because this is the Book of Changes, these lines can change and are known as moving lines:

Heaven changes to earth line: ———o———	earth changes to Heaven line: ———x———
⚊ ⚊ Becomes ⇓ ⚊ ⚊	⚊⚊⚊ Becomes ⇓ ⚊⚊⚊

With moving lines one hexagram becomes another – a change

| *The Simple* Hexagram *25* | ———o———
———o———
———o———
⚊ ⚊
⚊ ⚊
⚊⚊⚊ | Becomes ⇒ | ⚊ ⚊
⚊ ⚊
⚊ ⚊
⚊ ⚊
⚊ ⚊
⚊⚊⚊ | *Returning* Hexagram *24* |

These line groups are determined by tossing coins or dividing a group of yarrow stalks. The *I Ching* consists of 64 hexagrams with the possibility of 6 moving lines in each hexagram. Therefore, a typical reading may result in one hexagram and that hexagram changes to another hexagram.

The *I Ching* addresses our rational mind and it expresses itself in words and phrases. The *Tarot* deals with imagery. It is as if one addresses one side of the mind while the other addresses the other side of the mind (left and right brain → imagery vs. words).

Both can be abused. In addition, one of the reasons the *I Ching* is somewhat nice is hexagram four. In some translations, it is called foolishness. It tells the operator in so many words, "I have told you over and over, and you haven't listened. I am not going to tell you again."

As has been described here, almost anything can be used as a metaphysical tool. Some people may get this almost spiritual rush when they watch and hearing the Blue Angels at an air-show. While, someone else may get a similar effect from thunder and lightning.

Almost anything can be used. It is the one-point focus, intent, and the 'head space' (perceptions) of the user that determines how the tool works and the direction the tool usage goes. All of the previous tool examples may involve some one-point focus over a period of time.

It has been said in this book repeatedly that what ever you give to God/Love it will use. Any tool you mentally give to Love/Universe to help facilitate the reduction of ~~truth~~ within your mind/matrix (grow); Love will work with you. As mentioned previously, this may also mean when it comes time to make a quantum jump in your growth; God/Love may act through the tool. This tool then can become part of the communion mode between you and your Creator that you have set up.

Tools used for metaphysical purposes are there to help foster an internal choice. What is important are the choices. It is important to apply those choices through your daily life and not when you are only using the tool. That is why many of the tools mentioned above work better if you have learned some mental disciplines before hand (meditation, emptiness, stillness, etc.). This can be done before using the tool, using the tool, or in the choice of not using the tool.

And…like a child learning to walk, eventually the child must learn to let the chair go and walk on his own.

8.2 Resonant Conditions or "I got this vibe!"

*C*hanges of time' references have been touched upon periodically throughout this work. Changes of spatial references were also introduced. What also been touched upon repeatedly is how a matrix relationship can possess intrinsic qualities. The synthesis of these is two the matrix relationship of a *BTR* repeatedly changing the same amount of space, in the same amount of time, and how it can store energy…resonance? Resonance is a way for a system to store energy. Moreover, the energy that is stored can exceed the capabilities of the physical container, a glass shattering with a high note.[66]

The various qualities of this rate of change matrices (vibrations) become another example of the influence of Truth Matrix extending itself in a multitude of temporal forms or even in the same form but in a changing manner. Without the Truth Matrix, there would be nothing.

Resonant conditions are natural. They happen with the smaller *BTR*s (weak and strong nuclear plus electromagnetic) constantly. Many changes of atomic quantum states are changes in resonant conditions. Resonant conditions also can occur on the macro *BTR* level such as pendulum, planet, or galaxy rotation. Resonant conditions allow a *BTR* to have varied qualities different from the same relatively static *BTR*.

Resonant conditions pervade all physical and metaphysical form. The truth ringing of Chapters 1 and 4 are examples of a resonance of being when excited by truth. Since most *BTR*s are really *BTR*s within *BTR*s within *BTR*s, etc., the component *BTR*s can add or change the quality of the larger *BTR* resonance, producing harmonics or adding their own qualities to the larger resonance.

A musical note is a resonant condition at a specific frequency. However, an *A* (*440* cycles/second) from a signal generator sounds different from an *A* from a violin which sounds different from an *A* from a tuba. This is all due to harmonics created by the conditions producing the event – instrument's construction.

Many mystical or metaphysical thought systems state everything is a matter of vibration. This not only applies to physical matter but much of an immediate **Individual** reality reaction to other realities[67] is a question of resonance or dissonance.

"I can resonate with that." Or *"He gives off bad vibes."*

---

66 As touched on briefly in Chapter 1, Nikoli Tesla created a white noise generator and strapped it to the column of a large building's sub-basement in New York City. The result was New York's skyscrapers started resonating like tuning forks. Manhattan, which is on solid rock, started shaking as if in the throes of an earthquake. If he allowed this to continue, the buildings would have eventually destroyed themselves. They would not be able to contain the energy being stored in resonance.

67 With another **Individual** reality, a **Consensual** reality, **Actual** reality, etc.)

This, again, can bring us back to Chapters' 1, 3, and 4 with the truth resonating within your mind/being/matrix. This can occur physically as well. Some resonances will make you uncomfortable (chalk and chalkboard) while others may feel good (Reggae music).

Music is a reoccurring vibration. (As opposed to sound, this is not a reoccurring vibration.) Music is a sequence of resonant vibrations. Music is of the moment. It changes from moment to moment. This makes music one of the most valuable metaphysical or spiritual tools we have. Because music changes from moment to moment (and in the moment), we can use music, through focus, to help us exhibit a property of the Precious Eternal Moment of Creation. On the other hand, stated another way, music can introduce us to an aspect of the Truth Matrix that we may have not been aware of previously.

Co-join this with symbolic truths (verse); we can have a condition where an individual's focus is on the moment while priming – 'pumping' -- the mind/matrix with truth. Thereby, augmenting the effect the music will have.

8.3 – Applications of Previous Chapter Material and Music

*T*he true power of music lies in the mind of the listener or the musician; the ones using the tool. Listening to music involves a number of mental applications introduced earlier in the book. A brief list of these applications is:

1) *Homework & Lab Assignment 4*: Eye Exercise or 'Surfing' the Mechanism...
   a) Listening to music is doing *Exercise and Lab 4* (the eye exercise) with your ears.
   b) There is a constant change in cognition, which resets the mind.
2) **Meditation Exercises in Chapter 6...**
   a) All meditation is a one-point focus on an event. Music is an event. Therefore listening to music can be a meditation.
   b) Augment the listening with emptiness and the waiting exercises.
   c) Repetitive short 'bursts' of focus *vs.* maintaining a continual focus
   d) Introduced in many of Chapter 6's exercises and chants there can be a burst of emptiness conjoined with a waiting with the word/s. In some of the exercises, the individual fills this burst with a specific word or image.
3) **Exercises 1a and 3, the effect truth has within the mind...**
   a) These exercises introduced the effects Truth has when present within the mind.
   b) 'Pumping' specific truths through a mind augmented by the first two conditions can augment or give direction to their resultant mental change of state.
4) **Exercise 3 and Chapter 2, how a logic system can create something 'alien' to that logic system...**
   a) That which is 'alien' to the finite and temporal is automatically infinite and eternal, and *vice versa*.
   b) The mortal mind can be used to step out of mortal mind activity.
5) **Resonance conditions touched on earlier in this chapter.**
6) **What ever you give to Love, Love will use.** (touched on throughout the book)

Here is a repetition of this list covered in detail.

1) ⇒ *Homework & Lab Assignment 4*: Eye Exercise or 'Surfing' the Mechanism

As the eye and the mind coordinate, the information of the event goes through the cognition mechanism and takes a specific moment of time to do so. The mind/matrix is refocusing. Constantly moving the eyes before the cognition mechanism is completed, creates a condition of non-choice and no 'subjective event' in the mind/matrix.[68] The mind/matrix is constantly refocusing before it finishes a cycle. With listening to music, you are doing the eye-exercise with your ears. The mind is constantly refocusing on each note.

---

68 Remember the Cognition path is a high priority survival loop.

The result of doing this for an extended period of time is your mind/matrix starts over after you are done – resets. You are 'seeing' with the ears while resetting the mind. Herein is a major effect of listening to music; it is a release or stepping out of the mental processes.

2) ⇒ Meditation Exercises in Chapter 6

Chapter 6 states that it is hard to keep an empty mind or a blank mind indefinitely. However, it is much easier to do the blankness in short 'bursts'. Rather than to keep an empty mind and do it for 5 or 10 minutes, it is easier to do 'bursts' of blank, blank, empty, empty, empty.

When first emptying the mind, there is a focus on an initial effort to have an empty mind; and then, a focus on maintaining the emptiness. These repetitive 'bursts' can be seen as a repetitive initial effort (as opposed to making the effort to be empty and holding it).

Chapter 6 introduced the idea that with chanting and some meditations, you can use the words as the vehicles for this emptiness or blankness. With instrumental music, you can introduce the emptiness or blankness with each note or sets of notes -- chords.

In the case of music and with a singular instrument, the emptiness can also be initiated between the notes. This can also be done with multiple instruments and following a melody. Your mind introduces 'bursts' of emptiness between the notes of the melody. You can use the notes and words. Listening to music the music serves as a vector to one point focus -- meditation. This has numerous applications.

- ♦ Filling the mind with each note or word
- ♦ Emptying the mind with each note or word
- ♦ Emptying the mind between notes

For the beginner though, it may be easier to learn to do an empty focus with only instrumentals. That way there are no words to distract or to initiate any mentation.

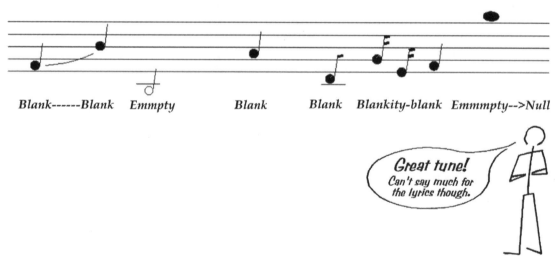

Figure 8-1, Music and Blank Mind

Be advised, that repetitive use of the mind's focus on emptiness is a similar use of the mind as the eye exercise of Chapter 4. It is also similar to the quick repetitive use of a word as was introduced with meditation in Chapter 6. And...a one-point focus of performing this act/event makes this a meditation. All of these are combined in one exercise.

3) ⇒ Exercises 1a and 3, the effect truth has within the mind

Through out *I AM A I* it has been mentioned that truth has an effect on the mind. From *Exercise and Lab 1.1* to 'pumping' truth through the mind or weaving thought forms, Truth can alter consciousness. Taking the two previous examples of how music can alter consciousness through a constant reset and having an empty mind for a window of time (a Δt), 'pumping' truths through that same altered mind will augment the effect of the previous two examples.

This is the power of verse. The one-point focus on the words of the music serve the same purpose as the one-point focus on the words of a chant (Chapter 6). In addition, it introduces to the mind a sequence of concepts that will alter consciousness depending on how much Truth is in these concepts – weaving thought forms.

4) $\Rightarrow$ Exercise 3 and Chapter 2, how a logic system can create something 'alien' to that logic system...

Remember that the concepts of infinite and finite or eternal and temporal are mutually exclusive. Anything created which is alien to a finite temporal mind – mortal mind, must be infinite and eternal related.

5) $\Rightarrow$ Resonance conditions touched on earlier in this chapter.

One can use one-point focus on each note or word, using the vibration like the 'mmmmmmmmm' part of OM. Listening to music, one can ride the vibrations of the music into one's self. Riding the music into your self adds another element to 2a).

Quick and slow tempos – various resonance conditions[69] -- have effects on us. Quick tempos tend to speed the mind up and engage it more while slow tempos tend to do the opposite.

There is a story about Pythagoras that the author recalls somewhere from college research a gazillion years ago. One time, when on the street, he saw a man taking firewood from a cart and stacking it against a house. He watched the man for a while then finally asked him what he was doing. He stated that he was angry. The house was where he lived with his wife and she was inside the house with her lover. He wanted revenge and to teach them a lesson. Down the road, a street musician was playing a martial song (a march).

The story goes that Pythagoras pulled back and watched the man some more. Then he walked over to the street musician, gave him some money, asked the musician to play something like a lullaby, and went back to watching the man.

Shortly, the man's actions slowed and then he stopped. He looked at the firewood; then, looked at the almost empty cart that carried it. He looked at the house and then at the firewood. Eventually, he started to pick up the firewood around the house and replaced it on the cart. This went on for a bit. Then Pythagoras asked him again what he was doing.

He said he realized he was probably better off without her and was at least glad he learned this about her. He also stated that the firewood cost money and he did not want to spend any more money on her. He was going to take the firewood to market and resell it.

Everything vibrates in storing energy be it *Music of the Spheres*[70] and its cosmic resonances with harmonics to white paint. When a frequency that is in harmonic to a resonant system enters that system, it will affect that system. This can occur on a physical level or metaphysical level.

Music can affect us on this level as well. There are so many layers to this one – music -- that covering them all would be prohibitive.

It is important to point this out though. This story is an example of the power of music tempo affects us subconsciously.

6) $\Rightarrow$ What ever you give to Love, Love will use.

There are many ways to build a house. Yet, every house must obey the laws of physics – of matter.

This God's Love arrangement allows us to custom design our own spiritual trip. Religious contemplatives agree; all spiritual journeys work with the same internal mechanics.

---

69 When two frequencies enter a non-linear amplifier (the ear) four frequencies result. The original two frequencies are there as well as the sum of the two frequencies and the difference between two frequencies (400hz and 600hz create 400hz, 600hz, 1000hz, and 200hz). This is one of many ways harmonics are created. (400hz is the first harmonic to 200hz.)

70 The vibrations emitted by celestial bodies like planets, stars, constellations, etc.

The individual changes the constructs and how they are applied -- the forms. The end is the same. Love dictates that we will be aware of our union with God. It is a closed system.[71] It is only a question of time, which does not exist from Love's reference.

There are many other ways to apply the material of the previous chapters to tools on a daily basis, without stopping everything to meditate. One way is to do the exercises while you are waiting for something (like the phone or in an elevator). Any situation that requires you to just sit and wait can be used. As mentioned earlier, the author learned to apply many of these exercises while in the army. There were many times the military had the author waiting.[72]

One application that has been introduced before can be when driving long distances or driving in areas that are familiar. You can be empty and waiting, while guiding the vehicle. Recognizing and applying that there should be no thought is appropriate can help cultivate your intuition…no thought is appropriate!

Sports are another mentioned application and are another way to be empty of mind. Focus must be on a total overall situation -- objective event -- or you 'blow it'. No thought can be entertained – no subjective event.

Using the exercises in this book in other daily applications is going to affect significantly your daily consciousness or individual awareness and growth. One-point focus combined with a single encompassing desire and a perception of a whole system, i.e. golf, archery, surfing, skiing, pool, etc. produces effects.

You, as a metaphysical student or operator, will also find that when you start using these things daily, you may notice that there is a direct relationship between thinking and 'screwing up'. When a person leaves the one-point focus of the *external* event and starts working with their internal event, they tend to blow it. Their focus becomes split between an 'objective event' and a 'subjective event'.

This cannot be stressed enough: Until you take your daily internal disciplines into everyday life -- whatever disciplines you have -- it will not mean a thing. You need to learn to 'take it to the street'.

There can be a form of 'peripheral vision' involved with the one-point focus both mentally and physically. Two examples of this are dancing and driving. Dancing will be touched on later in this chapter. The driving thing relates to what is already in your programming and storage (the 'back of the mind' or the subconscious) and driving works with direct cognition.

With the driving example, there is cognition of what is before you, and at the same time, 'subjective events' (mental/emotional sets) may be allowed through the mental lens array.

Cognition is guiding the driving, while the *Perceptional Lens Array* is working in a peripheral vision mode. This can mean the lens is not focused on anything in particular or it is multiplexing – short time here, short time there, short time here... Both allow an 'objective event' and a 'subjective event' through the lens array. One is switching time blocks of focus while the other is equivalent to looking past someone and not focusing the eyes on anything in the foreground or the background.

With the latter, perception is 'tweaked' open enough to allow focus on the occurrence of both events – a form of peripheral vision. It is kind of having a camera's focus set between two objects of separate distances. Because focus is set on neither object but somewhere in between, both objects are seen and have a blurred appearance or are not seen clearly.

As with the eyes or camera example, if mental focus becomes localized on either the foreground or background ('objective event' or 'subjective event') the other is blurred to us as it passes through the lens array.

Furthermore, as mentioned previously, there are many daily applications where the material of this book can be used. The imagination and motivations of you as the individual are

---

71 Due to God's All Encompassing Love.
72 "Hurry up and wait", is the military credo.

the only limit to the applications. Motivation, your individual intention,[73] will always be a major variable in any successful applications.

If motivations are orientated to the whole -- whatever you choose -- the inclusiveness of God's Love will use whatever you set up. You need to recognize that there are mechanics involved – relationships, connections, and karma. The inclusiveness of God's Love allows you to work out the details of your own personal applications using the specific mechanics and relationships of those applications. Why do this? Why use music to remember God?

Not being with God means pain. Pain involves a perception of other-ness. God is a complete union -- with no other-ness -- and there is no pain/perception. It is One; it is bliss, the Eternal moment of Creation, etc. There is no pain. The only time we have conscious pain is when we are not consciously participating in Creation within us. Pain cannot exist when we are in God.

It is as if the dichotomies set up the angst; in a duality, there is a tension. It is not being with God lies angst, anguish, and pain. Ironically, Absolute Love will not fight you and allows you to choose anguish, if that is what you want to be your primary focus. Love will reflect the mistaken thinking back on the thinker (Karma), but it will not fight your mind directly.

It is only a question of how long you want to be a masochist; how long do you want to be separate and in pain. How long do we want to be spiritual masochists? Whether, it is *1* lifetime or *50,000* lifetimes. From an Eternal reference point, it does not make any difference how long an individual wants to take to do this. The temporal end will be the same.

It can be seen that the affects of listening to music can go in a multitude of directions. Most of these directions involve the music listener as they are applying numerous mental metaphysical operations (whether they know it or not).

All of the above affects become augmented when done on an assembled group level, specifically, with live music. Music can have an effect on an individual level or a group level. The idea of using music to produce group mind focus and emptiness is at the core of all religious use of music, from shamanic use of drums, to musical religious chants (e.g. Gregorian), to church choirs, or to a 'Dead' concert.

Eliminate ~~truth~~ and there is only Truth. If a group of people is doing the same things in their mind (music effects stated previous) and no ~~truth~~ is enforced or re-enforced within that window of time on a group level, Truth is what remains. Because of this, a secular music event can turn spiritual without warning.

"Once and a while you can get shown the light, in the strangest of places if you look at it right."
Scarlet Begonias, Grateful Dead.

The audience affects the musician/music, which affects the audience, which affects the musician…a feedback loop. This can create a group experience.[74]

The effects of a combination of all these applications show up in gospel music. Prayers or heart-songs are bursts of heart or emotional energy united with a perception/idea/concept (as opposed to a burst of an empty mind). With religious music, the prayer is riding the music vector and the empty mind created by listening to the music.

8.4 - Usage: Active and Passive Applications

*A*ctive use of music is the instrumentalist/singer and in some respects the dancer (a dancer uses both active and passive elements of music). For the moment, we will look at the active use of music as being the musicians with one-point focus.

There are numerous approaches to this. One is using or riding the vibration/sound;[75] while the other, is being empty.

---

73 P_S, D_{Tp}, A_S, D_S, etc.
74 "They are not the best at what the do. They are the only ones that do what they do." Bill Graham, the promoter, about the Grateful Dead
75 Like riding the 'mmmmmmmm' part of *OM*

With the latter, the player can use the repetition, as in percussion, to foster reoccurring bursts of emptiness within the player as he or she plays. First, the musician must wait until each note is to occur; then, they can use the repetition and the percussion to do the empty bursts and blanking; to work with it, to ride the notes, etc. It works best with well-known songs (songs they have worked on and practiced so there is an automatic established cognitive link).

The musician's one-point focus is on the music and the song, and in-between when there are no words, there is only an emptiness to be filled by the music... Nothing, no thoughts are in the mind.

As to the words, it may be more effective if the words can slip into some kind of spiritual parallel, to something that is in reference to the whole.

Some musicians may argue that the notes to the music are not as important as the rests -- the quiet places in-between. Which can be referenced directly back to the *Tao Te Ching* again,

> "The use of the clay determines the pot.
> The usefulness of the pot is determined by where the clay is not."

It is the combination of is and is not, that determines all form.[76]

With musical improvisation, in some ways, the player must be like their own instrument. Their instrument is empty and silent until the player plays it. The player must be as empty as their instrument. Whatever is coming out, is coming out. Many musicians have talked about surprising themselves, by letting go and entering this kind of state. It all depends on where their head goes and how they put the notes together.

Each note can almost float into the stillness of the Now, into the stillness of the Eternal Moment of Creation that the note is manifesting. Because that Eternal Moment of Creation is happening all the time, and because music is from moment to moment, it is very useful for entering the Eternal moment. There is only the music.

There are also schools of thought that maintain that the note is always there; it is Eternal, and we tune into it. It has been known as the *Music of the Spheres*, the lost chord, the Word, or the Song of God. It is the music that never stops:

> "They're a band beyond description,
> Like Jehovah's favorite choir.
> People join hand in hand.
> While the music plays the band,
> Lord they're setting us on fire."[77]

Music is <u>perceived</u> as a vibration. It is very similar to any other physical law. Just because the individual does not see the law applying, it does not mean the law is not there. That perception of vibration has the ability to be applied at any moment in time, anywhere. A specific note has a specific frequency (vibration). The Music is <u>perceived</u> as particular frequencies or collections of vibrations.[78] The musician is an instrument reflecting this vibration.

Whatever instrument the player uses, it takes practice to be proficient. Practice with the instrument and with working inside the head. You have to work at it at first, as with everything else.

---

76 Where the *BTR*s are, and where the *BTR*s are not, the space between, or their matrix array.

77 Lyrics by John Barlowe, *The Music Never Stopped*, <u>Blues For Allah</u>, The Grateful Dead, Copyright 1975 by Ice Nine Publishing, Inc.

78 A side note: as one does mental exercises, you will begin to be aware of a ringing in your ears, specifically the left ear. As the consciousness and growth progresses, the ringing changes; it starts to develop into chords.

With the **passive aspect** of listening to music, it is possible to enter deeper consciousness states than the active. This is because you do not have to do any physical activity while listening; therefore, your mental focus is not split. Physical exertion can split your focus. In passive listening, part of the mind is not set aside for things like maintaining physical balance.[79] It is possible for you to let go, and dissolve -- so to speak -- into the music.

When working with the passive aspect of music, you should make yourself comfortable, but not too comfortable of a position. You do not want to go to sleep.

Whatever positions you do chose, it could be quite helpful for you co-join the event with a slow, deep breathing. This will be asked of you when you do a lab exercise. All this information is leading up to an exercise.

With passive use of music, each note is accompanied with focus and blankness -- with a 'burst' of emptiness. You ride the music out. All you are doing, is riding out each note, and existing quietly, waiting and being patient, until the song is done. No thought in the mind is appropriate until the music is done. In this way, the song acts like the kitchen timer in Chapter 6. The music itself becomes your objective time keeping mechanism.

It has been said how you can ride the notes and wait quietly. It also has been mentioned how each note is resounded in the empty mind. In addition, the influence that tempos have on people earlier in the chapter. The next thing to mention is a combination of usage with the drive-plateau concept.

This is a time of intense driving music, with an intense moment of focus followed by a plateau of soft quiet music, a release. The individual sinks into the emptiness of the soft slow notes. With some music or songs, it is possible to do both several times.

The music can leave an intense drive and then enter a plateau, then repeats. Therefore, the individual can go back and forth from this incredible moment of drive, to this stillness, to this drive, to this stillness. The author first learned about this mechanism when using the record album, the Moody Blues' *To Our Children's, Children's, Children*. They did that a lot in the first half of that album.

Jerry[80] used to do that a lot; the 'Dead' were masters of this. It can be almost like an orgasm when that plateau is reached. After an intense guitar riff, the music slows in tempo and very note is hanging in the air (and stillness) and in your mind at the same time.

The musician is an active vessel (like their instrument), while the listener is a passive vessel. Now we are going to cover a combination of both. Dance is an active and a passive form of music use. The mind is completely passive, in the listening mode, being there. As this is occurring, the body is in an active mode, physically expressing the music, through the mind of the dancer. There is an emptiness and music throughout. The mind is passive and open, while the body is expressing what is passing through the mind. The music is going all the way through you, to your tapping toes!

The deeper trance states tend to occur, though, when the individual is physically passive. The dance tends to be deeper the more passive it is, the more the dance is on the inside. Like doing the mantras, the most powerful mantra is the one done in stillness. This way the individual enters deeper consciousness. The same is with dance. The most powerful dance that is done is the 'dance in the stillness'.

There is no physical exertion or focus. A person does not have to do anything. An individual does not have to worry about gravity, laws of motion. You can enter stellar states by mentally 'dancing to the music'. To learn this though, physical dance can be an excellent introduction.

The author's personal preference is live music.[81] The author prefers not to have words or only a few words now and then to introduce ideas or concepts. This tends to be jazz, blues,

---

79 Given, you are standing.
80 Jerry Garcia, lead guitarist of The Grateful Dead

jam, improvisational rock, or spacey stuff with the drums like the 'Dead', when they really got 'out there'. If there are words, the author prefers the lyrics to have some kind of spiritual parallel.

A reminder: Whatever operation you are doing, maintain a disinterested-interest in it and the outcome. Do it with the recognition that the outcome is an unknown. Why boggle your brain with something you do not know? Just work with the mechanics of it now.

Again, for experimentation purposes, low emotional content is preferable. Maintain a balance between the head and the heart. Whatever metaphysical experiments you do, give them the **K.I.S.S.** An empty mind and one-point focus of desire is simple, simple-ness in the mind, and simple-ness in the heart. Music exercises can serve as a jumping board for the heart-song, such as the Psalms. Eventually, the Psalms and all these heart-songs evolve into non-verbal communion. These devotional songs/prayers eventually go beyond words and become non-verbal communion between you and your Creator.

However, one can use secular love songs as if talking to God or God is talking to you. St. John of the Cross talked about that. He would take secular love songs and translate it in his mind to a love song to God. He used them as a very important spiritual vehicle for him.

Therefore, when there are words, the words can be given a spiritual reference by the listener. An individual can take the words and slip them into a spiritual parallel through manipulation of their perceptions. You can use secular love songs and convert them to your heart songs[82] to God.

Exercise and Lab #13: Music and an Empty Mind

Because the book format allows the reader to work on their own, it will be left up to the reader to pick the music they want to work with.

Starting with drums can be helpful. Dance and move to the drums. Then, sit or lie in a relaxed position and, first, do a passive application of focus to music. This should be done for at least fifteen minutes.

Then, take a song -- any song -- that can slip in to a spiritual parallel. No attachment, and do either dance or sit. Do either one; it does not make any difference which; this is only an introduction.

Use the music and one-point focus to enter it. With live versions of some songs (like *Sugar Magnolia -- Sunshine Daydream)*, it is possible to really boogie with the song when musicians are singing. When the song gets into strong instrumental, the boogie can get wilder while the mind can get stiller and stiller. Either way, the individual can enter deeper states.

Because the body can never do what all the notes or sounds are doing, the mind can enter the music as the body starts to get still. The body would never be able to relate to all the notes that it hears. It tends to relate to the gestalt of the music, the feeling.

This assignment is for you to:

➢ *Pick four pieces of music: two instrumentals only and two with vocals. The pieces should be ten to twenty minutes long.*
➢ *Find a place where you will not be disturbed and get in a comfortable (but not too comfortable) position.*
➢ *Do a short period of slow deep breathing, set your intention for this exercise, turn the music on, and enter.*
➢ *Focus on emptiness, or if you use an effort, 'bursts of blankness' of mind with each instrumental note or progression.*
➢ *Do this passive aspect once for each piece of music.*
➢ *Do also an active exercise -- a dance -- for each piece.*

---

81 A feedback loop occurs between the listener and the player. The deeper the listener gets, can affect the players state.
82 Chapter 6.2, *Exercise 8C*, Devotional Chanting

➤ After each exercise, sit and be still for several minutes, and notice any thoughts or sensations and perhaps record them in your notebook or journal.

*******************  *******************

8.5 – Additional Mechanics and Exercises

$\mathbb{R}$emember the Formula of Effectiveness of Chapter 5. The longer you spend focusing over a change of time [$f(\Delta t)$], the more effective you will be in that focus. The effectiveness in this particular reference is a change of consciousness. The longer you focus, the more there is going to be a change inside you.

Also, remember in the formula relationship that as attachment approaches 0 (A_S), effectiveness can approach infinite. As the individual starts working with this idea, and is reducing truth within their mind/matrix, their effectiveness can approach infinite. This concept is the springboard for magic and miracles.

Doing these music exercises, you are opening up your *Perceptional Lens Array* and allowing a free flow from the event (the music) through an empty lens array, going through the cognitive, contacting knowledge. Done in a consistent manner, you can change your programming this way. In addition, the constant exercise of one-point focus will make your focus stronger too, as in lifting weights. Your growth comes in choosing to focus the lens and returning when you drift.

As mentioned previously, one of the nice things about music is that the songs predetermine the length of the exercise. Instead of using a timing device as mentioned in Chapter 6, one can use the length of the song as the timing device. And...as in Chapter 6, having a specific time window for an exercise can help bring your focus back. "I am going to do this exercise until the song (or album) is over." (thereby reducing D_S)

In terms of motivation/intention, remember that all you are doing with these exercises is just 'messing around' with the lens array; playing with it this way and that. You are using the cognitive input of what is happening and avoiding the lower part of your individual matrix. Recognize that there are consistent cause and effect relationships involved. Things will automatically begin to happen if you start to apply these relationships.

That is why this course is laid out like a science program. None of what is being done here is new. It has all been said before, in other ways, by probably thousands and thousands of people. *I AM A I* is just attempting to demystify it.

Metaphysics tends to have cryptic mystical and esoteric presentations. They do not call it the occult for nothing.

As you do these exercises, remember your sense of purpose and the motivational analysis. By remembering your sense of purpose, if you drift, it is easier to come back when you remember: "What am I doing this for? What do I want? For this block of time I am only doing this."

What you do not want can be just as important as what you do want. It is very useful to bring your focus back by realizing, "No, I don't want to do that, I want to do this right now." Do the exercise just to do it. You do not know where it is going.

Many music pieces can help you do this work. Some are geared specifically to help, while other music pieces this was never the intention.

Be advised that there are seven music albums that have mystical references; and, the lyrics consistently keep in this vein. Each of the seven albums has a general theme and is performed by the same group, The Moody Blues.

The albums are:

❖ *Days of Futures Past*, Theme: A day in the life of a spiritual pilgrim.
❖ *To Our Children's Children's Children*, Theme: The internal work and journey.
❖ *In Search of the Lost Chord*, Theme: The quest, cycles, and experimentation.
❖ *A Question of Balance*, Theme: The balance between mind and heart.

❖ *On the Threshold of a Dream*, Theme: The spiritual journey and the promise of 'something else'.
❖ *Every Good Boy Deserves Favor*, Theme: How what you are doing works into Mankind.
❖ *The Seventh Sojourn*, Theme: A completion of the previous material.

8.6 – Questions

1) What are the advantages to using instrumental music only?

2) What are active applications of music, passive, and combinations of the two?

3) Music is the most powerful _____.

4) How does listening to music affect the mind?

5) Tools are _____.

6) Skill dictates knowing when to _____.

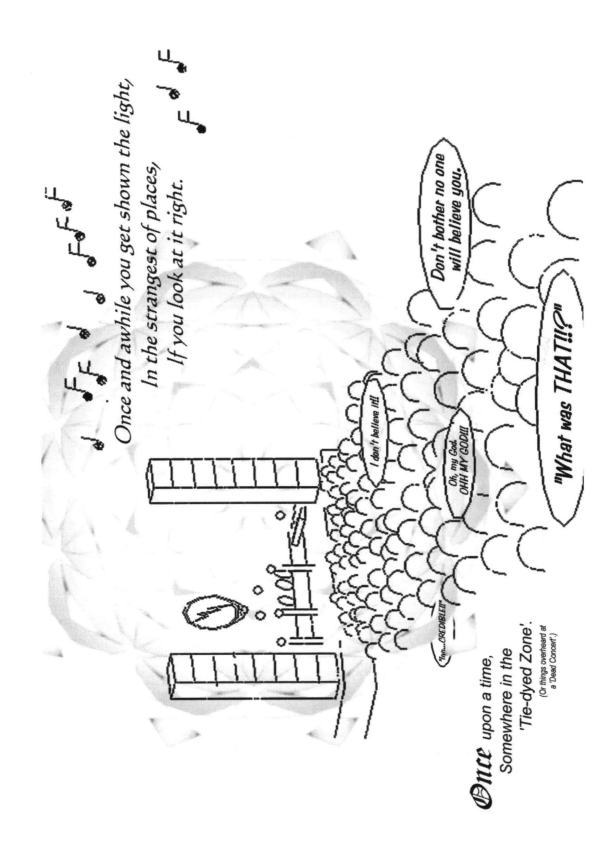

335

Chapter 9

Concerning Magic

9.1 – Review and Introduction

*T*he **first chapter** introduced using math logic mystically as an aide to religious thought. That chapter touches on how this is not a new idea by exposing you to Pythagoras and the roots of western sacred geometry. In addition, Chapter 1 touched on the strengths and weaknesses of the format of the book and previewed the rest of the book.

Exercise and Lab 1A introduces the effect truth has within the mind – 'truth ringing'. While *Exercise and Lab* 1B, exposes you to your mind being this science class's laboratory (along with *1A*). That exercise introduces the idea of the importance of maintaining a pristine 'lab'. *Exercise and Lab 2* introduces one-point focus on an event through artwork and has you make a chanting tool – make your own mandala or yantra.

The **second chapter** introduces the roots of math. This chapter combines that idea of math logic and mysticism into numerous postulates and theorems. Words are given specific definition and then treated like numbers. Within the postulates and theorems presented is an order of manifestation, from God to physical form. These postulates and theorems become the skeleton of the paradigm of this book and serve as an introduction to some universal ancient mystical concepts or axioms.

The **third chapter** takes the second chapter's presented skeleton and fleshes it out with laws of physics as they are viewed today. The chapter incorporates the current science paradigm and shows how it is a special case effect to the model introduced in Chapter 2. This chapter introduces concepts like the Correction, the Mirror, and Bubbles of Temporal/spatial Reference – *BTR*s. The last part of the chapter is an introduction to Eternal/temporal mechanics. How time can be ignored by the Eternal condition – time ignor-ance.

Exercise and Lab 3 -- Truth Perception – introduces thinking in parallels and the availability of truth within your immediate surroundings. This exercise introduces the concept (and advantages) of storing absolute or comprehensive truths in your 'mental attic'.

The **fourth chapter** completes the model of the book and gives temporal/physical form a mortal mind. This chapter conducts the information from previous chapters into the human condition and shows how truth and ~~truth~~ animate our mental form -- mind. Chapter 4 introduces the human mortal mind/matrix, its realities, its perceptional limits, and its basic operations (i.e. the relationships of its perceptual lens, to its *Storage*, to focus).

Exercise and Lab 4 introduces you to your cognitive mechanism, its high priority within your mental operations, and its capability to reset your mind. This exercise uses the temporal limit of the mortal mind to reset the mind.   While *Exercise and Lab 4.1* -- Time/Space Imagination Exercises -- gives you some tools to expand mentally your immediate perceptions.

Chapter 5 took the labels presented in Chapter 4, treated those labels as if they where numbers, and developed a mathematical formula. This formula determines the effectiveness of the interface between a mortal mind/matrix and the realities in which it finds itself immersed. The second part of the chapter exposes you to the front part of your individual perceptual lens – the relationship of your perceptions to your desires.

Exercise and Lab 5 -- How Do I See _____ -- exposes you to the relationship between your perceptions and your desires.

Chapter 6 uses concepts introduced in the previous chapters. This chapter introduced the concepts behind chanting and meditation and presented a multitude of forms meditation can take. The chapter familiarizes you with how you can become familiar with the basics of, or 'play' with, your mind/matrix operation.

Exercise and Labs 6-9 present hands-on exposure to some of these meditation concepts through breathing, chanting, and presents numerous options and variations.

The previous chapters are concerned with elementary operations of the mortal mind. **Chapter 7** introduces some intermediary workings of our mortal mind/matrix. This chapter tied into the last part of Chapter 3 with the time/space ignor-ance capabilities of *ESP*. The chapter introduced the role *ESP* plays in metaphysics and mysticism while giving examples of exercises that can be used to help cultivate that role. It defines all *ESP* as a form of telepathy. In addition, the chapter states telepathy or *ESP* are natural conditions or operations of our minds/matrices.

Exercise and Labs 10-12 present tools to help facilitate *ESP* expansion.

The **eighth chapter** is concerned with additional applications of the mortal mind/matrix mechanism.   The chapter discusses metaphysical and spiritual tools; their advantages and disadvantages; and, how music is one of the most useful of mystical tools available to us. That chapter exposes you to the various levels music affects the mind and being; and, it presents a number of applications.

Exercise and Lab 13 presents various ways you can mentally use the music tool.

This chapter concerns itself with advanced interfacing of the mortal mind/matrix with the Eternal Mind/Matrix.   It presents the necessary elements and their connections for advanced mystical/metaphysical applications. This chapter will consolidate previous chapters' information and return to *I AM A I*'s model overview.

In reference to learning magic, all the exercises and assignments given previously in this book are 'kid's stuff'. The previous material of this book just scratches the surface of the degree of self-discipline that is required for the 'magical art'.

Exercise and Lab 14: Energy Passage through the Body

This exercise is short and sweet. Sit in a comfortable position with your hands resting on your knees. The palm of your right hand should be facing up – "to Heaven", while the palm of your left hand should be facing down – "to earth".

Slowly breathe for a few minutes and relax. As you are doing this, notice how you feel. Notice how the energy in your body, arms, and hands feel. Another option of where to place your awareness might be; notice how the space – a cubic inch space -- just outside of your palms feels. How that space feels.

Relax, breath, and slowly get a feel for this position; and then, quickly reverse your hand positions. Your right hand palm is now down, while the palm of the left hand is facing up. Quickly flip your hands positions and notice the change you feel and what that change is like.

Now…sit with the hands in the opposite position for a while – left hand up and right hand down -- and notice what this feels like or what you feel outside the palms. After a few moments of observing again flip your hands quickly while noticing the changes.

> ➢ *Assignment: do this twice (four flips) at least three different times and allow at least 1 minute of time between flips to accumulate observations.*
> ➢ *Record any noticed changes in how you feel in your journal.*

If this exercise does what it is intended, you may understand why the *Mage* (Major Arcana *Tarot* card *1*) has his right hand to Heaven while his left is to earth.

9.3 -- Concerning the Love of God

A ll power comes from God. Bottom line: if an individual wishes to do **thaumaturgical**[1] magic, they must go to God/The Source/Whatever. In order to create, the magical operator must create like God (*Theorem 11B*). Therefore, the operator has to bring the Eternal Creative Moment into physical form the way God creates into form.

This may mean working or developing a thought matrix (a philosophy or construct relationship like Figures 9-1, 9-2, or 9-3). The first thing the magical operator has to do is establish a personal connection with the Eternal Creative Moment -- go to God -- within their self. God's Truth is the mage's power, anchor, and protection.

Then, magic can occur either actively or passively.

♦ Passively: This makes sense in so many ways. Physical form is an effect of the Mirror. The Mirror is there to reflect what is in our mind. The reflection of the Mirror – physical form – can be affected by changing what is in the mind, thereby the reflection – temporal/spatial form. Change what is in your mind and the 'reflection' changes.

♦ Actively: Connecting to the Mirror's Source – God – and thereby directly manipulating the Mirror's image or temporal/spatial form through a metaphysical framework – thought matrix.

Again; bottom line is if an individual wishes to do **thaumaturgical** magic or take it up as the religion it is, they must go to God/The Source/Whatever. All power comes from God. And…there is only One Source.

9.2 -- What is Magic and Its Paradoxes

T o begin with, the word *magic* has to be redefined. The original meaning of the word was "works of the magi". A magus was a priest of Zoroastrianism.[2] Since there are few true Zoroastrians[3] left, this word has to be redefined. What does this word *magic* mean?

The definition of magic in this book is "Manifesting a desire through the use of the will." If you think about this definition, this includes everything we do. Everything we do or manifest is through magic.

Because this definition includes everything we do, a magical operator's metaphysical/mystical/magical act will be paralleled to an architect's physical construction of a house in this chapter.

---

1 Thaumaturgy: "to work wonders"

2 It is interesting to note that the only other group of people (other than Jesus) that are represented in *the* traditional Christian nativity scene who knew something was 'going down', and were not given the knowledge of the event by an angel, were the Magi and their entourage. Angels informed Mary, Joseph, and the shepherds. The Magi were not informed this way. They knew 'something was going down' and wanted to be there for it.

3 There is a sect called Parsi that is a remnant of this religion.

Since the postulates and theorems state that there is only one Will and that is God's, all magic is through the Will of God. A Will shared with you. <u>All power comes from God</u>. A person endeavoring to be a mage must go to God to get the power.

All magic can be considered an act of creation,[4] an act of extending an idea from the operator's mind into physical form. There are essentially two basic levels of operation in which we 'manifest' through magic.

❑ One level -- the **mundane** -- most people are very familiar with, and do not even look at it as being magic. Picking up a pencil is a form of magic. It is manifesting a desire, to pick up a pencil. This is done through one *BTR,* directly affecting another *BTR,* usually through another *BTR.*

Watering the lawn, skipping rope, taking an aspirin, etc. are all acts of **mundane** magic. **Mundane** magic involves a low-level participation in the Eternal Act of Creation

The **mundane** form of magic also includes prestidigitation magic, the magic of illusion. Prestidigitationists are using physics and physical form matrices to create an illusion of non-physics. They use the laws of physical form to produce an effect that appears to defy the recognized truths we think know of physical form. This chapter is not concerned with this form of magic or illusion.

❑ The other level -- **thaumaturgical** -- is when higher vectors of delivery or operation are used to manifest form. The 'spell' or magical operation is also the use of the will to manifest a desire. This is done, however, without any <u>apparent</u> physical correlation being present. The *BTRs* involved have no *BTR* in common or *BTRs* acting as an intermediary. Thaumaturgy is what we usually think of as magic.

Thaumaturgical magic (using spells, *whammies*[5], the will, higher mental constructs of forms, matrices etc.) may involve tools, invocations, and rituals; or they may not. As with the postulates and theorems, **thaumaturgical** magic is essentially manifesting an idea/desire to physical form. Just as God goes from the Will, subtle and sublime, down to Creation – an extension of Self, the magical operation extends an idea from the self.

Thaumaturgical magic involves a higher level of active participation in the Eternal Act of Creation than **mundane**. The mechanics and matrices involved are on a metaphysical or mystical level.

Remember the Mirror introduced in Chapters 2 and 3. The function of the Mirror is to reflect ~~truth~~ back on the mind of Creation (in order for Creation to change its thinking). Those chapters state all physical form is an effect of and is related to the Mirror.

It naturally follows then that changing something in the mind will have an affect on physical form through the Mirror. All magic and most miracles work off this. (Just as changing an item on a blueprint before the house is built, automatically changes the actual house.)

<u>All power comes from God.</u> This applies to the **mundane** as well as thaumaturgy. Everything we do is through or by God's Will. Magic and miracle operators can be seen sometimes as using a form of telepathy. A communion or a communication with their temporal mind/matrix and God's Mind/Matrix (and its Eternal Moment of Creation) is involved.

Or...look at it another way: the lesser mortal matrix is sharing an idea with the greater Eternal Truth Matrix. Mystical Christianity and other contemplative disciplines refer to this form of telepathy (between Creator and Created) Communion with God. Once the idea is in the infinite mind – **Absolute** reality, it automatically becomes an **Actual** reality.

Thaumaturgical magic and miracles are a result of the operator's mortal mind/matrix being connected or in tangent some way with the Eternal Truth Mind/Matrix -- God. From

---

4 Made possible by the Eternal Moment of Creation; because we are participating in It.

5 Whammy is a grass roots expression for a spell casted by someone who may not have even studied magic. However, that person may be able to do one-point power focus. The individual is able to align <u>momentarily</u> their matrix to the Matrix to create an effect in physical form. "Whammied them." Many times this tends to occur with a strong focus and relatively strong single point emotional content. Somebody is upset and they mentally lash out.

there, through the Eternal Moment of Creation, the operator has access to the creation of everything. Magic and miracles are using the Creation Matrix to do the work (create).

Again, since all power comes from God, then the 'mage to be' must go to God to get the "power". That may include learning numerous schools of thought on how to 'go to God', raja yoga, devotional rites, other mental exercises, etc.

With magical and miracle operations, there are numerous paradoxes, ironies, or *Catch 22*'s. More so with magic than there are with miracles. These paradoxes are examples of how God's Loving Logic can fold things up to encompass everything. Contradictions appear; the end apparently negates the beginning, or questions the original premise.

This first paradox to magic is:

♦ Since all power comes from God.
♦ And, the operator must go to God to get the power.
♦ And, God is everything.

❖ **Paradox 1:** *Once you are in union with God, why bother with magic?*

These magical ironies and paradoxes will be touched on throughout this chapter.

Magic is a difficult subject to talk about. It is a very misunderstood religion. There is more myth about it than fact. What fact there is; usually, is not passed on. A quotation from the *Tao te Ching* expresses it very well.

*"Those who know do not talk,
And those who talk do not know".*

Why? This saying can be related to the last rule of the four rules governing the learning and the use of magic. They will be introduced briefly here.

1. *To Know*
2. *To Dare*
3. *To Will*
4. *To Keep Silent.*

Because of rule *4*, in order to grow in magic, one does not talk about what one has done. This, in itself, is a big obstacle for people who want to learn magic. Whenever we do something, our first inclination is to talk about it because it feels good to us.

Rule *4* is another example of the degree of self-discipline that is needed for the 'magical art'. Chapter 9.7 will go over these rules in depth.

Another reason magic and miracles are difficult to talk about is due to the limits of symbolic communications. In earlier chapters, it was touched how limited words are in discussing the metaphysical and spiritual subject matter. Not only is the word not the actuality, but for a communication to be complete, the listener must hold the same meanings to the symbols being used as the speaker (share a **Consensual** reality). Without this shared reality, there is no communication of ideas.

Due to the above reasons, what accurate information on magic that is available may be fractured or even appear to be misleading. The paradoxes in magic do not help.

Here is another magic paradox and it goes something like this:

♦ Because the sense of separation in our minds is a delusion,[6]

---

6 *Theorem 26A* and *32*

♦ Moreover, God's Correction through physical form is reflecting this delusional state back on us – the Mirror.

♦ In addition, the whole purpose of this is for us to correct this delusional state.

♦ And, the delusion correction entails choosing God and Truth instead of ~~truth~~. The basic premise of the 'Gita'

♦ Then, in the choosing the magic discipline to unite with God and whole without attachment to the result, the operator will have clear sailing. Every operation done is Karma-less and the Universe will fold time/space and start helping the operator.[7]

♦ In other words, only doing magic selflessly for the 'whole' is truly safe.

❖ **Paradox 2:** *The only safe magic you can do is that which fosters your (and everybody's) union with God's Love. You must do magic selflessly to preserve yourself.*

The magical operator becomes a subject of the Mirror and Karma if he or she chooses the magic discipline for anything other than God (i.e. self, division, or destruction). Karma becomes accelerated (because the operator has divisive perceptions, and because the operator is working on 'higher levels').[8]

If the operator is not careful, what that the operator is trying to achieve may end up as a dead-end or has twists to it that were not wanted. Although the operator has good intentions, one selfish motivation or ~~true~~ perception can give the **thaumaturgical** magic operation a right-angle twist. This is because the Universe and the magical operator (in some way) are working at cross-purposes. The operator is not working with all the laws of the way things are set up. The operator is trying to work against the existing system (not working with the truths), and so the system reflects this back on them.

In magic, this is referred to as the law of three. If destructive energies are used and the operator's intention is to the self, the 'payback' can be three times harder on the operator than the action is on the object of the spell.

The time folding aspect of this 'reflection' may not be immediately present. The effect can also occur over a time period. The selfish operator can create their own dead-ends. The operator's world can become narrower and narrower instead of expanding their spiritual horizons.

9.4 -- Concerning Magic Mechanics; Patterns and Parallels

$\mathcal{M}$any religious and mystical thought systems contain a duality of some sort and some combination involving them.[9] This dualism and their combination are reoccurring metaphysical themes. It has been expressed in many different ways:

♦ Heaven, Earth, and the Way of the *I Ching* and *Tao te Ching*.

♦ In the Zoroastrian construct or philosophy, all things were resolved into a conflict between two things: the creative fire (Ahura Mazda) and the darkness (Ahriman). It is believed that Zoroastrianism generated the concept of good and evil.

♦ Heaven, Hell, and earth in the Covenant religions.

♦ Brahma (the Creator), Shiva (the Destroyer), Vishnu (the Preserver) if the Hindu religions.

♦ Desire, desireless-ness, and Nirvana of Buddhism.

♦ Father, Son, and Holy Spirit

♦ Light, Dark, and Shadow

♦ Father Spirit, Mother Earth, and the Child – Mankind.

---

7 As Krishna told Arjuna in the *Bhagavad Gita* and Chapter 3: The Correction, The Mirror, and Instant Karma, Figure 3-7

8 This makes sense on the level that the operator is folding time/space to produce an effect. Therefore, the reflection of the operation will fold time/space, more than it normally does, to correct.

9 A *3-in-1, 1-in-3* concept.

- ◆ *I AM A I* uses Truth, ~~truth~~, and the Mirror. In addition it uses →
  - Creative Force, Destructive Force, and Form (or Intention)
  - God, Love, Logic
  - Mind, Heart, and Being

The unreal duality[10] within the mind of Man (and projected into the world) has been perceived in a multitude of ways. A harmonious, almost sexual, balance as in the *I Ching* and *Tao te Ching*, or a war between good and evil as in Zoroastrianism or Christianity. There are deities in some religions where it is their function to enact the duality -- one creates and one destroys, as in the Hindu tradition with Brahma and Shiva.

Between these various thought system, roles and relationships vary to such an extent that these relationships may not be entirely clear. This duality ambiguity and the mechanics between the two may be simplified if they are looked on as creative and destructive forces.

It may help if you remember that Truth and its Matrix spring from God's Love, which is not exclusive. From the Truth Matrix comes Creation.[11] Therefore, Truth is representative of the infinite Eternal Creative force -- creative. ~~Truth~~ is exclusive, not of God.[12] ~~Truth~~ can be considered divisive, finite, and temporal -- destructive.

The relationship between these two is very simple.

❑ **Creative forces**, because they can create, are independent forces -- they can stand-alone. This places them in column *2* of Figure 9-1 -- independent. They unite and encompass – God's Love.

❑ **Destructive forces** are dependent forces and cannot stand-alone; they need something to destroy. In fact, if totally isolated, left to themselves, and are not fed -- from outside of themselves, destructive forces will consume themselves. This places destructive forces in column *3* of Figure 9-1 -- dependent.

Theorem 24 states there is an element of Truth within the ~~truth~~. In fact, without that element of Truth there would be no ~~truth~~. Just as without the *real number* system, there can be no *imaginary number* system. Destructive forces can be seen as a 'special case' of creative forces. Instead of extending – creating, destructive forces are dis-extending.

The creative force springing from God's Love <u>does not exclude</u> the destructive -- Love creates even more from the destruction.

This can be seen in many different 'living' physical forms. What is all this leading to?

In the magic paradigm presented by *I AM A I*, there is no 'war' between the constructive (good?) and destructive (evil?). Without one, the other cannot stand. The dark cannot touch the light. One match will dispel the darkness, and the darkness has no power over it. In fact, it is the combination of light and dark -- the lighting of the match -- which allows perception to be possible. The shadows add a depth to the perception of forms.

In terms of magic, this means in a war between White magic and Black magic,[13] there is no contest. Such a concept arises only in stories and movies.

Typically, the idea of this type of conflict is thought to occur between a white magical operator and a black magical operator. The white magical operator's perception is relatively inclusive; it will not be the initiator of such a conflict. If such a conflict is to ensue, the operator of the destructive force, the black mage, usually initiates it.

<u>All power comes from God.</u> Since all power comes from God's Will and each one of us has God within us, a war between two magi is trying to pit God's Will against God's Will, trying to split God. God is a fundamental unity.[14] This act is not possible. God and Creation's Truth

---

10 *Theorems 26* and *26A*
11 *Postulate 5*
12 *Theorems 21* through *23*
13 Chapter 9.5, Concerning Magic Categories
14 *Postulates 1* through *5* and their theorems

along with the Mirror makes the two magical operators fighting idea non-sequitar. The *operations* will not completely work for either of them or 'blow-up in both their faces'.

If such a case arises, all a white magical operator has to do in such a situation is to forgive. Moreover, put no value or attachment to what the black magical operator is doing (or ignore them); while, being mindful of the Divine. With the white magical operator being non-exclusive and the black magical operator being exclusive, that leaves only one mage trying to split God.

If the white magical operator does not mentally/emotionally participate in this process/battle (is absolutely harmless in thought), the Correction -- the Mirror with the power of the Eternal Moment of Creation behind it -- will move against the black magical operator. The mirror will reflect the mistake to show that person the error of his/her ways.

In such a case, the worst thing a white magical operator can do to a black magical operator (one who is attacking him) is to forgive and ignore the black operator. This isolates the destructive force. The Mirror/Correction will reflect the forces that the black mage is using back on them.

Destructive forces are dependent; they must have something to consume. When the dark forces have nothing to consume – are isolated, they will consume themselves -- the black operator.

This idea is roughly equivalent to you declaring war, and only one side showing up (you) and all your weapons turning on you.

There is a side effect to this creative/destructive concept. Manipulation of creative energies does attract destructive energies. The reasoning for this is very simple: destructive energies are dependent and need something to destroy other than themselves in order to exist.

Within many philosophies, there are dark creatures (like demons), creatures of destruction. What are these destructive forces or, "What is a demon, Mama?"

Our bodies are gestalt entities; they are something more than the some total of the parts. In many schools of **thaumaturgical** magic, a demon is a gestalt being.

Chapter 4 mentions how we have developed thought/emotion sets within us. That chapter describes how we program our own emotions with our own relevant thoughts. These thought/emotion sets can be altruistic in nature (non-exclusive perceptions), self-centered (exclusive perceptions), or any combination.

Later, Chapter 7 describes how every thought we think is transmitted or extended. The volume (strength) of the transmission is proportional to the emotions and desires of the thinker.

Although there are many people in the world with different cultures and languages, many of our thought/emotion sets are very similar. You have a pride. I have pride. He/she/it has pride. In traditional **thaumaturgical** magic, our prideful mental/emotional set is equivalent to a one-cell animal.

Our physical bodies are composed of one-cell animals that become a gestalt -- something more than the one-cell animals. Accordingly, each cell of pride of every person on this planet (and the Universe) comprises a gestalt. This body of pride personified is Lucifer. The same is true of all the other self-centered/exclusive mental/emotional sets that we have: greed, anger, lust, envy, sloth, etc. They too, are cells that comprise other demons.[15]

Interactions with demons usually result in pride or fear within you. This is similar to most interactions with the *Ouija* board.

All demons are sustained by exclusive mental/emotional sets and are destructive or divisive in nature. How much truth inherent with those mental/emotional sets determines how much life/power the demon has.

---

15 A demon's biblical response to Jesus' inquiry as to the demon's identity, "I am legion." This is also one of the responses you get from the Ouija board when you ask it "Who are you?"

Here is another paradox around Black magic specifically:

❖ **Paradox 3:** *Before the black operator can have control over the 'demons' outside of self, he/she must control the 'demons' inside of self. Before one can gratify the baser self, one has to conquer the baser self.*

If the black magical operator does not do this, the demons within him/her will be their downfall. There was one black mage, who was infamous and wrote several books, by the name of Aleister Crowley. It was reported that, in order to conquer his pride, there was a time when he would slash his arm with a razor every time he said the word 'I'.

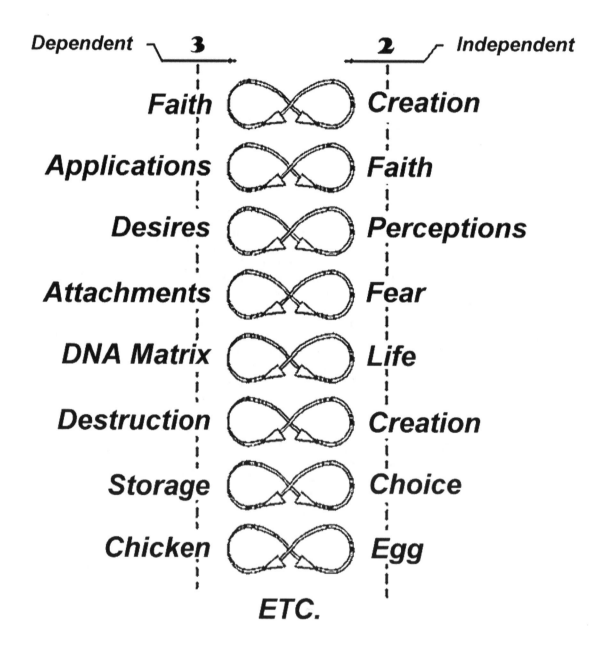

Figure 9-1, Three in One, One in Three Parallels

This is going off the 'deep end' a bit.

This concept of a demon being a gestalt being returns to another reason the magical operator does not talk about the operations. Whatever desire motivates talking, if self-centered, is part of a 'demon' in some schools of thought. If you are motivated by pride to talk, then you are listening to Lucifer within the presented paradigm. Most sane individuals would avoid such a relationship. Whatever this gestalt being comes across, it will try to destroy.

The fiction book *The Screwtape Letters* written by C. S. Lewis,[16] is a hilarious and very insightful book. The book is composed of letters from a greater demon to a lesser demon on how to tempt humans.

One of the recurring themes in the book is the true powerlessness of the demon. In that book, all the demon can do is distract the human so a person's mind is not on God – their Source. Distract the human with a thought of physical pleasure, fear, pride, or something of that nature. You putting your mind in the light dispel their darkness.

Since you are God's Creation, the demon cannot really hurt you[17] without your permission.[18] A demon can only distract you. It attempts to divert the attention of your mind from God.

At the same time, *The Screwtape Letters* is humorous and a relatively accurate in terms of its description of human foibles and weaknesses.

The interplay between the two forces (Creative and Destructive) is a complex dance. One form of the balance of the dance is that creating one thing can mean the destruction of another (as in the appearance of a new species in nature). Conversely, a new creation can spring from destruction (as in a mushroom rising from rotting forest loam and its break down of organic material to become nutrients for other organisms around it).

With the dance of creative and destructive forces, we have another counterpart of the 'three-in-one, one-in-three concept'.[19] Figure 9-1 shows a number of parallels to this idea. The figure illustrates numerous moebius' strips and the two columns of Figure 2-1; column 2 is independent while column 3 is dependent. Figure 9-1 illustrates how this concept extends into many different aspects of life, physical and metaphysical.

Magic's physical mechanics has more varied expressions – multitude of physical forms -- than the metaphysical mechanics – that is behind physical form.

Physical Mechanics

Physical form is totally neutral. A table is neutral. A chair is neutral. A cup is neutral. Whatever meaning these items have, is we give it. This is mentioned in *A Course in Miracles* and perceptual psychology. Physical form is the meeting ground where ~~truth~~ and Truth -- temporal/eternal -- exist together. Physical form is an arena where Truth reflects ~~true~~ thinking back on its source, back on Creation.

It is only in physical form that the concept of God can be called into question.

In Chapter 3, it was stated that the smallest bubbles of temporal/spatial reference that make up physical form are those that make up a nuclear particle – weak nuclear. The bubble of temporal reference of an atom is made up of these bubbles of temporal/spatial reference of its constituent particles, and so on. Up to molecules and to bubbles of temporal/spatial reference that are galaxies and nebulas, which are spatially measured in light years and are composed of the smaller *BTR*s. All of the above can be considered 'special applications' of weak nuclear *BTR*s arrays.

Of course, this is an over simplification. The number that makes up the variety of factors that determine matter, let alone the number of *BTR*s involved, would boggle our little

---

16 The Screwtape Letters, copyright 1959 by C. S. Lewis…

17 It can not 'hurt' who you really are in actuality.

18 Kind of like Dracula could not enter a house with out being invited in first.

19 Chapter 2.4, *Postulate 3* and Theorems

brain. What we perceive as matter or physical form is actually systems within systems within systems, matrices within matrices within matrices, *BTRs* within *BTRs*, etc.

A simple pebble is a system that is *pebble*. Within a *pebble,* there is a crystalline structure matrix that is determined by the constituent molecules (and its atomic matrices) and the pattern of forces (matrix of matrices interactions) between these molecules – electromagnetic interactions. This creates the *pebble's* particular material configuration and qualities. Within that matrix are more electromagnetic and the nuclear interactions matrices that determine the pebble's individual constituent elements (atoms). In addition, within each element, there is the electromagnetic matrix of charged particles that determines the qualities of the element in that energy state (solid, liquid, gas, or plasma) and so on.

Each matrix has forms of resonance (a stable form of change with reoccurring patterns). Each resonance involves an interaction of dualities within the matrix and stores energy. Just as, a single musical note or tone is a reoccurring change of state -- from two states -- within a system.[20]

Physical form is like a song within a song within a song, etc. Form can be seen as resonances within resonances, constantly changing, producing many different forms of harmonics. Starting from Truth/~~truth~~ through the Correction, down to the individual interactions of charged particles, the energy that initiates all resonance eventually can be traced to the Precious Eternal Moment of Creation.

Life can manipulate these bubbles of temporal/spatial reference resonances (because it originates and works from the Eternal Moment of Creation). It can change the song. We see this every day in nature. What we cannot see is how these systems are sustained on a very basic Eternal level.

The Eternal Moment of Creation orchestrates the song. It calls the song into being and can collapse temporal/spatial references, which changes the *BTR* relationships. The time-folding aspect of the Eternal Creative moment can edit the temporal song before the song is sung in any moment of time. It is a closed system in Love.

Because of this, and because it is at the source of these physical interactions it makes things like magic and miracles possible. This time ignor-ance idea is at the core of the apparent mystery of magic and miracles to a mortal mind.

One of the many physical confusions around life is life's many apparent forms, as opposed to it being intrinsically one thing. (There is only one Life, and that is God. It extends into and shares it with Creation.)

Physical life also involves, uses, and maintains systems within systems, etc. Each life system appears to be a gestalt of that system. Therefore, life has a digital or quantum appearance within a system. Either it is in the system or it is not. When life leaves the system, the system starts to break down into constituent systems – sub-lives/sub-matrices.

As in electromagnetic interactions, the photons that make visual perception possible have a specific quantum of energy. With a life system, there is a quantum of life within that system. As with quantum mechanics, the smallest quantum of life within physical form is in a DNA molecule.

Here is an irony with life and physical form. Life is the very source of physical form, yet it does not manifest until there are very subtle variations of conditions within the physical form matrices.[21]

Another paradox of life is that it is the very source of physical form and yet it seems to be the most fragile thing of physical form. Remove the 'life' conditions, and it is gone. It is there, and then it is not. It is there one moment, and then it is gone. Although the same form is there, the life that animated the form is gone.

Life is the subtlest and the strongest of all interactions; and, it is the 'force' at the core of all physical form. This idea gives the expression, "May the Force be with you" -- a real meaning.

---

20 The two states are the compression and rarefaction of air (of medium). The system: the transmission speed of a change of state through the air (or medium).
21 Figure 3-3, Life Manifesting into Physical Form, *A*

The amount of life in the bubble of temporal/spatial reference of a human can affect the amount of life within a bubble of temporal reference of a particle. This is why the results of some atomic particle experiments are different when a life focus -- a human -- is concentrated on or trying to define an aspect of an event. As mentioned in Chapter 3, until physics, physicists, or scientists recognize life as a viable interaction, they may have a hard time getting a universal field theory together.

The physical mechanics of magic involve the five basic interactions that make up the weave of physical form -- Chapter 3. However, Life is the 'woof' of these five basic weaves. It governs all the laws. It is at the beginning and end. Life is a physical form representative of the act of Eternal Creation – constantly extending itself.

All this only covers the **Actual** reality condition. As Chapter 4 states, there are other realities within physical form also. We -- as beings -- each have our **Individual** reality as well as we participate in a **Consensual** reality. In addition, since we are in physical form, there is some involvement of **Imaginary** reality somewhere. The interaction – matrix – developed by these realities' matrices and their constituent *BTR*s are what define our environmental forms, our bodies, our minds, and their interfacing.

With **Actual** reality matrices, because all the complex physical *BTR*s are *BTR*s in *BTR*s in *BTR*s…to that form, that means everything is eventually comprised of weak nuclear *BTR*s – a handful of quarks -- and their arrays -- matrices, any change on the weak nuclear *BTR* array level will reflect in the complex form. A change in the 'higher' automatically changes the 'lower'. Under this scenario, a chunk of steel can become a piece of wood, water, chicken feathers…by changing quark arrays.

The complexity of *BTR* changes occurring on this level is way beyond what our limited mortal mind can grasp. To an Eternal Mind that deals with infinities, within infinities, within infinities…with an Absolute Eternal Love/Mind/Matrix behind it; this is elementary. It is on this level that the Eternal Moment of Creation sustains physical/temporal form.

Metaphysical Mechanics

There are many philosophies – manifestation constructs – illustrating the process of from God into physical form. These philosophies assemble the Eternal Truth so the mortal mind can understand them. A mage works from some kind of truth philosophy – manifestation construct. This construct usually reflects how the truth is assembled within the mage's mind as well as representative of physical creation.

It is the Truth within these philosophies that are important, more so than the philosophies them selves. Why? Because, Truth is in its own construction – Matrix. Personal philosophies can change, when more Truth is learned; whereas, the Truth itself does not change.

Many metaphysical constructs have similar ideas and concepts (truths). One similarity that many of the philosophies tend to have is to show manifestation in parallel levels, kind of like an onion. The onion analogy is used repeatedly in metaphysics and spiritual thought.

Normally, the core of the onion determines the outside. Figure 9-2 illustrates an onion construct that shows manifestation from God to physical form with the outside being God (which does not exclude anything– a closed system), while the inside is a special temporal/spatial case. In Figure 9-2's construct, the higher determines the lower.

Figure 9-2 (similar to Figures 3-3, 4-3, and 4-8) only helps to give <u>an</u> idea of the arrangement. Please notice in Figure 9-2, the God, Love, Logic/Truth, and Creation circles all have one point in common -- a single point of tangency. Whereas the Causal (or Choice), Mental, Emotional, Etheric, and Physical circles, are presented with no single point in common. The rationale behind presenting Figures 9-2 and 9-3 is to illustrate to you some of the common philosophies and the relationships and/or connections between specific ideas within many mental constructs.

Figure 9-2 is only a <u>model</u> illustrating a flow from God to physical form. It is only meant to illustrate a point. In many ways, the labels of this construct are similar to the theosophists' construct.[22] There are other constructs -- philosophies. The Kabbalah[23] has several geometric constructs of the layers or levels from spiritual into form. Figure 9-3 inserts the constructs of this book into this Kabbalistic geometric construct.[24]

Figure 9-3 shows two ways the concepts of this book or some of the book's labels can be paralleled into that construct.[25] The left picture is reference to the human matrix[26] and the right pertains to physical form.[27] The Tree of Life figure illustrates an example of a fractured

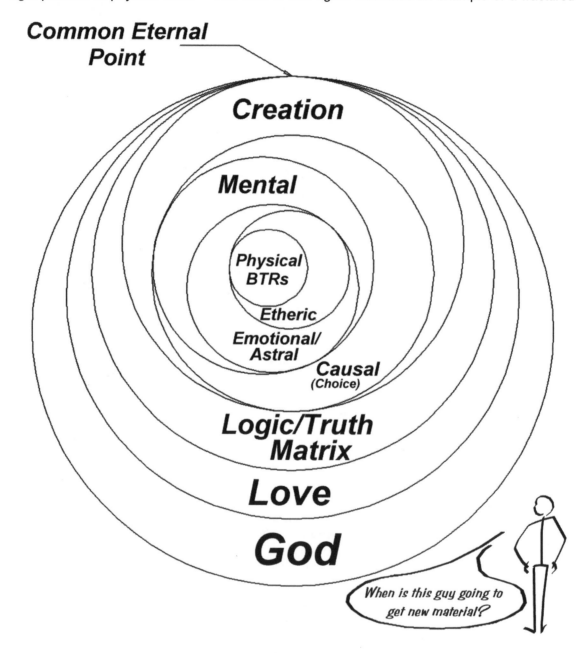

Figure 9-2, Manifestation Onion

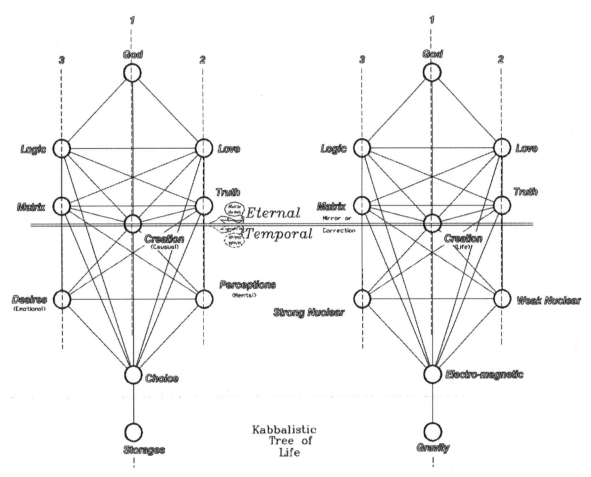

Figure 9-3, Parallels to the Kabbalah and the Tree of Life

symmetry between the physical and metaphysical.

The Tibetans have another construct of how God manifests form. Again, elements of these constructs are very similar.

In all of these philosophies and thought constructs, the higher determines the lower; an effect in the higher, automatically affects the lower. A change in thought produces a change in form. Just as, changing a dimension from ten feet to ten inches on a plan will affect an architect's house.

Remember the Correction, how Love compensated, and did not excluded the ~~truth~~/mis-creation. Around the ~~truth~~ are bubbles of temporal/spatial reference.[28] All this is representative of a closed system in God. Either Figures 9-2 or 9-3 can represent this closed system on a universal scale, or it can represent an enclosed system within that universe (a person).[29]

Figure 9-2 shows all bubbles of temporal/spatial reference contained within the Eternal Creation circle and become more localized or specialized with each decreasing circle. All are contained in God. This onion is shown inside out compared to a real onion. Instead of the core being on the inside (the seed element of the onion), everything is portrayed upside down and backwards…again.

God is represented on the outside in this instance because God is all encompassing. Some Kabbalistic drawings show the process going from out to in, while other mystical drawings show it going from in to out.

---

28 Figure 3-1

29 "As with Man, so it is with the universe, and vice versa."

<u>These all are only perceptional constructs.</u> Perceive it whatever way you need to for it to work for you.

Figure 9-2 presents:

♦   The outside circle is God, the Source, and the Will.
♦   The next circle is all encompassing Eternal Love.
♦   As Love is contained within the God circle, so is Logic/Truth Matrix contained within the Love circle. These three circles represent the first four postulates and their theorems.
♦   Contained within the Logic/Truth Matrix circle is the Creation circle -- the fifth and sixth postulates and their theorems.
♦   Inside Creation is the Causal circle, the realm of the seventh postulate and related theorems.
♦   Inside the Causal is the Mental circle
♦   Inside the Mental is the Astral or Emotional Circle
♦   Inside the Astral is the Etheric circle
♦   And, inside the Etheric is physical form

Figure 9-2 can be a symbol of one human system. When stable, the points of tangency of each circle in the system are in resonance with each other and their relative positions do not change that much. When we are in a mental/emotional reprogramming change, the relative positions of the points of tangency are in flux or change – the circles rotate.

The point is, from the Creative moment and Causal, there is a mind/matrix to image sequencing that manifests form. The higher has priority over the lower. When the mental construct changes, the form changes. As the blueprint changes, the house changes. This is important for the magical operation.

Figure 9-2 displays the inner circles, beginning with the Causal/Choice/mis-creation, are tangent to each other in a manner similar to the outer circles. The difference between the inner and outer circles is that the outer circles are tangent with one point in common while the inner circles are portrayed with no common point of tangency between them. It is as if the inner circles are copies of the outer circles, but the copies are skewed or rotated.

This again, brings us back to the mirror analogy.[30] The Mirror, or Correction, would be within (or be) the Causal circle for it was called into existence or caused by the ~~truth~~. There would also be some aspects of the Creation in this circle, for the mirror is working from the Eternal Moment of Creation. For the human, the Causal circle is where Choice resides.

Keeping with the mirror concept, the closest circle inside the Causal is very similar to the closest circle outside of the Creation's circle. Mental is equivalent to a mirror version of Logic/Truth. Again mirrored around Casual, emotional or Astral is like a distorted version of Love. Taking this analogy to the outermost and innermost circles, the Etheric and its effect, physical, is the source of everything we know within the realm of our five senses, which is kind of like a distorted image of God -- The Source of All.

Figure 9-2 shows physical form in the center. The circles where they are not connected at one point represent the separation/misalignment from the Mind of God. The points of tangency are *Storages* changing (Figure 4-3) as the perceptual lens of the individual human matrix focuses and refocuses. In fact, later in the chapter, common points of tangency in the inner circles will be mentioned when performing a magical operation.

How is the emotional and astral level the same? They are two different labels for the same level. Again, the form or nomenclature here is similar to a theosophical form. Astral is imagery and feeling with very little, or no, reason or thought. Most night dreams are astral in nature; they tend to form around specific wants.

The word *emotional* gives the idea of the astral level a more concrete handle for most people. However, there can be images (perceptions) involved that key (or are keyed by) the

---

30 Because the mirror's reflection is backward – skewed.

emotions or feelings. This particular arrangement (Mental, Astral/Emotional, Etheric, and Physical) is a recurring mystical theme. It can also be found in Kabbalistic thought. Although there are other terms in different systems, it is still just the emotional.

Etheric is what sustains physical form. In Chapter 3, Figures 3-2 and 3-3, it is represented as life energy. It is the one level just above physical form that sustains and holds physical form. Essentially, it is at the core of the smallest *BTR construction* and interaction. Etheric is a parallel of Creation's participation within physical existence on the most basic level.

Many mystical philosophies and thought frameworks present the physical body with an etheric body. The etheric field sticks out only about half an inch to an inch around any physical body.

The theory is that everything has an etheric field around it. When perceived, it appears the blue color of cigarette smoke that has not been inhaled. It has this iridescent-like, bright bluish color to it. Whereas, what people call the aura is more or less the physical, etheric, astral, and mental fields generated by that person's mind/matrix (desires/perceptions, emotion/thought, choices/*Storage*, etc.). Moreover, the aura can be representative of an individual's physical well being, influenced by an individual's physical body matrix.

The etheric field is easier to 'see' than the aura, and it is what sustains the physical form. When a person dies, the aura can leave -- there will be no mind/matrix activity or mental/emotion constructs. The body will still have an etheric field.

While the physical form still exists, an aspect of the etheric is present. As in Kirilian photography, where you can see the form of the whole leaf after you cut a part of the leaf off.

All this previous information in this section are examples of thought constructs and mystical philosophies. One of the patterns you are being exposed to in this book is a manifestation order in a parallel manner. However, they are not quite parallel. An ocean-fish relationship is an excellent analogy.

Look at seawater, which is made up of water (and other chemical compounds) and basic elements. Seawater can be considered a fluid chemical matrix. This fluid matrix has intrinsic properties (due to its composition).

Early life evolution started when cells would colonize and let the seawater pass through them to get nutrients. They would also us the same water currents to take away their waste. As these colonies became more and more complicated, they developed their own transfer fluid, which we call blood. Therefore, the blood of the fish is essentially a specialized form of seawater. Fish blood does what seawater does for coral, sponges, and other primitive life forms.

There is a matrix of ocean water the fish swims in; and then, there is this matrix of the very specialized ocean water inside of the fish. A fish in water is like seawater within seawater, or blood within blood. The fish parallel helps illustrate how one thing evolves from and is contained within the other.

These parallels and patterns are condensing as they manifest into physical form. The patterns become increasingly specialized, just as the fish's fluid matrix (blood) becomes a more specialized form of seawater.

The patterns, or weaves, of the metaphysical are present in every mathematical point in physical space, as are the patterns and weaves of physical laws. The metaphysical parallels, as with the seawater and fish blood, are going from the Eternal present, at the core of our being, infinite and unlimited, to temporary localized physical special applications (matter and us).

9.5 -- Concerning Magic Categories

*A*ll power comes from God. This applies to all types of magic, no matter what symbol system the operator uses. There is only One Source, although there may be a *perception* of multiple sources. How the power of the Eternal Creative Moment is magically used is categorized into five basic levels within this book: Black, White, Gray, Silver, and Gold.

The motivations/intentions of the operator[31] are a determining factor to what category of magic an 'operation' is. (How exclusive or inclusive are the operator's perceptions and desires.) These motivations can influence the predominant forces that are being wielded -- Creative or destructive.

In addition, the forces being used themselves – creative or destructive -- help define a magic's category.

Black Magic

Black magic deals with destructive forces primarily, with the effects of ~~truth~~. In Black magic, the perceptions and desires of the operator are <u>usually</u> limited in scope and focus. The operator's motivations are <u>usually</u> centered on the self while manipulating destructive forces.

It should be mentioned at this point that Black magic and Satanism are not the same thing. Satanism is a form of shamanic paganism that revolves around desire gratification while in the act of worshiping destruction.

Black magic is a manipulation of destructive forces to produce a desired effect without necessarily worshiping these destructive forces. A Catholic exorcism is an excellent example of a Black magic ritual.

Even if your perceptions have a broad background and you choose to work Black magic, only from the safety of God's protection, and only with His authority, will the destructive forces (demons[32]) even listen to what the operator has to say. When the operator is dealing in Black magic without the power and authority of God, 'demons' will not listen.

Unless the operator has God on their side, the 'demons' will laugh and ask, "Who the hell are you?" (Roughly speaking.) The 'demons' are not going to recognize the operator's authority; they will only recognize God's.

This makes it a gilt-edged priority for the Black magician to seek union with God. A Satanist tends to avoid this.

This brings up a number of interesting paradoxes around Black magic. As stated earlier, study of magic is full of ironies and paradoxes. Black magic has more bizarre paradoxes than the others do.

A. E. Waite hits the nail on the head in his book *Black Ceremonial Magic.*[33] In his book, there is a black grimoire (The Key of Solomon)[34]. The first chapter of this grimoire is *Concerning the Preparation of the Operator.* The first section of that chapter is entitled *Concerning the Love of God.* The content of the chapter is essentially, what has already been said here. Waite has a number of footnotes to that section and in those footnotes, he concludes (loosely quoted):

❖ **Paradox 4:** The *first paradox the Black magician must overcome is that he must be absolutely good to do evil. He must love his neighbor before he can bewitch them.*

The ritual to manifest Satan in that book is like something out of the Catholic liturgy. The operator is extolling God and crossing him/herself while trying to command Satan. The irony in all this is similar to *Paradox 1*:

❖ **Paradox 5:** If *the operator has to go initially to God, the primary Creative force, why bother dealing with secondary dependent destructive forces -- demons?*

What is wrong with this picture?

---

31 How their Perception/Desires Lens is focused – intention.
32 9.4 – Concerning Mechanics: Physical and Metaphysical -- Patterns and Parallels
33 A. E. Waite was one of the people who developed the Rider *Tarot* deck.
34 Authorship not clear. Some attribute it to Paracelsus, while others to a Hermes Trigamestos.

Since intent or motivation is a major variable here, there is a lot more Black magic in the world on the **mundane** level than one would first imagine. To hit someone over the head with a '2x4' is just as much an act of Black magic as a 'whammy' that produces the same results.

This is not saying to wish somebody ill were similar or the same as doing. Focusing on that wish and trying to make it real or extend it from the **Individual** reality into **Actual** reality is the magic. To work on extending a destructive/exclusive perception is Black magic.

However, just having the thought does have an effect on you through Choice and the Mirror; while, choosing to correct that thought also has an effect. *A Course in Miracles©* refers to them as killing thoughts, the thoughts of destruction and murder.

All self-centered mental/emotional sets boil down to some kind of thought of destruction or exclusion of something. The motivation is the same. What changes is the vector you are using to accomplish your motives. The energy is the same.

Remember, magic is manifesting a desire through the use of the will. A black mage manipulates destructive forces according to a specific desire. This may involve arranging a set conditions that fosters damage, destruction, or dissolution to a *BTR*.[35] The operator does this by manipulating (either directly or indirectly) the ocean of energy that manifests the *BTR and* its environment.

Because of parallels like matrices within matrices, systems within systems, seawater within seawater, etc., this reflects on war or conflict as a splash contest, a thing of the moment with no long-term consequences to the 'water'. While...the water itself is neutral.

Black magic is the category of the fool or the initiate, or the foolish initiate.

White Magic

In White magic, the perceptions and desires of the operator are <u>relatively</u> inclusive in scope and focus. The operator's motivations are usually healing and relatively altruistic (selfless) while manipulating constructive forces. It recognizes some kind of One Almighty Source and endeavors to work with it to manipulate a desire into matter.

As Black magic uses destructive forces, White magic uses creative forces. As Black magic revolves around desires toward self and gratification of self, White magic revolves around the concept of a whole and unity with the whole, selflessly. Sublimation of the self is co-joined with the recognition of an all-powerful deity.

The perceptional lens of the white operator is focused on that deity and whatever matrices, pantheons, philosophies, rites, etc. that is implied or has been associated with this deity (as the operator perceives it).

Most rites of world religions have an aspect of White magic in them. The Catholic mass starts being a devotional ritual between a group of individuals and the Creator. With the invocation of the sacrament and the petition of prayers, it becomes a White magic ritual because it involves a desire to affect physical form, to bring the 'higher' into the 'lower'.

White magic involves some deity recognition conjoined with some desire. Something the operator wants on earth, whether it is for crops, health, peace for all, etc. White magic tends to be the magic of most healers. It is subtler and less dramatic than black. The difference between Black and White is like planting a seed for growing a tree and planting a stick of dynamite to blow a tree up.

Both magics are still manifesting a desire using the will. With both forms, the operator is using God's Will within him/her. An operator is attempting to align their will -- their matrix -- with God and with the One Truth or the Truth Matrix. This means the operator, with both Black and White, must reduce as much ~~truth~~ (that which hinders the alignment) within their mind/matrix as possible.

---

35 Or, it may be to command a demon

White magic is the magic of harmlessness. It is the category of a priest and the priestess.

Gray Magic

Gray magic is a mixture of the two previous categories. The perceptions and desires of the gray operator are limited and they may be beginning to expand. This is the usual category of the early student or novice in magic. It is category where a student is first learning to do magic and mental exercises, while at the same time, still has a relatively large amount of ~~truth~~ within their mind/matrix.

A novice may have some altruistic aspirations, and yet, because he/she does not a grasp yet their own motivations, desires, or perceptions – see the whole picture, he or she can do some nasty stuff while learning. Some of the mechanics they have learned are applied towards the self and some of the mechanics they use is towards the whole.

Both Black and White recognizes a deity (one way or another), something beyond physical form. Gray can use the physical and metaphysical mechanics and their laws – truths -- behind form with a minimum of active deity recognition. If there is no complete recognition of a supreme deity, then the magic tends to stay in the gray level realm. Many forms (not all) of shamanism, witchcraft, and paganism may fall into this category.

Gray magic is the magic of the **mundane** also. An example of this is the architect building a house. Part of the act of building is just for the person, individual shelter or for the money. Part of the act involves the individual working with a whole. The number of destructive self-centered desires accompanying the act <u>may</u> be relatively low. Though a house was created, trees and the ground (in the form of rock and minerals – metals) were destroyed.

Building a house is an example of the individual matrix working with larger matrices to produce an effect (later). It is a form of Gray magic.

Many magic forms use ritual as a tool. How does the gray magic of an architect or engineer use rituals to produce Gray magic? Here are some simple draftsman rituals and refers back to before there were computers, before we were using CAD programs:

- Ritual number one: put your T-square down and put the paper on the edge of the T-square so it's 'true'.
- The draftsperson tapes up the corners and starts to make the frames and borders.

There may be all kinds of rituals involved with **mundane** magic, as with driving: fasten seat belts, look around, engage transmission, remove foot from brake, etc.

*Gray magic is the magic of the **mundane** or the **thaumaturgical** novice.*

Silver Magic

As stated earlier, with a Gray magic operation, there may be little or no recognition of a deity, a supreme deity, or one source. As in many **mundane** applications, there may little to no recognition of a system behind or beyond the *BTR* system the operator perceives himself or herself to be in.

Silver magic takes Gray the next step. In a Silver magic operation, the operator may have mixed desires and use mixed forces, but there is definitely deity recognition. Deity recognition involves something other than the individual; be it the nameless desert God, for the Whole, for Vishnu, for the Great Turtle, or "Use the Force, Luke". It does not make any difference. Silver magic involves a recognition of a connection with something greater than the mage.

Silver magic is another mixture of the first two categories. The perceptions and desires (motivations) of the operator are relatively inclusive in scope and focus, more so than with Gray. The operator's motivations are usually relatively altruistic. Yet, as in Gray, because the operator sees everything in physical form as a combination of dualities (creative and destructive forces), the operator uses both.

As can be seen, Silver magic can evolve from Gray. As the operator becomes more altruistic with magic, as one expands perceptions, and wants to do more for the whole, the Gray magic category tends to evolve into Silver. The Silver mage focuses on a significant reduction of ~~truth~~ participation in their mortal mind/matrix.

The difference between Gray magic and Silver magic is similar to the difference between early man's perceptions of the world and man today. We grew up from a Stone Age culture and evolved into a hi-tech culture. At one time, we had pantheons of unseen gods to explain the seen but we were limited to what it we could manifest in physical form.

The pantheon construct used by our technical expertise today is the unseen laws of physics and its logic -- math. Instead of gods, the laws of form comprise this pantheon. Therefore, we have a much greater influence in the variety of forms we can construct. We evolved into a broader or a more sophisticated understanding.

Silver magic involves a broader understanding of the subject matter; and, Silver magic may be much more controlled than Gray. By controlled, meaning, the operator has more control of self (coordinated). The operator has been removing ~~truth~~ from their mind/matrix over an extended period. Instead of just doing blind rituals or ceremonies in order to produce an effect, the Silver magic operator puts archetypes in their head and depends less on external symbolic items to remind the operator of the archetypes -- ritual magic.

Silver magic is the magic category of the high thaumaturge, a devote Wicca or shaman, or a magic initiate.

Gold Magic

In Gold magic, the perceptions and desires of the operator are even more inclusive – non-exclusive -- than White or Silver magic (if not Absolutely inclusive). The motivation of the mage is to be an instrument of God's Love. The major difference between Gold magic and the other categories of magic is this:

♦ With the other categories of magic there involves some perception of a lack – a desire.
♦ There is usually a sense of correction urgency around that perceived lack.
♦ The other categories attempt to rectify that perceived lack by filling it.
♦ Gold magic perceives no lack. There is nothing wrong. "God is in His Heaven and all is right with the world."

Because the Gold mage does not perceive any lack or need, there is no conscious effort on the part of the operator to fill a lack. It is a passive form of magic.[36]

The Gold mage's mortal mind/matrix has many points in common – in tangent (Figure 9-6) -- with the Eternal Mind/Matrix; in addition, the mage's motivations are centered on the Source. Because of this, physical form (through the mirror) starts arranging itself around the Gold mage's individual *BTR* in such a way to reflect the individual's mind (and therefore the Mind). This is not unusual; the mirror is constantly doing this.

What is unusual is that the mind/matrix of their bubble of temporal/spatial reference is relatively close to the Creator's Eternal Matrix in structure, and wonders start to happen around them automatically. The Eternal Moment of Creation is reflected out into the world through their eyes. Just the presence of the Gold mage is enough for this to occur.

When other bubbles of temporal/spatial reference (human matrixes/*BTRs*) enter the vicinity of a *BTR of* a Gold mage (same temporal/spatial reference), those people can become more aware of the presence of God. The mystic's bubble of temporal reference is reflecting back what is in his/her mind -- God.

That means, because of the Mirror, form itself is reflecting God. This happens with no effort on the mage's part (other than remembering God). The Eternal Creative moment is working with and through the individual, without any conscious effort to do so on their part. It is possible that any perceived lack brought to the Gold mage can be filled.

---

36 Beginning of chapter

An example of this is people would walk into a grove where the Buddha was and they would start feeling good – at peace. They could feel that he was there before they could see him. They could feel the Presence. They were entering an environment – Buddha's *BTR* -- that was reflecting the Buddha's mind.

A Gold mage may also be the one mage who is the most dangerous to be around for the non-spiritual. Why? Because they are working on advanced levels of Creation, the Mirror, and its time ignor-ance, the non-spiritual individual's karma may accelerate. The 'paybacks' or 'reflections' of what is in their mind may not be dampened through time. Every day may be 'Friday the thirteenth'.

Gold magic is the magic category of an adept, master, miracle worker, saint, or priest-king.

9.6 -- Concerning the Preparation of the Operator

A recommended prerequisite study to **thaumaturgical** magic is raja yoga. This is the yoga of the mind and mental disciplines. If you think the labs and homework assignments in this book are too much work, you should stay away from magic. As mentioned earlier, from an adept mage's viewpoint, all the exercises in this book are "beginner's shit". There is a tremendous amount of self-knowledge, self-discipline, and internal work to become a mage and most people do not choose this.

Raja yoga is a common recommended prerequisite to **thaumaturgical** magic practice. The magical operator needs to do mental disciplines and exercises, learn mental dexterity, to adjust the points of tangency inside them in order to work with the Source. They need to exercise their focus 'muscle' and learn coordination. For the beginner, this usually means a period of deep meditation before 'the work'. They must still their personal mental/emotional activity.

The difference between a normal person and a high magic adept (in terms of internal coordination) is the difference in physical coordination between a seven-year-old child and a proficient adult acrobat. If the operator does not know themselves and their motivations, he or she could be in for a world of pain. It would be like trying to do a back flip without preparation – a warm up.

The reader may notice there is only the one lab in this chapter.[37] That is because this chapter deals with advance applications and one should be familiar with the previous exercises in this book before even attempting a magical operation. Magic is not for everybody. Just like, being an electrician is not for everybody. With both, if you are not careful, you can be 'zapped'.

As mentioned earlier, the Mirror (the Correction) present within every bubble of temporal/spatial reference along with the Eternal Moment of Creation is what makes magic and miracles possible.

Earlier chapters stated that the function of the Mirror is to reflect mistaken thinking back on the mind of origin. The purpose: to correct the mistaken thinking and have that mind remember its union with God.

Because the sole purpose of the Mirror is to reflect what is in the mind back on Creation, a coordinated temporal mind/matrix can manipulate physical form (the reflection) by changing aspects of their mind/matrix. This is the magic or miracles base (in addition to God). This is what makes them possible.

Physical form is meant to reflect the temporal mind. The mind of a saint or mage is using (or participating in) this. As stated before, only an act done to promote the mindfulness of God (without attachment) is Karma-less. Since the Mirror is there to foster this -- the system is rigged. It is no wonder it is usually the very religious who produce the marvels.

---

37 Exercise and Lab 14: Energy Passage Through Your Body

All working religious, metaphysical, or mystical thought systems (constructs) share a consistent pattern. The elements of this pattern are:

1) There is Deity or a holistic recognition with a subsequent thought construct or philosophy.

2) If there is no deity recognition, there is at least recognition of an unseen reality – non-physical -- with a subsequent thought construct or philosophy.

3) Participation in this unseen reality is accomplished by:

a) Assimilating or working with attributes or truths of the Deity, the whole, or unseen reality.

b) Relinquishing attachment to, questioning of, or rejecting the seen reality

c) Doing both *a)* and *b)*.

4) In any successful spiritual quest, the last step will always be God's, The Eternal, The Infinite...

How thought systems or philosophies satisfy this pattern will depend on the mental constructs within an individual matrix system (how an individual/s programs their matrix/mind with whatever philosophy and discipline).

Keeping with the above common patterns and parallels in religious thought introduced, next is how the elements of these patterns relate to the magical operator's preparation.

1) There *is deity or a holistic recognition* -- The mage (no matter what beliefs or faith) must recognize something greater than him/her. It is through the greater that the lesser (mage) manipulates form.

When an individual physically creates, he or she works with a greater logic matrix than his or her own. An individual may not consciously recognize this matrix; but a working relationship exists in order to manifest into form.

2) If *there is no deity recognition, there is at the least recognition of an unseen reality* -- This unseen reality is what is being manipulated to produce the seen.

When an individual creates, there are some forms of cause and effect relationships within a system matrix/matrices constantly happening. This applies to physical existence (**Actual** reality) as well as metaphysical existence. There is an unseen system of laws of physics, biology, and chemistry represented in a symbolic logic matrix (mathematics) -- eternally constant.

Some examples of laws the architect's **mundane** (Gray magic) uses are: a symbolic logic matrix (mathematics); gravity, motion, stress (structure); manipulation of light, strengths, and frequencies emanating from a two-dimensional surfaces (paint); orchestration of the sequencing of electrical charges through a semi-conductor matrix (computer); and the laws of finance.

Many of the architect's systems may be unseen and yet the architect will work with such systems, presenting seen results. All of this can be done without 'thinking about God'. Which leads into:

3) One can participate in this unseen reality by:

a) *Assimilating or working with attributes of the deity or whole with its unseen reality* – Given unseen reality causes the seen; attributes or truths of the unseen must be applied to manipulate the seen.

In religious magic, the system the mage uses takes the form of a religious philosophy or some sort of a pantheon; some sort of cause and effect levels or relationships within the Universe. There may be a metaphysical recognition of gods, spirits, angels, demons, or self. It does not matter; there still is a system, an array of concepts.[38]   The mage's unseen metaphysical system incorporates or takes into account the Truth configuration of God manifesting into physical form.   This system is characterized in the operator by a symbolic thought construct/philosophy.   This thought system usually represents how the mage has programmed their human matrix.

For the mage, this means searching for absolute truths/archetypes and choosing to store them in their mortal mind/matrix.   If the novice does not have some kind of Truth perception exercise[39] and a perception expansion exercise[40] this may entail a lot of reading.   This truth storage is the beginning.   This storage of truths is in preparation for the mage to program in common elements between his personal mind/matrix and the Matrix.   This gives the mage a place to 'stand'.

Or…as it was said long ago, "Be ye perfect as your Father in Heaven is perfect".

> **b)** Relinquishing *attachment to the seen reality* – If **a** is not observed, then **b** must be observed.   If one is to learn a new perception system, the current system – the one in use – must be called into question.

There is a recurring element of purification within holistic/metaphysical/spiritual systems.   Depending on what system used, this purification concept can take many forms.   All of them relate to, in some way, a reduction of ~~truth~~ within mind/matrix's Choice and *Storage*. Many thought systems like Buddhism stress a non-attachment and/or a relinquishment of desire to the seen (which reduces ~~true~~ choices and therefore reduces ~~truth~~ in *Storage*).   At the same time, this will increase effectiveness working with the unseen.[41]

> **c)** *Doing both of the above* – The ideal is to do both **a** and **b** at the same time. This would help reduce ideological (thought construct) tensions/conflicts while learning and growing.

This is 'covering all the bases'.   The 'would be mage' must work within this presented outline framework.   The last statement in the outline is:

> **4)** *In any successful spiritual quest, the last step will always be God's, The Eternal, The Infinite...*

The "last step is God's" thing comes from the asymptotic nature of the way a finite approaches an infinite.   Finite approaches an infinite, but never reaches an infinite.   It is the Infinite that bridges the gap.

The finite is weak on infinity's parameters.   If a bridging is to occur, the infinite assimilates the finite.

The Chapter 10 will return to this outline pattern, when covering world religions.

9.7 -- Concerning the Four Rules of Magic

*I*nstead of looking at how God manifests an idea into physical form, let us look at how Man mundanely creates something into physical form.   Creation starts with an idea.[42]   With Man, it is usually a perception/desire relationship -- an idea; and wanting to bring that idea to form; to extend that idea.   Creation always starts somewhere in a mind first.

The idea might not be clear, but *something* is there.   In some cases, the individual may not even know what he or she wants to do.   Both unclear perception and strong desire are co-joined in that example.[43]

---

38 As in Chapter 9.4 - Concerning Mechanics; Patterns and Parallels
39 Chapter 3, *Exercise and Lab #3:* Truth Perception
40 Chapter 4, *Exercise and Lab #4:* Time/ space Imagination Exercises
41 Chapter 5, Formula of Effectiveness
42 Chapter 2.6 - *Postulate 5, Theorems 11(A & B), 15, 15(A), and 17*

Comparing how the architect creates a house to how a mage creates will help bring the magical operation concept down to more concrete terms. As stated, both contain an idea and a desire to do the idea. Then, as with the architect, there is a recognition involved; there is a recognition of a matrix of laws that determine physical forms and realities. Moreover, there is recognition that they are going to have to work through these matrix(s) or weave(s) -- represented by logic system(s) -- to make this idea real.

The four rules governing learning and the use of magic (introduced in the beginning of the chapter) are to be covered. They will be synthesized with the procedure the architect has to go through. We will periodically look at Figure 9-4 also, to help demonstrate the work of the mage.

TO KNOW

This has numerous parts. The first part of *To Know* usually involves some thought/logic system (a mental construct/philosophy containing Truth) to help them do so.[44] It not only means to study what others have done before (which is difficult because "Those who know don't talk"). In other words, one part of *To Know* means to go through some manner of schooling.

Another part of *To Know* also means the operator has already begun establishing the discipline for aligning himself or herself to the Source.

Concerning the first part, the architect's magic uses architectural logic and symbol system, mathematics. The idea has to be translated into mathematical concepts.[45] In the old days, it was thought everything had a true name -- know the name and you would have control of that thing.

Today this rationale has evolved to be an extension of Pythagorean thinking: everything can be expressed as numbers. Manipulating the physical form to numbers creates something that works (providing you are using the right numbers). Both are examples of magical thinking -- to control form through symbols and the logic behind the symbols.

Both the mage and the architect are using magical thinking. One is using symbols to key truths in the mind, and the truths will take care of the form. The other is using symbols to assembling ideas that have material existence according to the mathematical symbols of truth: dimensions, hardness, spatial arrangements, curing time, finances, labor, etc.

The architect must also recognize and be schooled in the laws of physics applicable to physical forms, the physical form itself, and its symbols. Some examples involve the basic physical materials to be used: What is concrete? What is it made out of? What is wood? What is iron? How does iron work different than concrete? How is it that, when you put the two of them together, they help each other? Etc.

In both cases (**thaumaturgical** and **mundane**), if the symbols are correctly applied, the form <u>must</u> follow. This process involves some degree of experience, through either education or other ways. This also means both must program their mind with the applicable truths.

The perception/desire (idea) that is wanted (in the particular magical operation) is then translated into some logic matrix of its own – mental construct, and visualized. The architect draws plans of what he wants to do. He tries to solidify the idea down, so to speak. With artists, and some artwork, this idea starts with plans and sketches or rehearsals. Then, there is other artwork, where the plan is extemporaneous. The artist is going to do something, but does not have any plan about it yet. They are going to do it as they go along. And...<u>that is</u> a plan.

For the mage, this may involve some constructed visualization (either actual as a picture or a visual construct within their mind). *To Know* also may mean developing some sort of ritual or an execution procedure.

---

43 Strong (D_S) with unclear (P_S)

44 As mentioned earlier, a world religion philosophy, any metaphysical viewpoint like theosophists or this book, a shamanic or witchcraft philosophy, etc.

45 A 4"x8 "x 10'-6" with a 2" notch on each end, suspended 12'-2" from the floor.

The architect's plan idea also includes sequencing of the work – an execution procedure.

It was stated earlier; and it is important to remember from the postulates and theorems, as well as Figure 9-2, that the higher always determines the lower. God determines the Love, Love determines the Logic, Logic determines the Truth Matrix, and the Truth Matrix determines the Creation. Just as the idea within your mind determines what the final form is going to be, the higher always determines the lower.

If the architect changes any aspect of their visualization of their mental construct/matrix/plan, the form changes. A contractor is reading the plans; the plan reads 10" instead of 10'. That one notation mark change in the plan matrix makes a major change in the physical form. The higher always determines the lower, and as the higher changes, the form changes.

All of which, of course, is in line with the thought system/logic matrix they are using. The architect is aligning their perceptual lens to using physics, math, and society. While the mage, is aligning their perceptual lens using a metaphysical thought system (both are priming their perceptual lens/matrix with, as well as, learning applications of relevant truths).

The architect has to arrange to plug the idea into a **Consensual** reality[46] in order to bring the idea into physical form. Much of the architect's plan construction is with that in mind. To weave or extend the idea (**Individual** reality) into **Absolute** and **Actual** reality (physics and materials) and then into a **Consensual** reality (culture), all which will build the house.

Another part of *To Know* means the operator has learned some form of internal coordination <u>and</u> has harmonized the discipline with their thought system/matrix. The mage must know about meditation, one-point focus, visualization, etc.

For effectiveness purposes, the operator's thought matrix/construct must be as encompassing – non-exclusive -- as possible. The more Absolute Truth that is in their mind/matrix, the better. This helps the operator's mortal mind matrix become tangent to the all-encompassing Loving Mind that comes from God.

From the telepathic/psychic reference, nourishing Truth in the human matrix fosters the necessary love bond between a mortal mind/matrix and the Mind/Matrix for the operation to be possible.

In both cases, for the mage as well as the architect, this entails a degree of self-discipline and practice beforehand.

To Know <u>also</u> means for the mage to know one's self. Why are you doing this? What are the operator's desires, intentions? What is one's motivation/intention for working with '*The Lathe of Heaven*'?[47] Just because a person <u>can</u> do something, does not necessarily mean, he or she <u>should</u> do it.

One imagination exercise is to recognize an individual perception/desire (a want), and then imagine you already have that perception/desire (got what you wanted). Then using your memories of previous gratified desires and you ask yourself, "Now what?"

As stated earlier, motivation or intention determines what category of magic the operator will be doing. In addition, it determines the nature of the operation's karmic reflection back on the operator, the Mirror's reaction to the action.

Remember the Formula of Effectiveness, and how your motivations factor into the formula.[48] Motivations can affect the effectiveness of the operation and the 'paybacks' -- this makes it a <u>very high priority</u> for the magical operator to know their motivations.

To summarize, *To Know* means to study – the universe as well as yourself, to have a plan, and to prepare your mind/matrix.

---

46 Banks, material yards (lumber, rock, hardware), zoning, etc.
47 A science fiction book by Ursula K. LeGuinn, copyright 1974
48 Chapter 5, Formula of Effectiveness

TO DARE

The second rule is *To Dare*. The operator dares to do the operation. It means to conquer any fear related to the operation. Part of this dare is to know that what the operator is about to do is very different from what he or she has done before.

Another part of the dare is to know that whatever is done that is not aimed at union with God is going to draw Karma. The Mirror will reflect the operator's thinking and actions back on them. As mentioned earlier, because the operator of magic is manipulating form on a Causal level, Karma can be accelerated. As a friend once said, "paybacks are a motherfucker".

Fear and its related perceptions are just as much an obstacle to the architect as it is to a mage, though on different levels. Fear is divisive. It divides and separates. There can be a number of reasons the architect may be afraid of bringing his/her idea to fruition. What if it does not work? Will I look like a fool? What am I going to eat? (If the project fails)... etc. The end result is the same. The fractured perception that fear generates hinders the architect from following through on the idea.

With the mage, the reasons and the thinking may be different, but the results are the same. The fearful perceptions that keep a mage from working may be: What if my motivations are not pure? What will be the repercussions to my act (including individual karmic consequences)? I am dealing with 'The Great Unknown' here.

For both, fear is a perceptual distraction that keeps them from focusing totally on their perceptual lens/matrix manifesting the idea. Therefore, they both must dare to do what they want to do.

TO WILL

To Will means to do it. When performing an operation, the magical operator is adjusting the circles of Figure 9-2 (elements of their human matrix) within him/herself. In some ways, it can be said, the operator is manipulating the mirrored image, of Figures 3-3, 3-7, 4-4, and 9-2 within themselves to affect the mirrored image outside.[49]

In reference to Figure 9-2, a mage creates a weave or pattern of tangency within their matrix to bring the power of the precious Eternal Moment of Creation into effect. The closer to one point tangency within the individual, the closer God's Creation comes into physical form. This is called a 'coordinated being' in magic. Depending on the skill and on the points of tangency, the results can vary from a simple manipulation of daily changes to the awesome.

The next section goes over the operation in depth.

TO KEEP SILENT

As stated in the beginning of this chapter, this rule explains why there is not that much factual information about magic. Silence was also a concept of the Pythagorean mystery schools.[50] Since Pythagoras spent some time with Zoroaster, the two schools having the same idea in common is not that surprising.

The introduction of this chapter also explains why there is so much misinformation about magic, because of this rule. For the most part, the people putting the information out do not know the subject matter. They may not know that talking fosters attachment. They are speaking from ignorance.

Why keep silent? Nobody likes a big mouth. Egoists are focused more on themselves than the work. About the only reason to talk about an accomplishment (other than for teaching purposes), is pride. ("Look what I did!" "Look what I did!") For the architect, this may only involve a lack of social graces. For the mage, it is much more serious.

Here is a partial list of reasons why a mage needs to keep silent.

❑ A mage must change their mind's programming or alter their mind's operation to perform a magical operation. Talking, being a choice and an act of creation alters their

---

49 Or, adjusting Figure 9-3 left, to affect 9-3 right.
50 Chapter 1.4 - Pythagoras and the Pythagorean Schools

programming. This program alteration can occur to such an extent that it can inhibit future operations. One reason for silence is be aware that talking fosters an attachment to what you are doing, and this can work against the effectiveness of the current and future operations.[51]

❑ Along with this reason for silence comes from a quote from Jesus, "Don't let the left hand know what the right hand is doing". This is very sound advice to an aspiring mage. If the right hand is the Truth Matrix and the left hand is their mortal mind/matrix, their temporal mind/matrix cannot grasp everything that the Truth Matrix is doing.[52]

What information the personal matrix does get is liable to be fractured or incomplete -- because the temporal matrix cannot perceive the whole picture.[53] Any conclusions or judgments the temporal matrix makes will tend to be wrong because it does not have complete information. For the mage, this means not only does he or she not talk about an operation after it is done, they do not even think about the performed operation as well!

Once the mage has operated, the mage must let go of the work (remember the effectiveness formula and the role of non-attachment). The operator must have faith (apply knowledge) and let the Truth Matrix do its stuff. To not 'let go', means the operator is still putting mental/emotional focus on the work with lack of faith (poorly applied). They are still attached.

This not only affects the outcome, but it may also bring the operation back on them. When the operator talks about an operation, that act brings their mental/emotional focus, with their life energy, back into the operation.

❑ Another reason is the demon's – a gestalt being -- relationship to self-centered perception/desire sets mentioned previously. This was introduced in Chapter 9.4 with the creative and destructive forces. Listening to these self-centered divisive thoughts is like listening to a demon.

❑ Another reason the operator does not talk about what he or she is doing inside him/herself is that, in the end, when we are dealing with magic and some of the higher metaphysical concepts, words become inadequate. The words are an attempt to share an idea between two temporal frames of references or individual realities (*BTRs*). For this to work, the people in communication must agree on the meaning of the words used. In addition, they must have certain ideas in common already for the words to have meaning.

It is very difficult to talk to a child about trigonometry if the child is just learning to count. The words and their usage are based on certain ideas that are not yet in the young mind. The words just do not work.

❑ There is a saying: "The sign of a good artist is to know when the painting is done." For the mage to talk about an operation is equivalent to an artist going back and touching up a picture that has been sold, framed, and is hanging on somebody's wall.

9.8 -- Concerning the Operation

$\mathcal{B}$ ecause the architect is dealing in several realities at once, his act of creation can be a relatively involved process. He has to align the idea in his mind to a number of other thought systems/truths/matrices -- realities. He not only has to work with **Absolute** and **Actual** realities/laws/truths and thought systems; he also has to work with **Consensual**, **Individual**, and perhaps some **Imaginary** realities/laws/truths (Figure 9-4). He must 'know' the truths/laws across a broad spectrum of realities.

---

51 (*A_S*), Formula of Effectiveness, Chapter 5
52 Chapter 3.1, Review of Chapter 2, qualities of the infinite and finite
53 Chapter 4.3 - Limits of the Perceptual Window

For the mage, the idea is the same and it still involves a lot of work, but the process is simpler. The magical operator needs only apply **Absolute** Reality and the other realities will automatically follow.

In terms of the architect, the idea within the human matrix of the architect is woven into the greater matrix of a whole system/s or reality/s as in Figure 9-4. It can also be said a lesser matrix/system (his mind) has interfaced or extended an idea into greater matrix/system/s.

Examples of this may be whether it is winter, and if the contractor can build in winter. Then, the contractor has to wait until summer, wait for a planetary system. As well as, the construction starts along the greater matrix/system lines, dealing with the nature of the matter and material itself. The greater matrix is what makes the idea work/manifest – **Actual** reality concepts.

The architect then puts energy into the assembly of systems and matrices (materials, knowledge, availability, labor, knowledge, etc.) That includes energy/money accumulated along reality matrix lines – **Consensual** reality concepts.

The idea of energy/money is used because money is a symbolic form of condensed energy within our physical world. Then the energy and/or money are matched with the idea -- the desire/perception -- and through the will of the architect; the house becomes actualized and manifested into form through this effort. Through these matrix systems: money, labor, material, and skills -- all used by the architect -- the house is built.

As said before, this involves putting the energy (focused life energy with the condensed energy/money) behind the house idea to assemble systems and sub-systems that work with the previously recognized greater mathematics/physics matrix (**Absolute** and **Actual** realities). This also includes what cultural matrix/s he may be occupying at the time (**Consensual**,

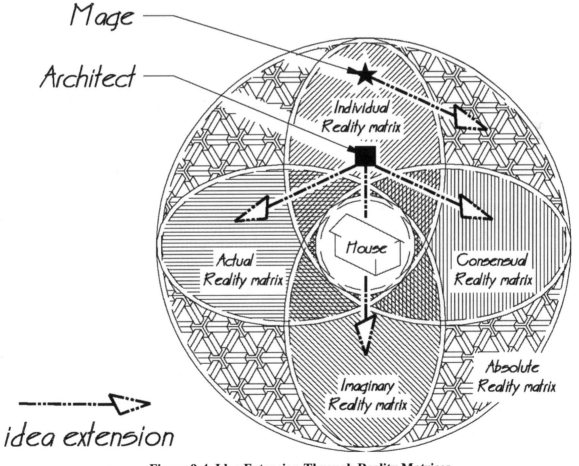

Figure 9-4, Idea Extension Through Reality Matrices

363

Individual and perhaps there may be a few **Imaginary** realities). He literally extends his vision -- the plans -- into these matrices. Once this done, as long as focus is maintained, <u>the matrices/systems build the house physically</u>, makes it real in **Actual** reality.

That is how an architect creates on a **mundane** level. The procedure is relatively similar (though simpler) on the **thaumaturgical** level. When working on **thaumaturgical** levels, the only systems the mage is working with are his matrix and the Truth Matrix. The magical operator <u>extends</u> their idea (**Individual** reality) onto the greater thought Matrix (**Absolute** Reality). This is why the operator needs to arrange their temporal matrix to be aligned with the Truth Matrix -- go to God.

The individual does this while maintaining a focus on the idea they wish to accomplish in their temporal matrix. For energy, they align the points of tangency in their perceptual lens/matrix to work with the Eternal Moment of Creation, as they perceive it (their thought system). Once this is done, the Absolute power of the Truth Matrix (with the Eternal Moment of Creation) collapses time/space and does all the work. <u>Once the idea is in **Absolute** Reality, it automatically effects **Actual** and all the other realities</u>. Again, the matrices do the work.

Instead of formulas and their mathematical relationships (symbols of physical truths) – as with the architect, the mage works with the archetypes (Truths) within their established system. Many established systems <u>perceive</u> the same Truths differently. This is why there is such variation in philosophies on, and uses of, magic. The symbology the mage uses is not important. It is the Truth that those symbols represent to the mage that is important, and consequently, the Matrix these 'Truths' already are in. If you are working with Truth, the Truth Matrix begins to effect.

As stated previously, none of these philosophy variations make much difference. What gives the magical operator the power to work is God, the Truth Matrix, and the Eternal Moment of Creation within them. Both the architect and the mage are working through the Eternal Moment of Creation. The thought system the magical operator uses is not important just as long as they use it to create the points of tangency (as in Figure 9-6) within themselves. A mage may use chants, prayer, music, etc. to maintain focus, to bring their internal points into tangency with **Absolute** reality; while, an architect manipulates Actual, **Individual**, **Consensual**, and **Imaginary** realities and aligns them.

It is the points of tangency within the operator that funnel the power of the Eternal Creative Moment/Matrix through to produce 'the work' into physical form. In other words, how

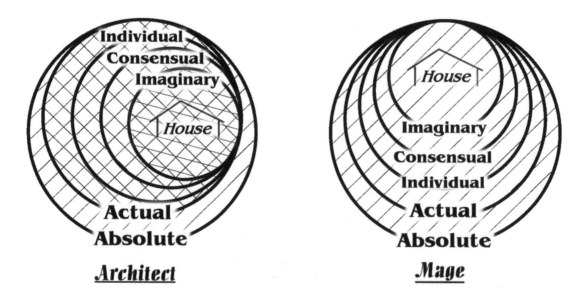

Figure 9-6 Reality Alignments

364

much (and what) Truth is in their temporal matrix determines how well the operator can connect to the Truth Matrix. As with the architect, if the operator makes the proper connections/alignment, the Matrix does the work.[54]

So how does the operator do this? First, stilling the mind/matrix and eliminating as much ~~truth~~ as possible and all non-relevant – to the operation -- truths is a beginning. Next, is weaving 'thought forms' -- this is the 'pumping' of specific truths through their matrix.[55] They may surround themselves with archetypal symbols to help remind them of these truths. This is done until their matrix is ringing on at least the third level, preferably the fourth level, or in very advanced applications, the fifth level.[56]

They then insert and maintain a thought construct of what they wish to accomplish – their intention -- along with these truths. This may be in way of an image, a concept, words, etc. All of this is done with one-point focus -- a mage cannot let the mind drift. No distractions must enter while performing the operation. Focus is maintained until there is a sense of completion.

As stated earlier, a mage may use rituals, chants, music, a tool (like fire), prayer, etc. to help maintain this one-point focus.

A reminder about ritual; beginners and novices usually use ritual. Beginners may surround themselves with religious symbols and things they feel are representative of the applicable truths involved and with what they want to achieve.

For White magic, this may involve inscribed characters or things that have symbolic meaning: crosses and sacrament, Kabbalistic writings, incense, knives, chalices, candles, etc. These are things that have a physical frame of reference which the operator perceives is in keeping with an metaphysical frame of reference and the desired outcome. These items are constant reminders of the truths that evoke the operation.

For Black magic, this also can mean some really nasty stuff: candles made from human fat, a cat that has fed on human flesh, skull of a patricide, skull of a goat that has had sexual intercourse with a human, etc.[57] Items not normally kept on your coffee table.

The ritual magic operator then takes these symbols and performs a predetermined symbolic operation with them: pray and take sacrament; work with the knife, the chalice, or the wand; sing a symbolic song or chant; etc.

What is the mage really doing? The symbols are reminders of universal archetypes/truths that the operator places into their mind -- concepts within the eternal Matrix are 'pumped' into the mortal matrix. In addition, the operator extends an image of the operator's desire into this Matrix.

The connections that make the operation work are all done in the mind of the operator. The things around the mage are just there to help the operator make that internal connection. They are only there to remind the operator. In the end, the only powers these things have are what they key in the mind of the mage. With proficiency and practice, the mage does not need the externals. An advanced initiate has learned how to make the connections inside themselves without the ritual paraphernalia.

This is why ritual magic is the magic of those who are learning. People who have not gotten the operation down yet perform it. In the end, the deeper into magic a student evolves, the more he or she must learn to let go of all planned ritual ceremony.

This applies to most **thaumaturgical** magic: White, Black, Gray, and Silver. Gold magic has no pre-established rituals. If there are any rituals at all, they are spontaneous and of the moment.[58]

---

54 Remember, one of the meanings of the root word, matre, is womb. Put the 'seed' in the womb, and the womb does the work.

55 Chapter 6.3, Additional Study: Zen and Slipping Between Thoughts.

56 Chapter 4.8, Ring My Bell

57 Items used in a ritual to invoke Satan in A. E. Waite's *Black Ceremonial Magic*.

58 Such as Jesus rubbing spit on the eyelids in order to heal blindness.

There is one minor exception to this paraphernalia thing: the pentacle, the pyramid, or any geometric figure that uses the golden section and pi. These figures are equivalent to neutral amplifiers. (Remember the golden section is the mathematical proportion in which life physically comes out of itself and pi is the proportion by which life physically contains itself).[59] Because these figures are based on mathematics that are, in turn, an effect of the life force, the physical presence of these mathematical proportions can resonate with the life force to some extent (although these figures are inanimate and they are totally neutral.).

These geometric figures are quite useful in the beginning while learning and they must be used with great care as the operator grows in magical skill. As with an operation without these figures, if the operator is not clear on his or her motivations, or has an attachment to the outcome, the paybacks may be surprising and regrettable. Everything can become accelerated and the affect on the operator can vary from a physical influence on their body to a psychotic episode. These figures are not to be used lightly.

To conclude, here is something the author learned as a child (grade school). At one time, the author was experimenting and playing with his body movement and control. The author would look at his arm and do all kinds of mental activity (visualizations) trying to move his arm. Sometimes this would go on for five minutes. No matter what mentation or imagery the author would use, if the author did not apply his neural matrix the arm would not move.

The magical operation is very similar to this. No matter what imagery or mentation is used, unless the greater Matrix is applied, the operation will not work. When it is applied, the magic student finds out that the actual operation is as easy as moving an arm or batting an eyelid. The reason behind this is simple if you recognize that the womb is a matrix. Plant a seed in it and the matrix/womb does the rest.

The predominant work involved in magic revolves around establishing the internal coordination. Just as it took you almost the first seven years of your life to coordinate and program your neural matrix (to learn physical coordination – move your arm), it takes a learning mage some time to coordinate and program their human matrix -- mortal mind.

9.9 – Concerning the *Law of Love* and Some Kind of Conclusion

*E*verything up to this point in the book helps illustrate and work with the Absolute Logic of Love. Much of this chapter deals with working within that Logic. The point is; if you work in the Love, the Logic automatically follows. You do not have to be 'schooled' in the Logic; it comes with the Love. Or…it is not important to know the Logic -- the information in this book, as long as you work with the Love.

The growth factor of magic is governed by Love. To be more specific, the *Law of Power and Responsibility* governs the growth factor of **thaumaturgical** magic. The law states simply: the more responsible you become with what power you have, the more power you will be given. The more you apply love, the more the Love is given to you.[60]

Karma and *Law of Power and Responsibility* helps keep **thaumaturgical** magic abuse to a minimum. It is one of the many ways that Love protects us from ourselves. When the operator has – within -- access to the Absolute Power, some form of governance or discipline is necessary to control that power. This introduces an irony or another paradox to magic study; growth truly begins in magical power in not doing something, being capable and yet not doing.

❖ **Paradox 6:** *You grow in magical power by not doing magic.*

This is a major *Catch-22* with magic and it revolves around its very usage. Given God/Creation/and everything else is a closed system by God's all-inclusive Love,[61] God's Perfect Love takes care of everything perfectly and leaves nothing to chance, then 'everything' is running perfectly.

---

59 Chapter 1.5 - Mysticism and Mathematics
60 The Peter Principle© states it another way: "Everybody rises to their own level of incompetence and stays there."
61 *Theorem 11A.* The God-Creation process is a closed system within God.

You may learn magical operations, but your growth in magic will be in <u>not</u> doing something and allowing God's Love to take care of things. Just because you can do something, does not necessarily mean you should. This adds another level of self-discipline to the magical art.

Therefore, another paradox in magic is to gain Absolute power, the operator uses the power minimally, if at all. They have done all the discipline needed for the work; but, are very careful about doing any work. This has been said in other ways:

- "God is in His Heaven and all is right with the world."
- "Don't mess with a good thing."
- "If it ain't broke, don't fix it."
- If you don't know what you're doing, "Leave it alone".

A person, who wishes to use magic and the laws that pertain to the use of magic, must know the *Law of Love* behind the Logic. The *Law of Love* expresses itself in a myriad of metaphysical laws, in different forms. It makes for overall safety guidelines. Karma is a reflection of the *Law of Love*, because it includes choices and then reflects the choices of a mistaken mind back on itself.

The *Law of Power and Responsibility* mentioned earlier, is the *Law of Love* at work: "As you become responsible with what power you have, the more power you are given". This ensures protection against misuse. An individual can misuse what they have, but they will not get any more power to misuse. Eventually, when you misuse magic, the only person you are going to hurt is yourself.

The *Law of Power and Responsibility* creates the ultimate paradox of magic; "He who has absolute power is he who refuses to control anything."[62] Because everything is Absolute Perfection under God's Love, the Gold operator does not do anything, consciously.

Another way to express this is:

❖ **Paradox 7:** *To achieve Absolute Power one must learn Absolute Harmlessness.*[63]

This makes the Gold magic operator the most harmless, and…the most dangerous. The operator perceives no need to do anything; everything is just appreciated and observed. When the operator does perceive a need (or a need is brought before them), Creation works with and through them, using him/her as a conduit to manifest.

As mentioned in a previous section, the gold mage is most dangerous because what is in the mind of the people around the mage is reflected back at them at an accelerated pace and in its purest form.

It is imperative that the magical operator knows him/herself when he/she starts doing magic. Know what your desires are -- long-term and short-term desires. What do you want out of life? This is one of many reasons the subject of motivations was covered in Chapter 5. The operator of magic needs to know the reason why they are performing an operation. What do you want when you are doing this operation? What is the reasoning here?

Implied with these long-term and short-term desires will be long term and short term perceptions. What are the individual's perceptions – tomorrow or a hundred years from now? What does the operator want to effect – what is right in front or the whole? What does the operator want of what is being seen – for self or whole? What are the attachments – vested interests?

Remember the Formula of Effectiveness of Chapter 5. To be effective in magic, the operator has to let go of their attachments. Attachments must be *0* or very small to be more effective. In doing magic, the operator has learned to take a 'disinterested-interest' to the *nth* degree, to the 'eyes of a child'.

---

62 Tao te Ching…
63 Harmlessness is a major theme of Mahavira and Jainism.

Earlier it was said altruistic motivations <u>tend</u> to protect the operator from mistakes. However, these altruistic motivations must be comprehensive in scope (large T_P and T_K). Whereas, if the student has selfish motivations, their mistakes will bounce back...quite hard.

That is Karma. Because the mage is using the Eternal Moment of Creation and its time/space folding capabilities, the reflection of the operation (Karma) can be accelerated. The paybacks can be real tough.

If you do want to work with God's Logic, it would be quite helpful if you study other philosophies, religious thoughts, and viewpoints such as theosophy, world religion, shamanic lore, philosophy, and physics. As you program your own personal matrix with Absolute Truths, keeping an open perspective and being as all encompassing as possible,[64] your thought system should envelop – not exclude -- other thought systems.

Included with this idea, are things you cannot immediately understand; and yet, you are aware they are there. To know you do not know. It is imperative to maintain as a non-exclusive mind (Love) and as open a 'mind's eye'[65] as possible.

Studying other philosophies and thought systems can help you to program your own personal mind/matrix (increases T_P and T_K). It is mandatory that you, as a student of magic, have a single desire for union with God, the Universe, the Whole, or whatever (keeping D_S down). From the Source, all power comes. It is only when the mage is coming from the reference of God's Truth, will the operator be protected from any ~~truth~~. If you are going to be a mage, you have to go to God. <u>*Bottom line*</u>.

All metaphysical beings will recognize God. It is only within the physical form (the effect of a mis-creation), can the question of God's existence be called into question. All metaphysical beings: demons, angels, spirits, etc. must and will recognize the Source.

Another thing the person who wishes to do magic must recognize is the relationship between Man and the universe. Specifically, the axiom: "As with Man, so with the Universe. As with the Universe, so with man." Recognize that we are not separate parts of creation. Mankind and the whole Universe are mirror images of each other. Mankind is part of it. As we change one part inside of ourselves, it can change the Universe. That was covered earlier. The correction is set up to mirror the mind of Man, and so its reflections are affected by the mind of Man.

The more a mage starts thinking of him/her as a separate part of the creation, the less they will grow.[66] The more the operator has of a sense of unity and less ego, the more they will grow. He or she is growing into the whole.

The *Right Angle Rule* introduced in Chapter 3 is another form of this Love. It governs magic and everything else and is relevant to many of the paradoxes. An aspect of the *Right Angle Rule* appears when mystical student does not know where they are or where they going and they focus on taking care of their own perceptual desire systems, to making themselves whole. Then, God takes care of the rest. This is an example of not seeking God, but taking care of your internal growth. In taking care of internal growth, God comes to you. You attain by not seeking to attain.

In other words, the student is not striving to go to God outside. They are striving to realign themselves, and God will come from the inside. This is a form of *Right Angle Rule*. Instead of trying to go out, you do not. You just work on it inside, and the 'out' comes to you. When you start recognizing parallels, working with them to expand the horizons (horizontal), God will take care of growth (vertical). You are the axis.

One example of this is in advance meditation, a light forms in the head.[67] The light tends to show up while an individual is doing a blank or empty mind discipline for an extended time. The light just appears. If a student focuses on the light, the light will go away. However,

---

64 This allows T_P to become T_K in their matrix, thereby increasing effectiveness.
65 Chapter 4.7, The Human Matrix, *Lab #4*, Imagination Exercise
66 They have increased $\mathcal{F}_P$ and $\mathcal{F}_C$, while decreasing T_K, T_P, and T_C in the formula.
67 Chapter 6.4, Road Signs: *I-B-1-a*

if the individual recognizes the light and keeps focus on the discipline (ignoring the light), the light will start to increase -- changing and getting brighter. To maintain the light within the mind, a person cannot focus on the light itself. This is a form of the *Right Angle Rule*. "You can't go that way directly. You've got to go this way, to go that way."

It has been said that if you really want to know something, or to perceive it truly, then do not look at it directly. Look at it from an angle. Look at it with a kind of with your peripheral vision, your whole vision.[68]

You are looking with the whole vision of the mind's eye, the mind's peripheral vision. All perception is in the mind. We use the sense organs as tools to facilitate the process. However, the senses are only tools. The information they give is assembled in the mind.

Given the operator learns the *Law of Love* and starts working in these Absolutes on a consistent level, everything else will follow. The individual does not have to do much else. The Creation Matrix does everything. The postulate flow of direction goes from God, to Love, to everything else.

You should recognize there are Logical laws within Love. Recognize there is a greater reasoning present, and recognize that there are limits to your own mortal temporal mind (your reasoning). You may not see all the reasons, but know the reasoning is there.

Perceiving this, the magical operator learns to get out of mentation -- learns to stop thinking. Necessity dictates this.

And...a disinterested-interest, always. To have maximum effect with everything that you do, a disinterested-interest must be cultivated. You may have to go in what appears to be the opposite direction to where you think you have to go.

There are many miscellaneous rules that go with ritual magic: the *Law of Sympathy*, *The Law of Similarity*, the *Law of Resonance*, plus others. The serious student can find out what those are in their studies. They are extensions of the subject matter of this chapter.

In the end, the true mage becomes a synthesis to all mystical thought.

In conclusion, there is so much work and so many paradoxes involved with magic (Black, White, Gray, or Silver); one should consider carefully this discipline. There are 'dangers' and benefits.

---

68 This is part of a recognized exercise for learning to see auras.

9.10 - Questions

1. All power comes from _____.

2. Magic is defined as _____.

3. What are the five categories of magic, and what determines the categories?

4. How does the mage generate the love bond necessary to telepathically commune with the Matrix?

5. Ritual magic is used by _____.

6. What is The *Law of Power and Responsibility*?

7. What is the difference between **mundane** and **thaumaturgical** magic?

8. A mage has a _____ being.

9. The actual magical operation itself is easy as _____.

10. What are the four rules governing the study and use of magic?

11. A traditional prerequisite study or discipline to the practice of magic is _____.

Chapter 10

Concerning World Religions and Miracles

10.1 - A World Religion Overview

*I*n Chapter 9, a brief outline introduced common elements present in most religious and metaphysical thought systems. That outline is repeated here as a review and as an introduction to this chapter.

1) There is Deity or a holistic recognition with a subsequent thought construct or philosophy.

2) If there is no deity recognition, there is at least recognition of an unseen reality with a subsequent thought construct or philosophy.

3) Participation in this unseen reality is accomplished by:

    a) Assimilating or working with attributes or truths of the Deity, the whole, or unseen reality.[1]

    b) Relinquishing attachment to, questioning of, or rejecting the seen reality.[2]

    c) Doing both *a)* and *b)*.

4) In any successful spiritual quest, the last step will always be God's, The Eternal, The Infinite...

All major world mystic thought systems contain elements of this outline to some degree or another. Each has its own thought constructs or philosophies just as each mystic has an individual thought construct or philosophy. Each philosophy/construct is a mental picture generated by the mortal mind/minds that attempts to paint a picture of 'that' which is beyond the mortal mind.

Some have *3a* as their primary focus or way to approach the 'unknown'. While others, have *3b* as their primary focus. For these thought systems to work though, they all must use *3c* somewhat.

Every philosophy or thought construct (including this book) is an attempt to reduce the Eternal and Infinite God into a package that the mortal mind can understand. The 'package' consists of a matrix of symbols that represent an **Absolute** reality. Many working religious or

---

1 $\Uparrow$ numerator to ∞ (T_K, T_P, T_C and F) of Chapter 5 formula.

2 $\Downarrow$ denominator to 0 ($\mathcal{F}_K$, $\mathcal{F}_P$, $\mathcal{F}_C$, D_S, and A_S)

<u>mystical</u> thought systems recognize this concept and the limits of words; they recognize the limits of the 'packaging'.

The difference between popular religions (as perceived by non-mystics) and mystical thought systems is that most mystical thought systems point out the limits of the 'box' – the mortal mind. They encourage the individuals to 'explore outside the box'.

While, most common religion thought systems are an attempt to put you and God in boxes. They attempt to 'package' God for a 'quick sell'. Buried deep within that 'package' one might find a working mystical thought system at its core.

Because the Infinite Eternal Mind can contain infinities within infinities of mortal (temporal/spatial) minds, the variety of attributes of the 'packages' are many and at times appear conflicting. Any serious spiritual pilgrim would be well advised to learn the core basics of the many world religions (or the teachings at their origin), to learn the core concepts in some of these 'packages'.

Using some of their spiritual methods – their disciplines, you can expand your perceptions (increase T_P, T_K, and T_C consequently), decrease ~~truth~~ within you, customize the methods of your spiritual journey, and increase your internal coordination.

Each world religion (and religious thought system, group as well as individual) is equivalent to a facet on a multifaceted jewel. To begin with, each jewel facet is a *two*-dimensional plane on a *three*-dimensional object. Right off, this implies that each 'plane' is missing a dimension. (This is roughly parallel to the limits of words and human cultural perceptions as well as mortal – finite/temporal -- perceptions, in reference to an Eternal Infinite God)

With the jewel analogy, there is no way that any one facet – two-dimensional surface -- is going to express the intrinsic nature of the whole jewel (diamond, sapphire, ruby, etc.) – a three-dimensional object. When looking at a jewel, some facets are not immediately visible – those opposite from your eyes. You may only be aware of these other facets by looking deep inside the jewel to see the light being reflected or bent by them.

You can, though, turn the jewel over, look at the whole jewel, and appreciate the multitude of facets; and, how they compliment the intrinsic nature of the jewel. One can appreciate the beauty of the whole. With this chapter, we are going to look at some of the facets of God's jewel, plus put previous chapter material together so the beauty of the whole can be appreciated.

World religion's mysticism can be broken down into two basic types: Covenant and Non-Covenant religions. The Covenant is a contract. Covenant mysticism is based on a contract made between God and Man. The Judaic, Christian, and Islamic religions are based on a contract that God originally made to Abraham and then later was extended to all Mankind.

Each mystical thought system (Covenant and non-Covenant) is a describable facet on this Indescribable Jewel.[3]

First, the Non-Covenant religions and then there will be a thumbnail Bible story – the Covenant.

10.2 - Non-Covenant World Religions

$\mathcal{M}$ ost Covenant and Non-Covenant religions are based on some individual making a 'shamanic journey'. What is a 'shamanic journey'? Given in any society and culture, there are sets of truths/laws that the individuals within the society or culture recognize. Because that society is a gestalt of mortal minds -- limited, their cultural perception will be limited also.

The shamanic journey involves a person questioning of the way things are perceived to be and that individual stepping outside the cultural **Consensual** reality in a quest for knowledge, understanding, or self -- **Individual** reality or **Actual** reality. They do a 'walkabout'. This 'walkabout' may or may not involve a physical movement of the individual. Meaning, the

---

3 As a side note, most world religions (Covenant and non-Covenant) use the common tool of music or sound to facilitate a personal religious experience.

'walkabout' involves more of an internal quest than an external. There may be an external element to this 'walkabout' – a physical removal from an environment. However, there maybe a quest of spirit in whatever environment one finds oneself (without physically traveling).

When that person 'returns', the perception of an **Absolute** reality (or the perception of the speaker's **Individual** reality experience of the **Absolute**) must be translated into a **Consensual** reality condition. That message, in turn, must then be applied or translated to each listener's **Individual** reality.

In this 'walkabout', an individual achieves some understanding; a comprehensive idea or concept is reached. Then it is taken back into the culture and assimilated or integrated into the original culture. Eventually, this understanding may become an organized religion.

The Allegory of the Cave in Plato's Republic describes the shamanic journey. In the *Allegory of the Cave*, a man leaves a **Consensual** reality – the cave – on a quest.

Figure 10-1, Allegory of the Cave

The Allegory of the Cave has a cave with a fire in the back, shadow puppeteers, and a wall to hide the puppeteers (Figure 10-1). A group of people is watching a 'play' of shadows cast on the wall of a cave by the puppeteers. Their heads are loosely chained so that cannot look at anything but the shadow play. There are discussions and guesses about the nature and quality of the shadows.

A man, within the group, wonders about his surroundings, tries to turn his head, and finds chains restrict his head movement. Exploring further, he finds his chains lift right off his head. The man looks around and finds an exit. The way is dark so he gropes his way out. Working his way out of the cave, the light is getting brighter until he is outside and the light is so bright it blinds him and hurts his eyes. As his eyes get used to this light, he sees this paradise and wonders around him – this great Truth.

He decides to enter the cave and tell everyone about the paradise outside of the dark cave. Then, as he reenters the cave, the man becomes blind again. This time, because his eyes are not used to the dark.

The man gropes his way back into the cave with chained people watching the shadow play. The man, in his exuberance, tries to remove people's chains for them and found the people would fight to the death to keep their chains on.

The man could do nothing for the people except freely walk around among them, point out that they were wearing chains, and they could remove these chains at any time they wanted.

This is the shamanic journey 'in a nutshell'.

Early Man 'walkabouts' usually involved bringing back something in nature, like an animal, that represents the 'nature of things'. They brought back a totem that represented a specific concept. The totem served as a spiritual translating or teaching device.

Over time, totems become gods. As complex civilizations evolved, the deities took on a half-human half-animal appearance. The 'natural order' started to acquire human qualities. Eventually, these deities took on a human appearance (even including some human weaknesses).

Mankind's perception of the Divine took on anthropomorphic qualities – projected human qualities.

World religion 'walkabouts' usually start out with an individual having a revelation or a series of mystical experiences about the nature of 'reality'. The individual then tries to express what has been experienced to people who have no reference to this 'reality'. Which usually means the message must be 'translated'.

The 'message' generally loses something in the translation. The predominant reasons for this are:

♦ Words are totally inadequate to the subject matter.

♦ It is roughly equivalent to an electrician talking about impedances and currents to an English teacher. Most people just do not have the same frame of reference for a complete communication of the subject matter.

♦ Another hurdle the returning mystic must face is not being believed.

Ironically, if the questor is bringing eternal truths that have never changed -- they have always been present, most people do not want to hear about it. The truth interferes too much with people's illusions and delusions. They do not want to hear it. [4]

Here begins the Bodhisattva's tears.

Another problem studying established religions arises. Because of the nature of the individual's source and where the individual is returning to -- the culture, many times the returning mystic communicates the information in culturally based – a **Consensual** reality -- allegories or parables.

Accordingly, over time, some of the original material is lost or becomes changed. Because, cultures change. Usually, the Divine starts taking on anthropomorphic characteristics (act or appear as human), again. [5] This multitude of translations or interpretations is another contributing reason that there are differences in philosophies around The Divine, even in the same religion.

---

4 " If I told you what it takes to reach the highest highs,
You'd laugh and say nothing is that simple.
And you've been told many times before
Messiahs pointed to the door,
And no one had the guts to leave the temple.
I'm free."
 (From the rock opera *Tommy* by The Who)
5 Example: Giving anthropomorphic gender references (sex) to God. The idea of sex related to the core of all physical creation, is non-sequitar. It is like giving sexual attributes to gravity.

The result is; that two hundred years after the original event, no established world religion bore any resemblance to that original event. Not one! God/Divine became altered and 'packaged' for the people.

Here is another major factor why many creeds between cultures and established world religions have a hard time agreeing. Most of their arguments are over the 'packaging'; which facet of the jewel is the jewel.

As stated previously, the people who have a mystical experience have to translate it into the perception of the culture that is being addressed; thereby, giving the experience to the culture. This gives the culture a 'handle' or reference to the nature of the 'Divine'.

God, being Love, will use whatever is given. This applies to whole cultures as well as the individual. If a culture's philosophy or mental construct is given to God, then that is what God will use to 'speak' to the people (which may involve a *4* event from the outline in the beginning of this chapter).

To understand the material *I AM A I* has presented and how it relates to the Non-Covenant religions, this chapter will review Chapter 1.4 - Pythagoras and the Pythagorean Schools – the Axial Age.[6] Remember; this is the 100-year period where the foundations of today's civilization were laid.

They will be cross-referenced to the previous spiritual outline.

❑ **Buddhism** → stresses the relationship between desire and suffering; remove desire and you remove suffering, *3b*. Established Buddhism works from the Four Noble Truths and the Eight-fold Path. These stress non-attachment and ridding oneself of desire and illusion. This references to information presented throughout *I AM A I* 's Chapters 4-9 -- a decrease of D_S, A_S, $\bcancel{T}_P$, and $\bcancel{T}_K$ -- with an attempt to increase T_P, and T_K.

❑ **Jainism** → primary tenet is absolute harmlessness. This relates directly to Chapter 9 and the need for the mage to become absolutely harmless to learn absolute power. This can also be related to *3b* and *3a* → *3c*.

❑ The **Bhagavad Gita** → has been referred to throughout this book and it communicates about what ever you have to do; do it to be in union with God -- with non-attachment to the outcome. Only this is karma-less. (Keeping D_S down and having only one D_{Tp} – God; while eliminating A_S; $[A_S \Rightarrow 0]$. This also reduces the ~~truth~~ being reflected back to you through the Mirror function – Chapter 5). This is predominately *3b* orientated.

❑ **Upanishads** → presents a multitude of mystical information – about the Oneness. It contains stresses on deep meditation (which reduces ~~truth~~ and cultivates an internal experience) -- Chapter 6, *3b* and some *3a* → *3c*.

❑ The **Tao te Ching**[7] → has been referred to throughout *I AM A I*. Like the *Upanishads*, it also presents a multitude of mystical information. Some consider it more lyrical than the *Upanishads*. It expresses mystical concepts through daily events or ideas. The universal concepts of the *Tao te Ching* (though there is little to no official Taoism now) are applied today throughout a multitude of world religion contemplatives.[8] Zen (an offshoot of Taoism) is involved with the meaninglessness of thought and slipping between the spaces of thought – Chapters 4 and 6; again predominately *3a* orientated and has some *3b* → *3c*.

❑ **Zoroaster's** → creation's apparent duality (and its nature) has been touched upon in Chapter 9, Concerning Magic. The manipulation of this duality is predominately *3a* oriented.

❑ **Second Isaiah** → Covenant orientated and is mentioned later this chapter. Most Covenant religions are *3a* orientated ("Be ye perfect..."). Most mystical Covenant schools also promote *3b*, which means *3c* is an element again.

---

6 Ignoring the one relatively non-spiritual reference -- Confucius

7 One of the few recommended books

8 Catholic contemplatives – monks – substitute the word *Way* with the word *Christ* and call the *Tao te Ching* 'the book'.

❑ **Pythagoras** → and Pythagorean thinking was introduced and used throughout *I AM A I*. The book is using math reasoning and relating it to the Divine. This is predominately **3a** orientated.

Just as *ESP* information becomes clothed by the mind that receives it,[9] so does Divine information become clothed by the culture receiving it?

Numerous Non-Covenant eastern mystical schools tend to focus primarily on **3b** of the outline. Many of these eastern religions have the mechanics of the **3b** down cold. While, **3a** may be a secondary focus. Most of these schools tend to center on the relinquishment, or being rid of, perceived attributes of the perceived **Actual**, **Individual**, and **Consensual** realties – the 'seen' reality.

10.3 - The Covenant

*T*he Covenant is a contract between a God and Man[10]. The God of the Covenant was known at the time of the Covenant's instigation as the Nameless One or the Nameless Desert God. Originally, the Covenant was with a single individual – Abraham -- and his progeny, his children's children's children... Later the Covenant was extended to all of Mankind. From this contract comes Judaism, Christianity, and Islam.

The Covenant is a two-sided contract with God; meaning God took an active posture in the agreement. Judaism, Christianity, and Islam add a depth to the relationship between the Creator and Man, beyond just the 'mechanics' of the situation.

This is not saying the other religions do not have the depth. What is being said is there is something slightly different here or the 'accent' is in a slightly different direction. With the Covenant, it appears a God takes a more active interest or participates more in the affairs of Man.

What is the Covenant and how did it come about? Abraham was a nomad with an extended family of people with him. In the times of the nomadic Abraham, there were cities with religious temples. Many of these temples had elaborate pantheons of gods and goddesses. It was the accepted practice at the time to give a god an offering in exchange for some desire. "God of _____, I will give you _____, if give me _____!" They would try to bargain with what they perceived to be divinity to obtain a specific desire.

God speaks through the language of the culture, so this is how Abraham was approached. One day the Nameless Desert God addressed Abraham through an intermediary named Melchizedek,[11] a priest-king; and a contract was made.

So right off, with the Covenant idea, instead of a man doing a 'walkabout' in the wilderness to find God, the Covenant involves a God coming out of the wilderness to talk to a man. In addition to this, instead of "God of _____, I will give you _____, if give me _____", the Covenant involves a God saying, "Abraham, have I got a deal for you".
The Judaic religion is the only contract religion in the world.

The essence of the contract was, "Abraham, if you worship me and follow my laws; I will take care of your children's, children's, children, as long as they follow my laws."

Covenant mysticism tends to have **3a** of the outline as its primary focus. While, **3b** is its secondary. The reason being, it involves following a set of laws/truths is an attempt to align with the law's truth matrix.

A large number of people are familiar with some aspect of Abraham and his progeny through the bible. And...what about God's intermediary in the Covenant, the priest-king Melchizedek? What is a priest-king (or priestess/queen)?

---

9 Chapters 4 and 7
10 Mankind
11 The 'Nameless and Formless' must have a form to bargain from.

♦   A priest (or priestess) serves as an intermediary between the Divine and the secular. They 'serve' God to the people; they act as a go-between. A priest-king is his own intermediary to the Divine.

♦   A king is one who rules. One who conquers or governs. A priest-king is one who has conquered himself; one who governs and rules their being.

♦   Therefore, a priest-king – priestess-queen -- is one who serves as his or her own intermediary to God and who has conquered their self.

Very little is known about Melchizedek. It is a relatively safe assumption that most of Abraham's s dialogs with God's angel were dialogs with Melchizedek. In addition, it is relatively safe assumption that Melchizedek went to Sodom and Gomorrah.

Sodom and Gomorrah served two functions in the Covenant.

❑   One function was to explain some 'rules' to Abraham; do not do what these people do – a *3b* concept.

❑   In addition, it drove home a point to Abraham; the absolute nature of Who he just made a 'deal' with. "I am God!"[12]

Melchizedek is referred to once more, later in the bible.

Here is a very condensed biblical version of what followed the 'deal' made with Abraham:

⇒   In terms of Abraham's children, Abraham had two sons. One son was from his wife, Sara -- Isaac. Another son was from Sara's maid, Hagar – Ishmael. Ishmael was born first. (Sara was technically past childbearing years and wanted Abraham to have progeny. Therefore, she had Hagar bear Abraham a son. Later, Sara became pregnant.)

It appears Isaac may have been a disciplinary problem. (Perhaps from being spoiled?) Because of tensions, Hagar and Ishmael – Abraham's first-born blood -- were expelled from this extended family and they leave the bible.

They are brought back and referenced to by Mohammed.

⇒   Isaac had two fraternal twin sons, Esau and Jacob. Esau, who was born first, appears to be the brawn of the two; while Jacob, appears to be the brains. To make a long story short: Jacob – a trickster in the bible -- fools Isaac and Esau into giving Jacob the mantle of the Covenant, birthright.

Jacob repents, changes his name to Israel, has twelve sons, and here begins the Twelve Tribes of Israel.

Like Ishmael, Esau leaves the bible and is also later brought back and referenced to by Mohammed.

⇒   Israel's sons having a 'falling out' and one is sold into slavery, Joseph. Over a number of years and after a series of tribulations, Joseph ends up with a 'cushy' government job in Egypt.

A famine occurs; Israel's sons go to Egypt to get some seed grain, finds Joseph, and eventually the whole family moves to Egypt. ("And...they lived happily ever after!")

⇒   In the womb of Egypt, this family became a hoard. The family group was divided by which of Israel's sons they could trace their ancestry to -- their tribe.

The first couple of hundred years the group had an easy time of it. Several hundred years later (as the group swelled in numbers), Abraham's progeny became a significant minority in Egypt, and suffered persecution.

---

12 God always speaks through the language of the culture. Part of the language of this region is violence (even to this day). This may explain the <u>apparent</u> violent nature of a Loving God.

One main reason is the Egyptians recognized numerous gods including the 'Nameless One', but the Israelites did not recognize any gods but their own.

Enter Moses.

$\Rightarrow$ With Moses, a number of major events or changes occurred with this family group. Moses does his first 'walkabout', comes back, acts as a midwife, and Judaism along with the nation of Israel is born.

One of the most significant things about Moses' first 'walkabout' is; when he came back, he came back with a name for the God of the Covenant – a name for the 'Nameless One'. The 'Nameless One' now has a name, *I Am*.

"Who shall I say sent me?
I Am.[13] That *I Am* sent you."

Later, people took the letters of *I Am That Am* (*JHVH*[14]), added the vowels of *Adonai* (Lord), and the name *Jehovah* is introduced.[15]

This group leaves Egypt, and a diverse group converges in one spot. Moses does his second 'walkabout', and comes back with a codified set of rules for the Covenant – the Ten Commandments.[16] In addition, with this codified set of rules, the Hebrew alphabet is introduced.[17] Moses also 'writes'/introduces five books. These books serve as guidelines that Judaism is based on.[18]

After some sever purging, the group/nation wanders around for forty years and consequently becomes a very tight-knit group.

$\Rightarrow$ The group was promised their own land by God. Joshua of Nun leads the group out of the nomadic state by grabbing some land, killing the previous owners, and the nomadic nation of Israel is on the map and enters an agricultural era.

$\Rightarrow$ A spiritual commune, of sorts, develops. There is no ruler like a king or emperor. God -- *I Am* -- was their ruler and their king. God's 'mouthpieces' were called Prophets.[19]

In terms of secular matters, when the time of leadership was needed or just to settle civil affairs, Judges were appointed.

This continued through numerous generations. Eventually, they started to look around at the neighbors. Abraham's progeny were surrounded by nations who had kings or rulers – central governments. The perceived advantages of a central government were public buildings, roads, public works, etc. After a while, the Hebrew people seeing other people had a king and not to be upstaged by the 'Joneses', asked God's prophet (Samuel) for a king.

Samuel's response was (paraphrased), Why do you want a king? A king will take your land, your money, your crops, your wife, your children, your freedom, and your life. I will do it; and…you'll be sorry!

$\Rightarrow$ So the prophet Samuel picked the biggest guy he could find and made him king, Saul.[20] Meanwhile, a shepherd who wrote songs to God and practiced with a sling[21] while watching sheep becomes a war hero.

---

13 Punctuation is the author's
14 Known as the Tetragrammaton in magic.
15 It was a stoning offense to say God's name -- heresy, but one could say *Jehovah*.
16 At this time, there still were no 'rules' written done for the Covenant.
17 Written by the 'finger of God'.
18 The Kabbalah in Chapter 9 is one of these books.
19 The 'works' measured the authenticity of a prophet as their words were validated by real events.
20 Mr. Big → a big guy?
21 To discourage predators.

History portrays Saul as not being very bright and he had made a series of bad decisions. Saul is rejected and the war hero is made king – David. David's songs (the Psalms) become part of the group's worship.

David is rejected as king over time due to his perchance for violence and carousing around. Eventually, David's son Solomon is picked as king. Solomon gives the people buildings and a Temple, which is what they originally wanted. Eventually, Solomon's works almost bankrupt the country..

⇒ As Samuel prophesied, the situation went downhill very quickly in time. To such an extent that kings were killing prophets. The prophets went 'underground'.

Many scholars recognize that two maybe three people wrote the book of Isaiah. It is the 2nd Isaiah[22] (a prophet – God's mouthpiece) that rejects the 'king system' and says (paraphrased): Okay, if you want a king, I (God) will give you a king. Your king will come in the tradition of the priest-king Melchizedek.[23]

Here begins the prophecies for Jesus and Christianity begins. A promise from God is made in the Covenant.

⇒ Essentially, Jesus lived a 'script' many people wrote over a period of hundreds of years. Even to the 22nd Psalm that he initiated while on the cross.[24]

There were a number of conditions Jesus had to meet to be the 'king' prophesied. Some of these conditions were to be killed and resurrected. Jesus could improvise around these conditions, and he could not avoid them.

Since Moses' time, the laws and rules of the Covenant went from the Ten Commandments to a vast tome of rules of 'dos' and 'don'ts'. One of the things Jesus did was reduce the Covenant's rules to two:

♦ Love God with your entire mind, entire heart, and entire soul.
♦ Do onto others as would have them do to you (extend this love).

This simplified things greatly.

Another thing that Jesus did was extend the Covenant beyond Abraham's descendants. The Covenant was not just for "the Children of Abraham" any more; it was for gentiles also. The Covenant was extended to all Mankind – Man. Anybody could embrace the Covenant.

In addition, dying the way he did (a priest-king with Love in his heart), Jesus left a metaphysical/mystical door open for all to follow. This 'mystical door' is at the core of most mystical Christianity. Leaving that door of Love open, changed things in the development of the relationship between the Creator and Mankind, as we perceive ourselves.

There is a metaphysical detail involving the conditions surrounding Jesus' death that is not commonly known.

Know it is impossible to kill a realized Child of God -- a priest-king -- without his/her permission. Because of their connection/communion with the One Mind, he/she can see if the death is what the culture needs to see or experience -- part of God's Story.

If it is not, he/she will not be there for the perpetrators. He/she can 'sidestep' the situation before it reaches them. If he/she sees that the death is necessary for the whole, he/she will walk into the situation fully knowing what is going to happen. When that person does this, one of two things can happen.

---

22 Axial Age

23 This is the only other place in the bible that Melchizedek is mentioned.

24 In Jesus' time, the rabbi would sing the first line of a psalm and the congregation would sing the rest. The first line of the 22nd psalm begins with, "My God, my God, why has thou forsaken me?" This psalm sings about the same things that were happening to Jesus at the time of his crucifixion (limbs being pulled from their sockets, life leaking out of his side, at the singer's feet the gambling for his clothes).

♦ If there is a sufficient block of time between the deathblow and the death itself, the Child *will* forgive them, as Jesus did. He even led his followers into a religious service (with the 22nd Psalm).

♦ If there is not a sufficient block of time between the deathblow and the death itself for forgiveness to occur, Creation will rise up against all responsible for such an act.

In other words, the act of murder directed toward God would cause the Mirror to reflect the act back on the perpetrators and <u>any</u> that helped facilitate the event.

This means <u>everybody</u>; the person who cooked the guards' breakfast or made their sandals, all the people in the governments – Rome and Judea, the carpenter who fashioned the timbers, the woodcutter who felled the tree, the people who made the road, the fisherman or baker that helped feed these people, etc.

This was starting to happen during the crucifixion; the sky turned dark and the ground started to shake. Then Jesus forgave and it subsided. If the deathblow to Jesus had been instantaneous, to say the shaking ground was just a prelude would be a gross understatement. Physical form itself – the Mirror -- would rise up against the 'act' and <u>anybody</u> that contributed to the act in <u>any</u> way.[25]

This is something that you could not escape; nor would you want to be around to see.

❑ Last but not least in the Covenant is Mohammed. Mohammed claimed to be in the line of prophets that contained Moses and Jesus. His claim was he was of the Covenant and for the children of Ishmael and Esau.

Islam teaches people to remember God throughout the day (Call to Prayer).

One of the reasons the Covenant must be looked at is its comprehensive nature. With Jesus, the Covenant changed as well as, who it applied to. Some examples are:

♦ Given: the two rules of the Covenant given by Jesus.
- Love God with your entire mind, entire heart, and entire soul.
- Do onto others as would have them do to you (extend this love).
♦ Given: there is only One Love.[26]
♦ Given: Jesus said, "Those who are not against me are with me."[27] (speaking as God's mouthpiece – prophet)

❖ Then: If you believe in a Loving Deity and you are not against the Covenant and you follow the two above rules, you are under the auspices of the Covenant whether you believe in the Covenant or not.

This illustrates how comprehensive the Covenant has become and how it is beyond most contemporary Judaic, Christian, and Islamic religious thought. Many of these exclusive religious sects underestimate God's Love with their exclusiveness.

Basically, the bible is a record of how God kept His side of the Covenant and how many of Abraham's descendants 'blew' theirs.

While in some of the stories, there is encouragement. A number of people in the bible kept their side of the Covenant; and consequently, God backed them.

There is one other thing in the bible to look at, the Creation myth in the book of Genesis. The Garden of Eden story has many different ways of being viewed. Here are two examples:

---

25 There is a story about a woman falsely accusing the Buddha of fostering her child. In the story, the ground opens up and swallows her.
26 Chapter 2, Postulates and Theorems
27 This is in two of the gospels. Jesus' followers wanted to beat and drive out somebody who was doing what Jesus was doing; but for a different God. Jesus' response was this statement.

❑ In the bible, it says God saw Adam was lonely and put Adam in a deep sleep, and…the bible never says anything equivalent to God woke Adam up. Assuming, he was not woken up; in this sleep, Adam – the Divine Androgyny -- dreamed he was split into two complimentary parts – two sexes. In his dream, he becomes a multitude and he dreams of being separated from God.[28] We all know dreams are not real. Adam's dream is not also.

With this Cosmic Dream idea, Covenant mysticism can border on Non-Covenant mysticism – the illusion of form. In addition, the argument of one life or reincarnation becomes moot. It does not matter if one life or many are dreamt. It is still a part of the dream.

❑ An ironic aspect about this creation myth is the role of the serpent. In this story, Lucifer takes the 'guise' of a serpent.[29] In many early man cultures, including Judaism, the serpent was the symbol of wisdom. Therefore, when Lucifer took the 'guise' of a serpent, he used the disguise of wisdom to tempt Eve to eat the fruit from the "tree of knowledge of good and evil". The choice to eat (live by) the knowledge of good and evil becomes the *first* judgment led on by an apparent wisdom.

What happened to the serpent/wisdom? The serpent/wisdom became 'cursed' and sentenced to moving along on its stomach at a crawl. Whenever the serpent/wisdom would raise his head, man would "crush him beneath his heal".

Things like Socrates given a cup of hemlock, Jesus nailed to a 'tree', and Gandhi gets a bullet for his work, etc.; tend to substantiate this idea.

Relating the Covenant to the jewel idea in the beginning of this chapter, the Covenant is like a special cut on top of the jewel. Covenant religions have some of the same issues as Non-Covenant religions. However, instead of like many religions being an observation of nature, the individual, or reality, the Covenant illustrates how the Divine can take on an active and interactive connection to the human condition.

10.4 - Miracles

*M*iracles are the highest form of mysticism – advanced metaphysics. The first miracle was Creation, the extension of God's Love. All other miracles are a variation of that first – are born of the Precious Moment of Creation, God's Love. They extend God either into form, or into the mind of the perceiver, or both.

The defining place where Gold magic of the previous chapter leaves off and miracles start is somewhat blurred. The major difference between the two is long-term intent of the operator. The miracle worker tends to be devoted to God more than a gold mage, and is more selfless. Miracle workers work from moment to moment in God. They are less concerned with long-term goals and are more concerned with doing God's work in the moment.

Where Gold magic ends, miracles begin. Or, more precisely, all Gold magic can be considered a miracle. However, not all miracles can be considered Gold magic. Miracles transcend all magic categories. The operator is not working with the perception/desire sets that are associated with Black, White, Gray, or Silver magic.

As with everything, the power of miracles stems from the Precious Moment of Eternal Creation – all power comes from God. The Eternal Moment of Creation *is/was/will be* the first miracle. Unlike most mages, the miracle worker's points of tangency within their matrix (which taps that power) are more stable. The gold mage may not always have their internal matrix in alignment to God for the 'work' to happen.

Whereas, because the miracle worker's matrix is more focused-on/aligned-with God, there is less conscious direction (and effort). The Eternal Moment of Creation flows through them automatically; and, the Mirror reflects this around them. Of course, all of this is according to what Love 'sees' is needed at that moment.

---

28 See Chapter 2.8, *Postulate 7*

29 A disguise, meaning; Lucifer and the serpent are not the same being.

Miracles are not the monopoly of any religion or group of saints. Saints of a multitude of religions have been doing such works all over the world and all through time.

Remember the Mirror. The Correction function of the Mirror is to reflect mistaken thinking back on itself. Though it is fueled by Love, it is totally neutral. It just reflects, for the sole purpose of the thinker to turn thinking and choices to God. With the analogy of the Mirror, physical[30] and temporal forms are perceived. Physical form is an effect of the Mirror. The Mirror is linked with the perceptions and desires of the perceiver, be it one person or a culture.

A person at one with God has the truest perception there can be. Truest perception meaning they see, that which is behind the form, rather than just the form. They perceive God and the Spirit/Truth underlying the form. The Mirror is neutral. This true perception, just as with the non-mystic's ~~true~~ perception, is also reflected back by the Mirror.

An example of how this may appear to a non-mystic is say, you walk out into a garden, and you see some roses. You see this beauty within nature from the roses in this garden and you have this quiet appreciation. Then, an individual who is at one – at-oned[31] -- with God comes into the same garden. As your bubble of temporal/spatial reference interacts with the mystic's bubble of temporal/spatial reference, those forms around you will reflect the mystic's *truer* perception.

Therefore, your perception may jump from just seeing the beauty of the garden to seeing something equivalent to the presence of Eden or Heaven everywhere. Because you are influenced by the bubble of temporal/spatial reference of a person who sees that in their mind, the form reflects this back and you happen to experience/perceive it also. Your physical existence is also part of the Mirror.

People see wonders around them; and from God's or the saint's reference point, it is only natural. If you walk into the influence of someone whose mind is on God, you end up walking into this reflection of the Loving Mind of God.

This is how it works with the saints. They do not seek to achieve anything. Things change around them. They do not see a need; Love's Mind fills any perceived need brought into their *BTR*, without individual effort on their part.

There are many examples of this kind of operation; one is the Buddha and the grove story. Another example occurred with the Christian St. Romuald after his death.[32] When Romuald was dug up from the grave (to be reburied in a newly constructed chapel) five years after his death, he was not decayed. The saint is not even alive, and yet there is no effort. His body appeared as it was when it was first laid in the ground, five years later.

This is very common with saints. They lived in a life they saw as Eternal, so when they die, their bodies -- which reflect what they saw -- take on Eternal attributes.

Another more recent example of this comes from India. It was reported when Paramahansa Yogananda died, his body lay in state for view for 21 days in tropical India. After that 21 days, his body had scientists stumped, because there was not one sign of corruption. It did not even start to rot. This illustrates how miracles are not just Christian manifestations.

This common theme has been repeated with saints everywhere. It is because the perception system of the individual, the saint, did not see or recognize corruption/destruction. Since the physical form reflects his or her mind, when they are gone, their form -- the only form left of them (body) -- reflects that Eternal beauty, that Eternal moment. It is influenced by that Eternal moment and does not rot.

10.5 - *A Course in Miracles*©

All through this book, the many limits of language have been expressed, specially concerning mystical/metaphysical subject matter. When entering metaphysics to the depth of miracles, language becomes totally inadequate. With miracles -- metaphysically --

---

30 And non-physical temporal forms being thoughts, emotions, desires, etc.
31 Atoned
32 First millennium *AD*, was the founder of the Camaldolese monastic order, and…who lived to be *150* years old.

you do them; you do not talk about them.

Since there is a book that instructs on this subject matter already, *A Course in Miracles*[33], this author is going to quit while ahead (take the easy way out). This 'course' has been referred to periodically throughout *I AM A I*.

How did *A Course in Miracles* come about? Two professors of medical psychology at Columbia University (Helen Schuman and William Thetford) united and started looking for 'a better way' in their profession. Helen started to have dreams and after three months, William suggested writing the images and dreams down. The very first thing she wrote was the Introduction to *A Course in Miracles*.

Unlike automatic writing, she could stop at any time; and when she started again, she would start where she left off.

Because of *ACIM's* physical authors — how the information was 'clothed', the book is laced with perceptual psychology.

First *ACIM's* Introduction will be cross-reference to *I AM A I's* material. Then, the first section of the first chapter of *ACIM* will be introduced. The rest of this chapter will cross-reference the information presented in *ACIM* to the information presented previously in *I AM A I*. Essentially, where *I AM A I* ends, *A Course in Miracles* begins.

The *ACIM* introduction and the first thing Helen wrote is:

Introduction

1.)   This is a course in miracles. It is a required course.

Only the time you take it is voluntary. Free will does not mean that you can establish the curriculum. It means only that you can elect what you want to take at a given time.

2.)   The course does not aim at teaching the meaning of love, for that is beyond what can be taught. It does aim, however, at removing the blocks to the awareness of love's presence, which is your natural inheritance.

The opposite of love is fear, but what is all encompassing can have no opposite.

3.)   This course can therefore be summed up very simply in this way:

Nothing real can be threatened.

Nothing unreal exists.

Herein lies the peace of God.

Commentary…Introduction

1.) Chapter 3 in this book states that God's inclusive Love insures *everything* is inside a closed system.

- Given: *Everything* is inside a closed system.
- Given: The Correction -- from God -- is aimed at Creation to turn its mind totally to God.
- Given: All power comes from God.
- Then: The outcome of the Correction is not in question. It will happen because it has the Infinite Eternal Power of God behind it. It is only a question of 'time'.

This is why material in *ACIM* is a required course. You will choose God in the end just because you will be tired of being a masochist. You will be tired of being separated from God.

---

33 The ideas represented herein are the personal interpretation of the author and are not necessarily endorsed by the copyright holder of *A Course in Miracle*®.

It may take one lifetime or a thousand, but the end result will be the same from an Eternal reference. And…from the Eternal reference, your choice has already happened.

2.) The non-exclusiveness of Love means there can be no opposite of it. Make something that is 'not-love' and Love will not exclude it; it becomes a part of Love.

There is no place, where Love is not. To work with love, you have to love. You do not talk about something beyond words; you do it and demonstrate it – apply it. This can relate to Chapter 4 -- how choice or application of the lens produces change in the individual's matrix. "Removing the blocks" can relate to **3b** of the outline in this chapter's beginning.

3.) This statement is implied in the postulates and theorems of Chapter 2. This paragraph also can be referenced to the duality delusion of *Theorem 26A*[34] and related to the prologue of the book, the Lotus Sutra.[35]

In addition, this something mentioned throughout this book. God's Truth cannot be affected in any way.

A Course in Miracles is a learning device – a tool, the same as *I AM A I*. *A Course in Miracles* has three major parts: a Text presents paradigm –a thought construct, a Student Workbook with 365 lessons -- applications, and a short Manual for Teachers.

I AM A I teaches that Truth works when applied independent of belief. The Student workbook, in which you do a lesson a day for a year, also can have an effect. You do not have to read the Text. You can pick up *ACIM's* paradigm while applying its truths from the workbook. *ACIM* works on the application of these truths on a daily basis. When applied, these truth applications will have an effect. Especially the early exercises, which have you question your current personal paradigm.

Be advised that *ACIM* has a definite Covenant orientation; the first person tense that is in *ACIM* implies Jesus is speaking. Yet, in the *Manual for Teachers* in the definition of terms, Jesus -- Christ, the text starts with, "There is no need for help to enter Heaven for you never left".

This is a contradiction to most fundamental Christian thought.

Next, the first chapter of *ACIM* (Meaning of Miracles) will be cross-referenced to the information that has been presented in *I AM A I*.

1.   There is no order of difficulty in miracles. One is not "harder" or "bigger" than another. They are all the same. All expressions of love are maximal.

Commentary…1

Since all miracles come from the first and only miracle -- Creation[36], of course there is no order of difficulty. All springs from the Eternal Moment of Creation and have the Infinite and Eternal power of God behind them. A perception of order of difficulty is just that, a perception, no more.[37]

Of course, all expressions of Love are maximal; from Absolute Love, to Absolute Logic, to Creation, and from Creation comes *everything* else.[38] It is impossible to do more than that.

---

34 The mis-creation has generated an unreal duality within Creation. or The duality does not exist. or The mis-creation has generated a delusion of duality within Creation.

35 "The mind has nothing to do with thinking because its fundamental source is empty. To discard false views, this is the great causal event."

36 Chapter 2, Postulates and Theorems

37 Chapter 4.3 - Limits of the Perceptual Window

38 *Postulates 2-5* and related theorems

This statement also relates to Chapter 9.8, Concerning the Operation. In that chapter, it talks about the magical mystical operation being as easy as moving an arm; Love's Truth Matrix does the work.

---

2.   Miracles as such do not matter. The only thing that matters is their Source, which is far beyond evaluation.

Commentary...2

Our perception of miracles is related to temporal form. From the Eternal reference, temporal form does not exist.[39] It does not matter. "Matter doesn't matter." God is the only important thing.

This statement relates to **Absolute** Reality[40] being the only reality. God is the only important thing here. Any evaluation made be a mortal mind/matrix towards God is going to 'fall short' of being complete; it will be missing a 'dimension'.[41]

---

3.   Miracles occur naturally as expressions of love. The real miracle is the love that inspires them. In this sense, everything that comes from love is a miracle.

Commentary...3

In *I AM A I*'s commentary of the first article (*Statement 1*) of the first chapter of *ACIM*, the commentary mentions the Eternal Moment of Creation is the first and only miracle. Chapter 2 of *I AM A I* states our ability to create is due to our participation in this Eternal Creation process.

Miracles flow out of the Truth Matrix, which is, in itself, an effect of Love (Chapter 2). Miracles, which are a true expression of the Eternal Moment of Creation within us, are an expression of this Love.

---

4.   All miracles mean life, and God is the Giver of life. His Voice will direct you very specifically. You will be told all you need to know.

Commentary...4

Life, the fifth interaction of physics, is a temporal effect of the eternal Creation Matrix...God.[42]

Consistent choices to choose God will open intuition and psychic facilities.[43] As an individual reprograms their matrix (along the greater Matrix lines), intuition/communion will tell the individual what is *right* and *true*.

---

5.   Miracles are habits, and should be involuntary. They should not be under conscious control. Consciously selected miracles can be misguided.

---

39 Theorems 21-23
40 Chapter 4.2, "What's Reality, Papa?"
41 Beginning of this chapter and the jewel analogy
42 Chapters 3 and 9
43 Chapter 7, Concerning *ESP* Events and Psychic Phenomenon

Commentary...5

Chapter 9 mentions the use of Gold magic having the same qualities of spontaneity and being without effort. When miracles are consciously selected, they tend to degrade from Miracles or Gold to Silver magic. Perceptions – other intentions -- other than the original true perception can be injected into the operation.

Chapters 4, 6, 7, and 9 use circles to illustrate points of tangency and how these tangency points can change within the being. The miracle worker's tangency points are more stable than a mage's through long-term practice and consequently effects tend to occur without conscious effort.

---

6.   Miracles are natural. When they do not occur, something has gone wrong.

Commentary...6

Chapter 7 says this of *ESP* and telepathy, which is the medium of miracles and magic. Miracles events flow Eternally from the Truth Matrix. If they are not happening, then Love's Logic -- Truth Matrix -- is not being truly used as God uses it – naturally. Something is blocking the 'flow'.

---

7.   Miracles are everyone's right, but purification is necessary first.

Commentary...7

As with number *statement 5*, the individual's mind/matrix must align to Truth. In addition, Chapters 4, 5, and 9 introduce the idea of how many working spiritual disciplines have a period of purification in common. They may have different philosophies; and, they are asking the individual to do the same things.

This purification usually involves a period of reducing ~~truth~~ within one's mortal mind/matrix. This may involve some *3b* of the outline in the beginning of this chapter. These previous chapters go on to say how the reduction of ~~truth~~ allows room for truth within a mortal mind/matrix.

In terms of miracles being everybody's right, of course, they are everybody's right; everybody has the Eternal Moment of Creation within them – you are God's Creation.

---

8.   Miracles are healing because they supply a lack; they are performed by those who
            temporarily have more for those who temporarily have less.

Commentary...8

The first part of this statement is in reference to a <u>perceived</u> lack, a perceived separation from God. They are healing, for they correct that perception.

How does one acquire (have) that which is inherent within one? Words can cloud as well as clarify. The second part of this statement may be more accurate if the words *temporarily remember* is substituted for the words *temporarily have* and *temporarily forgotten* for *temporarily have less*.

We all have the Eternal Moment of Creation with us. It is just that some remember and work with it and others have forgotten.

---

9.   Miracles are a kind of exchange. Like all expressions of love, which are always miraculous in the true sense, the exchange reverses the physical laws. They bring more love both to the giver and the receiver.

Commentary…9

The reference to physical laws in this sense would be a reference to the law of conservation of energy, which Chapter 3 has already introduced as having some 'glitches' (Coulomb's Law and quantum electrodynamics). *I AM A I* teaches that the physical laws are just a 'special case' of a metaphysical condition.

Working with Love is working with the whole; working as a whole team, so to speak. Look at it as the 'Universal Team'. As with teamwork, the more the team works together, the better the team and the individuals in the team become.

---

10.   The use of miracles as spectacles to induce belief is a misunderstanding of their purpose.

Commentary…10

This statement can also relate to *statement 5*. Personal belief in God comes from personal choice (the Mirror helps facilitates this). It involves the personal relationship between you and your Creator – your personal religion.

An attempt to induce personal belief first implies a perception of lack. To do miracles to induce belief is an attempt to 'correct' this 'lack', which means the operation is White or Silver magic and not of the miracle category.

To use miracles as 'special effects' to cause belief, is equivalent to winning an argument through proof. Argument is a form of conflict and is not a loving way to work. You are attempting to change someone instead of them changing themselves.

And…even though your argument may be impeccable or without flaw, it still does not mean someone will believe you.

---

11.   Prayer is the medium of miracles. It is a means of communication of the created with the Creator. Through prayer love is received, and through miracles love is expressed.

Commentary…11

Chapter 6 relates how prayers are the heart songs to your Creator. This statement refers to a song that is a form of communication or a communion, using the telepathic love bond of Chapter 7 as it was intended.

Love is expressed by miracles; miracles are an effect of the Creation Matrix, which is an expression of Absolute Love.

---

12.   Miracles are thoughts. Thoughts can represent the lower or bodily level of experience, or the higher or spiritual level of experience. One makes the physical, and the other creates the spiritual.

Commentary…12

Chapters 2 through 9 discuss the human temporal mind/matrix -- mortal mind -- (with its limits) and the Truth Matrix. A mortal temporal mind and an Eternal Mind are within each of us. The mortal mind is a weak distorted image of the Eternal Mind – a 'special case'.

Within our temporal mind/matrix, we can program thoughts of Eternal Truths instead of temporal thoughts of relative truths. The temporal thoughts of relative truths can contain ~~truths~~ within them.

This statement can also relate to Chapter 9 and the difference between how an architect creates and how a mage creates.

---

13.   Miracles are both beginnings and endings, and so they alter the temporal order. They are always affirmations of rebirth, which seem to go back but really go forward. They undo the past in the present, and thus release the future.

Commentary…13

This is in reference to Chapters 3, 7, and 9 and the time folding abilities of the Truth Matrix. When participating in miracles, we are participating in the Eternal Moment of Creation, which has access to any moment in time and is also at the birth or origin of our very being.

When working with and around the Eternal Moment of Creation, the concept of time is non-sequitar. In the model or paradigm presented in previous chapters, the past can be altered by future choices.

---

14.   Miracles bear witness to truth. They are convincing because they arise from conviction. Without conviction, they deteriorate into magic, which is mindless and therefore destructive; or rather, the uncreative use of mind.

Commentary…14

There is language problem here, a problem in 'packaging'. Part of the problem is *ACIM* has some word definitions that are different from this book. The first part of this statement is about miracles being an expression or an effect of Truth and the Matrix. In the second part of this statement, conviction in *I AM A I*, is a combination of Belief (Perception, Desire, Attachment, and Faith) and truth applications.

Cross-referencing to this book, the terms mind and mindless can be substituted with Mind and Mindless, Mind being the Eternal Mind and Mindless being the mortal mind. Chapter 9 mentions that all magic, except Gold, is controlled or guided by the temporal mind and instigated by temporal perceptions and desires. This makes the source of the first four categories of magic Mindless. (Even though the operator must go to the Mind to make an operation work, the original idea came from the mortal mind.) Gold magic and miracles on the other hand, are usually not under conscious control (see *statement 5*) and therefore are expressions of the Mind.

The term uncreative use of mind can also refer to mis-creative use of Mind of *Postulate 7* and the resultant theorems of Chapter 2.8.

---

15.   Each day should be devoted to miracles. The purpose of time is to enable you to learn how to use time constructively. It is thus a teaching device and a means to an end. Time will cease when it is no longer useful in facilitating learning.

Commentary…15

This relates to Chapters 4, 5, and 6 -- reprogramming the temporal mind/matrix. No matter what philosophy you develop, it is meaningless unless you apply it on a daily basis and it becomes a part of your daily life.

This statement also has reference to Chapters 3, 8, and 9: Love not being exclusive and using everything, including time as a tool. Time being a tool, like all tools there will be times when it is not needed.[44] When tools are not needed, they are set aside.

---

16.   Miracles are teaching devices for demonstrating it is as blessed to give as to receive. They simultaneously increase the strength of the giver and supply strength to the receiver.

Commentary…16

The power of Love and how it has generated a closed system has been referred to throughout this book. When Love is expressed, nobody looses or nothing is lost.

This statement also is related to previous *statement 9.*

---

17.   Miracles transcend the body. They are sudden shifts into invisibility, away from the bodily level. That is why they heal.

Commentary…17

The temporal, including the body, is related to a mistake in thinking by God's Creation…you. Eternal Creation, through miracles translating into temporal physical form, goes through the Correction setup to remedy the mistake in thinking.[45] This statement refers to how the Correction is aimed at something that transcends all bodily – temporal -- concerns.

This statement can also relate to the relationship between **Absolute** and **Actual** realities of Chapters 4 and 9; **Actual** must follow **Absolute**.

---

18.   A miracle is a service. It is the maximal-service you can render to another. It is a way of loving your neighbor as yourself. You recognize your own and your neighbor's worth simultaneously.

Commentary…18

The word service is the application of Love (**Absolute** Reality) to a **Consensual** reality of Chapter 4.

This statement also relates to unified or inclusive perceptions. Your source is your neighbor's source. Since there is only One Mind, you are your neighbor. "That which you do to the least of your brethren, you do to me." -- Jesus

---

19.   Miracles make minds one in God. They depend on cooperation because the Son-ship is the sum of all that God created. Miracles therefore reflect the laws of eternity, not of time.

---

*44*Chapter 8.1, The Nature of Tools
*45*Chapter 3.2, The Correction

Commentary...19

As its been repeated throughout this book, there is only One Eternal Mind. This statement can also relate to Chapters 7 and 9 (the One Mind, the nature of telepathy and magic, and the love bond), and the mechanics of the One mind within the Eternal moment of Creation.

The Son-ship here can be translated as God's Creation of *Postulate 5*. Miracles, being of Eternity, are of **Absolute** reality Eternal Truths not of **Actual** reality temporal related truths – of time.

---

20.   Miracles reawaken the awareness that the spirit, not the body, is the altar of truth. This is the recognition that leads to the healing power of the miracle.

Commentary...20

In this book, Chapter 2 stated from *I AM A I*'s reference that the words *spirit* and *truth* are interchangeable.[46] This is applicable to the first part of this statement.

The latter part of this statement refers to the Absolute Truth Matrix making itself known through the Cognitive Input – re-cognition -- and the mortal matrix's response to it (Chapters 1 and 4).

---

21.   Miracles are natural signs of forgiveness. Through miracles you accept God's forgiveness by extending it to others.

Commentary...21

This refers to developing an inclusive mind while reducing exclusive choices.[47] In forgiving, one is being inclusive and Truth is being extended. In doing such, you are aligning with the Truth Matrix with miracles as the result.

Later, in *ACIM*, the book refers to forgiveness as a correction measure for judgment and forgiveness is not needed with an inclusive mind. If no faults or errors are perceived (no ~~truth~~ chosen), there is nothing to forgive. No mistake is made.

---

22.   Miracles are associated with fear only because of the belief that darkness can hide. You believe that what your physical eyes cannot see does not exist. This leads to a denial of spiritual sight.

Commentary...22

This touches on fear of the unknown or attachments to the tangible (or the result of A_S).

This statement also refers to a denial of **Absolute** Reality, opening of the *Perceptual Lens Array*[48] to develop a non-exclusive mind, and the relationship or acceptance of **Absolute** Reality by an **Individual** reality.

---

23.   Miracles rearrange perception, and place all levels in true perspective. This is healing, because sickness comes from confusing the levels.

---

46 Chapter 2.5, *Postulate 4*, God's Logical Mind is a matrix of Absolute, Eternal Truth.
47 Chapter 4.5 - The *Perceptional Lens Array* Matrix
48 ibid.

Commentary...23

Applications of Truth rearrange the *Perceptual Lens Array* and reprogram the mind/matrix with Truth.[49] With the presence of Truth, there is no separation from God with a dis-ease -- disease (the mind/matrix influence on the body in Figure 4-4 [to the Body]).

---

24.   Miracles enable you to heal the sick and raise the dead because you made sickness and death yourself, and can therefore abolish both. You are a miracle, capable of creating in the likeness of your Creator. Everything else is your own nightmare, and does not exist. Only the creations of light are real.

Commentary...24

This statement relates to the previous statement and commentary. It also relates to Postulates and Theorems of Chapter 2.[50] Because sickness and death is a result of the 'mis-creation', it can be corrected by a correction in thinking or a cessation of mis-creation.

The last two sentences refer to the dream nature of physical form.[51] In addition, it has been stated repeatedly throughout this book that only **Absolute** reality and the Truth behind it is real.

---

25.   Miracles are part of an interlocking chain of forgiveness which, when completed, is the Atonement. Atonement works all the time and in all the dimensions of time.

Commentary...25

Atonement is at-One-ment of the Eternal God with the Truth Matrix, God's Creation, you, and involves the intrinsic quality of that union. The "chain of forgiveness" is the non-exclusive mind at work and practice.

In reference to the time aspect, refer to Chapter 3 and previous *statements 13* and *19* with commentaries.

---

26.   Miracles represent freedom from fear. "Atoning" means undoing." The undoing of fear is an essential part of the Atonement value of miracles.

Commentary...26

See *statement 25* with commentary. Of course, at-One-ment – Truth -- undoes an exclusive mind – ~~truth~~ (fear/attachments).[52] When one is at-One-ment with God -- Love, fear ceases to exist.

This statement also refers to 'undoing', which can be a form of ~~truth~~ removal -- purification.

---

27.   A miracle is a universal blessing from God through me to all my brothers. It is the privilege of the forgiven to forgive.

---

49 Chapters 4 -9
50 Specifically: *Theorem 15A*. Creation can Create like unto God. or Creation can extend God. Including, *Postulates* 6 and 7 with their theorems.
51 Chapters 2, 3, 9, & 10
52 Theorem 27B

Commentary…27

This involves the Eternal Moment of Creation and the proposed nature of the author of *ACIM* along with the mystical 'door' left open in the Covenant.

The second part of the statement is very similar to, "…and forgive us our trespasses as we forgive those who trespass against us…" Specifically, asking for an extension to you what you have already given.

This statement involves Mirror mechanics.[53] Also, see *statements 9, 13, 18, 21*, and *25* with commentaries.

---

28.   Miracles are a way of earning release from fear. Revelation induces a state in which fear has already been abolished. Miracles are thus a means and revelation is an end.

Commentary…28

Revelation is related to the cognitive mechanism of the temporal mind/matrix[54] working with Truth. Revelation is a form of Truth ringing.[55] When in Truth, the exclusive mind -- fear -- does not exist. Consequently, aspects of the Eternal Mind are being used.

In the end, cognition of God and your True Self is everything and leaves no room for fear – for anything else.

---

29.   Miracles praise God through you. They praise Him by honoring His creations, affirming their perfection. They heal because they deny body-identification and affirm spirit-identification.

Commentary…29

Imitation is the sincerest form of praise. To perform miracles is in imitation of God. Miracles honor Creation, because then, Creation is being itself.

The last part of this statement deals with the closed system and Truth correcting ~~truth~~.

---

30.   By recognizing spirit, miracles adjust the levels of perception and show them in proper alignment. This places spirit at the center, where it can communicate directly.

Commentary…30

See *statement 23* with commentary.

This statement can relate to reprogramming the temporal mind/matrix through cognition and Truth. This, in turn, adjusts the *Perceptional Lens Array*. Again, this statement also reflects back to *I AM A I*'s interchangeability of the words *truth* and *spirit*. Because of this, this statement could also read as, "By recognizing Truth…"

The last statement can also relate to the communion/intuition that results between mind/Mind from reprogramming with Truth.[56]

---

53 Chapter 3
54 Chapter 4, Realities and the Human Matrix
55 Chapter 4.8, Ring My Bell
56 Chapters 7 and 9

31.   Miracles should inspire gratitude, not awe. You should thank God for what you really are. The children of God are holy and the miracle honors their holiness, which can be hidden but never lost.

Commentary...31

The first part of this statement relates to the word *awe*, which has a meaning that can infer a fear (*statement 22*); where gratitude does not.

The second part of this statement hints at the indestructibility of Truth and Creation.

---

32.   I inspire all miracles, which are really intercessions. They intercede for your holiness and make your perceptions holy. By placing you beyond the physical laws, they raise you into the sphere of celestial order. In this order, you are perfect.

Commentary...32

The first sentence is in reference to the proposed author of *ACIM*, through the Covenant paradigm -- God's Creation, our true self.

The second sentence touches how truth alters perceptions.[57] This statement talks about how you are not your physical body. You are God's Creation and Love's Logic.[58]

---

33.   Miracles honor you because you are lovable. They dispel illusions about yourself and perceive the light in you. They thus atone for your errors by freeing you from your nightmares. By releasing your mind from the imprisonment of your illusions, they restore your sanity.

Commentary...33

The first part of this statement refers to who you <u>really</u> are. (see last statement)

The second part refers to Love and the inclusive Mind's effect (**Absolute** Reality) on **Individual** realities or bubbles of temporal/spatial reference.[59] Miracles being of Love/Truth, dispel ~~truth~~.[60] In dispelling ~~truth~~, the only thing left is truth.[61]

Not having Truth within the mind can be considered a spiritual un-sane condition.

---

34.   Miracles restore the mind to its fullness. By atoning for lack, they establish perfect protection. The spirit's strength leaves no room for intrusions.

Commentary...34

Miracles working from the One promote oneness. With at-One-ness – atone, indestructible Love recognizes no limits.

This statement references the truth's effect on an **Individual** reality. It also touches how it automatically affects the cessation of ~~truth~~ in our mind/matrix.

Truth's/Spirit's strength is Eternal and indomitable. See also *statements 25, 26,* and *33* with their commentaries.

---

57 A *3a* concept from the outline in the beginning of this chapter.
58 Postulate 6
59 Chapters 3, 4, 9, and the beginning of 10
60 Theorem 27B.   Truth corrects for untruth.
61 Chapters 4 and 5

35.   Miracles are expressions of love, but they may not always have observable effects.

Commentary…35

Truth, which comes from Love, is not directly perceived. This has been mentioned throughout this book. Miracles can work on the metaphysical level without readily perceivable physical effects.

---

36.   Miracles are examples of right thinking, aligning your perceptions with truth as God created it.

Commentary…36

This is in reference to reprogramming the individual's mortal mind/matrix *BTR* with Truth.[62] This is a **3a** condition in the outline of common religious elements presented in Chapters 9 and 10.

---

37.   A miracle is a correction introduced into false thinking by me. It acts as a catalyst, breaking up erroneous perception and reorganizing it properly. This places you under the Atonement principle, where perception is healed. Until this has occurred, knowledge of the Divine Order is impossible.

Commentary…37

See *statement 32* with commentary.

False thinking is ~~true~~ perceptions (F_P) based on ~~truth~~ known (F_K). This statement can refer to how a miracle can correct ~~true~~ perceptions. Perception is naturally healed with an at-One-ment. There is nothing to perceive.

The last sentence of this statement refers to until your fractured perception is healed the unity of the Divine Order will elude you.

---

38.   The Holy Spirit is the mechanism of miracles. He recognizes both God's creations and your illusions. He separates the true from the false by His ability to perceive totally rather than selectively.

Commentary…38

The Holy Spirit/Truth is the mechanism of Love.[63] Truth being of God's Love will not exclude anything.[64]

A portion of this statement anthropomorphizes (gives human qualities to) the mechanics between Truth and ~~truth~~. (This is not necessarily wrong, if that is what is necessary to get the point across.)

---

39.   The miracle dissolves error because the Holy Spirit identifies error as false or unreal. This is the same as saying that by perceiving light, darkness automatically disappears.

---

62 Chapters 4, 6, 7, and 9
63 Chapter 2
64 Definition of Terms -- Love

Commentary…39

    See the previous statement.

    This statement also refers the roles of creative and destructive forces.[65] Darkness has no effect on the light; yet, a single candle dispels the dark.

---

40.   The miracle acknowledges everyone as your brother and mine. It is a way of perceiving the universal mark of God.

Commentary…40

    This is the non-exclusive mind at work. This relates to there being only One Creation. What is done to one part is done to all. Or again, said another way, "That which you do to the least of your brethren, you do to me." …Jesus

---

41.   Wholeness is the perceptual content of miracles. They thus correct, or atone for, the faulty perception of lack.

Commentary…41

    This statement involves the non-exclusiveness of Love's Truth, the Correction, and how it applies to an **Individual** reality and its mortal matrix.

    This statement also refers the error of 'perception of lack' -- Chapter 9.

---

42.   A major contribution of miracles is their strength in releasing you from your false sense of isolation, deprivation, and lack.

Commentary…42

    Our sense of "isolation…lack" is part of the duality delusion.[66] As with *statement 41* and its commentary, this is an example of the non-exclusive Love correcting the exclusive thinking of our human matrix.

---

43.   Miracles arise from a miraculous state of mind, or a state of miracle-readiness.

Commentary…43

    This can relate to Gold magic and the result of extensive reprogramming of the mortal mind/matrix, along the lines of Truth.[67]

    This is also a reference to a way of life. A way of life whereby, miracles flow naturally (*statements 5* and *6* with commentaries)

---

44.   The miracle is an expression of an inner awareness of Christ and the acceptance of His Atonement.

---

[65] Chapter 9.7 - Creative and Destructive Forces
[66] *Theorem 32*
[67] Chapter 9.5 -- Concerning Magic Categories

Commentary...44

Language problems: the definition of Christ varies from person to person or from Christian religion to Christian religion.

I AM A I equates Christ as God's Holy Creation. Truth is inherent within all of us (as is the Christ/Creation) and the miracle is an expression of that. This includes the inherent at-One-ment that goes with this.

---

45.   A miracle is never lost. It may touch many people you have not even met, and produce undreamed of changes in situations of which you are not even aware.

Commentary...45

See *statement 35* and commentary.

The miracle is never lost for the concept *lost* is a temporal concept and miracles work outside of time. This statement also touches on the unlimited Eternal power of the Moment of Creation and the inclusiveness of Love <u>through all time</u> (as been said in various places throughout this book).

The last sentence also refers to the temporal/spatial perceptual limits of our human matrix.[68]

---

46.   The Holy Spirit is the highest communication medium. Miracles do not involve this type of communication, because they are temporary communication devices. When you return to your original form of communication with God by direct revelation, the need for miracles is over.

Commentary...46

The highest communication is the One Mind and its Truth/Spirit. Miracles being Divine 'audio-visual teaching aids' like all teaching aids, they are aimed at an individual to produce an application. It is the application that is important and not the 'teaching aid'.

With the advent of at-One-ment – communion with God, once this is restored, miracles -- the teaching aids -- are no longer necessary.

---

47.   The miracle is a learning device that lessens the need for time. It establishes an out-of-pattern time interval not under the usual laws of time. In this sense, it is timeless.

Commentary...47

The time ignor-ance of the Correction in Chapter 3.7, of Chapter 7, and is discussed with magic in Chapter 9.

---

48.   The miracle is the only device at your immediate disposal for controlling time. Only revelation transcends it, having nothing to do with time at all.

---

68 Chapter 4.3 - Limits of the Perceptual Window

Commentary...48

As with the previous statement, this refers to the time folding aspects of choices made in the individual matrix through the Correction and the use of time as a tool.

The second sentence can also refer to the use of the cognitive mechanism to know/be the Truth within you (ringing).[69]

---

49.   The miracle makes no distinction among degrees of misperception. It is a device for perception-correction, effective quite apart from either the degree or the direction of the error. This is its true indiscriminateness.

Commentary...49

See *statement 1* and commentary.

This relates to the Correction, the Inclusive Mind of God, and its Love with its non-exclusiveness. This statement also relates back to Truth corrects ~~truth~~.[70]

---

50.   The miracle compares what you have made with creation, accepting what is in accord with it as true, and rejecting what is out of accord as false.

Commentary...50

This is in reference the Correction, aligning the individual temporal mind/matrix with the Eternal Mind, and to ridding the temporal mind/matrix of ~~truth~~.

Because miracles are expressions of the Eternal Moment of Creation through God's Creation, God's Love/Logic is also present. Miracles defy the logic of the temporal mind since the temporal mind is limited by the ~~truth~~ it contains.

Once ~~truth~~ is removed from the human mind, miracles -- an expression of the very nature of things – manifest from the only thing left, God and His Beloved Creation.

******************** ☯ ********************

As it was it the beginning, so shall it be
World without end.
Glory be to GOD

---

69 Chapter 4.8, Ring My Bell
70 *Theorem 27B.*   Truth corrects for untruth.

10.4 Questions

1. What is the shamanic journey?

2. World religions are like _____ on a _____

3. World religions can be divided into _____ and _____ religions.

4. What is the Covenant and why is it important to other religions?

5. All _____ magic can be considered miracles.

6. What are the shaman's problems when returning from a 'walkabout'?

7. What is _____ can have no opposite.

8. What are the events that make up the Axial Age?

9. _____ should be natural.

10. Where did the Kabbalah come from?

11. Miracles ignore _____.

12. What constitutes a priest-king or priestess-queen?

13. Describe how the Axial Age events relate to *I AM A I* subject matter?

14. Who are the two parties involved in the Covenant?

We Have Met
the Enemy
and He Is
Us (Pogo, aka Walt Kelly)

Collage art 'stolen' from John Findley, Tex Arcana and from Robert Williams, The Low Brow Art of Robert Williams.

Epilogue

This book is only one finite language version of an Infinite and Eternal logic system, *I AM A I*'s approach was to give the text as much depth as possible. In addition, because this book is a finite version of the Absolute, it truly cannot be regarded as definitive.

In fact, if anyone says something like, "This is 'the book'", you can tell them "'The book' says that is bullshit!"

There is an anecdote involving Mark Twain. When Mark Twain was learning to be a pilot on the Mississippi river, and he asked an experienced pilot, "How can you travel, knowing there are all these tangles, wrecks, and bars are around you? How can you pilot this without crashing into something?"[1]

The pilot said, "Well, you don't have to know where every tangle or bramble is and where every sandbar is, and where every wreck is. You just have to know where it's clear sailing."

What *I AM A I* has been trying to do is point out where everything can be spiritual clear sailing, -- to paint a picture with words. In the apparent 'sea' of finite temporal chaos, the eternal and the infinite remains 'clear sailing' – it does not change.

Absolute Love has an Absolute Order – Logic – to it. This infinite Logic manifests in to the physical form -- finite -- with such intricacy it boggles the mortal mind. Just as, the whole Mississippi river would boggle any pilot. The pilot only knew one section of the river.

Looking at humanity as if it was one being growing up and observing the 'stages' it has gone through, one can see an evolution. Man's early stages can be likened to a child learning to interact in its environment. Man learned how to move through it. As the child matures into a teenager, it has a grasp of environment manipulation and navigation; it now must learn responsibility according to an established set of laws/truths. Man learned how to communicate – to talk.

Today's Man, like the teenager, has learned to tweak the environment. Now, Mankind must learn responsibility. Man must learn from the *Tao te Ching*, that there is a time to do and that there is a time not to do:

> "Use of clay determines a pot
> Use of the pot is determined where the clay is not."

To take this one step further, this book has given you numerous exercises that serve as a place to start in terms of self exploration. As you 'grow' spiritually, you learn as well that 'not doing something' can be more important than 'doing something'. This is the Way of the Dream.

Mankind has become knowledgeable, and some people are quite sophisticated in their knowledge. Unfortunately, most of the knowledge is of the temporal/spatial variety – physical – and quite limited at that.

One of the first priorities in acquiring knowledge should be to recognize your knowledge limits; recognize the extent of your ignorance – a mortal mind limit. This is why Socrates argued he was the wisest man in Greece.[2] He recognized his ignorance.

As long as a mortal mind's/minds' paradigm/philosophy/thought-matrix works with absolutes – comprehensives -- and eternal truths, the mortals' philosophy that houses this truth

---

[1] The Mississippi River was a tangle of sandbars, snags (log and wood accumulations), and previous shipwrecks – a navigators nightmare.

[2] The Oracle of Delphi agreed with Socrates. The Oracle of Delphi was asked by someone, "Is there anyone wiser than Socrates?" Instead of the usual cryptic response, the Oracles response was, "No."

is a convenience/conveyance to the Truth. Absolute Truth is already in a Matrix. God's Love has an Absolutely Logical Mind.

None of the concepts *I AM A I*'s words portray are new; they are ancient. We are dealing with eternals here. In addition, none of the words (or arrangement of words) in this book are the 'real thing'. It is in your applications/faith of the concepts that is everything.

It has been said throughout this book, "The map is not the terrain." The line on the map is not the street where you live. When you explore the street, you see the details the map missed. In the process of knowing the territory, the map will be put down eventually.

Ironically, though the Eternal laws/truths are ancient from a temporal reference, Truth has been largely ignored. Truth interferes too much with our illusions and delusions. Truth has been around 'forever'; and we ignore it except when it appears to serve us.

Moreover, ironically, the Eternal Love -- with Eternal patience -- awaits our attention. As gravity is within and without us, Loving Creation is at our core and surrounds us. Love is Eternally waiting for us to change our minds.

Eventually, you will rest in God's Eternal, Precious Moment. From the Eternal reference, you never left God. You are God's Creation, the 'Beloved of God'. In this, is your true identity, your spiritual invulnerability/security, and your serenity.

You are dreaming of being separated from God's Love. The Dreamtime does not effect Reality. Just as your body never left the room when you dream of other places, God's Peace has never left you.

You are Adam dreaming.
Wake up "Oh Holy Christ Child'!

Gazing past the planets, looking for total view
I've been lying here for hours.
You've got to make the journey out and in.
Wonders of a lifetime, right there before your eyes
Searching with this life of ours
You've got to make the journey out and in.
Out and in, out and in.
If you think it's a joke, that's all right
Do what you want to do
I've said my piece and I'll leave it all up to you. [3]

---

[3] Lyrics by Mike Pinder, *Out and In*, To Our Children's Children's Children, The Moody Blues, Copyright 1969 by Deram Music. Used by Permission

402

Appendix

A, Postulates and Theorems

B, Answers to Chapter Questions

C, Definitions of Terms

D, Figure 4.4, The Human Matrix and *Exercise and Lab 5* Worksheet

E, Mandalas and Mandala Templates

F, Index

Appendix A – Postulates and Theorems

POSTULATE 1	There is one God, the Source-less Source, the Formless Form. Absolute Will that is Eternal and Infinite in nature.

Theorems

1. God is the one source of Will.
   or
   There is no Will but God's.
   or
   God and Will are One.
2. God is the one Source of Eternal.
   or
   God and Eternity are One.
3. God is boundless and without limits.
3A. Will is boundless and without limits.
3B. Eternity is boundless and without limits.

POSTULATE 2	God's Absolute Will actualizes as an Absolute Eternal Love

Theorems

4. God and Love are One.
   or
   There is no Love but God's.
4A. Eternity and Love are One.
5. That which is not Love is not God.
5A. That which is not Love is not Eternal.

POSTULATE 3	God's Absolute Love has an Absolute, Logical, Eternal Mind.

Theorems

6. God and Logical Mind are One.
6A. Love and Logical Mind are One.
6B. Eternity and Logical Mind are One.
6C. Will, Love, and Logic are One in an Eternal God.
7. There is no Logic but God's.
7A. That which is not Love is not Logical and vice versa.

POSTULATE 4	God's Logical Mind is a matrix of Absolute, Eternal Truth.

Theorems

8. God and Truth are One.
   Plus all the counterpart corollaries that go with this:
   There is no Truth but God's.
   That which is not True is not God.

8A. Truth and Eternity are One.

or

That which is not Eternal is not True.

8B. That which is not True is not Real.

8C. That which is not Eternal is not Real.

9. Will, Love, Logic, and Truth are One in an Eternal God.

POSTULATE 5 **Creation is an Eternal effect of God's Truth matrix.**

or

Creation is an Eternal idea within the Mind of God.

Theorems

10. God and Creation are One.

10A. The God-Creation process occurs in Eternity.

or

The God-Creative process is Eternally occurring.

11. God is the one source of Creation.

11A. The God-Creation process is a closed system within God.

11B. The God-Creation process is the only Creative process.

12. Creation and Love are One.

or

Creation is Love.

12A. Creation is God's Logic.

12B. Creation is God's Truth.

12C. Creation is Reality.

13. Will, Love, Logic, and Truth are One in an Eternal God.

14. God Created like unto Himself.

or

To Create, God extended Himself.

15. The Only Creative process there is, is to extend God.

15A. Creation can Create like unto God.

or

Creation can extend God.

16. Creation did not Create God.

or

The God-Creation process is one way.

17. That which is Created never leaves the Creator.

or

Ideas do not leave the mind of their origin or source.

POSTULATE 6 **I am God's Creation.**

Theorems

18. God and I are One.

19. Will, Love, Logic, and Truth are One in an Eternal Me.

19A. I am God's Will.

19B. I am God's Love.

19C. I am God's Logic.

19D. I am God's Truth.

19E. I am Reality.

19F. I am Eternal.

19G. I am an extension of God.

20. I can extend God.

| **POSTULATE 7** | **God's Creation created/miscreated an untruth.** |

Theorems

21. The miscreation is not God.
22. The miscreation is not the Will of God.
22A. The miscreation is not God's Love.
22B. The miscreation is not God's Logic.
22C. The miscreation is not God's Truth.
22D. The miscreation is not God's Infinity.
22E. The miscreation is not Eternal.
> *or*

The miscreation is temporal.
23. The miscreation is not Real.
24. The untruth came from the Truth matrix.
> *or*

There is an element of Truth that caused the untruth.
25. The miscreation never left Creation.
26. The miscreation has generated a duality within Creation.
26A. The miscreation has generated an unreal duality within Creation.
> *or*

The duality does not exist.
> *or*

The miscreation has generated a delusion of duality within Creation.
27. God's Love did not exclude the miscreation.
> *or*

The miscreation was included within God's Love.
27A. God corrected for the untruth.
27B. Truth corrects for untruth.
28. The correction works outside of time.
> *or*

The correction (Eternal) and the miscreation (temporal) coexist.
28A. Truth and untruth coexist.
29. Physical form is related to or an aspect of the miscreation or untruth.
30. Truth coexists with physical form.
31. I miscreated an untruth.
32. I am/we are in a generated delusion of duality.

Appendix B - Answers to Chapter Questions

Chapter 1

1. By a response mechanism, 'ringing'.
2. (f)
3. Mathematics
4. Zoroaster
5. Anesthetic, chainsaw, sharp knife, and being insured couldn't hurt.
6. Colleges
7. An immortal soul
8. Applied and is independent of belief
9. Golden section and pi
10. The 'ringing' and silence of the first assignment. The union of mathematical logic and mysticism is not new. Most of the important information is in the following chapters.
11. Within that 100 year period, the foundations of today's civilization was laid. Within that 100 year period the Buddha, Mahavira (Jainism), the Tao te Ching was first put on paper, the Upanishads was put on paper, the Bhagavad Vita was put on paper, Confucius, Zoroaster, Pythagoras, and 2nd Isaiah (prophecies of Jesus) appeared.
12. Strike one tuning fork, and a tuning fork of the same frequency across a room will vibrate. Or, television and radio communication.
13. A symbolic thought system construct is a picture painted in words or numbers -- symbols. Both physics and metaphysics are mental symbolic constructs -- fabrications, created and used by Mankind, in order to help us relate to the 'universe'– a philosophical paradigm. Physics and metaphysics are only tools to help us understand and appreciate the actuality. Neither physics nor metaphysics constructs are the actuality.

Chapter 2

1. God, Love, Logic, Truth Matrix, then Creation
2. A few infinities
3. Creation of an untruth
4. Closed
5. God's Creation
6. Creation
7. Miscreated an untruth
8. Their source -- mind of origin
9. A mistake, the miscreation, untruth
10. Truth
11. Outside time and space
12. A duality delusion
13. Untruth
14. Truth, untruth
15. Have the power of God's Creation Matrix, infinite, to extend God
16. To extend God
17. Laws by which something works

Chapter 3

1. Did not exclude it
2. Bubble of Temporal Reference
3. Our thinking, our minds; through the Mirror
4. Karma
5. Weak nuclear, strong nuclear, electromagnetic, gravity, and life
6. Ignored or folded

7. Everywhere, by opening up perceptions
8. Love
9. Truth, Creation, Matrix
10. Our matrix begins to align to, or take on elements of the Truth Matrix
11. Parallel
12. The mirror image and the object it is reflecting
13. *BTRs*, within *BTRs*, within *BTRs or* matrices, within matrices, within matrices
14. Nowhere
15. Essay question
16. ~~Truth~~ to the mind of origin

Chapter 4

1. Perceptions and thoughts respectively
2. *Storage* matrix
3. Mortal mind matrix
4. All of them and **Individual** reality predominately
5. Cognitive input
6. Mortal mind
7. A camera or the eyeball
8. A plank raised above the ground
9. Truth applications
10. Perceptions, Desires, Faith, and Attachments
11. A viewfinder, to program knowledge, *or* facilitate the 'ringing'
12. The individual
13. **Absolute**
14. Time, space, processing capability, and information vector spectrum -- visible light
15. A *Perceptual Lens Array*
16. Cancels previous judgments
17. **Absolute**, **Actual**, **Individual**, **Consensual**, and **Imaginary**
18. Eternal Mind
19. Accept, reject, or make no choice -- wait

Chapter 5

1. Desires, Attachments, ~~true~~ perceptions, ~~true~~ choices, ~~true~~ knowledge
2. True perceptions, True choices, True Knowledge, Faith
3. Linked or one thing
4. How many times something is multiplied by itself
5. 1
6. As large as possible
7. As small as possible
8. The Mirror
9. (e)
10. ~~truth~~ participation
11. Essay Question
12. Essay Question

Chapter 6

1. Passive, Affirmation, and Devotional
2. ~~Truth~~ be it through knowledge (F_K), perceptions (F_P), choices (F_C), desires (D_S), attachments (A_S), or a combination of the above
3. *Perceptual Lens Array*
4. Focus over a change of time ($f\Delta t$)
5. (*b*)
6. Motivational analysis or pre-setting intention
7. A period of self observation

8. Increase truth participation
9. Truth
10. Essay question

Chapter 7

1. One Eternal Mind
2. Internally or through an external tool
3. A perception (words, images, etc.), a feeling, a knowing
4. Time and space
5. Telepathy
6. Premonitions: you, in the future, telling you, in the past, that something is about to come down. *Déjà vu*: accessing a future memory
7. Stilling the mind
8. Because it utilizes or is a communication within the One Mind of God. Something that is at the core of our being.
9. Preconceived ideas, attachments, beliefs
10. A 'disinterested-interest'
11. A love bond
12. They are temporal and finite in nature. Plus, they feel very similar to imagination.

Chapter 8

1. No extraneous perceptions are introduced through words.
2. Active: Instrument player, passive: listener, combination: dancer
3. Mystical tool
4. Resetting the mind, constant reuse of the cognitive input; can involve a focus over a change of time ($\int \Delta t$); emptying or stilling the perceptual lens array; reduction of ~~true~~ perceptions and choices (not T_P and not T_C); a reduction of desires and attachments (D_S and A_S).
5. Neutral
6. To not use a tool.

Chapter 9

1. God
2. Manifestation of a desire through the use of the will.
3. Black, White, Gray, Silver, and Gold. Motivations and forces brought to bear (creative or destructive).
4. By programming Truths into the human matrix
5. Beginners and novices
6. As you become responsible with the power you have, then you are given more power.
7. Vectors of application
8. Coordinated
9. Moving an arm
10. TO KNOW, TO DARE, TO WILL, TO KEEP SILENT
11. Raja Yoga

Chapter 10

1. A quest for answers
2. Facets on a jewel
3. Covenant and Non-Covenant
4. A contract with God; because of its comprehensiveness
5. Gold
6. Language, lack of common references, individual illusions and delusions
7. All encompassing
8. Foundation to civilization in the modern world was laid
9. Miracles
10. One of the five books of Moses

Appendix C - Definition of Terms[1]

Ability: The quality of being able to do something.

Absolute: All encompassing; no exceptions.

Attributes: A quality or characteristic of a person or a thing.

Cognition: The mental process or faculty by which knowledge is acquired.

Coordinated Being: One who has the same control over their mortal mind operations as most have over their body operations.

Create: To extend

Effect: Something brought about by a cause or agent; result

Eternal: Unaffected by time; timeless

Faith: Application of knowledge.

Gestalt: A physical, biological, psychological, or symbolic configuration or pattern of elements so unified as a whole that its properties cannot be derived from a simple summation of its parts.

Idea: A mental construct

Identity: The collective aspect of the set of characteristics by which a thing is definitively recognizable or known

Infinite: Having no boundaries or limits

Logic: A gestalt containing a pattern of interconnectedness.

Love : An Eternal, selfless state that is intrinsically not exclusive.

Magic: Manifesting a desire through the conscious use of will.

Matrix: 1. A situation or surrounding substance within which something else originates, develops, or is contained; 2. The womb -- mater: Important derivatives are: *mother, maternal, maternity, matriculate, matrix, matron, matrimony, metropolis, material, matter.*

Mind: A logic matrix that has awareness of self.

Miscreate: To create mistakenly.

Reality: An effect of truth.

Right Angle Rule: The effects of a choice are translated into a different direction (vector) than the original direction.

Self: Knowledge of existence.

Truth: Laws by which something works; spirit; mechanics of existence.

Will: An intrinsic ability, potential or actual

Appendix D Figure 4.4 and Exercise and Lab 5 Worksheet

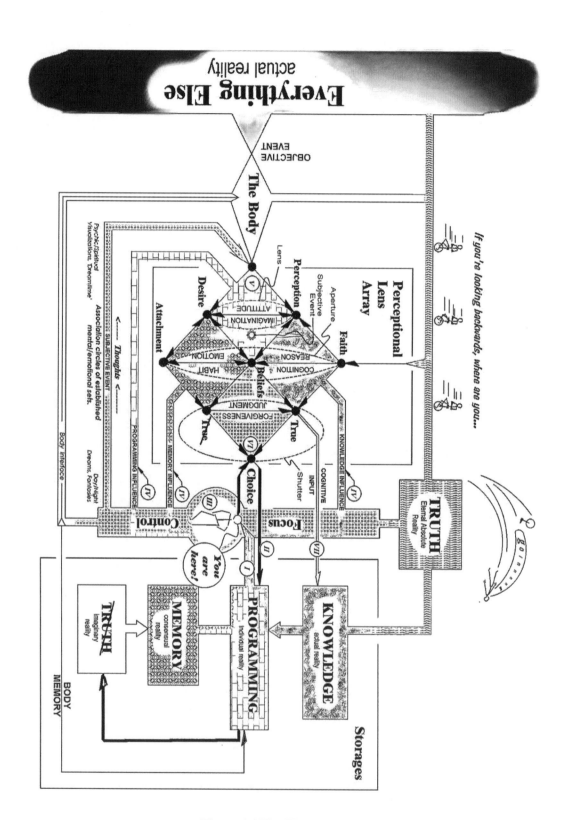

Figure 4.4 The Human Matrix

OBJECT:

SEE

WANT WANT WANT WANT WANT WANT WANT WANT WANT WANT WANT WANT

Exercise 5 Worksheet

Appendix E, Mandalas and Mandala Template

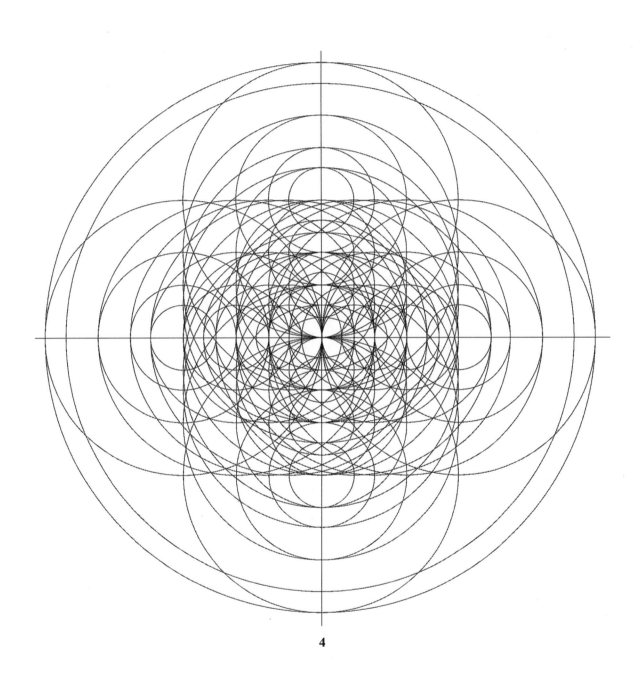

4

5 (Easy)

5 (Hard)

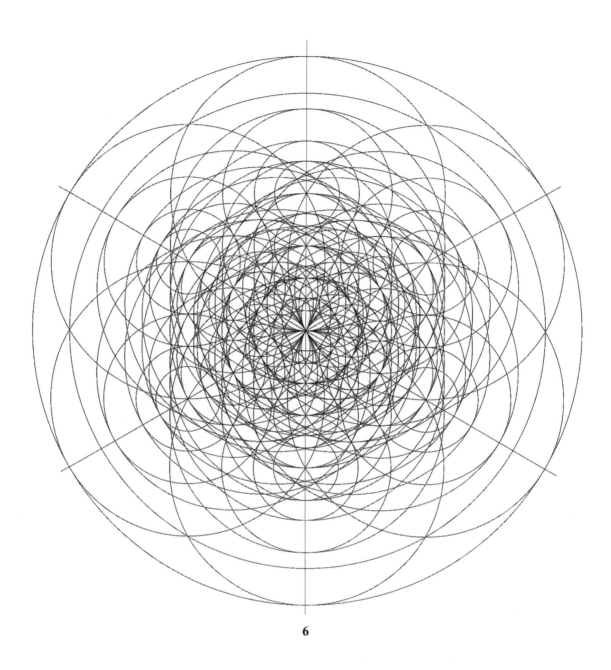

6

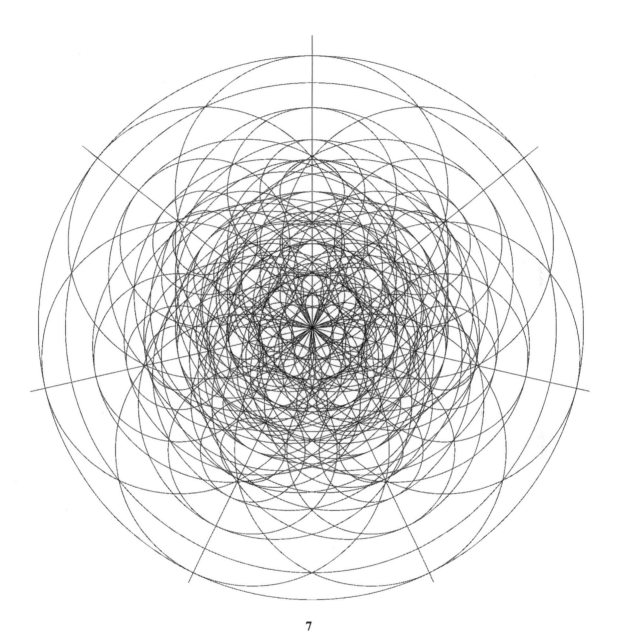

7

8

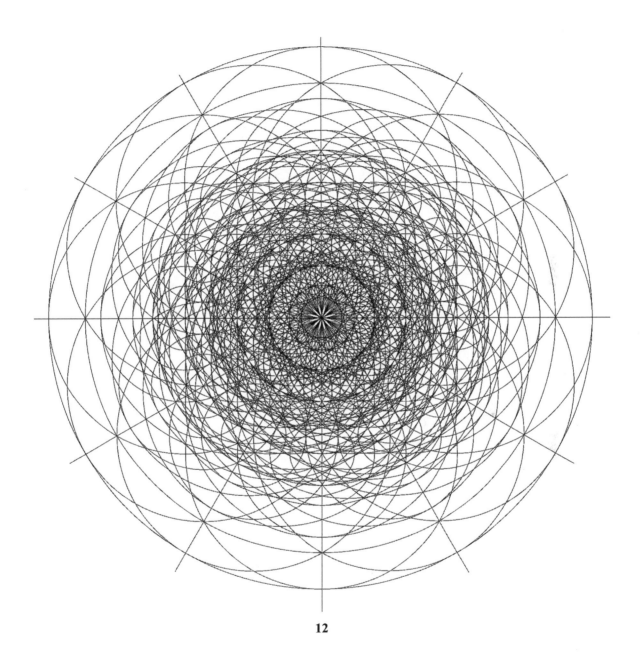

12

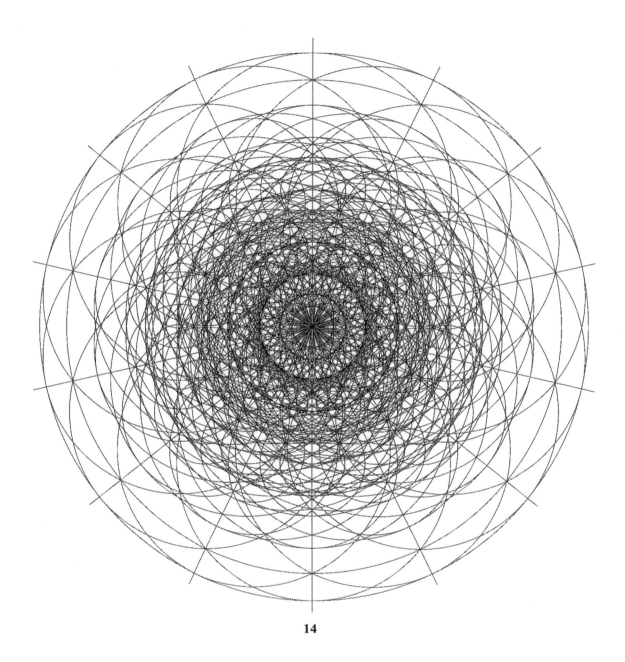

14

Appendix F: Index

xxxv

W

Y

Z

About the Author

When the author was very young, he would take his toys apart to see what made them work. As he got older, he turned that inquisitiveness to how his mind worked. Between the ages of 9-18 he learned or started 'playing' with a multitude of things such as: he could not trust my mind – 9 years old; the relationships of wants – desires – in everything we do (and changing his desires) – 9 years old; he learned the permanence of mathematics and science – 12-18 years old; there were 'glitches' in our – Mankind's -- perception of reality – 13 years old; he learned blank mind exercises – 11 years old; he learned truth perception in everyday objects – 15 years old; he learned to use music to aid blank mind exercises – 15 years old; and, he started to experiment with entering deep relaxation trance states – 15-18 years old.

The ages of 18-20 found Steven as a merchant seaman and he sailed the Pacific orient for a while before the selective service caught up with him. When a seaman, he learned about chanting and would do this on the deck of the ships he sailed and he also 'played' more with various trance states including self-hypnosis and sleep learning.

He entered the army at the age of twenty. The author turned the army experience into a serious metaphysical study and mental practice, mostly as a rebellion to the army ("They got my body, but they don't have my soul.") He started applying empty mind exercises to everything he did.

He began studying and doing exercises regularly in the *Tarot*, *I Ching*, thaumaturgical magic, music aided exercises, and learned raja yoga. Steve devised and performed numerous empirical experiments in the mystical/*ESP*/magic vein at this time and did many while he was doing his military chores

It was while in the army he was initiated into an intense period of internal schooling of thirteen months, which had distinct transitions/initiations through the 'schooling'. The schooling continued after his release from the army. The graduation from this school required his death. The age of twenty-three found Steven as a fourth level initiate, an adept.

Thinking it could not be that simple, he then studied the core concepts of world religions. The author found he could pick up books like *Tao te Ching*, *Upanishads*, or *Bhagavad Gita* and the majority of the time knew exactly what the books were expressing.

He has been in service to communities dedicated to growth, education, service, or of a spiritual nature most of the time since then. Fixing things is his version of "chopping wood and carrying water". The spectrum of these communities range from years working at Esalen Institute to years working for a Catholic monastery. Consequently, he has been exposed to a multitude of philosophies and thought systems.

He has taught workshops in *Mysticism and the Moody Blues*, *Magick: Preparation of the Operator*, and was a *Course in Miracles*© group discussion leader for a number of years. In addition, he has regularly taught an extracurricular quarter class titled an Introduction to the Mystic Arts (or Science) class at Heartwood Institute.

In the summer time, Steven can be found attending outdoor music festivals, applying *I AM A I*'s concepts.

Edwards Brothers Malloy
Oxnard, CA USA
September 11, 2014